Lecture Notes in Computer Science 16580

The series Lecture Notes in Computer Science (LNCS), including its subseries Lecture Notes in Artificial Intelligence (LNAI) and Lecture Notes in Bioinformatics (LNBI), has established itself as a medium for the publication of new developments in computer science and information technology research, teaching, and education.

LNCS enjoys close cooperation with the computer science R & D community, the series counts many renowned academics among its volume editors and paper authors, and collaborates with prestigious societies. Its mission is to serve this international community by providing an invaluable service, mainly focused on the publication of conference and workshop proceedings and postproceedings. LNCS commenced publication in 1973.

Alexander Raschke · Elvinia Riccobene ·
Klaus-Dieter Schewe · Bernhard Thalheim
Editors

Rigorous Methods in Theory and Practice

Essays Dedicated to Egon Börger on the Occasion of His 80th Birthday

Springer

Editors
Alexander Raschke
Universität Ulm
Ulm, Baden-Württemberg, Germany

Elvinia Riccobene
Università degli Studi di Milano
Milan, Italy

Klaus-Dieter Schewe
Linz, Austria

Bernhard Thalheim
Universität Kiel
Kiel, Germany

ISSN 0302-9743 ISSN 1611-3349 (electronic)
Lecture Notes in Computer Science
ISBN 978-3-032-24493-2 ISBN 978-3-032-24494-9 (eBook)
https://doi.org/10.1007/978-3-032-24494-9

This Springer imprint is published by the registered company Springer Nature Switzerland AG
The registered company address is: Gewerbestrasse 11, 6330 Cham, Switzerland

Preface

Tribute to Egon Börger on the Occasion of His 80th Birthday

Egon Börger was born on 13th May 1946 in Westfalia, Germany. He is widely recognized as a pioneer of rigorous hardware and software system design and analysis, a promoter of the Abstract State Machines (ASM) method, and the author of numerous foundational and applied monographs, as well as many journal and conference publications on rigorous state-based methods. He is also a co-founder of the ABZ conference series, dedicated to state-based formal methods. Throughout his career in the formal methods community, he has collaborated extensively with colleagues not only on Abstract State Machines but also on a variety of other methods and their applications, with the overarching goal of establishing software development as a true engineering discipline.

Egon Börger's strengths, which have contributed to his standing as a highly respected scientist, lie in his deep foundation in mathematics and logic, combined with an equally large interest in application problems. He has consistently used real-world problems not only to demonstrate the applicability of the methods he develops, but also as a source of scientifically relevant challenges that help refine, extend, and sharpen rigorous formal methods.

Recently, he published (together with Vincenzo Gervasi) a monograph on "Structures of Computing", in which, among others, they picked up the behavioural theory of reflective systems, i.e., systems that can on-the-fly modify their own behaviour, developed an easier usable extension to Abstract State Machines, and provided full specifications of reflection in functional and logic programming. Another monograph, published a few years earlier (together with Alexander Raschke), emphasised among others applications of a more general understanding of concurrency without reference to interleaving—the corresponding theory had been developed by Egon himself together with Klaus-Dieter Schewe—as well as applications of the concept of ambience, i.e., changing environments of systems.

The start of Egon Börger's academic career lies, however, not in the field of rigorous methods for systems development, but in philosophy and logic. He studied philosophy at the Université de Paris I (Sorbonne) and the Institut Supérieur de Philosophie in Louvain. He continued studying mathematical logic at the Westfälische Universität Münster, where the lively spirit of mathematical logic with a strong focus on the exploitation of logic for computing science aroused his interest in this area. Egon Börger became a renowned logician and theoretical computer scientist, and co-founder of the European Association for Computer Science Logic and its iconic CSL conference series. His monograph (together with Erich Grädel and Yuri Gurevich) on the classical decision problem is mandatory literature for all students in Logic.

In our tribute to Egon Börger's 75th birthday (see the Festschrift in LNCS 12750), we portrayed in more detail his contributions to logic, computation theory, and rigorous methods. We value Egon not only as an excellent scientist and inspiring mentor, but also as a virtuoso in bringing theoretical results into practical applications and, conversely, in drawing challenging scientific questions from real-world problems to advance knowledge to a higher level. Finally, we also appreciate Egon's open attitude and his ability to inspire people with his ideas. This has led to lasting friendships that have developed during scientific exchanges, and anyone who has ever visited him and his lovely wife in Tuscany can confirm their hospitality. With this Festschrift we want to express our special thanks to Egon.

May 2026

Alexander Raschke
Elvinia Riccobene
Klaus-Dieter Schewe
Bernhard Thalheim

Acknowledgement

We, Alexander Raschke, Elvinia Riccobene, Klaus-Dieter Schewe and Bernhard Thalheim, like to thank all contributors, authors and reviewers, to this Festschrift. This is a worthy birthday present for an inspiring scientist for all of us.

We are also grateful to Springer for giving us again the opportunity to express our appreciation for Egon through this Festschrift.

Organization

Reviewers of This Volume

Richard Banach
Christoph Beierle
Jonathan Bowen
Giuseppe Del Castillo
Guillaume Dupont
Flavio Ferrarotti
Marc Frappier
Angelo Gargantini
Vincenzo Gervasi
Régine Laleau
Michael Leuschel
Dominique Méry
Andreas Prinz
Alexander Raschke
Elvinia Riccobene
Gerhard Schellhorn
Klaus-Dieter Schewe
Neeraj Kumar Singh
Bernhard Thalheim
Wolf Zimmermann

Contents

Development of Computer Science and Rigorous Methods

Egon Börger's Contributions to Shaping Rigorous Methods 3
Hans Langmaack, Alexander Raschke, Klaus-Dieter Schewe, and Bernhard Thalheim

Formal Methods: Whence and Whither? 16
Jonathan P. Bowen

A Bibliometric Analysis of the Abstract State Machine Research Production and Community over the Years 30
Andrea Bombarda, Silvia Bonfanti, Angelo Gargantini, and Nico Pellegrinelli

Abstract State Machines

State-Based Implementation of Algebraic Data Types 49
Gerhard Schellhorn, Felix Pribyl, and Wolfgang Reif

Abstract State Machines for Security Assessment 76
Chiara Braghin and Elvinia Riccobene

Data in Distributed Computing 106
Andreas Prinz, Iulian Ober, and Edel Sherratt

A First Step Towards Agile Verification of Compilations 126
Wolf Zimmermann, Thomas Kühn, Edward Sabinus, and Mandy Weißbach

A Symbolic Execution Approach to Bounded Verification of Abstract State Machines 152
Giuseppe Del Castillo

Bridging Specification and Implementation in CoreASM Plugins 176
Vincenzo Gervasi and Federico Miraglia

Rigorous State-Based Methods

From Event-B to Lambdapi and TLA^+ 201
Yamine Ait-Ameur, Jean-Paul Bodeveix, Christophe Chen, Guillaume Dupont, Elie Fares, Mamoun Filali, Anne Grieu, Ismail Mendil, Marc Pantel, Peter Rivière, Neeraj Kumar Singh, and Guillaume Verdier

Design of Correct by Construction Algorithms by Double Checking Properties 223
Dominique Méry

Structure as Semantics: Impedance Modeling and Retrenchment in Cyber-Physical Systems 249
John Baugh, Richard Banach, and Eunsuk Kang

From Abstract State Machines to B: A Translation of a Medical Pillbox Model 273
Michael Leuschel

A Streamlined Semantics for TASTD 295
Diego de Azevedo Oliveira and Marc Frappier

Enhancing the Expressibility of ASM-Defined Classes of Algorithms with Event-B 317
Julien Cervelle, Frédéric Gervais, Pierre Valarcher, and Régine Laleau

Refinement-Centric Hazard Analysis with SHARCS: A Case Study Bridging Requirements and Formal Model 332
Asieh Salehi Fathabadi, Colin Snook, Thai Son Hoang, and Michael Butler

Logic and Theory of Computation

Capturing Quantum Algorithms by Quantum Abstract State Machines 357
Flavio Ferrarotti and Klaus-Dieter Schewe

Inductive Nonmonotonic Reasoning Based on Defeasible and Indefeasible Beliefs 377
Christoph Beierle, Alexander Hahn, Gabriele Kern-Isberner, and Lars-Phillip Spiegel

Non-deterministic Algorithms – Capture By Abstract State Machines 398
Klaus-Dieter Schewe and Flavio Ferrarotti

Modelling

Establishing Language-Backed Modelling 421
Bernhard Thalheim

Modeling and Implementing Human-Centered Digital Twins 445
Albert Fleischmann and Christian Stary

Author Index 469

Development of Computer Science and Rigorous Methods

Egon Börger's Contributions to Shaping Rigorous Methods

Hans Langmaack[1], Alexander Raschke[2], Klaus-Dieter Schewe[3](✉), and Bernhard Thalheim[1]

[1] Christian-Albrechts-Universität Kiel, Kiel, Germany
anm.ha.langmaack@t-online.de, bernhard.thalheim@email.uni-kiel.de
[2] Universität Ulm, Institut für Software Engineering und Programmiersprachen, Ulm, Germany
alexander.raschke@uni-ulm.de
[3] Institut Nationale Polytechnique de Toulouse/IRIT CNRS, Toulouse, France
kd.schewe@gmail.com

Hans Langmaack (born 1934) is one of Germany's earliest computer scientists, a doyen who has not only achieved a great deal, but whose wisdom can be beneficial in every respect. Like Egon Börger he received his initial scientific education in Münster as a mathematician, going on to earn a doctorate in complex analysis. With the emergence of computer science, he followed Friedrich L. Bauer and Klaus Samelson to Mainz and Munich. His first outstanding achievement, the co-development of a compiler for ALGOL60, determined his further professional career as a highly respected specialist in programming languages and compiler construction.

After an interlude at Purdue, USA, and his habilitation at Munich in matrix theory, he first worked in Saarbrücken and then, particularly fruitfully, in Kiel, where he co-established one of the first computer science degree programmes in Germany, with a well thought-out, deep mathematical foundation alongside numerous research projects, such as the ESPRIT project 'Provably Correct Systems' (ProCoS), a pioneering project in the field of rigorous methods.

The following interview with Hans Langmaack (HL) was conducted by Alexander Raschke (AR), Klaus-Dieter Schewe (KDS) and Bernhard Thalheim (BT).

AR. Professor Langmaack, thank you very much for your willingness to talk to us about the development of Computer Science, the field of rigorous methods, your experiences, and your relationship to Egon Börger. When did you first meet Egon Börger? Can you tell us a bit what were the most interesting topics at that time, in particular those you shared?

HL. The first time I met Egon Börger was at the 1983 FCT conference in Borgholm, which had been organised by Marek Karpinski. Egon Börger's Ph.D. supervisor, Professor Dieter Rödding from the logic school of the University of Münster, gave a survey presentation about "Modular Decomposition

A. Raschke et al. (Eds.): Egon Börger Festschrift, LNCS 16580, pp. 3–15, 2026.
https://doi.org/10.1007/978-3-032-24494-9_1

of Automata", which emphasised the close relationship between mathematical logic and computer science. After studying philosophy in Paris Egon Börger had returned in the mid 1960s to his home city Münster to continue studying logic at one of the most renowned logic institutions in Germany.

I had also been a student of Mathematics with Heinrich Behnke, Logic with Hans Hermes, and Theoretical Physics with Adolf Kratzer in Münster in the second half of the 1950s. My own first encounter with finite automata dated back to 1961/62, when Richard Büchi had been invited as guest professor to the University of Mainz. In Borgholm I gave a presentation about Hoare-like proof rules for ALGOL-like programs with finite procedure types. Egon Börger and I had many discussions about our common experiences during our studies in Münster, but we talked very little about computer science and logic.

KDS. When you met again at the beginning of the 1990s, Egon Börger had become a respected logician working on foundations of computation theory, and if I am right, this was also your main area. Gurevich's "New Thesis" about Evolving Algebras, which were later renamed to Abstract State Machines, was in "statu nascendi" and VDM, the first formal method, already existed for some years. Was there any indication that Gurevich's strengthening of Turing's thesis would impact on rigorous methods, in particular lead to something that is not only in the interest of mathematicians and theoretical computer scientists?

HL. Definitely yes. The experiences I gained from my studies of logic had already led to my conviction that Turing's thesis is accurate, i.e. every effective computation can be simulated by a Turing machine. In my book together with Albert A. Grau and Ursula Hill [5] we described a two-pass compiler for complete ALGOL60 (in ALGOL60 itself with arrays with practically unbounded limits), which led me to understand assignments $f(a_1, \ldots, a_n) := a_0$ in (turbo) ASMs as left-side indexed variables as in ALGOL60. When Egon Börger gave a presentation about ASMs at a ProCoS meeting in the mid 1990s, Hans Rischel and I could clarify some misunderstanding by pointing to this array idea in ALGOL60. Then in the late 1960s an ALGOL60 compiler according to a "specification in ALGOL60" [5] was installed at the Technical University of Munich, which in a way demonstrated the usefulness of (turbo) ASM specifications for industrial programming and development.

BT. When you met again in the early 1990s at the PDK conference, the circumstances had changed. You were involved in the ProCoS project dedicated to rigorous specification and verification [7], and Egon Börger was now promoting (turbo) ASMs. How did you see the upcoming ASMs, which after all came out of computation theory?

HL. My mathematical background lets me understand programs and processes as function definitions, which deliver for some input all kinds of quaint output.

Then it should be possible to use "classical" mathematical notation to represent such functions. I think this is what Yuri Gurevich, Egon Börger and their followers wanted to demonstrate. The stock of mathematical notation suffices, and it is not more complex than most terminology nowadays used in computer science.

AR. How did you see it that a renowned mathematician like Egon Börger was now so deeply interested in rigorous soft- and hardware development?

HL. Well, he was not the only one. Also other renowned mathematicians turned towards computers and their functioning and applicability. Maybe this still happened not often enough.

KDS. Egon Börger emphasised that ASMs follow rigorous mathematical methodology without being forced into the "straightjacket" of formal methods such as VDM or Z with too restricted rules about the systems development process. How did you see his position, which seems to be not in line with the ideas of ProCoS? I may add that I also made shocking experiences with the formal methods community, e.g. meeting researchers who openly declared their belief that with a formal specification and a few correctness proofs the work is done, and the rest is just dull, low-level encoding work. As you worked yourself also in mathematics and the theory of computing before entering the world of rigorous methods, how did you see the formal methods community?

HL. The ProCoS project (part I: 1989–91, part II: 1992–95, Working Group: 1994–97) followed the same mathematics-oriented ground idea as propagated by Egon Börger. Only at the beginning of the project a strict coordination regime under the direction of Dines Bjørner was applied, but it was oriented neither on VDM/Meta-IV nor on Z. Every development was strictly mathematically proven, but the composition and study of interface reports consumed a lot of time. So in ProCoS II we preferred mutual visits to Lyngby, Oxford, Oldenburg, and Kiel to develop proofs, which we understood by personal interaction. After Dines Bjørner moved to Macau, Anthony Hoare took over the lead of ProCoS II.

KDS. Let us talk a bit more about conflicts. Anthony Hoare was involved in ProCoS, and he was very outspoken about "declarativity" of formal methods, praising even the absence of any "dirty" computation aspect as highly desirable. Egon Börger cited and heavily criticised this in his ASM book. Instead, he emphasised the importance of different "levels of abstraction". How was the relationship to Dines Bjørner? After all, VDM is not as "declarative" as Hoare would like to have it.

HL. Sure, Anthony Hoare did not adhere to VDM, and he urged to move away from the software engineering project idea. During a visit to Houston in 1987 he got impressed by the automatic Boyer-Moore theorem prover, which was used by J Strother Moore to prove the correctness of the MicroGypsi compiler to the assembly language Piton and the machine language FM8502-ML, and the hardware description HDL of the FM8502 processor. The four groups participating in ProCoS wanted to achieve further results in this direction with stricter attention to the level of hardware and time; J Moore's "correctness stack" was to be extended to "the ProCoS tower".

Dines Bjørner held the Danish chair at the University of Kiel, and he taught VDM with its specification language Meta-IV. Among others this resulted in three Ph.D. theses by Reinhard Völler, Uwe Schmidt and Bernhard Steffen covering very successful industrial compilers. ProCoS II focused on proof obligations in temporal logic for the verification of hardware with timing problems. The algebraic proof technique, which was favoured by Anthony Hoare, led to impressive results with essential contributions by Markus Müller-Olm, Martin Fränzle and Burghard von Karger from the University of Kiel.

BT. There were also arguments between Dines Bjørner and Egon Börger. Do you have an explanation for these?

HL. My impression from personal talks was that Dines Bjørner, who by education is an electrical engineer, blamed Egon Börger for expecting too much epistemological knowledge and too much mathematical/logical understanding from his conversational partners. His own interest was in large industry-like projects, where very diverse skill sets of collaborators needed to be integrated so that everyone preserves a general overview.

To mediate this strained relationship, I wrote articles "An ALGOL-View on Turbo ASMs" [9] for an ASM workshop as well as "On Revival of ALGOL-Concepts in Modern Programming and Specification Languages" [10] for a Festcolloquium on the occasion of Dines Bjørner's 70th birthday. I highlighted that both Meta-IV and turbo ASMs tackle the same kind of problems, which already appeared in the block concept that Klaus Samelson introduced into ALGOL60 in 1959. Both Dines Bjørner and Egon Börger are highly esteemed colleagues, and computer science needs such researchers to raise the scientific standard of computer science. It should by now be undebatable that computer science had brought up questions outside the scope of established sciences.

AR. You were going on well with all these protagonists? How did you manage this?

HL. My personal view is that I was educated early to avoid disputes and at a pinch to take on the blame. This was, because my mother was a war widow with three children, and I as the oldest had to shoulder family responsibilities already at the age of eleven. There was no room for unnecessary arguments. This has become part of my nature. I have been commended by older colleagues because of my balancing attitude even towards "difficult" colleagues. In ProCoS I attracted students and contributors with highest intellectual skills, capable of coping with challenging tasks, whom I got to know from beginners' courses.

BT. According to you, computer science should be considered still a branch of mathematics. I would not deny that computer science has become a science in its own right, but clearly mathematical foundations are essential.

HL. I think that in a way Mathematics has dropped Computer Science, which was a mistake. According to my experiences from Saarbrücken and Kiel some Mathematics departments even try to keep mathematical logic at distance. This is, because logicians are suspected to only accept strictly formal proofs, i.e. proofs in a (Hilbert, Gentzen, natural deduction) calculus, whereas mathematicians haved learned to conduct proofs in less formalised way without losing exactness. I remember that the mathematicians were not amused, when in 1968 student groups demanded to start the curriculum with a course in mathematical logic that should precede the classical introductory courses in calculus and linear algebra, arguing that this would be easier to comprehend. This was not well received, in particular, as logic without sophisticated mathematical examples is even harder to digest.

However, I must confess that for me the knowledge in mathematical logic, which was compulsory for teachers' education, was far more useful for entering computer science than all my knowledge in "classical" mathematical fields. The ALGOL60 report had just been released, and in addition to my tasks as assistant in mathematics I was confronted with the obligation to build, together with Ursula Hill, an ALGOL60 compiler for the Siemens 2002 computer. I had no difficulty to understand to concepts for parameter transfer, because from Church's lambda calculus I knew about implicit renaming in case of clashes. When I got in contact with turbo ASMs I recognised the recurring ideas from ALGOL60, in particular, the absence (in essence) of typing obligations for formal procedure parameters, which enabled the simulation of "call by value" using "call by name". This is important to be mentioned, because nowadays the concepts of ALGOL60 are almost forgotten.

AR. How do you explain the seemingly decreasing interest in mathematical foundations in students and also in computer science researchers?

HL. Frankly, I do not know why people are not convinced about the importance of mathematics; there is no other discipline with such a clear conception of truth. Then today the school education in mathematics is not as good as in the 1950s, so students are not well prepared when they enter the university. Furthermore, I think that the number of mathematics teachers needed for the education of software engineers is hardly manageable with the current resources.

KDS. Is it not alarming, when large computer science communities, in particular in "Software Engineering", openly declare their aversion against mathematics? I have met computer scientists who claim that mathematics is too limited to enable the construction of a huge hanging bridge, which would require different non-mathematical methods.

HL. My advice is that programmers must learn (again) to integrate relevant comments into their programs, which are meant to enable comprehension. Such comments are the first step for a mathematically acceptable proof of correctness. Every loop and every procedure body requires a comment containing the proof-relevant invariant. Mathematical proofs are not sequences of formulae, but they contain a lot of text with arguments that allow any reader to accept the reasoning as correct. A completely formalised derivation in some calculus is not needed. Deep mathematical results that matured over decades or even centuries were never the result of complete formalisation. This has been accepted as accurate and should remain so.

BT. How do you see the development that mathematical education is more and more reduced in many computer science curricula around the world (outside Europe even worse than here)? For instance, we have currently a machine-learning hype, but there are many researchers without decent knowledge about probability theory and statistics. And for the hype on quantum computing it should be understood that linear algebra—I would also add here algebraic geometry—is highly important.

HL. I can only emphasise again that in my view computer scientists need decent knowledge about mathematics, so the promotion of mathematics is very important. As you say, probability theory and statistics are very important for machine learning. However, I am also astounded that in 2024 a larger group of DMV[1] members launched a request to reestablish machine learning within mathematics, because this would be the only way to guarantee an appropriate level in research and education. I doubt that in this way the various links to applications would be well supported. Nowadays, such disputes about ownership have increased, and like me you know examples from Kiel. During my active time, I have always tried to forge collaboration for mutual benefit.

I was first confronted with "learning circuits" in 1961 by a colloquium talk in Mainz given by Karl Steinbuch, who had been invited by Friedrich L. Bauer and Klaus Samelson, though Professor Bauer has never been a friend of Artificial Intelligence. In fact, since 1960 there have been so many promises by AI followed by deep disappointment, for which computer science as a whole had to carry the can. In the 1980s, this created open opposition from electrical engineering, and not only few "faculties of electrical and information engineering" were created.

[1] DMV (Deutsche Mathematiker Vereinigung) is a German association of mathematicians.

Fortunately, these trials were not overly successful, e.g. in Kiel the number of computer science students is still more than double the number of students in all other engineering institutes together. The Technical University of Munich pursued a different approach by creating a super faculty for mathematics, computer science and electrical and information engineering to foster better collaboration. Unfortunately, this had a negative impact on the visibility of mathematics and computer science, and on the exceptional position of Mathematics.

KDS. Rigorous methods such as ASMs target reliable hard- and software systems emphasising "blueprints" of systems to be built. This links to the discussions at the 1968 NATO-sponsored conference in Marktoberdorf, where for the first time ever the notion of "software engineering" was used. All discussants, though their opinions differed largely, agreed that rigorous specifications are necessary and their verification is indispensible. The general impression is that the field of Software Engineering to a large degree is even less precise than the programming methodology practiced in the 1960s, which motivated the 1968 conference focusing on the question how the "crisis" could be overcome or at least mitigated. What went wrong in the last 50 years, and what do you suggest could be done to correct the wrong development?

HL. I believe that Bauer, who coined the notion "software engineering", wanted to express his vision about the future development of computer science, and he was very confident that he could bring this to life. Whether it was discussed in his own research group I do not know, but outside it hardly was. I was in the group of Samelson, and software engineering was inessential. I already expressed my views on the importance of mathematical proofs and how it could become common practice, but I have not the power to let colleagues in software engineering gain the right insights.

AR. Your suggestion to write up "informal" proofs is what Egon Börger always emphasises: proving "in a mathematical way" what needs to be proven about specifications and systems, because a proof by a (dumb) machine would first require to make all implicit assumptions explicit.

HL. As I already said, this is how all deep mathematical results have been achieved. A complete formalisation, or precisely a proof in a calculus, would not have been possible.

BT. In all engineering disciplines, it is common practice to set and exploit standards, by means of which already verified quality can be exploited and costly maintenance can be avoided. In computer science, we often encounter incomprehension about what has already been achieved. How can computer science and in particular software engineering learn from the other disciplines?

HL. This is again the same complex of problems. If a standard is set and commonly accepted, it creates components with verified quality, as you say. That means that a big step towards a proof of correctness has already been made. In their studies, the nascent engineers are forced to think why their constructions work. Building a faulty machine, circuit or building is not acceptable and at the end also expensive. Engineers may not love mathematics, but there is nonetheless an insight about the necessity. In computer science there is a lack of understanding, and developing standards could contribute to mitigate this. They also can help to enforce a certain discipline, e.g. not creating all the time new notions for old concepts.

KDS. We now mentioned many times that methods should be rigorous, as in mathematics. For compiler construction, accurate methods have been developed. What can be done to ensure that scientific accuracy becomes omnipresent in software engineering?

HL. When I was a student in Münster, I learnt that comprehension is the result of precision. As long as I am not able to express precisely a result in mathematics or logic, I have not yet understood it completely. I remember well a visit of Donald Knuth to Schleswig-Holstein in the 1980s, which included giving a colloquium presentation at the University of Kiel. When asked what he considers to be the most essential contribution of computer science, he answered that it is the introduction of assignments, which after all provide the means for state changes. In a way, it is the same as what Yuri Gurevich and Egon Börger provide with ASMs: there are values that can be assigned to abstract locations, or named, if I use the terminology of ALGOL60. This is the first logic step; when it has been understood, it is easy to understand also Turing machines and ASMs.

BT. I may add here that it is a common mistake in software engineering not to talk explicitly about accompanying models. The context must be understood. What Knuth said is simply that you can only handle state changes, if you have a precise understanding of what state changes are. A colleague from Berlin once uttered that, in his opinion, computer science often took a wrong turn. Based on your experiences, how could this have been avoided? For instance, insights on programming languages gained from ALGOL, Modula and later Oberon are almost forgotten.

HL. The colleague is right, and there are many more examples of such wrong turns. I already mentioned that successors of ALGOL60 literally killed the good ideas of the language, a point where Friedrich L. Bauer concurs with Anthony Hoare. I was very pleased to see that the concepts in a way have been preserved in turbo ASMs.

BT. You have emphasised the important role of mathematics in computer science, and we all agree with you. However, should the mathematics taught to computer science students not be different? After all, the focus on analysis and linear algebra reflects the parallel developments in mathematics and physics over centuries.

HL. I agree, but I insist that the content of courses taught to computer science students must be genuine mathematics. I can imagine to start with discrete mathematics and logic as the basis, but most importantly, students need to appreciate the way of thinking and the culture of mathematics. Then there are optional other fields of mathematics that should be made compulsory for specific fields of specialisation. For instance, as already discussed knowledge about probability theory and statistics is essential for machine learning as is linear algebra. Analysis and in particular differential equations are required when dealing with hybrid systems. The list can be continued, as all fields of computer science link to some branch of mathematics covering necessary foundations.

AR. You published a series of articles referring to "Dijkstra's error" [11–13]? What exactly did you mean by this?

HL. Actually, it was Clement L. McGowan who introduced the parlance of *Dijkstra's "most recent" error* [14]. He found an inaccuracy (or at least an ambiguous formulation) in Dijkstra's work on "Recursive Programming" dealing with compiler construction for ALGOL60 [4] and a sufficient condition, under which this error in the run-time stack of a compiled ALGOL60 program cannot occur. Unfortunately, Dijkstra's inaccuracy was repeated in slightly modified form in several textbooks about compiler construction. In our book on ALGOL60 compilation [5] we already discovered that Dijkstra's run time stack behaves in a most interesting, names clashes avoiding way, different from Dijkstra's formulation in [4]. When working on our book [5] we had not yet recognised the problem in [4], which McGowan in his paper [14] showed up. McGowan's result was generalised by Peter Kandzia, who proved under which conditions the absence of "most recent" errors of an uninterpreted ALGOL60 program can be decided [6].

KDS. In ProCoS and related work on Occam and ALGOL60/68, also in joint work with Martin Fränzle or Ernst-Rüdiger Olderog there is always a focus on proofs, in particular correctness proofs. What do you think about the work of Egon Börger, Dean Rosenzweig, Gerhard Schellhorn and others on Prolog, Java, Occam, and other examples for correctness of compilers?

HL. I always asked myself the question, how a program problem can be considered as a mathematical problem. In many cases, these problems were shallow, but there were also problems that required a deeper mathematical investigation.

The research assistants I appointed in Kiel were all well-trained through mathematical logic lectures by Arnold Oberschelp, and with this background, I could expect them to cope with such problems. Concerning the work done by Egon Börger and others, the examples for compiler correctness you mention all qualify as mathematically interesting, and I have no doubts that the achieved results are correct.

BT. In particular, Egon Börger emphasises these large case studies as providing evidence for the easiness of the ASM method and its flexible notion of refinement. Would you agree? You also launched a sophisticated steam-boiler case study together with Jean-Raymond Abrial and Egon Börger [1]. There have been other cases, such as the Mondex electronic purse, where the ASM-based approach succeeded to complete the task.

HL. I appreciate very much that people propagating the ASM method, in particular Egon Börger, Robert Stärk and Joachim Schmid, cared intensively about industrial application projects and standardisation. Egon Börger even sought the discussion with standardisation committees and tried to support them. It does not come as a surprise that the mathematical flexibility emphasised by the ASM method shows advantages when dealing with realistic specification tasks.

I also appreciate the transition from ASMs to turbo ASMs, which in my view adds a control instrument. This is similar to the transition from ALGOL58 to ALGOL60 with the introduction of block structuring by Klaus Samelson. Every procedure body extended by a formal parameter list becomes a block. We know analogues such as introducing quantifiers in logic or lambda abstraction in the lambda calculus. In all cases implicit renaming is due to avoid clashes. Again, I see many similarities between the work on ALGOL60 and turbo ASMs.

Of course, there was also opposition. For instance, Kristen Nygaard launched a philippic against formal procedures in ALGOL60, which he condemned to be incomprehensible. This motivated his and Ole Jan Dahl's development of object-oriented programming with inheritance mechanism. In 2005 Wolfgang Goerigk showed that ALGOL60 programs with nested procedure declarations and formal procedure names that can be substituted by non-formal procedure names can be simulated in a structurally equivalent way (see [10]) by object-oriented Java programs, so the presumably incomprehensible ALGOL60 structures can also be found in Java. In this context an utterance of Anthony Hoare inflicts on myself: "ALGOL60 was an important progress compared to most of its successor programming languages". Same as Klaus Samelson's block structuring in ALGOL60 led to better understandable program structuring, Egon Börger's and Robert Stärk's turbo ASMs lead to insight-increasing structuring of specifications.

KDS. In your reflections on correctness proofs you mention that the correctness of the theorem prover is hardly ever addressed. Of course, there are limitations for tool-based proofs, which implies even more the importance of mathematics. What do you think would be a feasible approach?

HL. The problems around the effective, complete and correct application of automatic theorem provers are presumably too big to achieve always timely and reliable results. As I already said, I believe that the use of mathematical proofs is most likely the best option. This starts from system programmers adding meaningful justifying comments into programs, which can be seen as the first step towards verification. For this "classical" mathematics with emphasis on "informal" proofs remains most important. The best way to learn proper proving is to practice on existing approved examples, even if the propositions will never be needed. Such training of young brains should already start at school.

AR. If you look back at your pioneering years in computer science, many success stories and meanders and the coming and going of various themes, what do you recommend to young researchers in computer science concerning their education, positioning in the academic activities, paths to success and scientific seriousness?

HL. My general advice for students seeking their right career path is to listen to experienced men and women who anticipate future developments. For any personal, familial or financial problems a solution can usually be found, though it may be stressful. I would like to illustrate this advice by my own life experience: When I started my university studies, due to economic necessities I had to sacrifice all semester breaks to work hard on the farm of my mother. I compensated this double burden by becoming a "berserker"[2], so I concluded all my tasks without any help, but still surprisingly successful, because I insisted to understand everything by myself to compensate for the lack of time during semester breaks.

Originally I wanted to study mechanical engineering, for which it was mandatory to first complete a half-year course of practical work at an established machine building company. I was lucky to get accepted by a company in North Germany without the usual hard selection examinations. During a learning unit at a working lathe I made a geometric-mathematical observation, for which I was highly commended by the chief engineer, because I was the first ever student apprentice who made this discovery. For me this led to a crisis, and I wondered, if mechanical engineering would be the right field for me to "get to the bottom" of things. My renowned teacher ObStDir. Dr. phil. Dr. Ing. habil. H. Athen recommended that I should change direction and study mathematics in Münster. He personally knew most mathematics professors, in particular Heinrich Behnke, and Münster was away from home far enough so that I could not simply be called back home when a sudden need on the farm arose. My mother held my teacher in high esteem, so she endorsed my plans and let me go by November 1st, 1954.

In autumn 1959 Professor Friedrich L. Bauer from the University of Mainz asked in the name of his colleague Klaus Samelson [8]—both worked on large

[2] A berserker originally denotes a warrior of a legendary wild Germanic tribe, but it is also used as a metaphor for a very hard working person.

computers—whether Professor Behnke could recommend a mathematician as post-doctoral research fellow. Behnke first could not name a suitable candidate, so he openly asked in his Ph.D. seminar for those close to submit their Ph.D. thesis. I was the only one who shyly came forward, so I started my new endeavour in Mainz in June 1960. So far, my path had led me from mechanical engineering over a Ph.D. in pure mathematics with minors in theoretical physics and logic to computer science[3].

I collaborated with Ursula Hill to build the ALGOL60 compiler "ALCOR MAINZ 2002" for the Siemens 2002 mainframe computer. The compiler was released in 1962. We used the assembler language PROSA, but our specification was de facto written in some quasi-ALGOL60, which in my view follows the same ground idea as turbo ASMs—even the important explanation of name clashes in the ASM book [3, p.170] was already present in the ALGOL60 report [2]. This was followed by a book project on ALGOL compilation together with Albert A. Grau from Evanston and Ursula Hill [5]. In 1966/67 I spent a sabbatical at the Computer Science department of Purdue University in West Lafayette (Indiana, USA), where I taught a course on "Programming in Diverse Higher Programming Languages", in addition corrected the proofs of our book, which had already been finalised in Munich, and wrote up my habilitation thesis in mathematics. In autumn 1967, I habilitated at the Technical University of Munich. When in 1969 the German federal government endorsed the establishment of university degree programmes "Informatik", the first 40 full professor positions were created, and the necessary funding for 10 universities interested in these programmes was released. Soon afterwards, I was appointed as Professor at the University of the Saarland in Saarbrücken.

You asked me about paths to success, so here are a few thoughts on this. When I gave introductory courses in computer science, I memorised those students who seemed capable of handling challenging programming problems of mathematical nature. Then I tried to attrack these students for Master and Ph.D. theses, and I managed to procure the necessary funding. My success is mainly the success of my students.

As computer science professors were a small minority, I was elected as expert consultant for the DFG[4], and in this role I tried to foster cross-regional research programmes. In 1991 I was in charge of handling a funding application entitled "Deduction" by Wolfgang Bibel, a colleague from the Technical University of Darmstadt, which in my view was outstanding. As Wolfgang Bibel was logician, I also appointed Egon Börger, who was a highly respected logician, as member of the assessment panel. Egon Börger was rather sceptical, in particular concerning the objective to find proofs with artificial intelligence methods, but could be convinced that the envisioned methods were mathematically solid. The research

---

[3] The German name "Informatik" had firstly been coined by Karl Steinbuch in 1958, the discipline was hardly known, and it took until 1969 to establish the first university degree courses.

[4] DFG = Deutsche ForschungsGemeinschaft, the main funding association in Germany.

programme was endorsed and released remarkable results. It should be noted that representatives from arts and social sciences were rather open to research programmes in novel areas, but there was usually a strong opposition from representatives from engineering disciplines. We already talked about the reasons for this animosity, which at the end could not prevent computer science to grow and become a very important profession.

BT. We like to thank you again that you took the time for this interview.

References

1. Abrial, J.R., Börger, E., Langmaack, H.: The steam boiler case study: competition of formal program specification and development methods. In: Abrial, J.R., Börger, E., Langmaack, H. (eds.) Formal Methods for Industrial Applications. LNCS, vol. 1165, pp. 1–12. Springer, Cham (1995). https://doi.org/10.1007/BFB0027228
2. Backus, J.W., et al.: Report on the algorithmic language ALGOL60. Numer. Math. **2**, 106–136 (1960)
3. Börger, E., Stärk, R.F.: Abstract State Machines. A Method for High-Level System Design and Analysis. Springer, Cham (2003)
4. Dijkstra, E.W.: Recursive programming. Numer. Math. **2**, 312–318 (1960)
5. Grau, A.A., Hill, U., Langmaack, H.: Handbook for Automatic Computation I, Part b: Translation of ALGOL60, Grundlehren der mathematischen Wissenschaft, vol. 137. Springer, Heidelberg (1967)
6. Kandzia, P.: On the most recent property of ALGOL-like programs. In: Loeckx, J. (ed.) ICALP 1974. LNCS, vol. 14, pp. 97–111. Springer, Heidelberg (1974). https://doi.org/10.1007/3-540-06841-4_54
7. Langmaack, H.: The ProCoS approach to correct systems. Real Time Syst. **13**(3), 253–275 (1997). https://doi.org/10.1023/A:1007963427189
8. Langmaack, H.: Klaus Samelsons frühe Beiträge zur Informatikentwicklung - Historische Notiz. Inform. Spektrum **25**(2), 132–137 (2002). https://doi.org/10.1007/S002870200218
9. Langmaack, H.: An ALGOL-view on turbo ASM. In: Zimmermann, W., Thalheim, B. (eds.) ASM 2004. LNCS, vol. 3052, pp. 20–37. Springer, Heidelberg (2004). https://doi.org/10.1007/978-3-540-24773-9_3
10. Langmaack, H.: On revival of Algol-concepts in modern programming and specification languages. In: Jones, C.B., Liu, Z., Woodcock, J. (eds.) Formal Methods and Hybrid Real-Time Systems. LNCS, vol. 4700, pp. 414–434. Springer, Heidelberg (2007). https://doi.org/10.1007/978-3-540-75221-9_19
11. Langmaack, H.: Dijkstras fruchtbarer, folgenreicher Irrtum - Teil 1: Die Kopenhagener Diskussion und deren Folgen. Inform. Spektrum **33**(3), 302–308 (2010a). https://doi.org/10.1007/S00287-010-0433-7
12. Langmaack, H.: Dijkstras fruchtbarer, folgenreicher Irrtum - Teil 2: "Most recent"-Eigenschaft eines Programms. Inform. Spektrum **33**(4), 384–392 (2010b). https://doi.org/10.1007/S00287-010-0446-2
13. Langmaack, H.: Dijkstras fruchtbarer, folgenreicher Irrtum - Teil 3: Zu Laufzeitsystemkorrektheit und Auswirkungen von Dijkstras Aussage. Inform. Spektrum **33**(6), 634–646 (2010c). https://doi.org/10.1007/S00287-010-0466-Y
14. McGowan, C.L.: The "most recent" error: its causes and correction. In: Proceedings of ACM Conference on Proving Assertions About Programs, pp. 191–202. ACM (1972). https://doi.org/10.1145/800235.807085

Formal Methods: Whence and Whither?

Jonathan P. Bowen[1,2,3](✉)

[1] London South Bank University, London, UK
jonathan.bowen@lsbu.ac.uk
[2] Southwest University, Chongqing, China
[3] Museophile Limited, Oxford, UK
https://www.jpbowen.com

Abstract. Alan Turing arguably wrote the first paper on formal methods over 75 years ago. Since then, there have been claims and counterclaims about formal methods. Tool development has been slow, but aided by Moore's Law with the increasing power of computers. Although formal methods are not widespread in practical usage at a heavyweight level, their influence has crept into software engineering practice to the extent that they are no longer necessarily called formal methods in their use. In addition, in areas where safety and security are important, with the increasing use of computers in such applications, formal methods are a viable way to improve the reliability of such software-based systems. Their use in hardware, where a mistake can be very costly, is also important. This paper presents a personal exploration of the journey of formal methods to the present day and speculates on future directions, including the use of Artificial Intelligence.

Keywords: Formal Methods · History of Computing · Software Engineering · Artificial Intelligence · Generative AI · Z Notation · Theorem Proving

1 Introduction

This paper traces the trajectory of formal methods [52] in computer science, examining their historical origins, their practical application in industry, and their future direction in the age of Artificial Intelligence (AI). Beginning with the foundational work of Alan Turing in 1949 on checking a program formally [47], we explore the evolution of mathematical verification. We cover some common myths that have historically hindered the adoption of formal methods and counter them with evidence from industrial success stories, particularly the implementation of the iFACTS Air Traffic Control support software for National Air Traffic Services (NATS) in the UK using the formal Z notation [44] and SPARK Ada [4]. Finally, we consider where the field could be heading, discussing the convergence of formal methods with Generative AI (GenAI), Large Language Models (LLMs), and combined approaches to theorem proving, suggesting that we may be on the cusp of a renaissance in software correctness driven by these hybrid approaches.

A. Raschke et al. (Eds.): Egon Börger Festschrift, LNCS 16580, pp. 16–29, 2026.
https://doi.org/10.1007/978-3-032-24494-9_2

The reliability of software systems remains one of the critical challenges of the modern era. As once noted on a fridge magnet, "Failure is not an option... It comes bundled with the software!". While this is humorous, the implications for safety-critical systems, ranging from aviation to nuclear power, are potentially very serious.

Formal methods, the application of mathematical logic-based techniques [35] to the specification, development, and verification of software and hardware systems, have for several decades been proposed as a potential way to ease the "software crisis". Despite their rigourous foundations, they have often been viewed as a niche area by many practitioners in the software engineering field, relegated to use by academia or for applications where safety or security is very critical.

This paper provides a retrospective and prospective view of formal methods. We examine the "whence" – the historical roots from Aristotle to Turing – and the "whither" – the possible future integration with Artificial Intelligence (AI), specifically Generative AI (GenAI). We argue that the separation of practical and theoretical work, as lamented by the formal methods pioneer and colleague of Turing, Christopher Strachey (1916–1975), is contrived and ultimately detrimental; and that recent and continuing AI developments offer a path to unification with formal methods approaches.

2 Historical Foundations: The "Whence"

2.1 Early Roots and Turing's Contribution

While the logical foundations of formal methods can be traced back to Aristotle's logic and the desire to formalize reasoning, the application to computing has distinct 20th-century roots. In mathematics, it is typical to have simply stated theorems, by with potentially very deep and complex proofs. Consider Fermat's Last Theorem (c. 1637) – $a^n + b^n \neq c^n$ for integer $n > 2$ – postulated by the French mathematician Pierre de Fermat (1607–1665). This was finally proved bu Andrew Wiles around 358 years later in 1994–5, not a timescale acceptable in software development! Instead, in software verification, there are complicated specifications, potentially thousands of pages, and long programs with millions of lines of code, but with relatively shallow proofs compared to those developed by professional mathematicians.

Arguably, the first paper on formal methods was written by Alan Turing in 1949, titled "Checking a Large Routine" [47]. In this seminal work, presented at the EDSAC Inaugural Conference, Turing introduced the concept of making assertions about the various states that a machine can reach. He posited that the checker of a routine has to verify that:

1. The initial condition and the stopped condition agree with the claims made for the routine as a whole.
2. Each assertion in the flow is correct.
3. The process eventually comes to an end (termination).

Turing utilized a flow diagram with properties attached to edges, anticipating the later work of Floyd and Hoare by decades. As noted by Morris and Jones in their analysis of Turing's work [38], had Turing lived longer, the field of program proving might have developed much more rapidly, rather than requiring the ideas to be rediscovered in the late 1960s.

Reading Turing's paper now, it uses many of the terms that are common in formal methods today, such as "verification", "assertions", and even the "dashed" after states used in the Z notation:

> "In order to assist the checker, the programmer should make *assertions* about the various states that the machine can reach."
> "The checker has to *verify* that the [...] initial condition and the stopped condition agree with the claims that are made for the routine as a whole."
> "He has also to *verify* that each of the *assertions* ... is correct."
> "Finally the checker has to *verify* that the process comes to an end."

As is conventional in the Z notation nowadays, Turing notes that:

> "(i) a dashed letter indicates the value at the end of the process [...]
> (ii) an undashed letter represents the initial value of a quantity."

In 1951, Christopher Strachey wrote a letter to Alan Turing on his programming plans, developing on Turing's ideas and foreseeing future formal methods approaches to software specification and development:

> "[...] once the suitable notation is decided, all that would be necessary would be to type more or less ordinary mathematics and a special routine called, say, 'Programme' would convert this into the necessary instructions to make the machine carry out the operations indicated. This may sound rather Utopian, but I think it, or something like it, should be possible [ldots]"

But what of Turing's influence on program proving? Adruaan "Aad" van Wijngaarden (1916–1987), a Dutch mathematician and computer scientist, and an early advocate of a mathematical approach to computing, was at the Cambridge meeting where Turing presented his ideas, but that is no obvious influence on van Wijngaarden.

Robert Floyd rediscovered ideas similar to those of Turing, published in 1967 [20]. Tony Hoare developed these further, published in his classic 1969 paper presenting what has become known as "Hoare Logic" [28]. Had Turing lived longer, perhaps formal methods (in particular, program proving) would have developed more rapidly and with greater continuity, rather than being rediscovered. We explore these later developments in the next section.

2.2 The Evolution of Logic in Programming

More than a decade later after Turing, the field of program proving saw significant theoretical advancements. In 1967, Robert Floyd published "Assigning

Meaning to Programs" [20] and in 1969, Tony Hoare introduced his axiomatic basis for computer programming [28], which became know as "Hoare Logic". This approach, denoted by the triple $\{P\}C\{Q\}$, provides a mechanism to reason about program correctness using pre-conditions (P) and post-conditions (Q) for program code (C).

Despite these advances, a gap remained between theory and practice. Christopher Strachey, a pioneer in denotational semantics, observed that practical work is often "unsound and clumsy" due to a lack of understanding of fundamental design principles, while theoretical work is often "sterile" because it lacks contact with real computing [45]:

> "It has long been my personal view that the separation of practical and theoretical work is artificial and injurious. Much of the practical work done in computing, both in software and in hardware design, is unsound and clumsy because the people who do it have not any clear understanding of the fundamental design principles of their work. Most of the abstract mathematical and theoretical work is sterile because it has no point of contact with real computing."

3 From Mathematical Logic to Formal Methods

Consider a dictionary definition of "formal":

> **formal** /fm()l/ a. LME. [L formalis, f. forma: see FORM n., -AL.] 1 **a** Philos. Of or pertaining to the form or constitutive essence of a thing; essential. LME. **b** Pertaining to the specific form of an animal or plant. LME-L17. c Of or pertaining to the outward form, shape, appearance, arrangement, or external qualities of a thing. Formerly also (of knowledge), theoretical. M17. **d** *Logic. Concerned with the form, not the matter, of reasoning.* M19.

Of the four definitions of "formal" above (a–d), definition "d" from the 19th century is the closest to the meaning in the term "formal methods", concerning reasoning in logic.

Similarly, for the (abridged) dictionary definition of "method":

> **method** /methd/ n. LME. [L methodus f. Gk methodos pursuit of knowledge, mode of investigation, f. meta (see META-) + hodos way.] **I** Procedure for attaining an object. **1** ... **2** A mode of procedure; a (defined or systematic) way of doing a thing, esp. (w. specifying wd or wds) in accordance with a particular theory or as associated with a particular person. L16. ... **II** Systematic arrangement, order. **3** *The branch of logic that deals with the description and arrangement of arguments or propositions for the investigation or exposition of a truth.* M16. **4** Order in thinking or expressing thoughts; the orderly arrangement of ideas; gen. orderliness, regularity, or planning in doing anything. M16.

The third definition concerning logic from the 16th century is the closest to that meant in the term "formal methods".

As can be seen above, there is plenty of opportunity for the misunderstanding of the meaning of "formal methods" in a more general context.

One of the earliest books with "formal methods" in its title is a 1962 volume by the Dutch philosopher and logician, Evert Willem Beth (1908–1964) [5]. The full title is *Formal Methods: An Introduction to Symbolic Logic and to the Study of Effective Operations in Arithmetic and Logic.* Although this book is not about software, it does use the term "formal methods" with a meaning that is recognizable by the formal methods community of today.

The term "formal methods" was established in its computer science context by late 1970s, as the next more rigourous stage from structured design, establishing a mathematical basis. It involves formal specification and (optionally) proof, covering:

Validation: checking that the specification meets the requirements ("build the right thing"); and
Verification: checking that the implementation is correct with respect to a formal specification ("build it right").

It should be noted that the use of proof in a software engineering context is an outlier compared to most engineering disciplines. Engineers typically "calculate", for example, using mathematical formulae developed and "proved" previously (e.g., using Maxwell's equations).

There are a variety of ways to apply formal methods to computer-based systems, including:

Abstract Interpretation: approximating program behaviour to prove correctness or detect errors [18].
Model-Based Testing: generating test cases from a formal model [11,25].
Model Checking: exhaustively or symbolically verifying system behaviour against a formal specification [17].
Proof Assistants: tools for interactively constructing and verifying mathematical proofs (e.g., Isabelle/HOL [39]).
Refinement: systematically refining a high-level specification into a correct implementation (e.g., the B-Method [1]).
Static Analysis: analyzing program code meaning to detect errors or enforce constraints (e.g., as available in SPARK Ada [4]).
Verification: proving the correctness of a program using logical inference rules for reasoning [31].

There are also different levels at which formal methods can be used:

1. **Formal Specification:** Sometimes know as Formal Description Techniques (FDTs), such as Estelle, LOTOS (Language of Temporal Ordering Specification), SDL (Specification and Description Language) [48], and the Z notation [8,44].
   - Applicable for the system requirements;

  - Formal analysis and proofs are optional;
  - Can be used to aid testing;
  - Most cost-effective.
2. **Formal Verification:** VDM [33] and the B-Method [1] enable this approach.
  - The implemented program is produced in a more formal way;
  - Uses proof or refinement based on a formal specification;
  - This is significantly more costly than just using formal specification.
3. **Theorem Proving:** Isabelle/HOL [39], Lean [19], and PVS (Prototype Verification System) [40] are examples of theorem provers, sometimes also called proof assistants.
  - This involves the use of a theorem prover tool;
  - Allows formal machine-checked proofs;
  - A proof of the entire system is possible, but scaling is difficult;
  - The approach can be very expensive and hard.

The IEEE previously defined formal methods as follows:

1. A specification written and approved in accordance with established standards;
2. A specification written in a formal notation, often for use in proof of correctness.

The second definition above aligns with the meaning understood by the formal methods community, but the first could easily cause confusion in discussion with those not in this community. Further issues concerning formal methods misconceptions are discussed in the next section.

4 Myths and Misconceptions

By the 1990s, formal methods had established a presence but were surrounded by misconceptions regarding their difficulty and utility. In 1990, Anthony Hall published the "Seven Myths of Formal Methods" [24], attempting to correct the record. Five years later, Bowen and Hinchey added seven more [14].

4.1 Seven Myths of Formal Methods

In 1990, Anthony Hall proposed seven "myths" of formal methods, commonly held beliefs about the approach that are inaccurate in practice [24]:

1. **Perfection:** The belief that formal methods can guarantee software is perfect. (Fact: They increase confidence but do not eliminate all errors.)
2. **Proving:** The belief that they are all about program proving. (Fact: Specification is often more valuable than full proof.)
3. **Utility:** The belief that they are only useful for safety-critical systems. (Fact: They have been used in standard large systems like the IBM CICS transaction processing.)

4. **Mathematical Skills:** The belief that they require highly trained mathematicians. (Fact: Engineers can learn the necessary notations.)
5. **Cost:** The belief that they increase development cost. (Fact: Finding errors early reduces total lifecycle costs.)
6. **Users:** The belief that they are unacceptable to users. (Fact: They can help clarify requirements for users.)
7. **Scalability:** The belief that they are not used on real, large-scale software. (Fact: Various industrial examples exist.)

4.2 Seven More Myths of Formal Methods

Further myths were proposed in 1995 [14], including the ideas that formal methods delay the development process, lack tool support, replace traditional engineering design, only apply to software, or are simply not required. A persistent fallacy was the "all or nothing" approach – the belief that one must be dogmatic. In reality, a related paper on the "Ten Commandments of Formal Methods" [13] suggests a pragmatic approach. For example, "Thou shalt formalize but not over-formalize" and "Thou shalt guestimate costs."

4.3 Provably Correct Systems

During the 1990s, two European collaborative projects and a Working Group with a larger set of members investigated "Provably Correct Systems" ("ProCoS") [12]. The idea, influenced by the CLInc "Stack" of formally linked levels of abstraction, was to connect these abstract levels using a formal approach. The levels included: Requirements; Specification; Design; Programming; Compilation; Hardware. The investigation was based on the Occam programming language and the Transputer processor.

As is often the case with research, an unexpected result of the project was the Duration Calculus (DC), suited to specifying requirements involving timing in a succinct way. Later, the project also led to the 1998 book *Unifying Theories of Programming* (UTP) [29], connecting various formal semantic descriptions of programming languages. Both DC and UTP led to communities of researchers, dedicated conferences, etc.

When using various abstract levels for a system, there is little point unless there is a significant difference in the size of the various descriptions. For example:

- 15k lines of (informal) requirements
- 150k lines of (formal) specification
- 1.5 million lines of (formal refinement) design description
- 15 million lines of (formal) high-level program code
- 150 million machine instructions of low-level object code
- 1.5 billion transistors in digital hardware

At the lower levels, from the program code onwards, the description is always formal, even if the semantics are complex. The process of connecting levels can be automated (e.g., a compiler from program code to object code). At the higher levels, the introduction of formality is more flexible. In many cases, it is delayed until the production of program code. In a formal approach, it is introduced earlier, for example, at the specification level. This enables the possibility of formal refinement or at least a much more rigourous approach to testing. At any level, errors may be discovered. This may mean returning to modify higher levels of description. This is a much cheaper and faster process if it can be done at the higher levels. Introducing formality at these levels means that more errors are likely to be discovered earlier, potentially resulting in cost savings and higher reliability overall.

4.4 Case Studies

In the 1995 book *Applications of Formal Methods*, a number of case studies using formal methods were presented using different formal methods [26]; for example: Tektronix (Z notation [44]) – oscilloscopes; STV algorithm (VDM [33]) – voting; IBM CICS (B-Method [1]) – transaction processing; AAMP5 microprocessor (PVS [40]) – hardware; GEC Alsthom (B-Method) – railway software; A300/340 (Z notation) – airplane software. A follow-on book in 1999 [27] presented further examples: Motorola CAP DSP (ACL2); Radiation Therapy Machine (Z notation); ATC system (VDM); Railways (Prover Technology). Here we avoid introducing the formal methods used in detail, but provide key references for the various notations and approaches. An introduction to Z, VDM, Larch, temporal logic, CSP (Communicating Sequential Processes), and transition axioms was published in 1990 [50].

A 2001 book [21] presented the process of developing a formal specification for a unified case study by explicitly showing the questions raised when developing such a specification using a wide selection of different formal methods: Z notation [44], SAZ, B-Method [1], OMT, Action Systems, UML, VHDL, Estelle, SDL, E-LOTOS [16], JSD, CASL, Coq, and Petri Nets. This contrasts with many presentations where only the final specification of a system is provided, with little information on how this was derived. Further formal methods case study books have been published [7,23].

Formal methods have found their specific niche in the development of systems where safety or security is critical. This has sometimes been driven by the recommendation or even mandating of the use of formal methods in systems at the most critical levels in standards [15], often where human lives are at risk in the case of failure. In the next section, we present a significant industrial project providing critical national infrastructure that took a formal methods approach to minimise errors in the system.

5 Industrial Application: The NATS Case Study

To demonstrate the viability of formal methods in a critical industrial setting, we examine the case of National Air Traffic Services (NATS) in the United

Kingdom. NATS manages some of the busiest and most complex airspace in the world, handling approximately 2.5 million flights per year (pre-COVID).

5.1 iFACTS: Interim Future Area Control Tools Support

NATS pioneered the development of advanced air traffic control tools through the iFACTS (Interim Future Area Control Tools Support) project [49]. This system introduced electronic flight strips to replace paper strips and provided trajectory tools for prediction, deviation alerts, and conflict detection.

The development of iFACTS is a good example of successful formal methods application:

- **Specification:** The functional specification was written in the **Z notation** [44].
- **Algorithm Specification:** Complex mathematical algorithms were specified using Mathematica [51].
- **Implementation:** The critical code was implemented in **SPARK Ada**, an annotated subset of the Ada programming language that supports static verification [4].
- **Verification:** The project utilized the SPARK Examiner for rigourous checking, though full formal partial correctness proofs were not considered cost-effective; reliance was placed on Run-Time Exception (RTE) proofs.

5.2 Training and Tooling at NATS

A common barrier to entry is education. The experience on the iFACTS project demonstrated that training engineers is not an insurmountable barrier.

- **Z Training:** "Z Reader" training took only 3 days, with fluency achieved after one week on the job. "Z Writer" training took 3 days, with fluency after 3 months.
- **SPARK Training:** 57 people were trained. It was found that all SPARK coders were also effective Z readers.

Crucially, the tooling was adapted to the workforce. The Z specifications were written in Microsoft Word using add-ins, allowing engineers to work within a familiar environment while supporting type-checking (via *fuzz*) and cross-referencing.

5.3 Results

The iFACTS system has been in operation for airspace over England and Wales since 2011. It has enabled up to a 40% capacity increase in some sectors, and allows for up to 18 min of trajectory prediction. The project demonstrates that formal methods can be integrated into the full lifecycle – from requirements to code – without requiring every engineer to be a PhD mathematician.

6 The "Whither": Formal Methods and AI

As we look to the future (2026 and beyond), the landscape of formal methods has changed, with many formal methods now used less that they were. For example, the practical restriction of the Z notation [8] to use for formal specification with limited tools lead to the development of the B-Method [1] and then Event-B [2], with better tool support for refinement and program verification.

There is now the potential for formal methods to converge with the recent rapid advancements in Artificial Intelligence (AI). There has been an interest in the interplay of formal methods and AI for some time [41]. Discussions have included the applicability of formal methods to machine learning [34]. There are possibilities of reducing hallucination in Large Language Models LLMs) using iterative prompting guided by formal methods [32]. It may be that formal methods can be used with LLMs to produce trustworthy AI agents [53]. The recent development of Generative AI (GenAI) has created significant opportunities for further synergy.

6.1 Possible Convergence

Traditionally, there has been a dichotomy:

- **Formal Methods:** Rigorous, "correct by construction", based on precise language and proof assistants.
- **Machine Learning/AI:** Based on large learned models, statistical probability, and often "unreliable" or "hallucinating" outputs.

However, we are seeing the emergence of hybrid approaches. Just as deep neural networks have revolutionized pattern recognition, AI is now being applied to mathematical discovery and program proof [3,46].

6.2 From "Vibe Coding" to "Vibe Proving"

Recent research highlights the potential for AI to guide search in theorem proving. For example, systems like *Lean* (a proof assistant and associated functional programming language [19]) are being integrated with AI tools to suggest outline proofs, which are then rigourously checked by the formal system [30,36]. This addresses the "unreliability" of LLMs by using the formal system as a verifier of the AI's "intuition".

New concepts have emerged and may emerge:

- **Vibe Coding:** A colloquial term for AI-generated code that "feels" right but requires verification.
- **Vibe Proving:** Perhaps using AI to bridge gaps in formal proofs.

Publications in *Nature* regarding mathematical discoveries from program search [42] and the ideas of the Fields Medalist Terence Tao [46] suggest that we are entering a new and exciting era where AI fills in the steps of a proof, easing the use of formal verification in an interactive approach to proving both mathematics in general and programs in particular.

6.3 A New "AI Spring" for Formal Methods?

Just as AI experienced "winters" before its current boom, formal methods have seen cycles of hype and disillusionment. The integration with GenAI may trigger a "Formal Methods Spring". Tools like *DeepSeekMath* [43] and *LeanProgress* [30] indicate that the barrier to entry for formal proofs is lowering. Maybe we will see a unification where engineers calculate and prove properties of software with the same ease that civil engineers calculate loads, aided by intelligent assistants.

7 Conclusion

Formal methods have travelled a long path from Turing's manual checking of routines to industrial-scale automated verification in air traffic control. The myths that they are too difficult or too costly have been debunked by projects like iFACTS, which demonstrate that, with appropriate tooling and training, formal methods are viable and valuable.

The future lies in the symbiotic relationship between formal rigour and artificial intelligence. By leveraging AI to handle the tedious aspects of proof and specification, while retaining the mathematical certainty of formal methods for verification, it should be possible to achieve a level of software reliability previously thought impossible. As Théophile Gautier (1811–1872) wrote on art in 1856 [22]:

> Oui, l'œuvre sort plus belle
> D'une forme au travail
> Rebelle,
> Vers, marbre, onyx, émail.
> [Yes, the work comes out more beautiful from a material that resists the process, verse, marble, onyx, or enamel.]

In the context of this paper, software is that resistant material, and formal methods, potentially augmented by AI in the future, provide the chisel to shape it.

Acknowledgement. This paper is dedicated to Egon Börger on the occasion of his 80th birthday. I have known Egon since the 1990s, when he visited the Programming Research Group at Oxford University and presented his ideas on Abstract State Machines (ASM) [6,9,10]. ASM is a state-based approach to formal methods, like the B-Method [1] and the Z notation [8,44]. These three approaches have inspired the ABZ conference series, which continues to this day. This paper was developed from a talk delivered to the BCS-FACS Specialist Group as the annual 2025 Peter Landin Semantics Seminar in London [37]. Finally, thank you for the anonymous review comments, which were used to improve this final version of the paper.

References

1. Abrial, J.-R.: The B-Book: Assigning Programs to Meanings, Cambridge University Press (1996)
2. Abrial, J.-R.: Modeling in Event-B: System and Software Engineering, Cambridge University Press (2010)
3. Avigad, J.: Mathematics in the Age of AI. LMS/BCS-FACS Seminar, London Mathematical Society (2025). https://www.lms.ac.uk/events/lms-bcs-facs-seminar-jeremy-avigad
4. Barnes, J.: Spark: The Proven Approach to High Integrity Software. Altran Praxis, London (2012)
5. Beth, E.W.: Formal Methods: An Introduction to Symbolic Logic and to the Study of Effective Operations in Arithmetic and Logic, D. Reidel Publishing Company/Dordrecht-Holland (1962)
6. Börger, E., Stärk, R.: Abstract State Machines: A Method for High-Level System Design and Analysis, Springer (2003). https://doi.org/10.1007/978-3-642-18216-7
7. Boulanger, J.-L. (ed.): Formal Methods: Industrial Use from Model to the Code. Wiley, ISTE (2012)
8. Bowen, J.P.: The Z Notation: Whence the Cause and Whither the Course? In: Liu, Z., Zhang, Z. (eds.) SETSS 2014. LNCS, vol. 9506, pp. 103–151. Springer, Cham (2016). https://doi.org/10.1007/978-3-319-29628-9_3
9. Bowen, J.P.: Egon Börger and Alexander Raschke: Modeling companion for software practitioners. Formal Aspects Comput. **30**(6), 761–762 (2018). https://doi.org/10.1007/s00165-018-0472-4
10. Bowen, J.P.: Communities and Ancestors Associated with Egon Börger and ASM. In: Raschke, A., Riccobene, E., Schewe, K.-D. (eds.) Logic, Computation and Rigorous Methods. LNCS, vol. 12750, pp. 96–120. Springer, Cham (2021). https://doi.org/10.1007/978-3-030-76020-5_6
11. Bowen, J.P., Bogdanov, K., Clark, J.A., Harman, M., Hierons, R.M., Krause, P.: FORTEST: formal methods and testing. In: Proceedings of the 26th Annual International Computer Software and Applications (COMPSAC 2002). IEEE (2002). https://doi.org/10.1109/CMPSAC.2002.1044538
12. Bowen, J.P., et al.: Experiences from the European ProCoS Projects: Provably Correct Systems. Formal Aspects Comput. (2026). https://doi.org/10.1145/3803555
13. Bowen, J.P., Hinchey, M.G.: Ten commandments of formal methods. Computer **28**(4), 56–63 (1995). https://doi.org/10.1109/2.375178
14. Bowen, J.P., Hinchey, M.G.: Seven more myths of formal methods. IEEE Softw. **12**(4), 34–41 (1995). https://doi.org/10.1109/52.391826
15. Bowen, J.P., Stavridou, V.: Safety-critical systems, formal methods and standards. Softw. Eng. J. **8**(4), 189–209 (1993). https://doi.org/10.1049/sej.1993.0025
16. Clark, R.G., Moreira, A.M.: Use of E-LOTOS in adding formality to UML. J. Univ. Comput. Sci. **6**(11), 1071–1087 (2000). https://doi.org/10.3217/jucs-006-11-1071
17. Clarke, E.M.: Model checking. In: Ramesh, S., Sivakumar, G. (eds.) FSTTCS 1997. LNCS, vol. 1346, pp. 54–56. Springer, Heidelberg (1997). https://doi.org/10.1007/BFb0058022
18. Cousot, P.: Abstract interpretation. ACM Comput. Surv. (CSUR) **28**(2), 324–328 (1996). https://doi.org/10.1145/234528.234740
19. Moura, L., Ullrich, S.: The Lean 4 Theorem Prover and Programming Language. In: Platzer, A., Sutcliffe, G. (eds.) CADE 2021. LNCS (LNAI), vol. 12699, pp. 625–635. Springer, Cham (2021). https://doi.org/10.1007/978-3-030-79876-5_37

20. Floyd, R.W.: Assigning meaning to programs. In: Scharts, S.T. (ed.) Proceedings of Symposia in Applied Mathematics 19. Mathematical Aspects of Computer Science. American Mathematical Society, Providence (1967). https://doi.org/10.1007/978-94-011-1793-7_4 (republished in 1993)
21. Frappier, M., Habrias, H. (eds.): Software Specification Methods: An Overview Using a Case Study. FACIT. Springer, London (2001)
22. Gautier, T.: L'Art Moderne. Paris: M. Lévy Frères (1856). https://archive.org/details/lartmodernetho00gautuoft
23. Gnesi, S., Margaria, T.: Formal Methods for Industrial Critical Systems: A Survey of Applications. IEEE Computer Society Press, Wiley (2012)
24. Hall, J.A.: Seven myths of formal methods. IEEE Softw. **7**(5), 11–19 (1990). https://doi.org/10.1109/52.57887
25. Hierons, R.M., Bowen, J.P., Harman, M. (eds.): Formal Methods and Testing. LNCS, vol. 4949. Springer, Heidelberg (2008). https://doi.org/10.1007/978-3-540-78917-8
26. Hinchey, M.G., Bowen, J.P. (eds.): Applications of Formal Methods. Series in Computer Science. Hemel Hempstead: Prentice Hall (1995)
27. Hinchey, M.G., Bowen, J.P. (eds.): Industrial-Strength Formal Methods in Practice. FACIT. Springer, London (1999)
28. Hoare, C.A.R.: An axiomatic basis for computer programming. Commun. ACM **12**(10), 576–580 (1969). https://doi.org/10.1145/363235.363259
29. Hoare, C.A.R., He, J.: Unifying Theories of Programming. Series in Computer Science. Prentice Hall, Hemel Hempstead (1998)
30. Huang, S., et al.: LeanProgress: Guiding Search for Neural Theorem Proving via Proof Progress Prediction. arXiv (2025). https://doi.org/10.48550/arXiv.2502.17925
31. Jackson, M.: What can we expect from program verification? Computer **39**(10), 65–71 (2006). https://doi.org/10.1109/MC.2006.363
32. Jha, S., Jha, S.K., Lincoln, P., Bastian, N.D., Velasquez, A., Neema, S.: Dehallucinating large language models using formal methods guided iterative prompting. In: Proceedings of the 2023 IEEE International Conference on Assured Autonomy (ICAA), pp. 149–152. IEEE (2023). https://doi.org/10.1109/ICAA58325.2023.00029
33. Jones, C.B.: Systematic Software Development Using VDM. Series in Computer Science. Prentice Hall, Hemel Hempstead (1990)
34. Krichen, M., Mihoub, A., Alzahrani, M.Y., Adoni, W.Y.H., Nahhal, T.: Are formal methods applicable to machine learning and Artificial Intelligence? In: Proceedings of the 2nd International Conference of Smart Systems and Emerging Technologies (SMARTTECH), pp. 48–53. IEEE (2022). https://doi.org/10.1109/SMARTTECH54121.2022.00025
35. Liu, Z., Woodcock, J., Bowen, J.P.: From logic to programming. In: Bowen, J.P., Gomes, C., Liu, Z. (eds.) SETSS 2024. LNCS, vol. 15584, pp. 7–67. Springer, Singapore (2024). https://doi.org/10.1007/978-981-96-4656-2_2
36. Lu, J., et al.: Lean Finder: Semantic Search for Mathlib That Understands User Intents. arXiv (2025). https://doi.org/10.48550/arXiv.2510.15940
37. Monahan, B., Lines, K.: BCS FACS 2025 Landin Lecture - formal methods: whence and whither? FACS FACTS 2026(1), 90–95 (2026). https://www.bcs.org/media/veppnllv/facs-jan26.pdf#page=90
38. Morris, F.L., Jones, C.B.: An early program proof by Alan Turing. IEEE Ann. Hist. Comput. **6**(2), 139–143 (1984). https://doi.org/10.1109/MAHC.1984.10017

39. Nipkow, T., Wenzel, M., Paulson, L.C. (eds.): Isabelle/HOL. LNCS, vol. 2283. Springer, Heidelberg (2002). https://doi.org/10.1007/3-540-45949-9
40. Owre, S., Rushby, J.M., Shankar, N.: PVS: A prototype verification system. In: Kapur, D. (ed.) CADE 1992. LNCS, vol. 607, pp. 748–752. Springer, Heidelberg (1992). https://doi.org/10.1007/3-540-55602-8_217
41. Ramsay, A.: Formal Methods in Artificial Intelligence 6, (1988) Cambridge University Press
42. Romera-Paredes, B., et al.: Mathematical discoveries from program search and large language models. Nature **625**, 468–475 (2024). https://doi.org/10.1038/s41586-023-06924-6
43. Shao, Z., et al.: DeepSeekMath-V2: Towards Self-Verifiable Mathematical Reasoning. arXiv (2025). https://doi.org/10.48550/arXiv.2511.22570
44. Spivey, J.M.: The Z Reference Manual. Series in Computer Science, 2nd edn. Prentice Hall, Hemel Hempstead (1992)
45. Strachey, C.: The Strachey's Philosophy. Department of Computer Science, University of Oxford. https://www.cs.ox.ac.uk/activities/concurrency/courses/stracheys.html. Accessed 23 Dec 2025
46. Tao, T.: The Potential for AI in Science and Mathematics. Oxford Mathematics Public Lectures, Science Museum, London (2024). https://www.maths.ox.ac.uk/node/68243
47. Turing, A.M.: Checking a large routine. In: Report of a Conference on High Speed Automatic Calculating Machines, Cambridge University Mathematical Laboratory, pp. 67–69 (1949). https://turingarchive.kings.cam.ac.uk/checking-large-routine
48. Turner, K.J. (ed.): Using Formal Description Techniques: An Introduction to Estelle. Wiley, LOTOS and SDL. Wiley, New York (1993)
49. White, N.: The Use of Formal Methods on the iFACTS ATC project. AdaCore (2010). https://www.youtube.com/watch?v=IQMWVqQfm5A. Accessed 24 Dec 2025
50. Wing, J.M.: A specifier's introduction to formal methods. Computer **23**(9), 8–22 (1990). https://doi.org/10.1109/2.58215
51. Wolfram, S.: The Mathematica Book, 5th edn, Wolfram Media (2003)
52. Woodcock, J., Larsen, P.G., Bicarregui, J., Fitzgerald, J.: Formal methods: practice and experience. ACM Comput. Surv. (CSUR) **41**(4), 1–36 (2009). https://doi.org/10.1145/1592434.1592436
53. Zhang, Y., Cai, Y., Zuo, X., Luan, X., et al.: The fusion of Large Language Models and formal methods for trustworthy AI agents: a roadmap. arXiv (2024). https://doi.org/10.48550/arXiv.2412.06512

A Bibliometric Analysis of the Abstract State Machine Research Production and Community over the Years

Andrea Bombarda, Silvia Bonfanti, Angelo Gargantini(✉), and Nico Pellegrinelli

University of Bergamo, Bergamo, Italy
{andrea.bombarda,silvia.bonfanti,angelo.gargantini, nico.pellegrinelli}@unibg.it

Abstract. Abstract State Machines (ASMs) constitute a well-established formal method for system specification and modeling, with applications spanning software engineering, hardware design, and semantics. Despite their long-standing theoretical foundations and practical use, a systematic assessment of the current status and impact of ASMs within the scientific community remains limited. This paper presents a bibliometric study aimed at evaluating the evolution, visibility, and influence of the ASM formalism over time. Using data extracted from major scientific publication databases, we analyze publication trends, citation patterns, core venues, and collaboration networks related to ASM research. Quantitative indicators such as citation counts, h-index values, and co-authorship structures are employed to identify key contributions, influential authors, and emerging research directions. The results provide an evidence-based perspective on the maturity and dissemination of ASMs, highlighting periods of growth, stabilization, and thematic shifts. By demonstrating how bibliometric information can be used to assess the status of a formal method, this study contributes both to the understanding of ASMs and to the broader methodological discussion on evaluating research impact in formal methods.

Keywords: Abstract State Machines · bibliometric analysis

1 Introduction

Abstract State Machines (ASMs) have played a central role in the landscape of formal methods for more than three decades. Originally introduced as a mathematically precise yet practically oriented framework for system specification and modeling, ASMs have been applied to a wide range of domains, including software engineering, hardware design, programming language semantics, and the formalization of standards. Their distinguishing feature lies in the combination of rigorous formal foundations with a high level of abstraction, enabling faithful and executable models of complex systems. Since their introduction, ASMs

A. Raschke et al. (Eds.): Egon Börger Festschrift, LNCS 16580, pp. 30–46, 2026.
https://doi.org/10.1007/978-3-032-24494-9_3

have been the subject of extensive theoretical development and numerous applications in both academic and industrial contexts. The formalism has evolved through refinements of its semantic foundations, extensions to support refinement and verification, and integrations with tools and methodologies for model checking, testing, and validation. As a result, ASMs have contributed to shaping the broader discourse on executable specifications and the role of formal models in system development.

Despite this long-standing presence and continued use, a comprehensive, data-driven assessment of the evolution and impact of ASM research within the scientific community is still lacking. There exist papers, like [10] that focus more on personal history and contributions, so a general view of the ASM is outside of their scope. On the other hand, existing surveys and overviews typically focus on conceptual developments, applications, or specific subfields, but do not systematically analyze publication dynamics, citation behavior, or collaboration patterns over time. Such an analysis is increasingly relevant, as bibliometric methods have become a recognized means of studying the maturity, visibility, and influence of research areas across disciplines, including computer science and formal methods.

This paper addresses this gap by presenting a bibliometric study of the ASM literature. By analyzing data extracted from major scientific publication databases, we investigate publication trends, citation patterns, core venues, the most frequently used keywords, and co-authorship networks associated with ASM research. Quantitative indicators such as citation counts, h-index values, and collaboration structures are used to identify influential contributions, leading authors, and thematic developments. The goal is not to evaluate individual works in isolation, but rather to provide an aggregated, evidence-based perspective on how the ASM formalism has evolved and disseminated within the research community, starting from Egon Börger's work.

The remainder of this paper is structured as follows. Section 2 describes the general process we have adopted to conduct our bibliometrics analysis. Section 3 reports the queries we used, while Sect. 4 discusses how we cleaned the obtained datasets. Section 5 represents the core contribution of this work and reports the results of our analysis. Section 6 discusses on potential limitations and, finally, Sect. 7 concludes the paper.

2 Process

In this section, we briefly present the process we have followed to perform our bibliometrics analysis. When defining our process, we have tried to follow the Leiden Manifesto [20], which proposed ten principles for the measurement of research performance. These include that the process should be systematic, transparent, and aligned with the *purpose* of the evaluation (mapping a field, assessing impact, informing funding, etc.). Although our current endeavor cannot be considered a proper Systematic Literature Review (SLR), we have followed some standard guidelines for SLR [22].

1. **Clarify the purpose and scope.** Before collecting any data, we tried to explicit the goals of this research. We have listed a set of reasonable objectives of the bibliometric analysis:
   - *Temporal analysis*, to identify publication trends over the years;
   - *Identify influential authors, papers, institutions, countries, or venues.* For instance, we are interested to evaluate Egon's direct contribution in the field;
   - *By means of keywords*, to see if it is possible to detect emerging topics or declining themes.

   In order to pursue these goals, we have defined the scope by strictly limiting our research area to that of the Abstract State Machines (no other methods), with a temporal scope starting from its inception (we fixed 1993, the date of the Lipari guide [17]) to the current time, for papers written in English and published only in well-recognized international workshops, conferences, and journals.
2. **Choose appropriate data sources.** Different databases emphasize different disciplines and outputs. We initially considered the following databases: **Web of Science (WoS)**[1], which is very curated and has strong citation data, **Scopus**[2], which offers a broader coverage and more information about the indexed papers, **Google Scholar**[3], which is very broad but opaque and noisy (thus, usually not ideal for formal evaluation), **Lens**[4], which provides comprehensive and integrated coverage of scholarly publications and patents, and finally **ACM digital library**[5] and **IEEE Xplore digital library**[6], which overlapped significantly with the content of previously considered databases. At the end, by inspecting the results provided by each considered source, we decided to use only WoS, Scopus, and Lens.
3. **Construct and validate the search strategy.** During this step, we have built the queries. Possible queries may, for example, search in titles, abstracts, and keywords suitable terms. During this step, one should also use controlled vocabularies where available, include synonyms, acronyms and exclude irrelevant homonyms. Thus, to improve the paper detection rate, we have also checked spelling invariants and grammatical variants (like "Abstract State Machines" and the singular "Abstract State Machine"). To validate the queries, one should manually inspect a sample of retrieved records to be sure that the "gold standard" papers are included (*recall*), and also to check that irrelevant papers are filtered out (*precision*). This process is highly iterative, and in Sect. 3 we explain how we have carried out this step.
4. **Clean and normalize the data.** Since raw bibliometric data may always contain inconsistencies, we have introduced a step in which we try to clean

[1] https://www.webofscience.com/wos/.
[2] https://www.scopus.com/.
[3] https://scholar.google.com/.
[4] https://www.lens.org/.
[5] https://dl.acm.org/.
[6] https://ieeexplore.ieee.org/.

and normalize the data (e.g., checking author's name and removing duplicates). This step is explained in Sect. 4.

5. **Select appropriate bibliometric indicators and tools.** During this phase, we have identified interesting bibliometric indicators and search for tools supporting their computation. As expected, we focused on some core descriptive indicators (e.g., publication counts, growth trends, and citation counts). We were also interested in analyzing relational indicators (e.g., countries, co-authorships, and co-citations networks).
   The choice of indicators is highly dependent on the tools one can use to compute them. After evaluating several tools, we decided to use only Bibliometrix [4], an R tool which provides a comprehensive and reproducible framework for quantitative analysis of scientific literature, including performance indicators, science mapping, and network analysis.
6. **Interpret results with domain expertise.** During this step, we have executed our analysis scripts on the results obtained thanks to the execution of the queries against the identified datasets. Section 5 reports our results and our interpretation, providing a critical discussion. We identify publication and citation patterns, as well as relevant authors and countries.
7. **Address limitations and biases explicitly.** During this step, it is important to identify possible limitations and biases of the bibliometric study. Typical issues may be related with the database coverage, language and regional bias, or self-citation effects. Section 6 explicitly discusses on these limitations.
8. **Report results transparently.** To improve transparency and reproducibility, we provide the queries we used for each database in Sect. 3. Additionally, the results of our queries as well as any evaluation script are available online at https://github.com/asmeta/bibliometrics_for_asms.

3 Construct and Validate the Search Strategy

Constructing and validating a bibliometric search strategy begins with a clear conceptual definition of the research field, specifying its core topics, methods, and boundaries before any keywords are selected. In our case it was clear from the objectives and scope that we were looking for publications directly linked to Abstract State Machines. On this basis, a small set of seed publications (and authors)—such as those that are highly cited reviews or foundational papers—is assembled to represent the core of the field. Terminology is then systematically extracted from the titles, abstracts, and keywords of these seed publications in order to identify relevant concepts, synonyms, acronyms, and historical variants. In our case, the term "Abstract State Machine" (or "Machines") is common among all the publications of interest. However, the term "evolving algebras" has also been used in the past to refer to the same formalism. For instance, this term was used in [11], one of the first work written by Egon in 1991 about application of ASMs. Thus, we decided to run some preliminary search through the three selected publication databases. The results are reported in Table 1.

By briefly analyzing the results, we have found that query 1 to 4 were increasingly inclusive, but using a single dataset (e.g., Scopus) was not enough as some

Table 1. Number of documents for each query type.

		N. of documents		
Q	Query	Scopus	WoS	Lens
1	“abstract” “state” “machines” in Title	248	160	415
2	“abstract state machines” in Title	241	160	395
3	“abstract state machines” in (author) Keywords	663	208	47
4	“abstract state machines” in Abstract	733	296	719
5	“abstract state machines” in Title, Abstract, Keywords	851	401	911
6	“abstract state machines” in All fields	2810	602	1710
7	“evolving algebras” in Title	18	6	49
8	“evolving algebras” in Keywords	19	3	1
9	“evolving algebras” in Abstract	54	19	87
10	“evolving algebras” in Title, Abstract, Keywords	60	26	113
11	“evolving algebras” in All fields	781	26	247

foundational papers we knew were missing. For instance, Egon’s fundamental book [9] is not indexed by Scopus nor by WoS. However, we found that query 4 added too many out of scope papers. To be as (reasonably) inclusive as possible, we decided to consider three dataset (i.e., Scopus, Lens, and WoS). Instead, we noticed that query 5 and 6 were too broad and this would have required a lot of effort to exclude many papers in other ways, e.g., by manual inspection. For what concerns the term “evolving algebras”, we decided to adopt stricter queries (i.e., query 7 and 8) since we found that sometimes the term “evolving algebra attenuation” is used in other contexts.

Once we selected the queries to be used, we combined them into a unique query using OR/AND operators. More specifically, at the end, we decided to combine the queries in the following way: `Q2 OR Q3 OR Q7 OR Q8`

The disjunction of the queries is implemented differently across the three databases, as summarized in Table 2, which also reports the number of retrieved documents.

4 Clean and Normalize the Data

In this section, we report the process we have followed to clean and normalize the papers subject of our analysis.

First, thanks to the Bibliometrix library and an R script (available in our GitHub repository), we have merged all datasets obtained by WoS, Scopus, and Lens. During this process, we removed all entries without authors and all duplicates. To perform duplicate detection and ensure the consistency of the process, we also removed all entries without DOI. Finally, we manually removed out of scope papers.

Table 2. Search queries and results across different repositories

Repository	Executed Query	Documents Retrieved
Scopus	`(TITLE (''abstract state machines'') OR KEY (''abstract state machines'') OR TITLE (''evolving algebras'') OR KEY (''evolving algebras'')) AND PUBYEAR > 1993`	732
Web of Science (WoS)	`(((TI=(''abstract state machines'')) OR AK=(''abstract state machines'')) OR TI=(''evolving algebras'')) OR AK=(''evolving algebras'')) AND PY=(1993--2026)`	241
Lens	`(Title:(''abstract state machines'') OR Keyword:(''abstract state machines'') OR Title:(''evolving algebras'') OR Keyword:(''evolving algebras'')) AND Filters: Year Published=(1993--) AND Publication Type=(journal article, book, book chapter, conference proceedings article, conference proceedings)`	461

At the end of this cleaning and normalization process, we obtained 729 papers and we used them for our analysis.

5 Results

In this section, we present the results of our analysis and we provide our interpretation.

5.1 Documents

Types of Paper. Figure 1 illustrates the distribution of publication types within the curated dataset. Conference papers constitute the largest share, accounting for 340 publications, followed by journal articles with 197 entries. Books and book chapters are also well represented, each contributing 27 publications. In contrast, reviews (6 papers) and editorials (3 papers) appear only marginally. This distribution highlights a strong prevalence of peer-reviewed research outputs disseminated through conferences and journals, with a smaller but non-negligible contribution from long-form scholarly works.

This pattern reflects the typical dissemination practices of the formal methods community, where conferences play a central role in presenting novel theoretical results, methodological advances, and tool developments. The substantial number of journal articles indicates that a significant portion of ASM research has undergone further consolidation and maturation, often extending earlier conference contributions into more comprehensive studies. The presence of books and book chapters suggests an additional emphasis on foundational work, tutorials, and integrative perspectives, which are particularly important for a formalism such as Abstract State Machines that combines theory, methodology, and application. Notable examples of books which defined the basis of the ASM formalism are those contributed by Egon Börger, such as [9,23].

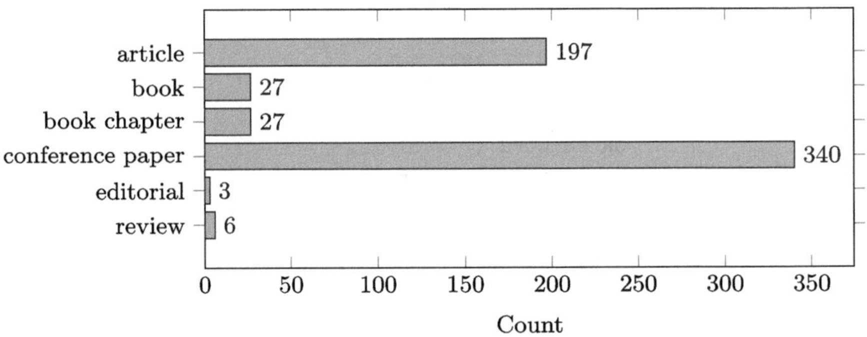

Fig. 1. Publication types.

Paper Citations. Figure 2 reports the ten most cited publications in the ASM corpus, ranked by total citation counts. The distribution shows a clear concentration of impact around a small set of foundational works, with citation values ranging from just over one hundred to nearly six hundred citations. This pattern is typical of mature research fields, where a limited number of seminal contributions establish core concepts, terminology, and methodological frameworks that continue to be referenced over long periods. The presence of both journal articles and books among the most cited works further indicates that ASM research has exerted influence through multiple dissemination channels, including archival venues and monographic treatments. Notably, three of the top-ten cited publications are authored or co-authored by Egon Börger [8,9,23], including the widely cited book [9] and key methodological paper on ASM refinement [8], highlighting his central role in shaping both the theoretical foundations and the practical adoption of the formalism. The prominence of these works in the citation ranking reflects not only their historical importance but also their continued relevance as reference points for subsequent research in the ASM community.

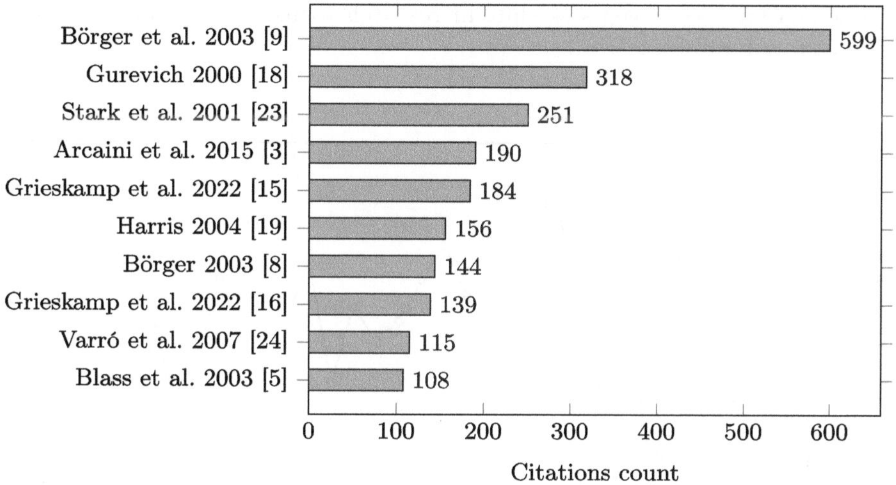

Fig. 2. Top 10 cited papers.

Annual Scientific Production. One interesting aspect, when analyzing the spreading of the use of ASMs, is the global scientific production over the years. The graph in Fig. 3 reports the number of papers published every year from 1993 to 2026. Here it is a plausible interpretation of the graph:

Early period (1993–1996): Scientific output is very low and fairly stable, with only a handful of papers published each year. This suggests the field was either emerging or had limited research activity. During these years Egon Börger started investigating on the ASM formalism while Yuri Gurevich had just published the Lipari Guide [17]. During this period, ASMs were referred to as *evolving algebras.*

Growth phase (1997–2000): There is a noticeable increase in publications, rising from around 10 papers per year to a first major peak around 2000 with around 40 papers. This indicates growing interest and expansion of research in the field.

Peak productivity (2001–2005): The number of papers fluctuates but remains high, culminating in a clear maximum around 2005, where annual production reaches its highest level (over 50 papers). This appears to be the most active and influential period for the field. It is, indeed, the period when Egon contributed its key papers on ASMs [9] and on their refinement [8]. This peak productivity demonstrates the strong impact of Egon Börger in the development of the ASM theory and adoption.

Gradual decline and stabilization (2006–2018): After the peak, publication output declines but stabilizes at a moderate level (roughly 30–45 papers per year). This suggests the field matured, with steady but less explosive research activity.

Recent decline (2019–2025): A sharp drop is observed after 2019, with very low publication counts in the early 2020s. This could reflect data incompleteness for recent years, a shift in research focus, or a genuine decline in interest or funding.

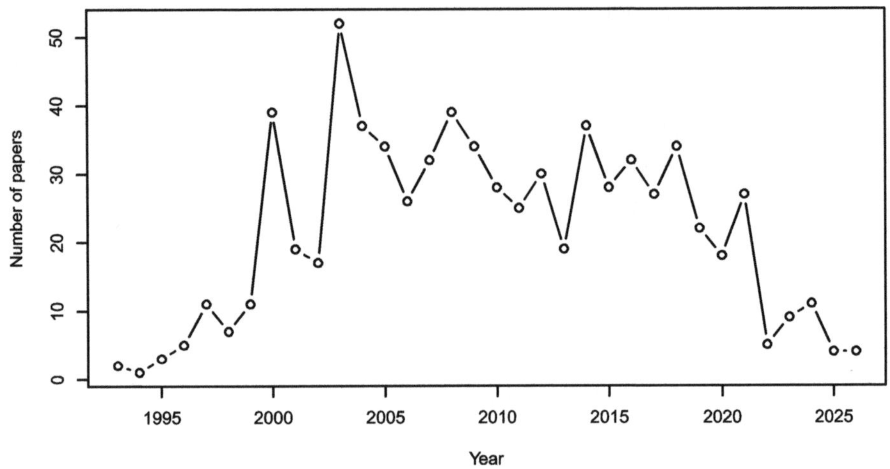

Fig. 3. Annual Scientific Production.

Most Relevant Sources. As discussed previously (see Fig. 1), the majority of publications on ASMs appear in conference proceedings or journals.

Table 3 provides an overview of the most relevant publication venues and is consistent with the distribution observed for publication types. Several of the most prominent sources, namely *Lecture Notes in Computer Science*, the *ACM International Conference Proceeding Series*, and the *ACM Symposium on Applied Computing*, publish conference proceedings, further confirming the central role of conferences within the formal methods community. In particular, the higher number of ASM-related contributions appears in the *Lecture Notes in Computer Science* (LNCS) series. By manually inspecting the LNCS entries, it is revealed that most contributions originate from the *International Workshop on Abstract State Machines*, the *International Conference on Rigorous State-Based Methods*, and the *International Symposium on Formal Methods.* The influence of Egon Börger's work is also clearly reflected in the publication venues, as two of the three most prominent conferences were either founded by him or strongly shaped by his contributions. By contrast, the remaining sources listed in Table 3 are peer-reviewed journals, indicating a sustained and significant presence of ASM-related research in established archival venues.

Most Used Keywords. Figure 4 depicts the temporal evolution of the ten most frequently used keywords in the ASM literature, grouped by semantic similarity. The distribution highlights the thematic continuity and gradual evolution of

Table 3. Top 10 most relevant sources

Source	Publication count
Lecture Notes in Computer Science	245
Science of Computer Programming	21
Theoretical Computer Science	13
Journal of Universal Computer Science	13
Electronic Notes in Theoretical Computer Science	12
ACM International Conference Proceeding Series	11
Communications In Computer and Information Science	11
Formal Aspects Of Computing	9
ACM Transactions on Computational Logic	7
ACM Symposium on Applied Computing	7

research topics over time. Foundational concepts such as semantics, theory, and refinement appear consistently throughout the entire time span, reflecting the strong theoretical grounding of Abstract State Machines since their inception. In particular, the persistent presence of semantics underscores the role of ASMs as a formal framework for precise system modeling and language definition.

At the same time, the figure reveals a clear shift toward more application-oriented and tool-supported themes. Keywords such as verification, model checking, and formal methods became increasingly prominent from the early 2000s onward, corresponding to the period in which ASMs were systematically integrated into verification workflows and formal analysis techniques. More recent years show the emergence and consolidation of keywords such as Asmeta [1,7], model transformation, and simulation, indicating a growing focus on tooling, automation, and practical adoption. Overall, the observed keyword trends mirror the historical trajectory of ASM research: from its early theoretical foundations, largely shaped by Egon Börger's seminal work, to a mature and diversified research area encompassing verification, tool support, and applied formal methods.

5.2 Authors

Corresponding Author's Countries. Figure 5 presents the distribution of the top ten countries according to the number of documents, ranked by the affiliation of the corresponding author. The results highlight a strong European concentration of ASM research, with Italy and Germany clearly leading the ranking, followed by Austria. This distribution reflects the historical roots and sustained development of the ASM community within Europe. At the same time, the presence of countries such as the United States, Canada, China, and the United Kingdom indicates a significant international dissemination of the formalism, confirming its adoption beyond its original geographical context.

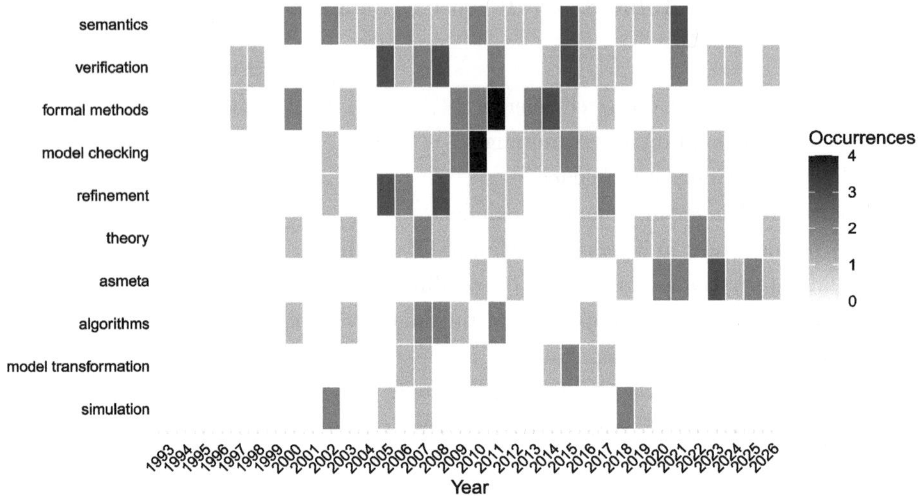

Fig. 4. The most used keywords.

This pattern highlights the role played by Egon Börger in shaping the ASM community. Several of the most productive countries (e.g., Italy, Germany, and France) correspond to regions where Börger has been academically active, has established long-term collaborations, or has directly contributed to the creation of research schools and conferences centered on ASMs. Overall, the geographical distribution shown in Fig. 5 underscores the enduring impact of Börger's work, which not only influenced individual contributions but also fostered an internationally distributed research community.

Most Relevant Authors. Figures 6 and 7 provide complementary perspectives on author prominence within the ASM research community, distinguishing between productivity and scientific impact. Figure 6 reports the top five authors ranked by number of contributions, highlighting a group of researchers who have been particularly active in terms of publication volume. The distribution shows a relatively balanced range of contributions, with no single author overwhelmingly dominating the ranking. This suggests ASM is a mature and collaborative research field in which sustained productivity is shared among several core contributors.

Figure 7 ranks authors by total citation counts, revealing a more pronounced differentiation in terms of impact. In this view, Egon Börger emerges as the most cited author by a substantial margin, followed by Yuri Gurevich and other key figures who have contributed foundational theoretical results and influential applications of the ASM formalism. While some authors appear in both rankings, the comparison between Figs. 6 and 7 clearly illustrates that productivity and citation impact do not necessarily coincide. High publication activity reflects sustained engagement with the field, whereas citation impact captures the long-term influence of seminal contributions. Taken together, these figures underscore

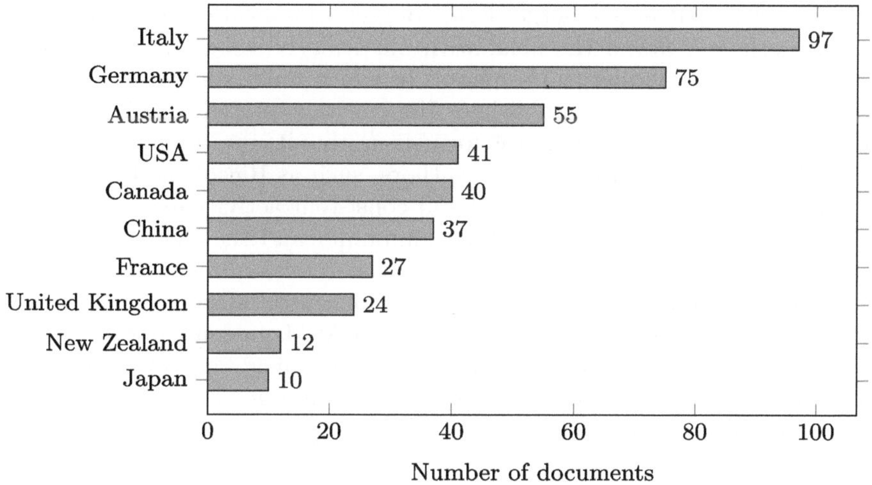

Fig. 5. Top 10 countries per contribution.

Börger's central role not only as a prolific contributor but, more importantly, as the principal intellectual force whose work has shaped the foundations, methodology, and enduring relevance of ASMs. Indeed, most of the authors reported in Figs. 6 and 7 started their work in the ASM field thanks to their collaboration with Egon Börger.

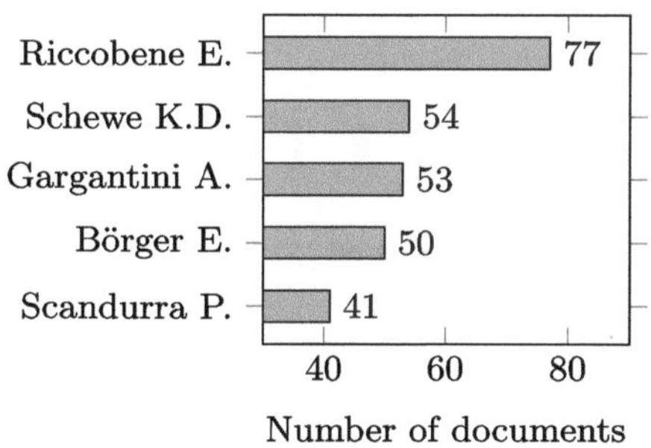

Fig. 6. Top 5 authors per contribution.

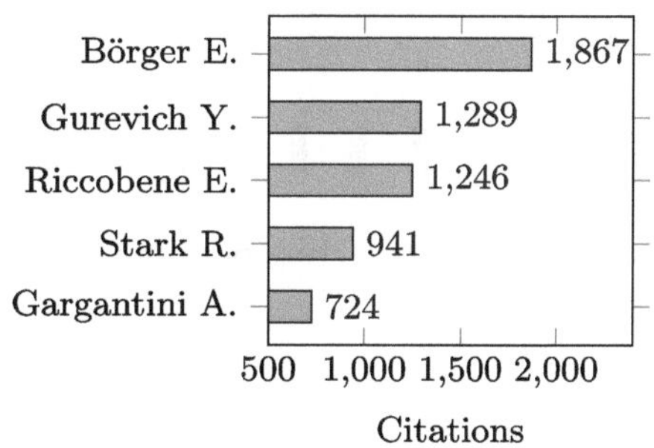

Fig. 7. Top 5 authors per citations.

Top-Authors' Productivity over the Time. Figure 8 illustrates the temporal distribution of publication activity for a selection of the top 5 most productive authors in the ASM community. Each row corresponds to an author, while the size of the bubbles indicates the number of publications produced in a given year. This visualization highlights both the continuity and the intensity of individual research contributions across the last three decades of ASM-related work.

Several clear patterns emerge. Egon Börger's publication activity is visible from the earliest years of the field, with particularly strong peaks around the early 2000s, corresponding to the period in which foundational works on ASM theory and refinement were published. His constant presence over time underscores his central role in shaping the formalism from its inception and guiding its methodological consolidation. Other authors, such as Riccobene E., Gargantini A., and Schewe K.D., show extended and consistent activity over later periods, reflecting the maturation of the ASM community and the emergence of stable research groups building upon the original theoretical framework. More recent contributors, including Scandurra P., exhibit concentrated activity in later years, indicating ongoing evolution and application of ASMs in contemporary research contexts. Overall, the figure conveys a picture of a field characterized by long-term continuity, generational overlap, and a clear lineage of influence originating from Börger's initial contributions.

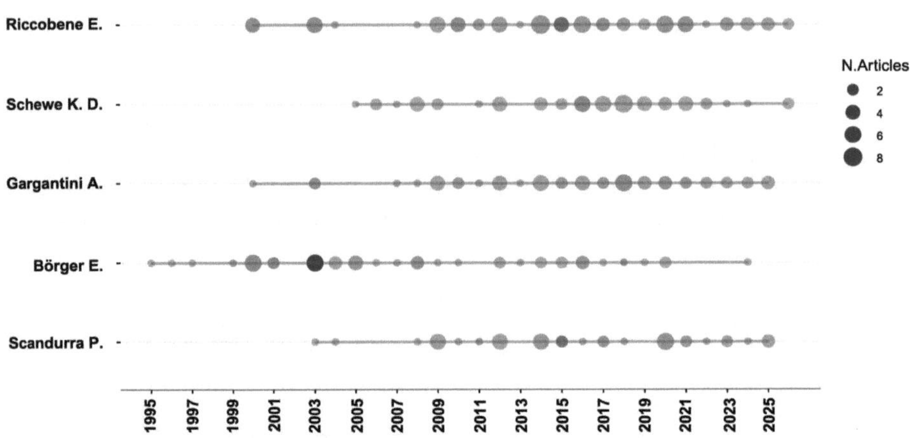

Fig. 8. Top 5 authors' productivity over time

6 Study Limitations

As with any bibliometric investigation, the results presented in this paper are subject to a number of limitations that should be taken into account when interpreting the findings.

First, our analysis is inherently dependent on the coverage and quality of the selected bibliographic databases, namely Web of Science, Scopus, and Lens. Although these sources are widely recognized and complementary in scope, none of them provides exhaustive coverage of all scientific outputs related to Abstract State Machines, as demonstrated by the fact that we needed to include all of them in our analysis. In particular, older publications, workshop proceedings, technical reports, and some foundational works may be underrepresented or inconsistently indexed, especially for the early years of ASM research.

Second, our search strategy and query formulation, while carefully constructed and validated, inevitably introduce a degree of bias. Despite including historical terminology such as *evolving algebras*, it is possible that we missed some relevant contributions due to variations in terminology, incomplete metadata, or differences in indexing practices across databases. More specifically, we observed that a substantial number of relevant publications do not include the search term "Abstract State Machines" in either the title or the keywords, but refer to it only within the abstract. For instance, in the Scopus database, we identified 143 additional documents that mention the term in the abstract but not in the title or keywords. While some of these records are out of scope or correspond to proceedings without author information, we identified 82 additional papers that were not included in our final analysis. Notably, several of these works were authored by researchers we identified among the most influential in the ASM community, including Riccobene [14], Schewe [21], Börger [12], Gargantini [6,13], and Scandurra [2], among others. We conjecture that these omissions are primarily due to the fact that, in such publications, Abstract State Machines are employed as a supporting technique rather than constituting the main focus of the work. Expanding the queries to include these works would have significantly increased the number of retrieved records (given that the same analysis should have been performed on all three used databases), at the cost of substantially reducing precision and requiring extensive manual filtering to exclude works in which ASMs play only a marginal or incidental role.

A limited number of papers not centrally focused on ASMs may still have been included and subsequently removed through manual inspection, introducing a small element of subjectivity into the cleaning process. Similarly, the data cleaning and normalization steps, although necessary to ensure consistency and reproducibility, may affect the final dataset. In particular, our decision to exclude records without authors or without a DOI improves duplicate removal accuracy and citation reliability, but may also lead to the exclusion of legitimate and important publications (especially older ones published before the widespread adoption of digital identifiers). As a consequence, citation-based indicators may favor more recent or better-indexed publications.

Our analysis considers citation-based metrics. These metrics themselves have well-known limitations. Citation counts do not capture the full intellectual or educational impact of a contribution. We did not consider the impact of self-citations. Moreover, citation practices vary across venues and over time, and highly cited works may benefit from cumulative advantage effects. While this study uses citation indicators to highlight influential contributions, these measures should be interpreted as proxies for impact rather than as definitive assessments of scientific value.

Finally, this study focuses primarily on quantitative bibliometric indicators and does not aim to provide a qualitative assessment of the scientific content of individual works. This limitation is especially relevant in a field such as formal methods, where long-term influence often extends beyond what can be captured through bibliographic data alone.

Despite these limitations, we believe that our analysis provides a meaningful and transparent overview of the evolution and impact of Abstract State Machine research, complementing existing qualitative works.

7 Conclusion

This paper presented a bibliometric analysis of the research landscape surrounding Abstract State Machines, with the aim of providing a data-driven perspective on the evolution, dissemination, and impact of the formalism over more than three decades. By integrating data from multiple bibliographic sources and applying our analysis process, we examined publication trends, citation patterns, core venues, author productivity, and geographical distribution within the ASM community.

The results highlight a research field that has undergone four main phases: emergence, growth, consolidation, and stabilization. Conference publications have played a central role in shaping the community, while journal articles and monographic works have contributed to the maturation and long-term consolidation of the formalism. Citation analyses further reveal a strong concentration of influence around a limited number of foundational contributions, reflecting the typical structure of a mature and well-defined research area.

Across all dimensions of the analysis, the enduring and central role of Egon Börger is evident. His contributions are prominently represented among the most cited works, the most influential publication venues, and the temporal evolution of research activity. Beyond quantitative indicators, the analysis also illustrates how Börger's work has acted as a catalyst for the formation of research groups, international collaborations, and successive generations of researchers who have extended and applied the ASM formalism in diverse contexts. In this sense, the bibliometric evidence presented in this paper confirms what is widely recognized within the community: ASM research is not only rooted in Börger's foundational ideas, but has been continuously shaped by his scientific leadership and mentorship.

References

1. Arcaini, P., Bombarda, A., Bonfanti, S., Gargantini, A., Riccobene, E., Scandurra, P.: The ASMETA Approach to Safety Assurance of Software Systems. In: Raschke, A., Riccobene, E., Schewe, K.-D. (eds.) Logic, Computation and Rigorous Methods. LNCS, vol. 12750, pp. 215–238. Springer, Cham (2021). https://doi.org/10.1007/978-3-030-76020-5_13
2. Arcaini, P., Gargantini, A., Riccobene, E., Scandurra, P.: Formal semantics for metamodel-based domain specific languages, pp. 216–241 (2012). https://doi.org/10.4018/978-1-4666-2092-6.ch008

3. Arcaini, P., Riccobene, E., Scandurra, P.: Modeling and analyzing mape-k feedback loops for self-adaptation. In: 2015 IEEE/ACM 10th International Symposium on Software Engineering for Adaptive and Self-Managing Systems, pp. 13–23 (2015). https://doi.org/10.1109/SEAMS.2015.10
4. Aria, M., Cuccurullo, C.: bibliometrix: an r-tool for comprehensive science mapping analysis. J. Informet. **11**(4), 959–975 (2017). https://doi.org/10.1016/j.joi.2017.08.007
5. Blass, A., Gurevich, Y.: Abstract state machines capture parallel algorithms. ACM Trans. Comput. Logic **4**(4), 578–651 (2003). https://doi.org/10.1145/937555.937561
6. Bombarda, A., Bonfanti, S., Gargantini, A.: formal MVC: a Pattern for the Integration of ASM Specifications in UI Development. In: Glässer, U., Creissac Campos, J., Méry, D., Palanque, P. (eds.) Rigorous State-Based Methods. ABZ 2023. Lecture Notes in Computer Science, vol. 14010. Springer, Cham (2023). https://doi.org/10.1007/978-3-031-33163-3_25
7. Bombarda, A., Bonfanti, S., Gargantini, A., Riccobene, E., Scandurra, P.: Asmeta tool set for rigorous system design. In: Platzer, A., Rozier, K.Y., Pradella, M., Rossi, M. (eds.) Formal Methods, pp. 492–517. Springer Nature Switzerland, Cham (2025)
8. Börger, E.: The ASM refinement method. Form. Asp. Comput. **15**(2–3), 237–257 (2003). https://doi.org/10.1007/s00165-003-0012-7
9. Börger, E., Stärk, R.: Abstract State Machines. Springer, Cham (2003). https://doi.org/10.1007/978-3-642-18216-7
10. Bowen, J.P.: Communities and Ancestors Associated with Egon Börger and ASM. In: Raschke, A., Riccobene, E., Schewe, K.-D. (eds.) Logic, Computation and Rigorous Methods. LNCS, vol. 12750, pp. 96–120. Springer, Cham (2021). https://doi.org/10.1007/978-3-030-76020-5_6
11. Börger, E., Riccobene, E.: Logical operational semantics of Parlog part I: And-Parallelism. In: Boley, H., Richter, M.M. (eds.) PDK 1991. LNCS, vol. 567, pp. 191–198. Springer, Heidelberg (1991). https://doi.org/10.1007/BFb0013530
12. Batory, D., Börger, E.: Modularizing theorems for software product lines: The jbook case study (2008). https://doi.org/10.3217/JUCS-014-12-2059, https://lib.jucs.org/article/29119/
13. Gargantini, A., Riccobene, E., Scandurra, P.: Model-driven language engineering: The asmeta case study, pp. 373–378 (2008). https://doi.org/10.1109/ICSEA.2008.62
14. Gargantini, A., Riccobene, E., Scandurra, P.: A model-driven validation & verification environment for embedded systems, pp. 241–244 (2008). https://doi.org/10.1109/SIES.2008.4577708
15. Grieskamp, W., Gurevich, Y., Schulte, W., Veanes, M.: Generating finite state machines from abstract state machines. In: Proceedings of the 2002 ACM SIGSOFT International Symposium on Software Testing and Analysis, pp. 112–122. ISSTA '02, Association for Computing Machinery, New York, NY, USA (2002). https://doi.org/10.1145/566172.566190
16. Grieskamp, W., Gurevich, Y., Schulte, W., Veanes, M.: Generating finite state machines from abstract state machines. SIGSOFT Softw. Eng. Notes **27**(4), 112–122 (2002). https://doi.org/10.1145/566171.566190
17. Gurevich, Y.: Evolving Algebras 1993: Lipari Guide, pp. 9–36. Oxford University Press, Inc., USA (1995). https://doi.org/10.5555/233976.233979

18. Gurevich, Y.: Sequential abstract-state machines capture sequential algorithms. ACM Trans. Comput. Logic **1**(1), 77–111 (2000). https://doi.org/10.1145/343369.343384
19. Harris, G.H.: Review of "abstract state machines: a method for high-level system design and analysis" by egon börger and robert stärk. springer-verlag 2003. SIGSOFT Softw. Eng. Notes **29**(2), 31–32 (2004). https://doi.org/10.1145/979743.979770
20. Hicks, D., Wouters, P., Waltman, L., de Rijcke, S., Rafols, I.: Bibliometrics: the leiden manifesto for research metrics. Nature **520**(7548), 429–431 (2015). https://doi.org/10.1038/520429a
21. Natschläger, C., Kossak, F., Schewe, K.D.: Deontic bpmn: a powerful extension of bpmn with a trusted model transformation. Softw. Syst. Model. **14**(2), 765–793 (2015). https://doi.org/10.1007/s10270-013-0329-5
22. Randles, R., Finnegan, A.: Guidelines for writing a systematic review. Nurse Educ. Today **125**, 105803 (2023). https://doi.org/10.1016/j.nedt.2023.105803
23. Stärk, R.F., Schmid, J., Börger, E.: Abstract State Machines, pp. 15–28. Springer, Cham (2001). https://doi.org/10.1007/978-3-642-59495-3_2
24. Varró, D., Balogh, A.: The model transformation language of the viatra2 framework. Sci. Comput. Program. **68**(3), 214–234 (2007). https://doi.org/10.1016/j.scico.2007.05.004. special Issue on Model Transformation

Abstract State Machines

State-Based Implementation of Algebraic Data Types

Gerhard Schellhorn(✉), Felix Pribyl, and Wolfgang Reif

Institute for Software and Systems Engineering, University of Augsburg, Augsburg, Germany
{schellhorn,reif}@informatik.uni-augsburg.de, f.pribyl@uni-a.de

Abstract. The construction of software systems by starting with an abstract specification and stepwise refinement has started out from two origins: one is algebraic refinement which allows to refine axiomatic descriptions of data types, the other is state-based refinement, which assumes that systems are given by a description of states and transitions. While there are various connections between the approaches, e.g. state-based specifications usually rely on algebraic types to describe their states, there seems to be no formalized concept so far, that allows to refine algebraic data types using a state-based implementation. This paper introduces state modules as such an approach, and defines proof obligations that are sufficient to prove its correctness. The approach is used to get a modular proof, that boolean formulas can be implemented as BDDs. It also allows to verify the standard implementation of free data types in functional languages. The concept has been implemented in the theorem prover KIV, and is currently integrated in KIV's code generator for Scala.

Keywords: Algebraic Refinement · State-Based Refinement · Interactive Verification · Immutable data types · KIV

1 Introduction

Concepts for verifying large software systems, such that the overall proof can be split into independent proofs for small components, have always been a major research topic of our group.

A key concept to achieve this are *modules*, that connect an abstract interface to an implementation, that can be verified to be a refinement of the interface. Other components then can rely on just the interface, when using the module.

Early work of our group was focused on algebraic refinement [24,25], where the interface as well as implementation are axiomatic specifications of algebraic data types.

Supported by the Deutsche Forschungsgemeinschaft (DFG), "Correct translation of abstract specifications to C-Code (VeriCode)" (grant RE828/26-1).

A. Raschke et al. (Eds.): Egon Börger Festschrift, LNCS 16580, pp. 49–75, 2026.
https://doi.org/10.1007/978-3-032-24494-9_4

It was then the ASM refinement concept introduced by Börger [5–7], that motivated us to investigate state-based refinement [26–28], where the central concept is a state that is updated by transitions.

Many of the case studies we have done had to develop and formalize state-based concepts of refinement [4,14,17,29–31].

This paper spans a bridge between the two worlds: it defines the concept that allows to implement an algebraic type with a state-based ASM and to show its correctness.

Section 2 gives some background on the specifications and programs used. It also gives an overview over algebraic and state based refinement. As an example, we show how sets can be refined with lists, one time using algebraic refinement, the other using state-based refinement.

Section 3 motivates and explains the concept using an example that was given as challenge 2 at the VerifyThis competition 2023 [38]. The challenge required to verify programs that encode boolean formulas as a reduced ordered binary decision diagram (ROBDD). We show that it is possible to structure the task as two independent problems: one is an algebraic proof that shows that boolean formulas can be transformed into semantically equivalent if-then-else formulas, where both are specified as simple algebraic data types. The other is that if-then-else formulas can be efficiently represented using a state-based representation with a graph (stored in the heap) as the state. To formally verify this, we introduce the concept of a *state module*.

Section 4 formally defines state modules and determines sufficient proof obligations. We show that these imply that any program using the exported algebraic data type is correctly implemented, if the exported operations are replaced by calls to the operations of the imported state machine.

Section 5 then gives two more examples: an implementation of lists with cons cells, which shows that standard implementations as they are done in functional languages can be realized using a state module.

A second example, that implements lists with *list objects* shows, that it is possible to implement algebraic types with objects, that have an identity.

Finally, Sect. 6 discusses limitations and concludes.

2 Background

Although we assume the reader to be familiar with many-sorted predicate-logic, we first reiterate some basic definitions to explain our expression-based setting and the semantics of data types. Figure 1 is a listing of the typical identifiers we use in the syntax.

Section 2.2 then defines the imperative programs used in implementations and gives a natural semantics. Both are sufficient to prove the correctness of the essential theorems given in Sect. 4.

We do not design the full setting used in KIV, which includes many more aspects, like polymorphic higher-order functions (with a semantics like in [16]), programs which may be concurrent, may throw exceptions or may have return statements. All these aspects have no real influence on the concept presented here. Nevertheless the concept has been implemented for this more general setting, and the specifications used in the web presentation [33] use these features.

Sections 2.3 and 2.4 then give an informal idea how algebraic refinement and state-based refinement work, by providing an example for each one.

Notation	Informal meaning
$s \in S$	Sort (type) of an expression
$x \in X_s$	Variable of sort S
$f : \underline{s} \to s \in F$	Function of type $s_1 \times \cdots \times s_n \to s$
e	Expression
$SIG = (S, F)$	Signature
$\varphi \in Fma(SIG, X)$	Formula: Expression of type *Bool*
$q : \underline{s}; \underline{s'} \to s \in Q$	Procedure with value parameter types $\underline{s}$, reference parameter types $\underline{s'}$ and return type s
$p \in Prog$	Program
$\mathcal{A} = ((A_s)_{s \in S}, (f^{\mathcal{A}})_{f \in F})$	Algebra with carrier sets A_s and functions f^A
$v : X \to A$	Valuation

Fig. 1. List of used notations and letters

2.1 Many-Sorted Predicate Logic and Algebraic Specifications

A signature $SIG = (S, F)$ consists of a set of sorts $s \in S$, where $Unit, Bool \in S$, and a set of typed functions $f : \underline{s} \to s \in F$. Here we underline a variable to denote a vector of $n \geq 0$ elements, i.e. $\underline{s} = s_1 \times \ldots \times s_n$. We assume that the boolean operations like $. \wedge . : Bool \times Bool \to Bool$ (the dots indicate infix notation) or $\mathtt{true} : Bool$ are always in the signature. Type *Unit* is assumed to be the 'void' type that indicates no result for programs and procedures (see below). It is typically not used in function types.

Let X_s be disjoint sets of variables for each sort s and $X = \bigcup_{s \in S} X_s$. We write $x : s$ if $x \in X_s$ has type s. Expressions over a signature and X include variables and well-typed function applications $f(\underline{e})$. A Formula $\varphi \in Fma(SIG, X)$ is an expression of type *Bool*. These also include equations $e_1 = e_2$ and quantified expressions $\forall\, x.\ \varphi$ and $\exists\, x.\ \varphi$. Free variables $free(e)$ are defined as usual.

An algebra $\mathcal{A}$ over a signature consists of a nonempty carrier set A_s for every sort s and functions $f^{\mathcal{A}} \in A_{\underline{s}} \to A_s$ for every function symbol, where $A_{s_1,\ldots,s_n} = A_{s_1} \times \cdots \times A_{s_n}$. It is assumed that the carrier set of booleans is always $A_{Bool} = \{\mathbf{tt}, \mathbf{ff}\}$, and that the predefined boolean operations have standard semantics (e.g. $true^{\mathcal{A}} = \mathbf{tt}$, $\mathbf{tt} \wedge^{\mathcal{A}} \mathbf{ff} = \mathbf{ff}$). The carrier set of the void type is assumed to have a single element: $A_{Unit} = \{\circ\}$. A valuation is a finite mapping from variables to values of the corresponding type ($v(x) \in A_s$, if $x \in X_s$). Given an expression of type s, an algebra $\mathcal{A}$ and a valuation v that maps at least the free variables of e ($free(e) \subseteq dom(v)$), the semantics $[\![e]\!]\mathcal{A}, v$ of an expression returns a value from A_s. It is defined recursively as usual.

The class $Alg(SIG, Ax, Gen)$ of algebras is defined relative to a set of axioms $Ax \subseteq Fma(SIG, X)$ and generation principles that it must satisfy. An algebra satisfies an axiom (written $\mathcal{A} \models \varphi$), iff $[\![\varphi]\!]\mathcal{A}, v = \mathbf{tt}$ for all valuations with $free(\varphi) \subseteq dom(v)$.

A generation principle has the form s **generatedby** C where $C \subseteq F$ is a finite set of constructor functions, that all have target sort s. It holds in an algebra, if the carrier set A_s contains only elements a that are the result of evaluating a constructor term ct ($a = [\![ct]\!]\mathcal{A}, v$) with some valuation. A constructor term ct is a quantifier-free expression of type s, that uses only the function symbols in C and no variables of type s. The generation principle implies a structural induction principle, that can be directly expressed as an axiom in higher-order logic.

As an example, for finite sets the constructors are $\varnothing$ and $s +\!\!+ a$, which adds an element to a set. Constructor terms are $\varnothing, \varnothing +\!\!+ a, \varnothing +\!\!+ a +\!\!+ b, \ldots$. The standard axioms are listed below:

$$s1 = s2 \leftrightarrow \forall\, a.\ a \in s1 \leftrightarrow a \in s2;$$

$$\neg\, a \in \varnothing; \qquad a \in s +\!\!+ b \leftrightarrow a = b \vee a \in s;$$

$$\#\varnothing = 0; \qquad \neg\, a \in s \rightarrow \#(s +\!\!+ a) = \#(s) + 1;$$

An important subclass are free data types, where different constructor terms always denote different elements. For these we use a shorthand definition. For example lists are defined as

$$\textbf{data}\ List = \texttt{[]} \mid . + .\ (\texttt{.head} : Elem;\ \texttt{.tail} : List)$$

The notation declares constructors `[]` (the empty list) and $a + x$ adding an element in front of a list with corresponding selectors x`.head` and x`.tail`. For such free data types standard axioms can be generated automatically, as listed below:

$$a + x \neq \texttt{[]}; \qquad a + x = b + y \leftrightarrow a = b \wedge x = y;$$

$$(a + x)\texttt{.head} = a; \qquad (a + x)\texttt{.tail} = x;$$

$$\#\texttt{[]} = 0; \qquad \#(a + x) = 0;$$

In general, the size (#) of a free data structure is the number of non-constant constructors of the constructor term.

2.2 Programs with a Natural Semantics

To define abstract programs, we use an extended signature $SIG = (S, F, Q)$, which adds a set of typed procedure symbols $q : \underline{s}; \underline{s'} \rightarrow s \in Q$. A procedure has value parameters of types $\underline{s}$, reference parameters of types $\underline{s'}$ and a return value of type s.

The semantics of a procedure is defined by procedure declarations of the form $q(\underline{x}; \underline{y}).p$ where p is a program. Programs $p \in \mathit{Prog}$ are defined by the grammar

$$\begin{aligned} P = \; & X \mid f(\underline{P}) \mid q(\underline{P}; \underline{X}) \mid X{:=}P \mid P = P \mid P; P \mid \\ & \textbf{while } P \textbf{ do } P \mid \textbf{if } P \textbf{ then } P \textbf{ else } P \mid \\ & \textbf{let } X = P \textbf{ in } P \mid \textbf{choose } x \textbf{ with } P \textbf{ in } P \textbf{ ifnone } P \end{aligned}$$

All programs have a type s (we write $p : s$), which is the type of the value they compute. Assignments and while loops compute an empty value $\circ$ of type *Unit*. Programs modify a state v, which is simply a valuation.

Note that this implies that abstract programs have a value semantics, which usually makes them much easier to verify than programs with a reference semantics where verification always has to consider side effects and aliasing. To explain how programs work we give a simple natural semantics, which is defined by rules that derive statements of the form $\langle p, v \rangle \Rightarrow (v', a)$. These read as: if program p is started in state v, where at least the free variables of p have a value ($\mathit{free}(p) \subseteq \mathit{dom}(v)$) then the program has a terminating run which ends in state v' and returns value a.

A statement is valid, if it is the conclusion of a *closed* derivation tree formed with the rules, i.e. a tree without any open premises. For a non-terminating program p, $\langle p, v \rangle \Rightarrow (v', a)$ is false for all v' and a, since no closed derivation tree can be constructed.

There are other possible semantics, e.g. one based on ASMs similar to the one of [36] or a small-step semantics. However, this would make the proofs more technically involved without gaining much insight.

The simplest rule of the semantics is for a variable, which computes the value it is mapped to and does not change the state:

$$\frac{}{\langle x, v \rangle \Rightarrow (v, v(x))} \; \mathrm{R(var)}$$

A function application evaluates its arguments sequentially from left to right and finally applies the function f^A to compute the final value:

$$\frac{\langle p_1, v_0 \rangle \Rightarrow (v_1, a_1) \;\; \langle p_2, v_1 \rangle \Rightarrow (v_2, a_2) \;\; \ldots \;\; \langle p_n, v_{n-1} \rangle \Rightarrow (v_n, a_n)}{\langle f(\underline{p}), v_0 \rangle \Rightarrow (v_n, f^A(\underline{a}))} \; \mathrm{R(app)}$$

Note that the evaluation of subexpressions may change the state by executing procedure calls and assignments as defined below, while applying f^A has no side effects.

Procedure calls $q(\underline{p}; \underline{z})$ expect pairwise different reference parameters $\underline{z}$. Therefore no aliasing is possible, and reference parameters can also be viewed as input-output parameters[1]. The rule for procedure calls requires a procedure declaration of the form $q(\underline{x}; \underline{y})$ $\{\mathit{body}\}$ to be given. The premises of the rule include

[1] This is true for the sequential setting we consider here. However, KIV in general also allows concurrent procedures with an interleaving semantics. For these the difference is relevant, since one thread must see updates to a common reference parameter by another thread immediately.

all of the ones for function calls (and one more), therefore we abbreviate them as $\langle \underline{p}, v_0 \rangle \Rightarrow (v_n, \underline{a})$. The type of *body* must be equal to the return type of q and the free variables *free*(*body*) must be a subset of the parameters $\underline{x}, \underline{y}$, which must all be different variables. The result of a procedure call is computed by executing the body:

$$\frac{\langle \underline{p}, v_0 \rangle \Rightarrow (v_n, \underline{a}) \quad \langle body, v_n\{\underline{x}, \underline{y} \mapsto \underline{a}, v_n(\underline{z})\} \rangle \Rightarrow (v', d)}{\langle q(\underline{p}; \underline{z}), v_0 \rangle \Rightarrow (v'\{\underline{x}, \underline{y} \mapsto v_n(\underline{x}), v_n(\underline{y})\}\{\underline{z} \mapsto v'(\underline{y})\}, d)} \text{ R(call)}$$

Like for a function call, the first premises evaluate the value parameters in order. Care must then be taken to respect the semantics of value and reference parameters: the last premise first binds the formal parameters $\underline{x}$ and $\underline{y}$ to the computed results for the value parameters ($\underline{a}$) and the current values stored in the reference parameters $\underline{z}$ of the call. It then executes the body, which computes a result value d and updates the values stored in $\underline{x}$ and $\underline{y}$ in the final state v'. Finally the final values computed in the formal reference parameters $\underline{y}$ are moved back to the reference parameters $\underline{z}$ of the call, while the (local) values $v'(\underline{x})$ are discarded and replaced with the global values before the call ($v_n(\underline{x})$). Note that if there is an overlap between $\underline{x}$ and $\underline{z}$, the relevant value is that of $\underline{z}$.

An assignment updates the value of x and returns the empty value $\circ$:

$$\frac{\langle p, v \rangle \Rightarrow (v', a)}{\langle x{:=}p, v \rangle \Rightarrow (v'\{x \mapsto a\}, \circ)} \text{ R(asg)}$$

Equality requires that both sides have the same type and computes a boolean result:

$$\frac{\langle p_1, v \rangle \Rightarrow (v'', a_1) \quad \langle p_2, v'' \rangle \Rightarrow (v', a_2)}{\langle p_1 = p_2, v \rangle \Rightarrow (v', a_1 = a_2)} \text{ R(eq)}$$

A compound executes sequentially. The first program should be of type *Unit*, the second program computes the final result:

$$\frac{\langle p_1, v \rangle \Rightarrow (v'', \circ) \quad \langle p_2, v'' \rangle \Rightarrow (v', a)}{\langle p_1; p_2, v \rangle \Rightarrow (v', a)} \text{ R(comp)}$$

An if-statement evaluates its test, which must be of type *Bool*, so the returned value is **tt** or **ff**. For the positive case the rule is

$$\frac{\langle p, v \rangle \Rightarrow (v'', \mathbf{tt}) \quad \langle p_1, v'' \rangle \Rightarrow (v', a)}{\langle \mathbf{if}\ p\ \mathbf{then}\ p_1\ \mathbf{else}\ p_2, v \rangle \Rightarrow (v', a)} \text{ R(ifpos)}$$

with a symmetric rule for the negative case. The types of p_1 and p_2 must be the same and are also the type of the value returned.

A while statement evaluates the test which again must be boolean. The body of the loop as well as the loop itself must be of type *Unit* and therefore compute the empty value $\circ$. If the test is positive we have:

$$\frac{\langle p, v \rangle \Rightarrow (v_1, \mathbf{tt}) \quad \langle p_1, v_1 \rangle \Rightarrow (v_2, \circ) \quad \langle \mathbf{while}\ p\ \mathbf{do}\ p_1, v_2 \rangle \Rightarrow (v', \circ)}{\langle \mathbf{while}\ p\ \mathbf{do}\ p_1, v \rangle \Rightarrow (v', \circ)} \text{ R(whilepos)}$$

The negative case is simply

$$\frac{\langle p, v\rangle \Rightarrow (v', \mathbf{ff})}{\langle \mathbf{while}\ p\ \mathbf{do}\ p_1, v\rangle \Rightarrow (v', \circ)}\ \text{R(whileneg)}$$

A let statement binds the local variable to the value computed by p (which must be of the same type). The final value is computed by the body p_1:

$$\frac{\langle p, v\rangle \Rightarrow (v_1, b) \quad \langle p_1, v_1\{x \mapsto b\}\rangle \Rightarrow (v_2, a)}{\langle \mathbf{let}\ x = p\ \mathbf{in}\ p_1, v\rangle \Rightarrow (v_2\{x \mapsto v_1(x)\}, a)}\ \text{R(let)}$$

Like for calls, binding x to the local value b temporarily overwrites x while the body executes and resets the variable to the previous value $v_1(x)$ afterwards.

Finally, the choose statement nondeterministically binds a local variable x to some value b such that the test p holds and executes the body p_1 with this binding. The test must have no side effects, but must be an ordinary quantifier-free expression (which are a subset of the programs). For these the state is unchanged and the value computed by the natural semantics is the same as the one computed by the standard expression semantics.

$$\frac{\langle p, v\{x \mapsto b\}\rangle \Rightarrow (v\{x \mapsto b\}, \mathbf{tt}) \quad \langle p_1, v\{x \mapsto b\}\rangle \Rightarrow (v_2, a)}{\langle \mathbf{choose}\ x\ \mathbf{with}\ p\ \mathbf{in}\ p_1\ \mathbf{ifnone}\ p_2, v\rangle \Rightarrow (v_2\{x \mapsto v(x)\}, a)}\ \text{R(choosepos)}$$

If there is no value b such that satisfies the test, then p_2 is executed:

$$\frac{\text{for all } b{:}\langle p, v\{x \mapsto b\}\rangle \Rightarrow (v\{x \mapsto b\}, \mathbf{ff}) \quad \langle p_2, v\rangle \Rightarrow (v', a)}{\langle \mathbf{choose}\ x\ \mathbf{with}\ p\ \mathbf{in}\ p_1\ \mathbf{ifnone}\ p_2, v\rangle \Rightarrow (v', a)}\ \text{R(chooseneg)}$$

The choose statement is used mainly for specification purposes, e.g. to choose a value such that some postcondition holds. Only specific instances can be translated to a program in a real programming language. Examples are choosing an element from a finite set (the **ifnone**-clause is executed when the set is empty) or choosing a fresh reference that is not yet allocated in the heap (which becomes 'alloc' in C, or creates a new object in an object-oriented language).

2.3 Algebraic Refinement

Algebraic Refinement is concerned with the refinement of algebras by other algebras. There is a vast literature on this topic and there are many variations. In particular the specification of algebras varies: the one we use here, uses full predicate-logic specifications [8,24,35] and classes of models. Other approaches use a single algebra, often the initial algebra relative to a specification with equations or horn clauses [12,13,15]. The concept is supported by many theorem provers, see e.g. [9,19,25].

Basically the idea is that an abstract algebra $\mathcal{A} \in Alg(ASIG)$ can be constructed from a concrete algebra $\mathcal{C} \in Alg(CSIG)$ by forming a quotient algebra: A subset of the elements of some carrier set C_s is selected (formally a *restriction predicate* $r : s \to Bool$ can be used to define the subset) and the elements of this subset are grouped into classes by an equivalence relation (an *equality predicate* $eq : s \times s \rightarrow Bool$ can be used for this purpose). The classes of elements formed then are shown to form the carrier set of an abstract algebra $\mathcal{A}$ by providing implementations of the functions from ASIG over the quotient algebra, that are compatible with the equivalence relation. The algebra is finally shown to obey the axioms that were used to define $\mathcal{A}$. We give a simple example, that is also available in the formal specifications online [33]. The example implements finite sets with lists.

Finite sets can be represented as a duplicate-free list with a restriction predicate $nodups : List \rightarrow Bool$, which tests, that the list has no duplicates. Lists which are a permutation of each other (an equality predicate $perm : List \times List \rightarrow Bool$ is defined) are put into the same class. Finally implementations of the operations on sets are provided (a membership test, a subset predicate, an equality test etc.) that work with duplicate free lists. For example $insert : s \times List \rightarrow List$ adds an element to the front of the List, if it is not already contained.

It must then be shown, that the implementations have the behavior specified by the axioms of sets. As an example, the axiom $a \in s +\!\!+ b \leftrightarrow a = b \vee a \in s$ must hold when using a duplicate-free list in place of set s, and calling the implementation of $\in$ and $+\!\!+$ on lists, and $isperm$ in place of equality. Congruence for the equality predicate must also be shown, i.e. $isperm$ must define an equivalence relation on duplicate free lists, that is compatible with function calls, e.g. calling the implementation of the membership test with an element and two lists which are permutations of each other, must yield the same boolean result. The web presentation [33] shows two instances of the set-list modules, one that is very similar to the one defined in [24] where functions had to be implemented by procedures that use output parameters instead of return values (the restriction and the equality predicate also had to be given as procedures), and another one, that uses polymorphic sets and lists, and implements some of the functions using a function or a procedure with a return value.

2.4 State-Based Systems and State-Based Refinement

State based systems use a very different approach to refinement: The standard idea there is that the system M is modeled to have a state that is updated by transitions resulting in runs of the system. A run starts in a initial state and executes a sequence of transitions (approaches differ in considering finite or infinite runs or both). The many approaches [1–3,7,10,11,18,22] that are possible, differ in how states and transitions are described, and what can be observed for a run.

States are often given as a tuple of values. A formal specification then typically defines a tuple of state variables $\underline{sv}$ with algebraic types, and the tuple of values they currently store is the state. Transitions can be given either by specifying contracts (pre- and postconditions), rules or programs, or by relations over the state. Observations can be some part of the state (some state variables are observable in each state of a run), or some of the rules (or all) applied in transitions are observable, since they produce visible results. Also whether runs terminate in final states is sometimes observable. Correct refinement of a system AM to a system CM is then typically based on the criterion, that the observations that can be made for any run of CM must also be possible as an observation of AM. In contrast, the state of each system is assumed to be hidden, so the state of AM can be different from the one of CM. Proving correctness of a refinement typically requires to split the runs into (ideally small, finite, often consisting of a single transition) segments, that can be shown to have the same observations. The proof typically needs an abstraction relation (or function) that shows that states are related at the start and end of these related segments, resulting in so-called commuting diagrams.

A simple example is data refinement [18], where the transitions are assumed to be calls of (named) system operations, which all have input and output (and all three are observable). In this case the operations of both AM and CM must be the same with the same input and output types. A simple example that parallels the one given above would be to have an abstract system that has a single set as state (represented as a variable s of type Set, together with transitions that add or delete an element from s, or test whether an element is in the set s. This system can be refined by one that has a duplicate free list $x : List$ as state and the same operations.

A data refinement of a state-based system (called an abstract state machine; ASM in KIV) that refines a set to a list is given as part of the specifications online [33]. Although the result looks somewhat similar to the algebraic refinement, there are some significant differences:

- Algebraic refinement is possible for operations like the union of two sets, while for data refinement (without changing the setting of the state being *one* variable of type set) it is not possible to add such an operation.
- Algebraic refinement proves that the specification of the abstract data type is consistent, if the concrete one is, since it constructs a model of the abstract one from the concrete one. Data refinement does not give such a guarantee: both algebraic specifications of lists and sets have to be consistent, for the refinement to be meaningful.
- Algebraic refinement however does allow functional implementations only, that are not allowed to mutate data structures, since the abstract functions that have to be implemented, are specified as mathematical functions, that can not mutate their arguments (and the arguments may still be used after the function call). In contrast, the transitions of a state-based system can mutate the state, since the old state is no longer needed after a transition.

3 A State Module for ROBDDS

3.1 Reduced Ordered Binary Decision Diagrams

The VerifyThis competition is a yearly workshop event, in which various verification challenges are posed to participiants with fixed time limits. Challenge 2 of the 2023 edition defines algorithms, that construct reduced ordered binary trees (ROBDD) from a boolean formula. An example (reproduced from the task description [38]) is given in Fig. 2.

The representation is a directed acyclic graph, where each node tests a variable. Given an interpretation of the used variable, each node represents a test for the variable to be true. If it is, the solid branch is followed, otherwise the dotted branch. Two leaf nodes indicate the final result.

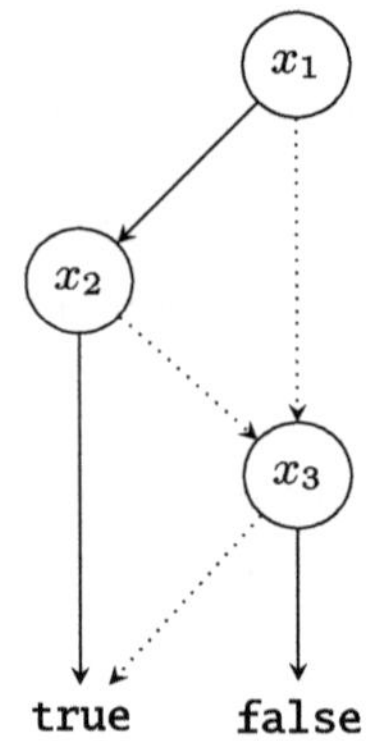

Fig. 2. ROBDD for the formula $(x_1 \wedge x_2) \vee x_3$.

The graph is *ordered*: variables are assumed to appear in ascending order. In the figure the order is indicated by the indices, the algorithms directly use integers. The graph is also *reduced*, i.e. the left and right subgraph of each node are never isomorphic. If two subgraphs were isomorphic, the case split on the variable does not matter, so the node with its two subgraphs can be replaced by one copy of the subgraph.

The Challenge also provides sample implementations in various programming languages, where the main procedures are $\texttt{and}(r_1,\ r_2)$ and $\texttt{not}(r)$. Given references r_1 and r_2 that point to ROBDDs (stored in the heap) for formulas φ_1 and φ_2 the first algorithm computes a reference to a ROBDD that represents $\varphi_1 \wedge \varphi_2$. Importantly, both algorithms are side-effect free, i.e. r_1 will still point to a graph that represents φ_1 after computing the new reference $\texttt{and}(r_1,\ r_2)$ that points to the conjunction. It, however, uses an extra map as a state that caches all nodes that the algorithm has already constructed: this allows to have an efficient test, whether two graphs are isomorphic, by simply comparing their two top-level nodes to be the same. The main verification task is to show the correctness of these operations implemented in a language of choice.

Of course it is possible, to verify the algorithms directly. However, from our perspective the algorithms mix two aspects, that can and should be separated in a clean solution, allowing for modular verification.

The first aspect is constructing a boolean formula as a semantically equivalent if-then-else formula (*IteFma*). This data type can be specified algebraically.

$$\begin{aligned}\textbf{data}\ \mathit{IteFma} = \ & \texttt{true}\\ \mid\ & \texttt{false}\\ \mid\ & \texttt{Ite}(\texttt{.var} : \mathit{Int};\ \texttt{.high} : \mathit{IteFma};\ \texttt{.low} : \mathit{IteFma})\ \textbf{with}\ \texttt{.ite?};\end{aligned}$$

where integers are used to denote variables (as specified in the challenge; a generic totally ordered type could of course be used as well). In the definition, predicate `.ite?` tests that an *IteFma* is constructed with `Ite` (so it is neither `true` nor `false`). The specification and verification of the core of the algorithm, then is a simple inductive proof using predicate logic, that we will detail in the next subsection. The other more difficult aspect is the implementation of the algebraic data type *IteFma* using a graph structure that optimally shares substructures. This is the task, for which we define a state module in Sect. 3.3.

3.2 Algebraic Verification in KIV

The main algorithms of the challenge are represented on the algebraic level as functions. $\wedge i$. : *IteFma* × *IteFma* → *IteFma* and $\neg i$: *IteFma* → *IteFma*. Their axioms are:

$$\texttt{mkIte}(i,\ ite1,\ ite2) = (ite1 = ite_2 \supset ite_1;\ \texttt{Ite}(i,\ ite_1,\ ite_2));$$

$$\neg i\ \texttt{true} = \texttt{false}; \qquad \neg i\ \texttt{false} = \texttt{true};$$

$$\neg i\ \texttt{Ite}(i,\ ite_1,\ ite_2) = \texttt{mkIte}(i, \neg i\ ite_1, \neg i\ ite_2);$$

$$\texttt{true}\ \wedge i\ ite = ite \qquad \texttt{false}\ \wedge i\ ite = \texttt{false};$$

$$ite\ \wedge i\ \texttt{true} = ite \qquad ite\ \wedge i\ \texttt{false} = \texttt{false};$$

$$\begin{aligned} & i_1 < i_2 \\ \rightarrow\ & \texttt{Ite}(i_1,\ ite_1,\ ite_2)\ \wedge i\ \texttt{Ite}(i_2,\ ite_3,\ ite_4) \\ & = \texttt{mkIte}(i_1,\ ite_1\ \wedge i\ \texttt{Ite}(i_2,\ ite_3,\ ite_4),\ ite_2\ \wedge i\ \texttt{Ite}(i_2,\ ite_3,\ ite_4)); \end{aligned}$$

$$\begin{aligned} & \texttt{Ite}(i,\ ite_1,\ ite_2)\ \wedge i\ \texttt{Ite}(i,\ ite_3,\ ite_4) \\ = \ & \texttt{mkIte}(i,\ ite_1\ \wedge i\ ite_3, ite_2\ \wedge i\ ite_4); \end{aligned}$$

$$\begin{aligned} & i_2 < i_1 \\ \rightarrow\ & \texttt{Ite}(i_1,\ ite_1,\ ite_2)\ \wedge i\ \texttt{Ite}(i_2,\ ite_3,\ ite_4) \\ & = \texttt{mkIte}(i_2,\ \texttt{Ite}(i_1,\ ite_1,\ ite_2)\ \wedge i\ ite_3,\ \texttt{Ite}(i_1,\ ite_1,\ ite_2)\ \wedge i\ ite_4); \end{aligned}$$

In the first axiom the formula $(\varphi \supset e_1; e_2)$ computes e_1 when the test is true, e_2 otherwise. Note that on this abstract level, the test necessary to ensure that the final formula is reduced is simple the equality test $ite_1 = ite_2$. This will be relevant for the final implementation of equality when using the graph based representation of IteFmas in the next section.

To prove the correctness of the two functions we have to show, that a) their result is always a reduced, ordered *IteFma*, when the inputs are, and b) the semantics of the constructed *IteFma* is the conjunction/negation of the semantics of the inputs.

To prove this we defined a predicate *redordered* : *IteFma* → *Bool* and an evaluation function: $[\![ite]\!]\ (\sigma)$ evaluates *ite* for an interpretation σ : *Int* → *Bool* of the variables. The axioms are straightforward:

$$\texttt{redordered(true)}; \qquad \texttt{redordered(false)};$$
$$\texttt{redordered(Ite}(i, ite_1, ite_2))$$
$$\leftrightarrow \quad \texttt{redordered}(ite_1) \wedge \texttt{redordered}(ite_2) \wedge ite_1 \neq ite_2$$
$$\wedge\ (ite_1\texttt{.ite?} \rightarrow i < ite_1\texttt{.var}) \wedge (ite_2\texttt{.ite?} \rightarrow i < ite_2\texttt{.var});$$

$$[\![\texttt{true}]\!]\ (\sigma); \qquad \neg[\![\texttt{false}]\!]\ (\sigma);$$
$$[\![\texttt{Ite}(i,\ ite_1,\ ite_2)]\!]\ (\sigma) \leftrightarrow (\sigma(i) \supset [\![ite_1]\!]\ (\sigma);\ [\![ite_2]\!]\ (\sigma));$$

With these definitions we can prove in KIV:

Theorem 1. *Correct construction of if-then-else formulas* The two functions $\wedge i$ and $\neg i$ are correct. They satisfy

$$\texttt{redordered}(ite_1) \wedge \texttt{redordered}(ite_2) \rightarrow \texttt{redordered}(ite_1\ \wedge i\ \ ite_2);$$
$$\texttt{redordered}(ite) \rightarrow \texttt{redordered}(\neg i\ ite);$$
$$[\![ite_1\ \ \wedge i\ \ ite_2]\!]\ (\sigma) \leftrightarrow\ [\![ite_1]\!]\ (\sigma)\ \wedge\ [\![ite_2]\!]\ (\sigma);$$
$$[\![\neg i\ ite]\!]\ (\sigma) \leftrightarrow \neg\ [\![ite]\!]\ (\sigma);$$

Proof. The proof of all four statements is by well-founded induction over the size of their inputs (for $\wedge i$ the sum of the two sizes decreases in the recursion). For the first two theorems the postcondition needs to be strengthened to ensure that the results computed by recursive calls use larger variables than the top-level. For $\wedge i$ the generalization is

$$\texttt{redordered}(ite_1) \wedge \texttt{redordered}(ite_2)$$
$$\rightarrow (\ \texttt{redordered}(ite_1\ \ \wedge i\ \ ite_2)$$
$$\wedge (\quad ite_1\texttt{.ite?} \wedge ite_2\texttt{.ite?} \wedge (ite_1 \wedge i\ ite_2)\texttt{.ite?}$$
$$\rightarrow \neg((ite_1 \wedge i\ ite_2).var < ite_1.var \wedge (ite_1 \wedge i\ ite_2).var < ite_2.var)) \quad \square$$

The proof required 57 interactions in KIV.

3.3 Implementing IteFmas with BDDs with a State Module

The original programs given by the challenge are implementations of functions $\wedge i$ and $\neg i$ that do not use abstract formulas of type *IteFma*, but directly use heap structures and a hashmap. This intertwines an efficient data representation of *IteFma* with the abstract algorithms of the previous section, so verification has to consider both aspects together. This section defines a state-based implementation of the algebraic type, which is now considered to be an interface to a state-based implementation.

The state module we define, specifies implementations for the primitive functions and predicates on *IteFma*: its constructors, selectors and the equality predicate. The abstract algorithms $\wedge i$ and $\neg i$ are kept as is (they form a standard recursive program), the full code just has to call the implementations of the primitive functions. The proof obligations that verify correctness of the state module, defined and verified in Section 4 have to guarantee, that replacing the interface of *IteFma* with the implementation is correct.

The representation of the data type *IteFma* is the same as in the original challenge. It becomes the state of an ASM, and we explain this state and the data types used first.

Heaps are a specialization of the algebraic type *Map*[*Key*, *Val*]. They map finitely many keys of type *Key* to values of type *Val*. Maps are constructed from the empty map (denoted $\varnothing$) by adding/overwriting key-value pairs with $map(k := v)$. Testing a key to be in the map is written $k \in map$. For a key in the map $map(k)$ returns the value stored. $\#map$ determines the number of keys in the map. The axioms for maps are:

$$map_1 = map_2 \leftrightarrow (\forall a.\ (a \in map_1 \leftrightarrow a \in map_2) \wedge map_1(a) = map_2(a))$$

$$\neg\ a \in \varnothing \qquad\qquad a \in map(b := d) \leftrightarrow a = b \vee a \in map$$

$$map(a := d)(a) = d \qquad\qquad a \neq b \rightarrow map(b := d)(a) = map(a)$$

$$\#\varnothing = 0; \qquad\qquad \neg\ a \in map \rightarrow \#map(a{:=}d) = \#map + 1;$$

The type of heaps specializes[2] maps by using the predefined type *Ref* of references as keys. These include the `null` pointer, which is not allowed to be used as a key. The heap type also has a predefined procedure

$$\textbf{alloc\#}(;\ h)\{\ \textbf{choose}\ ref\ \textbf{with}\ ref \notin h \wedge ref \neq \texttt{null}\ \textbf{in}\ \{\ h(ref){:=}v;\ ref\ \}\ \}$$

which allocates and returns a new reference (the value stored is unspecified). The notation $h(ref){:=}v$, that we also use in programs (and for maps) below, abbreviates $h{:=}h(ref := v)$. The heap that is used to represent BDDs stores nodes of type *Node*:

data *Node* = `L(.b` : *Bool*) **with** `.L?`
| `N(.var` : *Int*; `.high` : *Ref*; `.low` : *Ref*) **with** `.N?`;

and we write *Heap* as an abbreviation for *Map*[*Ref*, *Node*]. An additional map stores a reverse mapping for all non-leaf nodes of the graph constructed so far, Its keys are triples (*Int*, *Ref*, *Ref*) that are mapped to references as values *Ref*. In the following we will simply write *Map* instead of *Map*[(*Int*, *Ref*, *Ref*), *Ref*]. The full state of our implementation is

$$\textbf{state}\ h : Heap, map : Map, trueref : Ref, falseref : Ref;$$

It contains two references *trueref* and *falseref* that are initialized (in procedure **init#**) to point to the two preallocated nodes that store the constants `true` and `false`.

[2] Formally, the type is specified separately: KIV's code generator generates objects on the global heap for this type, and enforces that the heap is never copied or used as a component of another type. For *Map*, instead hash maps are generated.

A listing of the procedures defined by the ASM is given in Fig. 3. State variables used in the procedure bodies are implicitly part of the value or reference parameters (depending on the usage) and not explicitly listed, since they are not visible to an outside caller. They must be different from the parameters given explicitly.

```
init#()
  initialization
{ map := ∅; h := ∅;
  trueref := alloc#(; h);
  h(trueref) := L(true);
  falseref := alloc#(; h);
  h(falseref) := L(false); }

mkite#(i, ref_1, ref_2) : Ref
  pre ref_1 ∈ h ∧ ref_2 ∈ h;
{ if (i, ref_2, ref_2) ∈ map
  then map((i, ref_1, ref_2))
  else let ref = alloc#(; h) in {
         map(ref) := N(i, ref_1, ref_2);
         map((i, ref_1, ref_2)) := ref;
         ref } }

high#(ref) : Ref
  pre  ref ∈ h ∧ ref ≠ trueref
         ∧ ref ≠ falseref;
{ map(ref).high }

low#(ref) : Ref
  pre  ref ∈ h ∧ ref ≠ trueref
         ∧ ref ≠ falseref;
{ map(ref).low }

var#(ref) : Int
  pre  ref ∈ h ∧ ref ≠ trueref
         ∧ ref ≠ falseref;
{ map(ref).var }

isIte#(ref) : Bool
  pre ref ∈ h;
{ ref ≠ trueref ∧ ref ≠ falseref }

false#() : Ref { falseref }

true#() : Ref { trueref }
```

Fig. 3. Procedures implementing type *IteFma* in BDD-ASM.

BDD-ASM guarantees that *map* always stores a reverse mapping for all nodes allocated in the heap. The state module itself defines an abstraction relation, that associates an if-then-else formula with a reference in the heap, that stores the corresponding BDD. It also specifies the obvious mapping from the primitive functions defined on *IteFma* to the procedures of Fig. 3. Both the invariant and the abstraction relation will be formally specified in Sect. 4.1, after we specify the concept in general and have defined the necessary proof obligations that ensure correctness of the state module in the next section.

4 State Modules and Their Correctness

In this section we describe *state modules* and their correctness formally. We start with a formal definition, together with an explanation how the module described in the previous section realizes each component.

Definition 1. *Components of a State Module*

A State Module STMOD = (*Exp*, *ASM*, *Imp*, ρ, *abs*, π) consists of the following components:

- An algebraic specification *Exp*, the export specification. In our example this specification defines the type *IteFma*.
- An abstract state machine *ASM* (the import machine) that is used to implement the abstract data type. The machine has a state consisting of a tuple of state variables $\underline{sv}$ of types $\underline{\text{sty}}$. A valuation w assigns them some values $w(\underline{sv}) = \underline{st}$. It offers operations on the state as procedures: each procedure $q(\underline{x}; \underline{sv})$ has some inputs $\underline{x}$, modifies the state and returns an output value. The machine uses an import specification *Imp* to specify the algebraic types used by the state variables, inputs and outputs. In our BDD module, the ASM defines $\underline{sv} = h, map, trueref, falseref$ and the procedures shown in Fig. 3.
- A sort mapping ρ, that maps export sorts to import sorts. We use as to denote an export sort, and cs to denote the corresponding import sorts $cs = \rho(as)$. The two predefined sorts *Bool* and *Unit* cannot be mapped. Sorts not explicitly mapped are implicitly mapped by identity, i.e. they must be present in the import specification.
  For the BDD module we have $\rho(IteFma) = Ref$, no other sort is mapped.
- For every mapped sort as, an abstraction relation (a predicate) $abs_{as} : as \times cs \times \underline{sty} \rightarrow Bool$ that relates elements of the export type to its representation used by the import machine. For non-mapped sorts, the relation is identity, ignoring the state. We drop the index as in the following and write $abs(ax, cx, \underline{sv})$, since the type can be inferred from the type of variable $ax : as$. In the case of a nonmapped sort, the formula just abbreviates $ax = cx$. For the BDD module the abstraction relation *abs* is defined in Section 4.1.
- A mapping π, that maps some of the functions $f : \underline{as} \rightarrow as$ of the export spec that involve mapped export sorts to an implementing procedure $\pi(f)$ in the import machine. The type of procedure $\pi(f)$ is required to be $\rho(\underline{as}); \underline{sty} \rightarrow \rho(as)$, i.e. the procedure uses the corresponding input types, modifies the state and returns the corresponding output type. It is necessary to map at least constructors and non-constructively defined functions of the export specification. If an export operation has a constructive definition (e.g. a structural recursive definition) that is based on other functions, that are implemented, it is optional to provide an implementation for efficiency. For the BDD module all operations were implemented, we will see examples, where only some operations are implemented, in the next section.
- An implementation for equality on a mapped type as can be optionally provided as a procedure eq_{as} of type $\rho(as), \rho(as); \underline{sty} \rightarrow Bool$. If none is given, it defaults to equality on $\rho(as)$ (and ignores the state). This is the case for the BDD module, where the implementation is equality of references. Examples with a different implementation of equality are given in the next section.

To prove correctness, we now define a translation of programs over the export spec to programs that call the operations of the import machine. Roughly, we show that the behavior of both programs is the same, modulo the abstraction relation.

To define the translation formally, we assume that the export and import specification use two disjoint sets of variables $AX = \{ax_1, ax_2, \ldots\}$ and $CX = \{cx_1, cx_2, \ldots\}$, such that the sorts are compatible (if $ax_i : as$ then $cx_i : \rho(as)$) and that both variable sets do not involve $\underline{sv}$. Any program over the export specification then uses some variables $\underline{ax}$, which are a finite subset of AX.

Definition 2. *Translation of Programs*

Given a state module STMOD and an abstract program p, the translated program $\tau(p)$ is defined as follows:

- $\tau(ax_i) \stackrel{\text{def}}{=} cx_i$
- $\tau(f(\underline{p})) \stackrel{\text{def}}{=} \pi(f)(\tau(\underline{p}), \underline{sv})$
- $\tau(p_1 = p_2) \stackrel{\text{def}}{=} eq_{as}(\tau(p_1), \tau(p_2); \underline{sv})$ if an implementation of equality is given, $\tau(p_1) = \tau(p_2)$ otherwise.
- All other cases are defined homomorphically, e.g. $\tau(\textbf{if } p_1 \textbf{ then } p_2 \textbf{ else } p_3) \stackrel{\text{def}}{=} \textbf{if } \tau(p_1) \textbf{ then } \tau(p_2) \textbf{ else } \tau(p_3)$

If the type of p is as, then $\tau(p) : \rho(as)$. In particular the type does not change, if it is not mapped explicitly. If p uses variables from $\underline{ax}$, then $\tau(p)$ uses the corresponding variables $\underline{cx}$ and the state variables $\underline{sv}$.

To prove equivalence, we assume that initial states for both programs are related by the abstraction relation:

Definition 3. *Related States*

Given an Algebra $\mathcal{A} \in Alg(Exp \cup Imp)$, two states v and w with $dom(v) = \underline{ax}$ and $dom(w) = \underline{cx} \mathbin{\dot{\cup}} \underline{sv}$ are related by abs, written $v \stackrel{\text{abs}}{=} w$ iff $abs^{\mathcal{A}}(v(ax_i), w(cx_i), w(\underline{sv}))$ holds for all i.

Theorem 2. *Correctness of State Modules*

If the proof obligations given below hold, then for any two states with $v \stackrel{\text{abs}}{=} w$ and for every program p with $free(p) \subseteq dom(v)$

$$\langle p, v\rangle \Rightarrow (v', a) \text{ iff } \langle \tau(p), w\rangle \Rightarrow (w', c)$$

with $v' \stackrel{\text{abs}}{=} w'$ and $abs^{\mathcal{A}}(a, c, \underline{st})$

Informally: when started in two states related by the abstraction relation, the original program terminates iff the translated program does too, and both programs result in final states and result values, that are related again by the abstraction relation. In particular, if the result value is not of a mapped type, it is equal. To prove the theorem we define the following proof obligations:

Definition 4. *Proof Obligations*

For any f where $\pi(\mathrm{f}) = \mathrm{q}$ we have to prove

$$abs(ax_0, cx_0, \underline{sv}) \wedge abs(ax_1, cx_1, \underline{sv}) \wedge \ldots \wedge abs(ax_n, cx_n, \underline{sv})$$
$$\rightarrow \langle\!| cx{:=}q(\underline{cx}; \underline{sv}) |\!\rangle\, (abs(ax_0, cx_0, \underline{sv}) \wedge abs(f(ax_1, \ldots, ax_n), cx))$$

Here, a formula $\langle\!| p |\!\rangle\, \varphi$ has to be read as a weakest-precondition formula: it states, that program p (which must be of type $Unit$) terminates for every initial state and that all runs ensure that the postcondition φ holds at the end. Therefore, the proof obligation gives two guarantees: first, if the abstract inputs stored in $ax_1, \ldots ax_n$ are related to concrete inputs in $cx_1, \ldots cx_n$ then q terminates and its output cx is related to the result $f(ax_1, \ldots ax_n)$ of calling f. Second, if any two values a_0 and c_0 (stored as $v(ax_0)$ and $v(cx_0)$) are related before the call, the values are still related after the call even though the state has changed. In other words the state change preserves abstraction relations between *any* two related values a_0 and c_0.

Formally, we can prove:

Lemma 1. *Correctness of Function Application*
The proof obligation above guarantees: if

- $abs^{\mathcal{A}}(a_0, c_0, w(\underline{sv}))$ for some arbitrary a_0, c_0
- $v \stackrel{\text{abs}}{=} w$
- $abs^{\mathcal{A}}(\underline{a}, w(\underline{x}), w(\underline{sv}))$

all hold, then there is a closed derivation tree for conclusion $\langle q(\underline{x}; \underline{sv}), w\rangle \Rightarrow (w', d)$ that satisfies

- $abs^{\mathcal{A}}(a_0, c_0, w'(\underline{sv}))$
- $v \stackrel{\text{abs}}{=} w'$
- $abs^{\mathcal{A}}(f^{\mathcal{A}}(\underline{a}), d, w'(\underline{sv}))$

The proof of the lemma uses the soundness of the calculus applied to the proof obligation: Assume a call starts in an arbitrary state $v + w + \{cx \mapsto c\}$ that combines a state v with domain $ax_0, \ldots ax_n$, a state w with domain $cx_0, \ldots, cx_n, \underline{sv}$ and an (irrelevant) initial value c for cx, such that $v \stackrel{\text{abs}}{=} w$ holds. For such a state the precondition of the proof obligation is clearly satisfied.

This implies that the call will terminate and end in a state $v + w' + \{cx \mapsto d\}$ (note that the program does not change the variables of v) that satisfies the postcondition. The existence of a terminating run means that there is a closed derivation tree for $\langle cx{:=}q(\underline{x}; \underline{sv}), v + w + \{cx \mapsto c\}\rangle \Rightarrow (v + w' + \{cx \mapsto d\}, \circ)$ for some final state $v + w' + \{cx \mapsto d\}$. Removing the last step of this derivation which moves the computed value of the call to cx using rule R(asg), we get a closed derivation for $\langle q(\underline{x}; \underline{sv}), v + w + \{cx \mapsto c\}\rangle \Rightarrow (v + w' + \{cx \mapsto c\}, d)$. Since the call neither uses the variables from $dom(v)$ nor cx, they can be dropped using a simple coincidence lemma resulting in the closed derivation required by the lemma. Since the program also does not use cx_0 and ax_0, the derivation is independent of the two values these store in the initial state, and both values do not change.

Finally, the proof obligation asserts that the two postconditions hold in the final state $v + w' + \{cx \mapsto d\}$. The first of them establishes the first guarantee of the lemma by choosing $v(ax_0) = a_0$ and $w(cx_0) = c_0$. The second guarantee also follows by noting that we can choose the values stored in ax_0 and cx_0 to be any of $v(ax_i)$ and $w(cx_i)$ (for $i = 1 \ldots n$), which implies $abs^{\mathcal{A}}(a_i, c_i, w'(\underline{sv}))$, i.e. $v \stackrel{\text{abs}}{=} w'$. Finally, the second postcondition implies $abs^{\mathcal{A}}(f^{\mathcal{A}}(\underline{a}), d, w'(\underline{sv}))$.

With the lemma, we can now prove the main Theorem 2:

Proof. The proof is by induction over the size of a closed derivation (or equivalently, by fixpoint induction for the rules). The structure of both the abstract and the concrete derivation tree is the same, except that at function calls (rule R(app)), where the function call is translated to a procedure call the proof tree for the translated program attaches some derivation tree as given by Lemma 1. We prove a slightly generalized induction hypothesis, where additionally to the main theorem, we show, that given $abs^{\mathcal{A}}(a_0, c_0, w(\underline{sv}))$ for some arbitrary a_0 and c_0, $abs^{\mathcal{A}}(a_0, c_0, w'(\underline{sv}))$ also holds, similar to Lemma 1.

An induction step is necessary for each rule of the semantics as defined in Sect. 2.2. It assumes as its induction hypothesis that the generalized theorem already holds for all premises, and has to establish the generalized theorem for the conclusion. It can be assumed that the conclusions have the form $\langle p, v\rangle \Rightarrow (v', a)$ and $\langle \tau(p), w\rangle \Rightarrow (w', c)$ respectively (for some specific program) and that $v \stackrel{\text{abs}}{=} w$ holds. From this we must establish $v' \stackrel{\text{abs}}{=} w'$, $abs^{\mathcal{A}}(a_0, c_0, w'(\underline{sv}))$ and $abs^{\mathcal{A}}(a, c, w'(\underline{sv}))$ for the final state w' and computed values a and c.

For rule R(var) the step is trivial, since $v = v'$, $w = w'$, $a = v(x)$ and $c = w(x)$. For rule R(app) we have $p = f(\underline{p})$ and there are two cases: Either the function is not translated, then the rule in the concrete derivation tree is R(app) too. Otherwise we have $\tau(f) = q$ and the rule applied in the concrete derivation is R(call). In both cases the premises for the arguments guarantee that $v_i \stackrel{\text{abs}}{=} w_i$ and $abs^{\mathcal{A}}(a_i, c_i, w_i(\underline{sv}))$ hold for all $0 \leq i \leq n$ using the induction hypothesis. This already establishes $v_n \stackrel{\text{abs}}{=} w_n$. We however need to prove $abs^{\mathcal{A}}(a_i, c_i, w_n(\underline{sv}))$ for all i and the *last* state w_n after evaluating all arguments. Evaluating e.g. the second argument should not invalidate that *abs* holds for the already computed result of the first argument. The generalized induction hypothesis for all premises with indices bigger than i guarantees that this is indeed provable.

If f is not translated then all of its arguments are not from the implemented sorts, so a_i and c_i are equal for all i, and so is the result of applying f^A. In this case $v_n = v'$ and $w_n = w'$ which establishes $v' \stackrel{\text{abs}}{=} w'$. When $\tau(f) = q$ then Lemma 1 has to be applied using v_n and w_n as the states v and w before the call. The lemma establishes both $v' \stackrel{\text{abs}}{=} w'$ and $abs^{\mathcal{A}}(a, c, \underline{st'})$ for the states after the call. Note that this also has the generalized form which says that already computed values will also preserve *abs*.

For R(asg), where $p = x{:=}rhs$ we have $abs^{\mathcal{A}}(a, c, \underline{st'})$ for the values a and c and $v' \stackrel{\text{abs}}{=} w'$ for the two states v' and w' that result from evaluating the right hand side. This obviously implies $v'\{x \mapsto a\} \stackrel{\text{abs}}{=} w'\{x \mapsto c\}$ for the two states after the assignment. All other rules are fairly easy, as their premises already imply that *abs* is propagated to the final states and values. Note that the test of a conditional or while loop is never affected by τ, i.e. in both derivation trees the same boolean is computed. □

4.1 Verification of the BDD Module

Applying the general approach, we can now prove the module of the previous section:

Theorem 3. The proof obligations for the state module given in Sect. 3 hold for the implementation.

The proof has been done in KIV and is available online [33]. It splits into proving an invariant for the BDD-ASM, that ensures that the cache used is always the inverse mapping of what is stored in the heap. Formally:

$$
\begin{aligned}
&\mathit{inv}(\mathit{map},\ h,\ \mathit{trueref},\ \mathit{falseref}) \leftrightarrow \\
&\qquad \mathit{trueref} \in h \wedge \mathit{trueref} \neq \mathit{null} \wedge \mathit{map}(\mathit{trueref}) = \mathtt{L}(\mathtt{true}) \\
&\quad \wedge \mathit{falseref} \in h \wedge \mathit{falseref} \neq \mathit{null} \wedge \mathit{map}(\mathit{falseref}) = \mathtt{L}(\mathtt{false}) \\
&\quad \wedge (\forall\ \mathit{ref}.\ \mathit{ref} \neq \mathit{trueref} \wedge \mathit{ref} \neq \mathit{falseref} \wedge \mathit{ref} \in h \\
&\qquad \rightarrow \quad \mathit{map}(\mathit{ref})\mathtt{.N?} \\
&\qquad\qquad \wedge\ (\mathit{map}(\mathit{ref})\mathtt{.var}, \mathit{map}(\mathit{ref})\mathtt{.high}, \mathit{map}(\mathit{ref})\mathtt{.low}) \in \mathit{map} \\
&\qquad\qquad \wedge\ \mathit{ref} = \mathit{map}((\mathit{map}(\mathit{ref})\mathtt{.var}, \mathit{map}(\mathit{ref})\mathtt{.high}, \mathit{map}(\mathit{ref})\mathtt{.low}))) \\
&\quad \wedge (\forall\ i,\ \mathit{ref}_1,\ \mathit{ref}_2.\ (i,\ \mathit{ref}_1,\ \mathit{ref}_2) \in \mathit{map} \\
&\qquad \rightarrow \quad \mathit{map}((i,\ \mathit{ref}_1,\ \mathit{ref}_2)) \in h \\
&\qquad\qquad \wedge\ \mathit{map}(\mathit{map}((i, \mathit{ref}_1, \mathit{ref}_2))) = \mathtt{N}(i, \mathit{ref}_1, \mathit{ref}_2))
\end{aligned}
$$

Proving this invariant required 11 interactions.

To verify the state module itself, an abstraction relation $\mathit{abs}(\mathit{ref}, h, \mathit{ite})$ is defined, that relates the BDD stored at *ref* in the heap, with the if-then-else formula *ite*. It is defined as follows:

$$
\begin{aligned}
&\mathit{abs}(\mathit{ref}, h, \mathtt{false}) \leftrightarrow \mathit{ref} \in h \wedge \mathit{ref} \neq \mathit{null} \wedge \mathit{map}(\mathit{ref}) = \mathtt{L}(\mathtt{false}); \\
&\mathit{abs}(\mathit{ref}, h,\ \mathtt{true}\ ) \leftrightarrow \mathit{ref} \in h \wedge \mathit{ref} \neq \mathit{null} \wedge \mathit{map}(\mathit{ref}) = \mathtt{L}(\ \mathtt{true}\ ); \\
&\mathit{abs}(\mathit{ref},\ h,\ \mathtt{Ite}(i,\ \mathit{ite}_1,\ \mathit{ite}_2)) \\
&\quad \leftrightarrow \quad \mathit{ref} \in h \wedge \mathit{ref} \neq \mathit{null} \wedge \mathit{map}(\mathit{ref})\mathtt{.N?} \wedge \mathit{map}(\mathit{ref})\mathtt{.var} = i \\
&\qquad\quad \wedge\, \mathit{abs}(\mathit{map}(\mathit{ref})\mathtt{.high}, h, \mathit{ite}_1) \wedge \mathit{abs}(\mathit{map}(\mathit{ref})\mathtt{.low}, h, \mathit{ite}_2);
\end{aligned}
$$

As an example of a proof obligation, the one for the constructor `Ite` is:

$$
\begin{aligned}
&\qquad \mathit{abs}(\mathit{ref}_1, h, \mathit{ite}_1) \wedge\ \mathit{abs}(\mathit{ref}_2, h, \mathit{ite}_2) \wedge\ \mathit{abs}(\mathit{ref}_0, h, \mathit{ite}_0) \\
&\quad \wedge\ \mathit{inv}(\mathit{map},\ h,\ \mathit{trueref},\ \mathit{falseref}) \\
&\rightarrow \langle\!|\ \mathit{ref}{:=}\mathbf{BDD\_mkite\#}(i, \mathit{ref}_1, \mathit{ref}_2; \mathit{map}, h)\ |\!\rangle \\
&\qquad \langle\ \mathit{ite}{:=}\mathtt{Ite}(i, \mathit{ite}_1, \mathit{ite}_2)\ \rangle\ (\mathit{abs}(\mathit{ref}, h, \mathit{ite}) \wedge \mathit{abs}(\mathit{ref}_0, h, \mathit{ite}_0));
\end{aligned}
$$

It states that the procedure **BDD_mkite#**[3] called on a variable index i and two references ref_1 and ref_2 corresponding to ite_1 and ite_2 returns a reference *ite* that matches $\mathtt{Ite}(i, \mathit{ite}_1, \mathit{ite}_2)$. Additionally the proof obligation requires **BDD_mkite#** to preserve *abs* on an arbitrary reference ref_0 to ensure, that the operation does not break the abstraction for unrelated references previously returned by the ASM.

[3] Procedures defined in ASM in KIV get the name of the ASM, here 'BDD' as a prefix.

The proof obligations have rather simple proofs in KIV with 35 interactions total.

5 Examples of State Modules

This section discusses examples of two standard classes of implementations, that are instances of the refinement concept of state modules. The first class is the standard implementation of free data types, that is used in almost all functional languages as well as in Scala (for abstract classes with case classes as subclasses). Binary trees or abstract syntax trees for programming languages would all be suitable instances. To avoid the introduction of new types we just use the free data type of lists and the standard representation with cons-cells that underlies e.g. LISP in Sec. sec:list-conscell.

The second class is the object-oriented implementation of an algebraic type, which gives objects of a type an *identity*. A semantics where there is a difference between objects being identical or just being equal ("reference semantics") underlies all object-oriented programming languages, as well as specification languages like UML and Object-Z [34]. Again, to avoid introducing new types, we will use the type of lists, but an arbitrary data type is possible.

Both state modules are also shown in the web presentation [33].

5.1 Refining Lists with Cons Cells

The usual implementation of lists in functional languages is a null-terminated linked list of cons-cells in the heap. We define an ASM and a state module that refines the algebraic type *List* to this ASM. Its state is a heap similar to the one used in Section 3, except that the nodes stored in the heap are now cons-cells of type

$$\textbf{data}\ \mathit{Cell}\ =\ .\times.\ (\texttt{.val} : \mathit{Elem};\ \texttt{.nxt} : \mathit{Ref});$$
$$\textbf{state}\ h : \mathit{Heap};$$

The ASM implements all constructors and selectors of the *List* type as well as an empty initialization and an equality check shown in Fig. 4.

Note that in contrast to the one of Sect. 3 we must now use an implementation of the equality test that compares lists structurally, since there may now be two copies of the same list stored under different references.

The state module defines the obvious mapping from functions to implementing procedures and an abstraction relation

$$\textbf{abstraction relation}\ \lambda\ x,\ \mathit{ref}.\ (\texttt{ls}(\mathit{ref}, x) * \texttt{true})(h);$$

that makes use of a separation logic formula from KIV's library [30]. The predicate `ls` is also used in [23]. The formula states, that the heap can be split (expressed by the ∗-Operator) into two disjoint pieces. One is arbitrary (satisfies

init#() { }

nil#() : *Ref* { `null` }

cons#$(a, ref; h)$: *Ref*
{ **let** ref_0 = **alloc#**(; h) **in** { $h(ref_0) := a \times ref;\ ref_0$ } }

head#(ref, h) : A { $h(ref).val$ }

tail#(ref, h) : *Ref* { $h(ref)$`.nxt` }

equals#(ref_1, ref_2, h) : *Bool*
{ **if** $ref_1 = ref_2$ **then** `true`
else if $ref_1 =$ `null` $\vee\ ref_2 =$ `null` $\vee\ h(ref_1)$`.val` $\neq h(ref_2)$`.val`
then `false` **else** **equals#**$(h(ref_1)$`.nxt`, $h(ref_2)$`.nxt`, h) }

Fig. 4. ASM implementing lists with cons cells

`true`), the other stores an acyclic, null-terminated sequence of cons-cells with the same values as in x.

KIV again generates proof obligations, the one for cons-cells is:

$$\begin{array}{l}(\mathtt{ls}(ref, x) * \mathtt{true})(h) \wedge (\mathtt{ls}(ref_1, x_1) * \mathtt{true})(h) \\ \rightarrow \langle\!| \ ref_0 := \mathbf{cons\#}(a, ref; h) \ |\!\rangle \\ \quad \langle \ x_0 := a + x \ \rangle \ ((\mathtt{ls}(ref_0, x_0) * \mathtt{true})(h) \wedge (\mathtt{ls}(ref_1, x_1) * \mathtt{true})(h));\end{array}$$

One must show, that invoking cons on a reference *ref* representing a list x returns a reference ref_0, which represents the list $a + x$. At the same time the abstraction of another reference ref_1 to a list x_1 must not be broken by **cons#**. For the case $ref = ref_1$ this also implies, that *ref* stays a valid reference to x.

Optionally the state module can also refine other functions defined on lists to more efficient implementations. As an example the append function `app` : $List \times List \rightarrow List$ could be implemented algebraically using

$$\mathtt{app}(x, y) = (x = \mathtt{[]} \supset y; x\mathtt{.head} + \mathtt{app}(x\mathtt{.tail}, y))$$

but it is also possible to give an implementation in the state module (which is sometimes more efficient). We have done so, using an auxiliary procedure **copy#**

as follows:

$$
\begin{array}{l}
\textbf{copy\#}(\mathit{ref}; h; \mathit{ref}_1, \mathit{ref}_2) \\
\quad \{\ \mathit{ref}_1 := \textbf{alloc\#}(;\ h); h(\mathit{ref}_1) := h(\mathit{ref})\texttt{.val} \times \texttt{null}; \mathit{ref}_2 := \mathit{ref}_1; \\
\quad\quad \textbf{let}\ \mathit{ref}_3 = \texttt{null}\ \textbf{in while}\ h(\mathit{ref})\texttt{.nxt} \neq \texttt{null}\ \textbf{do}\ \{ \\
\quad\quad\quad \mathit{ref} := h(\mathit{ref})\texttt{.nxt}; \mathit{ref}_3 := \textbf{alloc\#}(;\ h); \\
\quad\quad\quad h(\mathit{ref}_3) := h(\mathit{ref})\texttt{.val} \times \texttt{null}; h(\mathit{ref}_2)\texttt{.nxt} := \mathit{ref}_3; \mathit{ref}_2 := \mathit{ref}_3\ \}\ \}
\end{array}
$$

$$
\begin{array}{l}
\textbf{append\#}(\mathit{ref}_1, \mathit{ref}_2; h) : \mathit{Ref} \\
\quad \{\ \textbf{if}\ \mathit{ref}_1 = \texttt{null}\ \textbf{then}\ \mathit{ref}_2\ \textbf{else let}\ \mathit{ref}_3 = \texttt{null}, \mathit{ref}_4 = \texttt{null}\ \textbf{in} \\
\quad\quad \{\ \textbf{copy\#}(\mathit{ref}_1; h; \mathit{ref}_3, \mathit{ref}_4); h(\mathit{ref}_4)\texttt{.nxt} := \mathit{ref}_2; \mathit{ref}_3\ \}\ \}
\end{array}
$$

copy# returns references to the beginning and end of a copy of the first list as output parameters and **append#** links the end of the copy to the beginning of the second list. While the second list can be reused, it is not possible to destructively update the last cell of the first list, because the caller may still use the reference ref_1 to the input list in further calls.

Proving the state module was quite simple. The most complex proof of a lemma for **copy#** needed 12 of 37 total interactions.

5.2 Refining Lists with List Objects

Another refinement made possible with state modules, is to implement an arbitrary algebraic type T as objects with an identity or reference. The representation uses a state that maps a type of identities Id to currently allocated objects of type T. In general we have

$$\textbf{state}\ \mathit{map} : \mathit{Map}[\mathit{Id}, T]$$

There is always a function that returns a new identity to allocate a new object. A special case is to use references (i.e. $\mathit{Id} = \mathit{Ref}$) as identities. Then the map is a heap with the **alloc#**(; h) procedure as used in Sect. 3.

In the example module of this section we will just use natural numbers (type Nat) as the type Id of identities. A counter is added to the state, and getting a new Id will increment the counter. The type T we implement is again lists, so we have

$$\textbf{state}\ \mathit{map} : \mathit{Map}[\mathit{Nat}, \mathit{List}], \mathit{maxId} : \mathit{Nat}$$

as the state of the implementation. Note that the implementation does not change the type of lists itself, it just adds an identity.

The implementations of an OO-ASM with this state are given in Fig. 5. The operations are implemented differently, showing some of the variations, that are possible.

The simplest implementation of an operation just allocates and returns a new identity, under which the function result of the algebraic operation is stored. The cons operation on lists is implemented by **cons#** in this way, and any operation on any data type can be schematically implemented in this way.

It is however possible to use other implementations that try not to create a new object every time the algebraic operation is called. A simple case is the implementation of constants like the one for the empty list: there OO-ASM preallocates the id 0 in the initialization routine **init#** to store the empty list, and every call to **nil#** returns the predefined id. This is the same strategy that was used for `true` and `false` in Sect. 3.

It is also possible to check, whether an object that is already created can be re-used as a return value. The technique of memoization that keeps a cache for every function (of arguments and results already computed) would be one example of such a reuse, the construction of BDDs in Sect. 3 is the extreme case, where every BDD node is re-used.

tail# shows a generic specification that allows reuse: if an id exists that already stores the tail of the input list x, it is possible to be reused, alternatively a new object is constructed. Again all operations could be schematically implemented in this way, allowing any concrete caches (e.g. an LRU cache) to be used in a standard state-based refinement of OO-ASM.

The implementation of equality with **equals#** checks $id_1 = id_2$ first for efficiency, and only compares the lists, if the identity is different. Just doing the

init#$(; map, maxId)$ $\{\ map := \varnothing(0 := []); maxId := 0\ \}$

nil#$()$: Nat $\{\ 0\ \}$

cons#$(a, id; map, maxId) : Nat$
pre $id \in map$;
$\{\ maxId := maxId + 1; map(maxId) := a + map(id); maxId\ \}$

head#$(id, map) : A$
pre $id \in map \wedge map(id) \neq []$;
$\{\ (mp(id))\texttt{.head}\ \}$

tail#$(id; map, maxId) : Nat$
pre $id \in map \wedge map(id) \neq []$;
$\{$ **choose** id_1 **with**
$id_1 \leq maxId \wedge map(id_1) = map(id)\texttt{.tail} \vee id_1 = maxId + 1$ **in**
if $id_1 = maxId + 1$
then $\{\ maxId := maxId + 1; map(id_1) := map(id)\texttt{.tail}\ \}$;
$id_1\ \}$

equals#$(id_1, id_2, map) : Bool$
pre $id_1 \in map \wedge id_2 \in map$;
$\{\ id_1 = id_2 \vee map(id_1) = map(id_2)\ \}$

Fig. 5. Implementation of List operations in OO-ASM

first check here would be incorrect, since we have no guarantee that each list is stored only once as in the ASM for BDDs in Sect. 3. A state-based refinement of OO-ASM could add hash-codes for the objects in order to increase the efficiency of equality tests. For example, case classes in Scala automatically define and use such hash codes.

The proof of the module uses an invariant for OO-ASM, that guarantees $map(0) = []$ and that all *id*s below *maxId* are used. The abstraction relation of the state module associates an *id* to a list x, if *map* has an according entry:

invariants $map(0) = [] \wedge (\forall\ id.\ id \in map \leftrightarrow id \leq maxId);$

abstraction relation $\lambda\ x, id.\ id \in map \wedge map(id) = x;$

The correctness proofs for the invariant and the state module are almost automatic (2 interactions).

6 Conclusion

We have defined the concept of state modules that bridges the gap between an algebraic specification of data types and a state-based implementation. The concept is useful to split the verification of algorithms into a conceptual part, and a data representation part as demonstrated with the BDD example.

The case studies we have shown in this paper were of a conceptual nature. We have not yet done complex case studies. The concept could be used to study what is usually called persistent (or immutable) data types like [37] based e.g. on tries [20] in programming languages, that offer an efficient representation of data structures, while the interface hides any mutation. Another concept that could be realized with a state module is memoization, where recently accessed objects are cached and reused to increase efficiency.

The concept has three limitations: first, to support concurrency, the implementing procedures must be implemented atomically, otherwise two concurrent calls might result in inconsistent updates on the state (concurrency is not considered in the simple semantics we give in this paper). However, proving an ASM to have atomic operations is already supported by our approach [4]. Second, mutating the abstract objects is not allowed, since this would cause side-effects on other variables. An example would be a mutating implementation of append on cons-cell lists, that does not copy the first list, but just links the second one to the end of the first. Third, garbage collection is necessary (at least in general) for the implementation: if a variable falls out of use in an abstract program using the algebraic data type, the portion of the state storing its representation can and should be freed. Therefore we currently plan to integrate the concept into KIV's code generator for Scala, but not into the one generating C code.

There are currently a number of object-oriented refinement ideas, e.g. the one of Dafny [21]: these allow a mutating append at the price, that their abstract specification of append is no longer purely algebraic. Side-effects then need to be considered when verifying programs over lists, using footprints (or formulas of separation logic).

We currently work on a concept of state modules, that allows side-effects, like using a mutating append, that also does not need garbage collection. Instead it requires help by the code generator, to ensure that these side-effects do not modify the semantics of code using algebraic lists. Some ideas towards this goal can be found in [32].

References

1. Abadi, M., Lamport, L.: The existence of refinement mappings. Theor. Comput. Sci. **2**, 253–284 (1991). Also appeared as SRC Research Report 29
2. Abrial, J.-R.: The B-Book: Assigning Programs to Meanings. Cambridge University Press, Cambridge (1996)
3. Abrial, J.-R.: Modeling in Event-B - System and Software Engineering. Cambridge University Press, Cambridge (2010)
4. Bodenmüller, S., Schellhorn, G., Bitterlich, M., Reif, W.: Flashix: modular verification of a concurrent and crash-safe flash file system. In: Raschke, A., Riccobene, E., Schewe, K.-D. (eds.) Logic, Computation and Rigorous Methods. LNCS, vol. 12750, pp. 239–265. Springer, Cham (2021). https://doi.org/10.1007/978-3-030-76020-5_14
5. Börger, E.: A logical operational semantics of full Prolog. In: Börger, E., Büning, H.K., Richter, M.M. (eds.) CSL 1989. LNCS, vol. 440, pp. 36–64. Springer, Heidelberg (1990a). https://doi.org/10.1007/3-540-52753-2_31
6. Börger, E.: A logical operational semantics of full Prolog. Part II: built-in predicates for database manipulation. In: Rovan, B. (ed.) MFCS 1990. LNCS, vol. 452, pp. 1–14. Springer, Heidelberg (1990b). https://doi.org/10.1007/BFb0029592
7. Börger, E.: The ASM refinement method. Formal Aspects Comput. **15**(1–2), 237–257 (2003)
8. Broy, M., Möller, B., Pepper, P., Wirsing, M.: Algebraic implementations preserve program correctness. Sci. Comput. Program. **7**, 35–53 (1986)
9. Chicli, L., Pottier, L., Simpson, C.: Mathematical quotients and quotient types in Coq. In: Geuvers, H., Wiedijk, F. (eds.) TYPES 2002. LNCS, vol. 2646, pp. 95–107. Springer, Heidelberg (2003). https://doi.org/10.1007/3-540-39185-1_6
10. de Roever, W., Engelhardt, K.: Data Refinement: Model-Oriented Proof Methods and their Comparison, vol. 47, Cambridge Tracts in Theoretical Computer Science. Cambridge University Press (1998)
11. Derrick, J., Boiten, E.: Refinement in Z and in object-Z: foundations and advanced applications. In: FACIT. Springer, Cham (2001)
12. Ehrig, H., Mahr, B.: Fundamentals of Algebraic Specification 1: Equations and Initial Semantics, vol. 6, Monographs in Theoretical Computer Science. Springer, Cham (1985)
13. Ehrig, H., Mahr, B.: Fundamentals of Algebraic Specification 2: Module Specifications and Constraints, vol. 21, Monographs in Theoretical Computer Science. Springer, Cham (1990)
14. Ernst, G., Pfähler, J., Schellhorn, G., Reif, W.: Modular, crash-safe refinement for ASMS with submachines. Sci. Comput. Program. **131**, 3–21 (2016)
15. Goguen, J.A.: An initial algebra approach to the specification, correctness and implementation of abstract data types. IBM Res. Rep. **6487** (1976)
16. Gordon, M.J.C., Melham, T.F.: Introduction to HOL: A Theorem Proving Environment for Higher Order Logic. Cambridge University Press, Cambridge (1993)

17. Haneberg, D., Moebius, N., Reif, W., Schellhorn, G., Stenzel, K.: Mondex: engineering a provable secure electronic purse. Int. J. Softw. Inf. **5**(1), 159–184 (2011). http://www.ijsi.org
18. He, J., Hoare, C.A.R., Sanders, J.W.: Data refinement refined resume. In: Robinet, B., Wilhelm, R. (eds.) ESOP 1986. LNCS, vol. 213, pp. 187–196. Springer, Heidelberg (1986). https://doi.org/10.1007/3-540-16442-1_14
19. Kaliszyk, C., Urban, C.: Quotients revisited for isabelle/hol. In: Proceedings of the 2011 ACM Symposium on Applied Computing, SAC '11, pp. 1639–1644. Association for Computing Machinery (2011)
20. Knuth, D.E.: The Art of Computer Programming, vol. 3: Searching and Sorting, pp. 492–507. Addison-Wesley, Boston (1998)
21. Ahmadi, R., Leino, K.R.M., Nummenmaa, J.: Automatic verification of dafny programs with traits. In: Proceedings Formal techniques for Java-like Programs. Association for Computing Machinery, New York (2015)
22. Lynch, N., Vaandrager, F.: Forward and backward simulations – Part I: untimed systems. Inf. Computat. **121**(2), 214–233 (1995)
23. O'Hearn, P., Reynolds, J., Yang, H.: Local reasoning about programs that alter data structures. In: Fribourg, L. (ed.) CSL 2001. LNCS, vol. 2142, pp. 1–19. Springer, Heidelberg (2001). https://doi.org/10.1007/3-540-44802-0_1
24. Reif, W.: Correctness of generic modules. In: Nerode, A., Taitslin, M. (eds.) LFCS 1992. LNCS, vol. 620, pp. 406–417. Springer, Heidelberg (1992a). https://doi.org/10.1007/BFb0023893
25. Reif, W.: Verification of large software systems. In: Shyamasundar, R. (ed.) FSTTCS 1992. LNCS, vol. 652, pp. 241–252. Springer, Heidelberg (1992b). https://doi.org/10.1007/3-540-56287-7_109
26. Schellhorn, G.: Verification of ASM refinements using generalized forward simulation. J. Univ. Comput. Sci. **7**(11), 952–979 (2001)
27. Schellhorn, G.: ASM refinement and generalizations of forward simulation in data refinement: a comparison. J. Theor. Comput. Sci. **336**(2–3), 403–435 (2005)
28. Schellhorn, G.: Completeness of fair ASM refinement. Sci. Comput. Program. **76**(9), 756–773 (2009)
29. Schellhorn, G., Ahrendt, W.: The WAM case study: verifying compiler correctness for Prolog with KIV. In: Bibel, W., Schmitt, P., (eds.) Automated Deduction — A Basis for Applications, vol. III: Applications, chapter 3: Automated Theorem Proving in Software Engineering, pp. 165–194. Kluwer Academic Publishers (1998)
30. Schellhorn, G., Bodenmüller, S., Bitterlich, M., Reif, W.: Separating separation logic—modular verification of red-black trees. In: Verified Software. Theories, Tools and Experiments, vol. 13800, LNCS, pp. 129–147. Springer, Cham (2022). https://doi.org/10.1007/978-3-031-25803-9_8
31. GSchellhorn, G., Bodenmüller, S., Reif, W.: Refinement and separation: modular verification of wandering trees. In: Herber, P., Wijs, A. (eds.) Integrated Formal Methods. iFM 2023. Lecture Notes in Computer Science, vol 14300. Springer, Cham (2024). https://doi.org/10.1007/978-3-031-47705-8_12
32. Schellhorn, G., Bodenmüller, S., Reif, W.: VeriCode: correct translation of abstract specifications to C code. In: Kosmatov, N., Kovács, L. (eds.) Integrated Formal Methods. IFM 2024. Lecture Notes in Computer Science, vol. 15234. Springer, Cham (2025). https://doi.org/10.1007/978-3-031-76554-4_4
33. Schellhorn, G., Pribyl, F., Reif, W.: Examples of verified state modules (2025). http://www.informatik.uni-augsburg.de/swt/projects/StateModules.html
34. Smith, G.: The object-Z specification language. In: Advanced on Formal Methods. Springer, Heidelberg (2000). https://doi.org/10.1007/978-1-4615-5265-9

35. Sperschneider, V., Antoniou, G.: Logic: A Foundation for Computer Science. Addison Wesley, Boston (1991)
36. Stärk, R.F., Schmid, J., Börger, E.: Java and the Java Virtual Machine: Definition, Verification, Validation. Springer, Heidelberg (2001)
37. Steindorfer, M.J., Vinju, J.J.: Optimizing hash-array mapped tries for fast and lean immutable JVM collections. In: Proceedings of the 2015 ACM SIGPLAN International Conference on Object-Oriented Programming, Systems, Languages, and Applications, pp. 783–800 (2015)
38. VerifyThis. Challenge 2—binary decision diagrams (2023). https://verifythis.github.io/onsite/archive/2023/challenges/Challenge%202.pdf

Abstract State Machines for Security Assessment

Chiara Braghin and Elvinia Riccobene(✉)

Computer Science Department, Università degli Studi di Milano,
via Celoria 18, Milan, Italy
{chiara.braghin,elvinia.riccobene}@unimi.it

Abstract. Security assessment demands rigorous, unambiguous models capable of capturing complex system behaviours and identifying subtle vulnerabilities. Traditional informal or semi-formal approaches often fall short in providing the precision and executability needed to analyze modern, highly dynamic systems. This paper argues for the central importance of formal methods in security assessment and positions Abstract State Machines (ASMs) as a particularly suitable formalism. ASMs offer mathematically precise yet flexible system specifications that scale from high-level designs to detailed operational models. Their executable nature enables systematic exploration of system states, automated checking of security properties, and early detection of design flaws. We demonstrate how ASMs can unify specification, validation, and analysis within a single coherent framework, thereby reducing ambiguity and improving the reliability of security evaluations. Through case studies, we illustrate how executable ASM models facilitate threat analysis and verification of critical security properties. The results highlight the utility of ASMs as a practical, expressive, and analytically powerful approach for advancing formal, model-based security assessment.

1 Introduction

The increasing complexity and ubiquity of distributed systems have heightened the need for rigorous and reliable methods to assess their security. Communication protocols, which govern the exchange of information across networks, and smart contracts, which encode and enforce agreements on blockchain platforms, both operate in adversarial environments where subtle design flaws can lead to severe vulnerabilities. Informal or semi-formal approaches to security assessment frequently prove insufficient, as they often fail to capture the full operational semantics of these systems or to expose corner cases that arise from intricate interactions among protocol components, execution environments, and potential attackers [3,31].

This work was partially supported by PRIN project SAFEST (G53D23002770006) and project SERICS (PE00000014) under the MUR National Recovery and Resilience Plan funded by the European Union - NextGenerationEU.

A. Raschke et al. (Eds.): Egon Börger Festschrift, LNCS 16580, pp. 76–105, 2026.
https://doi.org/10.1007/978-3-032-24494-9_5

In principle, formal methods offer a principled way to overcome these limitations by providing mathematically precise frameworks for specifying, analyzing, and verifying system behaviour. For example, in the field of protocol verification–an application domain that is significantly older than that of blockchain smart contracts–, formal methods have been very active over the last thirty years and have reached a fairly mature state [8,26,32]. Nevertheless, most available tools are not adopted by industry as widely as one might expect. Unfortunately, the uptake of formal methods is hindered by persistent myths and misconceptions, largely stemming from the math-like formalism and declarative logic-based notations adopted by many formal tools. These notations are often perceived as being far removed from the operational nature of software systems and from the way developers typically reason about program behavior; moreover, their heavy use of formal symbols and compact logical expressions may hinder readability, making them harder to grasp and thus discouraging designers and engineers from engaging with formal techniques. These tools often suffer from a number of recurring limitations. In particular, they rely on complex modelling languages that make model development error-prone, require verification processes involving substantial user interaction and detailed knowledge of tool internals, and produce results that are difficult to interpret or to relate back to the original protocol or source code.

In the plethora of formal methods, the *Abstract State Machine* (ASM) methodology [10,11] stands out for its expressive power, modularity, and faithfulness to real-world system semantics. ASMs model computations as transitions between well-defined states, enabling the representation of complex distributed behaviours at varying levels of abstraction without sacrificing precision. Their ability to serve as both high-level specifications and executable models makes them especially well suited for security assessment, where early validation and iterative refinement of system models are essential.

In the context of communication protocols, ASMs allow designers to capture message flows, cryptographic operations, and adversarial capabilities within a unified semantic framework. This facilitates systematic reasoning about confidentiality, integrity, authentication, and other security properties [31,37, 38]. When applied to blockchain-based smart contracts, ASMs provide a rigorous means of modelling contract logic, transaction execution, and underlying consensus mechanisms [43]. Because smart contracts execute autonomously and immutably, any flaw in their specification can lead to irreversible financial loss; thus, the precision and executability of ASM-based models offer a valuable way for identifying vulnerabilities before deployment [6].

This chapter explores how ASM-based modelling can be leveraged to assess the security of communication protocols and smart contracts. We examine how ASMs can support *security-by-design*, enabling the detection of design errors and security violations. By presenting methodological guidelines and illustrative examples, we aim to demonstrate the practical usefulness of ASMs as a formal and executable approach to security assessment across distinct yet related domains of distributed computation. Ultimately, ASMs provide a versatile foundation for bridging the gap between theoretical rigor and real-world applicability in the design and verification of secure systems.

The practical use of the ASMs is supported by ASMETA (ASM mETAmodelling) [5,9], a set of tools developed around the formal method to support model editing, validation and verification. Thus, ASM specifications of our illustrative case studies are written in `AsmetaL`, the textual notation of the ASMETA toolset.

The work presented here in the two application domains originated within our research activities at the University of Milan. Formal verification of security protocols and smart contract vulnerability detection were investigated within a common methodological framework. In both cases, the starting point was the definition of an ASMETA library capturing the fundamental concepts of the application domain. This library was then used to define ASM models for specific case studies and applications. Building on the positive results obtained through model analysis, and with the aim of further bridging the gap between specification languages and practical formal verification, dedicated specification and verification environments were developed. These environments support a security-by-design approach by combining domain-specific modelling front-ends with a transparent use of formal analysis tools. In particular, the front-end is based on domain-specific languages (DSLs) provided in both textual and graphical notations, while the back-end relies on formal verification tools that are invoked automatically, shielding users from their underlying complexity. Since this contribution is dedicated to Egon Börger, the founder of the ASM methodology, we primarily focus on the application of ASMs to security assessment in the two selected domains, leaving aside the integration with DSLs.

This chapter is organized as follows. Section 2 addresses the specification of security protocols and the verification of their security properties, illustrated through a well-known vulnerable protocol, the NeedhamSchroeder public-key protocol. The section introduces an ASM library of modeling primitives for cryptographic protocols and presents the security property schemas used in our approach. Section 3 addresses the specification and security assessment of Ethereum smart contracts, illustrated through a well-known vulnerable contract, the DAO smart contract. The section introduces an ASM library modelling the behaviour of the Ethereum Virtual Machine, presents the corresponding translation rules from Solidity to ASM, and discusses the types of properties and validation and verification techniques that can be applied. Section 4 concludes the chapter outlining current improvements of our research projects in the security assessment domain.

2 Security Protocols Domain

With the widespread use of the Internet and open networks, the world has become increasingly interconnected, and technology and data now play a central role in everyday life [21]. Much of this data, often sensitive, is exchanged through communication protocols.

To protect such exchanges, numerous security protocols have been developed to provide guarantees such as authentication and secrecy through cryptographic primitives. However, despite their apparent simplicity, security protocols are notoriously error-prone. Subtle vulnerabilities are difficult to detect without formal analysis and typically manifest only in the presence of a malicious adversary, rendering them invisible to traditional functional testing. As a result, many widely deployed protocols have been shown to be flawed years after their introduction. For these reasons, the formal verification of security protocols and the adoption of *security by design* principles have become essential [24].

Although research on protocol verification is well established, formal methods are still not widely adopted in industry. Their uptake is often hindered by complex modeling languages, steep learning curves, and verification results that are difficult to interpret or relate back to protocol specifications [19]. Moreover, despite the fact that protocol specifications frequently share common structural patterns, protocol models often need to be rebuilt from scratch. While several mature tools for automatic verification exist [8,26,32], many of the protocols analyzed to date have been treated primarily as isolated case studies tailored to specific tools.

With the work presented in [14], we laid the foundations for the long-term development of a user-friendly, ASM-based framework for the formal verification of security protocols. As a first step, we introduced a mathematically grounded set of templates that capture recurring patterns in security protocols and their associated security properties. In particular, we proposed an ASMETA-based cryptographic library comprising domain definitions, functions, and rule schemas for modeling security protocols.

Each protocol instantiates a common model template, while security goals are specified through temporal logic schemas that can be automatically verified using the `AsmetaSMV` model checker [4]. Protocol steps are expressed as agent state transitions governed by ASM rules, enabling complex interactions—such as message generation, nondeterministic choices, and adversary interleaving—to be modeled with clarity and precision. This semantic framework not only supports faithful protocol specifications but also enables direct model execution, facilitating trace exploration, test generation, and early validation of system behavior. Moreover, the resulting formalism can be read as pseudocode over abstract data, making it more accessible to practitioners.

We validated the approach on all historical protocols (e.g., the Needham-Schroeder public-key, Needham-Schroeder symmetric-key, SSL, Needham-Schroeder-Lowe, Woo-lam, BAN-Yahalom, Yahalom, Otway-Rees, and Denning-Sacco) documented in the works of Abadi and Needham [2] and often used as benchmarks [38]. The idea of pattern reuse has already been successfully applied to secure-by-construction cryptographic protocols, in which the verification process reuses smaller protocol components that have been previously proven correct and secure [7]. In contrast, the advantage of our approach lies in the executability of the models and in the ability to reproduce vulnerable execution paths.

A further key feature of our ASM/ASMETA-based approach is the explicit availability of an *adversary model*. Two intruder models are provided for validation and verification: a *passive* attacker, which merely eavesdrops on messages exchanged over the communication channel, and an *active* attacker, capable of intercepting, modifying, and crafting messages. Adversarial behavior is specified through ASM rules that execute concurrently with the protocol participants. By integrating the adversary within the same semantic framework, our approach enables systematic reasoning about security properties.

Another notable advantage of our approach is its extensibility. Owing to the inherent modularity and hierarchical structure of ASMs, protocol specifications and verification components can be incrementally refined or reused across different analyses. New cryptographic primitives, communication assumptions, or protocol roles can be seamlessly incorporated without modifying the core of the verification environment. This modularity is essential for addressing contemporary security challenges, where evolving protocol ecosystems require flexible yet dependable verification tools.

Among the industrial case studies, we applied our approach to IoT security protocols, including the Z-Wave and WPA3 protocols. The specification and verification of IoT protocols is a relatively recent topic in formal method research, and only a limited body of literature exists [25].

The Z-Wave protocol [44] was designed primarily for home automation, and claimed to be one of the most secure protocols for IoT devices communication. It was updated in 2016 with a new security layer (S2 Security), overcoming the shortcomings of the previous S0 security layer, which was found vulnerable [23]. Before our results in [15,28], which revealed a feasible Man-In-The-Middle (MITM) attack confirmed by the Z-Wave Alliance, the protocol lacked a rigorous approach to verification.

WPA3, introduced in 2018 to strengthen Wi-Fi network security over WPA2, has been shown to remain vulnerable in some implementations [41]. In [27,34], we present the first formal verification of WPA3's authentication protocol, SAE, as specified in the IEEE 802.11 standard [1, §12.4]. Using ASMs and ASMETA to model the protocol at the device level, we identified ambiguities, inconsistencies, and concrete security flaws that explain known attacks and reveal additional issues. These results led to more than 20 errata submitted to the IEEE 802.11 Working Group, most of which have been accepted and will appear in the next revision of the standard.

To strengthen the principle of security by design and to provide protocol designers with a simple and intuitive notation that facilitates both the construction of secure protocols and their translation into input models for the verification of key security properties, we developed the *Automatic Protocol Verifier* (AProVer) framework [16,27]. AProVer is a verification environment built upon the ASM methodology and is specifically designed to bridge the gap between high-level protocol specifications and automated verification tools by offering an executable formal semantics of protocol behaviour, together with an extensible infrastructure for the analysis of security goals. We briefly describe AProVer in Sect. 2.4, and refer the reader to [16,27] for an in-depth presentation.

In the following sections, we aim to illustrate our ASM/ASMETA-based approach to security protocol verification by means of a well-known vulnerable protocol, showing how it is modelled and how its associated security properties are analysed.

2.1 Background: Security Protocols and the NSPK Case Study

Communication protocols consist of a sequence of messages between two or more principals, each message sharing the following common structure:

$$\mathsf{M}.\ A \rightarrow B : \mathit{message\_payload}$$

where

- symbols A and B represent arbitrary *principals* (or *actors*) exchanging messages (the symbol S is usually used if the principal is a server), and the direction of the arrow specifies the *sender* and the *receiver* of the message.
- M is a *label* identifying the message, whereas *message_payload* specifies the message content.

In secure protocols, payloads can be partially or totally ciphered, either by symmetric-key encryption (in this case, K_{AB} is often used to specify a key shared between actors A and B, used both to encrypt and decrypt), or by asymmetric-key encryption (here, K_B and K_B^{-1} are used to specify a public and private key of B, respectively). Message payloads can contain other information, such as nonces (N), timestamps (T), etc.

To demonstrate our ASM-based security protocol specification, we consider the well-known NeedhamSchroeder public-key communication protocol [36] (NSPK, for short). It was introduced in 1978 for mutual authentication (here, we omit the exchanges with the certification authority to get the public keys). The protocol consists of a sequence of messages exchanged between two principals, A for *Alice* and B for *Bob*, with the goal of achieving mutual authentication. All messages are in the form described above.

Protocol:	*Legend*:
M1. $A \rightarrow B : \{A, N_A\}_{K_B}$	N_A, nonce generated by A
M2. $B \rightarrow A : \{N_A, N_B\}_{K_A}$	K_A, public key of A
M3. $A \rightarrow B : \{N_B\}_{K_B}$	$\{\dots\}_{K_A}$, encryption with K_A

In message M1, principal A sends to B a message containing her identity, A, and a nonce, N_A, to avoid replay attacks[1], that only B can decrypt with his private key. B's answer (message M2) is ciphered with A's public key and contains nonce N_A to authenticate B, and a nonce N_B to authenticate A with

[1] Reuse of old messages.

B. Since message M2 is encrypted with A's public key, she is the only one who can decrypt it, thus if B receives message M3 containing nonce N_B encrypted with his public key, A is authenticated, too.

In the terminology of security protocols, the *security goals* are often defined with respect to CIA (Confidentiality, Integrity, Authentication) triad: *confidentiality* or *integrity* of message payloads, or *entity authentication* (i.e., the process by which one entity is assured of the identity of a second entity that is participating to the same session of a protocol, thus, they share the same values of the protocol parameters, such as session keys, nonces, etc.).

In general, a secure protocol is used to communicate along an *insecure* network in an *untrusted* environment, such as Internet. That is, the communication channel is shared among possibly untrusted principals. This means that any arbitrary adversary E may try to subvert a protocol run. It is common to distinguish between *passive* and *active* attackers, which differ in the capabilities they have. The passive attacker is able to eavesdrop the channel, whereas an active attacker controls the network and can delete, inject, modify and intercept any message and is only limited by the constraints of the cryptographic methods used (i.e., the classical symbolic Dolev-Yao model [20] assuming perfect cryptography). In this fully untrusted scenario, it is also wrong to assume that an intended principal of the protocol always behaves honestly.

The NSPK protocol exhibits a well-known vulnerability, the Lowe attack [29]: if A starts a session of the protocol with a dishonest principal E, E may start a new session of the protocol with B to whom (s)he forwards all the messages (s)he receives from A, where (s)he just changes the key used to encrypt. As a consequence, B will think to run a protocol session with A and not with E (the solution is to add the identity of the intended receiver in message M2, i.e., $\{N_A, N_B, B\}_{K_A}$).

2.2 Modelling

Modelling Security Protocols Primitives in an ASMETA Library. We defined a set of *primitives* to capture the common structure of a security protocol in terms of ASM functions and domains using the `AsmetaL` notation. These primitives are provided in a predefined library, called `CryptoLibrary`, which can be imported into any ASM model of a specific protocol. The library offers a symbolic notation for specifying protocol actors, messages and their exchange, as well as the main cryptographic primitives [14]. We introduce here the main domains and functions.

The library defines four main types of actors, classified according to their roles within a protocol: the `Initiator`, which starts the protocol execution; the `Receiver`, which responds to messages received from the initiator; the `Intruder`, representing a potential adversary; and the `Server`, a trusted entity often acting as a key distributor. All these actors are modeled as ASM agents.

```
domain Initiator subsetof Agent
domain Receiver subsetof Agent
domain Intruder subsetof Agent
domain Server subsetof Agent
```

Each protocol message is uniquely identified by a label, which is contained in the domain `Message`; message labels are protocol-specific. Declaration of library domains as `subsetof Any` enable to declare a domain of `Any` kind and the definition of functions on such a generic domain. These domains are then customised according to the protocol, while the function signature can be imported from the library. Communication is handled using the function `protocolMessage` that associates the pair of principals (*sender*, *receiver*) with the label of the message they exchange[2].

```
domain Message subsetof Any
controlled protocolMessage: Prod(Agent,Agent)−> Message
```

A general domain `Knowledge` contains all the possible information contained in or derived from a message payload, and this knowledge is protocol-specific. Initial knowledge of an agent regarding private and public keys is specified by the functions `knowsAsymPrivKey` and `knowsAsymPubKey` (similar functions are defined in case of symmetric encryption); knowledge acquired by an agent during the protocol run is captured by the function `knowsField`. These functions need to be initialized in the specific protocol model.

```
enum domain Knowledge subsetof Any
controlled knowsAsymPubKey:Prod(Agent,Knowledge)−>Boolean
controlled knowsAsymPrivKey:Prod(Agent,Knowledge)−>Boolean
controlled knowsField:Prod(Agent,Knowledge)−>Boolean
```

`CryptoLibrary` contains encryption and decryption built-in primitives working with symmetric and asymmetric keys. For example, for asymmetric key encryption, `AsymPubKey` and `AsymPrivKey` are the sets of public and private asymmetric keys, and functions are used for encryption and decryption.

```
enum domain AsymPubKey subsetof Any
enum domain AsymPrivKey subsetof Any
static asymEnc: Prod(Message,AsymPubKey)−> Message
static asymDec: Prod(Message,AsymPrivKey)−> Boolean
```

In a communication protocol, principals exchange messages iteratively according to the definition of the protocol. We model honest actors behaviour as ASM control-state machines: each time an agent receives a new message, the content/knowledge in the message triggers an internal state change and possibly, if specified by the protocol, the sending of a new message. `Initiator`'s states are defined in the `StateInit` domain, `Receiver`'s states in the `StateRec` domain. The functions `initiatorState` and `receiverState` store the current state of the initiator and of the receiver, respectively.

```
domain StateInit subsetof Any
domain StateRec subsetof Any
controlled initiatorState: Initiator −> StateInit
controlled receiverState: Receiver −> StateRec
```

[2] `Prod` is the predefined operator for the Cartesian product of sets.

The program of an honest agent's consists of a number of protocol-dependent rules, each modeling the agent's internal computation upon receiving a message, its message sending and state change. They follow a pattern that is similar in all protocols, and are specified in the protocol's model.

Agents communicate with each other through messages. To verify the correctness of the protocol in case of attacks, the `CryptoLibrary` defines an intruder actor who controls the traffic (in accordance with Dolev-Yao model [20]), intercepts the communication, and understands the information that he/she can decrypt using the knowledge in his/her possession. Therefore, the communication between the two honest actors can be thought of as the communication between `Initiator` and `Intruder`, and between `Intruder` and `Receiver`. The intruder can operate in *passive* mode, i.e., as an eavesdropper saving all information transmitted in clear and those contained in message payloads that (s)he can decrypt; or in *active* mode: (s)he can craft messages by using information stolen and send fake messages (consistent with the protocol rules). This operation mode can be selected by the monitored function `chosenMode`, and the same protocol can be analyzed in the two passive/active intruder scenarios. Also, a legitimate actor of the protocol can have a malicious behaviour [14].

Mapping the NSPK Protocol Into a Model. As a general rule, a specific protocol model isobtained by customising the generic domains of the `CryptoLibrary`, and adding specific rules for agents.

In the case of the NSPK protocol, the model defines three running agents (no server is indeed involved) by adding suitable elements to the appropriate library domains:

```
static alice: Initiator
static bob: Receiver
static eve: Intruder
```

The `Message` types set identifies all kinds of protocol messages. We introduce a message type for each protocol message, distinguishing between clear and encrypted versions. For example, the message types `MSG_NA_NB` and `ENC_MSG_NA_NB` identify the message M2 containing two nonces (see the protocol in Sect. 2.1), in clear end encrypted form, respectively. An error message is added to identify messages not conforming with any protocol messages:

```
enum domain Message = {MSG_NA_IDA | MSG_NA_NB | MSG_NB |
                       ENC_MSG_NA_IDA | ENC_MSG_NA_NB |ENC_MSG_NB| ERROR} //Message tag name
```

The library `Knowledge` domain is defined as:

```
enum domain Knowledge = {NA | ID_A | NB | ID_B | // Fields Knowledge (Nonce,ID Certificate)
                         PRIVKA | PRIVKB | PRIVKE | // Private Keys
                         PUBKA | PUBKB | PUBKE } // Public Key
```

The NSPK protocol uses asymmetric cryptography, so encryption domains are the following:

```
enum domain AsymPubKey = {PUBKA | PUBKB | PUBKE}
enum domain AsymPrivKey = {PRIVKA | PRIVKB | PRIVKE }
```

Agents' states are defined as:

```
enum domain StateInit = {IDLE_A | WAIT_MSG2 | END_A} // Alice's internal state
enum domain StateRec = {WAIT_MSG1 | WAIT_MSG3 | END_B} // Bob's internal state
```

Code 1.1 shows the NSPK model. It is a multi-agent model comprising an `Initiator`, a `Receiver`, and the `Intruder`. The program associated with each agent (e.g., `r_agentARule` for the initiator `alice`) reflects the role that the agent plays during the protocol execution, with each rule modeling a specific action performed by the agent within a protocol run.

```
rule r_agentARule =
    par
        r_send_mess1[]
        r_send_mess3[]
    endpar
rule r_agentBRule =
    par
        r_send_mess2[]
        r_check_mess3[]
    endpar
rule r_agentERule =
    par
        r_replay_mess1[]
        r_replay_mess2[]
        r_replay_mess3[]
    endpar
main rule r_Main =
    par
        program(alice)
        program(bob)
        program(eve)
    endpar
```

```
default init s0:
  function initiatorState(alice)= IDLE_A
  function receiverState(bob)= WAIT_MSG1

  function knowsAsymPrivKey(alice,PRIVKA)= true
  function knowsAsymPrivKey(bob,PRIVKB)= true
  function knowsAsymPrivKey(eve,PRIVKE)= true

  function knowsAsymPubKey(alice,PUBKA)= true
  function knowsAsymPubKey(bob,PUBKB)= true
  function knowsAsymPubKey(eve,PUBKE)= true

  function knowsField(b in Receiver, f in Field)= false
  function knowsField(e in Intruder, f in Field)= false
  function knowsField(a in Initiator, f in Field)= false

  agent Initiator:
    r_agentARule[]
  agent Receiver:
    r_agentBRule[]
  agent Intruder:
    r_agentERule[]
```

Code 1.1. ASM model of the NSPK protocol.

As an example, the following rule in Code 1.2 models the action of Bob by receiving the first encrypted message from Alice. If he can decrypt the message with his private key `PRIVKB`, he saves into his knowledge the nonce `NA` and the sender identity `ID_A`, sends to the unsecured channel a message of type `MSG_NA_NB` encrypted with the sender public key `PUBKA`, and changes his internal state to `WAIT_MSG3`. Note that, according to its definition, the static function `asymEnc(m in Message, pub in AsymPubKey)`, on the parameters `m=MSG_NA_NB`, `pub=PUBKA`, yields `ENC_MSG_NA_NB`.

```
rule r_send_mess2 =
    if (receiverState(self)=WAIT_MSG1 and protocolMessage(eve,self)= ENC_MSG_NA_IDA) then
        if(knowsAsymPrivKey(self,PRIVKB)=true) and (asymDec(ENC_MSG_NA_IDA,PRIVKB)=true) then
                par
                    knowsField(self,NA):= true
                    knowsField(self,ID_A):= true
            knowsField(self,NB):= true
                    protocolMessage(self,eve):= asymEnc(MSG_NA_NB,PUBKA)
                receiverState(self):= WAIT_MSG3
                endpar endif endif
```

Code 1.2. Bob's reply to the Alice's sending of message M1 of NSPK protocol.

All other rules have a similar structure [14].

The intruder eve has rules to handle all possible behaviours (as eavesdropper and as message crafter) as described before. Thus, each `r_replay_messN` rule follows the same schema:

```
r_replay_messN =
   if(protocolMessage(alice,self)= TypeN and protocolMessage(self,bob)!=TypeN then
   if mode=PASSIVE then r_replay_messN_Passive[]
     else if mode=ACTIVE then r_replay_messN_Active[]
```

and the analyzer can express the expected behavior of the intruder in passive or active mode, consistently with the protocol rules.

Model initialization sets the initial states for honest agents, their keys' and initial knowledge.

2.3 Verification, Validation, and Security Assessment

To verify the protocol's security goals, in [15], we defined a set of CTL temporal logic formula schemas corresponding to the specification of the CIA triad, *confidentiality*, *integrity*, and *authentication* properties. These schemas involve knowledge functions, e.g., `knowsAsymPrivKey`, `knowsField`, which we identify by a function $\mathtt{f_k}$, and the piece of information `x` that must be protected. The parameters $\mathtt{f_k}$ and `x` are instantiated with the specific information knowledge under verification. The resulting CTL formulas are then verified by using the model checker `AsmetaSMV`, which integrates the use of the model checker NuSMV in ASMETA. In case a property does not hold, a counterexample is returned by the model checker, and thanks to the integration of the ASMETA tools, counterexamples obtained from false properties are given back as model *scenarios* that can be executed by the simulator `AsmetaS`.

Confidentiality. In security protocols, encryption ensures data confidentiality by restricting access to encrypted data to authorized actors who possess the correct decryption keys. *Confidentiality* of data `x` is assured if *there is not a state in the future in which* `Intruder` *knows* `x`:

$$\neg \boldsymbol{EF}(\mathtt{f}_k\mathtt{(Intruder,x)})$$

The confidentiality of the nonce N_B in the protocol NSPK should be guaranteed by the property:

$$\neg \boldsymbol{EF}(\mathtt{knowsField(eve,NB)})$$

The property verification fails, and Code 1.3 shows a scenario of the NSPK protocol model that reflects the counterexample reported by the model checker. This scenario is written in `Avalla`, the notation to specify scenarios in the ASMETA tool-set: the `set` command is used to assign values to monitored functions, the command `step` forces a step of the ASM execution, the `check` command is used to inspect location values in the current state of the underlying ASM. If `alice` initiates a protocol run with `bob` under the Dolev-Yao assumption of an active attacher `eve` controlling the traffic (line 4), upon a certain number (not reported here) of machine steps (lines 10–12), the protocol run ends with both agents `alice` and `bob` successfully completing the protocol (line 13), but also with the shared secret `NB` known by the attacker (line 14).

```
1   scenario NB_interception
2   load NS/NS.asm
3
4   set chosenMode:= ACTIVE;
5   step
6   check initiatorState(alice)= IDLE_A and receiverState(bob)= WAIT_MSG1;
7   step
8   check initiatorState(alice)=WAIT_MSG2 and receiverState(bob)=WAIT_MSG1 and asymEnc(MSG_NA_IDA,PUBKB)=true;
9   check protocolMessage(alice,eve)=ENC_MSG_NA_IDA;
10  step
11  .....
12  step
13  check initiatorState(alice)=END_A and receiverState(bob)=END_B;
14  check knownsField(eve,NB)= true;
```

Code 1.3. Scenario from the counterexample of the false confidentiality property.

This scenario reflects the well-known Lowe's attack on the protocol. Indeed, if message M2 of the original NSPK protocol (see Sect. 2.1) is patched –according to Lowe's improvement of this protocol– using message $\{N_A, N_B, B\}_{K_A}$, the property holds.

Field Integrity. This property requires that information exchanged between legitimate actors is not modified by an intruder during a protocol session, meaning that the received payload must match the sent one[3]. Field *integrity of* a message `m` is assured by proving that *there is not a state in the future in which an* `Intruder` *altered a field in position* `n` *of message* `m`:

$$\neg \boldsymbol{EF}(\texttt{messageField(Initiator,Intruder,n,m)!=messageField(Intruder,Receiver,n,m)})$$

In our NSPK protocol model, the integrity of a message m can be guaranteed by the property:

$$\neg \boldsymbol{EF}(\texttt{ messageField(alice,bob,n,m)!=messageField(eve,bob,n,m)})$$

There is no integrity violation in NSPK protocol, since the attacker does not modify any message along the channel, but can at most craft new messages based on his knowledge.

Entity Authentication. A principal proves their identity by demonstrating knowledge of a secret, which is not necessarily shared with other principals, without explicitly revealing that secret. Thus, if `x` is the secret shared by the two actors at the end of the protocol execution, authentication of entities is assured by proving that *if there is a state in the future in which* `Initiator` *and* `Receiver` *know* `x`, *then* `Intruder` *will never know* `x`.

$$\boldsymbol{EF}(\texttt{f}_k\texttt{(Receiver,x) and f}_k\texttt{(Initiator,x)}) \rightarrow \boldsymbol{AG}(\neg(\texttt{f}_k\texttt{(Intruder,x)}))$$

[3] This property specification requires the use of the `CryptoLibrary` function `messageField: Prod(Agent,Agent,FieldPosition,Message)->Knowledge`, which specifies the content of a specific message field; the domain `FieldPosition` is a set of integers used to enumerate the position of the content in a message.

In the NSPK protocol, the mutual authentication of principals A and B is given by both agents sharing the secret nonce N_B. In our model, we guarantee the mutual authentication by the property:

$$\boldsymbol{EF}(\texttt{knowsField(bob,NB) and knowsField(alice,NB)}) \rightarrow \boldsymbol{AG}(\neg(\texttt{knowsField(eve,NB)}))$$

The property verification fails, the nonce N_B is compromised and known by eve. The counterexample still reproduces the Lowe's attack.

Similar patterns can be used to guarantee further properties. We refer to [15] for further discussion.

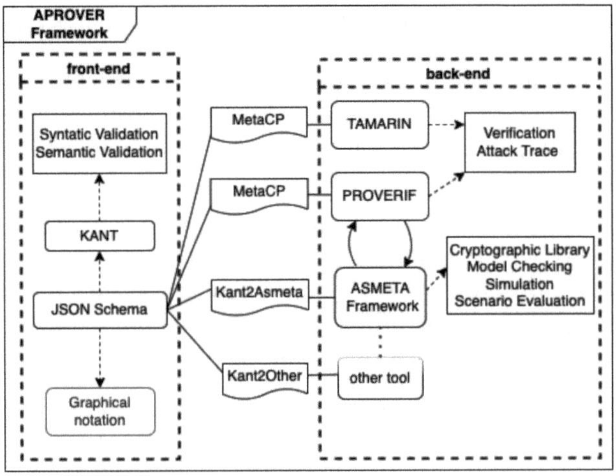

Fig. 1. AProVer Framework.

2.4 The AProVer Framework

The *Automatic Protocol Verifier* (AProVer) framework [16] is a security protocol verification environment built upon the ASM methodology and designed to support user-friendly protocol design. Its intuitive user interface, available in both textual and graphical forms, allows protocol features to be expressed through visual elements that users can compose via drag-and-drop interactions or through well-defined textual primitives. These graphical and textual protocol models are then automatically translated into input models for formal verification tools, enabling security assessment. In this way, AProVer bridges the gap between high-level protocol specifications and automated verification tools by providing an executable formal semantics of protocol behaviour together with an extensible infrastructure for the analysis of security goals. Its underlying philosophy is that protocol specifications should remain close to their conceptual design while still enabling tool-supported verification.

Figure 1 illustrates the overall architecture of AProVer, which consists of a modelling front end layered over multiple formal analysis and implementation back-end tools. The modelling front end provides two easy-to-use, concise, and intuitive notations for designing security protocols. Leveraging a model-driven software engineering (MDE) approach, we defined a domain-specific language (DSL) for protocol specification in terms of a metamodel, and subsequently developed both textual and graphical notations for it, with interchangeable models between the two representations.

The textual notation is the KANT language [16,17]. Its grammar definition is accompanied by an editor and a set of supporting tools that enable KANT models to be checked not only for syntactic correctness but also for consistency with a given semantic model. The latter is expressed through a collection of validation rules that capture both mandatory constraints and best-practice principles for designing security protocols. This checking mechanism is particularly important at design time, as it helps prevent common security errors (e.g., incorrect use of encryption keys) and warns designers about modelling choices that may lead to protocol vulnerabilities (e.g., omitting an explicit reference to a principal's identity within a message).

The graphical notation was designed [16] to be easily accessible through a web browser. As an example, Fig. 2 shows the Lowe's version of the NSPK protocol. A graphical model is stored in JSON format, and can be automatically translated into KANT program (although this feature is not yet mature). Indeed, the JSON structure was derived using Langium's[4] functionalities, which allow the generation of a syntax tree from the KANT grammar and its subsequent serialization into JSON. This process also enabled the definition of a corresponding JSON schema that conforms to all syntax tree requirements, thereby ensuring the syntactic correctness of the protocols produced by the GUI. DSL models can be translated into input models for the target back-end tools by defining suitable model transformations. For example, one transformation converts DSL specifications into TAMARIN [32] and *ProVerif* [8] models by mapping the JSON representation generated by the DSL to the XML format underlying MetaCP [33]. As primary back-end tools, ASMETA [5] has been integrated for model simulation and model checking, while *ProVerif* and TAMARIN are used for trace analysis. In the future, additional back-end tools may be incorporated into the AProVer framework by leveraging further model transformations.

The framework supports the specification of security properties using both state-based (by using ASM/ASMETA) and trace-based (by using ProVerif or Tamarin) formulations. Properties such as secrecy, agreement, or freshness can be encoded as invariants, temporal conditions, or reachability constraints. AProVer then employs state-space exploration, symbolic reasoning, or model-checking backends to determine whether any protocol execution violates these properties. Counterexamples, when found, are presented as concrete execution traces derived from the executable ASM model, providing valuable insight into the

[4] It is an open source language engineering tool that supports the MDE principles for DSL development and that has been used to develop KANT.

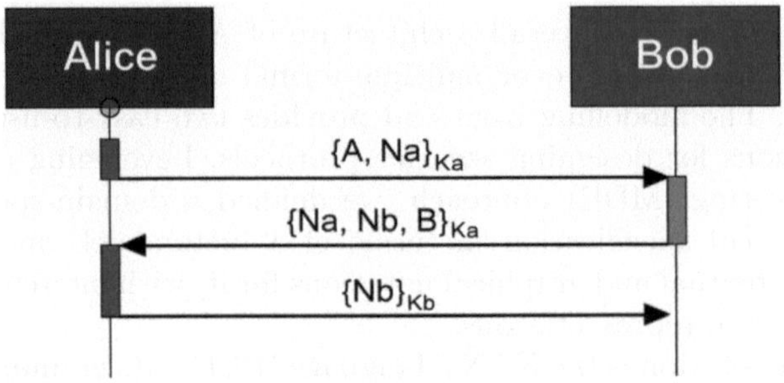

Fig. 2. The Lowe's version of the NSPK protocol in graphical notation.

cause of security weaknesses and guiding iterative refinement of the protocol design.

In summary, AProVer provides a unified, executable, and formally grounded environment for the analysis of communication protocols. Its combination of ASM-based modelling, explicit adversary semantics, and automated verification mechanisms makes it a powerful tool for uncovering subtle security flaws and validating protocol correctness. As communication systems grow in complexity and adversarial sophistication, frameworks such as AProVer highlight the importance of executable formal methods in securing the foundations of modern distributed computation.

3 Smart Contract Domain

Blockchain-based smart contracts have become a core technology for decentralized applications, particularly within the Ethereum ecosystem [42]. In Ethereum, smart contracts are typically written in Solidity, a high-level contract-oriented programming language designed for the platform and compiled into bytecode. This bytecode is executed by the Ethereum Virtual Machine (EVM), a decentralized runtime environment that runs on every participating node in the peer-to-peer blockchain network, ensuring consistent execution of contract logic across the system. Due to their immutable nature after deployment, errors and vulnerabilities in smart contracts may lead to irreversible financial losses and system-wide consequences.

From a system engineering perspective, smart contracts must satisfy a broad set of requirements, ranging from functional correctness to safety, robustness, and security. These requirements are not limited to the isolated behaviour of a single contract, but also concern its interaction with other contracts and its behaviour in the presence of exceptional execution flows. Consequently, security assessment must be addressed *at design time*, rather than being postponed to testing or post-deployment analysis.

In this context, we investigated the use of ASMs as a formal foundation for the specification and analysis of Ethereum smart contracts. We developed an ASM-based semantic model of the Ethereum Virtual Machine and of the core Solidity language primitives [12,40], providing a faithful abstraction of the Ethereum execution semantics in which smart contracts are executed as state transitions over a global blockchain state. In this model, the execution stack, function calls, and Ether transfers are explicitly represented, and Solidity contracts are systematically translated into ASM transition rules. This foundational formalisation enables reasoning about smart contracts at design time, independently of bytecode-level details, and supports both the verification of properties concerning the internal logic of a contract (*intra-contract properties*) and the analysis of its behaviour in the presence of interacting or malicious contracts (*inter-contract properties*). The model has been further refined to explicitly capture Ethereum exception handling and rollback semantics, which are essential to analyse vulnerabilities related to exception propagation and abnormal control flow [12]. More recently, to address scalability limitations of exhaustive verification, the approach has been complemented with symbolic execution techniques for ASM models [13].

The problem of ensuring correctness and security of Ethereum smart contracts has been extensively studied, and a wide range of analysis techniques has been proposed, including testing and fuzzing, bytecode-level analysis, symbolic execution, and formal verification [22,30,35]. Bytecode-based approaches are effective in practice, but often provide limited traceability to source-level design decisions. Conversely, several Solidity-level formal verification approaches aim at proving functional or security properties of smart contracts by reasoning directly on the source code or on formal specifications derived from it. While these approaches can provide strong correctness guarantees, they typically require the definition of explicit formal specifications expressed in dedicated verification languages or logical formalisms, which may increase the modelling effort and limit usability during early design stages. Similarly, the ASM approach adopted in this chapter also relies on the construction of explicit formal models. However, these models are expressed in the ASMETA framework using the `AsmetaL` specification language, which supports a concise and readable pseudo-code style closely reflecting the operational structure of the original Solidity programs. This reduces the conceptual gap between source-level reasoning and formal analysis, while still enabling rigorous verification. In addition, a common limitation of many existing approaches is the implicit or approximate treatment of contract interactions and exceptional behaviour, such as rollback semantics and adversarial contracts. In contrast, the ASM/ASMETA-based approach provides a uniform semantic setting in which the execution model of Ethereum, the behaviour of Solidity smart contracts, exceptional control flow, and malicious interactions are all modelled explicitly and within the same formal structure.

In the remainder of this chapter, we show how this modelling process framework can be systematically applied to specify Solidity smart contracts and to support security assessment. To this end, we consider a simplified version of the DAO smart contract, which is well known for its vulnerability to a reentrancy attack [39].

3.1 Background: Ethereum Smart Contracts and the DAO Case Study

Solidity is a high-level programming language designed for implementing smart contracts on the Ethereum blockchain. Its syntax and programming constructs are intentionally reminiscent of mainstream object-oriented languages, such as Java, including state variables, functions, conditional statements, and structured control flow. A Solidity contract can thus be intuitively understood as a class-like construct whose instances are deployed and executed within the blockchain.

A key feature of Solidity is the distinction between *state variables* and *local variables*. State variables are stored in the contract's persistent storage on the blockchain and retain their values across transactions; they can thus be viewed as global variables associated with the contract state. Local variables, instead, exist only during the execution of a function call and are discarded when the execution terminates. This distinction is central to the semantics and security of smart contracts.

Despite this syntactic resemblance to conventional programming languages, the execution model of Solidity programs differs substantially from that of traditional software systems. Smart contracts are executed by the Ethereum Virtual Machine (EVM), a distributed, stack-based virtual machine that operates as a replicated state machine across the blockchain network. Contract execution is triggered by transactions, which represent the atomic unit of computation in Ethereum and may involve the execution of multiple contract functions across different contracts. The EVM maintains a global state comprising account balances, contract code, and persistent storage; in particular, for each smart contract, the global state includes the values of its state variables stored on the blockchain. Function calls between contracts are executed as nested calls within the same transaction and are managed through an execution stack. These calls do not constitute independent transactions and their effects are committed only if the enclosing transaction completes successfully. To enforce atomicity, the EVM employs a rollback-based exception mechanism whereby execution failures, such as out-of-gas errors[5] or failed calls, revert the global state to a previously saved snapshot. This execution model prevents the persistence of partial state updates and is a key factor in the security of smart contracts, while also complicating reasoning about contract behaviour, since the effects of contract calls depend not

[5] In Ethereum, each transaction is associated with a bounded amount of *gas*, a unit that measures computational effort. Each instruction executed by the EVM consumes gas; if the available gas is exhausted, execution is aborted and the transaction is reverted.

only on local control flow but also on the success or failure of nested executions and on gas-related execution constraints.

To illustrate these concepts, we consider a simplified Solidity contract inspired by the historical DAO case, which models a decentralised fund-management scenario with deposit and withdrawal functionality. The contract, shown in Code 1.4, captures the essential elements required to discuss reentrancy vulnerabilities.

```
contract SimpleDAO {
    mapping(address => uint256) balances;

    function deposit() external payable {
        balances[msg.sender] += msg.value;}

    function withdraw(uint256 amount) {
        if (balances[msg.sender] >= amount) {
                msg.sender.call.value(amount);
                balances[msg.sender] -= amount;}}}
```

Code 1.4. A simplified DAO smart contract in Solidity.

The contract defines a single persistent state variable, `balances`, which associates each Ethereum address with a numeric value representing the amount of Ether owned by that address within the contract. In Ethereum, an address may correspond either to an externally owned account or to a smart contract, and the contents of `balances` are stored in the contract's persistent storage as part of the global blockchain state.

The function `deposit` allows users to transfer Ether to the contract. The function is marked as `payable`, meaning that it can receive Ether together with the call. The special variable `msg.sender` denotes the address of the entity that initiated the transaction, while `msg.value` denotes the amount of Ether transferred. Each invocation of `deposit` therefore increases the stored balance of the caller by the transferred amount.

The function `withdraw` implements the withdrawal logic. It first checks whether the caller has a sufficient balance and, if so, transfers the requested amount of Ether to the caller by performing an external call to `msg.sender`. The update of the stored balance is performed only after the external call has terminated, i.e., after all nested executions triggered by the call have completed.

When a smart contract transfers Ether to an address, the EVM determines how the recipient is handled. If the recipient address corresponds to an externally owned account, the transfer simply updates the account balance. If, instead, the recipient address corresponds to a smart contract, the EVM transfers control to that contract and executes one of its special handlers, known as the *fallback* or *receive* function, if present. This invocation is handled as a nested function call within the same transaction, and the fallback code is executed before control returns to the sending contract.

Since the internal balance is updated only after the external call, an attacker controlling the recipient contract can exploit this nested execution to re-enter the `withdraw` function multiple times before the balance is decreased. This ordering of operations, i.e., external interaction followed by state update, is the root cause of the reentrancy vulnerability. As will be shown in the following sections, this behaviour becomes explicit when the contract is modelled and analysed using Abstract State Machines, enabling precise reasoning about interaction-induced security violations. This example illustrates that understanding smart contract behaviour requires a precise formal specification of both Solidity constructs and the EVM execution mechanism.

3.2 Modelling

Modelling the Ethereum Virtual Machine as An ASMETA Library. In order to provide a precise semantic foundation for smart contract execution, we model the EVM as a reusable ASMETA library [12,18]. Following the ASM methodology, the EVM is described as a state-based system whose configurations represent the global blockchain state and whose transitions correspond to the execution of transactions and contract functions.

The library introduces a set of abstract domains and functions that capture the main entities involved in the Ethereum execution model. In particular, the abstract domain `User` represents Ethereum accounts. Accounts may correspond either to externally owned accounts or to smart contract accounts, and this distinction is captured by the derived function `is_contract`. In this way, the model explicitly distinguishes between accounts that simply hold Ether and accounts that are associated with executable code. The function `balance` associates the ether *balance* to each account. This function represents a core component of the Ethereum global state and is present for all accounts by default, independently of whether they correspond to users or smart contracts. As such, it models one of the fundamental state attributes maintained by the EVM and shared across all executions. Code 1.5 reports the corresponding fragment of the library defining Ethereum accounts and their basic attributes.

```
abstract domain User
domain MoneyAmount subsetof Integer

/* USER ATTRIBUTES */
dynamic controlled balance : User -> MoneyAmount
derived is_contract : User -> Boolean
```

Code 1.5. EVM library: Definition of Ethereum accounts.

The execution context of Ethereum transactions is modelled through the domain `StackLayer`, which represents the execution stack maintained by the EVM during the processing of a transaction. This stack captures nested invocations of smart contract functions triggered within the same transaction. In addition, the abstract domain `Function` is used to identify callable smart contract functions. Together, these domains provide the basis for representing control flow and function execution in the ASM model.

The dynamic state of the EVM execution stack is captured by a collection of controlled functions indexed by `StackLayer`. These functions record the information associated with each execution context. In particular, `executing_contract` and `executing_function` identify, respectively, the smart contract and the function currently being executed, while `instruction_pointer` denotes the position within the function body. Additional functions such as `sender`, `receiver`, and `amount` capture the transaction context, including the calling address, the callee address, and the amount of Ether transferred. In this way, each value of `StackLayer` corresponds to a stack frame on the EVM call stack, while the controlled function `current_layer` identifies the currently active frame, containing all the information required to suspend and resume execution across nested calls. Code 1.6 reports the corresponding fragment of the ASM library defining the execution stack and its associated state.

```
abstract domain Function
domain StackLayer subsetof Integer
domain InstructionPointer subsetof Integer

/* STACK MANAGEMENT */
dynamic controlled current_layer : StackLayer

/* STACK FRAME CONTENT 1 – TRANSACTION INFO */
dynamic controlled sender : StackLayer -> User
dynamic controlled receiver : StackLayer -> User
dynamic controlled amount : StackLayer -> MoneyAmount

/* STACK FRAME CONTENT 2 – SMART CONTRACT EXECUTION */
dynamic controlled executing_contract : StackLayer -> User
dynamic controlled executing_function : StackLayer -> Function
dynamic controlled instruction_pointer : StackLayer -> InstructionPointer
```

Code 1.6. EVM library: the EVM Execution Stack.

Transaction execution is modelled explicitly by the ASM rule `r_Transaction`, which abstracts both Ether transfers and function calls. When this rule is fired, a new execution context is created by incrementing `current_layer` and initialising the corresponding activation record. Control is then transferred to the callee function. Symmetrically, function termination is modelled by the rule `r_Ret`, which removes the current activation record and restores the previous execution context. This explicit representation of the execution stack makes nested contract calls and reentrant executions directly observable at the semantic level.

The execution model presented above abstracts from exception handling and assumes that contract executions complete successfully. This abstraction is sufficient to capture the core control-flow semantics of smart contracts, including nested calls and reentrancy patterns based on the ordering of external interactions and state updates. An extension of this baseline model, introduced in [12], refines the semantics by explicitly modelling Ethereum exception handling and rollback. In this refined model, state variables are indexed by a dedicated state-layer function, `global_state_layer`, which represents different versions of the contract's persistent storage during execution. This refinement makes the implicit rollback behaviour of the EVM explicit and enables the analysis of vulnerabilities related to failed calls, exception propagation, and out-of-gas conditions.

Overall, the EVM ASM library provides a uniform semantic core that abstracts from low-level bytecode details while faithfully capturing the execution mechanisms relevant to smart contract correctness and security. This library can be reused across different contract models and serves as the foundation on which Solidity smart contracts are systematically translated into ASM transition systems.

Mapping Solidity Constructs to ASM Models. Based on the ASMETA library modelling the Ethereum Virtual Machine, Solidity smart contracts are systematically translated into ASM models. The purpose of this translation is to obtain an executable semantic model that preserves the structure of the Solidity source code while making the execution behaviour explicit at the level of states and transitions.

Each Solidity contract is translated into an ASM model that instantiates the EVM library and introduces contract-specific elements. In particular, the contract itself is represented as an element of the abstract domain `User`, consistently with the EVM view of smart contracts as accounts endowed with code and persistent storage.

State variables declared at the contract level in Solidity are translated into controlled ASM functions representing the persistent storage of the contract. In the baseline model without exception handling, these functions directly represent the current values of the corresponding Solidity state variables. Local variables and function parameters, instead, are associated with a specific execution context and are therefore represented as controlled functions indexed by the domain `StackLayer`, with the controlled function `current_layer` identifying the currently active execution context.

Each Solidity function is mapped to a static element of the domain `Function` and to a corresponding ASM transition rule. The body of the rule is structured as a `switch` over the value of `instruction_pointer`, which identifies the next Solidity instruction to be executed. This representation reflects the stepwise execution semantics of the EVM and allows intermediate states to be observed and analysed.

External calls and Ether transfers appearing in Solidity code are translated into invocations of the EVM library rule `r_Transaction`, while function termination is modelled by the rule `r_Ret`. As a result, nested contract calls and reentrant executions arise naturally from the execution of the ASM model, without requiring any ad-hoc encoding of interaction patterns.

Fallback and receive functions are handled uniformly. If a Solidity contract defines such handlers, they are translated into corresponding ASM rules Otherwise, a default fallback rule is introduced, which simply transfers control back to the caller in the baseline model. The refined model with exception handling extends this behaviour as discussed previously.

Table 1. Mapping of Solidity constructs to ASM elements.

Solidity construct	ASM representation
Contract	Element of domain `User`
State variable	Controlled function (persistent state)
Local variable / parameter	Controlled function indexed by `StackLayer`
Mapping	ASM function over key type
Function	Static element of domain `Function` and ASM rule
Function body	`switch` on `instruction_pointer`
External call / Ether transfer	Invocation of `r_Transaction`
Return statement	Invocation of `r_Ret`
fallback / *receive* function	Dedicated ASM rule (or default rule)

For each smart contract, the ASM model includes a main rule that executes in parallel all rules corresponding to the contract's Solidity functions. Although these rules are enabled simultaneously, only the rule matching the function indicated by `executing_function(current_layer)` can effectively perform a state transition, thereby reflecting the function-dispatch mechanism of the EVM.

The mapping summarised in Table 1 can be illustrated by considering the DAO contract introduced in the previous section. The Solidity state variable `balances`, declared at contract level, is translated into a controlled ASM function representing the persistent storage of the contract, while function parameters such as `amount` are modelled as execution-scoped values indexed by the current execution layer.

The Solidity functions `deposit` and `withdraw` are mapped to static elements of the domain `Function` and to corresponding ASM transition rules. Within these rules, the sequence of Solidity instructions is encoded as a `switch` on the instruction pointer, making explicit the order in which balance checks, external calls, and state updates are executed.

In particular, the external call in the `withdraw` function is translated into an invocation of the EVM library rule `r_Transaction`, which creates a new execution context on the ASM stack and may trigger nested contract executions. Since this call precedes the update of the persistent state, the resulting ASM execution naturally exhibits the reentrancy behaviour discussed earlier. To make the translation concrete, Code 1.7 reports a simplified pseudo-ASM rule corresponding to the `withdraw` function of the DAO contract.

The rule mirrors the structure of the Solidity code and makes explicit the ordering of guards, external interactions, and state updates. As a consequence, nested calls and reentrant executions correspond to observable changes in the ASM state, rather than being implicit in the execution semantics. In this way, the translation preserves the structure and intent of the Solidity code while exposing its execution semantics in a form suitable for validation, verification, and security assessment.

```
rule r_Withdraw =
  if executing_function(current_layer) = withdraw then
    switch instruction_pointer(current_layer)
      case 0:
        if balances(sender(current_layer)) >= amount(current_layer) then
          instruction_pointer(current_layer) := 1
        else
          r_Ret
        endif
      case 1:
        r_Transaction(dao, sender(current_layer), amount(current_layer))
      case 2:
        balances(sender(current_layer)) :=
          balances(sender(current_layer)) − amount(current_layer)
      case 3:
        r_Ret
    endswitch
  endif
```

Code 1.7. Pseudo-ASM rule modelling the `withdraw` function of the DAO contract.

3.3 Verification, Validation, and Security Assessment

Once a Solidity smart contract has been translated into an ASM model, the model can be analysed by applying validation and verification techniques supported by the ASMETA toolset. In this setting, security assessment does not introduce a separate analysis method, but is obtained by verifying properties under different assumptions about the execution environment. For instance, a contract may first be analysed in isolation under the assumption of a benign environment (no adversarial reentrant calls), and subsequently analysed in the presence of explicitly modelled attacker contracts that can trigger malicious interaction patterns such as reentrancy or exception propagation.

Validation is concerned with checking whether the ASM model faithfully reflects the intended behaviour of the Solidity contract. This is typically achieved by simulating representative execution scenarios and inspecting intermediate model states. Thanks to the executable nature of ASMs, simulation allows one to observe the evolution of the execution stack, the values of state variables, and the effects of external calls, thereby increasing confidence in the correctness of the translation from Solidity to ASM.

Verification aims at establishing whether the ASM model satisfies formally stated properties for all possible executions. Properties are expressed as *invariants* or *temporal logic formulas*, expressed in CTL or LTL, and are checked against the transition system induced by the ASM model through model checking (via `AsmetaSMV`). Depending on how the execution environment is modelled, the same verification framework can be used to reason about functional correctness or about security.

Intra-contract properties capture requirements that depend solely on the internal logic of a smart contract and are verified on the ASM model of the contract executed in isolation. These properties implicitly assume a benign execution environment, in which calls to the contract do not exhibit adversarial behavior. In the DAO example, an intra-contract property can be informally stated as follows: whenever the `withdraw` function completes its execution, the persistent balance of the caller is decreased by the withdrawn amount. This property reflects the intended semantics of the contract and can be formalised as an invariant relating the value of the `balances` state variable before and after the execution of the corresponding ASM rule. Verification of such a property checks the correctness of the contract logic under the assumption that external calls do not interfere with the execution in unexpected ways.

Inter-contract properties arise when the correctness or security of a smart contract depends on its interaction with other contracts. In these cases, reasoning about the contract in isolation is insufficient, since security violations may manifest only under adversarial interaction patterns, where an attacker exploits the contract's exposed behaviour

Within the ASM framework, we address this situation by explicitly modelling the execution environment and introducing ASM models of interacting or malicious contracts. The resulting system is a multi-agent ASM in which the contract under analysis and its environment evolve together. In this setting, the attacker is not an external assumption, but an explicit agent whose behaviour represents a potentially hostile execution context. This avoids implicit assumptions about adversarial behaviour and allows security violations to be witnessed as concrete counterexample executions. By modelling the attacker explicitly, security properties can be stated and verified over the joint execution.

Modelling the Attacker. Inter-contract security properties require reasoning about the behaviour of a smart contract in the presence of potentially malicious interaction patterns. Within the ASM framework, this is achieved by explicitly modelling the execution environment and representing the attacker as an ASM agent interacting with the target contract through the same EVM execution mechanisms available to any other contract.

An attacker is modelled as a particular kind of smart contract whose behaviour is designed to exploit specific classes of vulnerabilities. To support systematic security analysis, we started to build a library of attacker models, each characterising a well-known vulnerability pattern and differing in the capabilities they assume [12]. From a modelling perspective, the attacker is not an external assumption, but an explicit component of the system, allowing security properties to be verified over the joint execution of the contract and its environment.

The ASM model of an attacker includes its own `r_Main` rule, which is executed whenever the current execution context corresponds to the attacker contract. The global `r_Main` rule orchestrates the execution of the target contract and the attacker contract within the same transaction by dispatching control to the rule associated with the contract that is currently active in the execution stack. The function `executing_contract(current_layer)` returns the contract whose code is being executed at the top of the stack. Depending on its value, `r_Main` invokes either the rule modelling the target contract or the rule modelling the attacker. In this way, control alternates between the two agents according to the

EVM call semantics, yielding a multi-agent ASM in which both contracts evolve within the same global state, as illustrated in Code 1.8.

```
main rule r_Main =
  if executing_contract(current_layer) = contractName then r_contractName[]
  else r_Attacker[]
  endif
```

Code 1.8. The attacker pseudo-ASM `r_Main` rule.

As illustrated in Code 1.8, the rule `r_Main` performs a dynamic dispatch based on the currently executing contract in the top execution layer. This reflects the EVM call semantics: execution alternates between the target contract and the attacker according to stack-based control transfer, while both manipulate the same global blockchain state. This mechanism enables the explicit modelling of external or nested calls, and reentrant control flow within a unified ASM framework.

The concrete behaviour of an attacker is specified by a set of attack rules that encode how the attacker reacts to interactions with the target contract. In the DAO scenario, the attacker exploits the reentrancy vulnerability by issuing reentrant calls to the `withdraw` function whenever control is transferred to it during an external call.

Code 1.9 reports the ASM rules defining the attacker behaviour for the DAO case. The rule `r_Attack` models the initial attack step, in which the attacker explicitly invokes the vulnerable `withdraw` function of the DAO contract. The rule `r_Fallback_attacker` models the malicious fallback behaviour: whenever the attacker receives Ether and its fallback is executed, it performs a further reentrant call to `withdraw` before the DAO state is updated. The rule `r_Attacker` combines these behaviours and is executed whenever the attacker contract is active. The parallel composition in `r_Attacker` reflects the fact that, depending on the current execution context, either the initial attack logic or the malicious fallback behaviour becomes enabled. Which rule actually progresses depends on the current stack frame (representing the active contract call) and on the associated `instruction_pointer`, which indicates the next instruction to be executed within that call. This mechanism mirrors the EVM's stack-based control flow and ensures that the attacker reacts precisely when control is transferred to it.

```
rule r_Attack =
  let ($cl = current_layer) in
    if executing_function($cl) = attack then
      switch instruction_pointer($cl)
        case 0:
          r_Transaction[attacker, dao, 10, withdraw]
        case 1:
          r_Ret[]
      endswitch
    endif
  endlet

rule r_Attacker =
  par
    r_Attack[]
    r_Fallback_attacker[]
  endpar
```

```
rule r_Fallback_attacker =
  let ($cl = current_layer) in
    if executing_function($cl) != attack then
      switch instruction_pointer($cl)
        case 0:
          r_Transaction[attacker, sender($cl), 10, withdraw]
        case 1:
          r_Ret[]
      endswitch
    endif
  endlet
```

Code 1.9. The DAO attacker: rules definition.

Despite its simplicity, this attacker model is sufficient to capture the essential adversarial interaction pattern underlying the DAO vulnerability. The reentrancy attack emerges from the explicit modelling of control transfer and nested calls, rather than from vulnerability-specific encodings. As a result, security violations are witnessed as concrete counterexample executions of the ASM model. The analyses described above are supported by the ASMETA toolset. Model validation is performed by simulating ASM models using `AsmetaS` and inspecting execution traces, which is particularly useful to explore representative interaction scenarios. Formal verification is carried out by translating ASM models into input for the symbolic model checker `AsmetaSMV`, allowing invariants and temporal logic properties to be exhaustively checked. In case a property is violated, the tool produces counterexample executions that explicitly exhibit the sequence of states and interactions leading to the violation.

In the DAO case, the reentrancy vulnerability can be characterized as the violation of a safety property over the execution stack. More precisely, the correct execution of the contract requires that a given user cannot have more than one active invocation of the `withdraw` function within the same transaction. In other words, once a call to `withdraw` is in progress, no further invocation of the same function for the same sender should be started before the first one completes. In the ASM model, each active function invocation corresponds to an element of the domain `StackLayer`. Therefore, overlapping executions of `withdraw` can be detected by the presence of two distinct stack layers, denoted by l_1 and l_2, both executing `withdraw` for the same sender. This requirement can be formalized as the following invariant:

$$\neg\exists l_1, l_2 \in \texttt{StackLayer} \;\middle|\; \begin{array}{l} (l_1 \neq l_2 \;\wedge \texttt{sender}(l_1) = \texttt{sender}(l_2) \wedge \\ \texttt{executing\_function}(l_1) = \texttt{withdraw} \wedge \\ \texttt{executing\_function}(l_2) = \texttt{withdraw}) \end{array}$$

In CTL notation, the model checker verifies the corresponding safety formula:

$$\boldsymbol{AG}\left(\neg\exists l_1 \neq l_2 \;\middle|\; \begin{array}{l} \texttt{sender}(l_1) = \texttt{sender}(l_2) \wedge \\ \texttt{executing\_function}(l_2) = \texttt{withdraw} \wedge \\ \texttt{executing\_function}(l_1) = \texttt{withdraw} \end{array}\right)$$

This property is inherently inter-contract: it holds when the DAO contract is executed in isolation, but it may be violated in the presence of an adversarial environment. Its violation, therefore, characterizes a system-level vulnerability arising from the interaction between the contract and an attacker. Verification of this property on the composed model (DAO contract together with the attacker agent) produces a counterexample execution in which control is transferred to the attacker during an external call, and the attacker re-enters the `withdraw` function before the previous invocation has completed. The resulting state contains two distinct stack layers executing `withdraw` for the same sender, thereby violating the invariant and formally capturing the reentrancy vulnerability.

4 Conclusion

This paper highlights the importance of formal methods for rigorous security assessment and demonstrates the suitability of Abstract State Machines as a foundation for this task. By providing precise and executable specifications, ASMs enable systematic analysis of system behaviour, automated verification of security properties, and early detection of design flaws. The presented case studies show that ASM-based modelling effectively supports threat analysis and security verification in complex systems, confirming ASMs as a practical and expressive approach to formal, model-based security assessment.

Regarding AProVer, master's students are currently working on several projects focused on (*i*) usability testing to evaluate the simplicity and effectiveness of the language, (*ii*) improving the front-end integration between the textual and graphical protocol design notations, (*iii*) refining the mapping from front-end models to the back-end ASMETA models used for model execution and model checking.

Concerning smart contracts, we have recently started developing a graphical interface for smart contract design in the context of tokenomics (i.e., the design and analysis of token-based economic mechanisms). We are also working on defining an ASM-based formal semantics for this graphical language and on mapping the resulting graphical models into formal ASM specifications suitable for security assessment.

Acknowledgement. The authors gratefully acknowledge Mario Lilli and Simone Valentini for their valuable and dedicated research contributions within their PhD projects at the University of Milan, which substantially supported the development, experimentation, and validation of the approaches presented in this paper.

References

1. IEEE Standard for Information Technology–Telecommunications and Information Exchange between Systems - Local and Metropolitan Area Networks–Specific Requirements - Part 11: Wireless LAN Medium Access Control (MAC) and Physical Layer (PHY) Specifications. IEEE Std 802.11-2020 (Revision of IEEE Std 802.11-2016), pp. 1–4379 (20210
2. Abadi, M., Needham, R.: Prudent engineering practice for cryptographic protocols. IEEE Trans. Software Eng. **22**(1), 6–15 (1996)
3. Anderson, R.: Security Engineering: A Guide to Building Dependable Distributed Systems. Wiley (2008)
4. Arcaini, P., Gargantini, A., Riccobene, E.: AsmetaSMV: A Way to Link High-Level ASM Models to Low-Level NuSMV Specifications. In: Frappier, M., Glässer, U., Khurshid, S., Laleau, R., Reeves, S. (eds.) ABZ 2010. LNCS, vol. 5977, pp. 61–74. Springer, Heidelberg (2010). https://doi.org/10.1007/978-3-642-11811-1_6
5. Arcaini, P., Gargantini, A., Riccobene, E., Scandurra, P.: A model-driven process for engineering a toolset for a formal method. Softw. Pract. Experience **41**(2), 155–166 (2011)

6. Atzei, N., Bartoletti, M., Cimoli, T.: A survey of attacks on ethereum smart contracts (sok). In: Proceedings of POST, pp. 164–186 (2017)
7. Benaissa, N., Méry, D.: Cryptographic Protocols Analysis in Event B. In: Pnueli, A., Virbitskaite, I., Voronkov, A. (eds.) PSI 2009. LNCS, vol. 5947, pp. 282–293. Springer, Heidelberg (2010). https://doi.org/10.1007/978-3-642-11486-1_24
8. Blanchet, B.: An efficient cryptographic protocol verifier based on prolog rules. In: Proceedings of IEEE Computer Security Foundations Workshop, pp. 82–96 (2001)
9. Bombarda, A., Bonfanti, S., Gargantini, A., Riccobene, E., Scandurra, P.: ASMETA tool set for rigorous system design. In: Platzer, A., Yvonne Rozier, K., Pradella, M., Rossi, M. (eds.) Formal Methods - 26th International Symposium, FM 2024, Milan, Italy, September 9–13, 2024, Proceedings, Part II, vol. 14934, Lecture Notes in Computer Science, pp. 492–517. Springer, Cham (2024). https://doi.org/10.1007/978-3-031-71177-0_28
10. Börger, E., Raschke, A.: Modeling Companion for Software Practitioners. Springer, Cham (2018)
11. Börger, E., Stärk, R.: Abstract State Machines: A Method for High-Level System Design and Analysis. Springer, Cham (2003)
12. Braghin, C., Riccobene, E., Valentini, S.: An ASM-based approach for security assessment of ethereum smart contracts. In: Proceedings of the 21st International Conference on Security and Cryptography - SECRYPT, pp. 334–344. INSTICC, SciTePress (2024)
13. Braghin, C., Del Castillo, G., Riccobene, E., Valentini, S.: Using symbolic model execution to detect vulnerabilities of smart contracts. In: Leuschel, M., Ishikawa, F. (eds.) Rigorous State-Based Methods, pages 31–51, Springer, Cham (2026)
14. Braghin, C., Lilli, M., Riccobene, E.: Towards ASM-Based Automated Formal Verification of Security Protocols. In: Raschke, A., Méry, D. (eds.) ABZ 2021. LNCS, vol. 12709, pp. 17–33. Springer, Cham (2021). https://doi.org/10.1007/978-3-030-77543-8_2
15. Braghin, C., Lilli, M., Riccobene, E.: A model-based approach for vulnerability analysis of IoT security protocols: The z-wave case study. Comput. Secur. **127**, 103037 (2023)
16. Braghin, C., Lilli, M., Riccobene, E.: Aprover front-end modelling language for designing security protocols. SN Comput. Sci. **6**(8), 992 (2025)
17. Braghin, C., Lilli, M., Riccobene, E., Baba, M.: Kant: a domain-specific language for modeling security protocols. In: José, F., Mayo, D., Ferreira Pires, L., Seidewitz, E. (eds.) Proceedings of the 12th International Conference on Model-Based Software and Systems Engineering, MODELSWARD 2024, Rome, Italy, February 21–23, 2024, pp. 62–73. SCITEPRESS (2024)
18. Braghin, C., Riccobene, E., Valentini, S.: Modeling and verification of smart contracts with abstract state machines. In: Proceedings of the 39th ACM/SIGAPP Symposium on Applied Computing, SAC '24, pp. 1425–1432, New York, NY, USA. Association for Computing Machinery (2024)
19. Davis, J., Clark, M., Cofer, D., et al.: Study on the barriers to the industrial adoption of formal methods. Lect. Notes Comput. Sci. **8187**, 63–77 (2013)
20. Dolev, D., Yao, A.: On the security of public key protocols. IEEE Trans. Inf. Theory **29**(2), 198–208 (1983)
21. Domo. Data never sleeps 6th (2017)
22. Feist, J., Greico, G., Groce, A.: Slither: a static analysis framework for smart contracts. In: Proceedings of the 2nd International Workshop on Emerging Trends in Software Engineering for Blockchain, WETSEB '19, pp. 8–15. IEEE Press (2019)

23. Fouladi, B., Ghanoun, S.: Security evaluation of the Z-Wave wireless protocol. In: Proceedings of Black Hat USA, pp. 1–2, (2013)
24. Haskins, B., Stecklein, J., Dick, B., Moroney, G., Lovell, R., Dabney, J.: 8.4.2 error cost escalation through the project life cycle. INCOSE Int. Symp. **14**, 1723–1737 (2004)
25. Hofer-Schmitz, K., Stojanović, B.: Towards formal verification of IoT protocols: a review. Comput. Netw. **174**, 107–233 (2020)
26. Kobeissi, N., Nicolas, G., Tiwari, M.: Verifpal: Cryptographic Protocol Analysis for the Real World. In: Bhargavan, K., Oswald, E., Prabhakaran, M. (eds.) INDOCRYPT 2020. LNCS, vol. 12578, pp. 151–202. Springer, Cham (2020). https://doi.org/10.1007/978-3-030-65277-7_8
27. Lilli, M.: APROVER: A Framework For The Development Of Security Protocols (2024). https://hdl.handle.net/2434/1039590
28. Lilli, M., Braghin, C., Riccobene, E.: Formal proof of a vulnerability in z-wave IoT protocol. In: di Vimercati, S.D.C., Samarati, P. (eds.) Proceedings of the 18th International Conference on Security and Cryptography, SECRYPT 2021, July 6–8, 2021, pp. 198–209. SCITEPRESS (2021)
29. Lowe, G.: An attack on the needham-schroeder public-key authentication protocol. Inf. Process. Lett. **56**, 131–133 (1995)
30. Luu, L., Chu, D.-H., Olickel, H., Saxena, P., Hobor, A.: Making smart contracts smarter. In: Proceedings of the 2016 ACM SIGSAC Conference on Computer and Communications Security, CCS '16, pp. 254–269, New York, NY, USA. Association for Computing Machinery (2016)
31. Meadows, C.: Applying formal methods to the analysis of a key management protocol. In: J. Comput. Secur. 5–36 (1996)
32. Meier, S., Schmidt, B., Cremers, C., Basin, D.: The TAMARIN Prover for the Symbolic Analysis of Security Protocols. In: Sharygina, N., Veith, H. (eds.) CAV 2013. LNCS, vol. 8044, pp. 696–701. Springer, Heidelberg (2013). https://doi.org/10.1007/978-3-642-39799-8_48
33. Metere, R., Arnaboldi, L.: Automating cryptographic protocol language generation from structured specifications. In: Hartmanns, A., Schaefer, I., Gnesi, S., Plat, N. (eds.) 10th IEEE/ACM International Conference on Formal Methods in Software Engineering, FormaliSE@ICSE 2022, pp. 91–101. ACM (2022)
34. Metere, R., Lilli, M., Arnaboldi, L., Riccobene, E.: What a mesh: formal security analysis of WPA3 SAE wireless authentication. arXiv:2603.23352 [cs.CR] (2026)
35. Mueller, B.: Smashing ethereum smart contracts for fun and ACTUAL profit. In: Proceedings of the 9th Annual HITB Security Conference (HITBSecConf). Hack In The Box (2018)
36. Needham, R.M., Schroeder, M.D.: Using encryption for authentication in large networks of computers. Commun. ACM **21**(12), 993–999 (1978)
37. Paulson, L.C.: The inductive approach to verifying cryptographic protocols. J. Comput. Secur. 85–128 (1998)
38. Schneider, S.: Verifying authentication protocols in CSP. IEEE Trans. Softw. Eng. **24**(9), 741–758 (1998)
39. Siegel,D.: Understanding The DAO Attack (2016). https://www.coindesk.com/learn/understanding-the-dao-attack/
40. Valentini, S., Braghin, C., Riccobene, E.: A modeling and verification framework for ethereum smart contracts. In: Bonfanti, S., Gargantini, A., Leuschel, M., Riccobene, E., Scandurra, P., (eds.) Rigorous State-Based Methods, pp. 201–207. Springer, Cham (2024). https://doi.org/10.1007/978-3-031-63790-2_13

41. Vanhoef, M., Ronen, E.: Dragonblood: analyzing the Dragonfly handshake of WPA3 and EAP-pwd. In: IEEE Symposium on Security & Privacy (SP). IEEE (2020)
42. Wood, G., et al.: Ethereum: a secure decentralised generalised transaction ledger. Ethereum Proj. Yellow Pap. **151**(2014), 1–32 (2014)
43. Wrigstad, T., et al.: Modeling blockchain smart contracts using abstract state machines. In: Proceedings of the ASM Workshop (2019)
44. Z-Wave Alliance. Z-Wave Protocol (2022)

Data in Distributed Computing

Andreas Prinz[1](✉), Iulian Ober[2], and Edel Sherratt[3]

[1] Department of ICT, University of Agder, Grimstad, Norway
Andreas.Prinz@UIA.no

[2] ISAE-Supaero, University of Toulouse, Toulouse, France
iulian.ober@isae-supaero.fr

[3] Department of Computer Science, Aberystwyth University, Aberystwyth, Wales SY23 3DB, UK
eds@aber.ac.uk

Abstract. Apart from the concurrency of distributed computing nodes, distributed computing involves concurrent interaction with data distributed across different physical places. An underlying synchronization behaviour aligns the distributed data. This paper begins by establishing that the behaviour of distributed programs depends as much on the behaviour of distributed data as it does on the behaviour of the computing nodes. For the final behaviour of the distributed system, the data behaviour needs to be described, preferably on the right level of abstraction. We introduce the concept of a memory policy. A memory policy describes the behaviour of each logical location, separately from the algorithm descriptions. We identify four common policies and compare how they are handled in databases, Java, and Abstract State Machines.

Keywords: distributed computation · distributed data · memory policy

1 Introduction

There is considerable overlap between distributed computing and concurrent computing. Often, concurrent computation is related to several computers that have access to the same shared memory. Distributed computing relates to several computers that have their own (physical) memory, and synchronize using message exchange [12]. This distinction seems clear enough, but it refers to physical memory places rather than to logical memory shared by the computers in which it is physically located. In this paper, distributed computing refers to several computers at different physical places that share logical memory that is (physically) available at those places.

Example 1. As an example, consider a distributed spreadsheet[1] with nine cells: a, b, c, d, the sum and product of a and b, and three conditions, see Fig. 1. We

[1] The sheet can be found at https://bit.ly/distributedSheet.

A. Raschke et al. (Eds.): Egon Börger Festschrift, LNCS 16580, pp. 106–125, 2026.
https://doi.org/10.1007/978-3-032-24494-9_6

	A	B	C	D	E	F	G
1		now	history 1	history 2	history 3	history 4	history 5
2	a	1	1	0	1	0	1
3	b	2	2	0	2	0	2
4	c	3	3	0	3	0	3
5	d	0	0	3	0	3	2
6	a+b	3	3	1	3	2	3
7	a*b	2	2	0	2	0	2
8	a>0 && a+b!=c	FALSE	FALSE	TRUE	FALSE	TRUE	FALSE
9	b>0 && a+b!=c	FALSE	FALSE	TRUE	FALSE	TRUE	FALSE
10	c>0 && a+b!=c	FALSE	FALSE	TRUE	FALSE	TRUE	FALSE

Fig. 1. Sample distributed spreadsheet.

have added a history of the values in the fields for our discussion. This sheet is shared across the world with multiple users changing the values of a and b according to their needs[2]. The value changes themselves can be the result of calculations that take place where the users are located. The sheet has implied calculations in the three derived cells and in the history cells[3].

The data distribution of the sheet can be implemented in various ways. The data can be stored in one physical place and then accessed by all the users. Alternatively, the data could be distributed with local copies for each user. In this case, there are many ways to synchronize these local copies. On the simpler side of the spectrum, one such possibility is to use timestamps[4] of the changes, such that later changes overwrite earlier changes. A more complex approach, which is actually used in production-grade applications such as Google Sheets, is to employ Operational Transformations [21]. This approach treats each user action as an operation that is transformed against concurrent operations from other users to ensure that the original intent of an edit is preserved. Unlike a simple 'last-writer-wins' policy, in this approach, the system does not merely store values but actively recalculates them to maintain a consistent logical state across all physical places.

Looking at the distributed computations going on at the different user places, it becomes clear that the speed of the calculations and the result of the computations, in particular the history cells, depend on the data distribution. Let's just imagine that two users change the value of a "at the same time", one of them making it 0 and the other making it 1. Ultimately, the conflict resolution

[2] In Example 2, we will consider concrete programs to be executed at different physical user places.

[3] The history is implemented as formulas of the kind *If the current history value needs to be updated and the next history element is already updated, then use the next value else use the current value.* For the cell `D2` the formula would be `=IF(AND(B2<>C2;C2<>D2;D2=E2);C2;D2)`.

[4] Distributed timestamps lead to a variety of problems related to the underlying model of time, as discussed in [17].

method[5] employed by the sheet determines which change wins and which number appears in the sheet. But this also means the history of at least one of the users will change as the new value of another user is inserted. If the changes in the history for the earlier user happen later than the other, then the history will not even be consistent.

Alternatively, the changes to the history cells can be bound to the time stamps of the value cells, such that the history is consistent. Note that here we focus on individual writes, not on groups of write events exemplified by, for example, database transactions. Obviously, different approaches to data handling can result in different values in the sheet even if the user behaviour and the code in the cells stay the same.

□ (*Example 1*)

A similar situation appears with distributed computing in general, where the distributed program can have varied results depending on the underlying data handling policies and rules. This paper considers situations where the algorithm (the code) is fixed but the underlying data handling can be changed.

Programming languages and formal models of computation must both take account of data handling in order to explain what happens when different computers access the same logical memory location.

For programming languages, a typical approach is to provide a memory model detailing the constraints that apply to shared memory access, where end users can select specific concrete constraints.

Formal models of computation typically provide an overview of all possible cases for the distribution of data. For example, Concurrent Abstract State Machines (CASM) [6] provide a very general model of distributed computing that subsumes many other formal models of data distribution. An adaptation or selection of a particular data distribution model is not considered to be part of the CASM model.

We continue this paper by discussing distributed data in Sect. 2 before defining computation at a level of abstraction that supports reasoning about distribution and concurrency (Sect. 3). This analysis reveals the need for a precise specification of distributed data handling, which is met by introducing memory policies to formalize data handling in distributed computing in Sect. 4. We apply the definition to the Java memory model (Sect. 5) and ASM (Sect. 6). In Sect. 7, we discuss some aspects of memory policies and Sect. 8 provides a summary of the paper.

2 Distributed Data

In distributed computations, there are several computing elements distributed at different physical places[6]. Each computing element includes an agent that

[5] Conflict resolution is achieved by operational transformation in Google Sheets. Alternative approaches include differential synchronization and conflict free replication.

[6] We avoid calling those physical places 'locations' because we use the word 'location' to mean an element of abstract memory accessed by a computation.

performs a computation by reading and writing data. A computing element has a physical place and some local data, The computing elements compute independently of each other, thereby reading and writing data. Physically, the elements use local data for their computations, while conceptually, some data items are considered to be the same logical data item even if they have different physical places.

Therefore, we consider distributed data conceptually as a set of data names (called locations) in different physical places, which is used by the computation, and where data names may have values in more than one physical place. Any modification (update) of the value at one physical place results in updates at the other physical places. Thus, distributed data is not just passive but has active behaviour. When computations are sequential [16], parallel [3,4], recursive [7,10], database [26], or distributed [15], they consider data as passive. Distributed data includes activity that synchronizes and aligns the different copies of data. This data activity is not visible in the algorithm describing the computation. However, it must be considered when reasoning about the behaviour.

The distributed spreadsheet example shows this: each user has an own sheet with own values in the sheet. Under the hood, all these local values are connected such that the impression emerges that all these local copies are values of the same data name. There is an underlying physical reality that includes the consistency algorithms at work behind the spreadsheet. We want to avoid this level of detail when looking at the spreadsheet. However, we must consider the implied local value updates.

Therefore, our view of distributed computation is on the conceptual level, where all local values are considered the same as long as they have the same data name (called location). We formalize this as follows.

We begin by defining the key concepts signature, interpretation, location, and write event (update) similar to [9], Chap. 2, pp 63–65. Let X be a fixed non-empty set of all possible values in the system (the superuniverse).

Definition 1 (signature and interpretation). *A signature Σ is a finite collection of function names, each with an arity. An interpretation of an n-ary function name is a function from X^n into X.*

Next, we define locations, which are storage places for data, like variables and database entries.

Definition 2. (location, [9], def 2.4.3, page 65). *A location $f(v_1, ..., v_n)$ is a function name f together with a (possibly empty) sequence of parameter values v_i (elements of X).*

Conceptually, a distributed location is an abstract memory element that can be physically realised at multiple physical places. Each physical realisation of a location has a value and can be read or updated by a computing element (at that place). Any modification of a local instance is propagated through all the physical realisations of the location. This behaviour is captured by the concept of a state below. Locations get (data) values using write events. Let T be an unspecified partially ordered domain of timestamps.

Definition 3 (write event). *A write event is an update as defined in [9], def 2.4.4, page 65, together with a timestamp. That is, it is a tuple (l, v, t), where l is a location, v is an element of X, and t is an element of T.*

At this point, timestamps are just an ordered set. The different agents in the computation have their own subsets of timestamps, and these subsets are totally ordered. In this way, the timestamps of all read and write events of each single agent are totally ordered because single agents are sequential.

By definition 1, an interpretation of a function name is a function. Therefore, it can be represented by a set of write events.

In the same way, we can use write events to define a *state* (defined in [9] as interpretations of function names) as a set of write events. This definition allows for several values of the same location, for example, due to different values of the same variable in different physical realisations.

Definition 4 (state). *A state S is a set of write events, at least one for each location. We write $S(l)$ for the write events of location l in S and $S_{max}(l)$ for the set of values of the time-maximal write events in $S(l)$, based on the time order. A state is consistent iff each location l has only one element in $S_{max}(l)$.*

Having a state means we can read the value of a location in a state.

Definition 5 (read event). *A read event is a tuple (l, S, v, t), where l is a location, S is a state, v is a value, and t is a timestamp. The state in the read event is called* ***source*** *of the read. The resulting value of the read event, v, called the* ***content*** *of the location l in S, ([9], def 2.4.3, page 65), is the value of a time-maximal write event of l in S, that is, $v \in S_{max}(l)$.*

Each read event is related to an agent (and thereby also to a place), which is given by the timestamp of the read. This is explained in detail in Sect. 3. The source of a read is completely open so far, a memory policy introduces conditions that constrain the **source**, see Sect. 4. Please note that, if the state is not consistent, the value of the read is not uniquely determined by the state, since the location has several applicable values in that state. If the state is consistent, the resulting value will be unique.

Lamport considers in [18] sequences of read and write events which are not directly connected as in process algebras, but where read events refer to earlier write events. This is similar to our definitions for write (Definition 3), read (Definition 5), and run (Definition 8).

3 Computations

We use in this section a conventional state-based framework for computations that is independent of the programming language[7]. The framework is defined at a level that enables comparison between Java programs and ASM programs.

We use read events and write events to define state changes as follows.

[7] We use the term programming language for all languages that allow execution on a computer.

Definition 6 (state change). *A state change sc is a set of read events and a set of write events. The change is effected by applying sc to a state S. The value v of each write event, (l, v, t) (Definition 3), in sc is determined by the program and may depend on the values of the read events in sc. By definition 5, the value of each read event in sc is the value of a time-maximal write event of l in S. Applying a state change sc to a state S means that S is the source of all read events in sc and the next state is the union of S and the write events of sc.*

A state change with a consistent set of write events is called a consistent state change.

Each computation step of *one agent* is a consistent state change. When several agents apply their state changes simultaneously, it can lead to inconsistent state changes and then also to inconsistent states.

In Abstract State Machines (ASM) [16], a state change is effected by applying an update set [9]. An update set does not include timestamps, and it does not explicitly include the read events.

Now we are ready to define computations, in particular sequential and distributed computations. We begin by defining programs.

Definition 7 (program). *A program is a static description of a computation, given by a collection of statements whose form and meaning depend on the language used.*

A program implies a signature Σ *(see definition 1), i.e. a structure for all (system)* states, *given by its* structural semantics[8], *where each system state is a set of write events as defined in Definition 4. In addition, a program has an* execution semantics[9], *which means that a program implies possible* system state changes. *In ASM, the state changes are given by the yields function as defined in [9], table 2.2, page 74.*

This way, a program does *not* directly imply a computation, but only state changes, see also Fig. 2. These state changes are orchestrated into computations by an underlying mechanism, which we call *memory policy*, discussed in detail in Sect. 4. Here we define computations in general.

Fig. 2. Execution framework: programs lead to state changes, which then lead to runs.

[8] To be precise, the semantics comes from the language in which the program is written. By the language semantics, the program implies the possible system states.
[9] The execution semantics again comes from the language.

Definition 8 (computation). *Let $\mathcal{A}$ be a set of pairs $(a, program(a))$ of agents $a \in A$ with a program each, called a multi-agent system, and let there be a consistent initial state I which includes write events for all locations with a time that is before all other times.*

A computation (also called run) of $\mathcal{A}$ starting with I is a set of state changes SC, where each state change $sc \in SC$ belongs to an agent a such that $sc \in semantics(program(a))$. The state changes are connected because the read events refer to write events. The possible connections between the read and write events are restricted by a memory policy MP, see Sect. 4. In addition, the timestamps of all read and write events of each single agent are totally ordered, because single agents are sequential.

In our definition, the initial state is attached to the computation, and not to the agent or the program. For sequential computations, it is possible to attach the initial state to the program, as there is only one program. For a distributed computation, the initial state has to be attached to the set of agents, i.e. to the computation.

It is important to see the difference between a (sequential) algorithm and a sequential computation. An algorithm is a syntactic entity, while a computation is a semantic entity. The algorithm can be run in a sequential environment, but it could also be run in a distributed environment. This decision is outside the algorithm, which only provides state changes.

Definition 8 is very general because it does not specify which data is read in the read events. Section 4 addresses this with the definition of memory policies.

We exemplify the definition of computation using ASM and Java. The *program structure* for Java is given by the Java syntax [14], and for ASM, the syntax is defined in [9].

The *system state* of a Java program is given by locations for an object of the *main* class and all its reachable objects as defined by the Java program. In addition, there are language-defined elements of the system state, e.g. a program counter, a method call stack, and a location for exceptions. For ASM, the system state contains locations for the values of functions - some of them defined by the program and some being predefined by the language ASM (e.g. '+' and '$\in$').

The *state changes* for the Java language are given in the language specification [14]. There is also a formal definition of them provided in [8]. The state changes implied by ASM are defined in [9] using the semantic function *yields* that, given a state and an ASM rule, yields the set of updates which when applied to the state give a new state.

By abstracting the language, we can consider Java and ASM as similar in the sense that both provide a way to write programs that then imply possible system states and a semantic relation *yields*. The *yields* function is independent of whether the computation is sequential or distributed, as it just defines state changes (computation steps).

The main benefit of definition 8 is that it defines distributed and concurrent computations in general terms. It is generally agreed that distributed computing should fulfil the following requirements [2,9,12,15,18,19].

- The individual agents are "sequential".
- The agents cooperate via information exchange.

In addition, the kind of information exchange can change the computation, which is acknowledged in [6] with the text: "IF the effects of such techniques are behaviorally relevant for the problem the programmer is asked to solve, THEN this should be described by a precise model through which the programmer can understand, check and justify that his code does what it is supposed to do." As we have seen, the information exchange is *not* directly part of the code, but it still influences the computation. It is at the system level, not the agent level. Therefore, we add another requirement as follows.

- The properties of the information exchange will influence the computation and therefore they must be made precise for the application.

In this paper, the first requirement is covered by the concept of computation (Definition 8), and the second is given by the concepts of read and write events (Definitions 3 and 5). The last item is given by the memory policy (Definition 10 in Sect. 4), which is a parameter to the distributed computation.

4 Memory Policies

In this section, we introduce the concept of memory policy (Sect. 4.1). We discuss some details in Sect. 7. The definition of computation (Definition 8) refers to memory policies to connect the read and write events of its state changes.

4.1 What is a Memory Policy?

When we defined computations (Definition 8), we made a difference between the state changes coming from the semantics of the code of individual agents and the orchestration of all these state changes into runs. With only one agent, this is trivial, as there is an interleaving of states and moves (state changes), where each state change starts with the previous state and ends in the next state.

The situation becomes different when we have several agents. The first simple case is that all data only exists once, which leads to interleaving, this time between different agents. If the data is distributed and might exist in several copies, then we need to agree on which runs are valid and which are not. This is done using a memory policy, which restricts the possible (order of) read and write events.

Shared memory enables interaction between different sequential computing agents. There are multiple ways in which shared memory can work, and we call each of these different ways a *memory policy*. A memory policy constrains which values can be read in a given state.

We start by introducing a relationship between events.

Definition 9 (before). *Write events and read events are ordered by a partial order called* ***before****. It captures the idea that there is a causal relationship between writing values and reading values. The order* ***before*** *must be consistent with the time: If the timestamps of two events are ordered, then the events are ordered in the same way in* ***before****.*

This way, **before** is a time relation, which also captures the causal order of events. The Java memory model calls this relation **happens-before** [19].

Causal consistency of computations is given by the following basic conditions: (1) it is not possible to read a value before it is written, and (2) it is not possible to read a value after it is overwritten. Obviously, these conditions are still informal, and we need to formulate them more precisely. This is done using a memory policy, which is similar to the Java memory model [19]. A similar idea called multistate semantics of concurrent and distributed runs was presented in [22].

A memory policy determines how the update propagates across the physical realisations, how conflicting updates are handled, and how 'reading the future' is prevented. A memory policy also maintains the higher level fiction, that an update applies simultaneously to all local instances.

Definition 10 (memory policy). *A memory policy is a consistency condition on the partial order* **before** *of the read and write events in a computation. It is related to the relation* source *as defined in definition 5, which connects each read with the state providing the value. The following conditions for the* ***before*** *relation are true for all memory policies because of causality.*

- **no-read-before-write** *No read is* ***before*** *any of the writes in its* source*, i.e., no read is* ***before*** *the corresponding write. It is also possible to consider a stronger condition* ***write-before-read*** *stating that all elements of* source *are* ***before*** *the read.*
- **read-last-value** *There is no other write to the same location between any read and its* source*, i.e., a last written value is read.*

Each memory policy can add more conditions depending on the concrete kind of relation between read and write events.

A memory policy resolves write conflicts, thereby protecting each location against simultaneous writes. Moreover, a memory policy can introduce value propagation mechanisms. In reality, this is realized by a memory manager, which orchestrates all writes at the different physical places of all logical locations. This is in contrast to sequential computation (e.g. in ASM), where a simultaneous write of two different values to the same location is inconsistent and treated as a special case.

4.2 Memory Policy Example

We extend the distributed spreadsheet Example 1 with code and use the resulting traces later to discuss what can happen in distributed computations.

Example 2. We consider three agents (humans or computers) working with the sheet from Example 1. They run the following algorithms (written in Java):

```
Agent AB: a=1; if (b>0 && a+b!=c) d=b;
Agent BC: b=2; if (c>0 && a+b!=c) d=c;
Agent CA: c=3; if (a>0 && a+b!=c) d=a;
```

All of the variables a, b, c, and d start with the value 0. We see that the traces for variables a, b, and c are simple, as they start with 0 and then have their final value at 1, 2, and 3, respectively. For d, we can have several different traces.

- one trace of length 1: 0
  This case happens when all the first actions of the three agents are executed first, and then all the second actions. It is also the result when the agents work in lock-step.
- three traces of length 2, namely $0 \rightarrow 1$, $0 \rightarrow 2$, and $0 \rightarrow 3$
  The case happens for example when agents AB and CA execute their first action, then CA executes its second action, then BC executes its first action and then the remaining actions are executed.
- six traces of length 3, namely $0 \rightarrow 1 \rightarrow 2$, $0 \rightarrow 1 \rightarrow 3$, $0 \rightarrow 2 \rightarrow 1$, and $0 \rightarrow 2 \rightarrow 3$, $0 \rightarrow 3 \rightarrow 1$, and $0 \rightarrow 3 \rightarrow 2$
  This case needs local copies of the variables. First, each agent executes its first activity locally. Then the new value of a is synchronized, and CA executes its second action. Then the new value of b is synchronized, and AB executes its second action. Finally, the new value of b is synchronized, and BC executes its second action.
- six traces of length 4, namely $0 \rightarrow 1 \rightarrow 2 \rightarrow 3$, $0 \rightarrow 1 \rightarrow 3 \rightarrow 2$, $0 \rightarrow 2 \rightarrow 1 \rightarrow 3$, and $0 \rightarrow 2 \rightarrow 3 \rightarrow 1$, $0 \rightarrow 3 \rightarrow 1 \rightarrow 2$, and $0 \rightarrow 3 \rightarrow 2 \rightarrow 1$
  This case also needs local copies of the variables. First, each agent executes its first activity locally. Then the new value of a is moved to CA, which executes its second action. Then the new value of b is moved to AB, which executes its second action. Finally, the new value of c is moved to BC, which executes its second action. Later, more synchronization is taking place.
  □ (*Example 2*)

4.3 Memory Policies and Databases

Databases are a natural place to look at the handling of distributed data. They support access to the same data items from distributed places. Are they memory policies? In our context, databases implement memory policies, but are not policies themselves.

A traditional SQL database implements a policy of a centralized memory, which conceptually means there is just one place of storage for the data. In some sense, such a policy tries to keep the sequential model for the distributed world. This policy is reflected in the well-known ACID properties of databases

(**A**tomicity, **C**onsistency, **I**solation, and **D**urability). There is a lot of theory about implementing ACID using an appropriate transaction manager, both in database literature and in ASM [5,24,27].

Modern noSQL databases like Cassandra [1,25] deviate from ACID because it is impossible to provide performance and consistency [13]. They use a different policy, commonly called BASE: **B**asically-**A**vailable, **S**oft-state, and **E**ventually-consistent. *Basically available* means that the system is able to respond to any incoming request. A system with *soft states* may keep changing states while it processes information. There may be some inconsistency in the system at times, but *eventual consistency* ensures that it will end up in a consistent state.

Cassandra uses replicated data on several nodes, given by a fixed replication factor. Each agent can access data by contacting one of the nodes. In the replicas, Cassandra keeps possibly different values for the same location. These are disambiguated using totally ordered timestamps. Conceptually, timestamps are based on a global clock that always advances and never provides the same timestamp.

Cassandra uses read- and write policies in order to adapt the level of data consistency. A policy indicates how many answers from replicas are needed for a successful read or write request. When reading, the receiver takes the value with the latest timestamp of all incoming values. Cassandra provides many different policies, but we will only look at the following three.

ONE It is enough with one received answer.
QUORUM We need answers from more than half of the replicas.
ALL We need answers from all replicas.

With policy ALL, we have only one conceptual storage for the data. Policy QUORUM provides consistency in the sense of ACID. Policy ONE allows inconsistent runs.

Example 3. We use the traces from Example 2.

SQL databases support traces of lengths 1 and 2. NoSQL databases support traces of lengths 1, 2, 3 and 4.

□ (*Example 3*)

5 Java Memory Model

In this section, we look at distributed data in the programming language Java.

We start by noticing that Java features sequential code, which might be executed in different places. These different computational places are connected using memory, which may or may not be distributed. The Java memory model [19] (JMM) describes how Java programs interact with memory (data). It is closely connected to the Java semantics [14], in this case, the sequential semantics of Java.

The JMM defines the consistency guarantees offered by the Java runtime for reads and writes of variables shared between threads. These consistency guarantees depend on the (partial) order of read and write events induced by the sequential programs executed by the threads, as well as on a set of *synchronization events*, which is considered to be totally ordered. In the absence of synchronization actions, the guarantees made by the JMM are very loose. The main purpose of the JMM is to guarantee sequential consistency[10] for correctly synchronized programs (i.e., data-race-free programs) while leaving enough room for compiler and runtime optimizations such as out-of-order execution, caches, etc. For sequential computations, synchronization does not make a difference.

The JMM does not *implement* the memory handling; rather, it provides *requirements* on allowed runs. Each implementation will have to include a memory manager to ensure that the requirements are met. In this paper, we do not consider the manager but focus on the memory model itself. This matches the general idea of the user who does not want to see the implementation details but the high-level handling of the situation.

In essence, the JMM defines two sets of memory policies, one for the general case (sequentially inconsistent) and one for synchronization (sequentially consistent). We observe that the synchronized case is a special case of the general case and that the data handling is separated from the computation. In a way, for a given piece of code, the JMM allows one to choose between a sequentially consistent execution of the code and a possibly inconsistent execution. The code stays the same. Only the policy of distributed data handling is changing.

The Java memory model includes the following conditions [19], which are constraints for the happens-before order which causally connects read and write events. For the details of the JMM we refer the reader to [14, 19].

Definition 11. (Java Memory Model *[19]***).**

1. *Each read of a variable x sees a write to x. All reads and writes of volatile variables are volatile actions.*
2. *Synchronization order is consistent with program order and mutual exclusion (i.e. the happens-before order is a partial order).*
3. *The execution obeys intra-thread consistency (i.e. each agent is sequential).*
4. *The execution obeys happens-before consistency. This means two things: (1) no read sees a write that is later than itself (i.e. we cannot see the future), and (2) there is no other write of the same variable between a read and the write it sees (i.e. we cannot see the past). The precise meaning of this condition is given in [19].*
5. *The execution obeys synchronization-order consistency (i.e. synchronized locations are sequentially consistent).*

The conditions in the JMM are very general and typically agreed upon when talking about distributed computation. The last condition in definition 11 distinguishes between synchronized and general locations.

[10] Sequential consistency [18] means that the result of any concurrent execution of a set of operation is the same as if the operations were executed in some sequential order, and the operations of each individual processor or agent appear in this sequence in the order specified by its program.

Example 4. We use the traces from Example 2.

JMM with synchronization supports the traces of lengths 1 and 2. JMM without synchronization adds the traces of lengths 3 and 4.

□ (*Example 4*)

6 Abstract State Machines

In this section, we consider distributed data in the formal programming model ASM. Abstract State Machines (ASM) as defined in [9,15] provide a general model of computation that includes distributed computations. The basic ASM framework provides a set of computation primitives that imply update sets (state changes). In the sequential case with just one agent, these state changes combine to form a run as a sequence of states, where the read events of a state change immediately precede the write events of that same state change. ASM does not consider timestamps of write events (only the location and new value) and does not consider individual read events (only the state used to read).

Concurrency (and distribution) are modelled using distributed ASMs (DASM) [15] and concurrent ASMs (CASM) [6]. The ASM model involves a global memory of all locations, so there is not much difference between concurrent and distributed computation as presented in the introduction.

6.1 Asynchronous Multi-agent (distributed) ASMs

A distributed ASM (DASM) [15] is a finite set of agents with a sequential ASM program for each given by *Module*(a) (called *program*(a) in definition 8). Based on this set, runs for DASM are defined.

Definition 12. ((global) DASM run [15]**).** *A partially ordered run of a DASM is a partially ordered set* $(M; \prec)$ *of moves* m *(rule applications) of its agents agent*(m) *with a state function* s *satisfying the following conditions:*

- *finite history: each move has only finitely many predecessors, i.e.* $\{m' \in M | m' \prec m\}$ *is finite for each* $m \in M$.
- *sequentiality of agents: for each agent* a *the set of its moves is linearly ordered, i.e. agent*(m) $=$ *agent*(m') *implies* $m \prec m'$ *or* $m' \prec m$.
- *coherence: each finite initial segment (downward closed subset)* I *of* $(M; \prec)$ *has an associated state* $s(I)$ *– think of it as the result of all moves in* I *– which for every maximal element* $m_{max} \in I$ *is the result of applying the state transition function of agent*(m_{max}) *in state* $s(I - \{m_{max}\})$.

The *source* of a read is not uniquely defined in case several agents are writing the same value in unordered moves. However, the following proposition (coherence condition) ensures that the *value* read is the same independent of the sequentialization in all cases.

Proposition 1. *All linearizations of the same finite initial segment of a DASM run have the same final state. [15]*

With the coherence condition, DASM runs are equivalent to interleaving runs, so the DASM view on data is global and sequential. This is also in line with the proof that DASM runs are equivalent to runs of recursive ASMs [7].

Example 5. We use the traces from Example 2.

DASMs support traces of lengths 1 and 2, but not longer traces because it does not support local copies.

□ (*Example 5*)

As DASM considers global data, it is not a distributed data approach even though it has distributed computation. Hence, it does not capture general distributed computation [23]. We see it also in the example above. DASM shows that the distribution of computation alone does not suffice; the distribution of data is also important.

For sequential consistency, only the existence of one proper sequentialization is needed, while for DASM, all sequentializations need to be OK. Centralized computations are sequentially consistent, but sequentially consistent runs are not always sequential (because some operations can be unordered) and not always centralized (because some read and write operations can be unordered).

6.2 Concurrent ASM

Concurrent ASMs (CASM) [6] are an important milestone for the general definition of distributed computation. In [6], it is proven that CASMs capture concurrent computations as given by a concurrency postulate.

CASMs are again defined by a finite set of agents, each agent a having an associated sequential ASM, $asm(a)$ (called $program(a)$ in definition 8). The agents may share some locations. CASM runs are defined as follows.

Definition 13. (CASM run [6]**).** *Let $\mathcal{A}$ be a set of pairs $(\alpha, asm(\alpha))$ of agents $\alpha \in A$ with sequential ASM $asm(\alpha)$. A concurrent run of $\mathcal{A}$ is a sequence $S_0, S_1, \ldots$ of states together with a sequence $A_0, A_1, \ldots$ of subsets of A such that each state S_{n+1} is obtained from S_n by applying to it the updates $\Delta(asm(\alpha), S_{j_\alpha})$ computed by the agents $\alpha \in A_n$ each of which started its current (internal) step by reading its input and shared locations in some preceding state S_{j_α} depending on α [and j_α is posterior to the previous step in which α performed an update]*[11]. *The run terminates in state S_n if the updates computed by the agents in A_n are inconsistent.*

[11] This condition is not included in the original definition but seems to be intended given other statements of [6]. Sequentiality of agents is a property of the definition of the runs (not of the algorithms), and therefore it has to be made explicit in CASM runs, which was not done. However, in the proof of the concurrent ASM thesis, the sequential nature of each agent is used, such that we can safely assume this condition. Without this condition, even runs with just one agent are not sequential.

With this definition, CASMs give up on interleaving and provide more possible runs than DASMs. Definition 13 allows a lot of freedom in the possible distributed runs. In particular, the state to read from is not unique, but allows several possible states to read from.

The data handling of CASM postulates a sequence of global states, which, per se, does not allow distributed data. However, the CASM reading policy allows delays in communication from writing to reading, i.e. it is possible to read an earlier value than the most recently written value. Still, locations are not completely independent as the sequentiality of states means that agents always write *all* their updates into the same global state.

Example 6. We use the traces from Example 2. Obviously, CASMs support the traces of lengths 1 and 2. Traces of length 3 are possible because we can run the agents in the following order: CA (c=3), AB (a=1), BC (b=2), CA (d=1), AB (d=2), where the last AB reads the state from after BC.

Traces of length 4 are not possible in CASM. This is due to the global state approach. Each agent writes its own variable before attempting to set d. Because of the global state, writes of the own variables are cumulative, and there will be a state that has all three variables a, b, and c set. The last agent to have set its variable cannot go back to before its own variable is set. Hence, it has all three of them and cannot set d because of the second condition.

□ (*Example 6*)

There are CASM runs that include shared memory, but there is no mechanism to enforce sharing. Interestingly, sharing happens when a variable is *not* written because then the current value is copied into the version visible to the agent, as in the example below.

Example 7. Let us look again at the code from Example 2. We let the agents not only write their variable but also copy the other two variables in parallel, symbolized by "|".

```
Agent AB: (a=1 | b=b | c=c); if (b>0 && a+b!=c) d=b;
Agent BC: (a=a | b=2 | c=c); if (c>0 && a+b!=c) d=c;
Agent CA: (a=a | b=b | c=3); if (a>0 && a+b!=c) d=a;
```

Now, the traces of length 4 are possible in CASM as follows. We write the state as a sequence of the values of a, b, c, d, with the initial state being 0000. AB makes a step leading to 1000, and CA makes a step leading to 1030. BC makes a step starting from 0000 and getting 0200. CA makes a step from 1030 to 1031. AB makes a step from 0200 to 0202. Finally, BC makes a step from 1031 to 1033.

Unfortunately, CASMs adds inconsistent traces that are not possible with previous approaches. In the example above, AB and CA cannot make their first step in sync because that introduces an inconsistency. This produces a trace where no variable whatsoever is updated.

□ (*Example 7*)

We see that the total order of the states in CASM is restrictive, as there are partial orders on moves that cannot be derived from a total order of states, but which would be valid in Java. Distributed computation lives by the idea that the state is distributed and that different agents may have different views of the state, unrelated by a total order.

6.3 Combining CASM and DASM

Both CASM and DASM work on the same kind of ASM code. DASM matches quite well with synchronized JMM, while CASM is more similar to unsynchronized JMM. As we have seen, the underlying model of computation is vastly different and runs are defined differently, such that it is not easily possible to combine CASM runs and DASM runs. This makes it hard to use the CASM model for some locations and the DASM model for other locations, which is possible in the JMM.

CASM runs are not sequentially consistent in general, but it would be possible to enforce sequential consistency for "synchronized" locations (to use the Java term). Still, the use of a sequence of global states is a serious restriction of the CASM approach.

In principle, sequential consistency could also be provided by defining a memory manager in CASM, but this turns things upside-down because normally, a memory manager implements a general handling of logical locations on top of a sequentially consistent handling of values at physical places. Interestingly, in [6], the Petrinet example needs sequential consistency, but the article does not explain how this restriction is enforced in CASM.

7 Discussion

Here we discuss some aspects of memory policies: why we need memory policies (Sect. 7.1), how to specify them (Sect. 7.2), and where to specify them (Sect. 7.3).

7.1 Why Do We Need a Memory Policy?

We have seen that distributed computations differ from sequential computations because they depend not only on the program that is run but also on the handling of shared memory. The same program can have different results depending on different shared memory access policies. We have shown this with the spreadsheet example. We had a look at different policies as follows.

- Java provides two levels of consistency in its memory model, which is given by regular and volatile variables. In this case, the difference in semantics is visible in the program itself by annotations to variable declarations.
- Abstract State Machines (ASM) provides DASM [15] and CASM [6], which are two different semantics definitions for distributed ASM runs involving the same programs.

- As an example from databases, Cassandra [1] provides several levels of possible shared data access, which all change the semantics of distributed programs running on top of Cassandra.

From these examples, we conclude that the principles of access to shared memory are an important factor in determining the semantics of a distributed program. Instead of defining shared memory with the exchanged messages, a memory policy provides an abstract definition of the possible interactions. This is in line with most approaches to distributed computations. This also means that a property like sequential consistency is a property of the memory policy, not of the algorithm. In this view, sequential consistency *is* a memory policy.

Message-based approaches to distributed systems like process algebras, e.g., the π-calculus [20], do not handle shared memory. This means that they do not need memory policies.

7.2 Which Memory Policies Do We Need?

From the distributed computation models studied in this paper, there are only a few meaningful memory model variants. We see four policy levels: lock-step, sequential consistency, global state, and general. In real systems, only variations of the general policy and of sequential consistency are used.

Lock-Step Policy. The first policy level is *lock-step computation*, where all agents work in parallel in each time step. Lock-step is effectively a restricted kind of sequential computation. In our example, it provides traces of length 1.

Sequential Consistency. This second policy level mimics *centralized memory* (each logical location has just one physical place: Definition 12) and provides traces of lengths 1 and 2. It is used in Java volatile locations, database ACID properties, DASM, Cassandra modes ALL and QUORUM, and sequential consistency.

By ensuring that any concurrent execution results in a state that could be reached if all the concurrent actions were performed in some sequential order, such memory management effectively maintains the sequential model for the distributed world. There is a lot of theory about implementing a memory manager for this level, both in database literature and in ASM [5,24,27].

Global State. The third policy level exists only in CASM (Definition 13). It provides traces of lengths 1, 2, and 3. The general idea is that, from some perspective, a system state in a distributed system can be seen as a global state. If we add reading from previous states, we should be settled. As the analysis in Sect. 6 shows, there are some unintended consequences of this idea. It is not possible to completely capture the distributed nature of assignments with a global state. It seems difficult to implement an effective memory manager for this approach and it is obviously not too different from the general policy.

General Policy. The final policy level is *general distribution* (Definition 11), as evidenced by general Java, database BASE properties, and Cassandra with mode ONE [1][12].

With the general policy, distributed computations cannot be captured using interleaving. Data is really distributed, and there are effects that are no longer sequential. A similar observation is true for the global state policy.

7.3 Where to Describe the Memory Policy?

From the languages and approaches discussed in this article, there are four general ways to express the memory policy as follows.

- The memory handling is expressed *implicitly* by the language. This applies to all ASM variants (DASM, CASM, CoreASM [11]) and also most theoretical approaches to concurrency (process algebras, sequential consistency).
- The memory handling can be expressed by specifying a *memory manager* as a program similar to the other agents. In this case, we need an underlying memory handling that is used by the memory handler. Typically, this underlying handling is sequential, and the handler is a singleton agent.
- The memory handling can be described in the concurrent program as *code annotations* to the memory locations (variables). This approach is used in Java by making variables volatile.
- The memory handling can be described *separately* as annotations to the memory locations (variables). Such an approach is used in noSQL databases as e.g. Cassandra [1]. Here, storage policies (ONE, ALL, ...) are selected for memory locations.

An *implicit* memory handling does not present a choice of different memory handlers. This means that the code in itself does not define the semantics, even if it is the same as in the case DASM versus CASM. This way, it defeats the credo presented in [6]: "IF the effects of such techniques are behaviorally relevant for the problem the programmer is asked to solve, THEN this should be described by a precise model through which the programmer can understand, check and justify that his code does what it is supposed to do."

It is certainly possible to specify the memory handling as a *memory manager*. However, a memory manager is a complex program, and it is not obvious what memory policy it implements based on the built-in memory handling for the memory handler itself. Moreover, it is not clear where this code would belong, as it is global to the system (being part of the underlying semantics of the run). As we are interested in a high-level view of distributed computation, we do not consider how to implement the memory policy, but rather how to define it[13].

12 Most of the memory modes of Cassandra fall into this category. They are similar in terms of memory handling but differ in terms of efficiency.

13 Please note that any implementation of a memory policy must be based on another, more basic, memory policy. For example, we can implement a distributed database system based on some properties of an underlying storage and messaging infrastructure. So we cannot get rid of the memory policy if we have distribution.

This leaves us with the last two options, which imply annotating logical locations with their policy either inside the program or in a dedicated memory policy description. Both have the same description, but for the separation of concerns, we argue that it is better to consider a dedicated specification to describe memory handling.

8 Summary and Conclusion

This paper has shown that distributed computation has two aspects: *processing* and *memory*. Both parts, the distribution of computation and the distribution of memory, have to be defined. Currently, the distribution of memory is often neglected.

We have shown that there are several ways to handle distributed memory, as evidenced by the two modes of the Java memory model, as well as DASM and CASM or Cassandra modes ALL and ONE. Choosing different handling leads to different behaviour even for the same program.

The concept of memory policies captures the nature of *memory* in distributed computations. Memory policies are consistency conditions on read and write events. The two main memory policies in practical use are sequential consistency and the general policy. The policy used should be specified separately per logical location, distinct from the distributed program.

References

1. Apache Software Foundation: Apache Cassandra 5.0 – Documentation (2026). https://cassandra.apache.org/doc/5.0/index.html
2. Best, E.: Semantics of Sequential and Parallel Programs. Prentice Hall (1996)
3. Blass, A., Gurevich, Y.: Abstract state machines capture parallel algorithms: Correction and extension. ACM Trans. Comput. Logic **9**(3) (2008). https://doi.org/10.1145/1352582.1352587
4. Blass, A., Gurevich, Y.: Abstract state machines capture parallel algorithms. ACM Trans. Comput. Logic (TOCL) **4**(4), 578–651 (2003). https://doi.org/10.1145/937555.937561
5. Börger, E., Schewe, K.D.: Specifying transaction control to serialize concurrent program executions. In: Ait Ameur, Y., Schewe, K.D. (eds.) Abstract State Machines, Alloy, B, TLA, VDM, and Z, pp. 142–157. Springer, Berlin Heidelberg, Berlin, Heidelberg (2014)
6. Börger, E., Schewe, K.D.: Concurrent abstract state machines. Acta Inf. **53**(5), 469–492 (2016). https://doi.org/10.1007/s00236-015-0249-7
7. Börger, E., Schewe, K.D.: A characterization of distributed ASMs with partial-order runs. In: Raschke, A., Méry, D., Houdek, F. (eds.) Rigorous State-Based Methods, pp. 78–92. Springer International Publishing, Cham (2020)
8. Börger, E., Schulte, W.: A Programmer Friendly Modular Definition of the Semantics of Java. In: Alves-Foss, J. (ed.) Formal Syntax and Semantics of Java. LNCS, vol. 1523, pp. 353–404. Springer, Heidelberg (1999). https://doi.org/10.1007/3-540-48737-9_10

9. Börger, E., Stärk, R.F.: Abstract State Machines. Springer, A Method for High-Level System Design and Analysis (2003)
10. Börger, E., Schewe, K.d.: A behavioural theory of recursive algorithms. Fundamenta Informaticae **177**, 1–37 (12 2020). https://doi.org/10.3233/FI-2020-1978
11. Farahbod, R., Gervasi, V., Glässer, U.: CoreASM: an extensible ASM execution engine. Fund. Inform. **77**(1–2), 71–103 (2007)
12. Ghosh, S.: Distributed Systems – An Algorithmic Approach. Chapman & Hall/CRC (2007)
13. Gilbert, S., Lynch, N.: Brewer's conjecture and the feasibility of consistent, available, partition-tolerant web services. SIGACT News **33**(2), 51–59 (2002). https://doi.org/10.1145/564585.564601
14. Gosling, J., Joy, B., Steele, G.L., Bracha, G., Buckley, A.: The Java Language Specification, Java SE 8 Edition. Addison-Wesley Professional, 1st edn. (2014)
15. Gurevich, Y.: Evolving algebras 1993: Lipari guide. In: Börger, E. (ed.) Specification and Validation Methods. Oxford University Press (1995)
16. Gurevich, Y.: Sequential abstract-state machines capture sequential algorithms. ACM Trans. Comp. Logic **1**(1), 77–111 (2000)
17. Lamport, L.: Time, clocks, and the ordering of events in a distributed system. Commun. ACM **21**(7), 558–565 (1978)
18. Lamport, L., Lynch, N.: Distributed Computing: Models and Methods, chap. Handbook of Theoretical Computer Science, pp. 1157–1199. Elsevier (1990)
19. Manson, J., Pugh, W., Adve, S.V.: The Java memory model. SIGPLAN Not. **40**(1), 378–391 (2005). https://doi.org/10.1145/1047659.1040336
20. Milner, R.: Communicating and Mobile Systems: The π-calculus. Cambridge University Press (1999). https://books.google.no/books?id=fMrCtQEACAAJ
21. Palmer, C.R., Cormack, G.V.: Operation transforms for a distributed shared spreadsheet. In: Proceedings of the 1998 ACM Conference on Computer Supported Cooperative Work, pp. 69–78. CSCW '98, Association for Computing Machinery, New York, NY, USA (1998). https://doi.org/10.1145/289444.289474
22. Prinz, A.: Distributed computing on distributed memory. In: System Analysis and Modeling. Languages, Methods, and Tools for Systems Engineering - 10th International Conference, SAM 2018, Copenhagen, Denmark, October 15-16, 2018, Proceedings, pp. 67–84 (2018). https://doi.org/10.1007/978-3-030-01042-3_5
23. Prinz, A., Sherratt, E.: Distributed ASM – pitfalls and solutions. In: Aït-Ameur, Y., Schewe, K.D. (eds.) Abstract State Machines, Alloy, B, TLA, VDM and Z – Proceedings of the 4th International Conference (ABZ 2014). LNCS, vol. 8477, pp. 210–215. Springer, Cham (2014). https://doi.org/10.1007/978-3-662-43652-3_18
24. Prinz, A., Thalheim, B.: Operational semantics of transactions. In: Proceedings of the 14th Australasian Database Conference - Vol. 17, pp. 169–179. ADC '03, Australian Computer Society, Inc., AUS (2003)
25. Rabl, T., Sadoghi, M., Jacobsen, H.A., Gómez-Villamor, S., Muntés-Mulero, V., Mankowskii, S.: Solving big data challenges for enterprise application performance management. PVLDB **5**(12), 1724–1735 (2012)
26. Schewe, K.D., Wang, Q.: A customised ASM thesis for database transformations. Acta Cyb. **19**(4), 765–805 (2010)
27. Weikum, G., Vossen, G.: Transactional Information Systems: Theory, Algorithms, and the Practice of Concurrency Control and Recovery. Morgan Kaufmann Publishers Inc., San Francisco, CA, USA (2001)

A First Step Towards Agile Verification of Compilations

Wolf Zimmermann(✉), Thomas Kühn, Edward Sabinus, and Mandy Weißbach

Institut für Informatik, Martin-Luther-Universität Halle-Wittenberg, 06120 Halle(Saale), Germany
{wolf.zimmermann,thomas.kuehn,edward.sabinus, mandy.weissbach}@informatik.uni-halle.de

Abstract. In practice, compilers are developed iteratively, starting from an initial version for a sub-language and continuously expanding. While in theory, the language is finished at some point, in practice, each language continues to grow alongside its specification, becoming too big to be verified as a whole.

Agile compiler development starts from an initial version of the programming language to be implemented, e.g., one that only accepts the smallest program. The initial version is iteratively extended, each introducing a new language concept. Our goal is to verify each version of the compiler such that proofs of all previous versions remain unchanged and valid. In this paper, we focus on verifying the compilation, i.e., verifying the transformations from a higher-level programming language to assembly code using intermediate languages. We examine the verification of the compilation of the initial version and discuss the engineering of the correctness proofs for *extensibility*, i.e., no revisions in the proof are necessary for subsequent iterations.

1 Introduction

The research groups of Gerhard Goos (Karlsruhe), Hans Langmaack (Kiel), and Friedrich v. Henke (Ulm) started the joint project *Verifix* in the early nineties. Its main goal was the development of techniques for the verification of compilers. The Karlsruhe group focused on approaches for verification of compilers developed by compiler generation toolchains. The Kiel group investigated an initial correct compiler using a bootstrap process leading to a verified compiler in binary code. The Ulm group checked the proofs by the other two groups. The first author, Wolf Zimmermann, worked as a postdoc in Karlsruhe within this project. Wolf Zimmermann met Egon Börger during a visit in Karlsruhe in the mid-nineties, where Börger proposed to employ *evolving algebras*[1] for the purpose of compiler verification. Thankfully, the first author followed this proposal, as Abstract State Machines were the key for the success not only of the *Verifix*

[1] Later renamed to *Abstract State Machines*.

A. Raschke et al. (Eds.): Egon Börger Festschrift, LNCS 16580, pp. 126–151, 2026.
https://doi.org/10.1007/978-3-032-24494-9_7

```
class MAIN is
  main is
  end -- main
end -- MAIN
```

Fig. 1. Sather-K program for the initial version.

project but also of the presented approach. *"Dear Egon, many thanks for this important hint"*.

The focus of *Verifix* was to develop methods for the formal verification of compilers. However, the process of compiler verification has not been considered. Such a process has been chosen by Schmid, Stärk, and Börger [21]. This work contains a coarse-grained iterative approach towards a correctness proof. It starts the correctness proof for an imperative core of *Java* and step-by-step extends this proof by procedures, classes and objects, exception handling, and concurrency. In particular, the correctness proofs of the first versions needed no revisions by the extensions.

This contribution is inspired by our recent work [24] where we propose very small steps. The idea follows the practical construction of compilers since compilers are developed iterativly [1,20]. The idea is to prove the correctness of the compilation along the iterative steps of the compiler development. The goal remains that the verification of later iterations does not require a revision of the correctness proofs of earlier iterations. In a certain sense, we propose agile verifications of agile-developed compilers.

We have chosen *Sather-K* because it is an object-oriented language that contains a sufficient number of different language concepts, such as parameterized classes with static call-by-name semantics, streams/iterators, polymorphic and monomorphic types, value classes and reference classes, subtype inheritance and include inheritance (analogous to module imports), assignable procedure/stream values, partial evaluation of procedures/streams. On the other hand, Sather-K is a language that is far less complex (the language report [8] has only 35 pages) than other languages, e.g. Java, C++, or C#. Although Sather-K is not a toy language, we argue that it is manageable and feasible to build a verified compiler. The MIPS assembly language was chosen as target language since it is well-documented and there exist emulators, such as, Spim [12] and QtSpim [13], where the latter supports debugging of MIPS assembly code. Currently, we have planned for 220 iterations. The agile compiler development starts with a compiler version that compiles the smallest program, cf. Fig. 1. Its execution starts with calling MAIN::*main* and ends after returning from *main*. Table 1 shows some of the first iterations. The complete iteration plan encompasses 220 versions, such as version 0.28 for *overloading (by number of parameters)*, version 0.61 introducing *stream (iterator) methods*, version 0.86 for *overloading with polymporphic types*, version 0.88 enabling *private features*, version 0.123 permits *exception blocks and fallbacks*, version 0.128 features *generic classes with multiple class parameters*, and version 0.186 introduces the *partial evaluation of methods*.

Table 1. First iterations in the development of the verified *Sather-K* compiler

Version	Added language feature
0.1	standard library for characters
...	...
0.6	call of builtin method for writing characters on standard output (as expression statement)
0.7	statement lists
0.8	single local variable declaration
0.9	assignment to local variable
0.10	reading access to local variable
0.11	list of local variable declarations
0.12	reference classes
0.13	(object) attribute declarations without initialization expressions
0.14	constructors
0.15	value classes
0.16	method declarations (parameter-less)
0.17	method calls (without arguments)
...	...

In this paper, we show the correctness of the compilation of the initial version of a Sather-K compiler. Compilation means the transformations used in the compiler. The correctness of the implementation of the compilation must be proven separately. The implementation correctness is not considered in this paper. We discuss the decisions in the proof engineering w.r.t. their extensibility.

Section 2 introduces Abstract State Machines inspired by the use in programming language semantics [19]. Section 3 introduces the ASM semantics of the source and intermediate languages used in the compiler required for the initial version. Section 4 introduces the steps in the compilations and verifies their correctness. Section 5 discusses related work.

2 Abstract State Machines

Table 2 shows the notations used throughout this paper.

In addition to the standard definition of Abstract State Machines [3], we use an order-sorted variant. In particular, the signature is an order-sorted signature according to [7]. Order-sorted signatures extend many-sorted signatures by the specification of a sub-sort relation $\sqsubseteq$. For simplicity, we assume that the reflexive transitive closure of $\sqsubseteq$ induces a lattice. The reflexive transitive closure is also denoted by $\sqsubseteq$. The lattice structure implies the requirements in [7]. Terms over an ordered-sorted signature are defined as usual. Additionally, any term of sort s is also a term of sort s' if $s \sqsubseteq s'$. The requirements in [7] imply that for each term t there is a *smallest* sort s such that t is of sort s. As usual, an *order-sorted*

Table 2. Notations and their meaning

$\Sigma \triangleq (S, \sqsubseteq, F)$	order-sorted signature with sorts S, sub-sort relation $\sqsubseteq$, operations F
$f : s_1 \times s_n \to s$	operation with parameter sorts $s_1, \ldots, s_n$ and result sort s
$\Sigma' \subseteq \Sigma$	Σ' is sub-signature of Σ
$t_1 \doteq_s t_2$	equality on terms for sort s; sort is omitted, if clear from context
t **is** s	type check (satisfied iff t is a term of sort s)
$\mathfrak{A} \triangleq ((A_s)_{s\in S}, [\![\cdot]\!]_A)$	Σ-Algebra
A_s	carrier set for sort s
$[\![f]\!]_A$	interpretation of operation f as function on corresponding carrier sets
$[t]_{\doteq}$	congruence class of t w.r.t. equality
$\mathfrak{A}\vert_{\Sigma'}$	restriction of Σ-algebra $\mathfrak{A}$ to signature $\Sigma' \subseteq \Sigma$
q	state of an Abstract State Machine
$q \models \varphi$	φ is satisfied by state q

abstract data type specifies axioms by (conditional) equations and inequations. We assume that for each term t of the smallest sort s, there is a subset C of the operation symbols with result sort s such that $t \doteq t'$ where t' is a term over C. In order to specify partial operations, we assume that there is a unique smallest sort UNDEF and a constructor $undef{:}\to \mathsf{UNDEF}$. Each other operation is (unless stated otherwise) *strict*, i.e., $f(t_1, \ldots, t_n) \doteq undef$ if $t_i \doteq undef$ for an $i \in \{1, \ldots, n\}$.

Order-sorted algebras $\mathfrak{A}$ are defined analogous to many-sorted algebras with the following additions:

(i) If $s \sqsubseteq s'$ then $A_s \subseteq A_{s'}$ for the carrier sets of sorts s and s', respectively.
(ii) If $f : s_1 \times \cdots s_n \to s \in F$, $f : s'_1 \times \cdots s'_n \to s' \in F$, and $s_i \sqsubseteq s'_i$ then $[\![f : s_1 \times \cdots \times s_n \to s]\!](x_1, \ldots, x_n) = [\![f : s'_1 \times \cdots \times s''_n \to s']\!](x_1, \ldots, x_n)$ for all $x_1 \in A_{s_1}, \ldots, x_n \in A_{s_n}$

Goguen and Meseguer [7] argue that order-sorted signatures enable subtype polymorphism and overloading. The notion of quotient term algebras is defined analogously to many-sorted algebras. Let $\Sigma' \triangleq (S', \sqsubset', F')$ be a sub-signature[2] of $\Sigma \triangleq (S, \sqsubseteq, F)$ and $\mathfrak{A} \triangleq (\Sigma, A, [\![.]\!]_A)$ be a $\Sigma - Algebra$. The restriction of $\mathfrak{A}$ to Σ' is the Σ'-algebra $\mathfrak{A}|_{\Sigma'} \triangleq (\Sigma', A', [\![.]\!]_{A'})$ such that $A'_s = A_s$ for each sort $s \in S'$ and $[\![f]\!]_{A'} = [\![f]\!]_A$ for each $f \in F'$.

The notion of a logical formula (and its interpretation) is as usual where equations and type checks are atomic formulas.

Let Σ be an order sorted-signature. An *Abstract State Machine* is a tuple $\mathcal{A} \triangleq (\Sigma, Q, I, R)$ where

(i) Σ is an order-sorted signature

[2] $\Sigma' \subseteq \Sigma$ iff $S' \subseteq S$, $\sqsubseteq' \ \subseteq \ \sqsubseteq$, and $F' \subseteq F$.

(ii) Q is the set of *states*, i.e., Σ-Algebras (with the same carrier sets)
(iii) $I \subseteq Q$ (set of *initial states*)
(iv) R is a finite set of transition rules **if** φ **then** $t{:=}t'$ where φ is a first-order logical formula and t, t' are Σ-terms of sorts s, s' respectively, with $s' \sqsubseteq s$.

The pair $t{:=}t'$ is called an *update.* A transition rule **if** φ **then** $t{:=}t'$ where φ is *activated in state* $q \in Q$ iff $q \models \varphi$. The set of activated rules in state q is denoted by *Activated*(q). The *update set in state* q is the set *Update*$(q) \triangleq \{t{:=}t' :$ **if** φ **then** $t{:=}t' \in \mathit{Activated}(q)\}$.

Two updates $f(t_1, \ldots, t_n){:=}t$, $f(t'_1, \ldots, t'_n){:=}t'$ are *consistent* in state q if $q \models t_i \doteq t'_i$, $i = 1, \ldots, n$ implies $q \models t \doteq t'$. Otherwise the updates are called *inconsistent.* A set of updates is *inconsistent,* iff it contains two inconsistent updates. Otherwise it is called *consistent.*

Let q be a state. Then the successor state *next*(q) is defined as follows:

$$\mathit{next}(q) \triangleq \begin{cases} q & \text{if } \mathit{Update}(q) \text{ is inconsistent} \\ q' & \text{otherwise} \end{cases}$$

where q' is defined as follows:

$$[\![f]\!]_{q'}(a_1, \ldots, a_n) \triangleq \begin{cases} [\![t]\!]_q & \text{if } f(t_1, \ldots, t_n) \in \mathit{Updates}(q) \text{ and} \\ & a_i = [\![t_i]\!]_q, i = 1, \ldots, n \\ [\![f]\!]_q(a_1, \ldots, a_n) & \text{otherwise} \end{cases}$$

Remark 1. Sometimes, we use the following notation:

if φ **then** u_1	is an abbreviation for	**if** φ **then** u_1
$\vdots$		$\vdots$
u_n		**if** φ **then** u_n

A *run* starting at state q_0 is an infinite sequence of states $\langle q_i | i \in \mathbb{N}\rangle$ such that $q_{i+1} = \mathit{next}(q_i)$, $i \in \mathbb{N}$. A *sub-run* is a sub-sequence of a run. A state q is *reachable* from q_0 iff it is an element of a run starting at q_0. We assume that the set Q is the set of all reachable states from an initial state $q_0 \in I$. A state q_j in a run $\langle q_i | i \in \mathbb{N}\rangle$ is *final* iff $q_k = q_j$ for all $k \geq j$.

There are two reasons for final states: An inconsistent update set or the updates do not change the state (in particular if it is empty).

A function symbol f is *dynamic* iff there are two reachable states $q, q' \in Q$ such that $[\![f]\!]_q \neq [\![f]\!]_{q'}$. Otherwise f is *static.* f is *directly dynamic* if there is a transition rule **if** φ **then** $f(t_1, \ldots, t_n){:=}t \in R$.

3 Semantics of Languages Used in the Compiler

For the verification of the compiler, the following intermediate languages are used [5]:

1. Source language semantics based on the source language concepts (language Sather-K_0)
2. Source language semantics based on the memory of the target language (language Sather-K_0^M)
3. Intermediate language based on basic-block graphs for each procedure. Basic block graphs represent the control-flow. The instructions are more fine-grained than those in the source language. The semantics of its operators is based on the target machine. (language IL_0)
4. Target tree: Basic blocks with machine instructions using eventually symbolic registers (language MIPS-TT_0)
5. Assembly language on the target machine (language $MIPS_0$)

Except Sather-K_0^M, each of these languages is used in a compiler.

The transformation from Sather-K_0 to Sather-K_0^M is the memory mapping. The transformation from Sather-K_0^M to IL_0 preserves the memory state space, but it transforms the source language to basic block graphs for each procedure. The languages IL_0, MIPS-TT_0, and $MIPS_0$ only have parameter-less procedures, i.e., there must be intermediate code for parameter passing. Furthermore, in IL_0 all values are atomic. The decomposition of non-atomic values must be explicitly implemented using intermediate language expressions. The transformation from IL_0 to MIPS-TT_0 is called *code selection* and specified as term-rewrite systems. The transformation from MIPS-TT_0 to $MIPS_0$ assigns registers to symbolic registers. In this paper, we consider the transformations from Sather-K_0 to Sather-K_0^M and the transformation from Sather-K_0^M to IL_0. For the other transformations, we refer to the results of the *Verifix*-project [23].

In this section, we introduce the formal semantics of the languages in Steps 1 to 3. The semantics of a language is based on its abstract syntax. The abstract syntax is a data structure that represents programs of a programming language. It may be extended by operations for the navigation within the programs. Furthermore, there are static functions modeling static semantic properties such as typing, static environments, control flow, and data-flow. Since these functions are static, they can be specified by axioms (using occurrences and abstract syntax trees). Note that the preparation for incremental correctness proofs requires incrementally defined languages.

Remark 2. In this work, we do not specify these axioms. Instead, the correctness proofs make some assumptions on the static semantics that must be proven using these axioms using a suitable calculus. Instead, we introduce the informal meaning of these operations.

3.1 Language Semantics Sather-K_0

The dynamic semantics of Sather-K_0 is based on the occurrence algebra of its abstract syntax [18]. For each production of the abstract syntax, there is a constructor yielding a term of the corresponding sort. For the semantics relevant

$prog:$	$\rightarrow \mathsf{PROG}$	$env = push(createEnv, frame(ip, nil, null))$
$ip:$	$\rightarrow \mathsf{OCC}$	$ip = first(prog, cls)$
$val:$	$\mathsf{OCC} \rightarrow \mathsf{LOC}$	$val(\varepsilon)) = null$
$env:$	$\rightarrow \mathsf{ENV}$	$val(o.i) = undef$
(a) Dynamic functions		(b) Axioms for the initial state

if CT **is** CALL **then** $env := push(env, procFrame)$
if CT **is** CALL **then** $ip := first(prog, CalledProc)$
if CT **is** RETURN **then** $env{:=}pop(env)$
if CT **is** RETURN **then** $ip{:=}getReturn(env)$
if CT **is** SKIP **then** $ip{:=}next(prog,ip)$
(c) State transition rules

$$\begin{aligned}
CT &\triangleq occ(prog, ip)\\
CalledProc &\triangleq proc(prog, ip)\\
Obj &\triangleq val(qual(prog, ip))\\
ProcFrame &\triangleq frame(CalledProc, next(prog, ip), Obj)
\end{aligned}$$

(d) Abbreviations

Fig. 2. Dynamic semantics of SATHER-K_0.

are the sorts that execute instructions and correspond to procedures. These are CALL for procedure calls, RETURN for procedure returns, SKIP for empty list of statements, PROC for procedures, and PROG for programs. Note that the program in Fig. 1 is the only program of SATHER-K_0. Occurrences are lists of natural numbers. ε denotes the empty list. The elements in the list are separated by a dot. These lists are used to refer to subterms (or nodes) in an abstract syntax tree (AST) where ε refers to the root of an abstract syntax tree. These references are defined by a function $occ : \mathsf{PROG} \times \mathsf{NAT}^* \rightarrow \mathsf{NODE}$. In addition, there is an occurrence $nil :\rightarrow \mathsf{OCC}$. It holds $occ(nil, p) = halt$ where $halt :\rightarrow \mathsf{HALT}$ is a constructor of sort HALT. Here, denotes $occ(p, o) \doteq undef$ iff occurrence o does not refer to a node in the abstract syntax tree p. Each of the above sorts is a subsort of NODE.

Remark 3. The introduction of the sort NODE ensures extensibility of the abstract syntax. Any new concept has a new sort C which is a sub-sort of NODE. Its dynamic semantics simply adds transition rules with guards $occ(prog, pc)$ **is** C.

The dynamic functions in Fig. 2(a) define the state space of the dynamic semantics, whereas *prog* is the abstract syntax tree of the program to be executed. The instruction pointer *ip* refers to the phrase to be executed in a state. Here, *val* denotes the reference or value of an object where the method is called. *Shared methods* have no such object, i.e., the reference is the *null* reference. LOC is the sort of such references. The sort ENV is the sort of environments. An *environment* is the calling stack of the currently executed procedures. Each element of the stack (called *frame*) contains the occurrence of the procedure, the return instruction, and the reference to the object where the procedure is being executed.

Remark 4. In subsequent versions, local variables of methods will be introduced. These must be included in the frame. The classical approach to model this is to include them in the constructor for frames. However, this would not be extensible. An extensible model introduces a constructor function *addLocalVar* that adds a local variable to a frame together with additional information required for the dynamic semantics. A function *getLocalVarInfo* can retrieve this information associated with a local variable. Both functions are easily extensible.

Sather-K defines that before calling the main method of the main class, all shared attributes must be initialized. If the initialization of a shared attribute of a class A uses a shared attribute of class B, then the shared attributes of B must be initialized before those of A. This initialization order must be acyclic. The language definition allows for using any topological order. The occurrence *cls* refers to any class with shared attributes without using shared attributes of other classes in their shared attribute initializations. If there are no shared attributes, then $cls = \varepsilon$. The latter represents the call of the `main` method, which is the instruction after the last shared attribute initialization. Since SATHER-K_0 has no shared attributes it is $cls = \varepsilon$, i.e., the main method is being called.

Figure 2(b) defines the axioms for the initial state. The environment has one frame, which is being used for maintaining the shared attributes in subsequent versions. The term *first*(*prog*, *cls*) denotes the very first instruction being executed. If $cls = \varepsilon$ this is the call $\mathsf{K} :: main$, where K is the main class. This is a qualified method call on *null*. The qualifier is the root of the abstract syntax tree.

Figure 2(c) shows the transition rules for qualified procedure calls and procedure returns. The frame stores the instruction to be executed after the call where $next(p, o)$ is the occurrence of the instruction to be executed after the instruction $occ(p, o)$. *Obj* is the reference of the object where the procedure is being called. If $CT = undef$, all guards are satisfied. Hence, the update set becomes inconsistent. It must be proven that this situation is avoided. The last instruction is a halting instruction (after return from the main method). There is no guard satisfied by the halting instruction, i.e., the update set is empty.

Remark 5. The initial states and the state transition rules are designed such that they are extensible. In particular, they shall not to be changed in subsequent versions. If $cls \neq \varepsilon$ then the execution of a program starts with the initialization of the first shared attribute of *occ*(*prog*, *cls*). The static function *next* yields the next instruction. If the last shared attribute is being initialized, *next* yields ε. Hence, the main method in the main class is called.

The transition rule for the procedure calls and returns are the classical ones modeling the last-in, first-out semantics of procedure calls. Hence, these transition rules need not to be changed in subsequent versions.

3.2 Language Semantics SATHER-K_0^M

The state space of the dynamic semantics is based on the runtime system, cf. Fig. 3. The environment *env* is mapped to the memory $mem : \mathsf{ADDR} \to \mathsf{BYTE}$

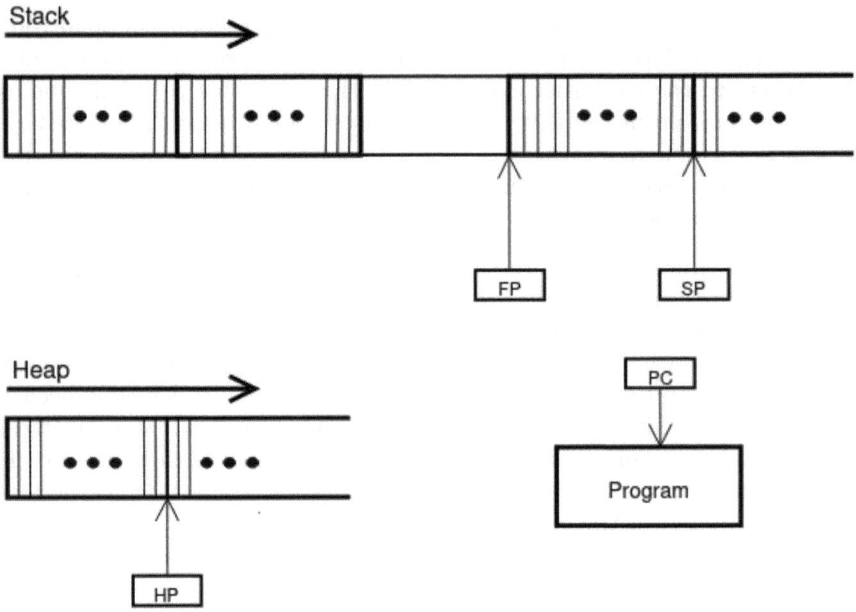

Fig. 3. Runtime system.

since MIPS has a byte-oriented memory. The environment is implemented as a stack of activation records allocated consecutively and non-overlapping in the memory. The *frame pointer fp* : ADDR contains the base address of the top activation record. The stack pointer *sp* : ADDR refers to the first free address after the top of the stack. Here, *bos* contains the address for the bottom of the stack and *gp* : ADDR the first address of the heap. Finally, *hp* is the heap pointer referring to the last address occupied by the heap. The runtime system keeps the heap disjoint from the stack. In MIPS the stack grows downwards and the heap grows upwards. The initial version does not require the heap since the initial Sather-K_0 has no instructions for creating objects.

The stack behaviour is implemented using the layout of activation records shown in Fig. 4(a). In particular, it shows the relative addresse for storing the base address of the callee, the return address (instruction after call), and *self* (the object where the method is being executed). For subsequent versions, the first-order memory stores the contents of the local variables and the second-order memory stores dynamic information that can be destroyed upon returning to the caller. The *size of a activation record for procedure p* is the size of the first-order memory. This is a static information.

The initial state allocates on the stack the first activation record and initializes the administrative information with the bottom of the stack *bos*, with the occurrence *nil*, and the address 0. Note that occurrences must be converted

≥ 12	first-order memory
8:	reference to *self*
4:	return address (instruction after caller)
0:	base address of caller's activation record
<0	second-order memory

(a) Memory layout of procedure activation records

$$
\begin{aligned}
&fp = bos - size(p, \varepsilon)\\
&sp = fp\\
&Mem(fp) = bos\\
&Mem(fp+4) = occtoval(nil)\\
&Mem(fp+8) = 0\\
&ip = first(prog, cls)
\end{aligned}
$$

(b) Axioms for the initial state

if CT **is** CALL $\wedge\ sp \geq min + FrameSize$ **then**
  $sp := sp - FrameSize$
  $fp := sp - FrameSize$
  $Store(sp - FrameSize, fp)$
  $Store(sp - FrameSize + 4), occtoval(next(prog, ip)))$
  $Store(fp - FrameSize + 8, QualAddr)$
  $ip := first(prog, CalledProc)$
endif

if CT **is** RETURN **then**
  $fp := Mem(fp)$
  $sp := fp + size(prog, ip)$
  $ip := valtoocc(Mem(fp + 4))$
endif

if CT **is** SKIP **then**
  $ip{:=}next(prog,ip)$
endif

(c) State transition rules

$$
\begin{aligned}
Store(a, v) \triangleq\ & mem(a) := byte(v, 0)\\
& mem(a+1) := byte(v, 1)\\
& mem(a+2) := byte(v, 2)\\
& mem(a+3) := byte(v, 3)\\
Mem(a) \triangleq\ & mkint32(mem(a+3), mem(a+2), mem(a+1), mem(a))\\
FrameSize \triangleq\ & size(occ(prog, CalledProc))\\
QualAddr \triangleq\ & obj(qual(prog, ip))
\end{aligned}
$$

(d) Abbreviations

Fig. 4. Dynamic semantics of SATHER-K_0^M.

to 32-bit words using the function *occtoval*. For this function, a precise definition is not required except that it is injective. For the correctness proof, it is only required that the function *valtoocc* be its inverse. The abbreviation $Mem(a)$ reads the word in the memory at addresses $a..a+3$ as little-endian representation. $Store(a, v)$ is the corresponding abbreviation for the updates storing a 32-Bit word in the memory. The last axiom for the initial state is the same as in SATHER-K_0.

Figure 4(c) shows the transition rules. The rule for procedure calls has an additional constraint that checks whether there is enough memory to allocate the activation record of the callee. If this is possible, the stack pointer and the frame pointer are updated to allocate the necessary space for the callee's activation record. The administrative information is stored in the callee's activation record: frame pointer of the caller, return address, and the address of *self*. The latter is defined by the qualifier of the call (abbreviation *QualAddr*). The transition rules for return restore the caller's frame pointer, the return address, and deallocate the current activation record.

The memory mapping implements the runtime stack without any restrictions. In particular, the transition rules in Fig. 4(c) remain unchanged for all subsequent versions. The following invariants are satisfied by SATHER-K_0^M

Theorem 1 (Invariants). For each run $\langle q_i \mid i \in \mathbb{N}\rangle$ of ASM $\mathcal{A}_{0.0}^{(2)}$ it holds:

- **i.** For all $i \in \mathbb{N}$: $q_i \models \mathit{fp}\%4 = 0$
- **ii.** For all $i \in \mathbb{N}$: $q_i \models \mathit{sp}\%4 = 0$
- **iii.** For all $i \in \mathbb{N}$: $q_i \models \forall j : \mathsf{NAT} \bullet \mathit{mem}(\mathit{succ}(j), \mathit{fp}) = \mathit{undef} \vee \mathit{mem}(\mathit{succ}(j), \mathit{fp}) + \mathit{size}(\mathit{CurProc}) < \mathit{mem}(j), \mathit{fp})$
- **iv.** For all $i \in \mathbb{N}$: $q_i \models \exists j : \mathsf{NAT} : \mathit{mem}(j+1, \mathit{fp}) = \mathit{bos}$
- **v.** For all $i \in \mathbb{N}$: $q_i \models \mathit{fp} \leq \mathit{sp}$
- **vi.** For all $i \in \mathbb{N}$: $q_i \models \mathit{mem}(i, \mathit{bos}) = \mathit{undef}$
- **vii.** For all $i \in \mathbb{N}$: $q_i \models \mathit{obj}(\mathit{qual}(\mathit{prog}, \varepsilon)) = 0$

$$\begin{aligned} &\text{where } \mathit{mem} : \mathsf{NAT} \times \mathsf{ADDR} \to \mathsf{VALUE} \\ &\mathit{mem}(\mathit{zero}, a) \quad = a \\ &\mathit{mem}(\mathit{succ}(n), a) = \mathit{mem}(n, \mathit{Mem}(a)) \end{aligned}$$

Properties (i) and (ii) mean that *fp* and *sp* are aligned according to the specification of MIPS. Property (iii) means that no two activation records overlap. Property (iv) means that tracking the base addresses of the activation records reaches the bottom of the stack. Property (v) means that the frame pointer never exceeds the stack pointer. Property (vii) means that the object address for calling main is 0 (i.e., there is no object).

Proof (Sketch). For the proof, it has to be shown that (i)–(vii) is satisfied by the initial states. Then, it has to be shown that if a state q satisfies the invariants, then $\mathit{next}(q)$ also satisfies the invariants. Due to lack of space, we show (iii). The proof distinguishes the cases by the guards of the transition rules. If q satisfies none of the guards or the update set $\mathit{Update}(q)$ is inconsistent, then $\mathit{next}(q) = q$. Hence, $\mathit{next}(q)$ also satisfies (iii). Otherwise, at most one of the guards is satisfied. A similar argument as above applies to the case $q \models \mathit{CT}$ **is** SKIP.

Consider the case $q \models \mathit{CT}$ **is** $\mathsf{CALL} \wedge \mathit{sp} \geq \mathit{min} + \mathit{FrameSize}$. The proof is in two steps:

(a) For all terms $n \in \mathcal{T}_{\mathsf{NAT}}$ it holds $[\![\mathit{Mem}(\mathit{succ}(n), \mathit{fp})]\!]_{\mathit{next}(q)} = [\![\mathit{Mem}(n, \mathit{fp})]\!]_q$
(b) $\mathit{next}(q) \models \mathit{mem}(\mathit{succ}(\mathit{zero}), \mathit{fp}) + \mathit{size}(\mathit{CurProc}) < \mathit{mem}(\mathit{zero}, \mathit{fp})$

(a) can be shown by induction on n and (b) can be directly shown using $\mathit{Update}(q)$. Together with the assumption that q satisfies (iii), (a) and (b) imply that $\mathit{next}(q)$ satisfies (iii).

$Instr$::=Skip()
$Instr$::=Push($Expr$)
$Instr$::=Pop($Expr$)
$Instr$::=IntStore($Expr$,$Expr$)
$Instr$::=AddrStore($Expr$,$Expr$)
$Instr$::=StoreBase($Expr$)
$Instr$::=StoreTopOfStack($Expr$)
$Instr$::=StoreBaseBotFrame($Expr$)
$Instr$::=Call($label$)
$Instr$::=Exit()
$Instr$::=Return()
$Expr$::=IntLoad($IntegerVal$)
$Expr$::=Base()
$Expr$::=TopOfStack()
$Expr$::=IntAdd($Expr$,$Expr$)
$Expr$::=IntLoadAddr($Expr$)
$Expr$::=AddrLoadAddr($Expr$)
$IntegerVal$::=IntegerLit(int)

(a) Tree grammar

$eval(\texttt{IntegerLit}(c)) = c$
$eval(\texttt{IntLoad}(l)) = eval(l)$
$eval(\texttt{Base}()) = fp$
$eval(\texttt{TopOfStack}()) = sp$
$eval(\texttt{IntAdd}(e_1, e_2)) = eval(e_1) + eval(e_2)$
$eval(\texttt{IntLoadAddr}(e)) = Mem(eval(e))$
$eval(\texttt{AddrLoadAddr}(e)) = Mem(eval(e))$

(b) Evaluation of expressions

$ilprog :\ \to$ IL
$fp :\ \to$ ADDR
$sp :\ \to$ ADDR
$mem :$ ADDR $\to$ BYTE
$ci\ \to$ LABEL $\times$ NAT

(c) Dynamic functions (state space)

$sp = bos$
$ci = \langle l0, 0\rangle$

(d) Initial state

if CI **is** IL_INSTR $\wedge \neg CI$ **is** IL_JUMP **then** $ci := next(ci)$
if CI **is** IL_PUSH **then** $sp := sp - eval(opd(CI))$
if CI **is** IL_POP **then** $sp := sp + eval(opd(CI))$
if CI **is** IL_INTSTORE **then** $Store(Dest, Src)$
if CI **is** IL_ADDRSTORE **then** $Store(Dest, Src)$
if CI **is** IL_STOREBASE **then** $fp := eval(opd(CI))$
if CI **is** IL_STORETOPOFSTACK **then** $sp := eval(opd(CI))$
if CI **is** IL_STOREBASEBOTFRAME **then** $fp := bot$
if CI **is** IL_CALL **then** $ci := \langle label(CI), 0\rangle$
if CI **is** IL_CALL **then** $Store(fp + 4, postoval(next(ci, ilprog)))$
if CI **is** IL_RETURN **then** $ci := valtopos(Mem(sp + 4))$

(e) State transition rules for instructions

$CI \triangleq getInstr(ilprog, ci)$
$Dest \triangleq dest(CI)$
$Src \triangleq src(CI)$

(f) Abbreviations

Fig. 5. The intermediate language IL_0.

3.3 Language Semantics IL_0

Intermediate languages are usually represented as basic block graphs for each procedure. A *basic block* is a sequence of instructions and associated with a unique *label*. A *program* is a set of procedures. Each procedure has a unique starting basic block. There is a unique basic block with label `main`.

The execution of a basic block starts with its first instruction and executes all its instructions in order of the sequence. The last instruction is either a conditional jump, a return, or an exit. The execution of the program starts with the basic block with label `main`.

Remark 6. This is the general structure of intermediate languages. They differ on the concrete definition of instructions. Hence, extensibility is achieved by adding instructions together with its dynamic semantics.

In this work, we assume that procedures have no parameters. Figure 5(a) shows the tree grammar for IL_0. Tree grammars derive trees (represented as a term) instead of strings. The tree grammar distinguishes *instructions* (trees that can be derived from the non-terminal *Instr*) and *expressions* (trees that can be derived from the non-terminal *Expr*). The non-terminal *IntegerVal* represents integer literals (defined as *int*). The call instruction has the label of the start block of the callee. Each of tree grammar rule defines a constructor. The result sorts are named with the operator name prefixed by $\mathsf{IL\_}$.

Expressions are *evaluated* (in the current state), cf. Fig. 5(b). It uses macros defined in Fig. 4. The infix operation + is the addition on 32-bit integers. Instructions are *executed* and change the state. Hence, their semantics is defined by transition rules; cf. Fig. 5(e). It uses the following five static functions: First, *opd* navigates to the child of unary operators. Second, *dest* navigates to the destination of store operations. Third, *src* navigates to the source of store-operations. Fourth, *getInstr* obtains the instruction in an IL program from the label and the instruction number. Finally, *next* determines the next instruction to be executed.

A pair $\langle label, i\rangle \in \mathsf{LABEL} \times \mathsf{NAT}$ refers to the i-th instruction of the basic block with label *label*. The function *valtopos* is defined analogously to *occtoval*, i.e., it maps the above pairs to values. The function *postoval* is the inverse of *valtopos*. The initial state starts with the execution of the basic block of shared attribute initializations. This phase ends with calling the main method. This first basic block has label *l0*. It is usual that *call instructions* are considered as non-jumps since after return from a call, the instruction after the call is being executed.

Figure 6 shows the result of the compilation of the program in Fig. 1 to IL. The instructions in lines (1)–(6) initialize the runtime stack such that the properties of the initial state of $\text{S}\small{\text{ATHER}}\text{-K}_0^M$ are satisfied, cf. Fig. 4(c). Line (7) allocates the space for the frame of `main` and Lines (8)–(9) store the frame pointer of the callee and *null* in the relative addresses 0 and 8, respectively. Line (10) changes the frame pointer to the frame pointer of the callee, which is equal to the stack pointer, cf. Fig. 3. Line (11) calls `main` (`l1` is the label of the start block

```
(1)  l0: Push(IntLoad(IntegerVal(12)))
(2)      StoreBase(TopOfStack)
(3)      StoreBaseBotFrame(Base)
(4)      AddrStore(IntAdd(Base,IntLoad(IntegerVal(8))),IntLoad(IntegerVal(0)))
(5)      AddrStore(IntAdd(Base,IntLoad(IntegerVal(4))),IntLoad(IntegerVal(-1)))
(6)      AddrStore(Base,IntLoad(IntegerVal(-1))
(7)      Push(IntLoad(IntegerVal(12)))
(8)      AddrStore(TopOfStack,Base)
(9)      AddrStore(IntAdd(TopOfStack,IntLoad(IntegerVal(8))),IntLoad(IntegerVal(0)))
(10)     StoreBase(TopOfStack)
(11)     Call(l1)
(12)     Pop(IntegerVal(IntLoad(12)))
(13)     Exit()
(14)
(15) l1: StoreTopOfStack(Base)
(16)     StoreBase(AddrLoadAddr(Base))
(17)     Return()
```

Fig. 6. Compilation result of the program in Fig. 1 to IL.

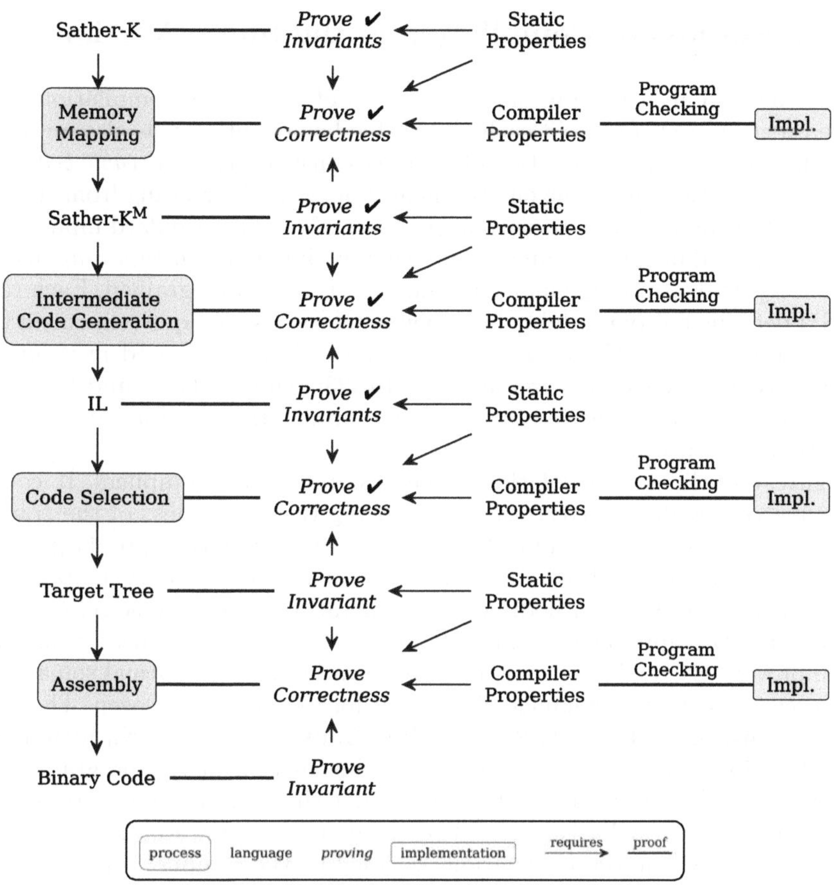

Fig. 7. Overview of the compilation process and corresponding correctness proofs.

of `main`). Note that the call instruction also stores the return address at relative address 4, cf. Fig. 5(e). After returning from a call, the stack deallocates the first-order memory of the callee (Line (12)). Then, the program terminates (Line (13)). The body of `main` is the skip statement. It is not necessary to generate code for skip statements. Thus, the basic block `l1` only contains the code for returning to the caller. Line (15) deallocates the second-order memory. Line (16) updates *fp* to the frame pointer of the callee. Hence, *fp* contains the base address of the caller and *sp* contains the base address of the callee. The `Return` instruction restores the return address, cf. Fig. 5(e).

Remark 7. The information of associating procedures to the labels of its start blocks with labels is provided by the compiler. The space required for allocating the first-order memory of an activation record is also computed by the compiler. Hence, the transformation does not hard code the number 12 but the activation record's size. In Sather-K_0^M this size equals 12.

4 Correctness of Compilation of the Initial Version

We use the notion of compilation correctness of *Verifix*: A compilation $\overline{\pi}$ of a source program π is *correct* iff each observable behaviour of π' is also an observable behaviour of π up to violation of resource constraints. *Observable behaviours* focus on interactions with the environment. For example, reading from standard input and writing to standard output are observable. The standard input stream and the standard output stream are modeled by dynamic constants *inp* and *out*, respectively. Programming language semantics is more fine-grained. Each run of an ASM defining a programming language semantics is a unique refinement of an observable behaviour. However, the semantics of languages used in a compiler have the dynamic constants *inp* and *out*. In [23], Zimmermann and Gaul show that correctness can be proved by simulation proofs. In particular, it shows that simulations are transitive.

Figure 7 outlines most of the correctness proofs for compilers. It consists of proving *compilation correctness*, i.e., proving the correctness of the transformation in the leftmost column. These proofs are simulation proofs proving a conditional refinement of ASM, cf. Theorem 2 for the memory mapping and Theorems 4–6 for the intermediate code generation. The code selection can be proven using the approach in [23]. [22] shows how the correctness of assembly can be proven. Each of the proofs may use invariants of the formal semantics of the source or the target language of the transformation to be proven. Theorem 1 shows the invariants for $\text{SATHER-K}^{M}_{0.0}$. Invariants for SATHER-K_0 include that the instruction pointer always refers to an instruction of the program if it is different from *nil*. Invariants for IL include that the current instruction *ci* refers to an instruction in a basic block. The correctness proves for the transformations may also depend on information provided by the compiler implementation (rightmost column). For example it must provide the relative addresses of local variables. For each of these local variables, non-overlapping memory must be allocated. In addition, it must not overlap with the memory allocated for the frame pointer, the return address, and *self*. It is not necessary to prove the correctness of the compiler implementation. Instead these properties are checked for their correctness. In general, the correctness of the implementation of transformations can be proven by *program checking* [6]. Finally, the correctness proof of a transformation may depend on static semantic properties. For example, it must be ensured that $next(o, p)$ also refers to an instruction in program p if occurrence o refers to an instruction in p. The static properties must be proven using static semantics of the language. The proofs are not state based but rely only on axioms. The properties required by the correctness of memory mapping are proven but not included in this article.

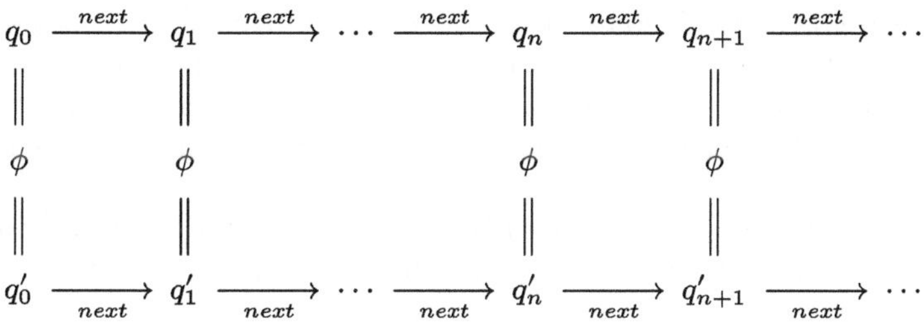

Fig. 8. Illustration of the 1:1-simulation.

$$
\begin{aligned}
&Inv_1 \triangleq addr(Obj) = QualAddr\\
&Inv_2 \triangleq \forall i : \mathsf{NAT} \bullet occtoval(getReturn(getFrame(i, env))) = Mem(mem(i, fp) + 4)\\
&Inv_3 \triangleq \forall i : \mathsf{NAT} \bullet addr(getSelf(getFrame(i, env))) = Mem(mem(i, fp) + 8)\\
&Inv_4 \triangleq mem(length(env), fp) = bos\\
&\text{where } getFrame : \mathsf{NAT} \times \mathsf{FRAME} \to \mathsf{ENV}\\
&\qquad getFrame(zero, e) \quad = top(e)\\
&\qquad getFrame(succ(n), e) = getFrame(n, pop(e))
\end{aligned}
$$

Fig. 9. Invariants for the simulation relation.

4.1 Correctness of Memory Mapping

We show that ASM Sather-K_0^M conditionally 1:1-simulates SM Sather-K_0:

Theorem 2. Let $\langle q'_i | i \in \mathbb{N}\rangle$ be a run of Sather-K_0^M then there is corresponding run $\langle q_i | i \in \mathbb{N}\rangle$ of SM Sather-K_0 such that there is a relation $\phi \subseteq Q' \times Q$ the following properties for each $(q', q) \in \phi$ are satisfied:

(i) $q' \not\models MemoryOverflow$
(ii) $[\![ip]\!]_{q'} = [\![ip]\!]_q$
(iii) $(next(q), \text{next}(q')) \in \phi$
(iv) If q' is an initial state, then q is an initial state

where $MemoryOverflow \triangleq CT\ \mathsf{is}\ \mathsf{CALL} \wedge sp < min + size(occ(prog, CalledProc))$.

Remark 8. Properties (ii)-(iv) define a 1:1-simulation, cf. Fig. 8. Property (i) restricts the 1:1-simulation up to the first state satisfying *MemoryOverlflow.* Note that if in a run $\langle q'_i | i \in \mathbb{N}\rangle$ be a run of Sather-K_0^M it holds $q_i \models MemoryOverlow$ then the update set is empty, i.e., $q_j = q_i$ for all $j \geq i$. Thus, (i)–(iv) can be considered as a conditional 1:1-simulation.

The relation ϕ is based on the memory mapping. The i-th stack frame of *env* corresponds to the i-th activation record in the memory. Figure 9 formally defines the relation ϕ as invariants on the simultaneous execution of the ASM Sather-K_0 and Sather-K_0^M. Inv_1 states the reference of the object where a procedure is being called is mapped to an address of this object. Inv_2 states that the relative address 4 of an activation record contains the return address of a frame. Inv_3 states that at relative address 8, the address of *self* is stored. Inv_4 defines that the number of activation records in the memory equals to number of frames in the environment.

For the simultaneous execution of SATHER-K_0 and SATHER-K_0^M we join the two ASMs and prove that the invariants in Fig. 9 are invariants of the joined ASM.

Definition 1 (Join ASMs). *Let* $\mathcal{A}_1 \triangleq (\Sigma_1, Q_1, I_1, R_1)$ *and* $\mathcal{A}_2 \triangleq (\Sigma_2, Q_2, I_2, R_2)$ *be two ASMs. The* join *of* $\mathcal{A}_1$ *and* $\mathcal{A}_2$ *is an ASM* $join(\mathcal{A}_1, \mathcal{A}_2) \triangleq (\Sigma_1 \cup \Sigma_2, Q, I, R_1 \cup R_2)$ *such that*

i $Q_1 = \{q|_{\Sigma_1} : q \in Q\}$ *and* $Q_2 = \{q|_{\Sigma_2} : q \in Q\}$
ii $I_1 = \{q|_{\Sigma_1} : q \in I\}$ *and* $I_2 = \{q|_{\Sigma_2} : q \in I\}$

The following Lemma shows that there is a 1:1-simulation between the ASMs and the joined ASM:

Lemma 1. $\mathcal{A}_1$ *and* $\mathcal{A}_2$ *be two ASMs. Let* $\langle q_i | i \in \mathbb{N}\rangle$ *be a run of* $join(\mathcal{A}_1, \mathcal{A}_2)$ *such that* $Update(q_i)$ *is consistent for all* $i \in \mathbb{N}$. *Then the sequence* $\langle q_i|_{\Sigma_1} | i \in \mathbb{N}\rangle$ *is a run of* $\mathcal{A}_1$ *and the sequence* $\langle q_i|_{\Sigma_2} | i \in \mathbb{N}\rangle$ *is a run of* $\mathcal{A}_2$.

Proof (Sketch). Definition 1(ii) implies that $q_o|_{\Sigma_1}$ is initial. Since the transition rules R_1 only update dynamic functions of Σ_1, it holds:
$next_{join(\mathcal{A}_1,\mathcal{A}_2)}(q_i)\big|_{\Sigma_1} = next_{\mathcal{A}_1}(q_i|_{\Sigma_1})$

Hence, the following theorem implies Theorem 2:

Theorem 3 (Invariants). The joined ASM $join$(SATHER-K_0, SATHER-K_0^M) satisfies:

i. $q \models Inv_k$, for $k = 1, 2, 3, 4$ and each initial state q.
ii. If $q \not\models MemoryOverflow$ and $q \models Inv_k$ then $next(q) \models Inv_k$, for $k = 1, 2, 3, 4$ and each reachable state q.

Proof. We focus on the proof of (ii). Let q be a reachable state such that $q \not\models MemoryOverflow$ and $q \models Inv_k$, $k = 1, 2, 3, 4$. If $Update(q) = \emptyset$ or $Update(q)$ is inconsistent, then $next(q) = q$. Thus, (ii) holds in this case. The remaining cases to be considered are $q \models CT$ **is** CALL, $q \models CT$ **is** RETURN, and $q \models CT$ **is** SKIP. The proof of the latter case argues similarly to the cases where $Update(q) = \emptyset$ or $Update(q)$ is inconsistent since $next(q)$ only differs in the interpretation of the instruction pointer ip.

Due to lack of space, we demonstrate the proof by proving Inv_3 for the case $q \models CT$ **is** CALL. Since $q \not\models MemoryOverflow$ it holds $q \models CT$ **is** CALL $\wedge\ sp \geq$

min + *FrameSize*. According to the transition rules in Fig. 2 and Fig. 4 it is

$$Update(q) = \left\{ \begin{array}{l} env := push(env, ProcFrame) \\ sp \ \ := sp - FrameSize \\ fp \ \ := fp - FrameSize \\ Store(sp - FrameSize, fp) \\ Store(sp - FrameSize + 4, occtoval(next(prog, ip))) \\ Store(sp - FrameSize + 8, QualAddr) \\ ip \ \ := first(prog, CalledProc) \end{array} \right\}$$

Thus, it holds

$$[\![env]\!]_{next(q)} = [\![push(env, ProcFrame)]\!]_q \quad (1)$$

$$[\![Mem(fp + 8)]\!]_{next(q)} = [\![QualAddr]\!]_q \quad (2)$$

Inv_3 is proven inductively over the sort NAT:
CASE 1: $i = zero$. Then it holds:

$[\![addr(getSelf(getFrame(zero, env)))]\!]_{next(q)}$	
$= [\![addr(getSelf(top(env)))]\!]_{next(q)}$	Def. *getFrame*, Fig. 9
$= [\![addr(getSelf(top(push(env, ProcFrame))))]\!]_q$	(1)
$= [\![addr(getSelf(ProcFrame))]\!]_q$	Axiom for stacks
$= [\![addr(getSelf(frame(CalledProc, next(prog, ip), Obj)))]\!]_q$	Def. *ProcFrame*, Fig. 2
$= [\![addr(Obj)]\!]_q$	Axiom for *getSelf*
$= [\![QualAddr)]\!]_q$	Invariant 1
$= [\![Mem(fp + 8)]\!]_{next(q)}$	(2)
$= [\![Mem(mem(zero, fp) + 8)]\!]_{next(q)}$	Def. *mem*, Theorem 1

CASE 2: $i = succ(n)$. Then it holds:

$[\![addr(getSelf(getFrame(succ(n), env)))]\!]_{q'}$	
$= [\![addr(getSelf(getFrame(n, pop(env))))]\!]_{q'}$	Def. *getFrame*, Fig. 9
$= [\![addr(getSelf(getFrame(n, pop(push(env, ProcFrame)))))]\!]_q$	(1)
$= [\![addr(getSelf(getFrame(n, env)))]\!]_q$	Axiom for Stacks
$= [\![Mem(mem(n, fp) + 8)]\!]_q$	$q \models Inv_3$
$= [\![Mem(mem(n, Mem(fp)) + 8)]\!]_{q'}$	(2)
$= [\![Mem(mem(succ(n), fp) + 8)]\!]_{q'}$	Def. *mem*, Theorem 1

Remark 9. The above proof is extensible. Adding a new language concept means extending SATHER-K$_i$ to the next version SATHER-K$_{i+1}$ by adding new static and dynamic functions, new axioms for the initial state, and new transition rules. The memory mapping may also be extended. Usually, this extension is a new sort CMD for the abstract syntax and by a transition rule with guard *CT* **is** CMD. If new dynamic functions are added, then there may be additional transition rules for guards *CT* **is** OLD, where OLD is a language concept in SATHER-K$_i$. For example, the latter is the case if exception handling is added.

SATHER-K$_i^M$ is extended analogously to the next version, SATHER-K$_{i+1}^M$, which in particular includes the memory mapping for the extension. For example, if reference classes are introduced, a heap is introduced to manage objects (which is also a source of a possible memory overflow). The abstract syntax, occurrences, etc., and the updates to the dynamic functions remain the same.

For the correctness proof, new invariants may be added for the extensions. The invariants of *join*(SATHER-K$_i$, Sather-K$_i^M$) are also invariants of the joined ASM *join*(SATHER-K$_{i+1}$, Sather-K$_{i+1}i^M$). Thus, the correctness proof of Version i is extended by the following proofs to obtain a correctness proof for Version $i+1$:

1. The new invariants are preserved by the transition rules of *join*(SATHER-K$_i$, SATHER-K$_i^M$)
2. The new invariants are preserved by the transition rules added to *join*(SATHER-K$_i$, SATHER-K$_i^M$)
3. The invariants of *join*(SATHER-K$_i$, Sather-K$_i^M$) are preserved by the new transition rules.

Each of these proofs are just new case distinctions that only need to be added to the correctness proofs (without revision) for Version i. In particular, Inv_i, $i = 1, 2, 3, 4$ are invariants for all subsequent versions.

4.2 Correctness of Intermediate Code Generation

The transformation to intermediate code transforms phrases to intermediate code according to recursively defined tree transformation rules. According to the general approach for the semantics of intermediate languages, the language semantics after memory mapping has the same state space except the program and the instruction pointers; see Fig. 4 and Fig. 5.

Definition 2 (Checkpoints). *Let p be a phrase that is transformed by a transformation rule, o be the occurrence of the first instruction of p, and $\langle l, i\rangle$ be the reference to the fist IL-instruction generated by the transformation rule. A pair $(q, q') \in Q_0^M \times Q_{IL}$ of states of the ASMs* SATHER-K$_0^M$ *and* IL$_i$ *is a* checkpoint *γ iff the following conditions are satisfied:*

i. $[\![ip]\!]_q = o$ *and* $[\![ci]\!]_{q'} = \langle l, i\rangle$
ii. $[\![ilprog]\!]_{q'} = compile([\![prog]\!]_q)$
iii. $[\![fp]\!]_q = [\![fp]\!]_q'$
iv. $[\![sp]\!]_q = [\![sp]\!]_q'$
v. $[\![bos]\!]_q = [\![bos]\!]_q'$
vi. $[\![mem]\!]_q = [\![mem]\!]_q'$
vii. $[\![occtoval(next(ip, prog))]\!]_q = [\![postoval(next(ci, ilprog))]\!]_{q'}$

Let p be a phrase in Sather-K. Then for *compile*(p) the following diagram must be proven:

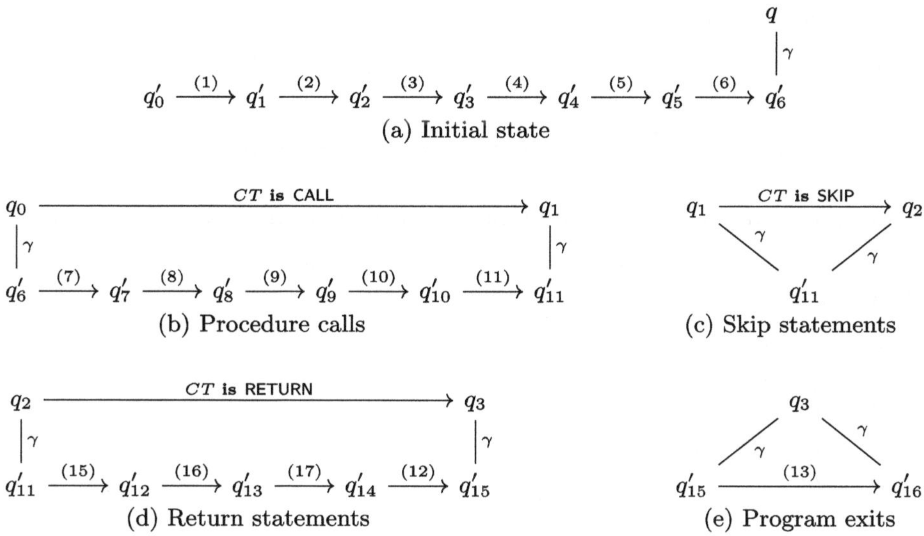

Fig. 10. Simulation relations for $\text{S}\small{\text{ATHER}}\text{-K}_0^M \mapsto \text{IL}_0$.

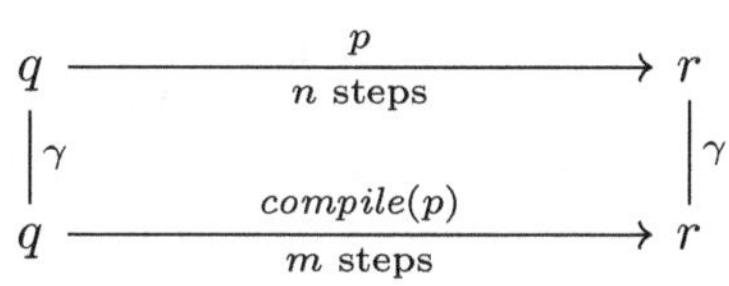

If this property is being satisfied for each transformation rule, then *compile*(*prog*) n-m-simulates *prog*. Zimmermann and Gaul [23] show that general n-m-simulations can be used to prove the correctness of compilations provided that the interactions with the environment between two consecutive checkpoints are equal for $\text{S}\small{\text{ATHER}}\text{-K}^M$ and IL.

Figure 10 shows that the semantics of the program in Fig. 6 n-m-simulates the semantics program in Fig. 1 after memory mapping. In particular simulations in Fig. 10(a)–(e) correspond to transformation rules.

Remark 10. Proving the correctness of the intermediate code generation a 1:1-simulation of the ASM after memory mapping and the ASM for IL is not possible. In particular there is no 1:1-simulation possible between IL_0 and $\text{S}\small{\text{ATHER}}\text{-K}_0^M$: The program semantics in Fig. 1 executes 3 steps until the program execution terminates. In contrast, the semantics of its compilation. cf. Fig. 6, executes 16 steps.

The code for the initialization of IL is:

```
(1)  l0: Push(IntLoad(IntegerVal(size(p,ε))))
(2)      StoreBase(TopOfStack)
(3)      StoreBaseBotFrame(Base)
(4)      AddrStore(IntAdd(Base,IntLoad(IntegerVal(8))),IntLoad(IntegerVal(0)))
(5)      AddrStore(IntAdd(Base,IntLoad(IntegerVal(4))),IntLoad(IntegerVal(-1)))
(6)      AddrStore(Base,IntLoad(IntegerVal(-1))
```

For the correctness a simulation analogous to Fig. 10(a) must be proven

Theorem 4 (Initial State). Let q'_6 be the state after the instruction (7) in IL. Then it holds

$$q'_6 \models fp = bos - size(p, \varepsilon)$$
$$q'_6 \models sp = fp$$
$$q'_6 \models Mem(fp) = bos$$
$$q'_6 \models Mem(fp + 4) = occtoval(nil)$$
$$Mem(fp + 8) = 0$$

Proof (Sketch). Executing the updates (starting from the initial state) of IL yields the above equalities.

Remark 11. This proof remains the same for all versions of the Sather-K compiler. This is the reason that we omit the version index in the theorem. The only difference is the value of $size(p, \varepsilon)$. This is the size required for the shared attributes + 12. Hence for Version 0 this size is 12. However, $size(p, \varepsilon)$ is determined by the static semantics. It can therefore be used as a kind of parameter in the above transformation and its proof. It can be detected statically that the total size of the shared attributes fits into the memory.

An analogous approach is chosen to define the transformation rule for procedure calls. The intermediate code for a (qualified) procedure call is:

```
(7)     Push(IntLoad(IntegerVal(FrameSize)))
(8)     AddrStore(TopOfStack,Base)
(9)     AddrStore(IntAdd(TopOfStack,IntLoad(IntegerVal(8))),Qual)
(10)    StoreBase(TopOfStack)
(11)    Call(label(CalledProc))
```

where *FrameSize* is the size of the first-order memory for the activation record of the callee, ***Qual*** is the IL-expression for computing the qualifier e of a qualified method call $e.m$, and *label*(*CalledProc*) is the label of the start block of the callee. The correctness of this transformation is proven analogous to the simulation in Fig. 10(b). It assumes the correctness of computing the reference to *self*, i.e., the correctness of the transformation for ***Qual*** .

Theorem 5 (Correctness of Qualified Procedure Calls). Let $(q_0, q'_6) \in \gamma$ be a checkpoint where $q_0 \models CT$ **is** CALL. Let $q_1 \triangleq next_{\text{SATHER-K}^M}(q_0)$ and $q'_{11} = next^5_{\text{IL}}(q'_6)$. If the IL-expression ***Qual*** evaluates to the address of the qualifier, i.e., $[\![eval(\textbf{Qual})]\!]_{q'_7} = [\![QualAddr]\!]_{q_0}$ then, $(q_1, q'_7) \in \gamma$ is a a checkpoint.

Proof (Sketch). According to Fig. 4(c) it holds for SATHER-K^M:

$$
\begin{aligned}
&[\![sp]\!]_{q_1} &&= [\![sp]\!]_{q_0} - \mathit{FrameSize}\\
&[\![fp]\!]_{q_1} &&= [\![fp]\!]_{q_0} - \mathit{FrameSize}\\
&[\![Mem(fp)]\!]_{q_1} &&= [\![fp]\!]_{q_0}\\
&[\![Mem(fp+4)]\!]_{q_1} &&= [\![occtoval(next(ip, prog))]\!]_{q_0}\\
&[\![Mem(fp+8)]\!]_{q_1} &&= [\![QualAddr]\!]_{q_0}\\
&[\![mem(a)]\!]_{q_1} &&= [\![mem(a)]\!]_{q_0} \quad \text{for all } a \geq [\![sp]\!]_{q_0} \text{ and for all } a \geq [\![sp]\!]_{q_0} + 12
\end{aligned}
$$

According to Fig. 5(e) it holds for IL:

$$
\begin{aligned}
&[\![sp]\!]_{q'_{11}} &&= [\![sp]\!]_{q'_6} - \mathit{FrameSize}\\
&[\![fp]\!]_{q'_{11}} &&= [\![fp]\!]_{q'_6} - \mathit{FrameSize}\\
&[\![Mem(fp)]\!]_{q'_{11}} &&= [\![fp]\!]_{q'_6}\\
&[\![Mem(fp+4)]\!]_{q'_{11}} &&= [\![postoval(next(ci, ilprog)]\!]_{q'_6}\\
&[\![Mem(fp+8)]\!]_{q'_{11}} &&= [\![eval(\mathtt{Qual})]\!]_{q'_6}\\
&[\![mem(a)]\!]_{q'_{11}} &&= [\![mem(a)]\!]_{q'_6} \quad \text{for all } a \geq [\![sp]\!]_{q'_6} \text{ and for all } a \geq [\![sp]\!]_{q'_6} + 12
\end{aligned}
$$

Using Definition 2 and $[\![eval(\mathtt{Qual})]\!]_{q'_7} = [\![QualAddr]\!]_{q_0}$ this shows that the pair (q_1, q'_{11}) also satisfies Definition 2. For example, it holds

$$
\begin{aligned}
[\![Mem(fp+8)]\!]_{q'_{11}} &= [\![eval(\mathtt{Qual})]\!]_{q'_6} && \text{see above property in IL}\\
&= [\![QualAddr]\!]_{q_0} && \text{since } [\![eval(\mathtt{Qual})]\!]_{q'_7} = [\![QualAddr]\!]_{q_0}\\
&= [\![Mem(fp+8)]\!]_{q_1} && \text{see above property in SATHER-K}^M
\end{aligned}
$$

The other properties can be proven similarly.

Remark 12. The correctness proof for the simulation of SATHER-K$_0$ by IL$_0$ can be completed by Theorem 1(vii) and by having *FrameSize* = 12. However, the above proof is valid for all subsequent versions of SATHER-K since it assumes the correctness of the transformation for the qualifier and it is parameterized by *FrameSize* (which is computed statically).

The transformation for procedure calls usually includes parameter passing. This is done after allocating memory on the stack via push, i.e. *fp* contains the base address of the caller and *sp* contains the base address of the callee. For simplicity, we omit parameter passing. This is an own transformation where SATHER-K$_0$ only knows empty parameter lists.

The transformation of the return from a procedure is similar to the call. Therefore, we omit the discussion of the return and its correctness proof (which is a simulation analogous to Fig. 10(c)). The proof for the simulation for SKIP, cf. Fig. 10(d) is straightforward since no dynamic function (except *ip* and *ci* changes its interpretation.

We finalize the correctness proof by proving the simulation in Fig. 10(f):

Theorem 6 (Program Termination). Let q_4 be a state of ASM SATHER-K^M satisfying $[\![ip]\!]_{q_4} = nil$ and q'_{16} be a state of ASM IL satisfying $q'_{16} \models CI$ **is** EXIT. If $(q_4, q'_{16}) \in \gamma$ is a checkpoint, then $(q_4, next(q'_{16}, ilprog)) \in \gamma$ is also a checkpoint.

Proof (Sketch). According to Fig. 5(e), it $Update_{\mathrm{IL}}(q'_{q_1 6}) = \emptyset$. Hence $next(q'_{16}, ilprog) = q'_{16}$. Thus, it is $(q_4, next(q'_{16}, ilprog) \in \gamma$.

Remark 13. The proof of the program termination (of finalization) is valid for all subsequent versions, provided that the update sets of $\mathsf{Sather\text{-}K}^M$ and IL are empty for all states satisfying the assumptions of Theorem 6. If a version $i+1$ adds new transition rule to $\mathsf{Sather\text{-}K}_i^M$ or IL then it must be checked that their guards are not satisfied by $ip = nil$ or CI **is** EXIT.

Thus, the proof sketch for the correctness of the transformation for SATHER-K_0^M to IL_0 is completed. It has been shown that the proofs for initialization, qualified method calls, method returns, skip statements, and program termination remain valid for all subsequent iterations. This has been achieved by parameterizations, assumptions on the correctness of sub-transformation, and proof obligation for transition rules to be added.

5 Related Work

The field of compiler verification was already successful, but we are not aware of any work that systematically investigates the construction process and adopts the iterative method for compiler construction. Each of the following works uses operational semantics and base their notion of correctness on preservation of an observable behaviour (with some variants).

The ProCos approach [11] uses proven algebraic identities that are applied in the compilation. They apply their approach to a small language based on Dijkstra's guarded commands. Their approach is based on the assumption that language concepts are orthogonal. However, language concepts are only orthogonal to some extent. Concepts such as exception handling, break- and continue statements, and explicit return statements influence the semantics of loops and procedure calls.

In *Verifix* [9] construction approaches towards realistic compilers are considered. Some proofs are checked using PVS [4]. *Verifix* allows that the target code may abort due to lack of resources, such as exceeding available memory. A complete back-end producing binary code for the DEC-Alpha processor family has been proven [23]. Approaches for correct parsing have been developed [10]. Otherwise, the correctness is based on an abstract syntax including correct static semantic properties. A fully verified compiler for a realistic language has not been developed.

Schmid, Stärk, and Börger proved the correctness of a compiler from Java to the Java Virtual Machine [21]. Their approach defines a stack of five sub-languages. In a certain sense, their approach is iterative with coarse-grained iteration cycles. The approach does not include machine checked proofs. The semantics are based on abstract syntax, including correct static semantic properties based on the Java language definition. The target code is Java Byte code, but not the binary. In particular, compilation to machine code of a target processor is not considered.

CompCert [14] is a fully verified compiler for a realistic sub-language of C that produces PowerPC assembly code. This sub-language has been extended [2]. Furthermore, the compiler includes now optimizations [16,17]. The correctness is proven completely with Coq, i.e., the correctness proof is fully checked by machine. It uses a similar notion of correctness as *Verifix*. It requires the notion of safe programs, which excludes undefined behaviour as well as violation of resource constraints. CompCert assume in their memory model that allocation of memory always succeeds [15]. However, real machines have finite memory, such that allocation can be rejected. The target code is the symbolic assembly code of the PowerPC. The proofs start with abstract syntax and static semantic properties. The correctness of parsing towards attributed abstract syntax trees is not considered.

Siek provides an incremental approach for compiler construction in Racket [20] using small-step increments. While these increments are much smaller than in other approaches, e.g. [21], our approach enables even smaller increments. Furthermore, Siek does not address the verification of a compiler, constructed by small-step increments.

As mentioned above, none of these works consider the process of construction of verified compilers using *small step iteration cycles*. For a small-step compiler verification, a semantics definition formalism that supports fine-grained iteration as well would be helpful. The approaches by Stärk, Schmid and Börger [21], Verifix [9], and CompCert [14] all use operational semantics. The Abstract State Machine approach used in [9,21] demonstrate that this base of semantic definition supports incremental construction of operational semantics that does not require changes in preceding versions. However, these works consider big step increments.

6 Conclusions

We have presented an extensible proof of the compilation of the initial version of *Sather-K*. One important lesson is to have a look into the complete language report. This must be done also for the implementation. For example, the procedure calling mechanism must be implemented and verified, although the initial version only needs to implement the call of *main*. Another important (preliminary) lesson is that the implementation and verification of the early compiler versions are much larger than later versions. For example, adding local variables to procedures do not require a re-configuration of the semantics and implementation of the procedure calls. It needs only to be proven that no local variable is associated with an address being used for managing the runtime stack. A third lesson being learned is that correctness proofs can be engineered by proving invariants, implying refinements of the language's semantics. In particular, there are also invariants on the languages. For example, it must be proven that the stack management in the memory correctly implements the calling stack of the procedures. These invariants must be engineered such that they are not invalidated by subsequent versions.

ASMs support this extensibility in two ways: First, it is straightforward to add new state transition rules for new language concepts. Second, it is also possible to extend the state space by adding new transition rules for the new dynamic functions. Thus, in both case, correctness proof extensions focus on these new transition rules.

References

1. Basil, V.R., Turner, A.J.: Iterative enhancement: a practical technique for software development. IEEE Trans. Softw. Eng. **SE-1**(4), 390–396 (1975)
2. Boldo, S., Jourdan, J.H., Leroy, X., Melquiond, G.: Verified compilation of floating-point computations. J. Autom. Reason. **54**, 135–163 (2015)
3. Börger, E., Stärk, R.: Abstract State Machines. Springer, Heidelberg (2003). https://doi.org/10.1007/978-3-642-18216-7
4. Dold, A., Vialard, V.: Formal verification of a compiler back-end generic checker program. In: Bjøner, D., Broy, M., Zamulin, A.V. (eds.) PSI 1999. LNCS, vol. 1755, pp. 470–480. Springer, Heidelberg (2000). https://doi.org/10.1007/3-540-46562-6_42
5. Glesner, S., Goos, G., Zimmermann, W.: Verifix: Konstruktion und architektur verifizierender übersetzer (verifix: construction and architecture of verifying compilers). IT-Inf. Technol. **46**(5), 265–276 (2004)
6. Goerigk, W., Gaul, T., Zimmermann, W.: Correct programs without proof? On checker based program verification. In: Tool Support for System Specification and Verification. Springer Series Advances in Computing Science, pp. 108–123. Springer, Cham (1999)
7. Goguen, J.A., Meseguer, J.: Order-sorted algebra i: equational deduction for multiple inheritance, overloading, exceptions and partial operations. Theoret. Comput. Sci. **105**(2), 217–273 (1992). https://doi.org/10.1016/0304-3975(92)90302-V
8. Goos, G.: Sather-k - the language. Softw.-Concepts Tools **18**(3), 91–109 (1997)
9. Goos, G., Zimmermann, W.: Verification of compilers. In: Correct System Design: Recent Insights and Advances, p. 201 (1999)
10. Heberle, A., Gaul, T., Goerigk, W., Goos, G., Zimmermann, W.: Construction of verified compiler front-ends with program-checking. In: Bjøner, D., Broy, M., Zamulin, A.V. (eds.) PSI 1999. LNCS, vol. 1755, pp. 481–492. Springer, Heidelberg (2000). https://doi.org/10.1007/3-540-46562-6_43
11. Hoare, C.A.R., Jifeng, H., Sampaio, A.: Normal form approach to compiler design. Acta Informatica **30**, 701–739 (1993)
12. Larus, J.: Assemblers, Linkers, and the SPIM Simulator, chap. Appendix. Morgan Kaufmann (2005)
13. Larus, J.: Qtspim (2019)
14. Leroy, X.: Formal verification of a realistic compiler. Commun. ACM **52**(7), 107–115 (2009)
15. Leroy, X., Appel, A.W., Blazy, S., Stewart, G.: The compcert memory model, version 2. Technical report, INRIA Paris-Rocquencourt (2012). https://inria.hal.science/hal-00703441v1/document
16. Monniaux, D., Six, C.: Formally verified loop-invariant code motion and assorted optimizations. ACM Trans. Embed. Comput. Syst. **22**(1), 1–27 (2022)
17. Mullen, E., Zuniga, D., Tatlock, Z., Grossman, D.: Verified peephole optimizations for compCert. In: Proceedings of the 37th ACM SIGPLAN Conference on Programming Language Design and Implementation, pp. 448–461 (2016)

18. Poetzsch-Heffter, A.: Developing efficient interpreters based on formal language specifications. In: Fritzson, P.A. (ed.) CC 1994. LNCS, vol. 786, pp. 233–247. Springer, Heidelberg (1994). https://doi.org/10.1007/3-540-57877-3_16
19. Raschke, A., Riccobene, E., Schewe, K.D. (eds.): Logic, Computation and Rigorous Methods. Springer, Cham (2021). https://doi.org/10.1007/978-3-030-76020-5
20. Siek, J.G.: Essentils of Compilation – An Incremental Approach in Racket. MIT Press, Cambridge (2023)
21. Stärk, R.F., Schmid, J., Börger, E.: Java and the Java Virtual Machine: Definition, Verification, Validation. Springer, Cham (2012)
22. Zimmermann, W.: On the correctness of transformations in compiler back-ends. In: Margaria, T., Steffen, B. (eds.) ISoLA 2004. LNCS, vol. 4313, pp. 74–95. Springer, Heidelberg (2006). https://doi.org/10.1007/11925040_6
23. Zimmermann, W., Gaul, T.: On the construction of correct compiler back-ends: an ASM-approach. J. Univers. Comput. Sci. **3**(5), 504–567 (1997)
24. Zimmermann, W., Kühn, T., Sabinus, E., Weißbach, M.: Small step incremental verification of compilers. In: Bonfanti, S., Gargantini, A., Leuschel, M., Riccobene, E., Scandurra, P. (eds.) ABZ 2024. LNCS, vol. 14759, pp. 262–269. Springer, Cham (2024). https://doi.org/10.1007/978-3-031-63790-2_21

A Symbolic Execution Approach to Bounded Verification of Abstract State Machines

Giuseppe Del Castillo(✉)

Munich, Germany
giuseppedelcastillo@acm.org

Abstract. This paper describes a method for verifying properties of bounded prefixes of Abstract State Machine (ASM) runs. The method applies symbolic execution to convert an ASM program into a single "n-step" ASM rule that computes the state S_n reached from an initial state S_0 after n execution steps. The resulting rule has the structure of a decision tree whose internal nodes are conditional rules and whose leaves define symbolic update sets. Such "decision tree"-shaped rules can be used to verify whether a given invariant holds in all run prefixes of length at most n, or to derive a formula characterising all initial states that can lead to a violation of the invariant within n steps.

This paper is a substantially expanded and improved version of a short paper presented at ABZ 2024 and extends that work to the broader context of bounded verification.

1 Introduction

Abstract State Machines (ASM) [7] are a well-established, rigorous state-based method for system design and analysis. The ASM method has been used to define the semantics of programming and modelling languages (Prolog, Java and UML state and activity diagrams, among others), specify and document hardware and software systems (including processor architectures, embedded control systems, communication protocols) and mathematically prove properties of the modelled languages and systems. In some cases, interactive theorem provers were used to formally verify proofs of properties of ASM models (see the Prolog-WAM case study [20] or the Verifix project addressing the construction of formally verified compilers [14]). An overview of this line of research can be found in [8]. Support for automated verification has been provided in ASM tools through interfaces to model checkers like SMV/NuSMV or Spin [2,11,17] and SMT solvers [3,4].

In this paper, we present a different approach to ASM verification, based on symbolic execution backed by an SMT solver. This method is limited to the verification of at most n steps of a sequential ASM run, where n is a fixed number ("bounded verification"), but is fully automatic, can be applied to ASM models with an infinite state space and generates human-readable simplified ASM rules,

A. Raschke et al. (Eds.): Egon Börger Festschrift, LNCS 16580, pp. 152–175, 2026.
https://doi.org/10.1007/978-3-032-24494-9_8

which can be inspected when looking for the cause of a property violation.[1] We also briefly introduce a tool implementing the techniques presented in this paper.

Symbolic execution is a classic technique that dates back to the 1970s [15, 22] and has started seeing renewed interest with the advent of SMT solvers, which have increased its practical applicability (see [5] for an overview). To the author's knowledge, the main works investigating symbolic execution of ASM are [16,19,21].[2] The work by Schellhorn et al. [21] is not about direct symbolic execution of ASM rules, but defines a relational encoding of rules into a logical formula and a logical calculus based on symbolic execution that can be used for verifying properties of ASM models using interactive theorem provers such as KIV. The work by Lezuo [16] is similar to ours in that it directly applies classic techniques of symbolic execution to ASM, but has a different focus, as it produces symbolic traces to perform translation validation on compiler-generated code, rather than a human-readable transformed ASM rule that can be executed. Finally, [19] applies symbolic execution to a timed variant of ASM for the purpose of estimating worst-case execution time.

The works by Arcaini et al. [3,4] are related to ours in that they use an SMT solver for ASM verification. They define a scheme for translating an ASM into an equivalent logical representation processable by the SMT solver. In contrast, our approach invokes the SMT solver dynamically during symbolic execution to simplify guards of conditionals in order to prune infeasible execution paths.

This paper is structured as follows: after summarising basic notions of ASM (Sect. 2), we define the symbolic execution scheme (Sect. 3) and show how to use it for bounded verification of sequential ASM runs (Sect. 4). Finally, we briefly introduce a tool that implements the techniques presented in this paper and discuss some limitations of the method and potential improvements (Sect. 5).

2 Basic Notions of Abstract State Machines

In this section we summarise essential notions of single-agent, deterministic ASM as defined in [7] and introduce some notation. Only the subset of ASM needed to define the symbolic execution method is presented, in particular: only static, controlled and derived functions are allowed; there are no logical formulas, but terms of *Boolean* type are used instead; there is no *undef*; `choose` and `import` rules are not supported. Furthermore, we use a many-sorted variant of the ASM language including the possibility of defining parametric sorts, such as *Set*(T) where T is any sort. We use the term "type" as a synonym for "sort" and do not

[1] The existing model checker based techniques are also fully automatic, but usually limited to finite state spaces. A notable exception is the partial support for nuXmv provided by the ASMETA tool set [6].

[2] Previous works such as the Verifix project [14] used symbolic execution techniques in an ad hoc manner, but did not address the systematic symbolic execution of ASM rules. Recently, [12] described a novel application of symbolic execution of control state ASM, but is not concerned with how to implement the symbolic execution.

provide any typing rules, as these are standard.[3] Besides the limitations mentioned above and the use of types, the semantics given in this section completely follows [7], even though the presentation is in part slightly different.[4]

We adopt the following notational conventions: f is used for function names (of any type), P for Boolean function names (predicate names); v for variables; t for terms (of any type); $\overline{t}$ for a tuple of terms $(t_1, \ldots, t_n)$; G, φ or ψ for Boolean terms; R for (transition) rules, r for rule names, P for the special rule called the "program"; T for types; $\mathcal{T}$ for the carrier set of type T; x for values, i.e. elements of carrier sets; $\overline{x}$ for a tuple of values $(x_1, \ldots, x_n)$; $l = (f, \overline{x})$ for a location; Σ for signatures; S for states; η for variable assignments (also called *environments*); U for update sets. Finally, the notation $t : T$ means "t is of type T".

2.1 Computational Model

Abstract State Machines formalise a state-based model of computation, where computations (*runs*) are finite or infinite sequences of *states* $S_0 \rightarrow S_1 \rightarrow \ldots$ starting from an initial state S_0, where each state S_{i+1} is obtained by updating the state S_i according to an *update set* U_i, which is computed by evaluating in state S_i a closed "main" transition rule P, called the *program*. In symbols: $S_{i+1} = S_i + U_i$ where $U_i = \{\!\{P\}\!\}_{\emptyset}^{S_i}$, if U_i is consistent and non-empty.[5] A run *terminates* in a final state S_n if either

- P yields no updates in S_n, i.e. $\{\!\{P\}\!\}_{\emptyset}^{S_n}$ is an empty update set (termination with success), or
- P yields conflicting updates in S_n, i.e. $\{\!\{P\}\!\}_{\emptyset}^{S_n}$ is an inconsistent update set (termination with failure).

If there is no such final state, the run is an infinite sequence of states.[6] The meaning of states, updates, update sets and transition rules is defined below.

[3] Strong typing is necessary for an effective use of SMT solvers to support symbolic execution. A type system for ASM that does not use *undef* to model partial functions, such as the one described in [23], while departing from the standard ASM definition, may facilitate the use of SMT solvers. Alternatively, it should be investigated how to fit *undef* into the type system without compromising the possibility of using SMT solvers efficiently. This problem is not addressed here and is left for future work.

[4] The most noticeable difference is that, given the absence of non-deterministic `choose` rules, the semantics of rules is defined as a *function* mapping rules to update sets, rather than as a *relation* (the "yields" relation of [7]).

[5] The unusual notation $\{\!\{\cdot\}\!\}$ is used here to refer to the semantics of terms and rules (evaluation) because the notation $[\![\cdot]\!]$ will be used later to denote *symbolic* evaluation. The semantics of a term t in state S under variable assignment η is a value $x = \{\!\{t\}\!\}_{\eta}^{S}$. Similarly, the semantics of a rule is an update set $U = \{\!\{R\}\!\}_{\eta}^{S}$. For the program P we take $\eta = \emptyset$, as P is closed. Definitions of $\{\!\{\cdot\}\!\}_{\eta}^{S}$ for terms and rules are given below.

[6] This is a natural notion of termination for deterministic, sequential systems. Other types of systems may require other termination criteria. For reactive systems, which normally do not terminate, one may stipulate that an empty update set—even in the absence of changes in the monitored functions defining the environment—does not cause termination, but an *empty move* (a transition from S_i to an identical S_{i+1}).

States. The *states* are algebras over a given *signature* Σ (Σ-algebras for short). A signature consists of a set of *basic types* and a set of *function names*. Each function name has a fixed arity n and function type $T_1, \ldots, T_n \to T$, where the T_i and T are basic types (written $f : T_1, \ldots, T_n \to T$; if f has arity 0, $f : \to T$ is shortened to $f : T$). A Σ-algebra (state) S consists of:

(i) a nonempty set $\mathcal{T}^S$ for each basic type T in Σ (the *carrier set* of basic type T in S; any element $x \in \mathcal{T}$ is called a *value* of type T, written $x : T$), and
(ii) a function $\mathbf{f}_S : \mathcal{T}_1^S \times \ldots \times \mathcal{T}_n^S \to \mathcal{T}^S$ for each function name $f : T_1, \ldots, T_n \to T$ in Σ (the *interpretation* of function name f in S).

A function name f in Σ can be declared to be of a given *kind*, which can be[7]:

- *static*, meaning that the interpretation of f is fixed and never changes during a run,
- *controlled*, meaning that the interpretation of f can change during a run due to updates resulting from the execution of transition rules (see below),
- *monitored*, meaning that the interpretation of f can change during a run in a way that is determined by the environment, or
- *derived*, meaning that the interpretation of f is defined by a computation rule in terms of other (static, controlled, or monitored) functions and can change during a run, but only as a consequence of changes in those functions.

Any signature Σ must contain basic types *Boolean* and *Set*(T) for any basic type T, static nullary function names (constants) *true* : *Boolean*, *false* : *Boolean*, the usual Boolean operators ($\neg$, $\wedge$, $\vee$, etc.) and equality ($= :\ T \times T \to \mathit{Boolean}$ for any T in Σ). Typically, Σ also includes at least a basic type *Integer* with the usual arithmetic operations, as well as any other type necessary for modelling the application at hand. Finally, a signature Σ may also contain a (possibly infinite but countable) number of *special constants*, i.e. static nullary function names of basic types denoting certain elements of the respective carrier set according to the usual conventions (e.g. $0, 1, \ldots$: *Integer*, $\emptyset_T$: *Set*(T)). These "background" types and function names have their standard interpretation in any state S.

When no ambiguity arises, the state S is not explicitly mentioned. In particular, we write $\mathcal{T}$ instead of $\mathcal{T}^S$ for carrier sets and $\mathbf{f}$ instead of $\mathbf{f}_S$ for static functions, as these never change during a run. The union of all carrier sets $\mathcal{T}$ is called the *superuniverse* $\mathcal{U}$ and any element $x \in \mathcal{U}$ is called a *value*.

Locations. If $f : T_1, \ldots, T_n \to T$ is a function name, a pair $l = (f, \overline{x})$ with $\overline{x} = (x_1, \ldots, x_n) \in \mathcal{T}_1 \times \ldots \times \mathcal{T}_n$ is called a *location*. Then, the *type* of l is T and the *value* of l in a state S is the element $x \in \mathcal{T}$ with $x = \mathbf{f}_S(\overline{x})$.

[7] The ASM method, as defined in [7], foresees further function kinds, such as *shared*, which are not supported by the symbolic execution method of this paper. Note that monitored functions are also not directly supported by the method, but in Sect. 5.2 some indications are given as to how they can be dealt with by means of a mapping.

Updates and Transitions. A transition transforms a state S into its *sequel state* S' by changing the interpretation of some controlled function names on a finite number of points (i.e., updating the values of a finite number of locations).

More precisely, a transition transforms S into $S' = S{+}U$ by firing a consistent update set U at S. An *update set* U is a finite set of *updates* of the form $((f,\overline{x}),y)$, where $(f,\overline{x})$ is the location to be updated and y is the new value of the location after the update. An update set U is called *consistent* if it does not contain any updates $((f,\overline{x}),y)$ and $((f,\overline{x}),y')$ with $y \neq y'$ (*conflicting updates*).

If U is a *consistent* update set, the sequel state $S' = S + U$ of S is the state S' in which the carrier sets are as in S and, for each controlled function name $f : T_1, \ldots, T_n \to T$ and $\overline{x} \in \mathcal{T}_1 \times \ldots \times \mathcal{T}_n$, the interpretation of f in S' is

$$\mathbf{f}_{S'}(\overline{x}) \;=\; \mathbf{f}_{S+U}(\overline{x}) = \begin{cases} y & \text{if } ((f,\overline{x}),y) \in U \\ \mathbf{f}_S(\overline{x}) & \text{otherwise.} \end{cases}$$

If U is *inconsistent*, there is no sequel state S' (the run terminates with failure).

2.2 ASM Language

Terms. Terms over a signature Σ include, as in (many-sorted) first-order logic, variables v and function applications $f(t_1, \ldots, t_n)$ for all t_i of the appropriate type (according to the type of f in Σ). If $n = 0$, $f()$ is abbreviated as f.

Due to their importance for symbolic execution, we add explicit *conditional terms*: for any terms G : *Boolean* ("guard") and t_1, t_2 of a same type T, there is a term "**if** G **then** t_1 **else** t_2" of type T. Finally, the term language includes let terms and quantifications $Q\, v \in t : \varphi$ over finite sets, where Q is $\forall$ or $\exists$, $v : T$ ranges over t : *Set(T)* and φ is a Boolean term in which v typically occurs free.

To summarise, the syntax of terms is as follows:

$t ::= f(t_1, \ldots, t_n)$	(function application)
$\mid$ **if** G **then** t_1 **else** t_2	(conditional term)
$\mid$ v	(variable)
$\mid$ **let** $v = t_1$ **in** t_2	(let term)
$\mid$ $\forall v \in t : \varphi$	(universal quantification)
$\mid$ $\exists v \in t : \varphi$	(existential quantification)

The semantics of a term $t : T$ in state S is a $\{\!\{t\}\!\}^S_\eta \in \mathcal{T}$ computed as in Table 1.

There is no distinct syntactic category for logical formulas in the ASM subset considered here. Instead, terms of *Boolean* type are used as formulas.

Table 1. ASM semantics: evaluation of terms and rules

Terms

$$\frac{\{\!\!\{t_i\}\!\!\}^S_\eta = x_i \quad \text{for all } i \in \{1,\dots,n\}}{\{\!\!\{f(t_1,\dots,t_n)\}\!\!\}^S_\eta = \mathbf{f}_S(x_1,\dots,x_n)} \qquad \frac{\eta(v) = x}{\{\!\!\{v\}\!\!\}^S_\eta = x}$$

$$\frac{\{\!\!\{G\}\!\!\}^S_\eta = \textbf{true}}{\{\!\!\{\texttt{if } G \texttt{ then } t_1 \texttt{ else } t_2\}\!\!\}^S_\eta = \{\!\!\{t_1\}\!\!\}^S_\eta} \qquad \frac{\{\!\!\{G\}\!\!\}^S_\eta = \textbf{false}}{\{\!\!\{\texttt{if } G \texttt{ then } t_1 \texttt{ else } t_2\}\!\!\}^S_\eta = \{\!\!\{t_2\}\!\!\}^S_\eta}$$

$$\frac{\{\!\!\{t_1\}\!\!\}^S_\eta = x}{\{\!\!\{\texttt{let } v \texttt{ = } t_1 \texttt{ in } t_2\}\!\!\}^S_\eta = \{\!\!\{t_2\}\!\!\}^S_{\eta[v\mapsto x]}}$$

$$\frac{\{\!\!\{t\}\!\!\}^S_\eta = \{x_1,\dots,x_n\}}{\{\!\!\{\forall v \in t : \varphi\}\!\!\}^S_\eta = \bigwedge_{i=1}^n \{\!\!\{\varphi\}\!\!\}^S_{\eta[v\mapsto x_i]}} \qquad \frac{\{\!\!\{t\}\!\!\}^S_\eta = \{x_1,\dots,x_n\}}{\{\!\!\{\exists v \in t : \varphi\}\!\!\}^S_\eta = \bigvee_{i=1}^n \{\!\!\{\varphi\}\!\!\}^S_{\eta[v\mapsto x_i]}}$$

Rules

$$\frac{\{\!\!\{t_i\}\!\!\}^S_\eta = x_i \quad \text{for all } i \in \{1,\dots,n\}}{\{\!\!\{f(t_1,\dots,t_n) := t\}\!\!\}^S_\eta = \{((f,(x_1,\dots,x_n)), \{\!\!\{t\}\!\!\}^S_\eta)\}} \qquad \frac{}{\{\!\!\{\texttt{skip}\}\!\!\}^S_\eta = \emptyset}$$

$$\frac{\{\!\!\{G\}\!\!\}^S_\eta = \textbf{true}}{\{\!\!\{\texttt{if } G \texttt{ then } R_1 \texttt{ else } R_2\}\!\!\}^S_\eta = \{\!\!\{R_1\}\!\!\}^S_\eta} \qquad \frac{\{\!\!\{G\}\!\!\}^S_\eta = \textbf{false}}{\{\!\!\{\texttt{if } G \texttt{ then } R_1 \texttt{ else } R_2\}\!\!\}^S_\eta = \{\!\!\{R_2\}\!\!\}^S_\eta}$$

$$\frac{\{\!\!\{R_1\}\!\!\}^S_\eta = U_1 \qquad \{\!\!\{R_2\}\!\!\}^S_\eta = U_2}{\{\!\!\{R_1 \texttt{ par } R_2\}\!\!\}^S_\eta = U_1 \cup U_2}$$

$$\frac{\{\!\!\{R_1\}\!\!\}^S_\eta = U_1 \qquad U_1 \text{ is inconsistent}}{\{\!\!\{R_1 \texttt{ seq } R_2\}\!\!\}^S_\eta = U_1}$$

$$\frac{\{\!\!\{R_1\}\!\!\}^S_\eta = U_1 \qquad U_1 \text{ is consistent} \qquad \{\!\!\{R_2\}\!\!\}^{S+U_1}_\eta = U_2}{\{\!\!\{R_1 \texttt{ seq } R_2\}\!\!\}^S_\eta = U_1 \oplus U_2}$$

$$\frac{\{\!\!\{R\}\!\!\}^S_\eta = \emptyset}{\{\!\!\{\texttt{iterate } R\}\!\!\}^S_\eta = \emptyset} \qquad \frac{\{\!\!\{R\}\!\!\}^S_\eta \neq \emptyset}{\{\!\!\{\texttt{iterate } R\}\!\!\}^S_\eta = \{\!\!\{R \texttt{ seq } (\texttt{iterate } R)\}\!\!\}^S_\eta}$$

$$\frac{\{\!\!\{t\}\!\!\}^S_\eta = x}{\{\!\!\{\texttt{let } v \texttt{ = } t \texttt{ in } R\}\!\!\}^S_\eta = \{\!\!\{R\}\!\!\}^S_{\eta[v\mapsto x]}}$$

$$\frac{\{x \in \{\!\!\{t\}\!\!\}^S_\eta \mid \{\!\!\{\varphi\}\!\!\}^S_{\eta[v\mapsto x]} = \textbf{true}\} = \{x_1,\dots,x_n\}}{\{\!\!\{\texttt{forall } v \in t \texttt{ with } \varphi \texttt{ do } R\}\!\!\}^S_\eta = \bigcup_{i=1}^n \{\!\!\{R\}\!\!\}^S_{\eta[v\mapsto x_i]}}$$

$$\frac{\{\!\!\{t_i\}\!\!\}^S_\eta = x_i \quad \text{for all } i \in \{1,\dots,n\} \qquad r \text{ declared as } r(v_1,\dots,v_n) = R}{\{\!\!\{r(t_1,\dots,t_n)\}\!\!\}^S_\eta = \{\!\!\{R\}\!\!\}^S_{\eta[v_1\mapsto x_1,\dots,v_n\mapsto x_n]}}$$

Transition Rules. The syntax of rules is as follows:

$R ::=$	`skip`	(empty rule)
$\mid$	$f(t_1, \ldots, t_n) := t$	(update rule)
$\mid$	`if` G `then` R_1 `else` R_2	(conditional rule)
$\mid$	R_1 `par` R_2	(parallel composition rule)
$\mid$	R_1 `seq` R_2	(sequential composition rule)
$\mid$	`iterate` R	(iteration rule)
$\mid$	`let` v `=` t `in` R	(let rule)
$\mid$	`forall` $v \in t$ `with` φ `do` R	(forall rule)
$\mid$	$r(t_1, \ldots, t_n)$	(call rule)

The semantics of a rule R in a state S is an update set $U = \{\!\!\{R\}\!\!\}_\eta^S$ determined as shown in Table 1, wherein $U_1 \oplus U_2$ denotes the composition of update sets:

$$U_1 \oplus U_2 = U_2 \cup \{(l, x) \in U_1 \mid \text{there is no } x' \text{ with } (l, x') \in U_2\}$$

The binary rule composition operators `par` and `seq` are associative. Therefore, "R_1 `par` R_2 `par` $R_3 \ldots$" or "R_1 `seq` R_2 `seq` $R_3 \ldots$" do not need parentheses. It is nevertheless assumed that `par` and `seq` are left-associative when parsed. The following syntactic abbreviations can be used:

`if` G `then` $R \equiv$ `if` G `then` R `else skip`
`while` (G) $R \equiv$ `iterate` (`if` G `then` R)

3 Basic Symbolic Execution: Rule Simplification

In this section, we define a symbolic execution framework for ASM by extending the definition of terms and rules to *partially evaluated* terms and rules and by refining their evaluation accordingly. The refined, symbolic evaluation mappings can be applied to a modified ASM that has the same signature as the original ASM to be verified, but with some functions and/or locations left uninterpreted ("symbolic"). In this way, the ASM program is transformed into a simplified "decision tree" form, which is later used for verification.

Throughout this section we assume that all functions are static or controlled. Derived and monitored functions will be discussed in Sect. 5.2.

3.1 Uninterpreted Locations and Functions

The starting point for symbolic execution is that the value of some or all locations $(f, \overline{x})$ of one or more function names f may be *unknown* in a given (initial) state.[8] We call such locations *uninterpreted locations* (or *symbolic locations*).

[8] We deliberately use the term "unknown" instead of "undefined" to avoid any confusion with the *undef* value normally used to model partial functions, which is an

If all locations $(f, \overline{x})$ of a given function name f are uninterpreted in S we say that f is *uninterpreted* (or *symbolic*).

Note that a location $(f, \overline{x})$ that is uninterpreted in S becomes interpreted in a sequel state $S' = S + U$ if there is an update of $(f, \overline{x})$ in U.

In this paper, we assume that only controlled function names, which represent the mutable state of the system being modelled, may be uninterpreted or have uninterpreted locations. Static function names, which define the operations on the data types forming the background of an ASM (such as *Boolean* or *Integer*) always have an interpretation in the sense of Sect. 2.1.

3.2 Symbolic States and Environments

To formalise the scenario described above, where states may be only partially defined (i.e. include symbolic functions and/or locations), the notion of *symbolic state* is introduced. A *symbolic state* S over a signature Σ consists of

(i) a nonempty set $\mathcal{T}$ for each basic type T in Σ, and
(ii) a function $\mathbf{f}_{\mathsf{S}} : \mathcal{T}_1 \times \ldots \times \mathcal{T}_n \rightarrow \mathit{PE\_TERM}_{\Sigma}(T)$ for each function name $f : T_1, \ldots, T_n \rightarrow T$ in Σ (the *symbolic interpretation* of f in S),

where $\mathit{PE\_TERM}_{\Sigma}(T)$ is the set of *partially evaluated terms* of type T over Σ, defined in Sect. 3.3 below, which extends the set $\mathit{TERM}_{\Sigma}(T)$ of terms over Σ with *value terms* of the form $\langle \text{val } x \rangle$, for $x \in \mathcal{T}$, and *symbolic location terms* of the form $\langle \text{initial } (f, \overline{x}) \rangle$. Intuitively, $\langle \text{initial } (f, \overline{x}) \rangle$ stands for the unknown initial value of the symbolic location $(f, \overline{x})$.

Notationally, a symbolic state S is distinguished from a state S by using a different font.

A symbolic state $\mathsf{S} = \mathit{symstate}(S, \{f_1, \ldots, f_m\})$ can be derived from a state S by making some function names $\{f_1, \ldots, f_m\}$ from the signature Σ of S symbolic, while keeping the interpretation of the other function names of Σ unchanged:

$$\mathbf{f}_{\mathsf{S}}(x_1, \ldots, x_n) = \begin{cases} \langle \text{val } \mathbf{f}_S(x_1, \ldots, x_n) \rangle & \text{if } f \notin \{f_1, \ldots, f_m\} \\ \langle \text{initial } (f, (x_1, \ldots, x_n)) \rangle & \text{if } f \in \{f_1, \ldots, f_m\}. \end{cases}$$

Symbolic Environments. Similarly, a variable assignment (environment) η mapping variables to values is replaced, in the symbolic execution framework, by a symbolic environment η mapping variables to partially evaluated terms.

---

element of the ASM superuniverse. A location $(f, \overline{x})$ with $f(\overline{x}) = \mathit{undef}$ is not uninterpreted: its value is known and equals *undef*. The question may arise how the two can be distinguished. In practice, a tool may need to provide some syntax to specify which locations of f are symbolic locations with "unknown value". The current implementation does not yet support this, but only allows the declaration of functions that are uninterpreted as a whole: these are simply the functions that are declared in the signature, but for which no definition is provided.

3.3 Partially Evaluated Terms

Partially evaluated terms (abbreviated "pe-terms") have the same structure as terms, but the base case of their recursive definition includes, in addition to nullary function names and variables, the value terms $\langle \text{val } x \rangle$ and the symbolic location terms $\langle \text{initial } (f, \overline{x}) \rangle$ already mentioned above:

$$
\begin{array}{lll}
t ::= & \ldots & \text{(all previously defined terms, see Sect. 2.2)} \\
| & \langle \text{val } x \rangle & \text{(value term)} \\
| & \langle \text{initial } (f, \overline{x}) \rangle & \text{(symbolic location term)}
\end{array}
$$

where $x \in \mathcal{T}$ is a value from a carrier set $\mathcal{T}$ of the original ASM and $(f, \overline{x})$ is a location (as defined in Sect. 2.1) where $f : T_1, \ldots, T_n \to T$ is a controlled function name in Σ and $\overline{x} \in \mathcal{T}_1 \times \ldots \times \mathcal{T}_n$. The set of partially evaluated terms of type T is referred to as $PE\_TERM_\Sigma(T)$. It includes value terms $\langle \text{val } x \rangle$ for all carrier set elements $x \in \mathcal{T}$ and symbolic location terms $\langle \text{initial } (f, \overline{x}) \rangle$ for all controlled function names f with codomain T.

The idea behind the above definition is that, when uninterpreted functions or locations are present, a term cannot always be fully evaluated to a concrete value. Some subterms may reduce to values, others to symbolic locations, and still others to forms that are neither values nor symbolic locations—or may not reduce at all. The goal is to simplify terms as much as possible. The definition of pe-terms is designed to reflect the structure of the symbolic evaluation's result.

Notationally, as $PE\_TERM_\Sigma(T)$ extends the regular terms $TERM_\Sigma(T)$ via the canonical inclusion $t \mapsto t$, we identify a term t and its corresponding pe-term, i.e. its image in $PE\_TERM_\Sigma(T)$, and refer to both simply as t.

3.4 Path Condition

The "path condition" is a standard notion in symbolic execution, characterised in [15] as the "accumulation of conditions which determines a unique control flow path through the program". In our setting, the path condition for an ASM subterm (or subrule) is the condition that holds in the branch of nested conditional terms (or rules) containing it. As this formula is a conjunction of the respective guards (for `then` branches) or negated guards (for `else` branches), we represent the path condition as a set of formulas Π, to be interpreted as conjunction.

In symbolic execution, a path condition is used as a constraint to guide the further execution of the given path. Accordingly, in our method, the evaluation of terms and rules does not only depend on a symbolic state S and variable assignment η, but also on a path condition Π.

3.5 Symbolic Evaluation of Partially Evaluated Terms

The *symbolic evaluation* ${}^{\Pi}[\![t]\!]^{\mathsf{S}}_{\eta}$ of a (pe-)term t in a symbolic state S with a closing variable assignment η under a path condition Π is defined in Table 2 as a set of deduction rules ("evaluation rules").[9] Since η is a closing variable assignment for t, i.e. it contains bindings for all variables that occur free in t, t can be treated—in combination with η—as closed ("t is closed under η").

The goal of the symbolic evaluation mapping ${}^{\sqcap}[\![t]\!]^{\mathsf{S}}_{\eta}$ is to reduce (pe-)term t to a simplified t' in a "decision tree" form consisting only of

1. conditional terms at the top (if any);
2. (possibly) application terms $f(\overline{t})$, where f is a static function name, between the conditional terms at the top and the leaves;
3. pe-terms of the form $\langle \text{val } x \rangle$ or $\langle \text{initial } (f, \overline{x}) \rangle$ as leaves.

In the best case, t' is a single node $\langle \text{val } x \rangle$, meaning that t can be *fully evaluated*. In the worst case, t cannot be reduced to the required decision tree form, i.e. the symbolic execution fails. This is explicitly indicated by evaluation rules stating in their consequence that, for the given t, ${}^{\sqcap}[\![t]\!]^{\mathsf{S}}_{\eta}$ is not defined (*failure rules*).

One of the main means of obtaining the decision tree form specified above is the use of *conditional-lifting rules*. These are evaluation rules by which a conditional term occurring within another term is "moved up" and specialised versions of that term become branches of the conditional.

For each term form there are one or more evaluation rules, which are briefly discussed below.

Values and Symbolic Locations. Two rules specify that value terms $\langle \text{val } x \rangle$ and symbolic location terms $\langle \text{initial } (f, \overline{x}) \rangle$ cannot be further reduced.

Function Application. There are five rules for function application terms:

- The first rule is for the case where all arguments are fully evaluated. In this case, the result is either a value term $\langle \text{val } x \rangle$ or, if $(f, \overline{x})$ is uninterpreted, a symbolic location term $\langle \text{initial } (f, \overline{x}) \rangle$.
- The second rule is the conditional-lifting rule.
- The third rule is for the case of non-Boolean terms $f(\overline{t})$, where f is a static function and not all arguments can be fully evaluated. These terms are kept as they are, with their arguments evaluated as much as possible.[10]
- The fourth rule is for Boolean terms, which are treated specially due to the essential role they play in symbolic execution. Whenever the guard of a conditional can be fully evaluated, one branch can be eliminated and the number of paths to be explored can be reduced substantially. Therefore, particular efforts must be made to try to evaluate Boolean terms fully. The operator

[9] The intention here is not to define a new logical calculus, but only to present the proposed symbolic execution method in a concise and precise manner. The formal definition of a notion of correctness for this method and the corresponding correctness proof are outside the scope of this paper and left for future work.

[10] These terms can be easily mapped to SMT solver terms, because static functions are "background" functions (see "States" subsection of Sect. 2.1 and last paragraph of Sect. 3.1) and correspond to the background functions of the SMT solver's theories.

Table 2. Symbolic evaluation of pe-terms

$$\frac{}{{}^{\Pi}[\![\langle \text{val } x\rangle]\!]^{\mathsf{S}}_{\eta} = \langle \text{val } x\rangle} \qquad \frac{}{{}^{\Pi}[\![\langle \text{initial } (f,\overline{x})\rangle]\!]^{\mathsf{S}}_{\eta} = \langle \text{initial } (f,\overline{x})\rangle}$$

$$\frac{{}^{\Pi}[\![t_i]\!]^{\mathsf{S}}_{\eta} = \langle \text{val } x_i\rangle \quad \text{for all } i \in \{1,\ldots,n\}}{{}^{\Pi}[\![f(t_1,\ldots,t_n)]\!]^{\mathsf{S}}_{\eta} = \mathbf{f}_{\mathsf{S}}(x_1,\ldots,x_n)}$$

$$\frac{{}^{\Pi}[\![t_i]\!]^{\mathsf{S}}_{\eta} = \texttt{if } G \texttt{ then } t_{i1} \texttt{ else } t_{i2} \qquad \text{for some } i \in \{1,\ldots,n\}}{\begin{array}{l}{}^{\Pi}[\![f(t_1,\ldots,t_i,\ldots,t_n)]\!]^{\mathsf{S}}_{\eta} = \\ \quad {}^{\Pi}[\![\texttt{if } G \texttt{ then } f(t_1,\ldots,t_{i1},\ldots,t_n) \texttt{ else } f(t_1,\ldots,t_{i2},\ldots,t_n)]\!]^{\mathsf{S}}_{\eta}\end{array}}$$

$$\frac{\begin{array}{llll} f : T_1,\ldots,T_n \to T & T \neq \mathit{Boolean} & f \text{ is static} & \text{all } t'_i \neq \texttt{if } \ldots \\ {}^{\Pi}[\![t_i]\!]^{\mathsf{S}}_{\eta} = t'_i \ \text{ for } i = 1,\ldots,n & & \multicolumn{2}{l}{t'_i \neq \langle \text{val } x_i\rangle \ \text{ for some } i \in \{1,\ldots,n\}}\end{array}}{{}^{\Pi}[\![f(t_1,\ldots,t_n)]\!]^{\mathsf{S}}_{\eta} = f(t'_1,\ldots,t'_n)}$$

$$\frac{\begin{array}{lll} f : T_1,\ldots,T_n \to \mathit{Boolean} & f \text{ is static} & \text{all } t'_i \neq \texttt{if } \ldots \\ {}^{\Pi}[\![t_i]\!]^{\mathsf{S}}_{\eta} = t'_i \ \text{ for } i = 1,\ldots,n & \multicolumn{2}{l}{t'_i \neq \langle \text{val } x_i\rangle \ \text{ for some } i \in \{1,\ldots,n\}}\end{array}}{{}^{\Pi}[\![f(t_1,\ldots,t_n)]\!]^{\mathsf{S}}_{\eta} = \mathsf{simplify\_formula}[\,\Pi, f(t'_1,\ldots,t'_n)\,]}$$

$$\frac{{}^{\Pi}[\![t_i]\!]^{\mathsf{S}}_{\eta} = t'_i \quad f \text{ is not static} \quad t'_i \neq \langle \text{val } x_i\rangle \text{ for some } i \in \{1,\ldots,n\} \quad \text{all } t'_i \neq \texttt{if } \ldots}{{}^{\Pi}[\![f(t_1,\ldots,t_n)]\!]^{\mathsf{S}}_{\eta} \ \text{ is not defined}}$$

$$\frac{{}^{\Pi}[\![G]\!]^{\mathsf{S}}_{\eta} = \langle \text{val } \mathbf{true}\rangle \ \text{ or } \ {}^{\Pi}[\![t_1]\!]^{\mathsf{S}}_{\eta} = {}^{\Pi}[\![t_2]\!]^{\mathsf{S}}_{\eta}}{{}^{\Pi}[\![\texttt{if } G \texttt{ then } t_1 \texttt{ else } t_2]\!]^{\mathsf{S}}_{\eta} = {}^{\Pi}[\![t_1]\!]^{\mathsf{S}}_{\eta}} \qquad \frac{{}^{\Pi}[\![G]\!]^{\mathsf{S}}_{\eta} = \langle \text{val } \mathbf{false}\rangle}{{}^{\Pi}[\![\texttt{if } G \texttt{ then } t_1 \texttt{ else } t_2]\!]^{\mathsf{S}}_{\eta} = {}^{\Pi}[\![t_2]\!]^{\mathsf{S}}_{\eta}}$$

$$\frac{{}^{\Pi}[\![G]\!]^{\mathsf{S}}_{\eta} = \texttt{if } G' \texttt{ then } G_1 \texttt{ else } G_2}{\begin{array}{l}{}^{\Pi}[\![\texttt{if } G \texttt{ then } t_1 \texttt{ else } t_2]\!]^{\mathsf{S}}_{\eta} = \\ \quad {}^{\Pi}[\![\texttt{if } G' \texttt{ then } (\texttt{if } G_1 \texttt{ then } t_1 \texttt{ else } t_2) \texttt{ else } (\texttt{if } G_2 \texttt{ then } t_1 \texttt{ else } t_2)]\!]^{\mathsf{S}}_{\eta}\end{array}}$$

$$\frac{{}^{\Pi}[\![G]\!]^{\mathsf{S}}_{\eta} = G' \qquad G' \notin \{\langle \text{val } \mathbf{true}\rangle, \langle \text{val } \mathbf{false}\rangle, \texttt{if } \ldots\} \qquad {}^{\Pi}[\![t_1]\!]^{\mathsf{S}}_{\eta} \neq {}^{\Pi}[\![t_2]\!]^{\mathsf{S}}_{\eta}}{{}^{\Pi}[\![\texttt{if } G \texttt{ then } t_1 \texttt{ else } t_2]\!]^{\mathsf{S}}_{\eta} = \texttt{if } G' \texttt{ then } {}^{\Pi\cup\{G'\}}[\![t_1]\!]^{\mathsf{S}}_{\eta} \texttt{ else } {}^{\Pi\cup\{\neg G'\}}[\![t_2]\!]^{\mathsf{S}}_{\eta}}$$

$$\frac{\eta(v) = t}{{}^{\Pi}[\![v]\!]^{\mathsf{S}}_{\eta} = {}^{\Pi}[\![t]\!]^{\mathsf{S}}_{\eta}} \qquad \frac{{}^{\Pi}[\![t_1]\!]^{\mathsf{S}}_{\eta} = t'_1}{{}^{\Pi}[\![\texttt{let } v \texttt{ = } t_1 \texttt{ in } t_2]\!]^{\mathsf{S}}_{\eta} = {}^{\Pi}[\![t_2]\!]^{\mathsf{S}}_{\eta[v \mapsto t'_1]}}$$

$$\frac{{}^{\Pi}[\![t]\!]^{\mathsf{S}}_{\eta} = \langle \text{val } \{x_1,\ldots,x_n\}\rangle}{{}^{\Pi}[\![\forall v \in t : \varphi]\!]^{\mathsf{S}}_{\eta} = \bigwedge_{i=1}^{n} {}^{\Pi}[\![\varphi]\!]^{\mathsf{S}}_{\eta[v\mapsto x_i]}} \qquad \frac{{}^{\Pi}[\![t]\!]^{\mathsf{S}}_{\eta} = \langle \text{val } \{x_1,\ldots,x_n\}\rangle}{{}^{\Pi}[\![\exists v \in t : \varphi]\!]^{\mathsf{S}}_{\eta} = \bigvee_{i=1}^{n} {}^{\Pi}[\![\varphi]\!]^{\mathsf{S}}_{\eta[v\mapsto x_i]}}$$

$$\frac{{}^{\Pi}[\![t]\!]^{\mathsf{S}}_{\eta} = \texttt{if } G \texttt{ then } t_1 \texttt{ else } t_2 \qquad Q \text{ is } \forall \text{ or } \exists}{{}^{\Pi}[\![Qv \in t : \varphi]\!]^{\mathsf{S}}_{\eta} = {}^{\Pi}[\![\texttt{if } G \texttt{ then } Qv \in t_1 : \varphi \texttt{ else } Qv \in t_2 : \varphi]\!]^{\mathsf{S}}_{\eta}}$$

$$\frac{{}^{\Pi}[\![t]\!]^{\mathsf{S}}_{\eta} \notin \{\langle \text{val } \ldots\rangle, \texttt{if } \ldots\} \qquad Q \text{ is } \forall \text{ or } \exists}{{}^{\Pi}[\![Qv \in t : \varphi]\!]^{\mathsf{S}}_{\eta} \ \text{ is not defined}}$$

simplify_formula[Π, φ] reduces, if possible, a Boolean term (formula) φ to ⟨val **true**⟩ or ⟨val **false**⟩ in view of the path condition Π:

$$\text{simplify\_formula}[\Pi, \varphi] = \begin{cases} \langle \text{val } \mathbf{true} \rangle & \text{if it can be proved that } \bigwedge_{\psi \in \Pi} \psi \Rightarrow \varphi \\ \langle \text{val } \mathbf{false} \rangle & \text{if it can be proved that } \bigwedge_{\psi \in \Pi} \psi \Rightarrow \neg\varphi \\ \varphi & \text{otherwise} \end{cases}$$

How simplify_formula tries to prove the formulas depends on the implementation. In our tool, described in Sect. 5.2 below, this is done by a combination of: directly checking whether $\varphi \in \Pi$, $\neg\varphi \in \Pi$, applying Boolean algebra rewrite rules (such as $\varphi \wedge \mathit{false} = \mathit{false}$, or $\mathit{true} \wedge \varphi = \varphi$), and invoking an SMT solver if the previous measures do not succeed.[11]

- The fifth rule is the failure rule. The symbolic evaluation of $t = f(t_1, \ldots, t_n)$ fails if f is a controlled function name and not all subterms t_i can be fully evaluated. Such a term is not allowed in the target decision tree form, because it is not possible to unambiguously associate it with a specific location. Therefore, we stipulate that the transformation fails in this case.[12]

Conditional. There are four rules for conditional terms:

- The first and second rules cover the cases where the conditional term can be eliminated, either because the guard can be fully evaluated (to **true** or **false**) or because the two branches—after evaluation—are equal.
- The third rule is a conditional-lifting rule that is applied when the guard is itself a conditional.
- The fourth rule is applied when the guard G cannot be fully evaluated: in this case, the conditional remains in place, but its `then` and `else` branches are evaluated symbolically with the path condition extended by G and $\neg G$, respectively. Note that this is the only evaluation rule that directly modifies the path condition (other rules do this indirectly by constructing a conditional, which is then evaluated).

---

11 Experiments showed that, while the SMT solver is decisive for the final simplification, the rewrite rules contribute substantially to reducing the number of SMT solver calls needed (which can be quite costly in terms of run time).

12 The reason for this restriction is to prevent the *aliasing* phenomenon, i.e., having different terms potentially referring to the same location.

The aliasing problem, i.e., determining whether two terms $f(\bar{t})$ and $f(\bar{t'})$ refer to the same location, is in general undecidable. Although methods for approximate alias analysis exist, they are quite complex and are only applicable to specific scenarios (such as arrays with integer indices).

Therefore, we decided to adopt a restrictive, but simple model. This limitation can be partially addressed using an "unfolding transformation" if the ranges of the arguments are finite, see Sect. 5.2.

Variable-Binding Terms. The rules for variables and let terms are straightforward and self-explanatory. With respect to quantifications:

- The first and second rules expand universal and existential quantifiers into conjunctions and disjunctions, respectively.[13]
- The third rule is the conditional-lifting rule.
- The fourth rule stipulates that the evaluation fails if the term defining the variable's range does not reduce to a concrete finite set value, because in this case the expansion rules cannot be applied.

Properties of the Mapping. To conclude this section, we mention some useful and/or interesting properties of the symbolic evaluation mapping for pe-terms:

1. If there are no uninterpreted locations, the symbolic state $\mathsf{S} = \mathit{symstate}(S, \emptyset)$ coincides with S for any state S and the symbolic evaluation $[\![\cdot]\!]$ yields the same result as the non-symbolic evaluation $\{\!\{\cdot\}\!\}$, wrapped in $\langle \mathrm{val}\ \cdot \rangle$:
$$^{\emptyset}[\![\, t \,]\!]_{\eta}^{\mathit{symstate}(S,\emptyset)} = \langle \mathrm{val}\ \{\!\{t\}\!\}_{\eta}^{S} \rangle.$$
2. The symbolic evaluation mapping eliminates all variable-binding terms (let, quantifications) by instantiating the variables with ground terms. Since the term t to be evaluated is closed under the variable assignment η, the resulting pe-term $t' = {}^{\sqcap}[\![t]\!]_{\eta}^{\mathsf{S}}$ does not contain any variables (either free or bound), i.e., it is a ground pe-term.
3. With the exception of the symbolic location terms, the reduced pe-term $t' = {}^{\sqcap}[\![t]\!]_{\eta}^{\mathsf{S}}$ consists only of static function applications (of which conditional terms are a special case) and constants (of which value terms are a special case). Therefore, the value of such a t' depends only on the values of the locations specified by the symbolic location terms that occur in it.

3.6 Symbolic Update Sets

For symbolic execution, update sets need to be replaced by symbolic update sets.

A *symbolic update set* U is defined as a finite set of *symbolic updates* of the form $((f, \overline{x}), t)$, where $(f, \overline{x})$ is the location to be updated and t is a ground pe-term in decision tree form to be associated to that location.

Transitions are defined accordingly. In the *sequel symbolic state* $\mathsf{S}' = \mathsf{S} + \mathsf{U}$ obtained by firing a symbolic update set U in symbolic state S, the symbolic interpretation of each controlled function name $f : T_1, \ldots, T_n \to T$ is

$$\mathbf{f}_{\mathsf{S}+\mathsf{U}}(\overline{x}) = \begin{cases} t & \text{if } ((f, \overline{x}), t) \in \mathsf{U} \\ \mathbf{f}_{\mathsf{S}}(\overline{x}) & \text{otherwise} \end{cases}$$

[13] In Table 2, the $\bigwedge$ and $\bigvee$ symbols have a different meaning than in Table 1, as they denote the construction of terms with the $\wedge$ and $\vee$ function symbols rather than the application of the $\wedge$ and $\vee$ functions.

for each $\overline{x} \in \mathcal{T}_1 \times \ldots \times \mathcal{T}_n$. This is a simple adaptation of the basic definition based on regular (non-symbolic) update sets, which was given in Sect. 2.1.

The issue of consistency is more subtle. Unlike regular (non-symbolic) update sets, the consistency of a symbolic update set U cannot always be determined from U alone. If there is, for each location $l = (f, \overline{x})$ that occurs on the left-hand side of a (symbolic) update in U, only one update of l in U, then U is consistent under all circumstances. Otherwise, its consistency depends on the state S and on the path condition Π.[14] Therefore, we introduce a new notion of consistency.

A symbolic update set U is called *provably* (S, Π)*-consistent* if, for all symbolic updates $((f, \overline{x}), t)$ and $((f, \overline{x}), t')$ of the same location $(f, \overline{x})$ in U, the condition ${}^{\Pi}[\![t = t']\!]^{\mathsf{S}}_{\emptyset} = \langle \text{val } \mathbf{true} \rangle$ holds. This is a conservative approximation of actual consistency: the definition requires that it can be proved that the formula $t = t'$ is always satisfied in symbolic state S under path condition Π.[15] Note that, if U is not provably (S, Π)-consistent, we must consider it potentially inconsistent and—in practice—treat it as inconsistent, i.e., causing termination with failure.

3.7 Partially Evaluated Transition Rules

Partially evaluated rules[16] ("pe-rules") have the same structure as rules, with an additional pe-rule of the form $\langle \text{upd } \mathsf{U} \rangle$ encapsulating a symbolic update set U:

$$
\begin{array}{rcll}
R & ::= & \ldots & \text{(all previously defined rules, see Sect. 2.2)} \\
 & | & \langle \text{upd } \mathsf{U} \rangle & \text{(symbolic update set rule)}
\end{array}
$$

The idea behind this definition is that it is not always possible to fully evaluate a pe-rule to a symbolic update set. However, if some of its subrules can be fully evaluated, they can be replaced by the special pe-rule $\langle \text{upd } \mathsf{U} \rangle$, which stands for the computed symbolic update set.

3.8 Symbolic Evaluation of Partially Evaluated Rules

The *symbolic evaluation* ${}^{\Pi}[\![R]\!]^{\mathsf{S}}_{\eta}$ of (pe-)rule R in a symbolic state S with a closing variable assignment[17] η under path condition Π is defined in Tables 3, 4 and 5.

The goal is to reduce the (pe-)rule R to a simplified R' in a "decision tree" form consisting only of

1. conditional rules as inner nodes (if any);
2. pe-rules of the form $\langle \text{upd } \mathsf{U} \rangle$, where U is a symbolic update set, as leaves.

---

[14] The environment η does not matter, as the pe-terms that appear on the right-hand sides of symbolic updates do not contain any variables.

[15] Nevertheless, this is a substantially better approximation than the one used in [10], where the symbolic update set was considered inconsistent whenever the conflicting t and t' were (structurally) different terms. With the new, improved definition, we can make use of the SMT solver to make the approximation as precise as possible.

[16] The term "rules" can stand for the ASM *transition rules* or for the *evaluation rules* of the symbolic execution scheme. We often use the term "rules" without further qualification, if it is clear from the context which kind of rules is meant.

[17] For explanations about the closing variable assignment, see Sect. 3.5, first paragraph.

Table 3. Symbolic evaluation of pe-rules (part 1: basic rules)

$$\frac{}{{}^{\Pi}[\![\mathtt{skip}]\!]^{\mathsf{S}}_{\eta} = \langle \text{upd } \emptyset \rangle} \qquad \frac{}{{}^{\Pi}[\![\langle \text{upd } \mathsf{U} \rangle]\!]^{\mathsf{S}}_{\eta} = \langle \text{upd } \mathsf{U} \rangle}$$

$$\frac{{}^{\Pi}[\![t_i]\!]^{\mathsf{S}}_{\eta} = \langle \text{val } x_i \rangle \quad \text{for all } i \in \{1, \ldots, n\}}{{}^{\Pi}[\![f(t_1, \ldots, t_n) := t]\!]^{\mathsf{S}}_{\eta} = \langle \text{upd } \{((f, (x_1, \ldots, x_n)), {}^{\Pi}[\![t]\!]^{\mathsf{S}}_{\eta})\} \rangle}$$

$$\frac{{}^{\Pi}[\![t_i]\!]^{\mathsf{S}}_{\eta} = \mathtt{if}\ G\ \mathtt{then}\ t_{i1}\ \mathtt{else}\ t_{i2} \qquad \text{for some } i \in \{1, \ldots, n\}}{\begin{array}{l}{}^{\Pi}[\![f(t_1, \ldots, t_i, \ldots, t_n) := t]\!]^{\mathsf{S}}_{\eta} = \\ \quad {}^{\Pi}[\![\mathtt{if}\ G\ \mathtt{then}\ f(t_1, \ldots, t_{i1}, \ldots, t_n) := t\ \mathtt{else}\ f(t_1, \ldots, t_{i2}, \ldots, t_n) := t]\!]^{\mathsf{S}}_{\eta}\end{array}}$$

$$\frac{{}^{\Pi}[\![t]\!]^{\mathsf{S}}_{\eta} = \mathtt{if}\ G\ \mathtt{then}\ t_1\ \mathtt{else}\ t_2}{{}^{\Pi}[\![f(t_1, \ldots, t_n) := t]\!]^{\mathsf{S}}_{\eta} = {}^{\Pi}[\![\mathtt{if}\ G\ \mathtt{then}\ f(t_1, \ldots, t_n) := t_1\ \mathtt{else}\ f(t_1, \ldots, t_n) := t_2]\!]^{\mathsf{S}}_{\eta}}$$

$$\frac{{}^{\Pi}[\![t_i]\!]^{\mathsf{S}}_{\eta} = t'_i \quad {}^{\Pi}[\![t]\!]^{\mathsf{S}}_{\eta} = t' \quad t'_i \neq \langle \text{val } x_i \rangle \text{ for some } i \in \{1, \ldots, n\} \quad \text{all } t'_i,\ t' \neq \mathtt{if} \ldots}{{}^{\Pi}[\![f(t_1, \ldots, t_n) := t]\!]^{\mathsf{S}}_{\eta} \ \text{ is not defined}}$$

$$\frac{{}^{\Pi}[\![G]\!]^{\mathsf{S}}_{\eta} = \langle \text{val } \mathbf{true} \rangle \ \text{ or } \ {}^{\Pi}[\![R_1]\!]^{\mathsf{S}}_{\eta} = {}^{\Pi}[\![R_2]\!]^{\mathsf{S}}_{\eta}}{{}^{\Pi}[\![\mathtt{if}\ G\ \mathtt{then}\ R_1\ \mathtt{else}\ R_2]\!]^{\mathsf{S}}_{\eta} = {}^{\Pi}[\![R_1]\!]^{\mathsf{S}}_{\eta}} \qquad \frac{{}^{\Pi}[\![G]\!]^{\mathsf{S}}_{\eta} = \langle \text{val } \mathbf{false} \rangle}{{}^{\Pi}[\![\mathtt{if}\ G\ \mathtt{then}\ R_1\ \mathtt{else}\ R_2]\!]^{\mathsf{S}}_{\eta} = {}^{\Pi}[\![R_2]\!]^{\mathsf{S}}_{\eta}}$$

$$\frac{{}^{\Pi}[\![G]\!]^{\mathsf{S}}_{\eta} = \mathtt{if}\ G'\ \mathtt{then}\ G_1\ \mathtt{else}\ G_2}{\begin{array}{l}{}^{\Pi}[\![\mathtt{if}\ G\ \mathtt{then}\ R_1\ \mathtt{else}\ R_2]\!]^{\mathsf{S}}_{\eta} = \\ \quad {}^{\Pi}[\![\mathtt{if}\ G'\ \mathtt{then}\ (\mathtt{if}\ G_1\ \mathtt{then}\ R_1\ \mathtt{else}\ R_2)\ \mathtt{else}\ (\mathtt{if}\ G_2\ \mathtt{then}\ R_1\ \mathtt{else}\ R_2)]\!]^{\mathsf{S}}_{\eta}\end{array}}$$

$$\frac{{}^{\Pi}[\![G]\!]^{\mathsf{S}}_{\eta} = G' \qquad G' \notin \{\langle \text{val } \mathbf{true} \rangle, \langle \text{val } \mathbf{false} \rangle, \mathtt{if} \ldots\} \qquad {}^{\Pi}[\![R_1]\!]^{\mathsf{S}}_{\eta} \neq {}^{\Pi}[\![R_2]\!]^{\mathsf{S}}_{\eta}}{{}^{\Pi}[\![\mathtt{if}\ G\ \mathtt{then}\ R_1\ \mathtt{else}\ R_2]\!]^{\mathsf{S}}_{\eta} = \mathtt{if}\ G'\ \mathtt{then}\ {}^{\Pi \cup \{G'\}}[\![R_1]\!]^{\mathsf{S}}_{\eta}\ \mathtt{else}\ {}^{\Pi \cup \{\neg G'\}}[\![R_2]\!]^{\mathsf{S}}_{\eta}}$$

$$\frac{{}^{\Pi}[\![R_1]\!]^{\mathsf{S}}_{\eta} = \langle \text{upd } \mathsf{U}_1 \rangle \qquad {}^{\Pi}[\![R_2]\!]^{\mathsf{S}}_{\eta} = \langle \text{upd } \mathsf{U}_2 \rangle}{{}^{\Pi}[\![R_1\ \mathtt{par}\ R_2]\!]^{\mathsf{S}}_{\eta} = \langle \text{upd } (\mathsf{U}_1 \cup \mathsf{U}_2) \rangle}$$

$$\frac{{}^{\Pi}[\![R_1]\!]^{\mathsf{S}}_{\eta} = \langle \text{upd } \mathsf{U}_1 \rangle \qquad {}^{\Pi}[\![R_2]\!]^{\mathsf{S}}_{\eta} = \mathtt{if}\ G_2\ \mathtt{then}\ R_{21}\ \mathtt{else}\ R_{22}}{{}^{\Pi}[\![R_1\ \mathtt{par}\ R_2]\!]^{\mathsf{S}}_{\eta} = {}^{\Pi}[\![\mathtt{if}\ G_2\ \mathtt{then}\ (\langle \text{upd } \mathsf{U}_1 \rangle\ \mathtt{par}\ R_{21})\ \mathtt{else}\ (\langle \text{upd } \mathsf{U}_1 \rangle\ \mathtt{par}\ R_{22})]\!]^{\mathsf{S}}_{\eta}}$$

$$\frac{{}^{\Pi}[\![R_1]\!]^{\mathsf{S}}_{\eta} = \mathtt{if}\ G_1\ \mathtt{then}\ R_{11}\ \mathtt{else}\ R_{12} \qquad (R_2 \text{ is any rule})}{{}^{\Pi}[\![R_1\ \mathtt{par}\ R_2]\!]^{\mathsf{S}}_{\eta} = {}^{\Pi}[\![\mathtt{if}\ G_1\ \mathtt{then}\ (R_{11}\ \mathtt{par}\ R_2)\ \mathtt{else}\ (R_{12}\ \mathtt{par}\ R_2)]\!]^{\mathsf{S}}_{\eta}}$$

Thus, for any R, ${}^{\Pi}[\![R]\!]^{\mathsf{S}}_{\eta}$ is either a symbolic update set $\langle \text{upd } \mathsf{U} \rangle$ or a conditional. The symbolic evaluation result ${}^{\Pi}[\![R]\!]^{\mathsf{S}}_{\eta}$ is a decision tree representing all possible execution paths, as specified by the nested conditional in the inner nodes, and the symbolic update sets in the leaves correspond to the cumulative state changes resulting from the execution of the respective path from root to leaf.

Table 4. Symbolic evaluation of pe-rules (part 2: `seq` and `iterate`)

$$\frac{{}^{\Pi}[\![R_1]\!]^{\mathsf{S}}_{\eta} = \langle \text{upd } \mathsf{U}_1 \rangle \qquad \mathsf{U}_1 \text{ is not provably } (\mathsf{S}, \Pi)\text{-consistent}}{{}^{\Pi}[\![R_1 \texttt{ seq } R_2]\!]^{\mathsf{S}}_{\eta} = \langle \text{upd } \mathsf{U}_1 \rangle}$$

$$\frac{{}^{\Pi}[\![R_1]\!]^{\mathsf{S}}_{\eta} = \langle \text{upd } \mathsf{U}_1 \rangle \qquad \mathsf{U}_1 \text{ is provably } (\mathsf{S}, \Pi)\text{-consistent} \qquad {}^{\Pi}[\![R_2]\!]^{\mathsf{S}+\mathsf{U}_1}_{\eta} = \langle \text{upd } \mathsf{U}_2 \rangle}{{}^{\Pi}[\![R_1 \texttt{ seq } R_2]\!]^{\mathsf{S}}_{\eta} = \langle \text{upd } (\mathsf{U}_1 \oplus \mathsf{U}_2) \rangle}$$

$$\frac{{}^{\Pi}[\![R_1]\!]^{\mathsf{S}}_{\eta} = \langle \text{upd } \mathsf{U}_1 \rangle \qquad {}^{\Pi}[\![R_2]\!]^{\mathsf{S}+\mathsf{U}_1}_{\eta} = \texttt{if } G_2 \texttt{ then } R_{21} \texttt{ else } R_{22}}{{}^{\Pi}[\![R_1 \texttt{ seq } R_2]\!]^{\mathsf{S}}_{\eta} = {}^{\Pi}[\![\texttt{if } G_2 \texttt{ then } (\langle \text{upd } \mathsf{U}_1 \rangle \texttt{ seq } R_{21}) \texttt{ else } (\langle \text{upd } \mathsf{U}_1 \rangle \texttt{ seq } R_{22})]\!]^{\mathsf{S}}_{\eta}}$$

$$\frac{{}^{\Pi}[\![R_1]\!]^{\mathsf{S}}_{\eta} = \texttt{if } G_1 \texttt{ then } R_{11} \texttt{ else } R_{12} \qquad (R_2 \text{ is any rule})}{{}^{\Pi}[\![R_1 \texttt{ seq } R_2]\!]^{\mathsf{S}}_{\eta} = {}^{\Pi}[\![\texttt{if } G_1 \texttt{ then } (R_{11} \texttt{ seq } R_2) \texttt{ else } (R_{12} \texttt{ seq } R_2)]\!]^{\mathsf{S}}_{\eta}}$$

$$\frac{{}^{\Pi}[\![R]\!]^{\mathsf{S}}_{\eta} = \langle \text{upd } \emptyset \rangle}{{}^{\Pi}[\![\texttt{iterate } R]\!]^{\mathsf{S}}_{\eta} = \langle \text{upd } \emptyset \rangle} \qquad \frac{{}^{\Pi}[\![R]\!]^{\mathsf{S}}_{\eta} \neq \langle \text{upd } \emptyset \rangle}{{}^{\Pi}[\![\texttt{iterate } R]\!]^{\mathsf{S}}_{\eta} = {}^{\Pi}[\![R \texttt{ seq } (\texttt{iterate } R)]\!]^{\mathsf{S}}_{\eta}}$$

The evaluation rules follow the same patterns already seen for the pe-terms, including the use of *conditional-lifting rules* and *failure rules* (see introductory paragraphs of Sect. 3.5).[18] Therefore, the rules will be discussed only briefly.

Two rules specify that `skip` and $\langle \text{upd } \mathsf{U} \rangle$ cannot be further reduced.

The evaluation rules for *update rules* are similar to a subset of the rules for application terms. In particular, the first rule (fully evaluated case) and the last rule (failure rule) are similar in both scenarios. However, there are two conditional-lifting rules for update rules (instead of one), addressing the left-hand side (second rule) and the right-hand side (third rule), respectively.

The rules for *conditionals* are completely analogous to those for terms.

For `par` and `seq`, the rules for the fully evaluated case are derived in a rather direct manner from the respective (non-symbolic) semantic rules of Table 1. The remaining cases are the conditional-lifting rules for R_1 `par` R_2 and R_1 `seq` R_2, where R_1 and/or R_2 are conditional rules. The rules for these cases were obtained by using the following semantic equivalences (where *op* is `par` or `seq`):

$$(\texttt{if } G_1 \texttt{ then } R_{11} \texttt{ else } R_{12})\, op\, R_2 \simeq \texttt{if } G_1 \texttt{ then } (R_{11}\, op\, R_2) \texttt{ else } (R_{12}\, op\, R_2)$$
$$R_1\, op\, (\texttt{if } G_2 \texttt{ then } R_{21} \texttt{ else } R_{22}) \simeq \texttt{if } G_2 \texttt{ then } (R_1\, op\, R_{21}) \texttt{ else } (R_1\, op\, R_{22})$$

Those rules rewrite, according to the above equivalences, the `par` or `seq` to a conditional rule, which is in turn evaluated symbolically.

The evaluation of the `iterate` rule is defined recursively in terms of `seq`.

Finally, for the variable-binding rules, the symbolic evaluation of the `let` rule and of the call rule are straightforward. The `forall` rule is treated by expanding

[18] Because a conditional-lifting rule is needed whenever a conditional occurs within any transition rule, the resulting proliferation of rules can make the symbolic execution scheme appear cumbersome. A potential simplification is discussed in Sect. 5.2.

Table 5. Symbolic evaluation of pe-rules (part 3: variable-binding rules)

$$\frac{{}^{\Pi}[\![t]\!]^{\mathsf{S}}_{\eta} = t'}{{}^{\Pi}[\![\texttt{let}\ v\ \texttt{=}\ t\ \texttt{in}\ R]\!]^{\mathsf{S}}_{\eta} = {}^{\Pi}[\![R]\!]^{\mathsf{S}}_{\eta[v\mapsto t']}}$$

$$\frac{{}^{\Pi}[\![t]\!]^{\mathsf{S}}_{\eta} = \langle \text{val } \{x_1, \ldots, x_n\}\rangle}{{}^{\Pi}[\![\texttt{forall}\ v \in t\ \texttt{with}\ \varphi\ \texttt{do}\ R]\!]^{\mathsf{S}}_{\eta} = {}^{\Pi}[\![\,\texttt{par}^{n}_{i=1}(\texttt{if}\ {}^{\Pi}[\![\varphi]\!]^{\mathsf{S}}_{\eta[v\mapsto x_i]}\ \texttt{then}\ {}^{\Pi}[\![R]\!]^{\mathsf{S}}_{\eta[v\mapsto x_i]})]\!]^{\mathsf{S}}_{\eta}}$$

$$\text{where } \texttt{par}^{n}_{i=1} R_i = \begin{cases} \texttt{skip} & \text{if } n = 0 \\ R_1 & \text{if } n = 1 \\ (\texttt{par}^{n-1}_{i=1} R_i)\ \texttt{par}\ R_n & \text{if } n \geq 2 \end{cases}$$

Additionally, there are a conditional-lifting rule and a failure rule for the `forall` rule analogous to those defined for quantification terms in Table 2.

$$\frac{{}^{\Pi}[\![t_i]\!]^{\mathsf{S}}_{\eta} = t'_i \text{ for all } i \in \{1, \ldots, n\} \qquad r \text{ declared as } r(v_1, \ldots, v_n) = R}{{}^{\Pi}[\![r(t_1, \ldots, t_n)]\!]^{\mathsf{S}}_{\eta} = {}^{\Pi}[\![R]\!]^{\mathsf{S}}_{\eta[v_1\mapsto t'_1, \ldots, v_n\mapsto t'_n]}}$$

it to a **par**-block in a similar manner as already seen for quantifiers (which were expanded to conjunctions or disjunctions).

Properties of the Mapping. Similar to the case of pe-terms, the symbolic evaluation mapping for pe-rules has the following properties:

1. If there are no uninterpreted locations, $\mathsf{S} = \mathit{symstate}(S, \emptyset)$ coincides with S for any state S and ${}^{\emptyset}[\![\, R\,]\!]^{\mathsf{S}}_{\eta} = \langle \text{upd } \{\!\!\{R\}\!\!\}^{S}_{\eta}\rangle$.
2. A pe-rule R' that is the result of symbolic evaluation (i.e., $R' = {}^{\Pi}[\![R]\!]^{\mathsf{S}}_{\eta}$ for some R) does not contain variables (in other words, R' is a ground pe-rule).
3. The update set of such a R' depends only on the values of the locations specified by the symbolic location terms that occur in it.

3.9 Conversion to ASM Transition Rule

After applying the transformation defined in Tables 3, 4 and 5, the generated pe-rule can be converted back to an equivalent ordinary ASM transition rule (as defined in Sect. 2.2), not containing any special $\langle$upd $\ldots\rangle$ pe-rules, nor any $\langle$val $\ldots\rangle$ and $\langle$initial$\ldots\rangle$ pe-terms. To achieve this, all $\langle$val $x\rangle$ pe-terms are replaced with ordinary terms that evaluate to x (e.g., *true*, *false* if x is Boolean, or special integer constants if x is an integer). All $\langle$initial $(f, (x_1, \ldots, x_n))\rangle$ pe-terms are replaced by corresponding function application terms $f(t_1, \ldots, t_n)$, where the t_i are terms that evaluate to x_i (see above). All $\langle$upd $\mathsf{U}\rangle$ pe-rules are similarly replaced by corresponding **par** blocks of update rules, each of which corresponds to a respective symbolic update in U.

4 Bounded Verification for Sequential ASM Runs

A first version of the symbolic execution scheme defined in detail in Sect. 3 was introduced in [10]—for a more limited subset of ASM—as a method to transform ASM rules with `seq` and `iterate` into basic ASM rules.

In [9], its scope of application was extended to enable (bounded) verification of (invariant) properties of models of smart contracts defined as sequential ASMs.

This symbolic execution approach to bounded verification, which was only sketched in [9], is described more precisely in this section.

4.1 Symbolic Execution of Sequential ASMs

For an ASM with program P, the state S_n of a sequential ASM run $S_0, S_1, \ldots$ starting in the initial state S_0 (see definition in Sect. 2.1, first paragraph) equals the state reached by executing P^n in S_0, where P^n is the program P iterated n times by means of the `seq` rule.[19] More precisely:

$$S_n = S_0 + \{\!\{P^n\}\!\}_{\emptyset}^{S_0}$$

where $P^0 := \texttt{skip}$, $P^1 := P$ and $P^{i+1} := P^i \texttt{ seq } P$ $(i \geq 1)$.

Therefore, to symbolically execute i steps of a sequential ASM run $(i \geq 0)$, we can use the symbolic evaluation rules defined in Sect. 3 to compute ${}^{\emptyset}[\![P^i]\!]_{\emptyset}^{\mathsf{S}_0}$ starting from an initial symbolic state S_0.

For a run prefix consisting of the first $n+1$ states $S_0, S_1, \ldots, S_n$ of the run, i.e., the first n steps, we may compute ${}^{\emptyset}[\![P^i]\!]_{\emptyset}^{\mathsf{S}_0}$ for $i = 0, \ldots, n$. However, for reasons of efficiency, instead of symbolically evaluating P^i from scratch for each i, we start from the previous symbolic evaluation result according to the following scheme: $\mathsf{P}_{\mathsf{S}_0}^0 := \langle \mathrm{upd}\ \emptyset \rangle$, $\mathsf{P}_{\mathsf{S}_0}^1 := {}^{\emptyset}[\![P]\!]_{\emptyset}^{\mathsf{S}_0}$ and $\mathsf{P}_{\mathsf{S}_0}^{i+1} := {}^{\emptyset}[\![\mathsf{P}_{\mathsf{S}_0}^i \texttt{ seq } P]\!]_{\emptyset}^{\mathsf{S}_0}$ $(1 \leq i \leq n)$.

4.2 Invariant Checking

The above construction can be used as a basis for verifying properties of (finite prefixes of) ASM sequential runs. We only consider the verification of properties that hold in a single state or, by extension, in a number of states of a run independently of what happens in other states of the same run. In practice, meaningful properties of this kind which one may want to verify are often *invariants*, i.e., properties that should hold in all states of all runs.[20]

In the rest of this section, we define a method for *bounded verification* of invariants based on the symbolic execution techniques of this paper. Bounded

[19] This is well-known from ASM theory, see for example [7], Sect. 4.1.1 (in particular Lemma 4.1.2), as well as Lemma 2.4.3 on page 67 in combination with the semantics of `seq`, consistent case (see Table 1).

[20] We have not yet considered the problem of how to apply the methods presented here to the verification of temporal logic formulas expressing relations between states of a same run. This is a subject for future work.

verification means in this context that the verification is limited to those states that can be reached from an initial state within a fixed number n of steps.

The starting point are the pe-rules $\mathsf{P}^0_{\mathsf{S}_0}, \mathsf{P}^1_{\mathsf{S}_0}, \ldots, \mathsf{P}^n_{\mathsf{S}_0}$, as defined at the end of Sect. 4.1. Since all these pe-rules have been obtained as a result of the application of the symbolic evaluation mapping $[\![\cdot]\!]$, they are in "decision tree" form, i.e. they have conditional rules as inner nodes and symbolic update sets $\langle \text{upd } \mathsf{U} \rangle$ as leaves.

The recursive function ${}^{\Pi}ivcs^{\mathsf{S}_0}_{\varphi}(R)$—where *ivcs* stands for "invariant violation conditions"—traverses a pe-rule R in decision tree form and returns a set of all conditions which, when met in initial state S_0, may lead to a violation of invariant φ after the execution of R (while Π is an auxiliary parameter that keeps track of the current path condition as the conditionals are traversed):

$$ {}^{\Pi}ivcs^{\mathsf{S}_0}_{\varphi}(\texttt{if } G \texttt{ then } R_1 \texttt{ else } R_2) := ({}^{\Pi\cup\{G\}}ivcs^{\mathsf{S}_0}_{\varphi}(R_1)) \cup ({}^{\Pi\cup\{\neg G\}}ivcs^{\mathsf{S}_0}_{\varphi}(R_2)) $$

$$ {}^{\Pi}ivcs^{\mathsf{S}_0}_{\varphi}(\langle \text{upd } \mathsf{U} \rangle) := \begin{cases} \emptyset & \text{if } {}^{\Pi}[\![\varphi]\!]^{\mathsf{S}_0 \oplus \mathsf{U}}_{\emptyset} = \langle \text{val } \mathbf{true} \rangle \\ \{\bigwedge_{\psi\in\Pi} \psi\} & \text{if } {}^{\Pi}[\![\varphi]\!]^{\mathsf{S}_0 \oplus \mathsf{U}}_{\emptyset} = \langle \text{val } \mathbf{false} \rangle \\ \{(\bigwedge_{\psi\in\Pi} \psi) \wedge \neg({}^{\Pi}[\![\varphi]\!]^{\mathsf{S}_0 \oplus \mathsf{U}}_{\emptyset})\} & \text{otherwise} \end{cases} $$

(note that the computed set of formulas is to be understood as a disjunction).[21]

The set of conditions leading to the violation of φ after exactly i steps (for the given program P and initial symbolic state S_0) can then be computed by

$$ ivcs_i := {}^{\emptyset}ivcs^{\mathsf{S}_0}_{\varphi}(\mathsf{P}^i_{\mathsf{S}_0}), $$

as $\mathsf{P}^i_{\mathsf{S}_0}$ corresponds to iterating i times the execution of P from initial state S_0.

If $ivcs_i = \emptyset$ for all $i \in \{0, \ldots, n\}$, then the invariant φ holds in all run prefixes of length at most n or, in other words, φ is never violated within n steps (including in the initial state, i.e., for $i = 0$). Otherwise, the formula

$$ ivc_{0\ldots n} := \bigvee_{i=0}^{n} (\bigvee_{\psi \in ivcs_i} \psi) $$

characterises the concrete initial states that may lead to an invariant violation within n steps (a subset of all concrete states represented by symbolic state S_0).

Note that this method is a conservative approximation, in the sense that:

- it can produce *false negatives*, i.e., results indicating that an invariant may be violated, even though it is actually never violated in any state reachable from the initial state within n steps: what "invariant may be violated" means in this context is that it cannot be proved that it is not violated;
- it produces *no false positives*: if the result is that the invariant is not violated within n steps, then this is actually true in all states that can be reached from any initial state represented by the symbolic state S_0 within n steps.

21 In order to relate the present definition to the terminology previously used in [9], it can be pointed out that, in the case distinction used to define ${}^{\Pi}ivcs^{\mathsf{S}_0}_{\varphi}(\langle \text{upd } \mathsf{U} \rangle)$, the first case corresponds to the *met* case, the second case to *definitely violated*, the third case to *possibly violated* (all three relative to the given path condition Π).

As usual when working with methods of this kind, when inspecting negative results to understand their cause, one would check whether they are in fact false negatives. Often the false negatives can be eliminated by modifying the ASM model and/or the properties to be verified, e.g., by strengthening preconditions.

5 Implementation, Limitations, Potential Improvements

5.1 Implementation

The techniques presented in this paper have been implemented in a prototype tool, which is publicly available at

https://github.com/constructum/asm-symbolic-execution

The tool is implemented in F# (an ML dialect for the .NET framework) and uses the Z3 SMT solver [18] via the .NET interface provided by Z3. The concrete syntax used for specifying ASM models, as well as the properties to be verified, is a subset of AsmetaL [13].[22] With respect to the techniques of this paper, the tool provides:

- a `-steps` i option that constructs the pe-rules $\mathsf{P}^i_{\mathsf{S}_0}$ as defined in Sect. 4.1;
- a `-invcheck` n option to check whether the specified invariants hold within the first n steps: this is an implementation of Sect. 4.2.[23]

5.2 Limitations and Potential Improvements

Nested Non-static Functions and Unfolding Transformation. The main limitation of the symbolic execution method presented in Sect. 3 is its inability to process terms of the form $f(t_1, \ldots, t_n)$ or update rules $f(t_1, \ldots, t_n) := t$ when f is a controlled function name and not all subterms t_i can be fully evaluated (see also Sect. 3.5, "Function Application", explanation about 5th rule, and footnote 12).

One way to overcome this limitation would be to discriminate between two terms $f(\overline{t})$ and $f(\overline{t'})$ potentially causing aliasing by generating conditionals that check equality of $\overline{t}$ and $\overline{t'}$ and have a branch for the "equal" case where $f(\overline{t})$ and $f(\overline{t'})$ are mapped to the same location and a branch for the "not equal" case where they denote different locations (and let the symbolic evaluation rules prune the branches, if possible). However, this would require a more complex symbolic execution framework where locations are not simply pairs $(f, \overline{x})$, where $\overline{x}$ is a tuple of values. Furthermore, such a method, while more general, would necessarily be approximate, would introduce uncertainty concerning the identity of locations and would generate more paths that are never taken (increasing the number of false negatives in the invariant verification).

[22] The language used in the first implementation, made for the ABZ 2024 paper [10], is a tiny subset of UASM [1]. In view of the current AsmetaL support, the use of this legacy language is deprecated and its support may be discontinued at some point.

[23] The n parameter can also be omitted: then, the number of steps is not limited and the execution (and search for invariant violations) continues until the user stops it.

A more limited, but simple and precise solution is to *unfold* the symbolic location terms that occur within $f(t_1,\ldots,t_n)$ if their range is a finite set $\{x_1,\ldots,x_n\}$, i.e. to replace any $\langle\text{initial } (g,\overline{y})\rangle$ occurring within $f(t_1,\ldots,t_n)$ by

$$\begin{array}{l}\texttt{if } \langle\text{initial } (g,\overline{y})\rangle = x_1 \texttt{ then } x_1 \texttt{ else}\\ \ldots\\ \texttt{if } \langle\text{initial } (g,\overline{y})\rangle = x_{n-1} \texttt{ then } x_{n-1} \texttt{ else } x_n.\end{array}$$

Such case distinctions can then be moved up by the conditional-lifting rules and their branches subsequently simplified by symbolic execution. Modifications of the evaluation rules are needed to avoid unnecessary unfolding and to prevent non-termination due to repeated unfolding of the symbolic location terms in the guards. Another (perhaps more efficient) approach to location unfolding was presented in [11]. Determining the best way to add unfolding to the symbolic execution framework requires further investigation.

Derived and Monitored Functions. The symbolic execution rules in Sect. 3 only cover static and controlled functions. *Derived functions* can be seen as macros and expanded, similar to call rules (see Table 5).[24] An approach to deal with *monitored functions* by representing them as uninterpreted functions with an additional *stage* parameter (corresponding to the index i of the state S_i of the run) is described in [9]. It is not yet clear whether this approach can serve as a basis for a more systematic treatment of monitored functions.

Simplification of the Symbolic Execution Scheme. As mentioned in footnote 18, the symbolic execution scheme may appear cumbersome due to the proliferation of conditional-lifting rules. This could be avoided by changing the representation of the symbolic execution result from a decision tree of nested conditional rules to a flat set of guarded symbolic update sets (G, U). In this way, the need for a case distinction between conditional rules and "symbolic update set rules" $\langle\text{upd } \mathsf{U}\rangle$ would disappear: $\langle\text{upd } \mathsf{U}\rangle$ could simply be represented as $(\langle\text{val } \mathbf{true}\rangle, \mathsf{U})$. Using this representation, the symbolic execution for `par` (as an example) could be defined by a single rule:

$$^{\sqcap}[\![R_1 \texttt{ par } R_2]\!]^{\mathsf{S}}_{\eta} = \left\{ (^{\sqcap}[\![G_1 \wedge G_2]\!]^{\mathsf{S}}_{\eta},\ \mathsf{U}_1 \cup \mathsf{U}_2) \;\middle|\; \begin{array}{l} (G_1, \mathsf{U}_1) \in {}^{\sqcap}[\![R_1]\!]^{\mathsf{S}}_{\eta},\\ (G_2, \mathsf{U}_2) \in {}^{\sqcap}[\![R_2]\!]^{\mathsf{S}}_{\eta},\\ ^{\sqcap}[\![G_1 \wedge G_2]\!]^{\mathsf{S}}_{\eta} \neq \langle\text{val } \mathbf{false}\rangle \end{array} \right\}$$

Note that such a change is not only a matter of notation, but leads to a different symbolic execution algorithm. A drawback of this alternative is that the resulting "flat set of paths" would depart from the structure of the original ASM program and be less human-readable than the "decision tree" rule. On the other hand, the symbolic execution scheme could be defined using fewer rules. It may be worth investigating whether one of the two approaches is more runtime-efficient.

---

[24] They are, in fact, implemented in the tool, despite not being described in this paper.

Directions for Future Work. The feasibility of the approach to bounded verification presented here has been validated with various experiments, most importantly those published in [9]. Future work should focus on improving its efficiency by applying and adapting state-of-the-art techniques from the fields of symbolic execution, model checking and automated verification.

Furthermore, it could be applied to extend the SMV-based model checking support for ASM [2,11] to support the `seq` construct by symbolically executing a single step to eliminate `seq` before applying the ASM to SMV mapping.

Finally, an important direction for future research is to extend the scope of the method presented here from mere counterexample-finding to actual proof by combining it with inductive reasoning techniques.

5.3 Conclusions

In this paper, we have presented a symbolic execution framework for sequential ASMs that enables automatic bounded verification backed by SMT solvers. By transforming rules into a simplified decision-tree form, our approach provides both a formal basis for invariant checking and human-readable feedback for model analysis. Future work should focus on covering a broader subset of ASM, improving runtime performance and supporting exhaustive verification in addition to counterexample-finding.

Acknowledgments. Thanks to the anonymous reviewer for the interesting remarks, including the suggestion concerning the simplification of the symbolic execution rules.

Disclosure of Interests. The author has no competing interests to declare that are relevant to the content of this article.

References

1. Arcaini, P., et al.: Unified syntax for abstract state machines. In: Butler, M., Schewe, K.D., Mashkoor, A., Biro, M. (eds.) Abstract State Machines, Alloy, B, TLA, VDM, and Z, pp. 231–236. Springer International Publishing, Cham (2016). https://doi.org/10.1007/978-3-319-33600-8_14
2. Arcaini, P., Gargantini, A., Riccobene, E.: AsmetaSMV: a way to link high-level ASM models to low-level NuSMV specifications. In: Frappier, M., Glässer, U., Khurshid, S., Laleau, R., Reeves, S. (eds.) Abstract State Machines, Alloy, B and Z, pp. 61–74. Springer Berlin Heidelberg, Berlin, Heidelberg (2010). https://doi.org/10.1007/978-3-642-11811-1_6
3. Arcaini, P., Gargantini, A., Riccobene, E.: Using SMT for dealing with nondeterminism in ASM-based runtime verification. Electron. Commun. EASST **70** (2014). https://doi.org/10.14279/tuj.eceasst.70.970, https://eceasst.org/index.php/eceasst/article/view/2168
4. Arcaini, P., Gargantini, A., Riccobene, E.: SMT for state-based formal methods: the ASM case study. In: Shankar, N., Dutertre, B. (eds.) Automated Formal Methods. Kalpa Publications in Computing, vol. 5, pp. 1–18. EasyChair (2018). http://doi.org/10.29007/djdz

5. Baldoni, R., Coppa, E., Cono D'Elia, D., Demetrescu, C., Finocchi, I.: A survey of symbolic execution techniques. ACM Comput. Surv. **51**(3) (2018). https://doi.org/10.1145/3182657
6. Bombarda, A., Bonfanti, S., Gargantini, A., Riccobene, E., Scandurra, P.: ASMETA tool set for rigorous system design. In: Platzer, A., Rozier, K.Y., Pradella, M., Rossi, M. (eds.) Formal Methods, pp. 492–517. Springer Nature Switzerland, Cham (2025). https://doi.org/10.1007/978-3-031-71177-0_28
7. Börger, E., Stärk, R.: Abstract State Machines. Springer, Berlin, Heidelberg (2003). https://doi.org/10.1007/978-3-642-18216-7
8. Börger, E.: The abstract state machines method for modular design and analysis of programming languages. J. Log. Comput. **27**(2), 417–439 (2017). https://doi.org/10.1093/logcom/exu077
9. Braghin, C., Del Castillo, G., Riccobene, E., Valentini, S.: Using symbolic model execution to detect vulnerabilities of smart contracts. In: Leuschel, M., Ishikawa, F. (eds.) 11th International Conference on Rigorous State-Based Methods, ABZ 2025. Lecture Notes in Computer Science, vol. 15728, pp. 31–51. Springer (2025). https://doi.org/10.1007/978-3-031-94533-5_3
10. Del Castillo, G.: Using symbolic execution to transform turbo abstract state machines into basic abstract state machines. In: 10th Int. Conf. on Rigorous State-Based Methods, ABZ 2024. Lecture Notes in Computer Science, vol. 14759, pp. 215–222. Springer (2024). https://doi.org/10.1007/978-3-031-63790-2_15
11. Del Castillo, G., Winter, K.: Model checking support for the ASM high-level language. In: Graf, S., Schwartzbach, M. (eds.) Tools and Algorithms for Construction and Analysis of Systems (TACAS 2000), pp. 331–346. Springer, Berlin, Heidelberg (2000). https://doi.org/10.1007/3-540-46419-0_23
12. Dorfmeister, D., Ferrarotti, F., Fischer, B., Haslinger, E., Ramler, R., Zimmermann, M.: An approach for safe and secure software protection supported by symbolic execution. In: Kotsis, G., Tjoa, A.M., Khalil, I., Moser, B., Mashkoor, A., Sametinger, J., Khan, M. (eds.) Database and Expert Systems Applications - DEXA 2023 Workshops, pp. 67–78. Springer Nature Switzerland, Cham (2023). https://doi.org/10.1007/978-3-031-39689-2_7
13. Gargantini, A., Riccobene, E., Scandurra, P.: A metamodel-based language and a simulation engine for abstract state machines. JUCS - J. Univers. Comput. Sci. **14**(12), 1949–1983 (2008). https://doi.org/10.3217/jucs-014-12-1949
14. Glesner, S., Goos, G., Zimmermann, W.: Verifix: Konstruktion und Architektur verifizierender Übersetzer (Verifix: Construction and architecture of verifying compilers). it - Information Technology **46**(5), 265–276 (2004). https://doi.org/10.1524/itit.46.5.265.44799
15. King, J.C.: Symbolic execution and program testing. Commun. ACM **19**(7), 385–394 (1976). https://doi.org/10.1145/360248.360252
16. Lezuo, R.: Scalable Translation Validation. Ph.D. thesis, Vienna University of Technology (2014). https://www.complang.tuwien.ac.at/tbfg
17. Ma, G.Z.S.: Model checking support for CoreASM: model checking distributed abstract state machines using Spin. Master's thesis, Simon Fraser University (2007). https://summit.sfu.ca/item/8056
18. de Moura, L., Bjørner, N.: Z3: An efficient SMT solver. In: Ramakrishnan, C.R., Rehof, J. (eds.) Tools and Algorithms for the Construction and Analysis of Systems (TACAS 2008), pp. 337–340. Springer Berlin Heidelberg, Berlin, Heidelberg (2008). https://doi.org/10.1007/978-3-540-78800-3_24

19. Paun, V.A., Monsuez, B., Baufreton, P.: Integration of symbolic execution into a formal abstract state machines based language. IFAC-PapersOnLine **50**(1), 11251–11256 (2017). https://doi.org/10.1016/j.ifacol.2017.08.1610, 20th IFAC World Congress
20. Schellhorn, G., Ahrendt, W.: The WAM case study: verifying compiler correctness for Prolog with KIV. In: Bibel, W., Schmitt, P.H. (eds.) Automated deduction - a basis for applications: volume 3 - applications. Kluwer Academic Publishers (1998)
21. Schellhorn, G., Ernst, G., Pfähler, J., Bodenmüller, S., Reif, W.: Symbolic execution for a clash-free subset of ASMs. Sci. Comput. Program. **158**, 21–40 (2018). https://doi.org/10.1016/j.scico.2017.08.014
22. Topor, R.W.: Interactive program verification using virtual programs. Ph.D. thesis, University of Edinburgh (1975). https://era.ed.ac.uk/handle/1842/6610
23. Zimmermann, W., Weißbach, M.: A framework for modeling the semantics of synchronous and asynchronous procedures with abstract state machines. Logic, Computation and Rigorous Methods: Essays Dedicated to Egon Börger on the Occasion of His 75th Birthday, pp. 326–352 (2021)

Bridging Specification and Implementation in CoreASM Plugins

Vincenzo Gervasi(✉) and Federico Miraglia

University of Pisa, Pisa, Italy
vincenzo.gervasi@unipi.it, f.miraglia3@studenti.unipi.it

Abstract. The definition of the CoreASM language in the early 2000s was a significant inflection point in the development of executable support for ASMs. Among other features, the language provided for user-defined extensions of both syntax and semantics, in order to provide specifiers with the linguistic tools needed to more faithfully express the behaviour of the specified system.

However, experience has shown that while the specification of CoreASM's plugins was approachable to third parties, the corresponding implementation (in the Java language) was too complex and at places fragile, so that only a small number of plug-ins have emerged from the community at large.

In this work, we introduce CoreL, a new language and corresponding transpiler to simplify the implementation of CoreASM's plugins by making their specification directly executable and embeddable in the language.

Keywords: Abstract State Machines · Extensibility · CoreASM · Domain Specific Language · CoreL

1 Introduction

It was Egon Börger, to whom the present volume is dedicated, that in March 2002—at a Dagstuhl Seminar on *Theory and Application of Abstract State Machines* [4]—suggested that with recent advancements in language and IDE technology, a more modern take on the design of executable support for ASMs might be overdue.

At the time there was no shortage of existing tools for executing ASM specifications, from the pioneering work based on Prolog [3,20] and on functional languages [13, Part III], to the mature implementations in the ASM Workbench [11,12], XASM [2] and AsmGofer [22]. The latter, in particular, had been used in the verification of the several models in the Java Book [23] (language semantics, compiler, bytecode verifier and virtual machine), so its usability in specifying a large-scale industrial project was well established. Unbeknownst to the authors at the time, a concurrent effort was ongoing at Microsoft to develop

A. Raschke et al. (Eds.): Egon Börger Festschrift, LNCS 16580, pp. 176–198, 2026.
https://doi.org/10.1007/978-3-032-24494-9_9

AsmL [19]: an ASM compiler based on .NET technology, which was later used in a number of internal verification projects.

Apparently, there was no need for yet another executable ASM version. Börger however argued convincingly[1] that there was still too much of a distance between what the available systems offered, and the way ASMs were being used in research. In particular, two issues were considered particularly delicate: maintaining strict adherence to formal ASM semantics (including its less usual aspects), and offering the expressive flexibility that had allowed researchers to come up with whatever construct was more suitable to a particular problem, using it freely in ASM specifications *in papers*.

All existing systems were extensible in their own way: AsmL could interoperate with all other .NET languages; AsmGofer was implemented by defining typical ASM behaviour in Gofer and was thus "immersed" in the latter, so that any Gofer expression could be used in a specification; XASM could invoke and be invoked by arbitrary C or C++ code, and so on. However, none of these systems could change the very syntax of its own source language, and most could not introduce new domains, universes, backgrounds except by encoding the desired properties with the data structures that were available to the base language.

As for semantics, all of the above systems took some liberty with the original definition, in order to accommodate their other stated goals. Among other issues, interaction with traditionally sequential languages (be it Gofer, C or any .NET language) inevitably exposed immediate side-effects incompatible with the regular handling of updates; multi-agent computation was absent or offloaded to the native language threading model; ASM's Turbo semantics was not implemented; no or limited support was available for partial updates or for handling conflicting updates.

The design choices by which CoreASM faithfully implemented the theoretical ASM semantics have been described elsewhere [14], and need not be repeated here. In the following, we will instead devote some attention to the issue of extensibility: how it was implemented, what experience has shown to have worked as expected or not, and will introduce a new tool, CoreL, to aid in the implementation of CoreASM plugins, with the goal of making language extensions according to domain-specific needs more practical.

The rest of the paper is structured as follows. In Sect. 2 we recall how CoreASM plugins have been specified and implemented, and discuss several problems that have emerged from experience with practical applications in the two decades since. In Sect. 3 we introduce CoreL, our proposed meta-language to address the problems we identified, and present its syntax and semantics, together with some note about its current implementation. Then, we discuss our results in

[1] According to the first author's recollection, the conversation happened one evening during the week-long seminar, around a pool table while a heated match was ongoing, and opposing Börger ideas would have distracted the first author from scoring that last decisive point—so on the whole, conceding the argument was found to be far more convenient.

Sect. 4, and conclude the work in Sect. 5, with a plan for future developments and research.

2 Implementing Extensions in CoreASM

After some initial discussion at the Dagstuhl seminar mentioned above with several participants, and especially with Börger, Glässer and Farahbod, it was decided to initiate a project on the design of a new ASM language (what would later become CoreASM), and that the first author would go visit Glässer and Farahbod at Simon Fraser University in Vancouver at the first opportunity—which presented itself in January-March 2003.

During the visit, the design of an interpreter for the language proceeded alongside theoretical discussions on what the "proper" way of implementing ASM semantics would be, especially on some subtler points of Turbo semantics regarding defeasible computations, the handling of inconsistent updates in multi-agent systems, and whether rules should be first-order values and thus represented in the ASM state, or rather a separate set of instructions defining a specific machine[2]. At the same time, architectural decisions on the implementations were being taken, e.g., using Java as implementation language for the CoreASM interpreter and its extensions, and the then-modern Eclipse IDE as hosting environment.

To further our extensibility goals, two kind of extensions were needed. The first, more technical in nature, were *architectural extensions* that would allow extension writers to customize the *behaviour* of the interpreter. This was obtained by designing the interpreter as a state machine[3] whose transitions included extension points into which external modules could be plugged. Examples of such extension points were: specification loading; parsing; selecting which agents to activate in a step; examining and altering update sets before application; etc. [16]. The second kind, of more direct interest for the present work, pertained to *language extensions*: the possibility to add new language constructs, specifying their syntax and semantics.

The various types of plugins used in CoreASM are listed in Table 1, with the first four interfaces being aimed at supporting language extensions and the second group of four constituing architectural extensions; the corresponding Java interface definitions are shown in Fig. 1.

During those few months of fruitful work, two critical methodological decisions were taken: (1) the specification of the language would be provided as an ASM, and (2) the most basic and traditional ASM constructs would be specified

[2] As a historical note, both the Lipari Guide [18] and the ASMBook [8] seemed to imply the second approach, akin to that of Turing in defining Turing Machines, whereas the first approach—which was ultimately chosen, although with some syntactical concession to the traditional notation which also guaranteed that the extension would be conservative—leaned more towards a von Neumann architecture.

[3] In fact, a Control State ASM [8].

Table 1. Plugin interfaces in CoreASM. Adapted from [14].

Plugin Interface	Extends	Description
Parser Plugin	Parser	provides additional grammar rules to the parser
Interpreter Plugin	Interpreter	provides new semantics to the Interpreter
Operator Provider	Parser, Interpreter	provides grammar rules for new operators along with their precedence levels and semantics
Vocabulary Extender	Abstract Storage	extends the state with additional functions, universes, and backgrounds
Aggregator	Abstract Storage	aggregates partial updates into basic updates
Scheduler Plugin	Scheduler	provides new scheduling policies for multi-agent ASMs
Extension Point Plugin	all components	extends the control state model of the engine
Package Plugin	plug-in system	packages multiple plugins in a named set

and implemented *exactly* as any other future or ad-hoc extension. Both decisions stemmed from the principle of *dogfooding* or "eating your own dog food": the practice of using a method or product in developing the same method or product, to ensure that the developers (or, in our case, the specifiers) have an opportunity to experience and test first-hand the workings of a system.

2.1 Specification Blessings...

To bootstrap the process, a set of ad-hoc notational conventions was defined, so that the specification of the language could be conveniently expressed by an ASM sitting at the *appropriate* level of abstraction for the problem, and unneeded encoding could be avoided.

The CoreASM interpreter follows a classical syntax-directed approach. An abstract syntax tree (AST) is built by the *parser* according to a set of *parsing rules* embodied by corresponding *productions*. Language extensions provide their own productions (by implementing the ParserPlugin interface), hence enriching the syntax accepted by the parser and thus the structure of the AST.

The AST consists of opaque *nodes* from a domain NODE, linked via the usual functions *first* : NODE → NODE (first child), *next* : NODE → NODE (next sibling), *parent* : NODE → NODE (parent, with the value being *undef* at the root). On each node, a number of "administrative" functions are defined, linking the node to the particular plugin and grammar rule that originated the node, as well as the specific token associated to the node. These are *class* : NODE → CLASS (grammar class, i.e., the non-terminal that generated the node), *grammarRule* : NODE → GRAMMARRULE (the actual syntactic production among the alternatives for the class), *token* : NODE → TOKEN (the actual lexical token for the node, e.g., a keyword, identifier, literal value), *pattern* : NODE → PATTERN (a symbolic name for the pattern used in specifying the plugin, see below), and *plugin* : NODE → PLUGIN associating the node to the plugin that provided the lexical and syntactic rules that originated the node.

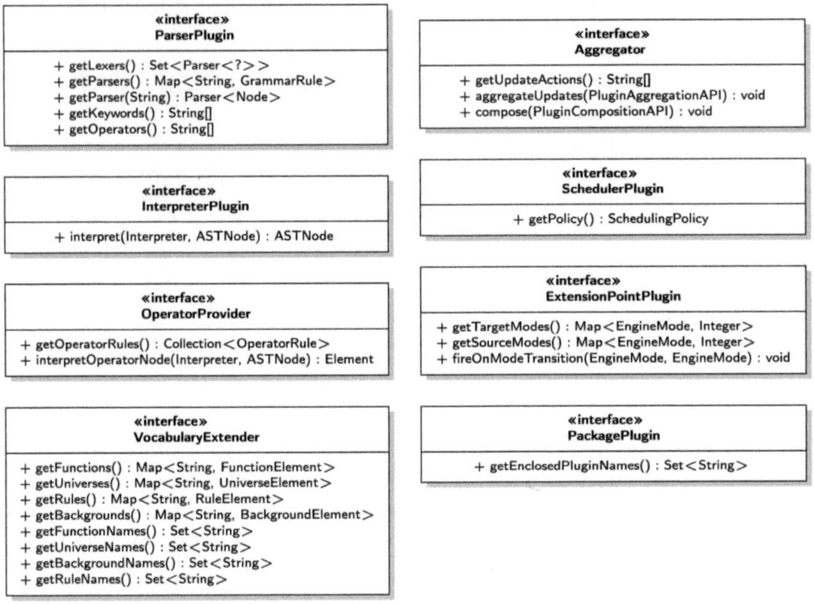

Fig. 1. Java interfaces for the various plug-in types. In the left column, interfaces that affect the CoreASM language syntax; in the right column, other architectural plugins.

The most important function is the *evaluation* of a node n, which we denote by $[\![n]\!]$. Formally,

$$[\![\cdot]\!] : \textsc{Node} \rightarrow \textsc{Loc} \times \mathit{Multiset}(\textsc{Update}) \times \textsc{Element}$$

where $\textsc{Loc}$ is the domain of locations (defined as usual by a function name with arguments, i.e., $\langle f, (a_1, \ldots, a_n)\rangle$; $\textsc{Update}$ is the domain of updates (defined as usual by a location and a value, i.e., $\langle l, v\rangle$, or possibly by an update instruction with arguments, generalizing the concept of partial updates [7, Ch. 4]); and $\textsc{Element}$ is the domain of all possible values (elements of universes that can appear in the ASM state). To simplify the notation, each element of the triple can be read by an accessor function, resp. $loc : \textsc{Node} \rightarrow \textsc{Loc}$, $updates : \textsc{Node} \rightarrow \mathit{Multiset}(\textsc{Update})$ and $value : \textsc{Node} \rightarrow \textsc{Element}$. Moreover, a boolean predicate $evaluated : \textsc{Node} \rightarrow \textsc{Boolean}$ defined as $evaluated(n) = ([\![n]\!] \neq undef)$ expresses the notion that a node has been evaluated. A well-known location $pos : \textsc{Node}$ holds at all times the node that is being evaluated.

The evaluation of a step of an ASM consists in cleaning the AST by setting $[\![n]\!] = undef$ on each node, setting pos to the root node $root$, and executing a specific set of rules derived from the plugins that are in use until $evaluated(root)$ becomes true[4].

[4] For multi-agent ASMs, this is performed for each agent's program.

The *specification* of a language plugin is provided by a set of pattern-action rules, which are themselves a form of extension of ASM syntax (in fact, they constitute an appropriate domain-specific level of abstraction for this particular problem). The general approach mirrors the one established by Stärk, Schmid and Börger in [23], but with several notational simplifications and a more streamlined tree navigation, which is succinctly expressed by the following macro:

Interpreter

ExecuteTree $\equiv$
  if $\neg evaluated(pos)$ **then**
    if $plugin(pos) \neq undef$ **then**
      let $R = pluginRule(plugin(pos))$ **in**
        R
    else
      KernelInterpreter
  else
    if $parent(pos) \neq undef$ **then**
      $pos := parent(pos)$

In essence, as long as the current node *pos* has not been fully evaluated, the interpreter repeatedly executes the ASM rules associated to the plugin that contributed the grammar rule that created *pos* at parsing time (or, for the very few cases that are native to the interpreter, such as the evaluation of `true` and `false`, the embedded set of rules given by KernelInterpreter). As soon as *pos* is evaluated, control is returned to the parent node, if any; if the root has been evaluated, the computation terminates (and the set of updates for the step is found at $updates(root)$).

The notation for pattern-action rules is as follows:

$$(\!| pattern |\!) \rightarrow action$$

where *action* is arbitrary ASM code (where assignments to *pos* or to $[\![pos]\!]$ implicitly control tree traversal), and *pattern* is a *grammar schema* representing both a BNF-style grammar rule, and the various stages of its evaluation. In particular, a *pattern* consists of a sequence of terminal (lexical) symbols and of various *binding placeholders*; for the latter we use the conventional names x (identifier), v (value), u (updates), l (location) for evaluated nodes, and $\boxed{e}$ (expression), $\boxed{r}$ (rule), $\boxed{l}$ (left-hand side) for unevaluated nodes[5]. We also use $\square$ for an unevaluated node of unspecified kind, and $\boxed{?}$ to indicate a node regardless of its state of evaluation. These placeholders corresponds to non-terminals in the grammar, and thus to nodes that are direct children of the top node. We use prefixed superscript greek letters to denote children nodes when needed.

These placeholders and location indicators are expanded in different ways in the *pattern* and in the *action*, as shown in Table 2; the whole pattern-action syntax is itself expanded as a traditional **if** - **then** rule.

[5] Notice that there is no unevaluated version of identifier nodes; an identifier as such always stands for itself.

Table 2. Expansion of placeholders in pattern-action rules.

placeholder	in *pattern*	in *action*
$^{\alpha}\cdot$, $^{\beta}\cdot$, etc.	$\mathit{first}(pos)$, $\mathit{next}(\mathit{first}(pos))$, etc.	
$^{\alpha}x$	$class(\alpha) = \mathsf{Id}$	$token(\alpha)$
$^{\alpha}v$	$value(\alpha) \neq undef$	$value(\alpha)$
$^{\alpha}u$	$updates(\alpha) \neq undef$	$updates(\alpha)$
$^{\alpha}l$	$loc(\alpha) \neq undef$	$loc(\alpha)$
$^{\alpha}\boxed{?}$	$class(\alpha) \neq \mathsf{Id}$	
$^{\alpha}\boxed{e}$, $^{\alpha}\boxed{r}$, $^{\alpha}\boxed{l}$, $^{\alpha}\Box$	$class(\alpha) \neq \mathsf{Id} \wedge \neg evaluated(\alpha)$	

With this convenient notation, the specification of a plugin can be expressed very directly. As a running example, let us consider the specification of the conditional **if - then - else** rule:

Conditional Rule

$(\!|$ **if** $^{\alpha}\boxed{e}$ **then** $^{\beta}\boxed{r}$ **else** $^{\gamma}\boxed{r}$ $|\!) \rightarrow pos := \alpha$
$(\!|$ **if** $^{\alpha}v$ **then** $^{\beta}\boxed{r}$ **else** $^{\gamma}\boxed{r}$ $|\!) \rightarrow$ **if** $v = \mathsf{true}$ **then** $pos := \beta$ **else** $pos := \gamma$
$(\!|$ **if** $^{\alpha}v$ **then** $^{\beta}u$ **else** $^{\gamma}\boxed{r}$ $|\!) \rightarrow [\![pos]\!] := (undef, u, undef)$
$(\!|$ **if** $^{\alpha}v$ **then** $^{\beta}\boxed{r}$ **else** $^{\gamma}u$ $|\!) \rightarrow [\![pos]\!] := (undef, u, undef)$

---

which, by the above substitutions, stands for the following:

1. a lexical addition of keywords `if`, `then` and `else` as terminals to the lexer;
2. a syntactic addition to the parser of a BNF production such as

$$Rule ::= \textbf{if } Expression \textbf{ then } Rule \textbf{ else } Rule$$

   This production will be marked with the identifier of the conditional rule plugin, and the same identifier will be assigned at parsing time to $plugin(c)$ for every node c in the AST produced by the production.
3. a semantics addition to the interpreter by providing the ASM rules (derived from the pattern-actions above) in Fig. 2; these rules will be retrieved as $pluginRule(plugin(c))$ where c is the root node of the **if - then - else** subtree.

As a further example, below is the specification for assignment (with error checking omitted for brevity); notice how the specification captures the non-determinism in the order of evaluation of lhs and rhs.

Assignment

$(\!|\, ^{\alpha}\boxed{?} := {}^{\beta}\boxed{?} \,|\!) \rightarrow$ **choose** $\tau \in \{\alpha, \beta\}$ **with** $\neg evaluated(\tau)$
    $pos := \tau$
  ifnone
    $[\![pos]\!] := (undef, \{\!|\langle loc(\alpha), value(\beta)\rangle|\!\}, undef)$

2.2 ... and Implementation Woes

The specification technique presented above served us well for specifying the entire CoreASM language according to [8], as detailed in [14], as well as a number of additional constructs: numbers of various sorts (naturals, integers, rationals, floating-point, complex) and corresponding mathematical functions; common container data types (collections, bags, lists, maps, multisets, queues, sets, stacks, strings, trees); concurrency (signals, counters, activations, mailboxes); I/O (console, simple debugging, file access, graphical plots); time (dates, times, time intervals); language utilities (control state ASMs, optional signatures and type checking, abstract macros, modules); etc.

Conditional Rule

if $class(first(pos)) \neq \mathsf{Id} \wedge \neg evaluated(first(pos))$
  and $class(next(first(pos))) \neq \mathsf{Id} \wedge \neg evaluated(next(first(pos)))$
  and $class(next(next(first(pos)))) \neq \mathsf{Id} \wedge \neg evaluated(next(next(first(pos))))$
 then $pos := first(pos)$
if $value(first(pos)) \neq undef$
  and $class(next(first(pos))) \neq \mathsf{Id} \wedge \neg evaluated(next(first(pos)))$
  and $class(next(next(first(pos)))) \neq \mathsf{Id} \wedge \neg evaluated(next(next(first(pos))))$
 then
  if $value(first(pos)) = \mathsf{true}$
   then $pos := next(first(pos))$
   else $pos := next(next(first(pos)))$
if $value(first(pos)) \neq undef$
  and $updates(next(first(pos))) \neq undef$
  and $class(next(next(first(pos)))) \neq \mathsf{Id} \wedge \neg evaluated(next(next(first(pos))))$
 then
  $value(pos) := undef$
  $updates(pos) := updates(next(first(pos)))$
  $loc(pos) := undef$
if $value(first(pos)) \neq undef$
  and $class(next(first(pos))) \neq \mathsf{Id} \wedge \neg evaluated(next(first(pos)))$
  and $updates(next(next(first(pos)))) \neq undef$
 then
  $value(pos) := undef$
  $updates(pos) := updates(next(next(first(pos))))$
  $loc(pos) := undef$

Fig. 2. Expanded ASM rules for the Conditional Rule.

The original implementation (in Java) of CoreASM was obtained largely by the manual but systematic translation of the pattern-action rules into Java code, thanks to the work of George Ma, Roozbeh Farahbod and others, and surprisingly few errors were introduced in this phase—proving that the specification technique was sound.

A few remarkable plugins have been developed externally, including support for aspect-oriented programming [9,10], interaction with Java code [17], scripting [1], ambients [6], grammars and parsing, graphs and related algorithms, and more. However, most of these efforts have seen the participation of at least one of the core developers of CoreASM, and after well over a decade, truly third-party, community-developed plugins have not materialized. This can only be interpreted as a failure to satisfy at least one of CoreASM's design goals.

With the benefit of hindsight, it appears that while conceptually the specification of a plugin may be clear, the effort required to write and integrate the corresponding Java code is not trivial. Despite some effort in documenting the process and providing examples [15], the task is still a significant challenge, mostly due to the large amount of administrative boilerplate code that has to be written in addition to the more "semantic" parts. Furthermore, the Java code needed for those semantic parts is closer to the expanded rules in Fig. 2 than to the original pattern-action rules, making the translation a delicate, albeit systematic, job.

For the Conditional rule presented above, two Java classes need to be developed:

1. a `ConditionalRuleNode` that extends `ASTNode` and represents the abstract syntax node generated by the **if** - **then** - **else** statement, and
2. a `ConditionalRulePlugin` that extends `Plugin` and implements the needed interfaces from Fig. 1, in our case `ParserPlugin` (to provide the syntax) and `InterpreterPlugin` (to provide the semantics).

The actual source code needed is shown in Appendix A, and its details need not concern us here. However, even a cursory look reveals that the actual semantics (in the `interpret()` method of `ConditionalRulePlugin`) is closely related to the pattern-action rules in their expanded form, but the machinery for properly setting up lexical and grammar rules, and interacting with the lexer and the parser at AST construction time, constitutes a rather large chunk of somewhat obscure code. Clearly a better approach is needed.

3 A Meta-language for Plugin Definition

Ideally, one would want a succinct notation such as the one in the pattern-action rules to suffice for the task. While this does not seem directly attainable at the moment, due to the needs of the Java implementation and legacy support, we can still design a *metalanguage* for implementing CoreASM plugins that is as close as possible to the specification given by the rules.

3.1 CoreL Design Principles

In designing the metalanguage, we adhered to a few design principles (and some aesthetic choices) that stemmed in part from practical considerations, in part from the desire to strike a more usable balance between universality and expressiveness. We list some of these design principles, together with their rationale, below.

ASCII Source. We wanted the source code for CoreL to be in plain text, to simplify editing and reuse proven parsing technology. This entails sacrificing fancy symbols, formats (e.g., bold for keywords), greek letters for locations in the AST, etc.

Java Actions. Since the *reason d'être* of plugins is to add to CoreASM semantics that cannot be readily expressed in CoreASM already, we kept Java as the "base" language for the action part. However, we enrich the language with ad-hoc macro substitutions to simplify the code.

Naming Conventions. The notational convention of using fixed, 1-letter identifiers (e.g., e, r, u etc.) to express both the kind of node and its state of evaluation worked well in the specification of plugins, and we wanted to maintain it.

Implicit Locations with Optional Naming. In patterns, locations were almost always assigned sequentially (α, β, etc.) according to the order of children in the AST. We opted then for implicit numerical indices, with the option for the specifier to provide a symbolic name instead[6], and with the default symbolic name being the 1-letter identifier mentioned above.

Separation of Concerns. Albeit in Java code both administrative information and semantics alike are implemented as methods of a single class inheriting from `Plugin` (e.g., `getVersionInfo()` vs. `interpret()`), in CoreL we want them to be clearly separated in the syntax.

Compilation into Java. For compatibility reasons, we want CoreL to generate plugins written in Java, which can then be compiled, and dynamically loaded into a CoreASM specification.

3.2 CoreL Syntax and Semantics

A plugin source code in CoreL is divided in a number of *stanzas*, each of which is prefixed by a header in bracket. The following stanzas are defined:

- `[plugin]` declares (*keyword*, *value*) pairs that describe the plugin as a whole, e.g., plugin name, author, version, etc. These are compiled into methods overloading those in the abstract superclass `Plugin`.
- `[vocabulary]` declares vocabulary additions by the plugin, i.e., functions, universes, backgrounds etc. These are then compiled into implementations of the `VocabularyExtender` interface.

[6] We found that this practice was often implemented in existing plugins. For example, the `ConditionalRuleNode` class in Appendix A.1 implemented methods `getGuard()`, `getIfRule()` and `getElseRule()` as more meaningful abbreviations for the various $next(next(first(pos)))$ that served exactly this purpose.

- `[operator]` declares new operators that can be used in expressions, including special properties such as their associativity (left or right) and their precedence with respect to other operators. This stanza is compiled into an implementation of the `OperatorProvider` and `ParserPlugin` interfaces.
- `[rule]` declares one or more pattern-action rules. This stanza—which is the more complex of the four—is compiled into an implementation of the `InterpreterPlugin` and `ParserPlugin`.

Example source code for the various stanzas is provided in Appendix B. Except for the general header `[plugin]`, stanzas can be repeated; the information provided in each is accumulated and merged in the resulting CoreASM plugin. We do not address at this time the remaining forms of plugins: those for partial updates aggregation, multi-agent scheduling policies and extension points in the interpreter lifecycle, are more specialized and of less frequent use, and require intimate knowledge of the interpreter's inner workings. Also, we do not address packaging plugins which are already quite easy to write (they consist of a single method returning a set of plugin names that should be imported when the package plugin is imported).

In writing plugins in CoreL, three special brackets denote scopes that are processed differently. Text enclosed in `(|...|)` (an ASCII representation of our $⦇\ldots⦈$) is processed as a *pattern*; text enclosed in `{|...|}` is treated as *enriched Java*—the curly braces hinting at their contents being program source code—and text enclosed in `[|...|]` is a *grammar rule*. Patterns and grammar rules are used only in `[rule]` stanzas, while enriched Java is used for all types of stanzas except `[plugin]`. CoreL's syntax consists thus of an outer language, describing the overall structure of a plugin, and of the three sub-languages for patterns, grammar rules and enriched Java. We present each of them in turn in the following.

Pattern. The pattern sub-language captures the ideas of the corresponding construct in the specification. Inside the pattern delimiters, symbols and keywords in FULL CAPS[7] are considered terminals. Any other symbol must be either a placeholder letter (Table 2)—with `x`, `u`, `v`, `l` keeping their usual meaning; `?`, `e`, `r`, `f`, `z` standing for $\boxed{?}$, $\boxed{e}$, $\boxed{r}$, $\boxed{l}$, and $\boxed{}$ respectively[8]—or a location indicator, in square brackets, placed immediately before a placeholder.

With these conventions, a specification pattern can be written almost identically in CoreL, e.g., $⦇\ \textbf{if}\ {}^{\alpha}v\ \textbf{then}\ {}^{\beta}\boxed{r}\ \textbf{else}\ {}^{\gamma}\boxed{r}\ ⦈$ becomes `(| IF [alpha]v THEN [beta]r ELSE [gamma]r |)` or more simply, given that locations are implicitly assigned, `(| IF v THEN r ELSE r |)`.

---

[7] While a poor substitute for bold type, full caps was considered visually more appealing than other alternatives. The actual keyword is the same word but in lower case, consistent with established ASM and CoreASM tradition.

[8] Given that `l` had been already used for l as location, we choose `f` (for *function*) as a key for $\boxed{l}$; we used `z` as a key for $\boxed{}$ given the limitations of the ASCII set.

In addition to generating appropriate matching conditions, each pattern produces a series of *bindings* for its placeholders. These bindings can then be used in the enriched Java part. In detail:

1. For each children of the AST node, a positional numeric binding is created, in left-to-right order. In our example, this creates bindings $\$1 = \mathit{first}(\mathit{pos})$, $\$2 = \mathit{next}(\$1)$, $\$3 = \mathit{next}(\$2)$.
2. For each occurrence of `?`, `e`, `r`, `f`, `z`, a binding identified by the same name with a consecutive order index appended is established, having as value the position of the corresponding node in the AST. In our example, this creates bindings $\$e1 = \$1$, $\$r1 = \$2$ and $\$r2 = \$3$.
3. the first occurrence of any `?`, `e`, `r`, `f`, `z`, if any, establishes a binding with the same name which is a synonym for the first of the indexed binding created above. In our example, bindings $\$v = \$v1$ and $\$r = \$r1$ are created. This is normally used only when there is only one instance of a given placeholder.
4. each location indicator is transformed into a binding with the given name, synonym with the corresponding positional binding. In our example, $\$alpha = \$1$, $\$beta = \$2$, and $\$gamma = \$3$.
5. Instances of `x`, `v`, `u`, `l` undergo a processing similar to that of points 2 and 3 above, but the value of the bindings is not the location of the corresponding node, but rather their associated "evaluated" content, i.e., *token*(), *value*(), *updates*() and *loc*() respectively.
6. three additional well-known bindings are established: $\$res$ is an assignable variable holding the results of the evaluation of an operator, $\$pos$ is an assignable variable holding the current node in the AST visit, and $\$[n]$ is a function which, when assigned, updates the triple $(loc, updates, value)$ of the argument node n.

Enriched Java. The enriched Java sub-language is treated by the CoreL transpiler as arbitrary text, which is copied into the output verbatim, except for substituting the various bindings above (all identified by a leading `$`) with their values. Some minor syntactic sugaring is performed as well, e.g., assignments of the form $\$[n] = (x, y, z)$ are translated into Java as n`.setNode(`x, y, z`)` (a method of the `ASTNode` class which in turn assigns to the various components of the triple).

At this stage, CoreL does not perform any static check on the contents of these sections (not even syntactic analysis), which is instead delegated to the Java compiler that will process the resulting code. Although missing in the current implementation, the translated code should include (in comments or as annotations) sufficient information to link the generated code back to the CoreL source, to ease debugging.

Grammar Rule. In most cases, the pattern section alone would suffice to describe the grammar of a construct; however, there may be situations in which a richer syntax such as EBNF is convenient to describe repetitions, alternatives or optional parts of a rule, especially when the *concrete syntax* is notationally richer than the *abstract syntax*. This is often the case in CoreASM, due to the multiple concrete variants of the same construct that have appeared in the literature (e.g., `par`/`endpar`, `if` with or without an `endif`, `seq` vs. `seqblock` vs. `step` etc.).

Hence, when CoreL processes a pattern the terminals are only collected to contribute to the list of keywords for the plugin, whereas the actual grammar production is provided in a separate segment between `[|` and `|]` immediately after the rule declaration. These productions are expressed in EBNF, with the added notational constraint that terminal keywords are written in upper case (but are then interpreted as lower case), whereas the lower case letters `x`, `e`, `r` and `f` are interpreted as the non-terminal classes Identifier, Expression, Rule and Expression[9]. If the grammar rule is omitted, the first pattern (after stripping location indicators) is used as grammar rule; this simplifies the notation in most regular cases.

Since the grammar rule is used in instructing the parser on how to build AST nodes, if the structure of the production does not match that in the patterns for the same rule, the pattern will not match, and the action will not be executed. Currently, the CoreL transpiler does not check the correspondence between the two.

Finally, the three sub-languages are bound together in a `[rule]` stanza by the construct `rule`:

```
rule tag [| grammar |] {
    (| pattern |) -> {| enriched Java |}
    ...
}
```

Notice that a stanza can contain multiple rules (each with a distinct tag and grammar), and a rule can contain multiple pattern-action pairs. At parsing time, the AST node created by a particular grammar production will be labeled with the corresponding tag, and at interpretation time when visiting a node with that tag, only patterns in the corresponding rules will be tested for matches.

3.3 CoreL Implementation

CoreL is implemented as a transpiler (from CoreL source to Java source); standard compiler technology is used to lexically separate the three sub-languages described above (pattern, enriched Java, grammar), which are then parsed by specialized parsers, and to parse the overall stanzas structure. The processing of most blocks revolves around collecting relevant information (e.g., list of rules, list of keywords, or list of predicates to check for a match, etc.), which is then passed on for macro-substitution to a *templating engine*. Macro substitution in templates happens in multiple stages. In the first stage, individual code fragments are substituted for corresponding placeholders in small-scale structures

[9] It may be observed that both `e` and `f` map to Expression. This is intentional; indeed, the difference is semantical and not grammatical: in `e` the *value* of the expression (rhs) is of interest, whereas in `f` the *location* of the expression (lhs), if any, is of interest.

(e.g., \$1 for *pos.getFirst*()). Then, the resulting chunk of code is replaced into method templates. Finally, these skeletons filled with the results of the first two stages are themselves used in a third stage for populating class-sized templates.

The template-based approach provides the flexibility to prepare multiple potential implementation, among which to choose based on specific circumstance (e.g., whether the plugin also defines new operators or not), and also allow customization options for advanced users—as well as freedom of experimentation for the developers of CoreL.

Finally, the full Java source code is automatically compiled by invoking a standard Java compiler, and the generated `.class` files are collected together with administrative information in a `.jar` archive, which is finally made available to the plugin author for installation into an instance of CoreASM or distribution through whichever means is suitable.

A prototype of the translator (for an earlier version of the language, with minor differences to the one we present here) has been developed in Rust by the second author as part of his M.Sc. thesis [21], and is currently being used to evaluate the expressiveness and user acceptance of the language.

As a critical part of the evaluation of the implementation, an effort is ongoing to assess how many of the standard CoreASM plugins could be rewritten in CoreL with identical functionality, and identify both limitations and improvement opportunities for the language.

4 Discussion

4.1 Aims and Limitations

The design of CoreL did not aim for additional functionality with respect to the current CoreASM plugin framework, but rather for increased expressiveness and a lower barrier to entry. In fact, if anything, CoreL is less powerful than native plugins, as currently only half of the plugin types in the CoreASM architecture are supported by the language. However, the plugin types that are currently supported are those that more closely align with one of the major goals of the ASM method as used in software specifications, namely that a specification should be at roughly the same level of abstraction as the problem that one is specifying: not more abstract (in order to avoid losing significant information by underspecification), nor too concrete (so that no unnatural encoding layer is introduced in the specification, making understanding and reasoning harder than it needs to be). In that, the ASM method—as eloquently argued by Börger in [5]—provides both a solid mathematical foundation and an adaptable linguistic expression, thus simplifying interaction, collaborative work, and ultimately validation of a specification.

While the CoreL specification for plugins (of the types that are supported) are clearly more concise and hopefully easier to understand than the corresponding implementations in Java, they still require some technical knowledge about CoreASM internals. Here, the aim of providing a freely extensible language has to come to terms with the need to keep the language executable, which has always been a defining feature of CoreASM. Some compromise are thus to be expected.

In our design, the technical knowledge needed is limited to certain key aspects, namely:

- the mechanism by which AST are navigated (by assigning to `$pos` and to `$[·]`);
- how to interact with values in the state (by methods of the `Element` class of which all sorts are subclasses);
- how to produce updates (by using the `Update` and `UpdateMultiset` classes);
- how to describe locations (by using the `Location` class).

All these are straightforward implementations of the corresponding theoretical concept, hence we expect that the effort required to familiarize with them, for a potential new plugin writer who already knows how ASMs work, should be rather limited.

4.2 Validation

Validating a language requires consideration of various separate facets. In our case, the major criterion is expressiveness, which we consider as a compromise between universality (whether the given language can express all possible useful behaviours) and effort (whether the specifications of such behaviours is not unduly complex and require too much effort to the specifier). In that sense, we already acknowledged above some limitations: namely, that only 4 out of 8 forms of plugins are supported, and even for those, the enriched Java sub-language only offers support for certain frequently used patterns. However, three considerations are in order. First, the forms of plugins that are currently supported are the most commonly used, as shown in Table 3 with reference to the 36 plugins that are distributed with CoreASM itself. Second, the stanza structure of CoreL provides an easy path towards expansion of the types of plugins supported by adding further stanzas with specialized syntax for each plugin type. Third, the action part of `[rule]` stanzas, written in enriched Java, is a strict superset—hence, a conservative extension—of the Java language that has been traditionally used in writing plugins; thus, expressive power is not diminished by providing the convenience macros described in Sect. 3.2.

As for effort, we already discussed how the system-level knowledge needed to be able to write plugins in CoreL is substantially less than that needed to be able to write native plugins in Java. We can additionally measure effort in terms of the size of code needed in Java and in CoreL to achieve identical functionality.

The code for the full[10] ConditionalRulePlugin in CoreL is 20 lines long, compared to 352 lines for the Java version: a reduction of around 94%. Similarly, the StackPlugin implementing the two rules **push** *value* **into** *stack* and

[10] This includes a conditional expression, in addition to the conditional rule that we discussed in our running example.

Table 3. Count (#) and percentage (%) of plugins in the CoreASM distribution implementing each interface. In the first group, interfaces currently supported by CoreL; in the second group, interfaces not currently supported by CoreL. Notice that many plugins support multiple interfaces.

Interface	#	%
ParserPlugin	34	94%
InterpreterPlugin	29	81%
OperatorProvider	7	19%
VocabularyExtender	17	47%
Aggregator	4	11%
Scheduler	1	3%
ExtensionPointPlugin	7	19%
PackagePlugin	2	6%
Total	36	100%

pull *value* **from** *stack* as well as the function *peek*(*stack*), is 40 lines long in CoreL versus 439 lines in Java, for a reduction of 91%.

More complex plugins, where the actual logic takes a larger share of the source code compared with boilerplate code, might exhibit smaller reduction ratios. However, even for those cases there is a clear advantage in size due to the domain-specific syntax and structure of CoreL.

Ultimately, the "proof is in the pudding" validation for a language consists in whether it will be adopted by its intended users, i.e., whether we will see an increased production of third-party plugins for CoreASM written in CoreL. This final and stronger form of validation will have to wait until CoreL's design and implementation are finalized, after further internal testing, and the transpiler is released to the wider public.

5 Conclusions

One of the main premises of the ASM method, as expounded by Börger and colleagues in [8], was that specifying a system in a language that is as close as possible to the essential nature of the problem, without extra layers of encoding to complicate reasoning, is the best strategy for managing complexity in large-scale, real-world problems. CoreASM aimed at providing a tool to support that philosophy, and at the same time at using the same principle in its own design. The effort was remarkably successful up to the design (which used ASM specifications), but then faced a challenging knowledge gap when translating those specifications into executable Java code. The process, although largely systematic, did in fact rely on a significant amount of extra encoding.

CoreL, introduced in the present work, was designed as a domain-specific language for the specification *and* implementation of CoreASM plugins. In fact, the CoreL transpiler automatically converts plugin specifications into executable Java code, ready for importing into CoreASM.

Specifications written in CoreL are slightly more concrete than the original ones, due to the need of bridging the ASM abstract state with the much more concrete set of Java types and methods, but not excessively so. More importantly, large amounts of boilerplate code, needed but largely unrelated to the abstract definition of language features that are desirable to express a certain behaviour—and thus might be usefully made into a plugin—can be avoided altogether.

Ultimately, user acceptance will tell if CoreL has striken the right balance between the needs of specification and implementation. We believe, however, that the language greatly lowers the barrier to plugin writing for new users, compared to the previous Java implementation.

The project is still at its early stages. While the sublanguages for writing new rules, operators and functions are substantially stable, we are still experimenting with convenient domain-specific sublanguages for the remaining features: in particular, partial update aggregation and agent scheduling seem to be the most promising targets.

Another potential venue for improvements lies in identifying common idioms used in the action part of [rule] stanzas, and providing shorthand syntax for those. In particular, we are experimenting with the typical non-deterministic evaluation pattern:

chooseλ **in** $\{\ldots\}$ **with** $\neg evaluated(\lambda)$ **do**
  $pos := \lambda$
ifnone
  ...

as well as with various type checks, type casts and error reporting, such as:

```
if (node.getValue() instanceof SomeUniverse) {
    SomeUniverse c=(SomeUniverse)node;
    /* other code */
} else {
    /* error reporting */
}
```

Finally, as CoreL stabilizes, we intend to rewrite as many standard plugins as possible in CoreL, as yet another application of the "dogfooding" principle. We believe the exercise will both prove CoreL viability as a DSL for CoreASM plugin writing, and suggest other improvements and shorthand notations to make coding practical, which is often one of the most decisive factors in furthering language adoption.

Disclosure of Interests. The authors have no competing interests to declare that are relevant to the content of this article.

A Example Source Code in Java

What follows is the actual source code for the Conditional Rule plugin from the CoreASM distribution, with some minor reformatting and simplification (we omit `package` and `import` statements, some comments, and the implementation of the `if-then-else` (ternary) operator. This implementation adds an optional `endif` keyword for compatibility with some historical use of the `if-then-else` rule.

A.1 ConditionalRuleNode.java

```
/**
 * ConditionalRuleNode is a node for conditional (ifThen) nodes.
 *
 * @author George Ma
 *
 */
public class ConditionalRuleNode extends ASTNode {
    private static final long serialVersionUID = 1L;

    /**
     * Creates a new ConditionalRuleNode
     */
    public ConditionalRuleNode(ScannerInfo info) {
        super(ConditionalRulePlugin.PLUGIN_NAME,
                ASTNode.RULE_CLASS,
                "ConditionalRule",
                null,
                info);
    }

    public ConditionalRuleNode(ConditionalRuleNode node) { super(node); }

    /**
     * Returns the node representing the guard of the conditional rule
     */
    public ASTNode getGuard() { return getFirst(); }

    /**
     * Returns the node representing the consequent of the conditional rule
     * (i.e. rule to execute if the guard is true)
     */
    public ASTNode getIfRule() { return getGuard().getNext(); }

    /**
     * Returns the node representing the 'else' part the conditional rule.
     * (i.e. rule to execute if the guard is false)
     * This value may be null.
     */
    public ASTNode getElseRule() { return getIfRule().getNext(); }
}
```

A.2 ConditionalRulePlugin.java

```
/**
 * Plugin for conditional rule
 *
 * @author George Ma, Roozbeh Farahbod
 *
```

```
 */
public class ConditionalRulePlugin extends Plugin
    implements ParserPlugin, InterpreterPlugin {

  public static final VersionInfo VERSION_INFO = new VersionInfo(0, 9, 1, "");

  public static final String PLUGIN_NAME = ConditionalRulePlugin.class.getSimpleName();

  private final String[] keywords = { "if", "then", "else", "endif" };
  private final String[] operators = {};

  private Map<String, GrammarRule> parsers = null;

  private final CompilerPlugin compilerPlugin = new CompilerConditionalRulePlugin(this);

  @Override
  public CompilerPlugin getCompilerPlugin() { return compilerPlugin; }

  @Override
  public String[] getKeywords() { return keywords; }

  @Override
  public String[] getOperators() { return operators; }

  @Override
  public ASTNode interpret(Interpreter interpreter, ASTNode pos) {

    if (pos instanceof ConditionalRuleNode) {
      ConditionalRuleNode conditionalNode = (ConditionalRuleNode) pos;

      if (!conditionalNode.getGuard().isEvaluated()) {
        return conditionalNode.getGuard();
      } else {
        if (!(conditionalNode.getGuard().getValue() instanceof BooleanElement))
          capi.error("Element used as guard within \"if\" is not a boolean.",
              conditionalNode.getGuard(),
                interpreter);
        if (conditionalNode.getGuard().getValue().equals(BooleanElement.TRUE)) {
          if (!conditionalNode.getIfRule().isEvaluated()) {
            return conditionalNode.getIfRule();
          } else {
            pos.setNode(null, conditionalNode.getIfRule().getUpdates(), null);
            return pos;
          }
        } else { // guard is false
          if (conditionalNode.getElseRule() == null) { // there is no else
            pos.setNode(null, new UpdateMultiset(), null);
            return pos;
          } else {
            if (!conditionalNode.getElseRule().isEvaluated()) {
              return conditionalNode.getElseRule();
            } else {
              pos.setNode(null, conditionalNode.getElseRule().getUpdates(), null);
              return pos;
            }
          }
        }
      }
    } else {
      return null;
    }
    return pos;
  }

  @Override
  public Set<Parser<? extends Object>> getLexers() { return Collections.emptySet(); }

  @Override
```

```
  public Parser<Node> getParser(String nonterminal) { return null; }

  @Override
  public Map<String, GrammarRule> getParsers() {
    if (parsers == null) {
      parsers = new HashMap<String, GrammarRule>();
      KernelServices kernel = (KernelServices) capi.getPlugin("Kernel").getPluginInterface();

      Parser<Node> ruleParser = kernel.getRuleParser();
      Parser<Node> guardParser = kernel.getGuardParser();

      ParserTools pTools = ParserTools.getInstance(capi);

      Parser<Node> condRuleParser = Parsers.array(
          new Parser[] {
              pTools.getKeywParser("if", PLUGIN_NAME),
              guardParser,
              pTools.getKeywParser("then", PLUGIN_NAME),
              ruleParser,
              Parsers.array(
                  pTools.getKeywParser("else", PLUGIN_NAME),
                  ruleParser).optional(),
              pTools.getKeywParser("endif", PLUGIN_NAME).optional()
          }).map(new ConditionalParseMap());
      parsers.put("Rule",
          new GrammarRule("ConditionalRule",
              "'if' Guard 'then' Rule ('else' Rule )? ('endif')?",
              condRuleParser, PLUGIN_NAME));
    }
    return parsers;
  }

  @Override
  public void initialize() {  }

  @Override
  public VersionInfo getVersionInfo() { return VERSION_INFO; }

  public static class ConditionalParseMap extends ArrayParseMap {
    String nextChildName = "guard";

    public ConditionalParseMap() { super(PLUGIN_NAME); }

    @Override
    public Node map(Object[] vals) {
      nextChildName = "guard";
      Node node = new ConditionalRuleNode(((Node) vals[0]).getScannerInfo());
      addChildren(node, vals);
      return node;
    }

    @Override
    public void addChild(Node parent, Node child) {
      if (child instanceof ASTNode)
        parent.addChild(nextChildName, child);
      else {
        String token = child.getToken();
        if (token.equals("then"))
          nextChildName = "rule";
        parent.addChild(child);
      }
    }
  }
}
```

B Example Source Code in CoreL

B.1 ConditionalRule.corel

The following is the full source code of the ConditionalPlugin written in CoreL. Compare with the Java source code in Appendix A.

```
[plugin]
    name: SampleConditionalPlugin
    author: FMiraglia
    version: 0.1.0
    package: sample.conditional

[rule]
rule ifRule [| IF e THEN r ELSE r |] {
    (| IF e THEN r ELSE r |) -> {| $pos=$e; |}
    (| IF v THEN r ELSE r |) -> {| if ($v.equals(BooleanElement.TRUE)) $pos=$r1;
                                   else $pos=$r2;
                                |}
    (| IF v THEN u ELSE r |) -> {| $[$pos]=(null, $u, null); |}
    (| IF v THEN r ELSE u |) -> {| $[$pos]=(null, $u, null); |}
}
```

B.2 Examples of Other Stanzas

The following are examples of CoreL stanzas for VocabularyExtender (here, adding a new background static function PI holding π) and for an OperatorProvider (here, adding an addition operation + between elements of the Number sort).

```
[vocabulary]
function PI {| $res = (NumberElement) Math.PI; |}

[operator]
operator "+": 750, left {|
    if ($1.getValue() instanceof NumberElement
            && $2.getValue() instanceof NumberElement) {
        NumberElement eL = (NumberElement) $1.getValue();
        NumberElement eR = (NumberElement) $2.getValue();
        $res = numberBackgroundElement.getNewValue(eL.value + eR.value);
    }
|}
```

References

1. Altenhofen, M., Farahbod, R.: Bârun: a scripting language for CoreASM. In: Frappier, M., Glässer, U., Khurshid, S., Laleau, R., Reeves, S. (eds.) ABZ 2010. LNCS, vol. 5977, pp. 47–60. Springer, Heidelberg (2010). https://doi.org/10.1007/978-3-642-11811-1_5
2. Anlauff, M.: XASM – an extensible, component-based abstract state machines language. In: Gurevich, Y., Kutter, P.W., Odersky, M., Thiele, L. (eds.) ASM 2000. LNCS, vol. 1912, pp. 69–90. Springer, Heidelberg (2000). https://doi.org/10.1007/3-540-44518-8_6
3. Beckert, B., Posegga, J.: lean*EA*: a lean evolving algebra compiler. In: Kleine Büning, H. (ed.) CSL 1995. LNCS, vol. 1092, pp. 64–85. Springer, Heidelberg (1996). https://doi.org/10.1007/3-540-61377-3_32

4. Blass, A.R., Börger, E., Gurevich, Y.: Theory and application of Abstract State Machines (Dagstuhl seminar 02101). Technical report. 336, Leibniz-Zentrum für Informatik, Schloss Dagstuhl (2002)
5. Börger, E.: The ASM ground model method as a foundation of requirements engineering. In: Dershowitz, N. (ed.) Verification: Theory and Practice. LNCS, vol. 2772, pp. 145–160. Springer, Heidelberg (2003). https://doi.org/10.1007/978-3-540-39910-0_6
6. Börger, E., Cisternino, A., Gervasi, V.: Ambient abstract state machines with applications. J. Comput. Syst. Sci. **78**(3), 939–959 (2012)
7. Börger, E., Gervasi, V.: Structures of Computing: A Guide to Practice-Oriented Theory. Springer, Cham (2024)
8. Börger, E., Stärk, R.: Abstract State Machines: A Method for High-Level System Design and Analysis. Springer, Cham (2003)
9. Dausend, M., Raschke, A.: Introducing aspect-oriented specification for abstract state machines. In: Ait Ameur, Y., Schewe, K.D. (eds.) Abstract State Machines, Alloy, B, TLA, VDM, and Z, pp. 174–187. Springer, Heidelberg (2014)
10. Dausend, M., Raschke, A.: Towards a comprehensive extension of abstract state machines for aspect-oriented specification. Sci. Comput. Program. **131**, 22–41 (2016)
11. Castillo, G.: Towards comprehensive tool support for abstract state machines: the ASM workbench tool environment and architecture. In: Hutter, D., Stephan, W., Traverso, P., Ullmann, M. (eds.) FM-Trends 1998. LNCS, vol. 1641, pp. 311–325. Springer, Heidelberg (1999). https://doi.org/10.1007/3-540-48257-1_21
12. Castillo, G.: The ASM workbench: a tool environment for computer-aided analysis and validation of abstract state machine models. In: Margaria, T., Yi, W. (eds.) TACAS 2001. LNCS, vol. 2031, pp. 578–581. Springer, Heidelberg (2001). https://doi.org/10.1007/3-540-45319-9_40
13. Diesen, D.: Specifying algorithms using evolving algebra. implementation of functional programming languages. Ph.D. thesis, Department of Informatics, University of Oslo (1995)
14. Farahbod, R.: CoreASM: an extensible modeling framework & tool environment for high-level design and analysis of distributed systems. Ph.D. thesis, School of Computing Science, Simon Fraser University, Vancouver (2009)
15. Farahbod, R.: How to write a CoreASM plug-in. Documentation distributed with the CoreASM source (2014)
16. Farahbod, R., Gervasi, V., Glässer, U., Ma, G.: CoreASM plug-in architecture. In: Abrial, J.-R., Glässer, U. (eds.) Rigorous Methods for Software Construction and Analysis. LNCS, vol. 5115, pp. 147–169. Springer, Heidelberg (2009). https://doi.org/10.1007/978-3-642-11447-2_10
17. Gervasi, V., Farahbod, R.: JASMine: accessing Java code from CoreASM. In: Abrial, J.-R., Glässer, U. (eds.) Rigorous Methods for Software Construction and Analysis. LNCS, vol. 5115, pp. 170–186. Springer, Heidelberg (2009). https://doi.org/10.1007/978-3-642-11447-2_11
18. Gurevich, Y.: Evolving algebras 1993: Lipari guide. In: Börger, E. (ed.) Specification and Validation Methods, pp. 9–36. Oxford University Press (1995)
19. Gurevich, Y., Schulte, W., Veanes, M.: Toward industrial strength abstract state machines. Technical report. MSR-TR-2001-98, Microsoft Research (2001)
20. Kappel, A.M.: Implementation of dynamic algebras with an application to prolog. Master's thesis, Computer Science Department, Universität Dortmund (1990)

21. Miraglia, F.: CoreL, a metalanguage for the definition of CoreASM plugins. Master's thesis, Dipartimento di Informatica, University of Pisa (2025)
22. Schmid, J.: Refinement and implementation techniques for abstract state machines. Ph.D. thesis, University of Ulm (2002)
23. Stärk, R.F., Schmid, J., Börger, E.: Java and the Java Virtual Machine: Definition, Verification, Validation. Springer, Cham (2001)

Rigorous State-Based Methods

From Event-B to Lambdapi and TLA$^+$

Yamine Ait-Ameur[1], Jean-Paul Bodeveix[1(✉)], Christophe Chen[1], Guillaume Dupont[1], Elie Fares[1,2], Mamoun Filali[1], Anne Grieu[1], Ismail Mendil[1], Marc Pantel[1], Peter Rivière[1], Neeraj Kumar Singh[1], and Guillaume Verdier[1]

[1] IRIT, Université de Toulouse, Toulouse, France
{yamine.ait-ameur,jean-paul.bodeveix,christophe.chen,guillaume.dupont, mamoun.filali,anne.grieu,ismail.mendil,marc.pantel,peter.riviere, neeraj.singh,guillaume.verdier}@irit.fr, efares@hct.ac.ae
[2] Higher Colleges of Technology, Ras Al Khaimah, UAE

Abstract. Our work focuses on the formal verification of Event-B proofs and on the transfer of models between Event-B and TLA$^+$. By using Lambdapi and TLA$^+$ proof system as our target frameworks, we aim to enhance interoperability across different set-theoretic proof environments, including B and its Atelier B framework. First, we use TLA$^+$ to express Event-B models and proof obligations, and TLA$^+$ proof system to translate Event-B proof trees. Second, we use Lambdapi to directly verify Event-B proofs built using Rodin. It relies on an embedding of the Event-B mathematical language in the proof system Lambdapi. It is grounded on the $\lambda\Pi$-calculus modulo rewriting, which facilitates the implementation of various logics and is already employed to enable interoperability between various proof systems.

Keywords: formal methods · B/Event-B · TLA$^+$ · set theory · proof systems · model translation

1 Introduction

Formal methods play an important role in the development of critical software and systems. They aim to rigorously specify behaviours and their properties and to prove their correctness. Among formal methods, we consider Event-B which offers a refinement-based development method which targets the upper levels of the development cycle. The proof platform Rodin [3] for Event-B [2] supports a large part of automatic proofs and helps users building non-automatic proofs via manual interaction. As for Event-B, the B-method [1], and TLA$^+$ [21] are theorem-proving frameworks based on set theory, which is well-suited for specifying reactive systems. The ICSPA[1] project proposes to study how to export these formalisms to a unique logical framework based on the $\lambda\Pi$-calculus modulo

[1] https://anr.fr/Projet-ANR-21-CE25-0015.

A. Raschke et al. (Eds.): Egon Börger Festschrift, LNCS 16580, pp. 201–222, 2026.
https://doi.org/10.1007/978-3-032-24494-9_10

rewriting, namely Lambdapi[2]/Lambdapi [5,13]. This framework is well-suited to represent various logical theories and reasoning on them. Our goal is to enhance confidence in the proofs produced by Atelier B [9] for the B method, Rodin [3] for Event-B and TLAPS [12] for TLA$^+$ as well as to facilitate interoperability among the corresponding set-based theories.

The B-Ware project [15] for Atelier B, along with its recent developments and the reconstruction of SMT proofs in Lambdapi [4,11], share the same goal of proof verification and interoperability through Lambdapi, but with different approaches. In the B-Ware project, proof obligations are translated into the platform Why3 [6,23], which employs automated provers to try to prove them. These proofs are then translated by Why3 to Lambdapi. So, proofs already made by Atelier B provers are not reused and the hints they may contain are lost. A closely related work is EB4EB [22], which also explores Event-B semantics. However, we believe EB4EB is better suited for addressing meta-level issues, such as defining the semantics of new constructs not currently supported by Event-B—e.g., liveness [21] or scheduling properties [19]. In contrast, our work is more focused on the exchange and the verification of proof developments.

This paper extends the work done in [16] which concerns TLA$^+$ only. Here, we extend the work to Lambdapi in order to facilitate the sharing of models and proofs between Event-B, Lambdapi and TLA$^+$. Section 2 provides a brief overview of the three considered formalisms, Event-B, TLA$^+$ and Lambdapi. Section 3 presents the translation of Event-B models and proofs into TLA$^+$. Section 4 presents the translation of Event-B proofs into Lambdapi. Finally, Sect. 5 concludes the paper.

2 Context

In this section, we provide a brief overview of Event-B, TLA$^+$ and Lambdapi, where we highlight the types and proof related aspects of the languages.

2.1 Event-B

This paragraph presents a succinct overview of the Event-B language and the Rodin platform as a proof environment. Following a brief introduction to the language, we present a simple example, along with an associated proof and its management within Rodin. For a more comprehensive overview of Event-B, please refer to [2].

Overview of the Event-B Language. An Event-B model is built from contexts and machines. Contexts describe data types as abstract sets, constants, axioms and derived theorems [7], characterizing the static structure of a system. Machines describe the behavioral aspect of a system through variables, invariants and guarded events updating variables while preserving the invariant

[2] https://deducteam.github.io/.

properties. Properties (axioms, theorems, invariants, guards, ...) are described using the Event-B mathematical language which defines first-order formulas over a typed set theory. An Event-B type is defined by the following grammar, where overlined type operators distinguish them from their expression counterpart[3].

$$\begin{array}{rll} t ::= & \overline{S} & \text{carrier sets (user defined abstract sets)} \\ \mid & \overline{\mathbb{Z}} & \text{integers} \\ \mid & \overline{\mathbb{B}} & \text{booleans} \\ \mid & t \overline{\times} t & \text{cartesian product} \\ \mid & \overline{\mathbb{P}}(t) & \text{powerset of types} \\ \mid & t_1 \overline{\leftrightarrow} t_2 = \overline{\mathbb{P}}(t_1 \overline{\times} t_2) & \text{binary relations} \end{array}$$

Although generic types are not directly accessible to the user, Event-B set operators are inherently generic. If we denote type variables by $\alpha, \beta, \ldots$, then the signatures of theses set operators can be considered as defined in Fig. 1[4] where o denotes a predicate.

operator	argument types	result type	comment
		Predicates	
$\in$	$\alpha, \overline{\mathbb{P}}(\alpha)$	o	set membership
$\subseteq$	$\overline{\mathbb{P}}(\alpha), \overline{\mathbb{P}}(\alpha)$	o	set containment
		Constants	
$\mathbb{Z}$		$\overline{\mathbb{P}}(\overline{\mathbb{Z}})$	set of integers
$\mathbb{N}$		$\overline{\mathbb{P}}(\overline{\mathbb{Z}})$	set of non negative integers
S		$\overline{\mathbb{P}}(\overline{S})$	user defined abstract sets
$\emptyset$		$\overline{\mathbb{P}}(\alpha)$	generic constant
		Unary Operators	
$\mathbb{P}$	$\overline{\mathbb{P}}(\alpha)$	$\overline{\mathbb{P}}(\overline{\mathbb{P}}(\alpha))$	powerset operator
		Binary Operators	
$\cup, \cap$	$\overline{\mathbb{P}}(\alpha), \overline{\mathbb{P}}(\alpha)$	$\overline{\mathbb{P}}(\alpha)$	set union, intersection
$\mapsto$	α, β	$\alpha \overline{\times} \beta$	ordered pair builder
$\times$	$\overline{\mathbb{P}}(\alpha), \overline{\mathbb{P}}(\beta)$	$\overline{\mathbb{P}}(\alpha \overline{\times} \beta)$	cartesian product
$\leftrightarrow$	$\overline{\mathbb{P}}(\alpha), \overline{\mathbb{P}}(\beta)$	$\overline{\mathbb{P}}(\alpha \overline{\leftrightarrow} \beta)$	binary relations
$\nrightarrow$	$\overline{\mathbb{P}}(\alpha), \overline{\mathbb{P}}(\beta)$	$\overline{\mathbb{P}}(\alpha \overline{\leftrightarrow} \beta)$	partial functions
$\lhd$	$\overline{\mathbb{P}}(\alpha), \alpha \overline{\leftrightarrow} \beta$	$\alpha \overline{\leftrightarrow} \beta$	domain restriction
$\Lleftarrow$	$\alpha \overline{\leftrightarrow} \beta, \alpha \overline{\leftrightarrow} \beta$	$\alpha \overline{\leftrightarrow} \beta$	relation overloading[a]
$\_(\_)$	$\alpha \overline{\leftrightarrow} \beta, \alpha$	β	function call

[a] $r_1 \Lleftarrow r_2 = \{x \mapsto y \mid x \mapsto y \in r_1 \land x \notin \mathrm{dom}(r_2)\} \cup r_2$. Thus $r \Lleftarrow \{x \mapsto v\}$ denotes r where the image of x becomes $\{v\}$.

Fig. 1. Signature of some Event-B operators

[3] Event-B uses the same syntax for both.

[4] We do not use the arrow do denote the result type intentionally.

We remark that it is not possible to form the union of sets with different types. Moreover, there is no specific type for functions. A function is modeled as a relation satisfying additional properties. Consequently, applying a function always generates a proof obligation for checking its well-formedness. This facilitates the manipulation of partial functions and simplifies the process of discharging the associated proof obligations.

Running Example. As a running example, we consider the well-known mutual exclusion problem (Fig. 2). Its static part is defined by the context `cMutex`, which introduces two abstract sets: a finite set of processes `Proc`, and an enumerated set of process states, `State`, containing the constants `In` and `Out`. The behavioral part of the model is represented by the machine `mMutex`. The machine's state is defined by the declared variable `state`, which is defined as a total function in the `invariant` clause, i.e. a relation associating each process in `Proc` with a unique state in `State`. This state must satisfy the mutual exclusion property. Initially, all processes are in the `Out` state. The `Enter` event changes the state of a process `p` to `In`[5] if no processes are in the `In` state. The event `Exit` changes the state of a process `p` from `In` back to `Out`.

```
context cMutex
sets
  Proc State
constants
  In Out
axioms
  @fin finite (Proc)
  @State partition (State,{In},{Out})
end
```

```
machine mMutex sees cMutex
variables state
invariants
 @state_ty state ∈ Proc → State
 @mutex ∀p1,p2· state(p1)=In ∧ state(p2)=In
     ⇒ p1 = p2
events
  event INITIALISATION
  then @i state := Proc × {Out} end
  event Enter any p where
    @p_ty p ∈ Proc
    @alone state⁻¹[{In}] = ∅
  then @enter state(p) := In end
  event Exit any p where
    @pIn state(p) = In
  then @exit state(p) := Out end
end
```

Fig. 2. The Mutex example in Event-B

Proof Obligations. The correctness of contexts and machines is established through the verification of their associated *proof obligations*, formal statements defined that must be proved. For example,

[5] Note that the action `state(p) := In` is defined as `state := state` $\Leftarrow\!\!\!+$ `{p` $\mapsto$ `In}`.

- The well-formedness of formulas should be proved by demonstrating that partially defined constructs are applied only when they are defined. For example, in the invariant `@mutex` of Fig. 2, the expression `state(p1)` is correct if the function state belongs to a set of functions and its argument `p1` is within its domain. This leads to a derived invariant.
- Contexts may include axioms tagged as theorems, which should derived logically as consequences of prior axioms and theorems.
- Machine events should preserve machine invariants: For example, the event `Enter` should preserve the invariant `mutex` of Fig. 2, which leads to the following proof obligation:

```
∀p,p1,p2·(state<+{p↦In})(p1)=In ∧ (state<+{p↦In})(p2)=In⇒p1=p2
```

From now on, we will focus solely on contexts. In fact, we can use a context to explicitly state this proof obligation, which would otherwise be automatically generated from the machine. So, we can reformulate the property as a theorem within a separate context (Listing 1.1). This context represents a more complex example of a context. It contains the previous context (an `extends` clause could be used), the variables and invariants of the machine, expressed as constants and axioms, and the proof obligation expressed as a theorem. Note that the overloading operator $\Leftarrow\!\!+$ is used to build the state obtained from updating the process `p`. Additionally, the `@pre` axiom encodes the guards of the `Mutex` event. While it could be incorporated within the theorem itself, it is declared an axiom here for improved readability, since it does not depend on the event parameter `p`.

Listing 1.1. Enter proof obligation as an Event-B context

```
context Mutex_enter_inv
sets
  Proc State // the set of processes and of process states
constants
  In Out // inside or outside the mutex section
  state  // the function mapping a process to its state
axioms
  @part  partition (State, {In}, {Out}) // defines State as an enumerated type
  @state  state ∈ Proc → State // state is a total function from Proc to State
  @inv ∀p1,p2 state(p1)=In ∧ state(p2)=In ⇒ p1=p2 // the mutex property
  @pre state⁻¹[{In}] = ∅ // the inverse image of the singleton is empty
  theorem @th ∀p,p1,p2· (state<+{p↦In})(p1)=In  (state<+{p↦In})(p2)=In ⇒ p1=p2
end
```

This context generates several proof obligations related to the well-formedness of the axiom `@inv` and the theorem `@th` (annotated with the `theorem` tag). Note that these proof obligations verify that the theorem logically follows from the axioms defined within the context.

Event-B Proof Trees. An Event-B proof is represented as a tree where each node is a *sequent* consisting of a goal and a list of hypotheses. The proof begins with a root sequent that contains the initial goal to be proved along with its hypotheses. The proof tree is constructed interactively by applying tactics. For a given sequent, a tactic produces a (possibly empty) set of new sequents, which become the children of the current node. The proof process concludes when all leaves are empty. Figure 3 illustrates an excerpt of a proof tree, where nodes are labeled by the applied tactic. Such proof tree can be described as follows:

- `Partition rewrite in hyp` introduces the definition of a partition to the hypotheses. In our example, this results in the additions of two hypotheses: `State={In ,Out}` and `In` $\neq$ `Out`.
- $\forall$ `goal` eliminates all leading universal quantifiers.
- $\Rightarrow$ `goal` applies to a goal with $\Rightarrow$ as the toplevel connector. It pushes the conjuncts of its left-hand side into the hypotheses.
- `ovr in (f` $\Leftarrow$ `{x` $\mapsto$ `v})(y)` splits the goal into two sub-goals based on whether `y=x` or not, and simplifies the goal accordingly: if `y=x`, the goal simplifies to v; Otherwise, the goals simplifies to `f(y)`
- `simplification rewrites` applies a database of hundreds of rules to rewrite hypotheses and the goal, satisfying the proof process.
- `eh with e1=e2` replaces every occurrence of `e1` with `e2` throughout the hypothesis and goals.
- `hyp` proves the goal if it (or some variants of it) is included in the hypotheses.

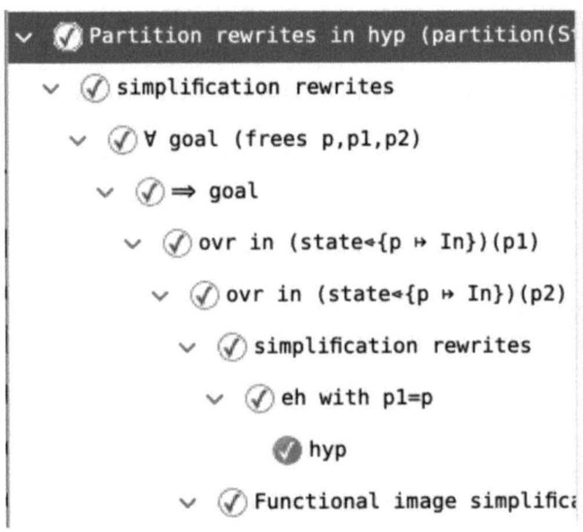

Fig. 3. Part of a Rodin Proof Tree

2.2 TLA$^+$

Overview of the TLA$^+$ Language. TLA$^+$ is a formal specification language developed by Leslie Lamport [21] for designing and verifying complex hardware and software systems, particularly those involving concurrency and distribution. Similar to Event-B, TLA$^+$ uses set theory and logic, and it additionally supports temporal reasoning to describe system behavior and identify errors before implementation. A TLA$^+$ + module can extend other modules, and like the Event-B modeling language, a TLA$^+$ + model combines static and behavioral properties within a single module. Static properties are expressed through constants, axioms (assumptions), and theorems, while behavioral properties are modeled using variables and actions that relate current and next (primed) values of variables, enabling the specification of system dynamics over time.

```
---- MODULE time ----
EXTENDS Naturals
CONSTANTS N
VARIABLES t
ASSUME N_ty N ∈ Nat \ {0}
Init ≜ t = 0
Next ≜ t' = IF t = N−1 THEN 0 ELSE t+1
======================
```

TLA$^+$ Proof Script Language. TLA$^+$ defines a textual proof script language [20]. A proved statement is characterized by an identifier, a formula or an assume-prove statement, and an optional tree structure[6]. The leaves of this tree comprise of definitions and/or facts (e.g., theorems) that support the proof. Each subtree represents a sequence of steps culminating in a `QED` step. Each step is associated with its own proof. TLA$^+$ provides proof constructs for building these steps. A proof can be either direct (`Obvious` and `By`) or needs multiple steps ending with a `QED` step. Some of the basic proof steps (specified by sub-classes of the class `Step`) include:

- The construct `WITNESS E` provides a value (E) for proving an existential goal.
- The construct `HAVE P` introduces a lemma stating the property `P`
- The construct `ASSUME H PROVE G` introduces a TLA$^+$ sequent, where `H` represents a sequence of either a variable declaration (using the `NEW` keyword) or a hypothesis. This construct can be viewed as a forward proof mechanism, as it allows assuming `H` and proving `G` based on that assumption.
- The `SUFFICES` construct introduces an intermediary step to discharge the current goal. After justifying this step, the proof continues with the newly introduced goal. Thus, `SUFFICES` can be viewed as a backward proof mechanism, as it helps to derive the goal by working backwards from the current step.

We illustrate the use of these constructs with the following excerpt, which is taken from the translation of the Rodin proof tree.

[6] The tree structure is optional; in such cases, the proof consists of a single named statement.

```
<1>3. SUFFICES ∀ p1 ∈ Proc, p2 ∈ Proc :
        FunImage(Overwrite(state, {⟨p, In⟩}), p1) = In
        ∧ FunImage(Overwrite(state, {⟨p, In⟩}), p2) = In ⇒ p1 = p2
  OBVIOUS
<1>4. SUFFICES
      ASSUME NEW CONSTANT p1 ∈ Proc, NEW CONSTANT p2 ∈ Proc
      PROVE  FunImage(Overwrite(state, {⟨p, In⟩}), p1)=In ∧ FunImage(Overwrite(state, {⟨p, In⟩}), p2)=In ⇒
          p1 = p2
  OBVIOUS
<1>5. SUFFICES
      ASSUME FunImage(Overwrite(state, {⟨p, In⟩}), p1)=In , FunImage(Overwrite(state, {⟨p, In⟩}), p2)=In
      PROVE p1 = p2
  OBVIOUS
```

2.3 Lambdapi

Lambdapi [13] is a proof assistant based on λΠ-calculus modulo theory, featuring dependent types and reasoning modulo user-defined rules. It doesn't impose a predefined logic, allowing users to define their own or choose from a repository of existing logics[7]. For example, one can consider first-order logic with classical axioms and definition of equality, which will be interesting for our purpose.

Overview of the Lambdapi Language. Lambdapi is built from terms of a dependent type lambda calculus defined by the following grammar:

`t ::=`	| `V`	variable
	| `TYPE`	sort of types
	| `Π (V:t), t`	dependent product
	| `λ (V:t), t`	abstraction
	| `let V ≔ t in t`	let construct
	| `t t`	application

As usual, `A→B` stands for `Π(x:A),B` when x is not free in B.

The main feature of Lambdapi is that it allows the definition of rewriting rules which are taken into account in the type system so that type checking is performed modulo the set of rules. It becomes possible to easily represent in Lambdapi languages incorporating their own set of rules. For example, we can encode β or η reduction on user defined terms. Given `app` and `lam` constructors for abstraction and application of an hypothetic object language, we can add the following β-reduction rule where $ variables are meta-variables matching any term: `rule (app (lam $F) $a) ↪ $F $a`
Here, the `lam` constructor is supposed to take a (meta-level) function as parameter, captured by $F. It is then called with the value of $a as parameter.

Encoding of Object Logics. In order to encode a logical framework, we introduce two declarations in Lambdapi: the type of formulas, `Prop` and a function π associating to each formula the type of its proofs. The following declarations introduce these symbols:

```
constant symbol Prop : TYPE;        // type of propositions
symbol π : Prop → TYPE;   // type of proofs
```

[7] https://github.com/Deducteam/lambdapi-logics.

Note that a type can be empty and the type of the proof of an invalid formula should be empty. We can now declare, in an axiomatic way, logical operators and their proof rules. Consider for example, the natural deduction rules for conjunction and implication operators:

$$\frac{p \quad q}{p \wedge q}\wedge_i \qquad \frac{p \wedge q}{p}\wedge_{e_1} \qquad \frac{p \wedge q}{q}\wedge_{e_2} \qquad \frac{\begin{matrix}[p]\\ \vdots \\ q\end{matrix}}{p \Rightarrow q}\Rightarrow_i \qquad \frac{p \quad p \Rightarrow q}{q}\Rightarrow_e$$

The introduction rule for implication $\Rightarrow_i$ reads as follows: if we can prove q by supposing p has a proof, then we have a proof of $p \Rightarrow q$. The operator signatures and the corresponding proof rules can be directly encoded in Lambdapi as follows:

```
constant symbol ∧ : Prop → Prop → Prop; // the operator signature
notation ∧ infix right 7; // declared as infix and right associative
constant symbol ⇒ : Prop → Prop → Prop; // the operator signature
notation ⇒ infix right 5; // declared as infix and right associative
constant symbol ∧i p q : π p → π q → π (p ∧ q); // encoding of each proof rule
constant symbol ∧e1 p q : π (p ∧ q) → π p;
constant symbol ∧e2 p q : π (p ∧ q) → π q;
constant symbol ⇒i p q : (π p → π q) → π (p ⇒ q);
constant symbol ⇒e p q : π p → π (p ⇒ q) → π q;
```

We can notice that rules for $\Rightarrow_i$ and $\Rightarrow_e$ come to use the proof of implication as a function mapping a proof of p to a proof of q (Curry-Howard correspondence). We can use a Lambdapi rewriting rule to encode this and replace $\Rightarrow$ proof rules by:

```
rule π ($p ⇒ $q) ↪ π $p → π $q;
```

which identifies a proof of $\$p \Rightarrow \$q$ with a mapping from proofs of $\$p$ to proofs of $\$q$.

Verification of confluence and termination of the rules is left to the user and can be performed by invoking external tools. Additionally, Lambdapi ensures that local confluence is preserved and issues warning for non-joinable critical pairs. It also checks type preservation by rewriting.

Lambdapi Proofs. In Lambdapi, a proof of a property is represented by a term whose type corresponds to that property. For example, using the previous encoding of the conjunction operator, we can demonstrate how to convert a proof of $p \wedge q$ into a proof of $q \wedge p$.

```
symbol and_comm (p q: Prop): π (p ∧ q) → π (q ∧ p) ≔
  λ (h : π (p ∧ q)), ∧i q p (∧e2 p q h) (∧e1 p q h);
```

However, constructing such a proof term directly can often be challenging. Lambdapi offers a limited set of tactics to assist in constructing the proof term. The same proof can also be constructed interactively as follows:

```
symbol and_comm (p q: Prop): π (p ∧ q) → π (q ∧ p) ≔
begin // enter  interactive  proof mode
  assume p q h; // adds to hypotheses p, q of type Prop and h of type π (p ∧ q)
  apply (∧ᵢ q p) // creates 2 sub−goals, one for each missing argument of ∧ᵢ
  { refine (∧ₑ₂ p q h); } // here we give the proof term for q
  { refine (∧ₑ₁ p q h); }; // and the proof term for p
end;
```

However, Lambdapi does not provide any decision procedure for propositional logic, linear arithmetic, ..., except a call to why3, but the proof term is not preserved. So, the translation of Rodin proofs to Lambdapi checkable proofs does not yield a direct mapping between Rodin and Lambdapi tactics.

3 Translating Event-B Models and Proofs to TLA$^+$

An Event-B [2] model consists of abstract and refined machines that describe the dynamics of a system using a symbolic labeled transition system. The machine state is represented by variables and invariants, ensuring the system preserves certain properties. Its behavior is governed by parameterized events that must preserve these invariants. Additionally, machines may reference contexts, which define static properties using carrier sets, constants, and axioms, organized hierarchically. Translating an Event-B machine involves first recursively translating all referenced contexts, then translating the machine itself. Both machines and contexts are mapped to separate TLA$^+$ modules [21].

3.1 Translating Contexts

Event-B contexts are translated in a hierarchical manner, with each context generating a corresponding TLA$^+$ module. Within this module, each Event-B set or constant is represented by a CONSTANT declaration, each axiom by an ASSUME declaration, and each theorem by a THEOREM declaration. For example, translating the context illustrated in Fig. 3.1 produces the following:

```
——————— MODULE cMutex1 ————————
EXTENDS Naturals, Integers, TLAPS, Relations, Partitions, FiniteSets
CONSTANTS State, Proc, In, Out
ASSUME In_ty ≜ In ∈ State // type synthesized by Rodin
ASSUME Out_ty ≜ Out ∈ State // type synthesized by Rodin
ASSUME fin ≜ IsFiniteSet(Proc)
ASSUME State ≜ Partition(State, ⟨{In}, {Out}⟩)
==========================================
```

3.2 Translating Event-B Formulas

Although TLA$^+$ is an untyped language, incorporating type information is essential for accurately translating Event-B formulas, as it defines the bounds for quantified variables. For instance, the formula: $\forall E \cdot 0 \in E \wedge (\forall x \cdot x \in E \Rightarrow x+1 \in E) \Rightarrow \mathbb{N} \subseteq$ E is first type-checked by Rodin which provides type annotations for all its quantified variables. It becomes:

$\forall E ⦂ \mathbb{P}(\mathbb{Z}) \cdot 0 \in E \wedge (\forall x ⦂ \mathbb{Z} \cdot x \in E \Rightarrow x+1 \in E) \Rightarrow \mathbb{N} \subseteq$ E where the terms on the right of the ⦂ operator are expressed in Event-B type language. The formula is then translated to TLA$^+$ by using the synthesized type information to bound the quantifiers:

```
∀ E ∈ SUBSET(Int): 0 ∈ E ∧ (∀ x ∈ Int: x ∈ E ⇒ x+1 ∈ E) ⇒ Nat ⊆ E
```

Rodin also infers type information for constants (based on context axioms), machine variables (derived from invariants), and event parameters (determined by event guards).

Formulas are classified into three categories: expressions, predicates, and actions. Expressions are further characterized by their assigned types.

Expressions. The primary challenge in translating Event-B expressions lies in the fact that most operators are relational, with no direct counterparts in TLA$^+$. Therefore, it is necessary to develop a library of TLA$^+$ operators, specifically designed to define all Event-B relational operators, commonly organized within the `Relation` module. A subset of these operators is presented here (closely aligned with the library provided by Lambdapi [17])[8].

```
-------------------- MODULE Relations -----------------
Rel(A,B) ≜ SUBSET (A × B)
Id(S) ≜ {r ∈ Rel(S,S) : ∀ c ∈ r: c[1] = c[2]}
Dom(R) ≜ {xy[1] : xy ∈ R }
Ran(R) ≜ {xy[2] : xy ∈ R }
Rev(R) ≜ {xy ∈ Ran(R) × Dom(R): ⟨xy[2],xy[1]⟩ ∈ R}
RestrictDom(R,D) ≜ { xy ∈ R : xy[1] ∈ D}
AntirestrictDom(R,D) ≜ { xy ∈ R : xy[1] ∉ D}
RestrictRan(R,D) ≜ { xy ∈ R : xy[2] ∈ D}
AntirestrictRan (R,D) ≜ { xy ∈ R : xy[2] ∉ D}
Overwrite(R,S) ≜ S ∪ AntirestrictDom(R,Dom(S))

PartialFunctions (D,R) ≜ {r ∈ Rel(D,R): ∀ e,x,y: ⟨e,x⟩∈ r ∧ ⟨e,y⟩∈ r ⇒ x=y}
TotalFunctions(D,R) ≜ {r ∈ PartialFunctions(D,R): Dom(r) = D}
PartialInjections (D,R) ≜ {r ∈ PartialFunctions(D,R): Rev(r) ∈ PartialFunctions (R,D)}
TotalInjections (D,R) ≜ TotalFunctions(D,R) ∩ PartialInjections (D,R)
```

We emphasize the `Overwrite(R,S)` operator, which takes two relations as arguments and returns a relation that includes pairs from S as well as

[8] We uses TLA$^+$ tuples $x = \langle x_1, \ldots, x_n \rangle$ where fields are accessed through $x[i]$.

pairs from R where the first projection has no corresponding image in S. The `Overwrite` operator is crucial for defining the semantics of function updates in machine actions. For instance, the Event-B assignment `f(x) := y` is translated in TLA$^+$ as: `f' = Overwrite(f, {⟨x,y⟩})`.

The second point concerns to partial functions (and by extension, total, injective, and surjective functions), which are encoded in TLA$^+$ as specific relations, similar to their representation in Event-B. As a result, TLA$^+$ functions are not directly used. While it is possible to identify relations that are actually functions and represent them as TLA$^+$ functions, thus enabling a more efficient translation to SMT, this approach would also require duplicating relational operators based on the nature of their arguments or introducing conversions during the translation. Such an approach would also complicate the translation of Event-B proof scripts to TLAPS [12].

Given this encoding, functional application in TLA$^+$ is defined using the `CHOOSE` operator, which means that the TLA$^+$ function call notation `f[x]` is not used. Instead, Event-B `f(x)` is encoded as follows:

```
RImage(R,S) ≜ {y ∈ Ran(R): ∃ x ∈ S: ⟨x,y⟩ ∈ R}
FunImage(R,c) ≜ CHOOSE i ∈ RImage(R,{c}): TRUE
```

However, this definition is not explicitly expanded to align the TLA$^+$ proof as closely as possible with the Rodin proof. It is only applied to the leaves of the TLA$^+$ proof tree, which are intended to be resolved by SMT calls. Otherwise, derived properties are used instead, such as the following, which can be proven within TLA$^+$:

```
THEOREM FunImageSingleton ≜
  ASSUME NEW S, NEW i PROVE ∀ c ∈ S: FunImage(S × {i},c) = i
```

In fact, it would be necessary to develop a TLA$^+$ library containing all the theorems used by Event-B proof rules.

Predicates. The translation of the predicate language is straightforward, since quantifier bounds are available through Rodin's type synthesis. However, built-in Event-B predicates (such as `finite` and `partition`) must be explicitly defined in TLA$^+$. For example, the `partition` is defined as follows:

```
Partition (S,s) ≜ S = UNION {s[i] : i ∈ DOMAIN s}
                  ∧ ∀ i ∈ DOMAIN s, j ∈ DOMAIN s: i # j ⇒ s[i] ∩ s[j]= ∅
```

Actions. Event-B actions are translated into TLA$^+$ actions, which are predicates that relate the current state to the next (primed) state of the module. Unchanged variables must be identified and explicitly declared. In our example, the deterministic assignment `state(p) := In` is translated into

```
ACT_Enter(p) ≜ ⟨state'⟩ = ⟨Overwrite(state,{⟨p, In⟩})⟩
```

3.3 Generation of Proof Obligations in TLA$^+$

In addition to translating the Event-B model, our plugin also generates proof obligations corresponding to Event-B ones [18] as TLA$^+$ theorems. The Event-B proof obligation generator provided by the Rodin platform [3] is not used here. Our plugin generates statements specific to TLA$^+$ that use named predicates (for example `Invariant` instead of the conjunction of individual formulas making the invariant) or the next-state operator. Furthermore, we generate generic proof scripts for TLAPS to facilitate automatic proof attempts. In the following, we detail some of the proof obligations generated by our approach.

WD Proof Obligations. Well-definedness proof obligations originate from the use of partially defined constructs, such as treating a relation as a function, determining the cardinality of a set, or selecting the minimum element of a set. The most common case involves function calls, where the proof obligation ensures that the relation belongs to a function space and that its argument resides within the relation's domain. These checks are derived from hypotheses inherited from referenced contexts, previous axioms (within contexts), invariants (within machines), prior guards, and quantified parameters (within events).

Feasibility Proof Obligations. Proof obligations are generated to ensure that when the invariants and guards hold, non-deterministic actions are feasible. Specifically, this requires that the before-after predicate must have at least one solution, and the corresponding set must be non-empty.

Theorem Proof Obligations. Theorems derived from axioms, invariants, and guards are translated into TLA$^+$ theorems. Their hypotheses comprise the relevant axioms, previously established theorems, and previous guards if they exist. When dealing with guards, hypotheses are quantified over typed event parameters. Outside of contexts, seen axioms are included directly into the TLA$^+$ model and do not need to be added to the theorem's hypotheses.

Invariant Preservation Proof Obligations. A proof obligation is generated for each declared invariant and event, ensuring that the event actions preserve the invariant.

For example, the preservation of the `mutex` invariant by the `Enter(p)` event results to the following theorem, where the TLA$^+$ prime operator is used to express that the invariant must be satisfied in the next state. Additionally, we assume that the previous invariants (such as `Inv_state_ty`) are preserved, as the corresponding theorem has already been established.

```
THEOREM PO_Next_Enter_mutex ≜ ∀ p ∈ Proc:
  Invariant  ∧ Inv_state_ty' ∧ _Enter(p) ⇒ Inv_mutex'
```

Automatic Proof of Proof Obligations. Automatically proving obligations in TLAPS is often challenging because users must provide all necessary theorems and definitions. While TLAPS implicitly injects the definitions and theorems related to standard TLA$^+$ modules (such as `Naturals`, `Sequences`, `FiniteSets`, etc.), and Event-B operators are fundamentally defined using relational operators. As a result, all these operators must be explicitly defined in TLA$^+$ and provided to TLAPS. However, even when these definitions are provided, proofs tend to fail because simplifying formulas to pure first-order logic results in proof goals that are too complex. This is why we have attempted to translate Rodin proofs.

3.4 Translating Rodin Proofs to TLA$^+$

Since automatically proving generated proof obligations is challenging, we propose to generate TLAPS proof scripts from the Rodin proof trees, utilizing the hints contained within them. To keep the TLA$^+$ proof synchronized with the Rodin proof, the translation of Event-B proof trees is performed through a recursive traversal of the tree. Each node leads to a corresponding TLA$^+$ proof script schema, where the proofs of the subtrees are inserted. The subgoals (and their hypotheses) are extracted from the Rodin proof tree and translated into TLA$^+$. Then, TLA$^+$ should prove that the goal of each node logically follows from the conjunction of its sub-node goals.

However, this general approach fails when the proofs that demonstrate the correctness of the rule instance, cannot be automated through SMT calls in TLA$^+$. In such cases, additional information—such as dedicated theorems, definitions to be unfolded, or intermediate goals—must be provided. These depend on the specific rule and its parameters, as indicated by the Rodin proof tree.

Translating Proofs of Rodin Proof Obligations. The following TLA$^+$ theorem is a direct translation of the proof tree built by the Rodin user for the proof obligation stating the preservation of the invariant `mutex` by the `Enter` event of the `Mutex1` machine (Listing 1.1). It is important to note that Rodin produces a self-contained proof obligation, which includes identifiers and axioms declared within the seen contexts (such as `Proc`, `State`, `In`, `Out`, etc.) and variables of the machine (in this case, `state`). Additionally, the state of the machine after the event is expressed using the Event-B `Overwrite` operator (lines 12–13). The statement of the theorem can be translated in TLA$^+$ as show in Listing 1.2. It is also self-contained and relies on a TLA$^+$ library for relational operators.

Listing 1.2. Mutual exclusion preservation in TLA$^+$

```
THEOREM Mutex1_Enter_mutex_INV_po ≜
  ASSUME NEW CONSTANT Proc, NEW CONSTANT State,
         NEW CONSTANT p ∈ Proc, NEW CONSTANT In ∈ State,
         NEW CONSTANT state ∈ SUBSET Proc × State,
```

```
        NEW CONSTANT Out ∈ State,
        RImage(Rev(state), {In}) = ∅ ,
        state ∈ TotalFunctions(Proc, State) ,
        ∀ p1 ∈ Proc, p2 ∈ Proc :
           FunImage(state, p1) = In ∧ FunImage(state, p2) = In ⇒ p1 = p2 ,
        Partition (State, ⟨{In}, {Out}⟩)
   PROVE ∀ p1 ∈ Proc, p2 ∈ Proc :
           FunImage(Overwrite(state, {⟨p, In⟩}), p1) = In
           ∧ FunImage(Overwrite(state, {⟨p, In⟩}), p2) = In ⇒ p1 = p2
```

Translating Rodin Proof Structure. Translating an Event-B proof tree involves recursively generating a TLAPS proof schema for each node. A node representing an Event-B proof rule is structured as follows:

$$\frac{C_1 : T_1, nH_1, H \vdash G_1 \quad \dots \quad C_k : T_k, nH_k, H \vdash G_k}{H \vdash G} R(p)$$

which states that applying rule R with input parameters p to the goal $H \vdash G$ generates k new sequents. Each of them using new constants C_i of type T_i and new hypotheses nH_i to solve the goal G_i. The generated TLAPS proof schema is then the following:

```
<N>  ASSUME H PROVE G (* current goal *)
  <N+1>1 ASSUME NEW CONSTANT C1 ∈ T1, H1 PROVE G1
       ... (* proof of G1 *)
  <N+1>k ASSUME NEW CONSTANT Cn ∈ Tk, Hk PROVE Gk
       ... (* proof of Gk *)
  <N+1>k+1 QED BY <N+1>1 ... <N+1>k (* try to prove H⇒G from subgoals *)
```

which means that given a proof for the k subgoals (marked with ...), we get a proof for the initial goal. TLA$^+$ will attempt to automatically prove the QED step.

The example given in Sect. 2.2 illustrates the translation of steps $\forall goal$ and $\Rightarrow goal$ from the Rodin proof tree in Fig. 3. The first step introduces the two typed quantified variables. The second step moves the left hand side of the $\Rightarrow$ connector to the assumptions.

The two script schemas aim to automatically verify the correctness of rule instances, ensuring that the conjunction of subgoals imply the initial goal. This automation typically succeeds for propositional and basic set reasoning. For more complex cases managed by Rodin through the use of domain-specific rules or theorems, we provide dedicated techniques in Sect. 3.4. They avoid trying to prove set-related formulas by reducing them to (often complex) first-order formulas.

Translating Rodin Tactics. As mentioned in the introduction, this work is preliminary, and achieving full coverage of the Event-B framework remains a long-term goal. Over many years, the Event-B has evolved to include more than 50 proof rules and over 500 simplification rules. Addressing these is essential to accurately preserve the structure of Event-B proofs.

Proof Rules. Here, we highlight one proof rules that illustrate the inherent challenges of translating Event-B proofs to TLA$^+$: Generalized Modus Ponens, which encapsulates a complex reasoning process. It uses many modus ponens-like rules, including the following two examples:

$$\frac{P, \varphi(\top) \vdash G}{P, \varphi(P) \vdash G} \qquad \frac{\varphi(\top) \vdash \neg G}{\varphi(G) \vdash \neg G}$$

where P is a predicate present in the list of hypotheses (left rule), $\varphi(\_)$ the list of (remaining for the left rule) hypotheses and G the current goal. Predicates of this list may contain P (left rule) or G (right rule) as a sub-formula. Applying one of these rules replaces P by $\top$ or G by $\bot$ in all the hypotheses. These rule applications are not explicitly traced, so the approach to handling this tactic is to let TLA$^+$ attempt to prove the resulting goal automatically.

Simplification Rules. An Event-B proof rule triggers a simplification procedure that applies numerous rewriting rules to the current goal and its hypotheses. However, the order in which these rules are applied is only available in debug mode via standard output, and the transformed sub-formulas are not specified. Even when the final formula is known, expecting an automatic proof in TLA$^+$ remains challenging. Therefore, it is essential to identify as many applied rules as possible to assist the TLA$^+$ prover. To illustrate potential approaches to this problem, we have selected one specific rule as an example: the rule `SIMP_MULTI_BINTER` removes duplicates in an intersection. It is specified as follows: $S \cap \ldots \cap T \cap \ldots \cap T \cap \ldots \cap U = S \cap \ldots \cap T \cap \ldots \cap$ U. It cannot be directly expressed as a TLA$^+$ theorem as it is in fact a rule schema. However, since we know the left and right terms, and the $\cap$ operator is a built-in TLA$^+$ operator, we can state the expected goal and expect an automatic proof[9].

```
THEOREM ints_SIMP_MULTI_BINTER ≜
    ASSUME NEW S, NEW T, NEW I, NEW U
    PROVE S ∩ T ∩ I ∩ T ∩ U = S ∩ T ∩ I ∩ U
    OBVIOUS
```

4 Translating Event-B Proofs to Lambdapi

In this section, we present the process of translating Event-B proofs into Lambdapi. This involves first translating Event-B formulas to Lambdapi. Then, the statement of a proof obligation is transformed to a Lambdapi formula, followed by the translation of its proof tree to a Lambdapi proof script.

4.1 Translating the Event-B Mathematical Language to Lambdapi

To express proofs constructed with the Rodin platform, we should first represent the mathematical language of Event-B in Lambdapi, i.e. a typed first-order

[9] It is indeed the case!.

set theory. As previously explained, the target logic must be axiomatised in Lambdapi. For this, we have made the choice to reuse some existing libraries [14], which provide axiomatizations for intuitionist propositional logic, first order quantifiers, equality, classical logic via the law of excluded middle, the Hilbert choice operator, and build Event-B on top of them by adding the axiomatization of set theory. As a consequence, we do not follow exactly the construction of the Event-B mathematical language as detailed in [3,8,12].

First-Order Logic with Equality in Lambdapi. Introducing first-order logic begins with the concept of data. To do this, we start by declaring a type for data types: `Set: TYPE`. This allows us to treat a concrete type as an object of type `Set`. Next, we define a function τ : `Set` $\rightarrow$ `TYPE`, which enables the use of concrete types as Lambdapi types. Given these declarations, we can declare the signature of quantifiers (Listing 1.3). These quantifiers accept a concrete type (a Set) as a parameter, which is marked as implicit using square brackets and a unary predicate.

Listing 1.3. Introduction of quantifiers

```
constant symbol Set: TYPE;
symbol τ: Set → TYPE;
constant symbol ∀ [a:Set] : (τ a → Prop) → Prop; notation ∀ quantifier;
constant symbol ∃ [a:Set] : (τ a → Prop) → Prop; notation ∃ quantifier;
```

To illustrate the use of these quantifiers, we introduce Leibnitz equality, which will be the first property we can express on user data. It is declared as generic, taking as implicit parameter the common type of its two arguments. It is specified by two axioms: reflexivity, ensuring each element is equal to itself, and an induction principle, which express that replacing an element with an equal one preserves provability.

Listing 1.4. Introduction of equality

```
symbol = [a] : τ a → τ a → Prop;
notation = infix 10;
symbol eq_refl [a] (x:τ a) : π (x = x);
symbol ind_eq [a] [x y:τ a]: π (x = y) → Π p, π (p y) → π (p x);
```

Proof rules for these quantifiers are the following, where x_0 is supposed to be a fresh variable:

$$\frac{P\ t}{\exists x \cdot\ P\ x}\exists_i \qquad \frac{(\exists x \cdot\ P\ x) \qquad (\forall x \cdot P\ x \Rightarrow Q)}{Q}\exists_e \qquad \frac{P\ x_0}{\forall x \cdot\ P\ x}\forall_i \qquad \frac{(\forall x \cdot\ P\ x) \qquad (P\ t \Rightarrow Q)}{Q}\forall_e$$

However, regarding implication, we do not encode $\forall$ rules directly. Instead, we apply the Curry-Howard isomorphism to implication, which interprets a proof of a $\forall$ formula as a function. This approach allows us to reuse the library provided by Lambdapi:

Listing 1.5. Quantifier rules

```
rule π (∀ $f) ↪ Π x, π ($f x); // the proof of a (∀ x) is a function
constant symbol ∃ᵢ [a] p (x:τ a) : π (p x) → π (∃ p);
symbol ∃ₑ [a] p : π (∃ p) → Π q, (Π x:τ a, π (p x) → π q) → π q;
rule ∃ₑ _ (∃ᵢ _ $x $px) _ $f ↪ $f $x $px; // proof simplification
```

Now, we can write some concrete formula, such as the symmetry of equality, and prove it using the induction principle `ind_eq`:

```
symbol eq_sym [a:Set]: π ('∀ (x:τ a), '∀ (y:τ a), x = y ⇒ y = x) ≔
begin
  assume a x y h; // ∀ rule is used here to extract x and y
  refine (ind_eq h (λ u, y = u) (eq_refl y));
end;
```

Translating Typed Set Theory of Event-B in Lambdapi. Event-B sets are seen as an abstract data type characterized by a single observer: set membership. Set operators are introduced as constructors. The application of the observer is defined via a Lambdapi rule. We start by defining, in Lambdapi, the type language of Event-B presented in Paragraph 2.1. Each type operator is interpreted as a `Set` constructor:

```
constant symbol σS: Set; // type of a carrier set S declared in a context
constant symbol σBOOL: Set;
constant symbol σℤ: Set;
 injective symbol σℙ: Set → Set;
 injective symbol σ×: Set → Set → Set; notation σ× infix left 24;
```

Set operators are then defined on this type language and their semantics given via the membership observer. Here, we provide a few rules:

```
symbol ∈ [T:Set] : τ T → τ(σℙ T) → Prop; // set membership signature
symbol ⊆ [T:Set] (e1 e2: τ(σℙ T)): Prop ≔ '∀ x, x ∈ e1 ⇒ x ∈ e2; // derived observer
constant symbol ∩ [T:Set]: τ(σℙ T) → τ(σℙ T) → τ(σℙ T); notation ∩ infix left 23;
rule $x ∈ $s1 ∩ $s2 ↪ $x ∈ $s1 ∧ $x ∈ $s2; // ∩ semantics
constant symbol ℙ [T:Set]: τ(σℙ T) → τ(σℙ(σℙ T)); // power−set signature
rule $e ∈ ℙ $S ↪ $e ⊆ $S; // power−set semantics
```

Relations and Functions. Event-B contains numerous operators about binary relations and defines functions as constrained relations. However, functions and relations are not distinguished by their type: they both behave as sets of ordered pairs. We give a few operator signatures and rules:

```
symbol rel (T1 T2: Set) ≔ τ (σℙ (T1 σ× T2)); // the type of relations
symbol ↔ [T1 T2:Set] (A:τ(σℙ T1)) (B: τ(σℙ T2)): τ(σℙ(σℙ(T1 σ× T2))) ≔ ℙ(A × B);
notation ↔ infix 11; // set of relations
constant symbol dom [T1 T2:Set]: rel T1 T2 → τ (σℙ T1); // domain of a relation
rule $x ∈ dom $r ↪ '∃ y, $x ↦ y ∈ $r; // semantics of dom
constant symbol ⇸ [T1 T2:Set]: τ (σℙ T1) → τ (σℙ T2) → τ (σℙ (σℙ (T1 σ× T2)));
notation ⇸ infix 11; // partial functions
// a partial function is a relation mapping each element to atmost one image
rule $f ∈ ($A⇸$B) ↪ ($f ∈ $A ↔ $B) ∧
    ('∀ x,'∀ y1,'∀ y2, x ↦ y1 ∈ $f ∧ x ↦ y2 ∈ $f ⇒ y1=y2);
```

Event-B defines function application $f(x)$ where f is typed as a relation that must belong to the set of partial functions, and x must be in its domain. As already stated, these properties are proved through the generation of proof obligations. In Lambdapi, function application is defined thanks to the Hilbert ϵ operator provided by the Lambdapi library. However, it would be necessary to transmit the welldefinedness proof to all theorems about function application, which is very hard to manage. Some axioms are thus added to overcome this problem. For example, proving $\mathtt{f(x)} = \mathtt{y} \Rightarrow \mathtt{x} \mapsto \mathtt{y} \in \mathtt{f}$ in Lambdapi would need such an hypothesis but is declared as an axiom for direct use.

4.2 Translating Rodin Proof Trees to Lambdapi

This section presents some of the options currently implemented and discusses issues encountered in the translation of Rodin proof trees to Lambdapi proof scripts. To illustrate our point, we present elements of the translation to Lambdapi of the proof of the mutex invariant preservation built using the Rodin platform (see Paragraph 2.1).

The global idea of the proof tree translation consists in maintaining a strong correspondence between proof steps in both systems. To achieve this, we use a map associating Event-B formulas used as hypotheses to a Lambdapi hypothesis number. Then, our goal is to generate a Lambdapi tactic for each Event-B proof step that faithfully reproduces the side effects of the original tactic. As mentioned in Paragraph 2.1, a tactic can create new proof nodes with new variables, new hypotheses and specific goals. From Lambdapi point of view, the correctness of the rule application must be proved.

Simple Tactics. Some of the Rodin tactics are quite direct to translate to Lambdapi. Some of them are presented in the following table:

Rodin rule	Lambdapi	Rodin rule	Lambdapi
$\dfrac{}{\Gamma, h : p \vdash p}$ (hyp)	refine h	$\dfrac{\Gamma, h : x_i \in T_i \vdash p}{\Gamma \vdash \forall x_1, \ldots, x_n \cdot p}$ ($\forall$goal)	assume $x_1 \ldots x_n$
$\dfrac{h : p, \Gamma \vdash q}{\Gamma \vdash p \Rightarrow q}$ ($\Rightarrow$ goal)	assume h	$\dfrac{\Gamma \vdash p \quad \Gamma \vdash q}{\Gamma \vdash p \wedge q}$ ($\wedge$goal)	apply $\wedge_i$ p q

Derived Rules. For several rules, we introduce theorems in Lambdapi to represent inference[10] or rewriting rules[11] of Rodin. For example, the Rodin rule `DERIV_IMP_IMP` : $P \Rightarrow (Q \Rightarrow R) \;\widehat{=}\; P \wedge Q \Rightarrow R$ is translated to the theorem:

```
symbol and_imp [p1 p2 q: Prop]: π (p1 ⇒ p2 ⇒ q) → π ((p1 ∧ p2) ⇒ q) ≔
begin assume p1 p2 q hi hc; refine (hi (∧e1 p1 p2 hc) (∧e2 p1 p2 hc)) end;
```

Its application allows extracting conjuncts from hypotheses.

[10] https://wiki.event-b.org/index.php/Inference_Rules.

[11] https://wiki.event-b.org/index.php/All_Rewrite_Rules.

N-ary Operators in Rodin. Some operators in Rodin are n-ary, like conjunction, while they are encoded as binary operators in Lambdapi. The current choice is to transform these n-ary expressions in nested binary expressions.

For instance, if the goal to prove is $P_1 \wedge P_2 \wedge P_3$, Rodin generates automatically three sub-goals. For Lambdapi to match this behavior, we build a composition of introduction terms so that its application will ask for the proof of n sub-goals. In presence of the three conjuncts, we generate the tactic `refine (∧ᵢ (P₁ ∧ (P₂ ∧ P₃)) _ ( ∧ᵢ P₂ P₃ _ _) )` which contains three holes, thus generating three sub-goals, as does Rodin tactic.

Advanced Transformations. Some Rodin tactics are rather complex and need specific attention. We point out one of them: the tactic *simplification rewrites* applies a data base of hundreds of equality or equivalence rules. The theorems of the database must be expressed and proved in Lambdapi and their application repeated as much as possible. Furthermore, as we have separated `Prop` from `Set`, equivalence rewriting must be proved as done by Coq `setoid-rewrite` [10], which needs generating a composition of theorem associated to the traversal of each logical connector. For the moment, a few simplifications are supported on if needed basis.

Transformation of the Mutex Invariant Preservation Proof. We have successfully produced a Lambdapi proof for this theorem. The Rodin proof tree contains 59 nodes and the resulting Lambdapi code is a 14 Kb file which is checked by Lambdapi in 0.5 s. The more complex tactic translation is linked to *simplification rewrites* which chains the application of several setoid-rewrite in order to transform $\text{state}^{-1}[\{\text{In}\}]$ into $\neg\text{In} \in \text{ran}(\text{state})$. A (small) part of the resulting proof term is given here:

```
have _H8 : π (¬(In ∈ (ran state ))) { // ¬In∈ran(state)
  refine (∧_{e1}
    (⇔_trans _ (((evb_add In ∅) ◁ (state ~)) = (@∅ (σState σ× σProc))) _
      (SIMP_RELIMAGE_EQUAL_EMPTY ((state ~)) ((evb_add In ∅)))
       ...));
  };
```

5 Conclusion

After a short presentation of Event-B, TLA$^+$ and Lambdapi, we have shown how Event-B models and proofs can be translated to TLA$^+$ and Lambdapi. The first transformation enables importing Event-B proofs and developments in TLA$^+$, while the second provides a way to formally check the correctness of Event-B proofs. Previous work about proof obligations mainly focused on verifying proof rules or translating theorem statements to facilitate the search for new proofs from scratch. In our approach, we can reuse the hints embedded within proofs built using Rodin. However, this work remains preliminary. Rodin prover uses hundreds of rewriting and (sometimes complex) deductions rules that should be taken into account in the translation. Furthermore, it relies on external provers (ad-hoc and SMT) whose proof traces should also be translated to Lambdapi. Lastly, Lambdapi itself currently lacks advanced tactics such as setoid rewriting, propositional solvers, and arithmetic solvers, which are still under development.

References

1. Abrial, J.R.: The B-Book - Assigning Programs to Meanings. Cambridge University Press (1996)
2. Abrial, J.R.: Modeling in Event-B: System and Software Engineering, 1st edn. Cambridge University Press, New York (2010)
3. Abrial, J.R., Butler, M., Hallerstede, S., Hoang, T.S., Mehta, F., Voisin, L.: Rodin: an open toolset for modelling and reasoning in Event-B. Int. J. Softw. Tools Technol. Transf. **12**(6), 447–466 (2010). https://doi.org/10.1007/s10009-010-0145-y
4. Alessio, C.: Reconstruction of TLAPS proofs solved by VeriT in lambdapi. In: Glässer, U., Campos, J.C., Méry, D., Palanque, P.A. (eds.) ABZ 2023. LNCS, vol. 14010, pp. 375–377. Springer, Cham (2023). https://doi.org/10.1007/978-3-031-33163-3_29
5. Assaf, A., et al.: Expressing theories in the λΠ-calculus modulo theory and in the Dedukti system. In: TYPES: Types for Proofs and Programs. Novi SAd, Serbia (2016). https://minesparis-psl.hal.science/hal-01441751
6. Bobot, F., Filliâtre, J.C., Marché, C., Paskevich, A.: Why3: Shepherd your herd of provers. In: Boogie 2011: First International Workshop on Intermediate Verification Languages (2012)
7. Bodeveix, J.-P., Filali, M.: Event-B formalization of event-B contexts. In: Raschke, A., Méry, D. (eds.) ABZ 2021. LNCS, vol. 12709, pp. 66–80. Springer, Cham (2021). https://doi.org/10.1007/978-3-030-77543-8_5
8. Christophe Métayer, L.V.: The Event-B mathematical language (2009). https://webarchive.southampton.ac.uk/deployeprints.ecs.soton.ac.uk/11/4/kernel_lang.pdf
9. CLEARSY: Atelier B Tool (2024). https://www.atelierb.eu/en/
10. Coen, C.S.: A semi-reflexive tactic for (sub-)equational reasoning. In: Filliâtre, J.-C., Paulin-Mohring, C., Werner, B. (eds.) TYPES 2004. LNCS, vol. 3839, pp. 98–114. Springer, Heidelberg (2006). https://doi.org/10.1007/11617990_7
11. Coltellacci, A., Dowek, G., Merz, S.: Reconstruction of SMT proofs with Lambdapi. In: Reger, G., Zohar, Y. (eds.) CEUR Workshop Proceedings, Montréal, Canada, vol. 3725, pp. 13–23 (2024). https://inria.hal.science/hal-04861898
12. Cousineau, D., Doligez, D., Lamport, L., Merz, S., Ricketts, D., Vanzetto, H.: TLA^+ proofs. In: Giannakopoulou, D., Méry, D. (eds.) FM 2012. LNCS, vol. 7436, pp. 147–154. Springer, Heidelberg (2012). https://doi.org/10.1007/978-3-642-32759-9_14
13. Cousineau, D., Dowek, G.: Embedding pure type systems in the lambda-pi-calculus modulo. In: Della Rocca, S.R. (ed.) TLCA 2007. LNCS, vol. 4583, pp. 102–117. Springer, Heidelberg (2007). https://doi.org/10.1007/978-3-540-73228-0_9
14. Deducteam: LambdaPi standard library (2026). https://github.com/Deducteam/lambdapi-stdlib. Accessed 29 Jan 2026

15. Delahaye, D., Dubois, C., Marché, C., Mentré, D.: The BWare project: building a proof platform for the automated verification of B proof obligations. In: Ait Ameur, Y., Schewe, K.D. (eds.) ABZ 2014, vol. 8477, pp. 290–293. Springer, Heidelberg (2014). https://doi.org/10.1007/978-3-662-43652-3_26
16. Grieu, A., Bodeveix, J., Filali, M.: Translating event-B models and development proofs to TLA+. In: Leuschel, M., Ishikawa, F. (eds.) ABZ 2025. LNCS, vol. 15728, pp. 124–142. Springer, Cham (2025). https://doi.org/10.1007/978-3-031-94533-5_8
17. Hansen, D., Leuschel, M.: Translating B to TLA$^+$ for validation with TLC. Sci. Comput. Program. **131**, 109–125 (2016). https://doi.org/10.1016/J.SCICO.2016.04.014
18. Hoang, T.S.: An introduction to the Event-B modelling method. In: Romanovsky, A., Thomas, M. (eds.) Industrial Deployment of System Engineering Methods, pp. 211–236. Springer (2013). http://www.springer.com/computer/swe/book/978-3-642-33169-5
19. Hudon, S., Hoang, T.S., Ostroff, J.S.: The Unit-B method: refinement guided by progress concerns. Softw. Syst. Model. **15**(4), 1091–1116 (2016). https://doi.org/10.1007/S10270-015-0456-2
20. Lamport, L.: TLA$^+$ version 2 a preliminary guide. https://lamport.azurewebsites.net/tla/tla2-guide.pdf. Accessed 18 Feb 2025
21. Lamport, L.: Specifying Systems: The TLA$^+$ Language and Tools for Hardware and Software Engineers. Addison-Wesley Longman Publishing Co. Inc, USA (2002)
22. Rivière, P., Singh, N.K., Aït-Ameur, Y.: Reflexive Event-B: semantics and correctness the EB4EB framework. IEEE Trans. Reliab. **73**(2), 835–850 (2024). https://doi.org/10.1109/TR.2022.3219649
23. Why3, a tool for deductive program verification, GNU LGPL 2.1

Design of Correct by Construction Algorithms by Double Checking Properties

Dominique Méry(✉)

LORIA & Université de Lorraine, Vandœuvre-lès-Nancy, France
dominique.mery@loria.fr

Abstract. Modeling languages such as Event-B and TLA$^+$ share common concepts, including set theory, states, invariance properties, actions, and events. The software environments supporting these languages provide interactive and automatic tools for proving verification conditions generated during model development. In this paper, we use the refinement of Event-B abstract machines to produce a PlusCal algorithm with inductive invariants which are then verified using the ToolBox TLA$^+$ environment by adapting inductive invariants of Event-B machines and checked during the refinement process. The refinement process, particularly the event merging, ensures the production of a final machine with a single event corresponding to the next relation. This relation is then exploited to produce a PlusCal algorithm, which is subsequently verified. The Event-B refinement process guides the analysis phase of algorithm design based on a contract, and TLA$^+$ validates the process itself by checking the inductive invariants inherited from the Event-B step. More precisely, a contract is transformed into an abstract Event-B machine (AEB) with one event prepost, which is transformed into a final Event-B machine (FEB) containing one event Calling, observing the call of an algorithm. We have derived an algorithm, A, from the event Calling. We have integrated it as a PlusCal algorithm with invariants derived from the full refinement chain of Event-B machines. We have checked it using the ToolBox TLA$^+$ tool. Cross-proofs using both Rodin and ToolBox TLA$^+$ definitively validate the correctness of the derived sequential algorithm.

Keywords: Event-B · TLA$^+$ · verification · modelling · correct-by-construction · semantics · sequential algorithms

1 Introduction

The correctness of sequential algorithms is an activity that has been widely studied through numerous works using techniques for proving total or partial correctness properties or absence of runtime errors, such as Hoare logic or Floyd

This work is supported by the grant ANR-19-CE25-0010 (The EBRP Plus Project https://www.irit.fr/EBRP/) from the Agence Nationale de la Recherche (ANR). The document is edited on May 13, 2026.

A. Raschke et al. (Eds.): Egon Börger Festschrift, LNCS 16580, pp. 223–248, 2026.
https://doi.org/10.1007/978-3-032-24494-9_11

method. These techniques were developed as soon as programs and computers appeared [23] and, as soon as they appeared, the question of finding an (inductive) invariant was an element that made these techniques complex to use. The development of verification tools such as model-checking techniques [6] or techniques using proof assistants [4,8,13] or even more sophisticated techniques such as those based on abstract interpretation [7] has made it possible to verify realistic algorithms and programs. To a certain extent, it's a question of finding out how the algorithm or program was constructed, and verification is seen as a *a posteriori* or *posthoc* step in writing an algorithm. However these techniques do not integrate the analysis phase corresponding to the discovery of inductive invariants as well as its checking. The gap between a (semi) formal statement of the contract and the resulting algorithm shoul be filled and may be wide. Another approach so-called *a priori*, promotes the idea of constructing an algorithm while constructing its correctness and implements the correct by construction methodology highlighting the refinement relationship between algorithms or programs, such as the B language for software [3], the Evenvent-B language for reactive systems [2], the refinement calculus [11,18].

In both approaches, the objective is to design a correct algorithm for a given contract using proof techniques and tools. Our idea is to combine the two approaches by using the *a priori* approach during the analysis phase to produce inductive invariants and a transition system corresponding to an algorithm, then to verify the algorithm produced using the second approach. In our case, we will use the Event-B language and the Rodin platform to derive a transition system that is correct by construction and satisfies the contract in question. Then we will use the TLA$^+$ language and its ToolBox TLA$^+$ platform to *replay* proofs of the inductive invariants generated from the intermediate Event-B models in the case of the transition system contained in the final event of the Event-B development. We make the following contributions in this paper:

- The development process of a sequential algorithm from a single event prepost modelling the contract to a single event next modelling a relational expression corresponding to a guarded command in a relational form according to the refinement.
- The relational expression is integrated as an implicit algorithm (init,next) which is translated into a TLA$^+$ module tla(eb3)(init,next))
- the relational guarded expression next is systematically translated into an algorithmic form using a systematic translation in Python.
- The algorithmic form is integrated as a PlusCal algorithm which is translated into a TLA$^+$ module tla(eb3)(PlusCal) enriched with the invariants of the Event-B machines. PlusCal is an algorithmic language associated with TLA$^+$ for expressing sequential or distributed algorithms translated by the platform ToolBox TLA$^+$ into TLA$^+$.
- The integration of Event-B (inductive) invariants in a TLA$^+$ module and the use of ToolBox TLA$^+$ for discharging proof obligations.
- A verification of Event-B constructions by ToolBox TLA$^+$.

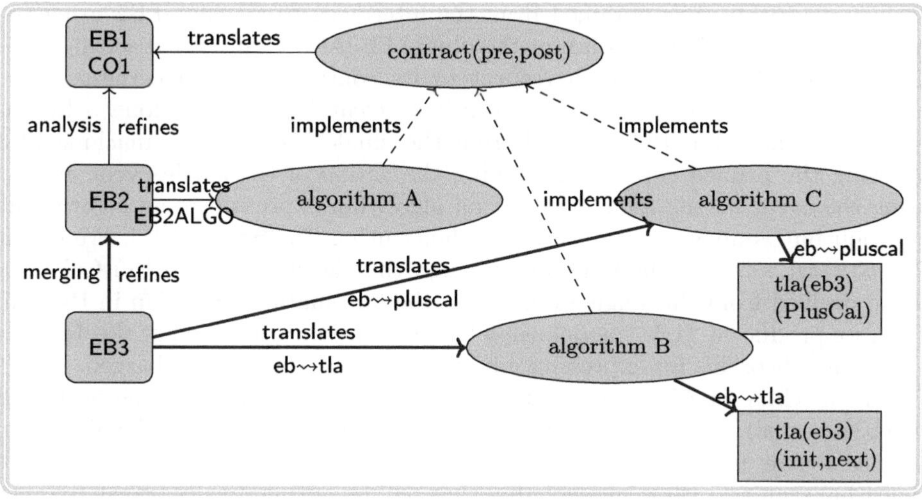

Fig. 1. Transformation and relationship among Event-B machines and TLA^+ specifications (blue for TLA^+ , pink for Event-B , yellow for algorithmic notations, blue lines for current transformations) (Color figure online)

Figure 1 illustrates various points we have dealt with. The process of developing a sequential algorithm begins by translating the contract into a machine EB1 with a single event and using a context where the problem is mathematically defined. The machine EB1 defines the *what* to compute. Then the analysis of the problem continues by refinement to obtain a machine EB2 made up of events which simulate the calculation or how to compute the specified function.. The machine EB2 can be translated into a pseudo-algorithm using the translation rules proposed by Abrial [2] and implemented by the EB2ALGO plugin [21]. The translation is based on two main rules for combining events, leading to a conditional structure or an iterative structure and no rule for sequential composition. These two rules are applied as often as necessary to obtain a structured algorithm. However, no proof of soundness of these rules has been given. The question of preserving semantics and therefore invariants is raised, and it is then necessary to validate the algorithmic solution obtained using other verification tools such as Frama-c [4] or DAFNY [13]. To a certain extent, the benefit of the refinement approach is lost, but the machine EB2 can be *further refined* to obtain only one event in the machine EB3. The meaning of EB3 is to observe the execution of the algorithm sought in the sense of *small-step* semantics [19]. With this strategy of pushing the refinement as far as possible, the invariants previously proven and preserved are maintained and the risks of mistranslation of a transition relation on the preserved concrete variables are reduced. Thus, the objectives of this work are to keep the benefit of the refinement, by continuing the refinement from EB2 with a view to obtaining a single-event machine EB3.

The algorithm A is obtained from the intermediate machine EB2 using the transformations of J.-R. Abrial (or the plugin EB2ALGO) and the resulting algorithm should be checked with respect to its contract: the correctness of the transformations of J.-R. Abrial is intuitively clear but not yet done. Alternatively, the algorithm B is derived from the single event of the machine EB3 by using the primed expression defining the action of the single event and by using the event initialisation. It is not an algorithm expressed in an algorithmic notation but is allows us to check invariants using ToolBox TLA^+ !. We call it $tla(eb3)(init, next)$ in the blue box. Finally, the algorithm C is a PlusCal algorithm derived from the single event using the automatic translation in Python. Then we produce a TLA^+ model using the translation to PlusCal of the ToolBox TLA^+ and theorems for expressing invariance are stated and discharged.

The machine EB3 is used to obtain two TLA^+ modules tla(eb3)(init,next) and tla(eb3)(pluscal). tla(eb3)(init,next) is an *implicit* TLA^+ version of the algorithm seen as a pair init and next and tla(eb3)(pluscal) is an explicit version of the algorithm seen as a PlusCal algorithm that will be automatically translated into a pair init and next by a feature of the ToolBox TLA^+ tool. Each of these two modules is enriched with invariants and mathematical properties extracted from the machines from EB1 to EB3. The chain of refinements from EB1 to EB2 and then to EB3 contains other machines linked by the relation of refinement, and the context CO1 defines sets, constants and properties of the problem being dealt with. The translation eb$\leadsto$tla is described and justified and the TLA^+ modules are verified using the ToolBox TLA^+ platform. The PlusCal algorithm is correct by construction and the invariants are obtained by refinement and validated by the ToolBox TLA^+ tool. The translation of the unique event of EB3 in the form of a PlusCal algorithm is justified using GKAT algebras [20,22].

Our document is organized as follow. Section A reports a short description of Event-B , TLA^+ , our small programming language and programming constructs. In Sect. 2, we give details on our approach to use the merging rule of refinement together with our Event-B models related to the development of sequential programs. Due to space limits, three examples are given in Sect. 3 and illustrate the idea to obtain the so-called final event in the last refinement machine. Section 4 transforms the relational term of the final event into a program of our programming language by justifying the translation using GKAT algebra. Using the generated program, we use TLA^+ for checking that invariants collected during the analysis phase are correct for the PlusCal algorithm. Section 5 is an assessment of our works and we give some feedbacks on the proof process. Section 6 gives possible extensions of this work.

2 First Step: Internalizing Events by Merging

We are now taking the first step in our work, which involves developing the machine EB1 (*prepost*) into the machine EB3 (*call*) via the machine EB2 (*small-steps*). In essence, the machine EB1 expresses the *what* in a single event (following C. Morgan [18] and the specification as action statement), and is a relation

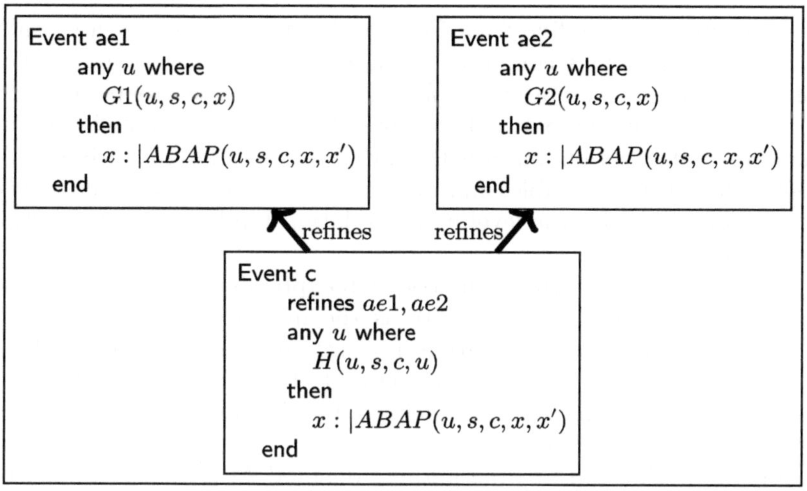

Fig. 2. Fusion of two events

between the initial values or pre-values and the final values or post-values. This relationship is derived from the contract noted pre/post in Fig. 1. The second machine, EB2, is obtained by a series of refinements which enable the calculation process to be implemented. This machine EB2 can be translated into an algorithm using the rules proposed by J.-R. Abrial's rules (see Chap. 15 - Development of sequential programs in [2]) for combining events into a conditional or into an iteration; the rules are implemented in the EB2ALGO tool [21]. The correctness of the algorithm obtained still needs to be proved, so we can use a tool like Frama-C [4,10] and the invariants discovered as we refine EB1 into EB2.

Let us consider a machine CM refining a machine AM. Every concrete event c in CM corresponds ,to an abstract event a and is linked by the relation refines and in a way, we could understand that the number of abstract events is less than the number of concrete events. This is not the case and it is possible to reduce the number of events per refinement by using event merging with very strong assumptions. Thus, by merging two abstract events a1 and a2, we obtain a concrete event c(a1 + a2) which refines the two events, but the condition is that the two abstract events have the same action. The condition is strong but allows us to merge and simplify the concrete models. This possibility requires strong conditions on the actions, which must be identical for all three events. As shown in the diagram in Fig. 2, the guards $G1$ and $G2$ are strengthened by the guard H and the verification condition is very simply the expression of this strengthening: $AX(s, c), I(s, c, x), H(v, s, c, y) \vdash G_1(s, c, x) \vee G_2(s, c, x)$. The conditions for applying this merging are very restrictive, but we will give an example of its application. Restrictions are due to the objective of simple proof obligations to check. In a case study, we used this merging to reduce a set of events to a single event.

Now, we propose to refine from EB2 to obtain events which are usable for merging them. An event e comprises a guard g(e) and an action a(e). For any level of abstraction n, we note a visible variable v and the events of the level n noted E(n). We will note a particular event called skip and is noted skip.n where n is the level of abstraction; Init.n is the initialisation of level n variables for v.n. v.n is generally a list of variables and we can decide to hide a variable of v.$(n-1)$ and is no more visible for the level n. The relationship between two abstraction levels is not the inclusion.

Finally, a level n also includes an assertion expressing the inductive invariant I.n(v.$(n-1)$, v.n)) for $n > 0$. I.0(v.0)) is the inductive invariant of the first abstraction level. An inductive invariant is a state property holding for the initial conditions and preserved by any observed event of the machine. In others words, it us a fixed)point of the operator defined by the initial conditions and the before-after relations of evets.

In summary, a level of abstraction n is denoted A(n) and is defined by the following tuple: $\mathsf{A}(n) = (\mathsf{v}.n, \mathsf{Init}.n, \mathsf{I}.n(\mathsf{v}.(n-1), \mathsf{v}.n), \mathsf{skip}.n, \mathsf{keep}.n, \mathsf{E}(\mathsf{n}))$. keep.$n$ is an event acting at level n and *keeping* the inductive invariant; it is mainly a methodological practise. In the case of A(0), I.n(v. 0) has no free variables of the previous level. We will denote $\mathsf{E}[0..m]$ the set of events of all levels from 0 to m and we will suppose that there is a maximal value m.

The relationship between the events is the refinement denoted $\xrightarrow{ref}$ and we will denote the structure of the events $(\mathsf{E}[0..m], \xrightarrow{ref})$.

The semantics of the refinement relation between two events ae and ce is expressed by the simulation relation with respect to the invariant of the level of ce denoted PO(ae, ce) (see Fig. 3). D. denotes the domain of variables values. The prime notation indicates the next values of a variable.

$$
\begin{array}{l}
TH(s,c), \mathsf{v}.(n-1), \mathsf{v}.n, \mathsf{v}.(n+1) \in \mathsf{D}. \vdash \\
\mathsf{I}.n(\mathsf{v}.(n-1), \mathsf{v}.n) \wedge \mathsf{I}.(n+1)(\mathsf{v}.(n), \mathsf{v}.(n+1)) \wedge \mathsf{ce}(\mathsf{v}.(n+1), \mathsf{v}.(n+1)') \\
\Rightarrow \\
\exists \mathsf{v}.(n-1)', \mathsf{v}.n'.\mathsf{ae}(\mathsf{v}.(n), \mathsf{v}.(n)') \wedge \mathsf{I}.(n+1)(\mathsf{v}.(n)', \mathsf{v}.(n+1)')
\end{array}
$$

Fig. 3. Proof obligation for refinement

The refinement relation $ae \xrightarrow{ref} ce$ is defined by PO(ae, ce) and means that the event ce *simulates* or *refines* ae. The structure of the events $(\mathsf{E}[0..m], \xrightarrow{ref})$ is assumed to be acyclic in our case. We discuss later the acyclicity property and its meaning. We are interested in two cases of refinement:

- the refinement of skip into several events at the more concrete level (splitting)
- the refinement of several events at the abstract level into a single concrete event (merging)

For the case of merging, the abstract events must have the same action acting on the abstract variables and the event resulting from the fusion is then with the same action and with, as a guard, the disjunction of the abstract guards. Thus, if we have events $\mathsf{ae1}, \ldots \mathsf{aep}$ with the common action $\mathsf{a(ae1)} = \ldots = \mathsf{a(aep)} = \mathsf{ca}$, then the concrete event of fusion is defined by the guard $\mathsf{g(ae1)} \vee \ldots \vee \mathsf{g(aep)}$ and by the action ca. The two levels retain the same variables.

Property 1. (Strategy for merging events)

Let be two events ae1 and ae2 such that the two guards are complementary (i.e. $\mathsf{g(ae1)} \Leftrightarrow \neg\mathsf{g(ae2)}$ or $\mathsf{g(ae2)} \Leftrightarrow \neg\mathsf{g(ae1)}$).

- Let cei be the event with the guard $\mathsf{g(aei)}$ and with the action $(\mathsf{g(ae1)} \Rightarrow \mathsf{a(ae1)}) \wedge (\mathsf{g(ae2} \Rightarrow \mathsf{a(ae2)})$. Then cei refines aei.
- Let ce be the event with the guard $\mathsf{g(ae1)} \vee \mathsf{g(ae2)}$. Then ce refines cei by fusion.

The property is important for getting finally one event in a final machine. The cost of this property is no penny since it is a way to combine events for using the merging rule. The set of events with the refinement is an acyclic graph with a first event pre/post and a final event call which is a lattice of events with a top event and a bottom event. Moreover, the event pre/post is refined by the event call. At this point, we have internalized the events and we have obtained a relational term relating the pre-values and post-values of the variables. The relational term can be directly transmated as a Next relation in a TLA^+ module or into an algorithm with the same semantics. It will be our second proposal after the next section. We are now showing what is possible on a case study, when following the first step (Sect. 2) and applying the property 1.

3 Examples of Algorithms

We illustrate the different stages of the methodology by presenting the various texts that make up the models relating to the development of a sequential algorithm from its contract. For each example, we provide the contract, the Event-B model and the TLA^+ model with proofs. The TLA^+ model contains a PlusCal version of the algorithm, the invariant associated with the partial correctness and the proof. We limit our work to partial correctness, but total correctness is a step that we can take with the TLAPS tool and which follows from the Event-B development, particularly with convergent events. The TLAPS tool and the TLA^+ modelling language will make it possible to extend this correctness processing to sequential algorithms. The reader can read the models in the current text or can get models from [14,15].

The logical variables x_0, x, x', x_f concern values of the variable x and the diagram below simply explains why we have introduced them. Natural semantics (nat) is given by the arrow having a label P *above* it to express the execution of P. When P is below, it refers to structural operational semantics (sos). The label pre/post indicates that the pre/post contract has to be established.

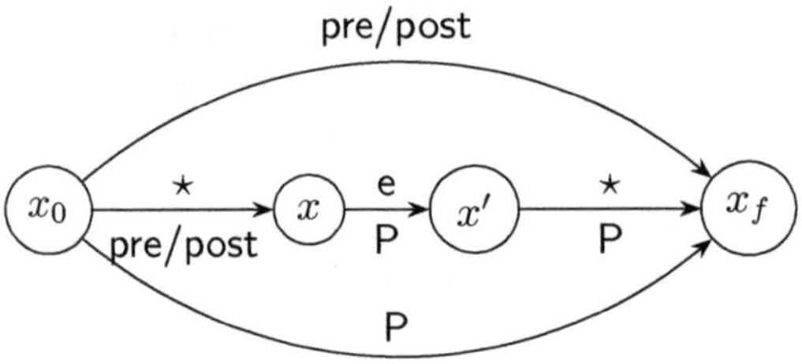

e represents an event observed when the program P is executed. The refinement begins by assuming that P exists but remains unknown and introduces the observed calculation steps in the form of events.

3.1 Incrementing a Positive Value

variables x
———
requires $x_0 \in \mathbb{N}$
ensures $x_f = x_0 + 1$
———

The contract expresses a relationship between the initial values of x, denoted x0, and the final value of x denoted x_f. This relationship simply expresses that the final value of the variable x denoted x_f is the value x_0+1. Obviously, we use the mathematical operator + and we aim to construct, by refinement, a set of events modelling the incrementation of x by 1.

The three components, namely ex1domain, ex1spec and ex1algo (see Fig. 4), are developed in the Rodin platform and form an analysis that allows us to derive a very simple algorithm that increases the initial value of x by 1.

```
CONTEXT ex1domain

 SETS L

 CONSTANTS x0 evt1 Done

 AXIOMS
  @axm1 x0 ∈ ℕ
  @axm2 partition(L, { evt1} , { Done} )
 END
```

From these components, we derive a PlusCal algorithm (automatically or systematically) and use the machine invariants to write a TLA+ module. We then add the correctness theorems.The TLAPS platform is used to translate the PlusCal algorithm into a list of definitions. The TLAPS prover verifies the theorems.

The Event-B model is giving a simple inductive invariant. The TLA module TLAPROOFINC.tla contains the PlusCal algorithm and the proofs. The files are available at https://mery54.github.io/mery/tla/. In this example, the algorithm is very simply obtained by translating the relation $x' = x + 1$ into the form of an assignment x := x + 1. The TLA$^+$ model is obtained very simply by translating the algorithm into a form of TLA$^+$ terms. The TLA$^+$ module is named TLAPROOFINC.tla.

The Event-B model has three levels ex1spec, ex1algo, ex1final. The two last machines are identical and do not require any transformation and it is a special case.

$$i1 \triangleq typeInt(x) \land pc \in \{"Lbl_1", "Done"\}$$
$$i2 \triangleq x \in x0..x0+1$$
$$i3 \triangleq pc = "Done" \Rightarrow x = x0+1$$
$$i4 \triangleq pc = "Lbl_1" \Rightarrow x = x0$$
$$InductiveInvariant \triangleq i1 \land i2 \land i3 \land i4$$

```
MACHINE ex1spec SEES ex1domain
 VARIABLES x done
 INVARIANTS
  @inv1 x ∈ ℤ ∧ done ∈ BOOL
  @inv2 done = TRUE ⇒ x = x0 + 1
 EVENTS
  EVENT INITIALISATION
      then
    @act1 done := FALSE
    @act2 x := x0
  end
  EVENT evt1
      where
    @grd1 done = FALSE
      then
    @act1 x := x0 + 1
    @act2 done := TRUE
  end
 END
```

```
MACHINE ex1algo REFINES ex1spec
  SEES ex1domain
 VARIABLES x pc
 INVARIANTS
  @inv1 pc ∈ L
  @inv3 pc = evt1 ⇒ x = x0
  @inv2 pc = Done ⇒ x = x0 + 1
  @inv5 pc = Done ⇔ done = TRUE
  @inv4 pc = evt1 ⇔ done = FALSE
 EVENTS
  EVENT INITIALISATION
      then
    @act1 x := x0
    @act2 pc := evt1
  end
  EVENT evt1 REFINES evt1
      where
    @grd2 pc = evt1
      then
    @act3 pc := Done
    @act4 x := x + 1
  end
 END
```

Fig. 4. Machines ex1spec and ex1algo

```
MODULE TLAPROOFINC
EXTENDS Naturals, Integers, TLAPS
--------------------------------
CONSTANTS x0
--------------------------------
(* auxiliary definitions *)
typeInt(u) ≜ u ∈ Int
pre(u) ≜ u ∈ Nat
--------------------------------
(* PlusCal algorithm *)
(*
--algorithm inc {
  VARIABLES x = x0;
  {
  evt1 : x := x + 1;
  }
}
*)
--------------------------------
(* INVARIANTS *)
i1 ≜ typeInt(x) ∧ pc ∈ {"evt1","Done"}
i2 ≜ x ∈ x0..x0 + 1
i3 ≜ pc = "Done" ⇒ x = x0 + 1
i4 ≜ pc = "evt1" ⇒ x = x0
InductiveIn VARIANT ≜ i1 ∧ i2 ∧ i3 ∧ i4
--------------------------------
THEOREMS Invariance ≜ Spec ⇒ [] InductiveInvariant
--------------------------------
```

3.2 Maximum of Two Integer Values

The contract expresses a relationship between the initial values of a, denoted a_0, b, denoted b_0 and the final value of r denoted r_f. This relationship simply expresses that the final value of the variable r denoted r_f is the maximum of a_0 and b_0.

variables a, b, r
———————
requires $a_0, b_0, r_0 \in \mathbb{Z}$
ensures $r_f = maximum(a_0, b_0)$
———————

Obviously, we use the mathematical operator maximum and we aim to construct, by refinement, a set of events modelling the assignment of r by the maximum of a and b.

The two axioms, designated as *req1* and *req2*, establish the (pre-) conditions on the data, specifically any two integers. The maximum function is defined by a list of axioms and can be implemented by the $\leq$ operator.

CONTEXT $m0$

CONSTANTS $a0\ b0\ maximum$

AXIOMS
$@req1\ a0 \in \mathbb{Z}$
$@req2\ b0 \in \mathbb{Z}$
$@axm3\ maximum \in \mathbb{Z} \times \mathbb{Z} \rightarrow \mathbb{Z}$
$@axm4\ \forall i, j.\ i \in \mathbb{Z} \wedge j \in \mathbb{Z} \wedge i \leq j \Rightarrow maximum(i \mapsto j) = j$
$@axm5\ \forall i, j.\ i \in \mathbb{Z} \wedge j \in \mathbb{Z} \wedge i > j \Rightarrow maximum(i \mapsto j) = i$
END

The problem is specified by machine *m1*, which has a single event that calculates and stores the maximum in the variable r. The variable done models the end of the calculation. The algorithm knows that done is TRUE at the end of the calculation. The term maximum($a \mapsto b$) denotes the *mathematical* value to be *calculated*, and the refinement will progressively replace the term on the right with a *calculated* value or a value resulting from the *calculation* process itself. The m1 machine expresses a relation between a concrete value contained in r and an abstract or mathematical value denoted maximum($a \mapsto b$) (Table 1).

Table 1. Description of the machines for computing the maximum of two integers

Components	Explanations of components
m0	Constants of our problem which are derived from the contract
m1	Statement of the relationship between the initial values of a and b and the variable r which should contain the maximum of a and b. Moreover, the variables a and b are not modified by the process
m2	The event max is refined into two events according to the sign of a and b
m3	The two events of *m2* are respectively refined by an event which has a form internalising the effect of the events
m4	The actions of each are combined by conjunction with disjunct ion of actions of *m3*. The two events are now sharing the same action but with the correct guard
m5	The final refinement is obtained by applying now the merging rule

The event max is used to observe the calculation of the value maximum of the two values a0 and b0. We then use a transformation of the internalised part to produce an algorithmic expression. Leading to the following PlusCal algorithm (see [14] for the TLA module TLAPROOFMAX2.tla). In Fig. 5 the event *max* in the machine $m5$ is obtained by the merging rule and is corresponding to a conditional statement. The transformation is explained in next Sect. 4 (see [14] for the file TLAPROOFMAX2.tla). The PlusCal algorithm is given:

```
MACHINE m1 SEES m0
 VARIABLES a b r done
 INVARIANTS
  @inv1 a ∈ ℤ ∧ b ∈ ℤ ∧ r ∈ ℤ
  @inv2 done ∈ BOOL
  @inv4 a = a0 ∧ b = b0
  @inv3 done = TRUE
       ⇒ r = maximum(a0 ↦ b0)
 EVENTS
  EVENT INITIALISATION
     then
    @act1 a := a0
    @act2 b := b0
    @act3 done := FALSE
    @act4 r :∈ ℤ
  end
  EVENT max
     where
    @grd1 done = FALSE
     then
    @act1 done := TRUE
    @act2 r := maximum(a ↦ b)
  end
 END
```

```
machine m5 REFINES m4 SEES m0
 VARIABLES a b r done
 INVARIANTS
  theorem @inv1 a = a0 ∧ b = b0
  theorem @inv2 done = TRUE
              ⇒ r = maximum(a0 ↦ b0)
 EVENTS
  EVENT INITIALISATION
     then
    @act1 a := a0
    @act2 b := b0
    @act3 done := FALSE
    @act4 r :∈ ℤ
  end
  EVENT max
  REFINES max − a0 max − b0
     where
    @grd1 done = FALSE
     then
    @act1 a, b, r, done :|
       (done′ = TRUE
       ∧ (a ≤ b ⇒ r′ = b)
       ∧ ( a > b ⇒ r′ = a)
       )
  end
 END
```

Fig. 5. Event-B Machines for the maximum of two integer values

Listing 1.1. PlusCal algorithm for maximum of two integer values

```
--algorithm maximum {
variables a=a0,b=b0,r;
{
w1: if (a < b) {
     r := b;}
     else {
     r := a;
     };
     }
   }
```

3.3 Summing a List of Integer Values

variables $n, v, r, done$

requires $\begin{cases} n_0 \in \mathbb{N} \\ n_0 \neq 0 \\ v_0 \in 1..n_0 \rightarrow \mathbb{Z} \\ r_0 \in \mathbb{Z} \\ done_0 \in \mathbb{BOOL} \end{cases}$

ensures $\begin{pmatrix} r_f = \sum_{k=1}^{n_0} v_0(k) \\ done_f = TRUE \end{pmatrix}$

The contract expresses a relationship between the initial values of n, v and done, denoted n_0, v_0, $done_0$ and the final value of r denoted r_f. This relationship simply expresses that the final value of the variable r denoted r_f is the sum $\sum_{k=1}^{n_0} v_0(k)$. Obviously, we use the mathematical sequence u defining the partial sums of v_0 and we aim to construct, by refinement, a set of events modelling the calculation of u. The context S0 defines the sequence u.

The refinement process starts by the specification namely S1 and leads to the machine S7 which is containing the event final internalizing the computation of the sum.

CONTEXT $S0$
CONSTANTS $n0\ v0\ u$
AXIOMS
$@pre1\ n0 \in \mathbb{N}$
$@pre2\ n0 \neq 0$
$@pre5\ v0 \in 1..n0 \rightarrow \mathbb{Z}$
$@axm1\ u \in 0..n0 \rightarrow \mathbb{Z}$
$@axm2\ u(0) = 0$
$@axm3\ \forall k.\ k \in 1..n0$
$\quad \Rightarrow u(k) = u(k-1) + v0(k)$
end

EVENT $final$ REFINES $final$
where
$@grd2\ done = FALSE$
then
$@act1\ r, i, cu, n, v, done\ :|\ ($
$\quad (i = n$
$\quad \Rightarrow (r' = cu \wedge cu' = cu \wedge i' = i$
$\quad\quad \wedge n' = n \wedge v' = v \wedge done' = TRUE))$
$\quad \wedge (i < n$
$\quad \Rightarrow r' = r \wedge cu' = cu + v(i+1) \wedge i' = i + 1$
$\quad\quad \wedge n' = n \wedge v' = v \wedge done' = done)$
$)$
end

The property 4 is applied for producing the following while program which is a PlusCal algorithm. It is then included into a TLA$^+$ module for checking the correctness of its invariance properties.

Listing 1.2. PlusCal algorithm for summing a vector

```
  --algorithm sumvect  {
variables  n=n0,v=v0,i=0,cu=0,r;
{
w1:while (i # n) {
  w2:cu:=cu+v[i+1]; i:=i+1;
};
w3:r:=cu;
}}
```

The file TLAPROOFVECTSUM.tla is available at [14].

Property 1 is applied and Rodin confirms the soundness of the refinement. The last machine contains only one event which contains the *next* relation of the computing process. Next section proposes a systematic step for generating a (PlusCal) algorithm from the *next* relation.

4 Second Step: Transformations of Generalized Substitutions Using Guarded Kleene Algebra with Tests

4.1 The Guarded Kleene Algebra with Tests

Kleene Algebra with Tests (KAT) [12] combines Kleene Algebra (KA) with Boolean Algebra (BA) and allows dealing with modelling fundamental constructs that arise in programs as sequencing, conditional branching, iteration, ... The main idea is to propose a representation for generating a regular language of traces. In a recent serie of works [22], GKAT is introduced as a fragment of KAT which is a propositional abstraction of imperative while programs. The language GKAT is a restriction of full KAT, but sufficiently expressive to model typical imperative programs. We borrow the definition of GKAT from [22] and make precise the syntax of different constructs. We define the programming language denoted $\mathcal{PL}$ in Sect. A.

Definition 1. [22]

The syntax of GKAT is parameterized by abstract sets of actions Σ and primitive tests T, where Σ and T are disjoint and nonempty, and T is finite. p and q are standing for actions, and t stands for primitive tests. The language consists of Boolean expressions, BExp, and GKAT expressions, Exp, as defined by the following grammar:

$b, c \in BExp ::=$		$e, f, g \in Exp ::=$	
$\|0$	**false**	$\|p \in \Sigma$	**do** p
$\|1$	**true**	$\|b \in BExp$	**assert** b
$\|t \in T$	t	$\|ef$	$e; f$
$\|bc$	b **and** c	$\|e +_b f$	**if** b **then** e **else** f
$\|b + c$	b **or** c	$\|e^{(b)}$	**while** b **do** e
$\|\bar{b}$	**not**b		

At denotes the set of atoms, which define the equivalence class of an expression of the form $c_1.c_2 \ldots c_n \in BExp$ with $c_i \in \{t_i, \overline{t_i}\}$. Each atom represents a truth assignment on T. The interpretation of an expression $e \in Exp$ ($[\![e]\!]$) is a set of *guarded string GS* and GS is the set of finite words $At.(\Sigma.At)^{\star})$.

Intuitively, a non-empty string $\alpha_0 p_1 \alpha_1 \ldots p_n \alpha_n \in GS$ describes a trace of an abstract program: the α_i describe the state of the system at various points in time, starting from an initial state α_0 and ending in a final state α_n , while the actions $p_i \in \Sigma$ are the transitions triggered between the various states. The interpretation $[\![.]\!]$ is defined as the composition of an homomorphism $\varphi(\in \mathsf{Exp} \rightarrow \mathsf{KExp})$ and $[\![K]\!](\in \mathsf{KExp} \rightarrow 2^{GS})$ which is stated as follow $[\![.]\!] = [\![K]\!] \circ \varphi$. The interpretation is providing a language model for each expression e in *Exp*. For instance, $\varphi(e{+_b}f) = be + \bar{b}f$ and **if** b **then** e **else** f is $e +_b f$.

A GKAT expression can be interpreted as a binary relation and an interpretation i is defined as a triple $(State, eval, sat)$ where

- *State* is a set of states
- *eval* is assigning a binary relation $eval(p) \subseteq State \times State$ for each $p \in \Sigma$.
- *sat* is assigning a set $sat(t) \subseteq State$ for each $t \in T$.

The relational model for GKAT expressions is defined as follow. The relational interpretation of e (or p or b) denoted $\mathcal{R}_i(e)$ is a subset of $State \times State$ and is defined as the smallest binary relation satisfying rules:

$$\frac{(s, s') \in eval(p))}{(s, s') \in \mathcal{R}_i(p)}\ R1 \qquad \frac{s \in sat(b)}{(s, s) \in \mathcal{R}_i(b)}\ R2 \qquad \frac{(s, s') \in \mathcal{R}_i(e), (s', s'') \in \mathcal{R}_i(f)}{(s, s'') \in \mathcal{R}_i(e; f)}\ R3$$

$$\frac{s \in sat(b), (s, s') \in \mathcal{R}_i(e)}{(s, s') \in \mathcal{R}_i(e +_b f)}\ R4 \qquad \frac{s \in sat(\bar{b}), (s, s') \in \mathcal{R}_i(f)}{(s, s') \in \mathcal{R}_i(e +_b f)}\ R5$$

$$\frac{s \in sat(b), (s, s') \in \mathcal{R}_i(e), (s', s") \in \mathcal{R}_i(e^{(b)})}{(s, s") \in \mathcal{R}_i(e^{(b)})}\ R6 \qquad \frac{s \in sat(\bar{b})}{(s, s) \in \mathcal{R}_i(e^{(b)})}\ R7$$

These rules are close to the big-step semantics style [19] and we give these rules to show how the programming language can be made abstract. Theorem 2.4 in [22] is recalling that the language model is sound and complete for the relational model. It means that $[\![e]\!] = [\![f]\!] \iff \forall i.\mathcal{R}_i(e) = \mathcal{R}_i(f)$. Our programming language $\mathcal{PL}$ can be modelled in GKAT with actions defined by simple statements as `x:=e` and primitive tests as comparisons. More precisely we can define $\Sigma = \{\mathtt{x} := \mathtt{e} | \mathtt{x} \in Var \wedge e \in AExp\}$ where $AExp$ is the set of arithmetic expressions and $T = \{\mathtt{a\ op\ b} | \mathtt{op} \in Relop \wedge a, b \in AExp\}$ where $Relop$ the set of relational operators. A set of axioms is proposed as for instance $e +_b e = e$ or $e^{(b)} = ee^{(b)} + 1$. GKAT is equipped with a set of equational axioms which is sound (Theorem 3.3 cite [22]). We do not give more details on GKAT algebras and we are using the equational calculus for deriving a term corresponding to a program in our programming language from the relational expression *inside* the last event of our development.

The relational interpretation of a GKAT term e is given by the expression $calR_i(e)$ with the interpretation $i = (State, eval, sat)$. This associates a relation on the set of states *State*. The idea is to associate a term with a relation constructed during refinement and appearing in the final event of the last machine. We keep the sets Σ and T that have been given as examples, and in particular, we give ourselves the assignment terms $\mathtt{x} := \mathtt{e}$ and the classical conditions of an algorithmic language for T.

Definition 2. *(mapping of a binary relation)*
A binary relation R on State can be mapped to a GKAT term e for the interpretation i, if $\mathcal{R}_i(e) = R$ *and we write* $map_i(R) = e$

For instance, the machine S1 of the example (3.3) *Summing a list of integer values* has two events namely init and final1. The GKAT term $\mathcal{GK}[\![S1]\!]$ is defined as init.final1. The interpretation is simply that the event final1 is appearing after the event init. Now the question is to use the relational calculus for structuring the relation term for the event $final7$ (final event of the level 7). We define the following predicates and actions:

- $sat(t) = \{s | s \in State \wedge s(i) < s(n)\}$
- $sat(\bar{t}) = \{s | s \in State \wedge s(i) \geq s(n)\}$
- $eval(e) = \{(s, s') | s, s' \in State \wedge s'(r) = s(cu) \wedge s'(cu) = s(cu) \wedge s'(i) = s(i) \wedge s'(n) = s(n) \wedge s'(v) = s(v) \wedge s'(done) = TRUE\}$
- $eval(f) = \{(s, s') | s, s' \in State \wedge s'(r) = s(cu) \wedge s'(cu) = s(cu) + s(v)(i+1) \wedge s'(i) = s(i) + 1 \wedge s'(n) = s(n) \wedge s'(v) = s(v) \wedge s'(done) = s(done)\}$
- $x = (r, i, cu, n, v, done)$
- $sat(d) = \{s | s \in State \wedge s(d) = TRUE\}$
- $sat(in) = \{s | s \in State \wedge r \in Z \wedge s(i) = 0 \wedge s(cu) = 0 \wedge s(v) = v0 \wedge s(n) = n0 \wedge s(d) = FALSE\}$

We derive the following term from the expression *final7* $\bar{d}.(f)^{(t)}.e.d$ and it is equivalent to $(f)^{(t)}$. e which is **while** t **do** $f; e$. It means that, for each relational expression R(x,x'), one can assign a GKAT term e satisfying the semantical interpretation i $\mathcal{R}_i(e)(s,s') = R(x,x')$ where $s(x) = x$ and $s'(x) = x'$. Following the Definition 2, $map_i(final7) = \bar{d}.(f)^{(t)}.e.d =$ **while** t **do** $f;e$. The final set is to add the initialisation in to obtain the term $in.$**while** t **do** $f;e$. The body of the loop is f and is obtained by mapping according to our assumption. The term d is mapping the relation (TRUE,TRUE) for the variable done of the machines. d or $\bar{\mathsf{d}}$ are expressing the control of the loop and finally are disappearing when the structures are apprearing. In fact, they are playing the role of hidden or implicit variables. We are considering the different properties that we can use for deriving a program from a relational term.

4.2 Mapping Events to Programming Constructs

We consider the case of a relational expression of the form $x' = E(x)$, which may or may not be translated into a programming language. We therefore define the term $f = \mathtt{x} := \mathtt{e(x)}$, which corresponds to the following semantic relation $\mathcal{R}_i(f)(s,s') \stackrel{def}{=} x' = e(x)$.

Property 2. Assignment

$f = \mathtt{x} := \mathtt{e(x)}$ is a sound program for the interpretation i: $\mathcal{R}_i(f)(s,s') \stackrel{def}{=} x' = e(x)$ where the generalized substitution is $x : |(x' = e(x)))$.

In the same way, two relationships can be structured using a complementary condition to produce a conditional program. However, the transformation should be guided to avoid a confusion with conditions of an iteration. At this point, we should use the variable called done which is introduced at the first machine. The variable done exresses the control of the iteration and we should introduce a new variable done2 for controling another iteration but we will discuss the question of nested structure in the next subsection. The next property assumes that neither A nor B modify the variable done.

Property 3. Conditional

Let a be a sound program for the interpretation i: $\mathcal{R}_i(a)(s,s') \stackrel{def}{=} A(x,x')$ and b be a sound program for the interpretation i: $\mathcal{R}_i(b)(s,s') \stackrel{def}{=} B(x,x')$. Let g be a sound test for the interpretation i: $\mathcal{R}_i(g)(s,s') \stackrel{def}{=} G(x)$. We assume that the variable done remained false while choosing one of the branch. Then $a +_g b$ is a sound program for the interpretation i: $\neg done \wedge done' \wedge (G(x) \Rightarrow A(x,x')) \wedge (\neg G(x) \Rightarrow B(x,x'))$.

The property 3 expresses a program using two notations $x : |A(x,x')$ and $x : |B(x,x')$ which express specifications. Obviously the goal of the refinement is to reduce at much as possible those expressions to a *computable* statement. In our case, we re-apply the transformation on A and B. Now we consider the transformation for getting an iteration.

Property 4. Iteration

Let a be a sound program for the interpretation i: $\mathcal{R}_i(a)(s,s') \stackrel{def}{=} A(x,x')$ and b be a sound program for the interpretation i: $\mathcal{R}_i(b)(s,s') \stackrel{def}{=} B(x,x')$, g a sound test for the interpretation i: $\mathcal{R}_i(g)(s,s') \stackrel{def}{=} G(x)$. We assume that the relational expression is $\neg done \wedge (G(x) \Rightarrow A(x,x')) \wedge (\neg G(x) \Rightarrow done' \wedge B(x,x'))$. Then the following GKAT expression $w = (a)^g; b$ is a sound program for the interpretation i.

The status of done is changing while we have transformed our relational expression into a GKAT expression. It is clear that the variable done is no more usefull for expressing the control.

Now we apply the properties for our example to get a complete processing of the case studies.

Example 1. (3.1) In the case of one assignment, the GKAT expression is simply $init.[\mathtt{x} := \mathtt{x} + 1]$ where $sat(init) = \{x0 | x0 \in \mathbb{N}\}$.

Example 2. (3.2)
The computing of the maximal values of two integer values is applying the conditional property and we obtain $init(maxb +_b maxa)$ where $sat(init) = \{(a0, b0, FALSE)\}$, $\mathcal{R}_i(maxa)(s,s') \stackrel{def}{=} \bar{c}.r := a$, $\mathcal{R}_i(maxb)(s,s') \stackrel{def}{=} c.r := b$, $eval(c) = \{(s,s) | s(a) \leq s(b)\}$.

Example 3. (3.3)
Summing a list of integer values is now considering the iteration property and we obtain $inita^{(c)}b$ where $sat(init) = \{(n0, v0, FALSE, 0, 0, ?)\}$, $\mathcal{R}_i(a)(s,s') \stackrel{def}{=} cu := cu + v(i+1); i := i+1$, $\mathcal{R}_i(b)(s,s') \stackrel{def}{=} c.r := cu; done := TRUE$, $eval(c) = \{(s,s) | s(i) < s(n)\}$.

We justified the translation of the events final into an algorithm by using GKAT algebra. We also used the TLAPM tool to prove the constructed algorithms. In short, we validated proofs of invariants verified by Rodin.

4.3 Structure with Mapping

We have developed simple examples where the body of the loop was straightforwardly translated into an algorithmic expression, essentially assignments. In general, the body of the loop can consist of some assignments or one conditional or a sequence of these elements. The insertion sort algorithm, which inserts the value t(i) in the right place between 0 and i, is a good example. The function `insertion` shifts the values as long as the value v is smaller than the current value of the array t and it can be developed from a contract characterizing the functionalities of the insertion algorithm or it can be retrieved in our library including Event-B models as well as TLA^+ modules. We need to simplify the development process and to promote the reusability of existing algorithms in our reasoning. We illustrate the ideas of reusability by considering a simple case study, which is the creation of a table of the first n squares (

0	1	2	3	4	5
0	1	4	9	16	25

for $n = 5$). First at all, we have to build an array a of values satisfying the condition that $\forall i.i \in dom(a) \Rightarrow a(i) = i * i$ or equivalently, the result r is set to a at the end of the process.

The contract is stating that the result r_f is set to a where a is defining the planned computed list of n_0 square values. n_0 is the input values. The context LP0 lists the usefull mathematical notations and the machine LP6 completes the refinement by merging the events into a unique event final_lp which contains the relational term which is then translated into a GKAT term: $lp \stackrel{def}{=} \bar{d}.in.p^{(c)}.q.d$ where

```
variables r,n
________
requires
  n0 ∈ ℕ
  r0 ∈ 0..n0 → ℤ
ensures
  rf = a
________
```

- $State = (done, r, aa, i) \rightarrow BOOL \times (0..n0 \twoheadrightarrow \mathbb{Z} \times \mathbb{Z}) \times (0..n0 \twoheadrightarrow \mathbb{Z} \times \mathbb{Z}) \times \mathbb{Z})$
- $sat(in) = \{(FALSE, ?, \varnothing, 0)\}$
- $\mathcal{R}_i(d)(s, s') \stackrel{def}{=} \{(s, s')|s, s' \in State \wedge s' = s \wedge s(d) = TRUE\}$
- $\mathcal{R}_i(p)(s, s') \stackrel{def}{=} \{(s, s')|s, s' \in State \wedge s'(i) = s(i) + 1 \wedge s'aa) = s(aa) \cup \{i + 1 \mapsto power2(i + 1)\}$
- $\mathcal{R}_i(r)(s, s') \stackrel{def}{=} \{(s, s')|s, s' \in State \wedge s'(r) = s(aa)\}$
- $\mathcal{R}_i(c)(s, s') \stackrel{def}{=} \{(s, s')|s, s' \in State \wedge s' = s \wedge s(i) < n0\}$

```
CONTEXT LP0
 CONSTANTS n0 a power2
 AXIOMS
  @axm1 n0 ∈ ℕ
  @axm2 a ∈ 0..n0 → ℕ
  @axm3 ∀ k. k ∈ 0..n0
            ⇒ a(k) = k ∗ k
  @axm4 power2 ∈ ℕ → ℕ
  @axm5 ∀ n. n ∈ 0..n0
            ⇒ power2(n) = a(n)
          // pre/post for power2P6
```

The function power2 is defined in the context and is used in the machines LP1 to LP7 to give the specification, i.e. the what.
The development of the function power2 is carried out very easily and leads to the machine POWER28 whose event final_power2 carries out the calculation of the function power2. We apply the same technique to extract an iteration from the relational term of the event final_power28 of the machine POWER28. $power2 \stackrel{def}{=} \bar{d}.in2.u^{(v)}.w.d$ where

- $State = (ok, r, k, cv, cw) \rightarrow BOOL \times \mathbb{Z} \times \mathbb{Z}) \times \mathbb{Z} \times \mathbb{Z}$
- $sat(in2) = \{(FALSE, 0, 0, 0, 0)\}$
- $\mathcal{R}_i(ok)(s, s') \stackrel{def}{=} \{(s, s')|s, s' \in State \wedge s' = s \wedge s(ok) = TRUE\}$
- $\mathcal{R}_i(u)(s, s') \stackrel{def}{=} \{(s, s')|s, s' \in State \wedge s'(k) = s(k) + 1 \wedge s'(cv) = s(cv) + s(cw) + 1 \wedge s'(cw) = s(cw) + 2\}$

- $\mathcal{R}_i(w)(s,s') \stackrel{def}{=} \{(s,s')|s,s' \in State \wedge s'(r) = s(cv)\}$
- $\mathcal{R}_i(v)(s,s') \stackrel{def}{=} \{(s,s')|s,s' \in State \wedge s' = s \wedge s(k) < x\}$

EVENT $final\_lp$ REFINES $computing5\ power5$
where
@$grd1\ done = FALSE$
then
@$act1\ i, r, aa, done$:|
$(i = n0 \Rightarrow done' = TRUE \wedge r' = aa)$
$\wedge\ (i < n0 \Rightarrow i' = i+1 \wedge aa' = aa \cup \{i+1 \mapsto power2(i+1)\})$
end

EVENT $final\_power2$ REFINES $computing\ step$
where
@$grd1\ ok = FALSE$
then
@$act1\ r,\ k,\ cv,\ cw,\ ok$:|
$(k = x \Rightarrow r' = cv \wedge ok' = TRUE \wedge k' = k \wedge cv' = cv \wedge cw' = cw)$
$\wedge$
$(k < x \Rightarrow r' = r \wedge ok' = ok \wedge k' = k+1 \wedge cv' = cv + cw + 1 \wedge cw' = cw + 2)$
end

We summarise the various stages followed and the different models developed with the Rodin platform:

$lp \stackrel{def}{=} in.p^{(c)}.q$ defines the following iteration

```
i := 0; aa(0) := 0;
while i < n0 do
   aa(i + 1) : = power2(i + 1);
   i := i + 1                      ;
od
r := aa
```

$power2 \stackrel{def}{=} in2.u^{(v)}.w$ defines the iteration

```
k := 0; cv := 0; cw := 0;
while k < x do
   cv := cv + cw + 1; cw := cw + 2;
   k := k + 1                      ;
od
r := cv
```

The function power2 had been developed to use the EB2ALGO plugin and we simply continued the refinement process to obtain the event final_power28. It is clear that the call to the function power2 must be legitimate and it is clear that a proof obligation must necessarily be produced and verified.

5 Assessment

Summary. We have presented work validating the development of sequential algorithms using the correct-by-construction paradigm. Our approach is to co-model the development of sequential algorithms using the modelling language and its tool among Event-B and TLA$^+$ by considering the most appropriate for the task at hand. Our methodology based on Event-B and Rodin produces a sequence of checked Event-B machines, starting with a machine with a single event prepost and ending with a machine with a single event final . This approach capitalises on a very expressive inductive invariant, and the translation of each final event is validated by the transformation via GKAT algebra. This activity leads to the creation of an algorithm that is translated into PlusCal. Finally, the process continues with a verification of the invariant collected from the Event-B machines using TLAPM and the automatic translation of the PlusCal algorithm into a sequence of TLA$^+$ definitions.

Proofs Learning Process. We have not mentioned the proof work, either with Rodin or with ToolBox TLA$^+$, because we're very familiar with the Rodin platform and less with ToolBox TLA$^+$. However, we had to learn the ToolBox TLA$^+$ proof tool from scratch, which require us to write more details and adapt to the rigour of Lamport's proof style. The set-theoretical languages are not identical and we have to mind the user on the two different languages and styles. Event-B is using a typed set-theoretical dialect focusing on sets with generalized substitution as updating operation of states and functions are functional relations. TLA$^+$ is an untyped set-theoretical dialect focusing on total functions and is using a definition mechanism with a special notation for variables namely primed and unprimed instance of variable; it provides a way to specify set of traces according to TLA$^+$. Both languages have advantages and are supported by tools. We have used Event-B entities for a first expression of the contract and the collection of invariants appearing during the progressive and safe refinement. A first comment is that TLA$^+$ is providing modules for organizing a list of definitions with a proof style supporting the statement of (temporal) specification, theorems and proofs. However, Event-B and its environment Rodin generate a list of proof obligations that make the proof of inductive invariants more efficient and we have translated the proof obligations in the TLA$^+$ module. The lemmas are defined as follows:

- eventipoj is the proof obligation called `eventi/invj/INV` which is listed in the tool Rodin .
- eventipoj is defined as a lemma.
- proof of eventipoj is duplicated and is generally automatic in ToolBox TLA$^+$.

The proof process in Rodin is driven by refinement and by the progressive discovery of invariants; the proof process in ToolBox TLA$^+$ is a checking of the inductive invariants obtained from the Event-B models. We use Event-B for discovering the inductive invariants and the last Event-B machine and then we move to TLA$^+$ for verifying two TLA$^+$ specifications derived from the last Event-B machine according to our Fig. 1. The list of case studies should be increased and it is clear that the proof effort remains important.

Semantics Preserving Transformations. The learning process for ToolBox TLA$^+$ was facilitated by the *SM* mode[1].The TLA$^+$ modules with the proofs are avail-

[1] A call to our friend Stephan Merz when we encountered issues with TLAPM. His scientific and geographical proximity enabled us to progress more easily.

able on the link [17], just as the Event-B machines are available on the link [16,17]. Validation with TLAPM corrected an invariant that had been incorrectly extracted from the Event-B machines.The advantage of first running a phase with Rodin and then a phase with TLAPM is that the invariant is, in principle, correct, except for one translation error. It is clear that Rodin's refinement relation ensures the systematic development of sequential algorithms. We know that obtaining a single final event containing an algorithm defined as a guarded command is the key point. This guarded command is defined as a relationship between the pre-values and post-values of variables. We have placed the models developed on two links for the TLA$^+$ [16] models and for the Event-B [17] models. In addition to using the tools of the two languages, we also wanted to give a stricter version of the preservation of the semantics of the model noted EB2 in an algorithm according to the rules of J.-R. Abrial and the tool EB2ALGO [21]. It therefore seemed important to us to continue the refinement as far as possible and to internalise the relationship made up of all the events into a single event. This single event is obtained by refinement and all that remains is to focus on restructuring the relationship into an algorithm using GKAT algebras.

6 Conclusion and Future Works

In the previous section, we assess our works and our difficulties when integrating both modelling languages. We have mentioned the work of translating models into TLA$^+$ [9] and this will undoubtedly be a step extending this translation in order to facilitate the work that we have done partly interactively. We have studied the feasibility of such an approach. We can also enrich the proof process of TLA$^+$ with Event-B strategies to simplify the proof process. A preliminary tool for translating the last Event-B models into a PlusCal has been sketched in a programming project and is under develoment. Future works will improve the translation of Event-B models into TLA$^+$ modules and will extend the use of GKAT terms to improve the analysis of models and algorithms.

A Summary on the Two Modelling Languages and Programming Constructs

A.1 Summary on Event-B

Event-B is a correct-by-construction, stated-based formal modelling language for system design [2]. First-order logic (FOL) and set theory underpin the Event-B modelling language. The design process consists of a series of refinements of an abstract model (specification) leading to a final concrete model. Refinement progressively contributes to add design decisions to the system. We are not considering the refinement relation in this paper. Three components define Event-B models: *Contexts*, *Machines*, and *Theories*. However, we will not use *Theories* and will not describe this concept.

A *Context* (Fig. 6) is the static part of a model. It is used to set up definitions, axioms, and theorems needed to describe required concepts. *Carrier*

MACHINE
  a
REFINES
  am
SEES
  co
VARIABLES
  x
INVARIANTS
  $I(s, c, x)$
THEOREMS
  $S(s, c, x)$
VARIANT
  $V(s, c, x)$
EVENTS
Event INIT
  BEGIN
    $x :|(IP(c, s, x'))$
  END ...
Event e
  ANY α
  WHERE
    $G(s, c, \alpha, x)$
  THEN
    $x :|(P(s, c, \alpha, x, x'))$
  ENDEND

CONTEXTS
  co
EXTENDS
  aco
SETS
  s
CONSTANTS
  c
AXIOMS

$$AX(s,c) = \left[\begin{array}{l} \ldots \\ ax : ax(s,c) \\ \ldots \end{array}\right.$$

THEOREMS

$$TH(s,c) = \left[\begin{array}{l} \ldots \\ th : th(s,c) \\ \ldots \end{array}\right.$$

END

(1) *Theorems(AX)* $AX(s, c) \vdash th(s, c)$
(2) *Theorems(TH)* $AX(s, c), I(s, c, x) \vdash S(s, c, x)$
(3) *Initialisation(INIT)*
  $AX(s, c), IP(s, c, x') \vdash I(s, c, x')$
(4) *Invariant(INV)*
  $AX(s, c), I(x), G(s, c, \alpha, x), P(s, c, \alpha, x, x')$
  $\vdash I(s, c, x')$
(5) *Feasibility(FIS)*
  $AX(s, c), I(s, c, x), G(s, c, \alpha, x)$
  $\vdash \exists x' \cdot P(s, c, \alpha, x, x')$

Fig. 6. Event-B structures: Context & Machine and Proof Obligations

sets s defining algebraically new types (possibly constrained in axioms or other extending contexts), *constants* c, *axioms* $AX(s, c)$, and *theorems* $TH(s, c)$ are introduced.

A *machine* (Fig. 6) describes the dynamic part of a model as a transition system. A set of possibly parameterised and/or guarded events (transitions) modifying a set of state variables (state) represents the core concepts of a machine. *Variables* x, *invariants* $I(s, c, x)$, *theorems* $S(s, c, x)$, *variants* $V(x)$, and *events* e (possibly guarded by G and/or parameterised by α) are defined in a machine. *Invariants* and *theorems* formalise system safety properties while *variants* define convergence properties (reachability).

Before-After Predicates (BAP) express state variables changes using prime notation x' to record the new value of a variable x after a change. The *"becomes such that"* :| substitution is used to define the next (transition or event) value of a state variable. We write $x :| P(c, s, \alpha, x, x')$ to express that the next value of x (denoted by x') satisfies the predicate $P(s, c, \alpha, x, x')$ defined on before and after values of variable x. When a parameter α is involved in a variable the *BAP* is expressed as $x :\mid P(s, c, \alpha, x, x')$.

To establish the correctness of an Event-B machine, POs (automatically generated from the calculus of substitutions) need to be proved.

The main POs, relevant for this paper, are listed in the table of Fig. 6. They require to demonstrate the context and machine theorems (1,2), initialisation (3), invariant preservation (4), event feasibility (5).

Rodin[2] is an open source, Eclipse-based Integrated Development Environment for modelling in Event-B. It offers resources for model editing, automatic PO generation, project management, refinement, proof, model checking, model animation, and code generation. Event-B's theories extension is available in the form of a plug-in, developed for the Rodin platform. Many provers like predicate provers, SMT solvers, are plugged into Rodin.

A.2 Summary TLA$^+$

TLA/TLA$^+$ is a modelling language based on set theory and the temporal logic of actions. It is extended by a PlusCal concurrent programming language which is present in the texts as specialised comments. A dedicated environment supports this language and provides an editor, a model-checker and a prover. The main target of TLA/TLA$^+$ concerns distributed algorithms, but the language can also be used to describe reactive systems. TLA/TLA$^+$ allows you to describe both the system and its specification in assertional form. Another UNITY framework [5], proposed by Chandy and Misra, can also be used to model distributed algorithms. However, it uses a simple programming language based on the notion of actions and a separate temporal language.

An action is defined as a relationship between the before and after values of variables called flexible variables. This notation is also used in eventb, but the semantics of traces is implicit. Finally, TLA/TLA$^+$ provides a means of defining fairness hypotheses and equity assumptions on actions to express specific modelling situations. A specification of Φ is given by a list of flexible variables x, initial conditions Init(x), the transition relation Next(x,x') and a liveness expression LIVE: $\Phi \stackrel{def}{=} \mathsf{Init}(x) \wedge \Box[\mathsf{Next}]_x \wedge \mathsf{LIVE}$ where $[\mathsf{Next}]_x$ stands for $\mathsf{Next} \vee x = x'$ and means that each *transition* step is either a *system* step or a *stuttering* step. Abadi and Lamport [1] add an important dimension for a methodology that incorporates refinement over traces. Since TLA/TLA$^+$ is expressing any entity as a logical one, refinement of traces is defined by some logical conditions.

A TLA$^+$ model is defined by a collection of definitions as set-theoretical notations, predicates, actions as relations, specification or temporal properties as *safety* ($\Box$) properties or *liveness* ($\leadsto$) properties. The structure of a TLA/TLA$^+$ model is based on syntactical entities called *modules*. A module is a syntactical structure listing declarations (constants, variables), definitions ($name \triangleq expressions$), specifications ($name \triangleq Init \wedge [Next]_{vars}$ where $Init$

[2] http://www.event-b.org/index.html.

defines the initial conditions of the variables *vars* and *Next* defines the next relation of a given system). In fact, a module is a comprehensive entity that defines concepts and presents theorems, which must be proven. A proof is a structured expression that states the text of the proof and can be verified by the dedicated tool, namely TLAPM. Finally, an algorithm can be expressed in a format called PlusCal, which is the ideal way to describe sequential processes that communicate via shared variables. PlusCal is an algorithmic language immersed in TLA$^+$ via a comment with a header of the form `(* -algorithm ...*)`. The advantage of the PlusCal language is that you can use the features of TLA$^+$ without having to master the translation of an algorithm into TLA$^+$.

A.3 Programming Constructs

Programming constructs are classical constructs as assignment ($\mathsf{v} := \mathsf{f}_{ell,\ell'}(\mathsf{v})$), skip statement skip, conditional statement (if cond(v) S_1 else S_2 fi) and iterative statement r (while cond(v) do S od). We use these constructs for expressing programs or algorithms which are annotated possibly by labels.

```
ℓ0 :
k := 0;
ℓ1 :
co := 0;
ℓ2 :
while (k < n) do
  ℓ3 :
    if (k %2  ==  0)
  ℓ4 :
      co := co + k + 1;
    fi;
  ℓ5 :
    k := k + 1;
od;
  ℓ6 :
ro := co;
  ℓ5 :
```

There different ways to annotate algorithms. One can assign a label $\ell \in L$ to each statement:

- $\mathsf{v} := \mathsf{f}_{ell,\ell'}(\mathsf{v})$ is labelled as follow
  ℓ :
  $\mathsf{v} := \mathsf{f}_{\ell,\ell'}(\mathsf{v})$;
- if cond(v) S_1 else S_2 fi is labelled as follow
  ℓ :
  if cond(v) S_1 else S_2 fi
- while cond(v) do S od is labelled as follow
  ℓ :
  while cond(v) do S od

The annotation process uses one label at most one time. For instance, the following annotation of a small algorithm is a small example in the left box.

Each pair of successive labels ℓ, ℓ' is interpreted by a condition denoted $\mathsf{cond}_{\ell,\ell'}(v)$ and an assignment $\mathsf{v} := \mathsf{f}_{\ell,\ell'}(\mathsf{v})$. A flowchart can be derived following the expression: $\textcircled{\ell} \xrightarrow{\mathsf{cond}_{\ell,\ell'}(v) \rightarrow \mathsf{v}:=\mathsf{f}_{\ell,\ell'}(\mathsf{v})} \textcircled{\ell'}$. In our paper, we assume that the programming language is $\mathcal{P}$ and one can derive a flowchart from the annotated algorithmic notation. Moreover, we use a program of $\mathcal{P}$ as a (sequential) PlusCal program and later in the text Sect. 4, we will reformulate what is a program. We do not define a specific language for expressing contracts and we are using either the Event-B modelling language or the TLA$^+$ language.

References

1. Abadi, M., Lamport, L.: The existence of refinement mappings. Theor. Comput. Sci. **82**(2), 253–284 (1991). https://doi.org/10.1016/0304-3975(91)90224-P
2. Abrial, J.R.: Modeling in Event-B: System and Software Engineering. Cambridge University Press (2010)
3. Abrial, J.: The B-Book - Assigning Programs to Meanings. Cambridge University Press (1996). https://doi.org/10.1017/CBO9780511624162
4. Baudin, P., et al.: The dogged pursuit of bug-free C programs: the FRAMA-C software analysis platform. Commun. ACM **64**(8), 56–68 (2021). https://doi.org/10.1145/3470569
5. Chandy, K.M., Misra, J.: Parallel Program Design A Foundation. Addison-Wesley Publishing Company (1988). iSBN 0-201-05866-9
6. Clarke, E.M., Henzinger, T.A., Veith, H., Bloem, R. (eds.): Handbook of Model Checking. Springer, Cham (2018)
7. Cousot, P.: Abstract Interpretation. The MIT Press (2021). iSBN 9780262044905
8. Filliâtre, J.C., Paskevich, A.: Why3 – where programs meet provers. In: LNCS. LNCS, vol. 7792. Springer, Rome (2013). https://inria.hal.science/hal-00789533
9. Hansen, D., Leuschel, M.: Translating B to TLA+ for validation with TLC. Sci. Comput. Program. **131**, 109–125 (2016). https://doi.org/10.1016/j.scico.2016.04.014, https://www.sciencedirect.com/science/article/pii/S0167642316300235. Abstract State Machines, Alloy, B, TLA, VDM and Z (ABZ 2014)
10. Kosmatov, N., Prevosto, V., Signoles, J. (eds.): Guide to Software Verification with Frama-C Core Components, Usages, and Applications. Springer, Cham (2024)
11. Kourie, D.G., Watson, B.W.: The Correctness-by-Construction Approach to Programming Book. Springer, Cham (2012). https://doi.org/10.1007/978-3-642-27919-5
12. Kozen, D.: Kleene algebra with tests. ACM Trans. Program. Lang. Syst. **19**(3), 427–443 (1997). https://doi.org/10.1145/256167.256195
13. Leino, R.: The Dafny programming and verification language (2024). https://dafny.org
14. Méry, D.: TLA^+Corner. https://mery54.github.io/mery/tla/
15. Méry, D.: Event-B corner (2025). https://mery54.github.io/mery/eventb/
16. Méry, D.: Modelling with Event-B (2025). https://mery54.github.io/mery/eventb
17. Méry, D.: Modelling with TLA^+ (2025). https://mery54.github.io/mery/tla
18. Morgan, C.: Programming from Specifications. Prentice Hall International Series in Computer Science, 2nd edn. Prentice Hall (1994)
19. Plotkin, G.D.: A structural approach to operational semantics. Technical report DAIMI FN-19, Aarhus University, Department of Computer Science (1981)
20. Rooduijn, J., Kozen, D., Silva, A.: A cyclic proof system for guarded Kleene algebra with tests (full version) (2024). https://arxiv.org/abs/2405.07505
21. Singh, N.K.: EB2ALGO (2024). Plugin Rodin
22. Smolka, S., Foster, N., Hsu, J., Kappé, T., Kozen, D., Silva, A.: Guarded Kleene algebra with tests: verification of uninterpreted programs in nearly linear time. Proc. ACM Program. Lang. **4**(POPL), 1–28 (2019). https://doi.org/10.1145/3371129
23. Turing, A.: On checking a large routine. In: Conference on High-Speed Automatic Calculating Machines. University Mathematical Laboratory, Cambridge (1949)

Structure as Semantics: Impedance Modeling and Retrenchment in Cyber-Physical Systems

John Baugh[1], Richard Banach[2](✉), and Eunsuk Kang[3]

[1] North Carolina State University, Raleigh, NC 27695, USA
jwb@ncsu.edu
[2] The University of Manchester, Manchester M13 9PL, UK
richard.banach@manchester.ac.uk
[3] Carnegie Mellon University, Pittsburgh, PA 15213, USA
eunsukk@andrew.cmu.edu

Abstract. We address a gap in CPS verification: current methods focus on temporal behavior but give little support for reasoning about *physical structure* and its interface guarantees. We render structure as first class by using *impedance* as the interface semantics, so models from different formalisms can be compared on equal terms and design steps judged by their boundary effect. This algebraic view suits state-based tools, enabling reasoning about physics without solving differential equations. We mechanize the approach in Alloy, deriving composition theorems for series-parallel networks and recovering standard circuit laws. A case study shows how impedance-based contracts support stepwise design via *retrenchment*, with bounded approximations that preserve boundary behavior. The method applies across physical domains, providing a uniform interface semantics for CPS models and tools.

Keywords: Cyber-physical systems · impedance modeling · interface semantics · retrenchment · refinement · Alloy · formal verification

1 Introduction

Cyber-Physical Systems (CPS) represent an increasingly important class of systems in engineering and computing, with applications spanning transportation, infrastructure, robotics, and manufacturing [4,7,36,38]. These systems combine discrete computational logic with continuous physical processes. Ensuring their correctness requires methods that support reasoning not only about software but also about physics and their interaction [1,15,35].

Accounting for this interaction has typically proceeded in one of two ways. One is the use of hybrid automata or similar frameworks in which continuous behavior, governed by differential equations, is punctuated by discrete transitions. This offers a unified behavioral semantics at the level of traces and reachability, and connects well with verification tools. The other is to discretize that

A. Raschke et al. (Eds.): Egon Börger Festschrift, LNCS 16580, pp. 249–272, 2026.
https://doi.org/10.1007/978-3-032-24494-9_12

behavior entirely and reason within a purely symbolic or state-based formalism, where verification techniques are well developed and tooling is mature.

Both approaches are useful, but neither treats *physical structure* as a first-class semantic concern. Differential equations capture behavior with greater precision, yet offer little guidance for principled modeling, transformation, or reuse; they are downstream of those structural choices. Engineering workflows, by contrast, rely on transforming models—abstracting, refining, or reconfiguring components—while preserving the properties that matter. This raises a basic question: what counts as a valid transformation, and how should we characterize the equivalence classes it respects, for example, equality of external behavior at system interfaces?

These questions are difficult to answer with trace semantics alone. Distinct internal structures can give rise to the same external behavior, and many internal differences may not matter from the standpoint of interaction with the environment. To address this, we suggest a shift in perspective: to regard physical structure—defined by interconnections and constitutive relationships—as a form of semantics.

We formalize this perspective by taking **impedance** as the interface semantics and **retrenchment** as the mechanism for controlled deviation. Impedance enables comparison of models that differ internally yet interact with their environment in the same way. Structural transformations are evaluated by their effect on the impedance, bounded by a *quantified* deviation. Retrenchment provides the language to quantify and constrain that deviation, turning design approximations into statements with bounds (e.g., parameter intervals, admissible shifts in poles and zeros, or frequency-window tolerances).

This combination is versatile: (i) it is not tied to a particular formalism, so it supports reasoning across series-parallel networks [2,22], linear graphs [24, 37,39], bond graphs [21,31,32], and other interconnection schemes [25,41]; and (ii) it is compatible with mature state-based formalisms such as ASM, Alloy, B, TLA$^+$, VDM, and Z [33] that support reasoning over standard numerical domains. In control-theoretic terms, it mirrors the move from time-domain differential operators to algebraic transfer functions in the complex s-plane, via the Laplace transform, where differentiation and integration become multiplication and division by functions of s.

Our aim in this paper is to show how impedance modeling and retrenchment, taken together, provide a foundation for reasoning about physical structure and behavior in CPS. We work with structure as semantics, using impedance to compare models, and use retrenchment to make approximations explicit and bounded. The goal is a simple formal discipline: transformations have stated conditions; preservation means the same impedance on a declared domain; deviations are recorded as quantitative tolerances. This places common engineering steps inside a precise semantics, in the spirit of principled, semantically grounded modeling to which Egon Börger's work on Abstract State Machines has contributed so deeply [20].

Paper Organization. Section 2 introduces the structural impedance semantics that treats interconnection and constitutive laws as the meaning at an interface. Section 3 presents a finite, state-based mechanization in Alloy and derives composition results for series-parallel networks. Section 4 formulates bounded-deviation steps via retrenchment, with illustrative tolerance and component library substitution examples. Section 5 reports on checks and cross-validation against symbolic and numerical calculations, and discusses limitations. Section 6 situates the approach within CPS modeling and verification. Section 7 summarizes contributions and outlines directions for extending structure-as-semantics across richer interconnection formalisms.

2 Structural Impedance Semantics

This section develops the central idea that *impedance* can serve as a semantics for physical structure, a meaning that allows different models to be compared on equal terms, independent of how they are realized internally. We begin with the effort-flow view of external behavior, then define impedance-based equivalence and the algebraic laws it obeys. The approach is illustrated on a simple series RC network whose impedance provides the canonical example.

2.1 Interfaces and Effort-Flow Behavior

Every physical component interacts with its environment through an *interface* carrying two complementary variables: an *effort* (such as voltage, force, or pressure) and a *flow* (such as current, velocity, or volumetric flux). Their product is power. The observable behavior of a system is the relation between these quantities at its ports.

Figure 1 illustrates the single-port interface convention used here: a system driven by an ideal source at a boundary port that carries the pair $(E_{\text{in}}, F_{\text{in}})$. We follow the common across/through terminology, treating effort as the across variable and flow as the through variable; the instantaneous power into the system is $E_{\text{in}}F_{\text{in}}$.

The source shown is purely conceptual, representing any admissible boundary condition; our concern is with the system's response relation, not with the realization of the driving source itself.

For linear, time-invariant components this relation is linear:

$$e = z * f$$

in the time domain, or, under Laplace transform and zero stored energy,

$$E(s) = Z(s)\,F(s).$$

Here $Z(s)$ is the *impedance* and $Y(s) = 1/Z(s)$ its admittance. Either can serve as the model's external *meaning*: the function that relates boundary effort and flow. Internal equations of motion (ODEs, DAEs, or state realizations) are one way to realize the same external relation; they are not part of the semantic layer.

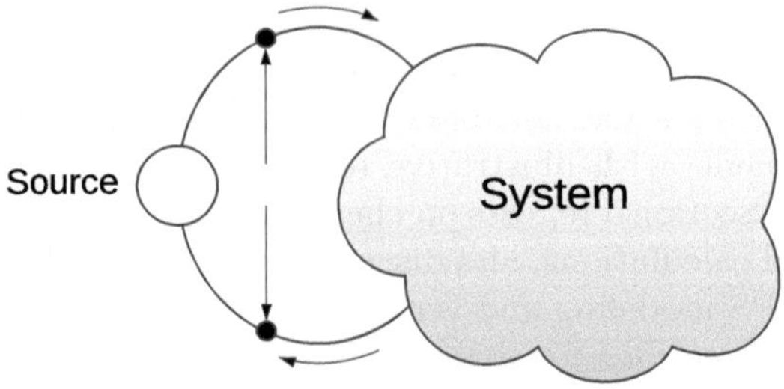

Fig. 1. Single-port interface view. An ideal source drives a system through a boundary port labeled with effort and flow.

2.2 Equivalence via Impedance

Two models are *equivalent* when they induce the same effort-flow relation at their boundary over a declared analysis domain S. We compare models extensionally, not by internal states. This permits cross-formalism reasoning: a series-parallel network, a linear graph, or a bond graph can all be considered equivalent if they exhibit the same mapping $E(s) \mapsto F(s)$.

For concreteness, we mechanize the series-parallel class of two-terminal networks used in our examples.

2.3 Syntax of Structures

Let Net be generated by the grammar

$$N ::= R(r) \mid L(\ell) \mid C(c) \mid N \bullet N \mid N \parallel N,$$

where $r, \ell, c \in \mathbb{R}_{>0}$. The operators $\bullet$ and $\parallel$ denote series and parallel composition, respectively.

2.4 Semantic Domain and Impedance Map

Let F be a field containing $\mathbb{R}$ (specialized later to $F = \mathbb{C}$), and let $S \subseteq F$ be an *admissible domain* on which all denominators below are nonzero; for steady-state sinusoidal analysis we take $S = \{ j\omega : \omega > 0 \}$. The impedance of $N \in \mathsf{Net}$ is the function $[\![N]\!] : S \to F$ defined recursively by

$$\begin{aligned}
[\![R(r)]\!](s) &= r, \\
[\![L(\ell)]\!](s) &= \ell\, s, \\
[\![C(c)]\!](s) &= \frac{1}{c\, s}, \\
[\![A \bullet B]\!](s) &= [\![A]\!](s) + [\![B]\!](s), \\
[\![A \parallel B]\!](s) &= \frac{[\![A]\!](s)\, [\![B]\!](s)}{[\![A]\!](s) + [\![B]\!](s)}.
\end{aligned}$$

Side conditions on S ensure all denominators in the parallel rule are nonzero.

2.5 Equivalence (Preservation Obligation)

For $A, B \in \mathsf{Net}$ and domain S,

$$A \equiv_S \mathrm{B} \iff \forall s \in S : [\![A]\!](s) = [\![B]\!](s).$$

A structure-preserving rewrite is valid on S if it maps A to B with $A \equiv_S B$. In this sense, algebraic laws such as series or parallel commutativity are verified by equality of impedances on the declared guard.

2.6 Basic Transformation Laws

For all $A, B, C \in \mathsf{Net}$ and all $s \in S$:

$$\begin{aligned}\text{Series commutativity: } & [\![A \bullet B]\!] = [\![B \bullet A]\!].\\ \text{Series associativity: } & [\![(A \bullet B) \bullet C]\!] = [\![A \bullet (B \bullet C)]\!].\\ \text{Parallel commutativity: } & [\![A \parallel B]\!] = [\![B \parallel A]\!].\\ \text{Parallel associativity: } & [\![(A \parallel B) \parallel C]\!] = [\![A \parallel (B \parallel C)]\!],\end{aligned}$$

all interpreted where denominators are nonzero on S. These serve as the canonical *structure-preserving transformations.*

2.7 Running Example: Series *RC*

A resistor R in series with a capacitor C, shown in Fig. 2, has impedance

$$Z(s) \;=\; R + \frac{1}{sC}.$$

Restricting to $s = j\omega$ with $1/j = -j$ and $\omega > 0$ gives

$$Z(j\omega) \;=\; R - \frac{j}{\omega C}.$$

The guard $S = \{j\omega : \omega > 0\}$ excludes the singularity at $\omega = 0$, where the capacitor is open-circuited. The external behavior is therefore completely determined by the pair (R, C). Recalling that we restrict to steady-state sinusoidal analysis, for which $S = \{\, j\omega : \omega > 0 \,\}$, exact preservation of an arbitrary model A's boundary behavior by another model B means $[\![A]\!](j\omega) = [\![B]\!](j\omega)$ for all $\omega > 0$.

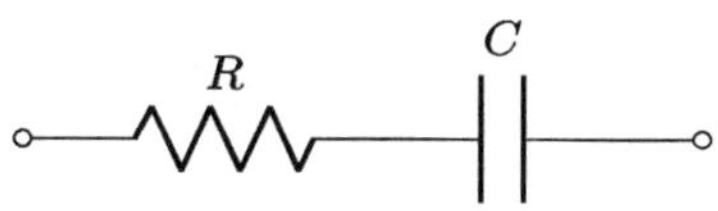

Fig. 2. Series *RC* between two terminals corresponding to $R \bullet C$.

This simple case already captures the structure of more elaborate examples. The real and imaginary parts correspond to dissipative and reactive behavior; their combination forms the external impedance seen at the port. Later sections introduce tolerance and interval variants of R and C, leading to bounded enclosures for $Z(j\omega)$ and quantitative *retrenchment* clauses.

2.8 What the Semantics is (and is Not)

By *structural impedance semantics* we mean a congruent, compositional interface semantics that maps a port-typed interconnection (the structure) to its boundary impedance—possibly multiport, frequency-dependent, or interval-valued—using series/parallel composition laws and context closure, so that design and proof proceed entirely by reasoning on the boundary.

The semantic object compared is the external effort-flow mapping Z, not an internal differential equation. Internal dynamics are merely one realization that induces the same Z. This makes the semantics compatible with state-based formalisms that support reasoning over numerical domains. Transformations appear as guarded rewrites whose preservation conditions reduce to algebraic equalities over the reals.

In short, the semantics tells us exactly what aspects of a physical model we are declaring to be significant: its interface behavior, not its internal realization. This matters because CPS modeling tools vary widely in how they describe continuous dynamics, but they all agree on the boundary quantities that govern interaction. The impedance semantics gives a common algebraic target—one that survives abstraction, structural rewriting, discretization, or even translation into a finite-state setting.

What the semantics does *not* do is replace differential equations or provide a new physical theory. It simply identifies the interface quantity that is preserved (or intentionally relaxed) by a transformation, and turns that into a concrete obligation. In this sense, it plays the same role that trace semantics plays for software refinement, but for physical structure: it supplies the glue that lets disparate descriptions be compared and composed.

2.9 Cross-Domain Analogy

The same structural semantics appears in many energy domains once effort and flow variables are reinterpreted (cf. the *analog computer* viewpoint of Feynman et al. [27]). For instance, in mechanics effort is force and flow is velocity; the analog of resistance is damping, and the analog of capacitance is compliance (spring constant). A pair of springs in series satisfies

$$\frac{1}{k_{\text{eq}}} = \frac{1}{k_1} + \frac{1}{k_2},$$

which is the same algebra as two capacitors in series. Such correspondences make the impedance semantics portable across physical domains and provide a unifying algebraic view of structure.

3 Alloy Modeling of Structural Semantics

The denotational view of Sect. 2 provides an algebraic meaning for networks: each structure denotes an impedance function $[\![N]\!] : S \to F$ that maps frequency to a complex value. To make this semantics executable and inspectable, we encode it in Alloy, a lightweight modeling language with a SAT-based analyzer that explores finite instances within a user-declared scope [30]. Alloy provides a declarative relational logic with built-in integers, and its Analyzer reduces assertions to SAT, automatically producing satisfying instances or counterexamples.

3.1 Alloy as Executable Approximation

Before turning to the model, it is important to distinguish two levels of semantics. The real-valued impedance semantics of Sect. 2 is the *ideal* domain in which preservation and equivalence are defined. Alloy provides a *finite approximation* of that semantics: numeric expressions are interpreted over bounded integers, and division at capacitive leaves uses the Analyzer's floor semantics. For algebraic obligations (series/parallel laws, commutativity, associativity), this approximation is exact, because no division is required in the check. For impedance bounds involving capacitors, we enforce sound, division-free inequalities, ensuring that every Alloy instance faithfully under-approximates its real-valued counterpart.

To make this concrete, we encode the series–parallel syntax and its impedance equations as relational constraints over these bounded integers. Within this setting, Alloy can check equivalence obligations, generate counterexamples, and, as a byproduct, perform *structural synthesis.*

The analysis is not a numerical simulation but a structural check over all configurations within a chosen scope. The *small-scope hypothesis* [6,29] suggests that most structural flaws have small witnesses, and the SAT-based engine can search the corresponding space effectively. This makes structural impedance semantics mechanically inspectable, rather than purely paper-based.

3.2 Basic Syntax

Here, we briefly introduce the basic syntax of Alloy. A more complete language description can be found in [30].

The Alloy keyword **`sig`** introduces a *signature*, which defines a set of elements in the universe. A signature may contain one or more *fields*, each introducing a relation that maps the elements of the signature to the field expression.

The **`extends`** keyword creates a subtyping relationship; an **`abstract`** signature has no elements except those belonging to its extensions, and **`one sig`** introduces a signature that contains only one element.

An Alloy **`fact`** is a set of constraints that holds for every satisfying instance of the model. A *predicate* (**`pred`**) is a parameterized encapsulation of constraints that can be reused across the model. A *function* (**`fun`**) returns an expression given zero or more parameters.

3.3 Core Signatures and Tree Structure

Returning to structural semantics, the Alloy model mirrors the abstract grammar of networks defined in Sect. 2. Each network node carries an impedance Z of type `Complex`; internal nodes connect subtrees; leaves carry component parameters. The `tree` constraint ensures acyclicity, enforcing the intended series-parallel structure rather than arbitrary graphs.

Listing 1.1. Core Alloy signatures.

```
// A complex number has real and imaginary parts
sig Complex {
  re, im: one Int
}

// Every network node has an impedance Z
abstract sig Node {
  Z: one Complex
}

// Binary operator nodes: the network is a tree
abstract sig Binary extends Node {
  left, right: one Node
}
{ left != right }

fun children: Node→Node { left + right }
fact { tree[children] }

// Internal nodes: series or parallel
sig Series, Parallel extends Binary {}

// Leaf nodes: components with a coefficient
abstract sig Component extends Node {
  val: one Int
}
{ val > 0 }

sig R, L, C extends Component {}
```

Figure 3 illustrates the corresponding metamodel automatically rendered by the Alloy Analyzer. Series and parallel nodes are binary; all nodes are linked to a single `Complex` impedance object. This schema constitutes the structural part of the semantics.

3.4 Leaf Laws and Propagation to Z

Each component imposes a simple algebraic form on its impedance: resistors contribute real positive terms, inductors positive imaginary terms, and capacitors negative imaginary terms. We evaluate on the imaginary axis ($s = j\omega$): a purely oscillatory input yields a complex impedance, with Z.re capturing the resistive part and Z.im the reactive part.

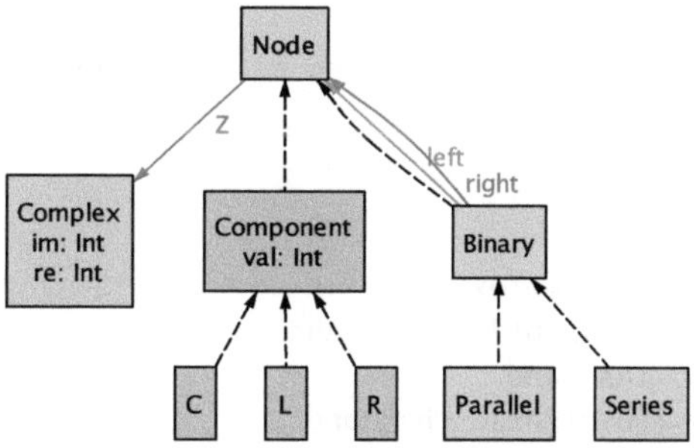

Fig. 3. A metamodel of the core Alloy signatures. Each dotted edge represents a subset relationship (i.e., **extends**), and a labeled edge represents a user-defined relation.

Listing 1.2. Leaf shapes on the imaginary axis ($s = j\omega$).

```
fact LeafShapes {
  all r: R | Z[r].im = 0 and Z[r].re > 0          // resistor
  all l: L | Z[l].re = 0 and Z[l].im > 0          // inductor
  all c: C | Z[c].re = 0 and Z[c].im < 0          // capacitor
}
```

The capacitor requires special handling because its impedance involves a reciprocal. To reduce explicit division and keep most arithmetic structural, we store its value as the inverse capacitance $D = 1/C$, so $1/(sC)$ becomes D/s. Consequently, each capacitor's numeric field `c.val` represents D rather than C, and the imaginary component of its impedance is computed as $-D/\omega$.

Listing 1.3. Leaf values.

```
// Global parameter: analysis frequency
one sig Params {
  omega: one Int
}
{ omega > 0 }

// Leaf values (numerical law)
fact LeafValues {
  all r: R | Z[r].re = r.val
  all l: L | Z[l].im = mul[Params.omega, l.val]
  all c: C | Z[c].im = negate[div[c.val, Params.omega]]
}
```

Series and parallel combinations follow the usual algebraic rules. In composition we avoid division by expressing the parallel rule via the product identity $Z\,(Z_a + Z_b) = Z_a\,Z_b$; the only divisions occur in leaf evaluation.

Listing 1.4. Series and parallel combination rules.

```
fact SeriesRule {
  all n: Series |
```

```
    some rhs: Complex |
      add[Z[n.left], Z[n.right], rhs] and eq[Z[n], rhs]
}

fact ParallelRule {
  all n: Parallel |
    some _sum, lhs, rhs: Complex |
      add[Z[n.left], Z[n.right], _sum] and
      mul[Z[n], _sum, lhs] and
      mul[Z[n.left], Z[n.right], rhs] and
      eq[lhs, rhs]
}
```

These facts constitute a literal mechanization of the mapping $[\![\cdot]\!]$ from Sect. 2. The representation is faithful for all points where denominators of the rational laws are nonzero. With the structural and numerical rules in place, we can now express the algebraic preservation laws as Alloy assertions.

3.5 Transformation Obligations as Assertions

Structure-preserving transformations become Alloy **assert** statements. For example, the commutativity of series composition is encoded as follows.

Listing 1.5. Representative transformation check.

```
assert SeriesComm {
  all a,b: Node |
    some s1, s2: Series |
      left[s1]=a and right[s1]=b and
      left[s2]=b and right[s2]=a implies
      Z[s1] = Z[s2]
}
check SeriesComm for 5 but 7 Complex, 6 Node, 6 Int
```

The **check** command tells Alloy to search for a counterexample to `SeriesComm` within a finite, user-given scope. For example, `for 5 but 7 Complex, 6 Node, 6 Int` means: explore all models whose signatures contain at most 5 atoms (except for `Complex`, `Node`, and `Int`, which are capped at 7, 6, and 6 atoms respectively). Alloy then performs a bounded but exhaustive search over this space. A successful check, indicated by the absence of any counterexample, would imply that the commutativity obligation holds for all structures within the explored scope. On the other hand, a counterexample instance, if it exists, would describe a particular structural configuration where equality fails.

Before working through larger examples, it is useful to clarify the status of Alloy's integer arithmetic and the role of explicit guards.

3.6 Guards, Partiality, and Arithmetic Soundness

Because the impedance algebra involves partial operations (e.g., division by ω), guard conditions must be stated explicitly in the formalization. In Alloy, these guards are written directly as constraints on each analysis state. Since Alloy's arithmetic is bounded and integral, all proofs and counterexamples occur within a finite domain of small integers, and every analysis state is a sampled frequency with integer-valued parameters.

Within this guarded domain, the integer model should be read as a finite, coarse sampling of the intended real-valued semantics. Any difference Alloy finds corresponds to a real semantic difference at the sampled frequency: if two structures yield distinct impedances under the bounded integer interpretation, then their real-valued impedances also differ at that state. The converse does *not* hold. Integer truncation and finite sampling can collapse nearby real-valued behaviors, so Alloy may report two structures as indistinguishable even though they differ outside the chosen scope or below the truncation granularity.

In this sense, the arithmetic is a sound *detector of differences* but not a completeness guarantee for equivalence. Section 4 later extends this finite analysis by introducing bounded intervals that summarize entire parameter ranges and make the loss of precision explicit in the form of quantified budgets using retrenchment.

3.7 Example: RLC Series Circuit

We model Example 3.4 from Ch. 10 of Chua et al. [22], which analyzes a standard series *RLC* network in the Laplace domain. In our notation,

$$N \;=\; R(6) \;\bullet\; L(1) \;\bullet\; C(25),$$

where R, L, and C denote the resistor, inductor, and capacitor (represented by its inverse parameter $D = 1/C$). Evaluated on the imaginary axis, the impedance function has the form

$$Z(j\omega) \;=\; R + j\big(\omega L - D/\omega\big),$$

whose imaginary part crosses zero at $\omega_0 = \sqrt{D/L} = 5$, the expected resonance frequency.

The Alloy fragment below declares this two-level series topology and, within a finite scope for ω, symbolically computes the same impedance relation.

Listing 1.6. RLC series circuit (Chua example).

```
pred RLC_topology [r: R, l: L, c: C, s1, s2: Series] {
  left[s1] = r and right[s1] = l
  left[s2] = s1 and right[s2] = c
  R = r and L = l and C = c
  Series = s1 + s2 and no Parallel
}
pred RLC_series [w: Int] {
  Params.omega = w
  some r: R, l: L, c: C, s1, s2: Series |
    RLC_topology[r, l, c, s1, s2] and
```

```
    r.val = 6 and l.val = 1 and c.val = 25
}
run RLC_series for 3 but 7 Complex, 5 Node, 6 Int
```

When the above **run** command is executed, the Analyzer reproduces the expected qualitative pattern of the impedance (constant real part and sign change in the imaginary component at $\omega_0 = 3$) confirming that the encoded semantics faithfully captures the analytic behavior; the tool further visualizes the generated instance as a graph diagram to aid in comprehension (Fig. 4).

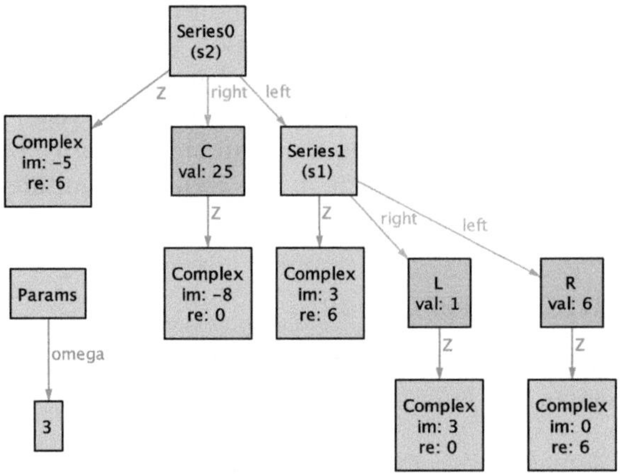

Fig. 4. A visualization of an instance representing the RLC series circuit with $\omega_0 = 3$.

3.8 Synthesis by Impedance Box Specification

The same encoding supports synthesis by treating the impedance box as a specification. The predicate inBox defines rectangular bounds in the complex plane.

Listing 1.7. Specification of a target impedance box.

```
pred inBox [c: Complex, re_lo, re_hi, im_lo, im_hi: Int] {
  c.re ≥ re_lo and c.re ≤ re_hi
  c.im ≥ im_lo and c.im ≤ im_hi
}

pred synth {
  some n: Node | Params.omega = 5 and inBox[Z[n], 6, 6, 0, 0]
}
run synth for 3 but 6 Complex, 5 Node, 7 Int
```

Given the above **run** command, Alloy enumerates candidate network topologies (up to the specified scope) to generate an instance whose impedance evaluates to 6 when $\omega = 5$. These amount to: a single R(6); a parallel pair followed by a series resistor $(R_1 \parallel R_2) \bullet R_3$; and other configurations that are algebraically equivalent to these. The model checker thus doubles as a symbolic search engine for structure-preserving solutions.

3.9 Extending to Multiple Analysis States

So far ω has been fixed globally. To move beyond single-frequency evaluation, we introduce a small set of analysis states:

```
sig State { omega: Int } { omega > 0 }
```

Each impedance becomes a two-dimensional relation `Z[node, s]`. Unlike temporal traces, these states are independent frequency samples. A total order over `State` aids inspection in Alloy's instance viewer: one can "scroll" through frequency slices to observe how each box moves in the complex plane. Multi-ω analysis is the foundation for synthesis tasks based on desired frequency responses.

3.10 Synthesis by Frequency Behavior: Low-Pass Filter

Introducing `State` allows specifications to span multiple frequencies rather than a single operating point. Our goal is to synthesize a simple *low-pass* network directly from its frequency behavior. Instead of prescribing a topology, we constrain the impedance trend: at low frequency the imaginary part should be large (capacitive), at high frequency smaller (more resistive), while the real part remains roughly constant, thereby suppressing unwanted high-frequency content (e.g., noise and interference in radar systems).

The following predicates express this requirement over two analysis states, representing $\omega = 6$ and $\omega = 24$.

Listing 1.8. Low-pass synthesis by behavior over two frequencies.

```
pred RC_series [root: Series] {
  some r: R, c: C {
    left[root] = r
    right[root] = c
    r.val = 2
    c.val = 48      // recall: 48 = 1/C
    isRooted[root]
  }
}

pred isLowPass [n: Node, s0, s1: State, Z_re, Z_lo, Z_hi: Int] {
  inBox[Z[n].s0, Z_re, Z_re, min[Int], Z_lo]   // low freq: larger |Im|
  inBox[Z[n].s1, Z_re, Z_re, Z_hi, max[Int]]   // high freq: smaller |Im|
}

pred synthLowPass {
  some n: Node |
    let s0 = so/first, s1 = s0.next |
```

```
        no_strays[n] and
        s0.omega = 6 and s1.omega = 24 and
        isLowPass[n, s0, s1, 2, -7, -3]
}
run synthLowPass for 3 but 12 Complex, 5 Node, 7 Int, exactly 2 State
```

Alloy searches the space of admissible interconnections and finds a network whose impedance decreases in magnitude as frequency increases, consistent with low-pass behavior. One solution is the series composition $C(42) \bullet R(2)$, satisfying $Z(6) = 2 - j7$ and $Z(24) = 2 - j1$. No topology is assumed in advance; the impedance boxes alone suffice to characterize and synthesize the desired behavior. Constraining `#L = 0` rules out inductors and reduces search time.

3.11 Discussion and Limits

These examples show how impedance-based semantics can be executed in a state-based tool: Alloy checks structural equivalence, finds counterexamples, and synthesizes networks satisfying interface specifications. Within Alloy's bounded-integer semantics, the treatment is *structurally exact* but *numerically approximate*: Although counterexamples confirm the failure of the stated property over any domain including the domain that is tested, confirmation of the property over the tested domain can only *suggest*, but not guarantee, its validity over a larger domain.

Other mature state-based frameworks, such as B and Event-B (Rodin), ASM, and ProB, support reasoning over richer numeric domains through symbolic proof and SMT back-ends, although their power is often constrained somewhat by being targeted at transition systems executing over real time, or some abstraction of real time (such as a sequence of states in succession). Despite this, the approaches mentioned are sufficient for the algebraic reasoning required here, since the impedance semantics needs only field properties of $\mathbb{R}$ or $\mathbb{Q}$ over rational functions, and not limits or continuity. In that spectrum, Alloy provides a lightweight and executable member, emphasizing exploration and synthesis rather than absolute verification via symbolic proof.

The next section moves from exact identities to controlled approximations via *retrenchment*: per-frequency boxes, deviation bounds, and quantified interface guarantees.

4 Retrenchment: Bounded Deviation at the Interface

Exact preservation ($Z_A \equiv Z_B$) may be too strong. For example, component tolerances, operating-point linearization, and library rounding all introduce small, intentional mismatches. Rather than stating only the ideal, we attach an explicit, auditable *tolerance* at the interface. We capture such departures from the ideal with *retrenchment* [10,12–14].

Retrenchment, as described in the cited references, is intended for the real time (or abstraction of real time) state-based point of view. As such, it suffers from a similar mismatch to the frequency domain, and need for a better fit to it, as do the state-based verification approaches mentioned above.

Briefly, retrenchment arose as an attempt to characterize deviation from exact preservation of a refinement (or gluing, or retrieve) relation between the state spaces of a step of a formal refinement of an abstract state-based transition model to a concrete one. The deviation was captured via a number of relations (as discussed in the next section). In the early days of experimentation with the concept, e.g. [12,13], these were combined in various ways in the main retrenchment proof obligation, in order to capture the deviation at issue. This line culminated in [14]. After some time, the concept was reappraised and simplified in [10], still for the time-oriented state-based point of view. None of these variants is ideal for the purpose here.

4.1 Clauses and Reading

Formulated in a way more suitable for the frequency domain needed in this paper, a retrenchment step from A to B over an admissible domain S_{guard} is recorded with:

WITHIN : Preconditions and guards (frequency band, side conditions).
RETRIEVE : The ideal relation (the refinement target), typically $Z_A(s) = Z_B(s)$ for all $s \in S_{\text{guard}}$.
OUTPUT : What is actually compared at the interface (e.g. $Z_A(s)$ inside a tolerance set around $Z_B(s)$).
CONCEDES : A quantitative budget that bounds the deviation permitted by the step.

Exact preservation is the degenerate case OUTPUT $\equiv$ RETRIEVE and CONCEDES $\equiv$ OUTPUT. In approximate steps, CONCEDES is the engineering "ledger entry."

Unlike the time domain oriented state-based versions, there is no proof obligation that is required to hold featuring the above clauses in the present frequency domain adaptation of retrenchment. However, like the state-based versions, there are straightforward composition laws for successive retrenchment steps.

For the retrenchment formulations mentioned earlier, composition was studied extensively in [11]. Here though, because CONCEDES records facts about *any* acceptable OUTPUT, the way the composition laws work in the present formulation is a little different.

Thus if A, B, and C are systems, with a retrenchment from A to B, captured using $W_{\text{A,B}}$, $R_{\text{A,B}}$, $O_{\text{A,B}}$, $C_{\text{A,B}}$, (in an obvious notation), and a retrenchment from B to C, captured using $W_{\text{B,C}}$, $R_{\text{B,C}}$, $O_{\text{B,C}}$, $C_{\text{B,C}}$, then these can be composed to yield a retrenchment from A to C, captured using:

$$W_{\mathrm{A,C}} \equiv (\exists\blacklozenge_B \bullet W_{\mathrm{A,B}} \wedge W_{\mathrm{B,C}})$$
$$R_{\mathrm{A,C}} \equiv (\exists\blacklozenge_B \bullet R_{\mathrm{A,B}} \wedge R_{\mathrm{B,C}})$$
$$O_{\mathrm{A,C}} \equiv (\exists\blacklozenge_B \bullet O_{\mathrm{A,B}} \wedge O_{\mathrm{B,C}})$$
$$C_{\mathrm{A,C}} \equiv (\exists\blacklozenge_B \bullet C_{\mathrm{A,B}} \wedge C_{\mathrm{B,C}})$$

This differs from the formulations in [11] in that the law for $C_{\mathrm{A,C}}$ is purely conjunctive. Also, in the above, the '$\exists\blacklozenge_B$' refers to the existential quantification of any constants or variables that are relevant exclusively to B. The composition is evidently associative.

4.2 Two Illustrative Steps

(i) Resistor Tolerance. Replacing a nominal $R(r)$ by a manufactured part $R(r')$ with $r' \in [r(1-\delta), r(1+\delta)]$ is:

$$\begin{aligned}
\textsc{Within}: &\ s \in S_{\mathrm{guard}},\ r > 0,\ \delta \in [0,1),\\
\textsc{Retrieve}: &\ r' = r,\\
\textsc{Output}: &\ Z_A(s) = r \in [\,r(1-\delta),\, r(1+\delta)\,] =: \widehat{Z}_B(s),\\
\textsc{Concedes}: &\ \mathrm{width}(\widehat{Z}_B) = 2r\delta \quad (\text{equivalently } |r - r'| \le r\delta).
\end{aligned}$$

The impedance is real and independent of s, so the box is constant on S_{guard}.

(ii) Series of Two Capacitors (or Two Springs).

With $[\![C(c)]\!](s) = \frac{1}{cs}$ and c_{eq} s.t. $\frac{1}{c_{\mathrm{eq}}} = \frac{1}{c_1} + \frac{1}{c_2}$,

$$\textsc{Within}:\ s \in S_{\mathrm{guard}},\ s \neq 0,\ c_1, c_2 > 0, \qquad \textsc{Retrieve}:\ \frac{1}{c_1 s} + \frac{1}{c_2 s} = \frac{1}{c_{\mathrm{eq}} s}.$$

If a single library element $\tilde{c}$ is chosen instead,

$$\textsc{Output}:\ \left|\frac{1}{c_1 s} + \frac{1}{c_2 s} - \frac{1}{\tilde{c} s}\right| = \frac{\left|\frac{1}{c_1} + \frac{1}{c_2} - \frac{1}{\tilde{c}}\right|}{|s|}, \qquad \textsc{Concedes}:\ \frac{\left|\frac{1}{c_1} + \frac{1}{c_2} - \frac{1}{\tilde{c}}\right|}{|s|} \le \varepsilon(s).$$

High frequencies (large $|s|$) tighten the bound; low frequencies loosen it.

4.3 Choosing the Guard S_{guard}

The guard states where the algebraic semantics is well-defined and relevant:

AC band: $S_{\mathrm{guard}} = \{\, j\omega : \omega \in [\omega_{\min}, \omega_{\max}]\,\}$; Half-plane: $\Re(s) \ge 0$ minus poles;
Structural side-conditions: $s \neq 0$, $[\![A]\!] + [\![B]\!] \neq 0$ for parallel subterms.

Narrower guards usually admit tighter Concedes budgets.

4.4 Local Retrenchment via Interval Semantics

We model component uncertainty directly and push it to the interface. Let

$$r \in [r^-, r^+], \quad \ell \in [\ell^-, \ell^+], \quad c \in [c^-, c^+], \quad s \in S_{\text{guard}}.$$

Pointwise (in s) interval semantics at the boundary is:

$$[\![R([r^-, r^+])]\!] = [r^-, r^+], \quad [\![L([\ell^-, \ell^+])]\!] = s \cdot [\ell^-, \ell^+], \quad [\![C([c^-, c^+])]\!] = \left[\frac{1}{c^+ s}, \frac{1}{c^- s}\right].$$

A *retrieve* relation that glues a concrete interval model $Z_C^\sharp : S \to \mathcal{I}(\mathbb{C})$ to an abstract point model $Z_A : S \to \mathbb{C}$ is:

$$R(c, a) \ : \ \forall s \in S_{\text{guard}} : \ Z_A(s) \in Z_C^\sharp(s).$$

Retrenchment then asserts WITHIN S_{guard} and records a budget, e.g. $\text{width}\big(Z_C^\sharp(s)\big) \le \varepsilon(s)$. Crucially, we perform *structural rewrites symbolically* and introduce intervals only at the interface, avoiding dependency blow-up inside the algebra.

4.5 Integer Semantics and Division-Free Bounds

Our Alloy mechanization uses integer arithmetic with a frequency parameter $\omega > 0$ in each `State`. Capacitor leaves implement

$$\Im Z_C(\omega) = -\left\lfloor \frac{D}{\omega} \right\rfloor, \quad \text{with } D = \frac{1}{C} \in \mathbb{Z}_{>0},$$

so *floor* semantics appears at the leaves. The tolerance information for a single RC configuration is packaged into a singleton record.

Listing 1.9. RC Box: tolerance parameters for a single RC configuration.

```
one sig RCBox {
  R0, Rmin, Rmax: Int,
  D0, DMin, DMax: Int      // (D = 1/C)
} {
  0 ≤ Rmin and Rmin ≤ R0 and R0 ≤ Rmax
  0 ≤ DMin and DMin ≤ D0 and D0 ≤ DMax
}
```

Mathematically, this corresponds to fixing a tolerance "RC box" with $\Re Z \in [R_{\min}, R_{\max}]$ and $D \in [D_{\min}, D_{\max}]$, and then deriving the corresponding bounds on $\Im Z$ for each $\omega > 0$.

We eliminate explicit division in membership tests via the standard property of floor:

$$\forall d \in \mathbb{Z}, \ \forall \omega > 0 : \qquad q = \lfloor d/\omega \rfloor \iff q\,\omega \le d < (q+1)\,\omega.$$

Because d is integral, the strict upper bound is equivalent to

$$d \le (q+1)\omega - 1 = q\omega + (\omega - 1).$$

Thus, for a tolerance "RC box" with real and imaginary bounds

$$\Re Z \in [R_{\min}, R_{\max}], \qquad \Im Z \in \big[-\lfloor D_{\max}/\omega \rfloor, -\lfloor D_{\min}/\omega \rfloor\big],$$

the equivalent *division-free* test is

$$R_{\min} \le \Re Z \le R_{\max}, \qquad -D_{\max} \le \omega \Im Z \le -D_{\min} + (\omega - 1),$$

which is exact for a series *RC* (and other linear sums) and avoids integer truncation mismatches.

In Alloy, we capture this as a predicate inRCBox[z, s, box], parameterized by an explicit box.

Listing 1.10. Division-free membership test for the RC box.

```
pred inRCBox [z: Complex, s: State, box: RCBox] {
  s.omega > 0
  re[z] ≥ box.Rmin and re[z] ≤ box.Rmax
  mul[im[z], s.omega] ≥ negate[box.DMax]
  mul[im[z], s.omega] ≤ negate[box.DMin] + (s.omega - 1)
}
```

In subsequent RC examples we use the unique instance RCBox, with the understanding that the underlying bounds come from the fixed record RCBox.

4.6 Lightweight Alloy Obligations (RC Running Example)

We use small *safety* assertions rather than existential "witness" assertions, so scopes without components do not spuriously fail checks. Below are representative obligations; the core model defines Within_RC, RC_nominal, RC_interval, and the division-free inRCBox predicate described above.

Listing 1.11. Alloy safety obligations for nominal and interval RC configurations.

```
// Any nominal RC (R0,D0) lies inside its RCBox at every admissible state.
assert RC_NominalInside_AllStates {
  all s: State | Within_RC[s] implies
    all root: Series, r: R, c: C |
      RC_nominal[root, r, c] implies inRCBox[root.Z.s, s, RCBox]
}

// Nominal RC is inside the same RCBox at two ordered analysis states.
assert RC_Nominal_Safety_2States {
  let s0 = so/first, s1 = s0.next |
    Within_RC[s0] and Within_RC[s1] implies
      all root: Series, r: R, c: C |
        RC_nominal[root, r, c] implies
          inRCBox[root.Z.s0, s0, RCBox] and
```

```
        inRCBox[root.Z.s1, s1, RCBox]
}

// Any RC whose parameters lie in RCBox (interval case) also stays inside
// RCBox at both ordered analysis states.
assert RC_Interval_Safety_2States {
  let s0 = so/first, s1 = s0.next |
    Within_RC[s0] and Within_RC[s1] implies
      all root: Series, r: R, c: C |
        RC_interval[root, r, c] implies
          inRCBox[root.Z.s0, s0, RCBox] and
          inRCBox[root.Z.s1, s1, RCBox]
}
```

In practice, we run checks with `0 L` to eliminate inductors in RC-focused assertions. All three assertions pass under modest scopes (e.g., `for 3 but 12 Complex, 5 Node, 0 L, 7 Int, 2 State`).

Widths as CONCEDES *Budgets.* On each `State` with $\omega > 0$ the box widths are

$$w_{\Re} = R_{\max} - R_{\min}, \qquad w_{\Im} = \left\lfloor \frac{D_{\max}}{\omega} \right\rfloor - \left\lfloor \frac{D_{\min}}{\omega} \right\rfloor,$$

and these serve directly as per-frequency CONCEDES quantities.

Retrenchment localizes approximation to the interface: structure gives the algebra; the algebra yields $Z(\cdot)$; and any deviation is recorded as an explicit, frequency-dependent budget. The Alloy harness shows these obligations are small, composable, and compatible with integer semantics.

5 Evaluation and Discussion

Symbolic and Numerical Cross-checks. The impedance semantics and retrenchment pattern were mechanized in Alloy and cross-checked against symbolic and numerical approaches. Alloy successfully discharged preservation and bounded-deviation obligations for representative RC networks, confirming that the semantics can be realized in a finite, state-based setting. Independent spot checks in Isabelle/HOL [34] verified the corresponding algebraic identities, while simulations in Julia [16] at sampled frequencies reproduced the same boundary impedances, providing an empirical validation of the formal results. Together these demonstrate coherence across formal, symbolic, and numerical domains.

Alternative Numeric Encodings. Our Alloy model uses bounded integers with floor division, which keeps analysis lightweight and makes the impedance semantics executable without introducing new numeric theories. Other encodings are possible. One could introduce a rational type or a small field-like numeric structure, providing exact algebra for the impedance laws and eliminating truncation effects at capacitive leaves. Such encodings offer richer arithmetic at the cost of increased solver time. Alloy and its SMT-backed extensions provide only integer arithmetic as a numeric theory; they do not support real arithmetic or expose bitvector or uninterpreted-function theories at the user level. Nonetheless, a type with field-like properties would better match the algebraic needs of impedance networks and could support a wider class of transformations and retrenchment steps.

Dependency and Interval Limitations. A continuing challenge is the treatment of dependency in interval arithmetic. The inversion strategy used here (computing pointwise numeric responses and enclosing them afterward) avoids the usual dependency blow-up but only for monotone, linear compositions. Nonmonotone or coupled systems will require richer enclosures (e.g., affine or symbolic) and tighter reasoning about shared uncertainty to preserve soundness under retrenchment.

Linear Systems. The perspective in this paper is formulated around Linear Time-Invariant (LTI) systems, reflecting the fact that CPS analysis and control are most often carried out on linearized models around operating points. Impedance semantics is naturally suited to this setting: series/parallel composition and frequency-domain reasoning are linear constructions, and transfer-function equivalence is expressed directly at the interface. Retrenchment then provides a way to record the gap between a nonlinear plant and its linear surrogate: the WITHIN clause delimits the operating region of the linearization, and the CONCEDES clause records the allowed deviation. Nonlinear dynamics and global behaviors are not treated here; the focus is on the LTI core that underpins most practical CPS workflows.

6 Related Work

A long line of work treats *structure* itself as a semantic concern. Börger's Abstract State Machines [19], algebraic specification, and categorical approaches to systems all highlight the semantic importance of structural relationships. In the physical domain, bond graphs and port-Hamiltonian models express this through conservation principles and interconnection rules that determine system behavior. Our use of impedance belongs to this tradition: it takes the boundary effort-flow relation as the semantic object and evaluates transformations by how they preserve (or intentionally relax) that interface behavior. A recent survey by Bliudze et al. [17] echoes this structural viewpoint, identifying CPS design as a sequence of modeling, discretization, and simulation steps rooted in physical interconnection structure. Their emphasis on structural equational models and linear/bond-graph semantics aligns closely with our motivation for providing a precise, algebraic interface semantics.

A second line of work concerns the integration of continuous and discrete dynamics. Hybrid automata [5,28], differential dynamic logic and KeYmaera X [35], Hybrid Event-B [8,9], set-based reachability analysis [3], and statistical model checkers such as UPPAAL SMC [23] provide expressive formalisms for reasoning about trajectories, invariants, reachability, and switching. Our contribution is orthogonal: we do not analyze trajectories or flows, but provide a denotational interface model that can sit alongside such formalisms, supplying a structural equivalence and approximation relation that is independent of the internal dynamics.

Finally, engineering practice relies heavily on simulation-centric frameworks such as the Modelica language and standard library [26,40], the Functional Mock-up Interface (FMI) for co-simulation [18], and Simulink/Stateflow development tools by MathWorks Inc. These environments provide executable models of continuous-time behavior, but they do not by themselves offer structural guarantees across transformations or abstractions. Impedance-based semantics offers a complementary notion of correctness: it isolates the boundary quantity that must be preserved across refactoring, code generation, discretization, or component substitution, providing a lightweight alternative to trajectory-level validation.

7 Conclusions

This work rests on two simple observations about CPS modeling and verification:

1. Starting from differential equations undermines physical reasoning at the interface.
2. Impedance provides the interface semantics that all physical models must agree on.

These observations clarify the role of structural semantics in CPS. Differential equations describe behavior but do not, on their own, express the physical constraints that arise from interconnection, energy conservation, and component-level structure. Impedance recovers this missing interface layer and provides the common quantity that any physical description must satisfy. This makes it possible to reason about transformations, abstractions, and approximations in a way that is independent of the modeling formalism, yet grounded in the physics that governs system interaction.

Why it Matters. We demonstrate that state-based methods can reason about physical semantics directly, not by simulation but by algebraic structure. This opens the door for symbolic verification tools to engage with the physics of CPS design in a principled, semantics-driven way, bridging the gap between what engineers simulate and what formal methods can prove.

Future Directions. A natural next step is to generalize the structural impedance semantics beyond series-parallel networks to bond graphs and linear graphs, making explicit the correspondence between different interconnection schemes and showing how they preserve (or transform) impedance at the interface. Extending the approach in this way would help unify multiple CPS modeling paradigms under a common algebraic semantics and test how structural equivalence principles scale to more complex networks.

Another direction is to move beyond steady-state sinusoidal response. The present work interprets $Z(s)$ on the imaginary axis $s = j\omega$, focusing on frequency-response behavior. More generally, impedance is given by an analytic function in the right half-plane where the Laplace transform (which underpins all such frequency domain approaches in the engineering world) is defined. Allowing the analysis domain S to range over this half-plane, or other judiciously chosen portions of it, rather than just the imaginary axis, would connect the same structural semantics to transient behavior and initial conditions via the inverse transform. Developing that link to the time-domain view common in CPS verification remains an open direction for future work.

References

1. Abrial, J.R., Su, W., Zhu, H.: Formalizing hybrid systems with Event-B. In: Abstract State Machines, Alloy, B, VDM, and Z - Third International Conference, ABZ 2012, Pisa, Italy, 18-21 June 2012. Proceedings. Lecture Notes in Computer Science, vol. 7316, pp. 178–193. Springer (2012)
2. Alexander, C.K., Sadiku, M.N.: Fundamentals of Electric Circuits. McGraw-Hill, 4th edn. (2009)
3. Althoff, M., Frehse, G., Girard, A.: Set propagation techniques for reachability analysis. Ann. Rev. Control Robot. Autonomous Syst. **4**(1), 369–395 (2021)
4. Alur, R.: Principles of Cyber-Physical Systems. MIT Press, Cambridge, MA (2015)
5. Alur, R., et al.: The algorithmic analysis of hybrid systems. Theoret. Comput. Sci. **138**(1), 3–34 (1995)
6. Andoni, A., Daniliuc, D., Khurshid, S.: Evaluating the "small scope hypothesis". Tech. Rep. MIT-LCS-TR-921, MIT CSAIL, Cambridge, MA, USA (2003)
7. Baheti, R., Gill, H.: Cyber-physical systems. In: Samad, T., Annaswamy, A. (eds.) The Impact of Control Technology: Overview, Success Stories, and Research Challenges. IEEE Control Systems Society (2011)
8. Banach, R., Butler, M., Qin, S., Verma, N., Zhu, H.: Core hybrid event-B I: single hybrid event-B machines. Sci. Comp. Prog. **105**, 92–123 (2015)
9. Banach, R., Butler, M., Qin, S., Zhu, H.: Core hybrid event-B II: multiple cooperating hybrid event-B machines. Sci. Comp. Prog. **139**, 1–35 (2017)
10. Banach, R.: Graded refinement, retrenchment, and simulation. ACM Trans. Softw. Eng. Methodol. **32**(2) (2023)
11. Banach, R., Jeske, C., Poppleton, M.: Composition mechanisms for retrenchment. J. Logic Algebraic Program. **75**, 209–229 (2008)
12. Banach, R., Poppleton, M.: Retrenchment: an engineering variation on refinement. In: International Conference of B Users, pp. 129–147. Springer (1998)
13. Banach, R., Poppleton, M.: Sharp retrenchment, modulated refinement and simulation. Formal Aspects Comput. **11**, 498–540 (1999)
14. Banach, R., Poppleton, M., Jeske, C., Stepney, S.: Engineering and theoretical underpinnings of retrenchment. Sci. Comput. Program. **67**(2), 301–329 (2007)
15. Banach, R., Su, W.: Cyberphysical systems: a behind-the-scenes foundational view. In: Models: Concepts, Theory, Logic, Reasoning and Semantics, pp. 177–201 (2018)

16. Bezanson, J., Edelman, A., Karpinski, S., Shah, V.B.: Julia: a fresh approach to numerical computing. SIAM Rev. **59**(1), 65–98 (2017)
17. Bliudze, S., Furic, S., Sifakis, J., Viel, A.: Rigorous design of cyber-physical systems. Softw. Syst. Model. (SoSyM) **18**(3), 1613–1636 (2019)
18. Blochwitz, T., et al.: The functional mockup interface for tool independent exchange of simulation models. In: Proceedings of the 8th International Modelica Conference, pp. 105–114. Linköping University Press (2011)
19. Börger, E., Stärk, R.: Abstract State Machines: A Method for High-Level System Design and Analysis. Springer, Berlin Heidelberg (2003)
20. Börger, E.: The abstract state machines method for high-level system design and analysis. In: Formal Methods: State of the Art and New Directions, pp. 79–116. Springer (2009)
21. Borutzky, W.: Bond Graph Methodology. Springer (2010)
22. Chua, L.O., Desoer, C.A., Kuh, E.S.: Linear and Nonlinear Circuits. McGraw Hill (1987)
23. David, A., Larsen, K.G., Legay, A., Mikučionis, M., Poulsen, D.B.: Uppaal SMC tutorial. Int. J. Softw. Tools Technol. Transfer **17**(4), 397–415 (2015)
24. De Silva, C.W.: Modeling of Dynamic Systems with Engineering Applications. CRC Press, 2nd edn. (2023)
25. Duindam, V., Macchelli, A., Stramigioli, S., Bruyninckx, H.: Modeling and control of complex physical systems: the port-hamiltonian approach. Springer (2009)
26. Elmqvist, H., Mattsson, S., Otter, M.: Modelica — a language for physical system modeling, visualization and interaction. In: Proceedings of the 1999 IEEE International Symposium on Computer Aided Control System Design (Cat. No.99TH8404), pp. 630–639 (1999)
27. Feynman, R.P., Leighton, R.B., Sands, M.: The Feynman Lectures on Physics: The New, Millennium Basic Books, New York (2010)
28. Henzinger, T.A.: The theory of hybrid automata. In: Proceedings 11th Annual IEEE Symposium on Logic in Computer Science, pp. 278–292. IEEE (1996)
29. Jackson, D., Damon, C.: Elements of style: analyzing a software design feature with a counterexample detector. IEEE Trans. Softw. Eng. **22**(7), 484–495 (1996)
30. Jackson, D.: Software Abstractions: Logic, Language, and Analysis. The MIT Press (2012)
31. Karnopp, D., Margolis, D., Rosenberg, R.: System Dynamics: Modeling, Simulation, and Control of Mechatronic Systems. Wiley, 5th edn. (2012)
32. Kypuros, J.: Dynamics and Control with Bond Graph Modeling. CRC (2013)
33. Leuschel, M., Ishikawa, F. (eds.): Rigorous State-Based Methods: 11th International Conference, ABZ 2025, Düsseldorf, Germany, 10–13 June 2025, Proceedings. Lecture Notes in Computer Science, Springer, Cham (2025)
34. Nipkow, T., Wenzel, M., Paulson, L.C.: Isabelle/HOL: a proof assistant for higher-order logic. Springer (2002)
35. Platzer, A.: Logical Foundations of Cyber-Physical Systems. Springer (2018)
36. Rajkumar, R., Lee, I., Sha, L., Stankovic, J.: Cyber-physical systems: the next computing revolution. Proc. IEEE **98**(1), 136–148 (2010)
37. Rowell, D., Wormley, D.N.: System Dynamics: An Introduction. Prentice Hall (1997)
38. Seshia, S.A.: Explorations in cyber-physical systems education. Commun. ACM **65**(5), 60–69 (2022)
39. Shearer, J.L., Murphy, A.T., Richardson, H.H.: Introduction to System Dynamics. Addison-Wesley (1967)

40. Tiller, M.: Introduction to Physical Modeling with Modelica. Kluwer Academic Publishers, USA (2001)
41. Wellstead, P.: Introduction to Physical System Modelling. Academic Press (1979)

From Abstract State Machines to B: A Translation of a Medical Pillbox Model

Michael Leuschel(✉)

Faculty of Mathematics and Natural Sciences, Heinrich Heine University Düsseldorf, Düsseldorf, Germany
michael.leuschel@hhu.de

Abstract. We systematically translate a formal model developed for an existing case study from ASM to B. During the translation of the original model developed for ASMETA to a B model for PROB, we gained insights about practical differences between ASM and B that were not discussed in earlier works (which focused on the partial update problem). In particular, we uncovered subtle issues in the translation of the ASM choose operator and various ASM data types. We also show the complementary, added value of the B tooling for this case study, for animation, visualisation and model checking. For the latter, the PROB tool uncovered a well-definedness issue. While the issue is not a problem in the original ASM model, the problem does manifest itself in the C++ code generated from the original ASM model.

1 Introduction

Within state-based formal methods, the states of a system are modelled as mathematical entities, and the models contain explicit operations which can inspect and modify the state. The family of state-based formal methods encompasses the B [1] and Event-B [2] methods, ASMs (Abstract State Machines) [10,11], as well as Z [33], TLA$^+$ [22], Alloy [19] and VDM [20].

ASMs have been used since 1989 to model computational systems of different kinds; various tools have been built to simulate or validate such models [5,8,15]. The B-method has been used for over twenty-five years [12] for developing safety critical systems.

In this article, we are interested in studying the similarities and differences between ASMs and the B and Event-B methods, with a stronger focus on practical modelling and tool support. Indeed, in earlier work, Leuschel and Börger [26] have developed a theoretical, systematic translation from a subset of ASMs to Event-B. This translation focusses on the partial update problem and generates valid but non-idiomatic Event-B models. Other works address the translation of ASM's partial updates to B or a relational setting [29–31]. These works did not study the full scope of ASM modelling as used in practice. In this paper, we thus performed a manual translation of a full ASM model written for ASMETA [8] to a B model. While the translation is not automated, it covers a larger range of

A. Raschke et al. (Eds.): Egon Börger Festschrift, LNCS 16580, pp. 273–294, 2026.
https://doi.org/10.1007/978-3-032-24494-9_13

language features, leading to new insights. We hope that this article is beneficial both to B or ASM practitioners who want to learn more about the other formalism, and who may be interested in applying tools from the other formalisms to their problem.

Our starting point is the tutorial article [8] about ASMETA, which presents an ASM model of a medical pillbox. The model is used to illustrate ASMs in general and the ASMETA tool in particular. In the present article, we translate it to a classical B model, thereby uncovering and discussing various subtle differences between ASMs and B, and also showcase the B tools to provide additional validation over that presented in [8].

2 The Pillbox ASM Model

The syntax and semantics of ASMs is defined in [11, Ch.2.4]. ASMs are defined as rules that transform structures of a given signature, their 'states'. The ASM model of a medical pillbox in Listing 2.1 was developed by Bombarda et al. [8] to showcase the ASMETA toolset. In essence, the model covers the following aspects:

- The pillbox has three drawers (`drawer1`, `drawer2`, and `drawer3`), each drawer containing multiple pills of some drug (specified in the `drug` variable).
- Each drawer has information about the time at which the respective pills need to be taken in the `time_consumption` variable. The `drug_index` variable keeps track of how many pills have been taken for each drawer, so that the next deadline can be determined.
- Each drawer has an LED light, that can be ON or OFF (`drawerLed`). An LED light that is on informs the patient that the next pill from this drawer needs to be taken. The invariant `inv_drawer1` stipulates that only one LED light can be on at the same time.
- There are auxiliary variables `isPillTobeTaken` and the timers, while the interaction with the patient is modelled by the (only) monitored variable `isPillTaken`

```
// Full Pill-Box specification, including TimeLibrary
// including timers and multiple deadlines for each drawer.
//
asm pillbox_final
import ../STDL/StandardLibrary
import ../STDL/CTLLibrary
import ../STDL/TimeLibrarySimple

signature:
    //*********************************************
    // DOMAINS
    //*********************************************
    abstract domain Drawer
    enum domain LedLights = {OFF | ON }
    enum domain Drugs = {TYLENOL | ASPIRINE | MOMENT}
    //*********************************************
    // MONITORED AND CONTROLLED FUNCTIONS
    //*********************************************
    dynamic monitored isPillTaken: Drawer -> Boolean
```

```
    dynamic controlled drawerLed: Drawer -> LedLights
    dynamic controlled time_consumption: Drawer -> Seq(Integer)
    dynamic controlled drug: Drawer -> Drugs
    dynamic controlled drugIndex: Drawer -> Natural
    dynamic controlled isPillTobeTaken: Drawer -> Boolean
    static tenMinutes: Timer
    //**********************************************
    // DERIVED FUNCTIONS
    //**********************************************
    // Functions checking the status of a Led
    derived isOn: Drawer -> Boolean
    derived isOff: Drawer -> Boolean
    derived areOthersOn: Drawer -> Boolean
    // It is true when the pill has to be taken
    derived pillDeadlineHit: Drawer -> Boolean
    // It is true if there is any other pill in that drawer still to be
        taken
    derived isThereAnyOtherDeadline: Drawer -> Boolean
    //**********************************************
    // STATIC FUNCTIONS
    //**********************************************
    static drawer1: Drawer
    static drawer2: Drawer
    static drawer3: Drawer

definitions:
    //**********************************************
    // STATIC AND DERIVED FUNCTIONS DEFINITIONS
    //**********************************************
    function isOn($d in Drawer) = (drawerLed($d) = ON)
    function isOff($d in Drawer) = (drawerLed($d) = OFF)
    function areOthersOn($d in Drawer) = switch($d)
            case drawer1 : isOn(drawer2) or isOn(drawer3)
            case drawer2 : isOn(drawer1) or isOn(drawer3)
            case drawer3 : isOn(drawer2) or isOn(drawer1)
        endswitch

    function pillDeadlineHit ($d in Drawer) = (at(time_consumption($d),
        drugIndex($d))<=mCurrTimeSecs)
    function isThereAnyOtherDeadline ($d in Drawer) = (drugIndex($d)<iton(
        length(time_consumption($d))))
    //**********************************************
    // RULE DEFINITIONS
    //**********************************************
    // Rule to reset the Drawer due to one of the possible reasons (
        Timeout, Pill taken, etc.)
    rule r_reset($drawer in Drawer) = par
            drawerLed($drawer) := OFF
            drugIndex($drawer) := drugIndex($drawer) + 1n
            isPillTobeTaken($drawer):= false
        endpar

    // Rule to set the led red ON when the pill has to be taken
    rule r_pillToBeTaken($drawer in Drawer) = par
            if isOff($drawer) then r_reset_timer[tenMinutes] endif
            drawerLed($drawer) := ON
        endpar

    // System evolution starting from the ON State
    rule r_take($drawer in Drawer) = if isOn($drawer) then
            // The pill has been taken, or the timer expires
            if expired(tenMinutes) or isPillTaken($drawer) then
                r_reset[$drawer] endif
        endif

    // Non-determinism: Only a single light is to be on at a time, so
        choose randomly one drawer
    rule r_choosePillToTake = choose $drawer in Drawer with
```

```
            isPillTobeTaken($drawer) and isOff($drawer) and not
                areOthersOn($drawer) do
                r_pillToBeTaken[$drawer]

    // Set the status for other drawers
    rule r_setOtherDrawers = forall $drawer in Drawer do par
            if pillDeadlineHit($drawer) and isOff($drawer) then
                isPillTobeTaken($drawer):= true endif
            // Handle the evolution of the System when the LED is in ON
                state
            // The pill has been taken, or the timer expires
            if (isThereAnyOtherDeadline($drawer)) then r_take[$drawer]
                endif
        endpar
    //**************************************************
    // INVARIANTS
    //**************************************************
    invariant inv_drawer1 over Drawer: (forall $d in Drawer with isOn($d)
        implies not areOthersOn($d))
    //**************************************************
    // MAIN Rule
    //**************************************************
    main rule r_Main = par
            // Non-determistic choice of the pill
            r_choosePillToTake[]
            // Handle other states
            r_setOtherDrawers[]
        endpar

default init s0:
    // Turn-off all the led of the Drawers
    function drawerLed($drawer in Drawer) = OFF

    // Initialization of the time consumption
    function time_consumption($drawer in Drawer) = switch($drawer)
            case drawer1 : [60, 1200, 1800]
            case drawer2 : [2400, 3000, 3600]
            case drawer3 : [180, 1200, 1800]
        endswitch

    // Insert a drug in each drawer
    function drug($drawer in Drawer) = switch($drawer)
            case drawer1 : TYLENOL
            case drawer2 : ASPIRINE
            case drawer3 : MOMENT
        endswitch

    function isPillTobeTaken($drawer in Drawer) = false

    // Every drawer has an index starting from 0
    function drugIndex($drawer in Drawer) = 0n

    // Timer initialization
    function duration($t in Timer) = 600
    function start($t in Timer) = currentTime($t)
```

Listing 2.1. ASM model `pillbox_final.asm` by Bombarda et al. [8]

3 Translating the ASM Machine to B

We now describe how the ASM machine in Listing 2.1 was manually translated to a B machine. We start with basic data types and then proceed to constants, variables, complex values, and on to ASM rules and partial updates.

3.1 New Domains and Enumerated, Deferred Sets

The enum signatures **LedLights** and **Drugs** can be translated directly to B enumerated sets, declared in the **SETS** section of a B machine. The abstract signature **Drawer** gets translated into a deferred set in B, which is just declared without explicitly listing its members:

```
SETS
    Drawer; // abstract domain Drawer
    LedLights = {OFF , ON }; // enum domain LedLights = {OFF | ON }
    Drugs = {TYLENOL, ASPIRINE, MOMENT}; // enum domain Drugs = {TYLENOL |
        ASPIRINE | MOMENT}
```

Listing 3.2. Enumerated and Deferred Sets in B

The ASM model also declares the static functions **drawer1**, **drawer2**, and **drawer3**. These get translated to B constants, declared in the **CONSTANTS** section and where the following typing and additional axioms are provided in the **PROPERTIES** section:

```
  {drawer1,drawer2,drawer3} <: Drawer &
  Drawer = {drawer1,drawer2,drawer3} & card({drawer1,drawer2,drawer3})=3
```

Listing 3.3. Translation of Individual Drawers in PROPERTIES

Observe that the second line stipulates that the three drawers partition the domain **Drawer**. Without this line, all three drawers could be identical and there could also be additional drawers. The fact that all three drawers are distinct is *not* written explicitly in the ASM model, but the underlying tools (animation, model checking) treat it as such.[1]

We can translate enum domains to enumerated sets, abstract domains to deferred sets, static functions of abstract domain to constants, (possibly) adding disjointness axioms.

3.2 Controlled Functions to Constants and Variables

Static functions are all translated as constants while dynamic ones are mapped to B variables. Let us first examine dynamic controlled functions. Take for example

```
dynamic controlled drawerLed: Drawer -> LedLights
dynamic controlled time_consumption: Drawer -> Seq(Integer)
```

Listing 3.4. Dynamic Controlled Functions

```
  drawerLed: Drawer --> LedLights &
  time_consumption: Drawer --> seq(INTEGER) &
```

Listing 3.5. B Invariants for Dynamic Controlled Functions

The initial value is specified in the INITIALISATION section as follows:

[1] Private communication by Angelo Gargantini, December 11th 2025.

```
drawerLed := Drawer * {OFF} ||  // Cartesian product
time_consumption := {drawer1 |-> [60, 1200, 1800],
                     drawer2 |-> [2400, 3000, 3600],
                     drawer3 |-> [180, 1200, 1800] } ||
```

Listing 3.6. Initialising the Variables

Observe that in B a function is a set, and as such, we can use set operators (like the Cartesian product * above) or set literals (instead of using the switch statement like in the ASM model).

Static functions are translated to B constants, while dynamic ones to B variables.

3.3 Derived Functions

In ASM one can declare functions as derived, as done for the following two functions in Listing 2.1:

```
derived isOn: Drawer -> Boolean
derived isOff: Drawer -> Boolean
...
function isOn($d in Drawer) = (drawerLed($d) = ON)
function isOff($d in Drawer) = (drawerLed($d) = OFF)
```

Listing 3.7. Derived Functions `isOn` and `isOff`

This is useful to define state that can be derived from regular state variables, because one does not have to explicitly update the derived functions (they automatically return an updated value when the variables change). For tools like model checking this is also useful, as their value does not have to be stored in the state space. B does not directly have this concept, but we can use B's definitions to that effect:

```
isOn(d) == (drawerLed(d) = ON);
isOff(d) == (drawerLed(d) = OFF);
```

Listing 3.8. B Definitions for Derived Functions

Definitions are implemented by textual replacement in tools like ATELIER-B [14,23]. In other words, they are macros with all of their problems, see Sect. 3.3 in [25]. For example, when not using parentheses in the definition bodies, textual replacement can result in unexpected changes of priorities. Another issue is *variable capture*, when the definition's locally quantified variables clash with identifiers in the actual arguments of the definition call. PROB [27] does warn about variable capture, and an automatic ASM to B conversion tool would have to be careful here to properly rename identifiers. Compared to the ASM versions, we also have no typing of the derived functions (which means B definitions can be polymorphic, but also means that we get less type safety). In the future, we plan to extend the B language with proper hygienic macros [17], which then would be identical in spirit to the derived functions in ASMs.

Derived functions can be translated to B definitions, taking care to avoid issues with variable capture and operator precedence.

3.4 Data Values

Data Values: Sequences. In B sequences are just a special case of a function, which in turn are sets of pairs. E.g., the sequence $[2,4]$ is represented by the set $\{1 \mapsto 2, 2 \mapsto 4\}$. As such, all operators on functions, sets, and relations are available for sequences. E.g., to obtain the second element of a sequence s, we can simply use function application: $s(2)$. This is used in the translation of the `pillDeadlineHit` function to B, where we translate the ASM `at` operator in `(at(time_consumption($d),drugIndex($d))<=mCurrTimeSecs)` to function application:

```
pillDeadlineHit(d) == time_consumption(d)(drugIndex(d)) <= mCurrTimeSecs
    ;
```

Listing 3.9. Sequence Operators as B Function Operators

However, note that sequence indexes start at 1 and not 0 in B. This means that we had to adapt, e.g., the initialisation of the `drugIndex` variable.

ASM sequences simply become B sequences and some special ASM operators are no longer required. Care must be taken with adapting the indexes to start at 1 and not 0.

Data Values: Naturals and Integers. In the ASM framework, the universes `Int` and `Nat` are distinct, while in B, naturals are a subset of the integers. ASM libraries therefore, provide conversion functions like `iton` to convert integers to natural numbers, which is used in `isThereAnyOtherDeadline`. The B translation does not require this conversion function:

```
isThereAnyOtherDeadline(d) == (drugIndex(d)<(size(time_consumption(d))));
```

Listing 3.10. Translation without Natural Number to Integer Conversion

Note, that we could have used a lambda function $\lambda x.(x \in \mathbb{N}|x)$ for `iton` and detect illegal conversions as well-definedness errors. Finally, note that the ASM model in Listing 2.1 uses special literals 0n and 1n for natural numbers, which become 0 and 1 in our translation.

Naturals can be mapped to integers; conversion functions either disappear or can be modelled by lambda abstractions like $\lambda x.(x \in \mathbb{N}|x)$ for `iton`.

3.5 The Initialisation

The ASM initialisation was translated directly to the B `INITIALISATION` section. It was convenient to use B set notations for functions and sequences. Take, for example, the following ASM switch statement to initialise the `drug` variable:

```
function drug($drawer in Drawer) = switch($drawer)
        case drawer1 : TYLENOL
        case drawer2 : ASPIRINE
        case drawer3 : MOMENT
    endswitch
```

Listing 3.11. Initialisation in ASM using switch

In B this becomes the following assignment using a set literal (see Listing 3.6 for another example):

```
drug := {drawer1 |-> TYLENOL, drawer2 |-> ASPIRINE, drawer3 |-> MOMENT}
```

Listing 3.12. Initialisation in B with a Set Extension

3.6 The Main Rule and Subsidiary Rules

ASMs have one main rule which stipulates the evolution of the state machine.

```
main rule r_Main = par
        // Non-determistic choice of the pill
        r_choosePillToTake[]
        // Handle other states
        r_setOtherDrawers[]
    endpar
```

Listing 3.13. ASM main Rule

In B, as originally defined by Abrial in his book [1], we can have multiple operations within a machine. However, operations within a machine are *not* allowed to call each other. One is only allowed to call operations from subsidiary B machines (e.g., included via the `INCLUDES` directive). Luckily, the B language, as supported by Atelier-B, has a concept of local operations [14]. These are operations that act like they come from a different machine and can be called by operations of the same machine. The above ASM rule can thus be translated to B by defining a regular B operation `r_Main` in the `OPERATIONS` section and defining all other subsidiary operations like `r_choosePillToTake` or `r_setOtherDrawers` in the `LOCAL_OPERATIONS` section.

Thanks to the `LOCAL_OPERATIONS` clause we can translate the main ASM rule as a regular B operation and all other ASM rules as local operations.

3.7 The choose Operator

The pillbox model uses the `choose` operator to non-deterministically select a drawer, in case the deadlines of several drawers have expired. The pillbox will then later light the LED for that drawer, instructing the patient to take the medication from that drawer first.

```
rule r_choosePillToTake = choose $drawer in Drawer with
        isPillTobeTaken($drawer) and isOff($drawer) and not
            areOthersOn($drawer) do
            r_pillToBeTaken[$drawer]
```

Listing 3.14. choose in ASM

As the B language also has a non-deterministic choice in the form of the `ANY` statement, one would think that the above ASM code can be easily translated to B as follows:

```
r_choosePillToTake = ANY drawer WHERE drawer : Drawer &
   isPillTobeTaken(drawer)=TRUE & isOff(drawer) & not(areOthersOn(drawer)
   )
 THEN  r_pillToBeTaken(drawer) END;
```

Listing 3.15. Incorrect Translation to `ANY`

During validation of the translation, it turned out that this B code behaved differently from the ASM code. Indeed, when no drawer `d` satisfies the predicate `isPillTobeTaken(d) and isOff(d) and not areOthersOn(d)`, the ASM rule does nothing, i.e., it behaves like the B's `skip` statement. [2] The `ANY` statement, however, is not enabled and blocks the entire surrounding operation. In other words, the predicate of the `ANY` statement acts like a guard which propagates to the top-level operation (`r_main`). To mimic the semantics of the ASM choose operator we need to translate the above ASM code as follows:

```
 r_choosePillToTake =
   LET cands BE
       cands = {drawer| drawer : Drawer & isPillTobeTaken(drawer)=TRUE &
                        isOff(drawer) & not (areOthersOn(drawer)) }
   IN IF cands /= {} THEN
        ANY drawer WHERE drawer:cands THEN r_pillToBeTaken(drawer) END
      END
   END;
```

Listing 3.16. Corrected Translation of choose to `ANY`, `LET`, and `IF`

Note that ProB also offers the `CHOOSE` external function, which has a different semantics to the `choose` operator in ASMs. `CHOOSE` is a mathematical function, selecting an element from a set. As such, `CHOOSE` is deterministic: for the same input it will always select the same element. The operator was added to ProB's standard library to enable translating TLA$^+$ [22] to B (see [16]).

The `choose` operator was not directly translated in [26] but first eliminated using rewriting rules within ASM. As such the first author of [26] did not notice this discrepancy between the ASM and B semantics.

The ASM choose operator is not directly equivalent to B's `ANY` statement. It generally needs to be translated using a combination of `LET`, `IF` and `ANY` statements.

[2] Skip is the default behaviour in Asmeta. It is possible to specify an optional `ifnone P` annotation.

3.8 Parallel Updates

Operators like if-then-else are easy to translate to B, as we have the equivalent `IF-THEN-ELSE` substitution at our disposal. Similarly, for the ASM `par` operator we have the parallel substitution operator `||` in B. Still, here the translation is much more complex. Indeed, the semantics of parallel updates is quite different in ASM and B (see [26]).

In B one cannot concurrently update the same variable. As such, `f(i) := x` cannot be executed in parallel with `f(j) := 1`. In ASM, such an update is allowed, but for the update to be consistent either $i \neq j$ or $x = 1$ must hold. The translation in [26] from ASM to Event-B introduced a generic scheme using update functions.[3] We have adapted the scheme and have proceeded as follows:

- Check syntactically which variables can be updated in parallel (in our case these are `drawerLed` and `isPillTobeTaken`).
- All variables which are not updated in parallel can be directly assigned in the B translation.
- For variables updated in parallel, we
  - do not perform the assignment directly, but compute an update set (e.g., $\{i \mapsto x\}$ and $\{j \mapsto 1\}$ above) and
  - return the update set for each operation.
  - At the end of the main rule we merge and apply the updates in one go.

Take the following ASM rule from Listing 2.1:

```
rule r_pillToBeTaken($drawer in Drawer) = par
        if isOff($drawer) then r_reset_timer[tenMinutes] endif
        drawerLed($drawer) := ON
    endpar
```

Listing 3.17. Concurrent Updates in r_pillToBeTaken

In the main rule and all dependent rules we have (potential) parallel updates to the two variables `drawerLed` and `isPillTobeTaken`. Note that `r_reset_timer` does not assign to any variables. Hence, the above ASM rule gets translated to the following B local operation:

```
    Delta_drawerLed <-- r_pillToBeTaken(drawer) = PRE drawer:Drawer THEN
        IF isOff(drawer) THEN r_reset_timer(tenMinutes) END
        ||
        Delta_drawerLed := {drawer |-> ON}
    END;
```

Listing 3.18. Concurrent Updates in r_pillToBeTaken

The main rule of our B machine then merges all updates using the relational override operator `$<$+`. Note that we do not do a consistency check in the main operation itself; this will be done by the invariant, which checks that the new values of `drawerLed` and `isPillTobeTaken` are functions (an inconsistent ASM update would result in a relation which is not a function).

[3] See also [29,30] for an alternate approach using clash freedom checks.

```
par_updates <-- r_Main = VAR dDelta1, dDelta2, iDelta1, iDelta2 IN
    BEGIN
      dDelta1 <-- r_choosePillToTake ||
      dDelta2,iDelta1,iDelta2 <-- r_setOtherDrawers
    END
    ;
    BEGIN
       drawerLed := drawerLed <+ (dDelta1 \/ dDelta2) ||
       isPillTobeTaken := isPillTobeTaken <+ (iDelta1 \/ iDelta2) ||
       par_updates := ((dDelta1 \/ dDelta2), (iDelta1 \/ iDelta2) )
    END
END;
```

Listing 3.19. Merging Parallel Updates in the main Operation

Note that the addition of the `par_updates` result value is not necessary; it is just as additional information to be displayed in the ProB animator.

While the translation in Listing 3.18 for `r_pillToBeTaken` was still relatively straightforward, the scheme gets a bit more involved when combining parallel updates with the ASM `forall` operator. Here we need to move the parallel updates into a B set comprehension or lambda abstraction to encode the `forall`:

```
rule r_setOtherDrawers = forall $drawer in Drawer do par
    if pillDeadlineHit($drawer) and isOff($drawer) then
        isPillTobeTaken($drawer):= true endif
    if (isThereAnyOtherDeadline($drawer)) then r_take[$drawer] endif
  endpar
```

Listing 3.20. An ASM forall with Parallel Updates

```
dDelta, iDelta1, iDelta2 <-- r_setOtherDrawers =
BEGIN
    iDelta1 := %drawer.(drawer:Drawer & pillDeadlineHit(drawer) &
        isOff(drawer) | TRUE)
    ||
    LET other BE other = {drawer| isThereAnyOtherDeadline(drawer)}
    IN
      dDelta,iDelta2 <-- r_take(other)
    END
END;
```

Listing 3.21. Translating forall with Parallel Updates

Observe how we had to merge parallel updates using B's lambda abstraction (the percentage sign stands for lambda) to compute `iDelta1`. Also note, how we pass the set of parallel update candidates `other` to the operation call `r_take`. Indeed, in B we cannot perform multiple parallel calls to the same operation. This has to be emulated by passing a set of instances as an additional argument. An alternative would have been to unfold the `forall` into a list of parallel updates. But this is only possible when the list is bounded and statically known (which is the case here), and would require updating the translation whenever the set of drawers changes (e.g., when adding an additional drawer to the pillbox).

An alternate approach to translating ASM's parallel updates to a relational encoding (thus compatible with B) is presented in [29,30]. See also [31] which presents an extension of Event-B and discusses partial updates (in Sect. 4). See also earlier discussions about the partial update problem in [32].

Converting parallel updates to B is not straightforward. It requires determining which variables are updated in parallel, passing update sets as return values of local operations, merging and applying the update in the main rule. Furthermore, for parallel updates in the scope of forall statements, we need to pass additional arguments to inner operation calls.

3.9 Encoding Monitored Variables and Updates to Them

ASM provides the feature to annotate variables as monitored, meaning they are not controlled by the abstract state machine, but by the environment. In the pillbox case study this is the `isPillTaken` function, which indicates whether an available pill is taken by the patient or not:

```
dynamic monitored isPillTaken: Drawer -> Boolean
```

Listing 3.22. Monitored Variable

The semantics (at least as far as AsmetaSMV [5] is concerned[4]), is that a transition of an ASM machine consist of a single execution of the main rule, directly followed by an arbitrary update of the monitored variables. The intermediate state is not visible (at least to the AsmetaSMV model checker).

B does not have the notion of monitored variables: all variables are explicitly controlled. But one can emulate monitored variables using non-deterministic assignments within environment operations (or events in Event-B).

Note that in the B translation, we have decided not to automatically execute the updates to the monitored `isPillTaken` variable after every execution of the main rule. We have preferred to leave the environment updates in a separate B operation:

```
ENV_toggle_isPillTaken(d,newval) =
 SELECT d:Drawer & newval = bool(isPillTaken(d)=FALSE) THEN
  isPillTaken(d) := newval // negate the entry
 END;
```

Listing 3.23. Updating Monitored Variable

This enables the user more fine-grained control about the updates in the animator. It also enables us to link buttons in the visualisation with incremental updates of the monitored variables (see Sect. 5). Also, as long as we do not use the next state operator in LTL or CTL formulas and our formulas are not sensitive to non-atomic changes of the monitored variables, this encoding is almost identical to automatically executing updates to monitored variables after the main rule:

- as the update is non-deterministic in ASM, there is always the option that the update does not modify the monitored variables. Hence, two successive execution of the main rule in B have a corresponding counterpart in ASM.

[4] Derived by the author by experimenting with CTL formulas using next state operators.

– as two or more updates in B (using `ENV_toggle_isPillTaken`) can be mimicked by a single non-deterministic choice, such executions in B also have a counterpart in ASM (but without the intermediate states).

One could argue that some of the values of `isPillTaken` (allowed by ASM's full non-determinism) do not make sense: i.e., a pill cannot be taken by the patient if none is available in the pillbox. In B we could filter out such "nonsense" behaviour and more precisely model the behaviour of the environment (i.e., the patient here).

Monitored variables can be translated to B variables which are non-deterministically updated by an environment operation. One can decide to exactly emulate the ASM semantics and execute these updates after each main rule. But it may make sense to allow independent evolution of the environment and the main machine, for user convenience and for more precise animation, simulation or verification (Table 1).

3.10 Summary

Table 1. Overview of Translation Rules from ASM to B

ASM	B Translation	Details
enum domain	`SETS`	Sect. 3.1 (enumerated)
abstract domain	`SETS`	Sect. 3.1 (deferred)
static controlled	`CONSTANTS`	Sect. 3.2
dynamic controlled	`VARIABLES`	Sect. 3.2
derived	`DEFINITIONS`	Sect. 3.3
dynamic monitored	`VARIABLES`	Sect. 3.9
main rule	`OPERATIONS`	Sect. 3.6
subsidiary rules	`LOCAL_OPERATIONS`	Sect. 3.6
default init	`INITIALISATION`	Sect. 3.5
choose operator	`LET-IF-ANY`	Sect. 3.7
parallel updates	$\|\|$ + Δ-updates	Sect. 3.8
forall operator	set comprehension / λ	Sect. 3.8
`Int`	`INTEGER`	
`Nat`	`NATURAL`	Sect. 3.4 (type $\mathbb{Z}$ in B)
`Boolean`	`BOOL`	
`String`	`STRING`	
`Seq`	`seq`	Sect. 3.4 (indexes start at 1)

4 Undefinedness vs Well-Definedness

With the above translation scheme, we managed to fully translate the ASM `pillbox_final` model to a B model. The validity of the translation could be checked by animating the B model with ProB and comparing it with Asmeta animations. Note that it took a while to get a faithful translation. E.g., early versions would unexpectedly deadlock in B, related to the blocking of the `ANY` substitution used to translate choose (see Sect. 3.7).

After fixing the translation scheme, one issue remained: ProB reported a well-definedness error on the B translation (see Fig. 1). And indeed, the treatment of well-definedness in ASM and B is quite different. In ASMs, every function can take the value `undef`. All functions are total; so, if one accesses an array out of bounds one gets `undef` as result. This result can be further manipulated; e.g., adding 1 to `undef` yields `undef` and the comparison `undef < 10` yields false.

The approach of the B-method is very different. B uses well-definedness (WD) proof obligations (POs) [4] for all formulas under consideration. These POs can be generated by the Rodin platform [3], by Atelier-B (where they are called WD-lemmas), and by ProB [24]. If they are discharged, we know that the corresponding formulas are well-defined and that we can safely apply inferences rules of two-valued logic. More details about this can be found in [6,24,28].

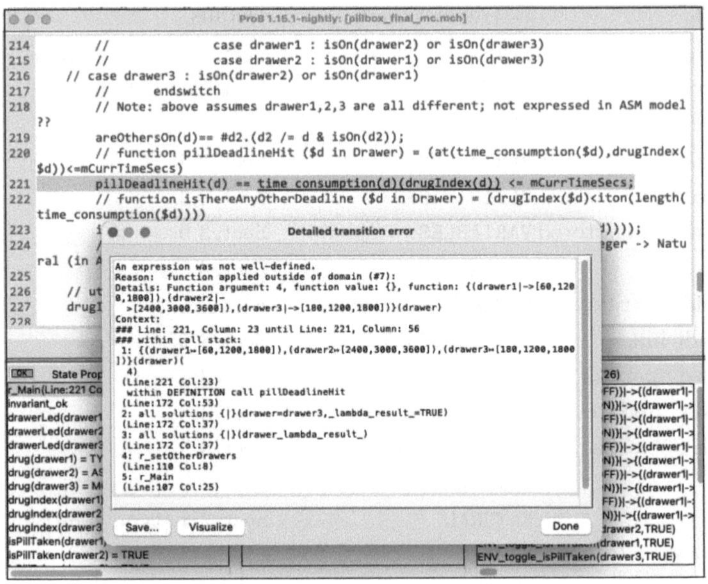

Fig. 1. Well-definedness Error Found by ProB in B model of ASM Pillbox

ProB reported the WD error in Fig. 1 for an out-of-bounds access after the last pill was taken from a drawer in the following piece of code:

```
pillDeadlineHit(d) == time_consumption(d)(drugIndex(d)) <= mCurrTimeSecs;
```

Listing 4.24. WD Issue in pillDeadlineHit

Indeed, when all drugs have been taken in a drawer d, the value of `drugIndex(d)` is not in the domain of `time_consumption`. This is an error in B, but simply `undef` in ASM.

The error in the model can be found either by model checking or by animating long enough. One can also use PROB's WD prover [24], which warns about one undischarged proof obligation:

```
WD-PO [r_setOtherDrawers] not discharged: drugIndex(drawer) : dom(time_consumption(drawer))
 ### File: pillbox_final_mc.mch
 ### Line: 221, Column: 23 until 56
 ### within: DEFINITION call of pillDeadlineHit at Line: 172 Column: 53 until Line: 172 Column: 75 in file: pillbox_final_mc.mch
```

Listing 4.25. WD Warning by ProB's WD-Prover

We have fixed the issue in our translation by adding an explicit bounds check `drugIndexWD` as follows:

```
    pillDeadlineHit(d) == drugIndexWD(d) & time_consumption(d)(drugIndex(d)) <= mCurrTimeSecs;
    // utility for B, to check if the drugIndex access is not out-of-bounds
    drugIndexWD(d) == drugIndex(d):dom(time_consumption(d));
```

Listing 4.26. WD Issue in pillDeadlineHit

In ASMs, we get `undef` for `pillDeadlineHit(d)` after the last pill has been taken, which makes the guard in `r_setOtherDrawers` false, and here leads to reasonable behaviour. It is probably still a good idea to adapt the ASM model in a similar fashion to the B model. Indeed, what happens if we use `pillDeadlineHit` inside a negation or temporal logic formula? Here, it is far from clear what the correct value of not(`undef`) should be. Furthermore, while the ASM tools can gracefully deal with out-of-bounds accesses, real programming languages like C++ do not. Hence, when translating the ASM rule `pillDeadlineHit` to C++, one has to add safeguards like Listing 4.26. Maybe surprisingly, such a safeguard is *not* present in the C++ code from [8], generated using [9]:

```
bool pillbox_final::pillDeadlineHit(Drawer* _d){return (time_consumption[0][_d][drugIndex[0][_d]] <= mCurrTimeSecs);}
```

Listing 4.27. C++ Translation of `pillDeadlineHit`

As you can see, the code generator has translated access to `time_consumption` using an "unsafe" array access of C++. Hence, when `drugIndex` becomes 3, we have undefined behaviour, which can result in crashes, wrong behaviour, or security risks. When compiling the code from [8] with more stringent compile-time flags we get this error message when `drugIndex` becomes 3:

```
==53544==ERROR: AddressSanitizer: heap-buffer-overflow on address 0x602000
    00015c at pc 0x0001008129dc bp 0x00016f5f0ff0 sp 0x00016f5f0fe8
READ of size 4 at 0x60200000015c thread T0
    #0 0x0001008129d8 in pillbox_final::pillDeadlineHit(
        pillbox_finalnamespace::Drawer*)+0x76c (a.out:arm64+0x1000069d8)
    #1 0x000100811f34 in pillbox_final::r_setOtherDrawers()+0x308 (a.out:
        arm64+0x100005f34)
    #2 0x000100813740 in pillbox_final::r_Main()+0x12c (a.out:arm64+0x1000
        07740)
    #3 0x0001008237b4 in main+0x214c (a.out:arm64+0x1000177b4)
    #4 0x000190b19d50  (<unknown module>)
```

Listing 4.28. C++ Error when using fsanitize=address,undefined Compile Flag

So, either the C++ code generator [9] needs to be adapted to treat **undef** values or one would need to run a well-definedness check similar to B before doing the code generation from an ASM machine.

☞ *Verdict: Well-Definedness.* While B's concept of well-definedness puts more burden on the modeler, the end result is more robust and can be more easily translated to safe code in a regular programming language.

5 Validating the Case Study with ProB

Animation. Figure 2 shows a screenshot of the ProB2-UI [7], validating our B translation of the pillbox case study. In the upper left-hand corner you can see the operations pane, where all available operations are pre-computed. You can see here that two executions of the main rule `r_Main` are possible (due to the choose operator in `r_choosePillToTake`: either the pill from drawer 1 or from drawer 3 can be chosen).

The fact that we have one main rule in the original ASM makes animation less user-friendly; we only see that `r_Main` got executed along with the update set. In ASMETA's animator we do not see what exactly happened within an ASM rule execution; we only see the effect of the entire rule (see Fig. 5 in [8]). However, by right-clicking in ProB2-UI on the `r_Main` transition and selecting "Show Details" one can inspect the exact behaviour of each rule execution (seeing which subsidiary local operations got called and what their effects were). This is a relatively new feature of ProB, which is particularly useful for ASM models with their complex main rules.

In the lower right-hand corner we can see the current history, while in the lower left-hand corner, we can inspect the list of saved traces (aka scenarios) and replay them. This is similar in concept to the Avalla traces from [8].[5] The visualisation in the lower middle pane is explained below in Sect. 5.

Animation with ProB generated traces which correspond to ASMETA traces. ProB provides a few additional features, like inspecting the details of a rule execution, backtracking the animation and showing all available transitions in the operations view. Avalla's ASMETA traces provide a few features not available in ProB.

[5] The Avalla traces have a few features like **step until** or directly setting variables which are not currently present in ProB's traces.

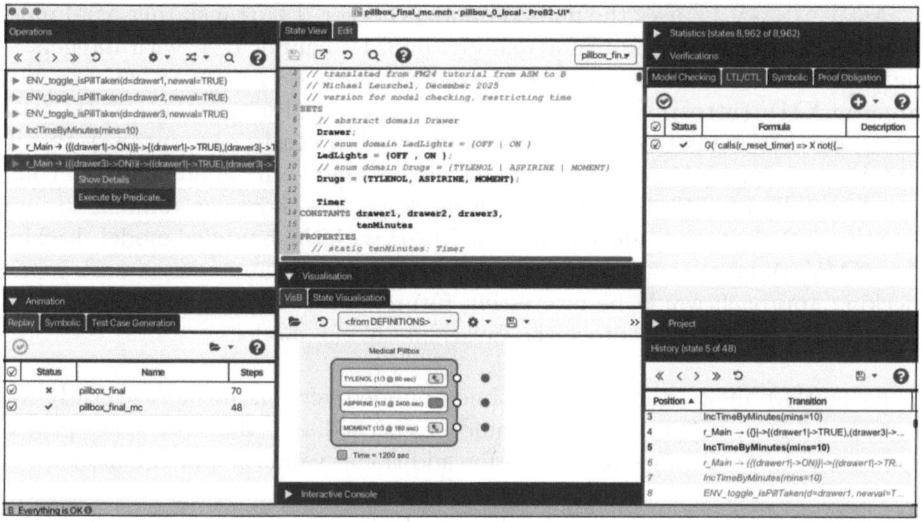

Fig. 2. ProB2-UI Screenshot

Model Checking. The state space of the `pillbox_final` ASM model and thus also of the B translation is infinite, due to the unbounded time variable `mCurrTimeSecs`. To make explicit model checking feasible, we restricted the maximal time value to the last pill deadline plus 10 minutes. We also restricted time evolutions to 10-minute steps. This leads to a B model with 8692 states and 43154 transitions. Checking the invariants, the well-definedness and the absence of deadlocks for this model takes 9.5 s (on a MacBook Air with M2 processor using ProB 1.15.1-final).

Once the state space has been constructed, we can for example generate projection diagrams [21] to check that the behaviour of the model is as expected (e.g., we projected the state space onto the status of the LED lights, which confirms that only one light can be on at any one time and that when changing the light from one drawer to another, we must encounter an intermediate state where all lights are off).

The feature to inspect the details of transition ("Show Details" in Fig. 2) can also be used within LTL properties, using the new `calls` operator. An atomic LTL proposition `calls(Op)` is true if the next transition calls the operation Op, either directly or via inner operation calls. Here is an example property which we can express using that new operator:

```
G(  calls(r_reset_timer) => X not({expired(tenMinutes)}))
```

Listing 5.29. LTL Property using `calls` Operator

In the upper right-hand part of Fig. 2 you can see that this LTL property was successfully checked.

AsmetaSMV [5] uses the nuSMV model checker [13], translating ASM models to SMV specifications. Unfortunately, nuSMV cannot deal with integers so the `pillbox_final` model cannot be checked with it. AsmetaSMV can also target nuXMV (https://nuxmv.fbk.eu), which can deal with integers.[6] Unfortunately, nuXMV cannot deal with sequences (used in `time_consumption`). But [8] contains a simpler `pillbox_time` model with a single pill, where this tool could be successfully used for bounded model checking. It is, however, difficult to compare the explicit state model checking of ProB with the bounded model checking of nuXMV. A more systematic comparison of the pros and cons of each model checking approach would be interesting future work. Another avenue would be to use the Atelier-B to prove the invariants of the model.

Exhaustive model checking of a time-bounded version of the case study was possible. LTL and CTL properties could be checked, and the state space projection visualisation features are useful for additional validation of the model.

Visualisation. VisB [35] is a visualisation feature available in ProB based on SVG (Scalable Vector Graphics). Below in Listing 5.30 you see the description of the visualisation used for the pillbox. The definition on line 1 defines the SVG file to be used for the visualisation, which can be seen on the left of Fig. 3. Note that the original draft of the SVG file was generated using ChatGPT, and then extended with additional objects by hand. Also `id` attributes were added, so that VisB can access and update the objects. This annotation can be expressed directly in B itself, via special definitions starting with the prefix `VISB_SVG`. B records are used to specify updates of attributes to existing SVG objects (with matching `id` attribute). For example, the definition `VISB_SVG_UPDATES5` below updates the text field of the SVG text object with id `Time_Text`. You can see the effect of the updates in the right of Fig. 3, for a particular state of the B model. Below we also specify tooltips via the title attribute (a VisB feature). In the full B model we also specify events that are triggered when clicking on various SVG objects (e.g., to influence the monitored variables).

```
1  DEFINITIONS
2     VISB_SVG_FILE == "pillbox_final_chatgpt.svg";
3     VISB_SVG_UPDATES1 == (drawer_updates(drawer1,"#f00"),
4                           drawer_updates(drawer2,"#f00"),
5                           drawer_updates(drawer3,"#f00"));
6     drawer_updates(d,col) ==
7         rec(`id`:("LED",d),
8             fill: IF drawerLed(d) = ON THEN col ELSE "white" END,
9             title: ```drawerLed(${d})=${drawerLed(d)}```);
10    defaults == (0..10)*{-1}; // default time to avoid WD error
11    VISB_SVG_UPDATES2 == {(d).d:Drawer |
12        rec(`id`:("Drug",d),
13            text:```${drug(d)} (${drugIndex(d)}/${size(time_consumption(d))
                 } @ ${(defaults<+time_consumption(d))(drugIndex(d))} sec)
                 ```)};
14   VISB_SVG_UPDATES3 == {(d).d:Drawer |
15   (rec(`id`:("isPillTobeTaken",d),
16   fill: IF isPillTobeTaken(d)=TRUE THEN "#eee" ELSE "#aaa" END)
                   ,
```

[6] Thanks to Silvia Bonfanti for making this available.
```

```
        rec('id':("Pill",d),
            visibility:isPillTobeTaken(d)))};
    VISB_SVG_UPDATES4 == (isPillTaken_updates(drawer1),
                          isPillTaken_updates(drawer2),
                          isPillTaken_updates(drawer3));
    isPillTaken_updates(d) ==
        rec('id':("isPillTaken",d),
            fill: IF isPillTaken(d)=TRUE THEN "#ff1" ELSE "gray" END,
            title: '''isPillTaken(${d})=${isPillTaken(d)}''');
    VISB_SVG_UPDATES5 == rec('id':"Time_Text", text:'''Time = ${
        mCurrTimeSecs} sec''');
```

Listing 5.30. VisB Visualisation of Pillbox

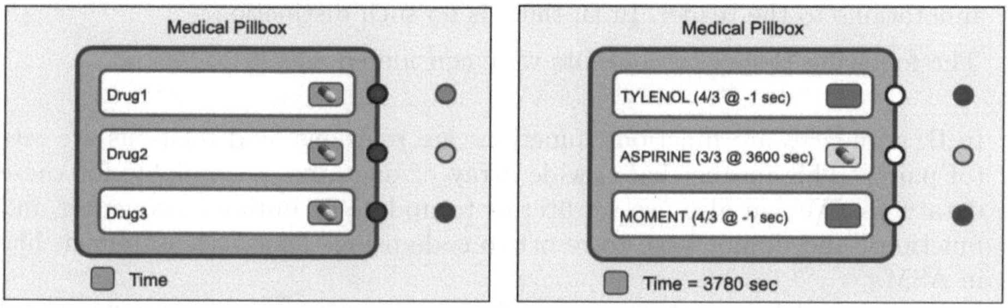

Fig. 3. Raw SVG File one the Left and VisB Visualisation of a State of the Pillbox on the Right

We can also export a trace as an HTML file [34], thus enabling a user without knowledge of B and without access to ProB to inspect the behaviour or the model. One such trace is available at the following websites:

`https://stups.hhu-hosting.de//models/asm2b/`
`https://doi.org/10.5281/zenodo.18757165`

Even though the data values of the model are not complex, the visualisation was still very helpful to get quick feedback about the state of the model and spot unexpected behaviour much more quickly.

6 Conclusion

We managed to translate the ASM pillbox case study from ASM to B, keeping the original rule structure intact. The result can be validated with B tools such as ProB, and the animation traces coincide with those from Asmeta. The manual translation from ASM to B has provided several new insights. For instance, we found surprising differences between ASM's `choose` operator and the `ANY` substitution in B. The separation of natural numbers from integers in ASMs was another surprise to the author. Finally, we found out that sequences in ASMs are not treated like functions (requiring special operators like `at`) and their indexes start at 0 (and not at 1 like in B).

We found the following concepts specific to ASMs very useful:

- The concept of derived functions in ASM is better than B's definitions (which are macros). Derived functions do not suffer from variable capture and carry typing information.
- The distinction between controlled and monitored variables provides clear annotations to the reader. In B, there is no such distinction.

The following B-specific concepts were considered useful:

- In B, sequences are functions, functions are relations, and relations are sets (of pairs). This means that a wide array of operators is available for these datatypes. We can also use set literals to update or initialise sequences and functions, and do not have to resort to code using the switch statement like in ASM.
- In B we do not have just one main rule (aka operation), but can have several operations. This can lead to easier animation and better system modelling (e.g., precise modelling of the environment updates).

The following language-specific aspects are also noteworthy:

- The distinction between integers and natural numbers in ASMs leads to stronger type checks, but requires special literals (0n vs 0) and conversion functions. For this case study, there was no benefit in this separation.
- The more flexible parallel updates in ASMs can be tricky to translate right to B (or similar formalisms). Parallel updates can be convenient, but may come at the cost of clarity. In Listing 2.1 it is not immediately clear which variables are updated in parallel.
- The approach of ASMs with the special `undef` value can be convenient for modelling, but may hide unexpected errors. As we have seen, in this case study, a subtle error in the ASM code C++ generator [9] lay undetected but was uncovered by B's approach to well-definedness.

Acknowledgements. I would like to thank Silvia Bonfanti, Angelo Gargantini for their very valuable feedback on Asmeta and AsmetaSMV. I am very grateful to Jan Gruteser, who provided helpful suggestions and corrections. Anonymous referees also provided very useful corrections. OpenAI GPT OSS 120B OSKI.nrw was used to diagnose the C++ code generated from the ASM model, and ChatGPT was used to produce the initial SVG for the visualisation.

This article is the practical counterpart to the work done [26] with Egon Börger during his visit as Humboldt Professor. It is my pleasure to dedicate this article to his Festschrift.

References

1. Abrial, J.-R.: The B-Book. Cambridge University Press (1996)
2. Abrial, J.-R.: Modeling in Event-B: System and Software Engineering. Cambridge University Press (2010)
3. Abrial, J.-R., Butler, M., Hallerstede, S., Voisin, L.: An open extensible tool environment for Event-B. In: Liu, Z., He, J. (eds.) ICFEM 2006. LNCS, vol. 4260, pp. 588–605. Springer, Heidelberg (2006). https://doi.org/10.1007/11901433_32
4. Abrial, J.-R., Mussat, L.: On using conditional definitions in formal theories. In: Bert, D., Bowen, J.P., Henson, M.C., Robinson, K. (eds.) ZB 2002. LNCS, vol. 2272, pp. 242–269. Springer, Heidelberg (2002). https://doi.org/10.1007/3-540-45648-1_13
5. Arcaini, P., Gargantini, A., Riccobene, E.: Asmetasmv: a way to link high-level ASM models to low-level NuSMV specifications. In: Proceedings ABZ'10, pp. 61–74 (2010)
6. Behm, P., Burdy, L., Meynadier, J.-M.: Well defined B. In: Bert, D. (ed.) B 1998. LNCS, vol. 1393, pp. 29–45. Springer, Heidelberg (1998). https://doi.org/10.1007/BFb0053354
7. Bendisposto, J., et al.: ProB2-UI: a java-based user interface for ProB. In: Lluch Lafuente, A., Mavridou, A. (eds.) FMICS 2021. LNCS, vol. 12863, pp. 193–201. Springer, Cham (2021). https://doi.org/10.1007/978-3-030-85248-1_12
8. Bombarda, A., Bonfanti, S., Gargantini, A., Riccobene, E., Scandurra, P.: ASMETA tool set for rigorous system design. In: Proceedings FM'2024 Part II, LNCS 14934, pp. 492–517 (2024)
9. Bonfanti, S., Gargantini, A., Mashkoor, A.: Design and validation of a C++ code generator from abstract state machines specifications. J. Softw. Evol. Process. **32**(2) (2020)
10. Börger, E.: Abstract State Machines. Springer-Verlag (2003)
11. Börger, E., Stärk, R.F.: Abstract State Machines. A Method for High-Level System Design and Analysis. Springer (2003)
12. Butler, M., Körner, P., Krings, S., Lecomte, T., Leuschel, M., Mejia, L.-F., Voisin, L.: The first twenty-five years of industrial use of the B-method. In: ter Beek, M.H., Ničković, D. (eds.) FMICS 2020. LNCS, vol. 12327, pp. 189–209. Springer, Cham (2020). https://doi.org/10.1007/978-3-030-58298-2_8
13. Cimatti, A., et al.: NuSMV Version 2: An OpenSource tool for symbolic model checking. In: Proceedings CAV 2002, Copenhagen, Denmark, vol. 2404 of LNCS. Springer (2002)
14. ClearSy. Atelier B, User and Reference Manuals. Aix-en-Provence, France (2009). http://www.atelierb.eu/
15. Farahbod, R., Gervasi, V., Glässer, U.: CoreASM: an extensible ASM execution engine. Fundam. Inform. **77**(1–2), 71–103 (2007)
16. Hansen, D., Leuschel, M.: Translating TLA+ to B for validation with ProB. In: Proceedings iFM'2012, LNCS 7321, pp. 24–38. Springer (2012)
17. Herman, D., Wand, M.: A theory of hygienic macros. In: Drossopoulou, S. (ed.) ESOP 2008. LNCS, vol. 4960, pp. 48–62. Springer, Heidelberg (2008). https://doi.org/10.1007/978-3-540-78739-6_4
18. Hörne, T., van der Poll, J.A.: Planning as model checking: the performance of ProB vs NuSMV. In: Botha, R., Cilliers, C., (eds.), SAICSIT Conf., vol. 338 of ACM International Conference Proceeding Series, pp. 114–123. ACM (2008)

19. Jackson, D.: Alloy: a lightweight object modelling notation. ACM Trans. Softw. Eng. Methodol. **11**, 256–290 (2002)
20. Jones, C.B.: Systematic Software Development using VDM. Prentice-Hall (1986)
21. Ladenberger, L., Leuschel, M.: Mastering the visualization of larger state spaces with projection diagrams. In: Butler, M., Conchon, S., Zaïdi, F. (eds.) ICFEM 2015. LNCS, vol. 9407, pp. 153–169. Springer, Cham (2015). https://doi.org/10.1007/978-3-319-25423-4_10
22. Lamport, L.: Specifying Systems. The TLA+ Language and Tools for Hardware and Software Engineers. Addison-Wesley (2002)
23. Lecomte, T., Deharbe, D., Prun, E., Mottin, E.: Applying a formal method in industry: a 25-year trajectory. In: Cavalheiro, S., Fiadeiro, J. (eds.) SBMF 2017. LNCS, vol. 10623, pp. 70–87. Springer, Cham (2017). https://doi.org/10.1007/978-3-319-70848-5_6
24. Leuschel, M.: Fast and effective well-definedness checking. In: Dongol, B., Troubitsyna, E. (eds.) IFM 2020. LNCS, vol. 12546, pp. 63–81. Springer, Cham (2020). https://doi.org/10.1007/978-3-030-63461-2_4
25. Leuschel, M.: Spot the difference: a detailed comparison between B and event-B. In: Raschke, A., Riccobene, E., Schewe, K.-D. (eds.) Logic, Computation and Rigorous Methods. LNCS, vol. 12750, pp. 147–172. Springer, Cham (2021). https://doi.org/10.1007/978-3-030-76020-5_9
26. Leuschel, M., Börger, E.: A compact encoding of sequential ASMs in Event-B. In: Butler, M., Schewe, K.-D., Mashkoor, A., Biro, M. (eds.) ABZ 2016. LNCS, vol. 9675, pp. 119–134. Springer, Cham (2016). https://doi.org/10.1007/978-3-319-33600-8_7
27. Leuschel, M., Butler, M.J.: ProB: an automated analysis toolset for the B method. STTT **10**(2), 185–203 (2008)
28. Métayer, C., Voisin, L.: The Event-B mathematical language. http://wiki.event-b.org/index.php/Event-B_Mathematical_Language (2009)
29. Schellhorn, G., Ernst, G., Pfähler, J., Bodenmüller, S., Reif, W.: Symbolic execution for a clash-free subset of ASMs. Sci. Comput. Program. **158**, 21–40 (2018)
30. Schellhorn, G., Ernst, G., Pfähler, J., Reif, W.: A relational encoding for a clash-free subset of ASMs. In: Butler, M., Schewe, K.-D., Mashkoor, A., Biro, M. (eds.) ABZ 2016. LNCS, vol. 9675, pp. 237–243. Springer, Cham (2016). https://doi.org/10.1007/978-3-319-33600-8_15
31. Schewe, K.-D.: Extensions to hybrid event-B to support concurrency in cyber-physical systems. In: Abdelwahed, E.H., Bellatreche, L., Golfarelli, M., Méry, D., Ordonez, C. (eds.) MEDI 2018. LNCS, vol. 11163, pp. 418–433. Springer, Cham (2018). https://doi.org/10.1007/978-3-030-00856-7_28
32. Schewe, K., Wang, Q.: Partial updates in complex-value databases. In: Heimbürger, A., Kiyoki, Y., Tokuda, T., Jaakkola, H., Yoshida, N., (eds.), Proceedings EJC 2010, vol. 225 of Frontiers in Artificial Intelligence and Applications, pp. 37–56. IOS Press (2010)
33. Spivey, J.M.: The Z Notation: a reference manual. Prentice-Hall (1992). https://github.com/Spivoxity/zrm
34. Vu, F., Happe, C., Leuschel, M.: Generating interactive documents for domain-specific validation of formal models. Int. J. Softw. Tools Technol. Transfer (2024)
35. Werth, M., Leuschel, M.: VisB: a lightweight tool to visualize formal models with SVG graphics. In: Raschke, A., Méry, D., Houdek, F. (eds.) ABZ 2020. LNCS, vol. 12071, pp. 260–265. Springer, Cham (2020). https://doi.org/10.1007/978-3-030-48077-6_21

A Streamlined Semantics for TASTD

Diego de Azevedo Oliveira and Marc Frappier(✉)

CRICUS, Université de Sherbrooke, Sherbrooke, Canada
{Diego.De.Azevedo.Oliveira,Marc.Frappier}@USherbrooke.ca

Abstract. Timed Algebraic State-Transition Diagram (TASTD) is a graphical notation that allows for the combination of extended hierarchical state machines with process algebra operators. It supports the specification of real-time constraints using a global clock, timing operators and user-defined clocks. This paper proposes a simplified semantics for TASTD. The operational semantics of TASTD is defined in a tabular representation, identifying commonalities between operators, in order to facilitate its understanding and analysis. The semantics of parallel operators is simplified, removing the obligation of commutativity of actions in a synchronization and a flow; non-deterministic choice between the two possible sequential execution of actions in a parallel composition is used.

Keywords: ASTD · real-time model · case study · TASTD · formal method

1 Introduction

ASTD (Algebraic State-Transition Diagram) [1] is a graphical notation that combines process algebra operators drawn from CSP [2,3] and a variant of extended hierarchical state machines [4,5] inspired from Statecharts [6]. Timed ASTD (TASTD) [7,8] is a real-time extension for ASTD, integrating concepts from time extensions that have been proposed for several well-known languages like Statecharts, with MATLAB Stateflow [9], automata, with timed automata [10], process algebra, with Timed CSP [11,12] and Stateful Timed CSP [13]. TASTD takes advantage of the strengths of these notations: graphical representation, hierarchy, orthogonality, compositionality, and abstraction. It has been successfully applied in case studies for intrusion detection [14–16] and control systems [17,18].

This paper introduces a simplified semantics for TASTD, compared to the one introduced in [7,8]. Its operational semantics is defined in a simpler manner, represented by tabular expression, identifying commonalities between operators, in order to facilitate its understanding and analysis. The semantics of parallel operators is simplified, removing the obligation of commutativity of actions in a synchronization and a flow; non-deterministic choice between the two possible sequential execution of actions in a parallel composition is used.

This article is structured as follows. Section 2 presents TASTD and its semantics. Section 4 discusses related work. Section 5 concludes the paper.

A. Raschke et al. (Eds.): Egon Börger Festschrift, LNCS 16580, pp. 295–316, 2026.
https://doi.org/10.1007/978-3-032-24494-9_14

2 TASTD

In this section, we first provide a summary of the ASTD notation, and we then define its time extension, TASTD. The semantics of the extended language is introduced.

2.1 Conventions

When defining a mathematical structure M of type $(a_1 : T_1, \ldots, a_n : T_n)$, we simply write $(a_1, \ldots, a_n)$ and introduce the types $T_1, \ldots, T_n$ and additional constraints in the text following the declaration. We refer to a component a_i of M as $M.a_i$. We use the B notation [19] to write our mathematical descriptions.

- $f \in D_1 \rightarrow D_2$ is a total function from D_1 to D_2.
- $f \in D_1 \nrightarrow D_2$ is a partial function from D_1 to D_2.
- $\text{dom}(r) = \{d \mid \exists d' \cdot (d, d') \in r\}$ is the domain of relation r.
- $r[D] = \{d' \mid \exists d \cdot d \in D \wedge (d, d') \in r\}$ is the set of images of elements of D by relation r.
- $D \lhd r = \{(d, d') \mid (d, d') \in r \wedge d \in D\}$ is the domain restriction of relation r with set D.
- $r \trianglerighteq D = \{(d, d') \mid (d, d') \in r \wedge d' \notin D\}$ is the negative range restriction of relation r with set D.
- $r_1 \circ r_2 = \{(d, d') \mid \exists d'' \cdot (d, d'') \in r_1 \wedge (d'', d') \in r_2\}$ is the relational composition of relations r_1 and r_2. Note that the symbol ";" is used in B for both relational composition and statement composition. To avoid any confusion, we will use "$\circ$" for relational composition and ";" for statement composition.
- $\beta_1 ; \beta_2 = \{(d, d') \mid (d, d') \in \beta_1 \circ \beta_2 \wedge \beta_1[\{d\}] \subseteq \text{dom}(\beta_2)\}$ denotes the sequential composition of actions β_1 and β_2. In this paper, actions are represented by relations. Operator ";" is monotonic with respect to B refinement. It is also called demonic composition in relational semantics of programs [20,21].
- "$\frown$" is list concatenation.

$\mathbb{T} = \mathbb{R}_{\geq 0}$ is the set of timestamps (*i.e.*, clock values) given by non-negative real numbers. $\mathbb{B} = \{\mathsf{true}, \mathsf{false}\}$ is the set of Boolean values. Var is a set of variables. We assume in the sequel that each variable declaration in a specification uses a variable distinct from the variables of all the other declarations, in order to avoid shadowing and to simplify the semantic definitions; shadowing is taken into account in [8]. $\mathsf{Env} = \mathsf{Var} \nrightarrow \mathsf{Type}$ is the set of *environments*: An environment is a partial function that maps variables in Var to their values in Type, which denotes the union of all types available. The substitution of free occurrences of variable x by expression v in expression w is noted $w([x := v])$, which can be generalized to an arbitrary environment e, and noted $w([e])$, and denoting simultaneous substitution. β denotes an action that modifies variables of an ASTD. We assume that a relational semantics is available for the action language, and we write $\beta(e, e')$ for the relation between the initial value e and final values e' induced by the execution of action β.

2.2 The ASTD Notation

ASTD is graphical notation. We provide here its abstract syntax. There are 10 types of primary ASTD, and 6 types of secondary ASTD which are defined in terms of primary ASTD. The primary ASTD types are listed in Table 1: automaton "Aut", sequence " ", interrupt "$\triangle$", persistent guard "$\Rightarrow_p$", choice "$|$", Kleene closure "$\star$", generalized parallel (*i.e.*, synchronization) "$|[]|$", flow "⫛", quantified choice "$|:$", quantified parallel "$|[]|:$", and ASTD call. The guard ASTD, which was in the original ASTD definition [1], is now a secondary ASTD defined using a persistent guard ASTD. elem is the elementary ASTD type that is used solely to type elementary states of an automaton.

There are three kinds of variables in an ASTD specification: i) ASTD parameters, denoted by P, whose values are specified when an ASTD is called, and can be modified during execution; ii) ASTD attributes, denoted by V, play the same role as attributes in a class definition of a programming language, and define part of the state of an ASTD; iii) quantified variables, which are introduced by quantified ASTD operator quantified choice and quantified generalized parallel; they are read-only.

We do not detail here the syntax of actions. Actions of executable ASTD specifications are written in C++, because this is the language in which cASTD [15], the compiler of the ASTD notation, generates an executable implementation. Actions can also be written using the generalized substitution language of B [19] or the action language of Event-B [22].

All ASTD types share common characteristics, which we define in a general (abstract) type ASTD, from which the primary and secondary ASTD types inherit:

$$\mathsf{ASTD} \triangleq (n, P, V, \beta_{init}, \beta_{astd})$$

Each ASTD has a name n, a list of parameter declarations P, a list of attribute declarations V, an action β_{init} that initializes the attributes of V, and an action β_{astd} that is executed on each transition of the ASTD. Each ASTD type includes a notion of *initial* state and *final* states, which will be defined in Sect. 3.

2.3 Primary ASTD Types

Automaton. An automaton ASTD $(\mathsf{Aut}, \Sigma, Q, \nu, \delta, F, q_0, \zeta)$ is an extension of traditional automata and also represent OR states of Statecharts. $\Sigma \subseteq \mathsf{Event}$ is the alphabet. An event $\sigma \in \Sigma$ has a label and parameters; $\alpha(\sigma)$ returns the label of σ. The special event step is an element of Σ that can be used to label transitions. It denotes a transition that can be triggered by the passage of time, whereas the other elements of Σ are events submitted by the environment of the ASTD. step is drawn from Stateflow. It is tested for execution on a periodical basis; this period is defined as a parameter of the ASTD specification. $Q \subseteq \mathsf{Name}$ is the set of automaton states. $\nu \in Q \rightarrow \mathsf{ASTD}$ maps each state to its sub-ASTD, which can be elementary (noted elem) or complex (*i.e.*, of any ASTD type). δ is the set of transitions. A transition from q_1 to q_2 is labelled with the usual Statecharts notation $\sigma[g]/\beta_{tr}$, which denotes that when guard g holds, event σ

can be accepted and action β_{tr} is executed. The abstract syntax of a transition is $\delta(\eta, \sigma, g, \beta_{tr}, \mathit{final?})$. η denotes an arrow (edge) between $q_1, q_2 \in Q$. A transition (loc, q_1, q_2) denotes a local transition from q_1 to q_2. *final?* is a Boolean: when *final?* $=$ true, the source of the transition is decorated with a bullet (i.e., $\bullet$); it indicates that the transition can be fired only if n_1 is final. $F \subseteq Q$ is the set of final states, which is partitioned into SF and DF: SF is the set of *shallow* final states, while DF denotes the set of *deep* final states, with $DF \subseteq \mathrm{dom}(\nu \rhd \{\mathsf{elem}\}$. Function $\mathcal{F}$ defined in Fig. 6 determines how these two types of final states are used. A shallow final is final irrespective of its inner state; a deep final state is final if its inner state is also final. Like in extended state machines, an automaton state can also have action declarations, given by $\zeta \in Q \to (\beta_{in}, \beta_{out}, \beta_{stay})$, which maps each state name to its actions: β_{in} is executed when a transition enters the state; β_{out} is executed when a transition leaves the state; β_{stay} is executed when a transition loops on the state, or is executed within the state.

Sequence. A sequence ASTD starts its execution with ASTD A_1. When A_1 is in a final state, A_2 is enabled to start its execution, but A_1 is still enabled to execute an event (*i.e.,* A_1 is not disabled when it is in a final state, until A_2 starts its execution). Thus, when A_1 is final and both A_1 and A_2 can execute an event, the choice between them is nondeterministic. When A_2 executes its first event, A_1 becomes disabled and stops its execution.

Interrupt. An interrupt $(\Delta, A_1, A_2, \beta_{int})$ is similar to a sequence, but A_2 can start its execution without waiting for A_1 to be in a final state. A_1 can be interrupted at any point (including its initial state). If both A_1 and A_2 can execute an event, then the choice between them is nondeterministic. Action β_{int} is executed on the first event of A_2 that interrupts A_1. A_1 is disabled after being interrupted by A_2. A_2 does not have to be executed; thus, when A_1 is in a final state, then the interrupt is also in a final state, which differs from a sequence, where A_2 has to be executed after A_1. Contrary to CSP's interrupt operator, A_2 is not disabled when A_1 reaches a final state.

Persistent Guard. A persistent guard $(\Rightarrow_p, g, A_1)$ checks that condition g is satisfied on the execution of each event of A_1. A choice $(|, A_1, A_2)$ allows the first event to choose between executing A_1 or A_2; when the choice is made, the unchosen ASTD is disabled, and the chosen ASTD continues the execution.

Kleene Closure. A Kleene closure $(\star, A_1)$ allows for looping on A_1: it executes A_1, and it can restart A_1 from its initial state when A_1 is in a final state. When A_1 is in a final state, and the next event can be executed both from the initial state of A_1 and its current final state, the choice between them is nondeterministic.

Flow. A flow $A = (\pitchfork, A_1, A_2)$ is inspired by the AND state of Statecharts; it executes an event on A_1 and A_2 whenever possible. More precisely, a flow A

executes an event σ iff either A_1, A_2, or both A_1 and A_2 can execute it. The order in which A_1 and A_2 are executed is nondeterministic; thus the final values of attributes in A, A_1 and A_2 depend on the order of execution of A_1 and A_2. This semantics of flow differs from its original semantics introduced in [8], where the execution of the actions of A_1 and A_2 needs to be commutative. This turned out to be hard to used in practice. Using a non-deterministic choice between the two ordering allows for an implementation to use one of the execution order. Thus, the compiler cASTD can select one ordering, or the user can specify one in the ASTD editor eASTD, and this one is tested first for execution.

Generalized Parallel. The generalized parallel [3] $(|[]|, \Delta, A_1, A_2)$ synchronizes the execution of A_1 and A_2 on events σ whose label $\alpha(\sigma)$ belong to Δ. Note that Δ is a set of event labels, thus, contrary to CSP, the synchronization cannot be restricted to a subset of the parameters of σ. To execute an event σ such that $\alpha(\sigma) \in \Delta$, both A_1 and A_2 must be able to execute it; otherwise, the event is refused. As with the flow operator $\pitchfork$, the order in which the actions of A_1 and A_2 are executed is nondeterministic. When $\alpha(\sigma) \notin \Delta$, then either A_1 or A_2 execute σ; if both can execute σ, then the choice between them is nondeterministic. If Δ is empty, then the parameterized synchronisation is an interleave, abbreviated as $|||$. CSP's $\|$ is defined as $(|[]|, \alpha(A_1) \cap \alpha(A_2), A_1, A_2)$.

We can draw an analogy between these three operators $\pitchfork$, $|[]|$, $|||$ and Boolean operators. Operator $|[]|$ acts like a conjunction: $(|[]|, \{\alpha(\sigma)\}, E_1, E_2)$ can execute an event σ iff both E_1 and E_2 can execute it. It expresses a conjunction of ordering constraints on σ given by E_1 and E_2. It is a *hard* synchronisation. Operator $\pitchfork$ acts like an inclusive "or": $(\pitchfork, E_1, E_2)$ can execute an event σ iff either E_1, or E_2, or both E_1 and E_2 can execute it. It is a *soft* synchronisation. Operator $|||$ looks like an exclusive "or": $(|||, E_1, E_2)$ will execute σ on either E_1 or E_2, but on only one of them; if both E_1 and E_2 can execute σ, then one of them is nondeterministically chosen.

Quantified Choice. A quantified choice $(|:, x, T, A_1)$ is similar to an existential quantification in first-order logic. It declares a local variable $x \in T$ whose scope is A_1. The value of x is chosen when the first event of A_1 is executed and it cannot be modified afterwards. A quantified generalized parallel $(|[]|:, x, T, \Delta, A_1)$ instantiates one copy $A_1(\![x := c]\!)$ for each value $c \in T$, and composes them with $|[\Delta]|$; hence it denotes the n-ary ASTD $|[\Delta]|_{c \in T} A_1(\![x := c]\!)$.

2.4 Distinctions with CSP

Termination in CSP is represented by the execution of the special process SKIP, which ends the execution of a process, and enables the execution of its successor when used within a sequential composition. In comparison, an ASTD does not terminate; if it is in a final state, it enables its successor within a sequential composition or a new iteration within a closure. When an ASTD is in a final state, it can still execute events, whereas a CSP process that has executed SKIP can no longer execute events. A final state in an automaton with no outgoing transition can simulate the behaviour of SKIP. Final states are determined by function $\mathcal{F}$ defined in Fig. 6. $\mathcal{F}$ is recursively defined over the structure of an ASTD. The semantics of TASTD does not contain internal transitions τ and ✓ used in CSP. This provides for a simpler semantics of observable transitions and easier code generation.

2.5 Graphical Representation

Figure 1 illustrate the main elements of the graphical representation of an ASTD, where *Type* denote the ASTD type and Z the components specific to an ASTD type (*e.g.*, the guard predicate). s0 is an elementary initial state, while A1 is a complex initial state which contains an ASTD also named A1. s1 is an elementary final state, and shallow by definition. A2 is a complex shallow final state, whereas A3 is a complex deep final state. B is a sequence ASTD, represented by a white arrow, which denotes that B1 is executed before B2. C is an interrupt ASTD, represented by a black arrow, which denotes that C1 is interrupted by C2.

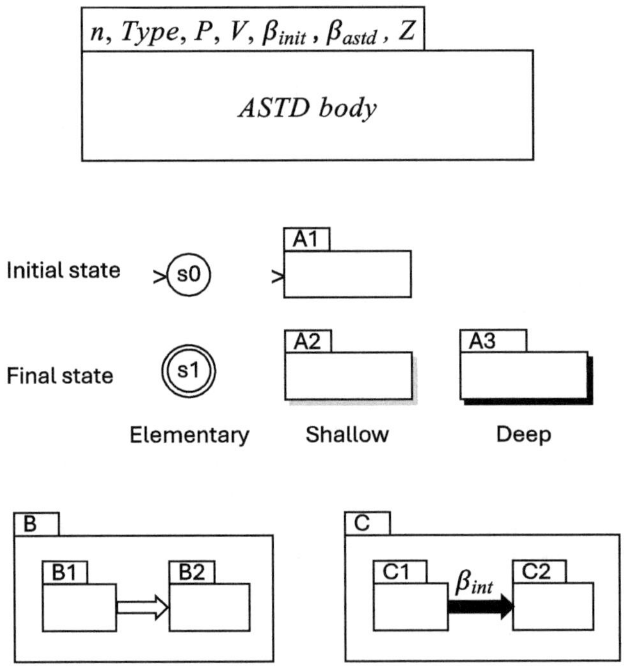

Fig. 1. The main elements of the graphical representation of an ASTD.

2.6 Secondary ASTD Type

A secondary ASTD type can be defined by a composition of primary ASTD types. There is currently a single secondary type, the guard operator of the CSP notation. A guard $(\Rightarrow, g, A)$ is defined using a persistent guard; it checks that the condition g is satisfied on the execution of the first event of A, like CSP's guard; the guard is ignored for the subsequent events. A guard is formally defined as follows.

$$(n, \Rightarrow, P, V, \beta_{init}, \beta_{astd}, g, A) \triangleq \\ (n, \Rightarrow_p, P, V \frown (b : \mathbb{B}), (\beta_{init}; b := \mathsf{false}), (\beta_{astd}; b := \mathsf{true}), g \vee b, A)$$

It uses a persistent guard $g \vee b$ on a local Boolean variable b, initialized to false, and set to true after the first event is executed. Hence, the persistent guard always holds after executing the first event.

2.7 TASTD Types

TASTD introduces five types to deal with time constraints: delay, persistent delay, timeout, persistent timeout, and timed interrupt. They are defined in terms of primary ASTDs.

Delay. A delay (Delay, d, A) will wait d units of time before accepting the first event of ASTD A. The execution of subsequent events are not subject to the delay. A delay is represented by a guard that checks that at least d units of time have elapsed since the last event has been executed. The elapsed time is represented by the difference between the current system time cst and the last event execution time t. These two variables are predefined in the ASTD notation.

$$(n, \mathsf{Delay}, P, V, \beta_{init}, \beta_{astd}, d, A) \triangleq (n, \Rightarrow, P, V, \beta_{init}, \beta_{astd}, \mathsf{cst} - \mathsf{t} > d, A)$$

Persistent Delay. A persistent delay (PDelay, d, A) will apply the delay d to the execution of each event of A. A persistent delay is represented by a persistent guard in a manner similar to the delay.

$$(n, \mathsf{PDelay}, P, V, \beta_{init}, \beta_{astd}, d, A) \triangleq (n, \Rightarrow_p, P, V, \beta_{init}, \beta_{astd}, \mathsf{cst} - \mathsf{t} > d, A)$$

Timeout. A timeout $(\mathsf{TO}, d, \beta_{to}, A_1, A_2)$ must execute its first event on A_1 within d units of time, otherwise A_1 is disabled, and A_2 takes over and executes the subsequent events. If A_1 succeeds in executing the first event within d, then A_2 is disabled, and A_1 continues the execution without any further time constraint. Action β_{to} is executed when a timeout occurs. A timeout is easier to define using its graphical representation provided in Fig. 2. The timeout n is represented by an interrupt n on n_1 and n_2. n_1 is a guard on A_1 checking that no more than d units of time have elapsed since the last executed event. This ensure that the first event of A_1 must occurs before d units of time; otherwise the guard is false and n_1 is disabled. A boolean b is added to list of variable declarations of n and initialized to false. The execution of the first event of A_1 sets b to true by the ASTD action of A_1. This disables the execution of n_2, because n_2 is a guard checking that d units of time have elapsed and that A_1 has not executed its first event. n_2 is applied to a choice n_3 between a step event in automaton n_4 and A_2. So either step or the first event of A_2 can interrupt A_1. After executing step, n_4 enables A_2. Action β_{to} is executed when the interrupt occurs.

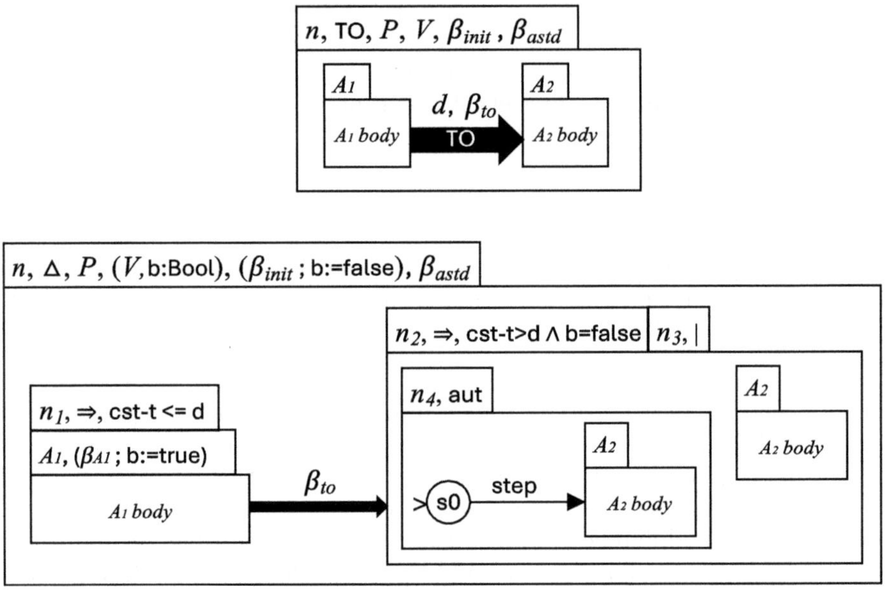

Fig. 2. At the bottom, the ASTD defining a timeout $(n, \mathsf{TO}, P, V, \beta_{init}, \beta_{astd}, d, \beta_{to}, A_1, A_2)$ illustrated at the top

Persistent Timeout. A persistent timeout $(\mathsf{PTO}, d, \beta_{to}, A_1, A_2)$ will apply d to each event of A_1; if d is missed, then A_2 takes over, and A_1 is disabled. A persistent timeout is defined in a similar fashion in Fig. 3 as the timeout. A persistent guard is used in n_1, so that the time out is checked on each event execution of A_1. There is no need to declare a boolean in that case.

Timed Interrupt. A timed interrupt $(\mathsf{TI}, d, \beta_{to}, A_1, A_2)$ executes A_1 for up to d units of time; execution is transferred to A_2 after d, and A_1 is disabled. Action β_{to} is executed when the interrupt occurs. A time interrupt is also defined in a similar fashion in Fig. 4 as a timeout. n declares a timestamp variable ts which is initialized to the last event execution time t. n_1 is a persistent guard that

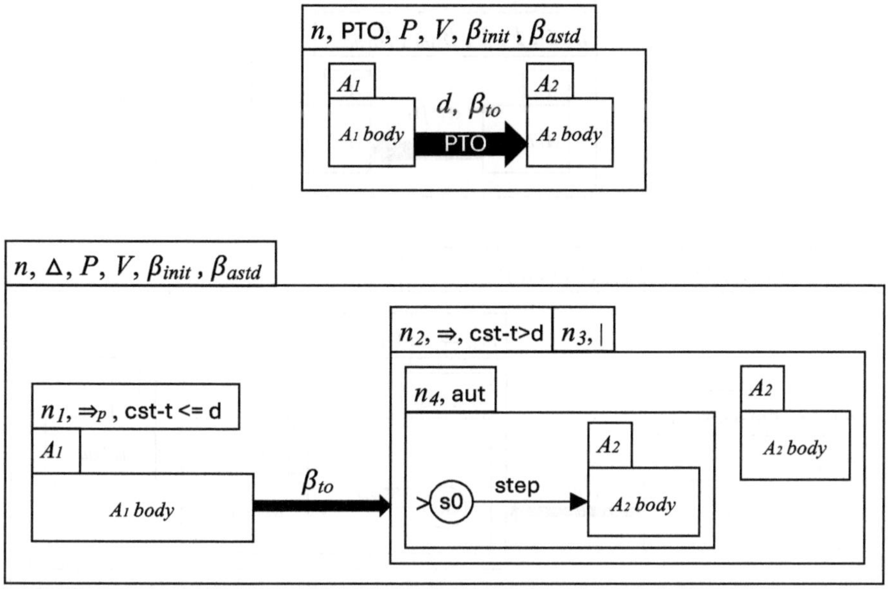

Fig. 3. At the bottom, the ASTD defining a persistent timeout $(n, \mathsf{PTO}, P, V, \beta_{init}, \beta_{astd}, d, \beta_{to}, A_1, A_2)$ illustrated at the top

allows A_1 to execute for d units of time. When that time is up, the guard of n_2 is enabled, allowing a step event or the first event of A_2 to execute.

3 TASTD Semantics

In this section, we introduce the modifications made to adapt the operational semantics of ASTDs [1] to deal with time. This semantics is defined using inference rules in the Plotkin style [23].

3.1 Transition System

The semantics of a TASTD $a(P)$, where P are the parameters of a, consists of a labelled transition system (LTS) $\mathcal{L}$, which is a subset of $\mathcal{S} \times \Sigma \times \mathcal{S}$, where $\mathcal{S} \triangleq \mathsf{S}_a \times \mathbb{T} \times \mathsf{Env}$, and S_a is the set of states of ASTD a that shall be inductively defined in the sequel (see Table 1). The LTS represents a set of transitions of the form $(s, \mathsf{t}, p) \xrightarrow{\sigma} (s', \mathsf{t}', p')$ denoting that a TASTD can execute event σ from state s and move to state s'. Symbols p, p' respectively denote the before (p) and after (p') values of the ASTD parameters P, meaning that ASTD parameters can be modified during execution. Symbols t, t' respectively denote the time at which states s, s' were reached; hence, they denote the timestamp of the *last executed event*. The value of t for the system's initial state is some timestamp, which represents the system start time. The timestamp t of a state s is needed

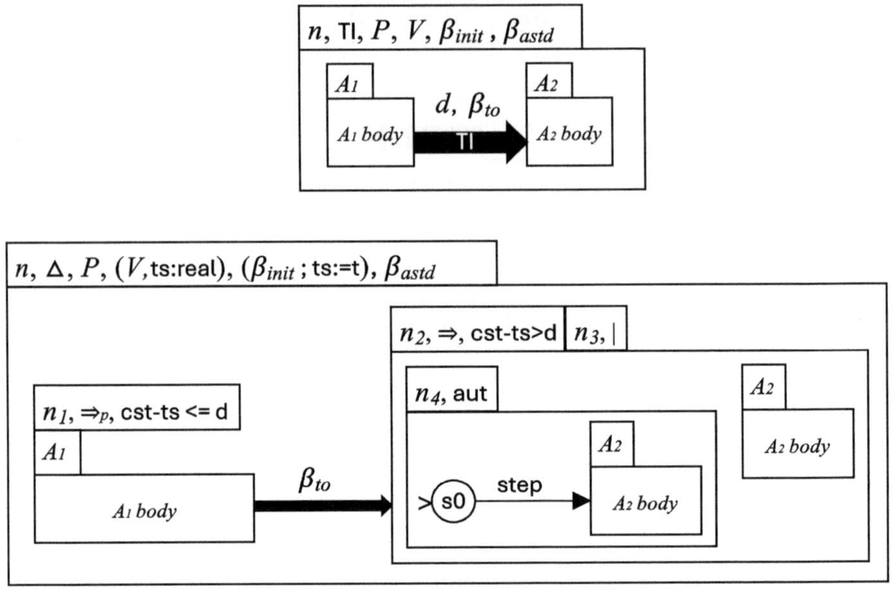

Fig. 4. At the bottom, the ASTD defining a timed interrupt $(n, \mathsf{TI}, P, V, \beta_{init}, \beta_{astd}, d, \beta_{to}, A_1, A_2)$ illustrated at the top.

when deciding on various time operators. For instance, a timeout is evaluated with respect to the last event executed. TASTD time operators simulate clocks, relying on the time of the last event executed for that purpose. Thus, when using a TASTD operator, there is no need to define a clock to specify time constraints. However, clocks can be declared as TASTD attributes and used to specify arbitrary time constraints. A state s contains its own attributes declared within the ASTD and control values that represent the behaviour of various ASTD operators.

A TASTD state includes a timestamp that denotes the time at which the state was reached. TASTD rely on the availability of a global clock called cst, which stands for *current system time*. It is used in various time operators to represent time constraints and simulate clocks. In ASTD, a transition can be triggered only by external events. In TASTD, a transition can be triggered by the passage of time; such a transition is labelled by a special event called step, drawn from Stateflow; it also corresponds to time transition in timed automaton. Automaton transitions can be labelled with step, and some time operators implicitly include step transitions. When implementing a TASTD, the executability of a time-triggered transition is checked on a periodical basis, according to the desired time granularity required to match system time constraints.

The semantics of TASTDs is designed for generating executable code. It differs from the semantics of timed automata and timed CSP, where there are transitions on external events σ of the form $s \xrightarrow{\sigma} s'$ and transitions on the passage of time with d units $s \xrightarrow{d} s'$, which are more suitable for model-checking. A TASTD transition $(s, t, p) \xrightarrow{\sigma} (s', t', p')$ corresponds to two successive transitions $s \xrightarrow{t'-t} s$ and $s \xrightarrow{\sigma} s'$ in timed automata.

Because ASTD can declare local variables, and that a nested ASTD can use variables declared in its enclosing ASTDs, we use environments in an auxiliary transition relation called $\mathcal{L}_a$ which is used to define $\mathcal{L}$. Suppose that a_2 is a sub-TASTD of a_1. a_1 may declare variables that a_2 can use and modify. Thus, the behaviour of a_2 depends on the variables declared in its enclosing ASTD a_1. A transition of $\mathcal{L}_a$ has the following form:

$$s \xrightarrow{\sigma, \mathsf{t}, e, e'}_a s'$$

where σ is the event executed, e, e' are environments respectively containing the before and after values of variables in the ASTDs enclosing ASTD a. These variables could be ASTD parameters, attributes, or quantified variables introduced by quantified operators like choice and generalized parallel. The time of the last executed event is denoted by timestamp t.

The initial state of a system whose main ASTD is a, called with parameter values p is

$$(\mathcal{I}(a, \mathsf{cst}, p), \mathsf{cst}, p)$$

We distinguish between a system state and an ASTD state. A *system state* (s, t, p) is made of the state of its main ASTD a, the last event execution time t and the values p of the parameters of a. $\mathcal{I}$ is a function that returns the initial state of an ASTD (see Fig. 6). $\mathcal{I}$ receives the current system time cst to initialize the local clocks of sub-ASTDs of a that must deal with local time constraints, *i.e.*,, generalized parallel and flow.

The following main inference rule connects $\mathcal{L}$ to $\mathcal{L}_a$:

$$\mathsf{env}\ \frac{s \xrightarrow{\sigma, \mathsf{t}, p, p'}_a s'}{(s, \mathsf{t}, p) \xrightarrow{\sigma}_a (s', \mathsf{cst}, p')}$$

It states that a transition in $\mathcal{L}$ is proved by proving a transition in $\mathcal{L}_a$ using the before values p of the parameters P of a, their final values p', and the last event execution time t. The current system time cst is stored in the global state as the new last event execution time. The operational semantics of ASTD is inductively defined on $\mathcal{L}_a$ for each ASTD type.

3.2 ASTD States

The type S_a of a state s of an ASTD a depends on the type of a. This differs from the process algebra style, where a state is given by a process term. In the sequel, for the sake of convenience and concision, we define $\mathsf{S}_{A_0} \triangleq \{\bot\}$, such that $s \in \mathsf{S}_{A_0}$ denotes an undefined state $s = \bot$, which means that the corresponding ASTD is not initialized, and thus has not started its execution. In Table 1, we define a state structure for each ASTD type. Each state contains the values v of its ASTD attributes. One must not confuse a state $q \in Q$ of an automaton with the state of an ASTD. The state $s \in \mathsf{S}_a$ of an automaton a contains more information than q; q is just a label for a node in an automaton, as in traditional automata. s constain all the information necessary to define $\mathcal{L}_a$. In particular, each state s contains the values $v \in \mathsf{Env}$ of attributes V declared in a, as well as other control information to define operator behaviour. The state of an automaton is given by both q and the state s of its sub-ASTD $\nu(q)$; when q is elementary, then $\nu(q) = \mathsf{elem}$ and $s = \mathsf{elem}_\circ$. We omit in Table 1 the definition of history states h, drawn from Statecharts; details can be found in [8]. State component i in a sequence and an interrupt indicates which ASTD A_i it is currently executing. The sub-state s of choice and closure is undefined ($s \in \mathsf{S}_{A_0}$) in their initial state. Flow and general parallel contain the states s_i and last event execution time t_i of each of their sub-ASTD A_i, which means that their operands have their own local clock to deal with time constraints. Quantified choice stores the value v_x of its quantified variable x, which is undefined (*i.e.*, $v_x = \varnothing \wedge s \in A_0$) in its initial state. Functions f and u of a quantified general parallel respectively contain the current states and the last event execution time of their instances, while t records the time where the instances become available for execution, and is used to initialize $u(d)$ when instance $d \in T$ is started.

Table 1. Primary ASTD types and their state structure for defining $\mathcal{L}_a$

Syntax ASTD Type	Semantics ASTD State	Description
elem	$\mathsf{elem}_\circ$	state of an elementary automaton state
$(\mathsf{Aut}, \Sigma, Q, \delta, F, q_0, \zeta, \nu)$	$(\mathsf{Aut}_\circ, v, q, s)$	$q \in Q,\ s \in \mathsf{S}_{a.\nu(q)}$
		$i \in 1..2 \wedge s \in \mathsf{S}_{A_i}$
$(\vartriangle, \beta_{int}, A_1, A_2)$	$(\vartriangle_\circ, v, i, s)$	$i \in 1..2 \wedge s \in \mathsf{S}_{A_i}$
$(\Rightarrow_p, g, A_1)$	$(\Rightarrow_{p\,\circ}, v, s)$	$s \in \mathsf{S}_{A_1}$
$(\mid, A_1, A_2)$	$(\mid_\circ, v, i, s)$	$i \in 0..2 \wedge s \in \mathsf{S}_{A_i}$
$(\star, A_1)$	$(\star_\circ, v, s)$	$i \in 0..1 \wedge s \in \mathsf{S}_{A_i}$
$(\pitchfork, A_1, A_2)$	$(\pitchfork_\circ, v, s_1, t_1, s_2, t_2)$	$s_i \in \mathsf{S}_{A_i} \wedge t_i \in \mathbb{T}$
$(\lvert[\,]\rvert, \Delta, A_1, A_2)$	$(\lvert[\,]\rvert_\circ, v, s_1, t_1, s_2, t_2)$	$s_i \in \mathsf{S}_{A_i} \wedge t_i \in \mathbb{T}$
$(\mid:, x, T, A_1)$	$(\mid:_\circ, v, v_x, s)$	$v_x \in \{x\} \mathrel{+\!\!\!\rightarrow} T$ $i \in 0..1 \wedge s \in \mathsf{S}_{A_i}$
$(\lvert[\,]\rvert:, x, T, \Delta, A_1)$	$(\lvert[\,]\rvert:_\circ, v, t, f, u)$	$t \in \mathbb{T}$ $f \in T \mathrel{+\!\!\!\rightarrow} \mathsf{S}_{A_1}$ $u \in T \mathrel{+\!\!\!\rightarrow} \mathbb{T}$

3.3 ASTD Initial States and Final States

Function $\mathcal{I}(a,t,e)$ defined in Fig. 5 returns the initial state of ASTD a using last event execution time t and environment e that provides the current values of variables declared in ASTDs enclosing a. Function $\mathcal{F}(a,s)$ defined in Fig. 6 returns true if state s of ASTD a is final. Function final does not depend on the values of the variables or the last event execution time; it depends essentially on the state of the leaf ASTDs in a, which are automata. When a sub-ASTD A_i of an ASTD a is not initialized, then its initial state $\mathcal{I}(a.A_i, \_, \_)$ is used to determine if a is final.

$$
\begin{array}{l}
\mathcal{I}(a : \mathsf{ASTD}, t : \mathbb{T}, e : \mathsf{Env}) : \mathsf{S}_a \triangleq \\
\quad \textbf{let } v \text{ be such that } a.\beta_{init}(e,v), \\
\qquad e' = v \cup e \textbf{ in} \\
\quad \textbf{match } a \textbf{ with} \\
\begin{array}{rl}
& \mathsf{elem} : \mathsf{elem}_\circ \\
(\mathsf{Aut}, \Sigma, Q, \delta, F, q_0, \zeta, \nu) : & (\mathsf{Aut}_\circ, v, q_0, \mathcal{I}(\nu(q_0), t, e')) \\
(\Rightarrow, A_1, A_2) : & (\Rightarrow_\circ, v, 1, \mathcal{I}(a.A_1, t, e')) \\
(\Delta, A_1, A_2, \beta_{int}) : & (\Delta_\circ, v, 1, \mathcal{I}(a.A_1, t, e')) \\
(\Rightarrow_p, g, A_1) : & (\Rightarrow_{p\circ}, v, \mathcal{I}(a.A_1, t, e')) \\
(|, A_1, A_2) : & (|_\circ, v, 0, \bot) \\
(\star, A_1) : & (\star_\circ, v, \bot) \\
(\pitchfork, A_1, A_2) : & (\pitchfork_\circ, v, \mathcal{I}(a.A_1, t, e'), t, \mathcal{I}(a.A_2, t, e'), t) \\
(|[\,]|, \Delta, A_1, A_2) : & (|[\,]|_\circ, v, \mathcal{I}(a.A_1, t, e'), t, \mathcal{I}(a.A_2, t, e'), t) \\
(|:, x, T, A_1) : & (|:_\circ, v, \varnothing, \bot) \\
(|[\,]|:, x, T, \Delta, A_1) : & (|[\,]|:_\circ, v, t, \varnothing, \varnothing)
\end{array}
\end{array}
$$

Fig. 5. Function $\mathcal{I}$ that returns the initial state of an ASTD.

3.4 Inference Rules

Rule r_1 describes a transition between local states of an automaton.

$$
\mathsf{r}_1 \; \frac{
\begin{array}{l}
(1)\ a.\delta((\mathsf{loc}, q_1, q_2), \sigma', g, \beta_{tr}, \mathit{final?}) \\
(2)\ (\sigma' = \sigma \ \wedge \ (\mathit{final?} \Rightarrow \mathcal{F}(a.\nu(q_1), s)) \ \wedge \ g)(\![e]\!) \\
(3)\ \textbf{if } q_1 = q_2 \\
(4)\quad \textbf{then } \beta = \beta_{tr} \ ; \ a.\zeta(q_1).\beta_{stay} \ ; \ a.\beta_{astd} \\
(5)\quad \textbf{else } \beta = a.\zeta(q_1).\beta_{out} \ ; \ \beta_{tr} \ ; \ a.\zeta(q_2).\beta_{in} \ ; \ a.\beta_{astd} \\
(6)\ \beta(e \cup v, e' \cup v')
\end{array}
}{
(\mathsf{Aut}_\circ, q_1, v, s_1) \xrightarrow{\sigma,t,e,e'}_a (\mathsf{Aut}_\circ, q_2, v', \mathcal{I}(a.\nu(q_2), t, e'))
}
$$

Hypothesis (1) indicates that there is a transition from q_1 to q_2 labeled with σ' in automaton a. Hypothesis (2) checks that the transition label σ', which may contain variables, matches the event σ to be executed, after applying the

$$
\begin{array}{l}
\mathcal{F}(a : \mathsf{ASTD}, s' : \mathsf{S}_a) : \mathbb{B} \triangleq \\
\textbf{match } s' \textbf{ with} \\
\quad \begin{array}{rl}
(\mathsf{Aut}_\circ, v, q, h, s) : & q \in a.SF \vee (q \in a.DF \wedge \mathcal{F}(a.\nu(q), s)) \\
(\Rightarrow_\circ, v, i, s) : & \textbf{if } i = 1 \textbf{ then} \\
 & \quad \mathcal{F}(a.A_1, s) \wedge \mathcal{F}(a.A_2, \mathcal{I}(a.A_2, \_, \_)) \\
 & \textbf{else } \mathcal{F}(a.A_2, s) \\
(\Delta_\circ, v, i, s) : & \mathcal{F}(a.A_i, s) \\
(\Rightarrow_{p\circ}, v, s) : & \mathcal{F}(a.A_1, s) \\
(|_\circ, v, i, s) : & \textbf{if } i = 0 \textbf{ then} \\
 & \quad \mathcal{F}(a.A_1, \mathcal{I}(a.A_1, \_, \_)) \vee \mathcal{F}(a.A_2, \mathcal{I}(a.A_2, \_, \_)) \\
 & \textbf{else } \mathcal{F}(a.A_i, s) \\
(\star_\circ, v, s) : & s = \bot \vee \mathcal{F}(a.A_1, s) \\
(|\![\,]\!|_\circ, v, s_1, t_1, s_2, t_2) : & \mathcal{F}(a.A_1, s_1) \wedge \mathcal{F}(a.A_2, s_2) \\
(|[\,]|_\circ, v, s_1, t_1, s_2, t_2) : & \mathcal{F}(a.A_1, s_1) \wedge \mathcal{F}(a.A_2, s_2) \\
(|:_\circ, v, v_x, s) : & \textbf{if } s = \bot \textbf{ then} \\
 & \quad \mathcal{F}(a.A_1, \mathcal{I}(a.A_1, \_, \_)) \\
 & \textbf{else } \mathcal{F}(a.A_i, s) \\
(|[\,]|:_\circ, v, t, f, u) : & (\forall c \in \mathrm{dom}(f) \cdot \mathcal{F}(a.A_1, f(c))) \wedge \\
 & (\mathrm{dom}(f) \neq T \Rightarrow \mathcal{F}(a.A_1, \mathcal{I}(a.A_1, \_, \_))
\end{array}
\end{array}
$$

Fig. 6. Boolean function $\mathcal{F}$ that determines if an ASTD state is final.

environment e as a substitution; it also checks that q_1 is in a final state if the transition is marked as final, and that its guard holds. Hypotheses (4) to (6) determine the action to execute. The state and transition actions are executed before the astd action β_{astd}. The traditional semi-colon ";" is used to indicate sequential composition of actions. If $q_1 = q_2$, the stay action β_{stay} is executed, followed by the transition action β_{tr}; otherwise, the exit, transition and entry actions are executed.

The other rules for Aut, , Δ, $\Rightarrow_p$, $|$ and $\star$ are defined following general form below, and compactly represented in tabular format in Table 2.

$$
\mathsf{r}_2..\mathsf{r}_{11}\ \frac{\begin{array}{l}(1)\ s_1 \xrightarrow{\sigma,t,e\cup v,e_2}_{a.A_i} s' \\ (2)\ \beta(e_2, e_3) \\ (3)\ e' = \mathrm{dom}(e) \lhd e_3 \quad \wedge \quad v' = \mathrm{dom}(v) \lhd e_3 \\ (4)\ \Theta\end{array}}{(\mathsf{A}_\circ, v, \gamma, s_1) \xrightarrow{\sigma,t,e,e'}_a (\mathsf{A}_\circ, v', \gamma', s')}
$$

Hypothesis (1) indicates that the new state s' of sub-ASTD $a.A_i$ is determined by the execution of $a.A_i$ from state s_1 under environment $e \cup v$ on event σ with last event execution time t. e_2 contains the new (intermediate) values of e and v. Hypothesis (2) indicates that action β is executed on e_2, producing the final values e', v' stored in e_3; thus, this means that actions are executed bottom-up in an ASTD hierarchy. Θ is a condition that depends on the particular case that the rule is dealing with. γ and γ' denote the current state q in an automaton, or i in ASTD types , Δ and $|$. Table 2 provides a compact representation of the rules that follow this pattern and defines the values of γ,

γ', A_i, s_1, β and Θ of this rule pattern, and it allows for an easy comparison of the rules.

Table 2. Inference rules for Aut, , $\triangle$, $\Rightarrow_p$, $|$ and $\star$

r	Type	γ	γ'	A_i	s_1	β	Θ
r_2	Aut	q	q	$a.\nu(q)$	s	$a.\zeta(q).\beta_{stay}$; $a.\beta_{astd}$	
r_3		i	i	$a.A_i$	s	$a.\beta_{astd}$	$i : 1..2$
r_4		1	2	$a.A_2$	$\mathcal{I}(a.A_2, t, e_1)$	$a.\beta_{astd}$	$\mathcal{F}(a.A_1, s)$
r_5	$\triangle$	i	i	$a.A_i$	s	$a.\beta_{astd}$	$i : 1..2$
r_6	$\triangle$	1	2	$a.A_2$	$\mathcal{I}(a.A_2, t, e_1)$	$a.\beta_{int}$; $a.\beta_{astd}$	
r_7	$|$	0	i	$a.A_i$	$\mathcal{I}(a.A_i, t, e_1)$	$a.\beta_{astd}$	$i \in 1..2$
r_8	$|$	i	i	$a.A_i$	s	$a.\beta_{astd}$	$i \in 1..2$
r_9	$\Rightarrow_p$			$a.A_1$	s	$a.\beta_{astd}$	$g(\llbracket e \rrbracket)$
r_{10}	$\star$			$a.A_1$	$\mathcal{I}(a.A_1, t, e_1)$	$a.\beta_{astd}$	$\mathcal{F}(a, (\star_\circ, v, s))$
r_{11}	$\star$			$a.A_1$	s	$a.\beta_{astd}$	

Inference Rules for Flow. A flow ASTD $(\pitchfork, A_1, A_2)$ tries to execute both A_1 and A_2. Rule r_{12} deals with the case where one ASTD, noted A_{ok}, can execute the event, but not the other (A_{ko}), which is denoted by $s_{ko} \not\xrightarrow{\sigma, t_{ko}, e_1, -}_{a.A_{ko}}$. Hypothesis (1) matches $\{A_1, A_2\}$ with $\{A_{ok}, A_{ko}\}$, allowing to write a single rule for either A_1 or A_2 executing the event. Rule r_{13} deals with the case where both A_1 and A_2 can execute the event. Hypothesis (1) states that the order in which they are executed is non-deterministic, by allowing either A_1 or A_2 to execute first; i denotes the first ASTD to execute and j denotes the second ASTD. Hypothesis (2) executes the first ASTD i, followed by the second ASTD j using the values of the variables e_1 obtained after executing the first ASTD. Note that the last event execution times used to compute a transition in each sub-ASTD A_1 and A_2 are the ones stored in the flow state, represented respectively by t_1 and t_2. These values are updated with cst when they execute.

$$\mathsf{r}_{12}\ \frac{\begin{array}{l}(1)\ \{(A_1, s_1, t_1, s'_1, t'_1), (A_2, s_2, t_2, s'_2, t'_2)\} = \{(A_{ok}, s_{ok}, t_{ok}, s'_{ok}, \mathsf{cst}), (A_{ko}, s_{ko}, t_{ko}, s_{ko}, t_{ko})\} \\ (2)\ s_{ok} \xrightarrow{\sigma, t_{ok}, e \cup v, e_1}_{a.A_{ok}} s'_{ok} \ \wedge\ s_{ko} \not\xrightarrow{\sigma, t_{ko}, e_1, -}_{a.A_{ko}} \\ (3)\ \beta_{astd}(e_1, e_2) \ \wedge\ e' = \mathrm{dom}(e) \lhd e_2 \ \wedge\ v' = \mathrm{dom}(v) \lhd e_2\end{array}}{(\pitchfork_\circ, v, s_1, t_1, s_2, t_2) \xrightarrow{\sigma, -, e, e'}_a (\pitchfork_\circ, v', s'_1, t'_1, s'_2, t'_2)}$$

$$\mathsf{r}_{13}\ \frac{\begin{array}{l}(1)\ \{(A_1, s_1, t_1, s'_1), (A_2, s_2, t_2, s'_2)\} = \{(A_i, s_i, t_i, s'_i), (A_j, s_j, t_j, s'_j)\} \\ (2)\ s_i \xrightarrow{\sigma, t_i, e \cup v, e_1}_{a.A_i} s'_i \quad \wedge \quad s_j \xrightarrow{\sigma, t_j, e_1, e_2}_{a.A_j} s'_j \\ (3)\ \beta_{astd}(e_2, e_3) \quad \wedge \quad e' = \mathrm{dom}(e) \lhd e_3 \quad \wedge \quad v' = \mathrm{dom}(v) \lhd e_3\end{array}}{(\pitchfork_\circ, v, s_1, t_1, s_2, t_2) \xrightarrow{\sigma, \_, e, e'}_a (\pitchfork_\circ, v', s'_1, \mathsf{cst}, s'_2, \mathsf{cst})}$$

Inference Rules for Generalized Parallel. The rules for a generalized parallel $(|[]|, \Delta, A_1, A_2)$ are very similar to a flow, except that events for which synchronization is required are specified using Δ. Thus, if the label $\alpha(\sigma)$ of σ is not in Δ (rule r_{14}), then only one of A_1, A_2 is allowed to execute; if both can execute σ, then one is chosen non-deterministically. If $\alpha(\sigma) \in \Delta$ (rule r_{15}), then a transition occurs iff both A_1 and A_2 can execute it. A_i denotes the first to execute, while A_j executes after A_i from the environment e_1 computed by A_i (hypothesis (2)). The order in which A_1 and A_2 are executed is non-deterministic (hypothesis (1) and (2)).

$$\mathsf{r}_{14}\ \frac{\begin{array}{l}(1)\ \{(A_1, s_1, t_1, s'_1, t'_1), (A_2, s_2, t_2, s'_2, t'_2)\} = \{(A_{ok}, s_{ok}, t_{ok}, s'_{ok}, \mathsf{cst}), (A_{ko}, s_{ko}, t_{ko}, s_{ko}, t_{ko})\} \\ (2)\ \alpha(\sigma) \notin \Delta \quad \wedge \quad s_{ok} \xrightarrow{\sigma, t_{ok}, e \cup v, e_1}_{a.A_{ok}} s'_{ok} \\ (3)\ \beta_{astd}(e_1, e_2) \quad \wedge \quad e' = \mathrm{dom}(e) \lhd e_2 \quad \wedge \quad v' = \mathrm{dom}(v) \lhd e_2\end{array}}{(|[]|_\circ, v, s_1, t_1, s_2, t_2) \xrightarrow{\sigma, \_, e, e'}_a (|[]|_\circ, v', s'_1, t'_1, s'_2, t'_2)}$$

$$\mathsf{r}_{15}\ \frac{\begin{array}{l}(1)\ \{(A_1, s_1, t_1, s'_1), (A_2, s_2, t_2, s'_2)\} = \{(A_i, s_i, t_i, s'_i), (A_j, s_j, t_j, s'_j)\} \\ (2)\ \alpha(\sigma) \in \Delta \quad \wedge \quad s_i \xrightarrow{\sigma, t_i, e \cup v, e_1}_{a.A_i} s'_i \quad \wedge \quad s_j \xrightarrow{\sigma, t_j, e_1, e_2}_{a.A_j} s'_j \\ (3)\ \beta_{astd}(e_2, e_3) \quad \wedge \quad e' = \mathrm{dom}(e) \lhd e_3 \quad \wedge \quad v' = \mathrm{dom}(v) \lhd e_3\end{array}}{(|[]|_\circ, v, s_1, t_1, s_2, t_2) \xrightarrow{\sigma, \_, e, e'}_a (|[]|_\circ, v', s'_1, \mathsf{cst}, s'_2, \mathsf{cst})}$$

Inference Rules for Quantified Choice. Rule r_{16} deals with the case where a quantified choice $(|:, x, T, A_1)$ has not started its execution, and it allows for the non-deterministic choice of a value d for x such that its sub-ASTD A_1 can execute a transition with d. Rule 17 caters for the other transitions once the value of x is chosen.

$$\mathsf{r}_{16}\ \frac{\begin{array}{l}(1)\ d \in a.T \quad \wedge \quad \mathcal{I}(a.A_1, t, e \cup v) \xrightarrow{\sigma, t, e \cup v \cup \{x \mapsto d\}, e_1}_{a.A_1} s' \\ (2)\ \beta_{astd}(e_1, e_2) \quad \wedge \quad e' = \mathrm{dom}(e) \lhd e_2 \quad \wedge \quad v' = \mathrm{dom}(v) \lhd e_2\end{array}}{(|:\ _\circ, v, v_x, s) \xrightarrow{\sigma, t, e, e'}_a (|:\ _\circ, v', \{x \mapsto d\}, s')}$$

$$\mathsf{r}_{17}\ \frac{\begin{array}{l}(1)\ s \xrightarrow{\sigma, t, e \cup v \cup v_x, e_1}_{a.A_1} s' \\ (2)\ \beta_{astd}(e_1, e_2) \quad \wedge \quad e' = \mathrm{dom}(e) \lhd e_2 \quad \wedge \quad v' = \mathrm{dom}(v) \lhd e_2\end{array}}{(|:\ _\circ, v, v_x, s) \xrightarrow{\sigma, t, e, e'}_a (|:\ _\circ, v', v_x, s')}$$

Inference Rules for Quantified Generalized Parallel. A quantified generalized parallel $(|[]|:, x, T, \Delta, A_1)$ executes one copy of A_1 for each value d of T. Since f and u are initialized to $\varnothing$, f' and u' denote their extension with initialization values for elements of T not started yet. They are used in rules r_{18} and r_{19} and defined as follows:

$$
\begin{aligned}
f' &= f \;\cup\; (T - dom(f)) \times \mathcal{I}(a.A_1, t, e \cup v)\\
u' &= u \;\cup\; (T - dom(u)) \times \{t\}
\end{aligned}
$$

The last event execution to start each instance of A_1 is the one used to initialized the quantified ASTD. Rule r_{18} deals with the case where there is no synchronization and only one instance executes the event; the last event execution time t used is the one stored in the state of the quantified generalized parallel $(|[]|:_\circ, v, t, f, u)$, not the one given in $\xrightarrow{\sigma,\_,e,e'}_a$, represented by an "_".

$$
\mathsf{r}_{18}\;\frac{\begin{array}{l}(1)\ \alpha(\sigma) \notin \Delta \;\;\wedge\;\; d \in T \;\;\wedge\;\; f'(d) \xrightarrow{\sigma, u'(d), e \cup v \cup \{x \mapsto d\}, e_1}_{a.A_1} s'\\ (2)\ \beta_{astd}(e_1, e_2) \;\;\wedge\;\; e' = \mathrm{dom}(e) \lhd e_2 \;\;\wedge\;\; v' = \mathrm{dom}(v) \lhd e_2\end{array}}{(|[]|:_\circ, v, t, f, u) \xrightarrow{\sigma,\_,e,e'}_a (|[]|:_\circ, v', t, f \Leftarrow \{d \mapsto s'\}, u \Leftarrow \{d \mapsto \mathsf{cst}\})}
$$

Rule r_{19} deals with the case of synchronization, thus, each instance must be able to execute the event (hyp. (2)). It non-deterministically picks a permutation p of T which denotes the order in which the instances of A_1 are executed (hyp. (1)). g is a function that records the intermediate values of e and v during the execution of the k instances, with $g(0)$ denoting their initial values, and $g(k)$ their final values (hyp. (3)). f'' denote the states of the instances after their execution.

$$
\mathsf{r}_{19}\;\frac{\begin{array}{l}(1)\ \alpha(\sigma) \in \Delta \;\;\wedge\;\; k = |T| \;\;\wedge\;\; p \in \pi(T)\\ (2)\ \forall d \in T \cdot f'(d) \xrightarrow{\sigma, u'(d), e \cup v \cup \{x \mapsto d\}, \_}_{a.A_1} \_\\ (3)\ g \in 0..k \twoheadrightarrow \mathsf{Env} \;\;\wedge\;\; g(0) = e \cup v \;\;\wedge\;\; g(k) = e_1\\ (4)\ \forall i \in 1..k \cdot f'(p(i)) \xrightarrow{\sigma, u(p(i)), g(i-1) \Leftarrow \{x \mapsto p(i)\}, g(i)}_{a.A_1} f''(p(i))\\ (5)\ \beta_{astd}(e_1, e_2) \;\;\wedge\;\; e' = \mathrm{dom}(e) \lhd e_2 \;\;\wedge\;\; v' = \mathrm{dom}(v) \lhd e_2\end{array}}{(|[]|:_\circ, v, t, f, u) \xrightarrow{\sigma,\_,e,e'}_a (|[]|:_\circ, v', t, f'', T \times \{\mathsf{cst}\})}
$$

4 Related Work

The ASTD notation was designed to specify control and monitoring systems in an abstract, compositional manner and to automatically generate an efficient implementation from a specification. It is inspired by process algebras like CSP to freely compose behaviours using operators. CSP does not allow for state variables, but Stateful Timed CSP (STCSP) [24] does. TASTD supports all the time operators of STCSP. TASTD offers a more modular approach to specify actions and attributes than STCSP: variables are global in STCSP, while they are local in an ASTD declaration. On the other hand, CSP and STCSP are well supported by model checking tools like FDR [25] and PAT [26]. Given its rich language, we still have to evaluate how easy it will be to develop model checking tools for TASTD specifications. Using automata to specify the basic behaviour of systems is an advantage over textual notations like CSP and STCSP. RoboSim is a graphical tool for modelling and verifying software simulation of robots. It uses *tock*-CSP [27] as its semantics. *tock*-CSP does not provide quantified operators such as quantified synchronisation, quantified choice or flow, as provided in ASTDs. In the semantics of *tock*-CSP, the passage of one unit of time is denoted by a transition labeled with special event *tock*, so time is discrete. In STCSP, time is densed; the passage of $i \in \mathbb{R}$ units of time is represented by a transition $\xrightarrow{i}$. In TASTD, time is also densed; there is no transition labeled with a duration as in STCSP; the time elapsed between two states is represented by $(s, \mathsf{t}, p) \xrightarrow{\sigma} (s', \mathsf{t}', p')$, so the duration is $\mathsf{t}' - \mathsf{t}$, but it also includes the execution time of σ. Events are instantaneous in *tock*-CSP and STCSP.

Timed automata are graphical notations that offer limited support for specification composition. However, they are more amenable to model checking and well supported by sophisticated tools like UPPAAL [28]. In several works, including [29–31], pattern diagrams for timed automata have been proposed to aid in the modelling of high-level system designs. The work in [30] uses patterns based on UML Statecharts, while [31] proposes patterns from time-proven compositional constructs in Timed CSP/TCOZ, and UML activity diagrams are proposed in [29]. Alternatively, TASTD offers those patterns as TASTD types, thus making them algebraic and compositional, and the use of Statecharts-like boxes makes their application modular and transparent. TASTD supports all the basic features of Stateflow [9], and it can simulate all Stateflow operators. It is also efficiently executable like Stateflow models. Stateflow does not support compositional specifications like TASTD does through its algebraic approach. In particular, Stateflow does not support quantified operators like interleaving and choice, which are very useful to model systems where there are an arbitrary number of instances of a given state machine that represent a component. These operators are handy in cybersecurity when modeling attacks that can target, for instance, all the computers of a network. One can model an attack on a machine and quantify over the IP address of the machines to recognise attacks on a whole network all at once [14]. Thanks to shared variables, correlation can be done between attacks spread on several machines, and better top-level decisions can be easily specified [1,14].

The algebraic approach of TASTDs allows for more modularity than in model-based notations like B [19], Event-B [32] and ASM [33]. On the other hand, this syntactic richness entails a more complex semantics, hence the need to have a simple description of it, which is the main objective of this paper. Moreover, these model-based notations offer rich refinement and proof theories, well supported by tools, that TASTD should draw from in the future. Some refinement patterns exist for ASTD [34,35]. It remains to be investigated how adequate they are for refining TASTD specifications. In [36], an approach for proving invariants for a subset of the ASTD notation is defined. Attributes can be defined using the mathematical language of classical B or Event-B, and actions can be written using the rich generalized substitution language of classical B. Proof obligations are generated and can be discharged using Event-B provers. These proof obligations can also be discharged using an Event-B metamodel of the ASTD language introduced in [37] using Rodin [38] and its theory plugin [39,40]. This work is the first complete formal mechanization of the ASTD operational semantics. Translation of ASTDs into B has been proposed in [41] and formally proved correct using COQ in [42] for the formal semantics of automata. In this paper, we omit the declaration of invariants, as they are properties of a specification, and do not affect its behaviour.

5 Conclusion

This paper proposes a simplified description of TASTD, a time extension of the ASTD notation. Its tabular presentation is more concise and easier to understand than its previous version. Non-deterministic choice is used for the choice of an execution order between actions in a flow and a synchronization. TASTD operators are defined in terms of primary ASTDs.

The main advantages of modelling with TASTD in comparison with other comparable methods are the following. The algebraic approach allows for the decomposition of a specification into very small components which are easier to analyse and understand. In particular, the behaviour of an event that affects several components can be separately specified in each component. The synchronisation and flow operators can be used to indicate how these components interact over these events (i.e., hard or soft synchronisation). Communication by shared attributes permits to simplify automata of a specification and reduce the number of automaton states. The graphical nature of TASTD allows for an easier understanding of a specification. Automata and process algebra operators make it easier to understand the ordering relationship between events. TASTD provides a simple, modular approach to deal with time requirements. TASTD, with its compiler cASTD, can generate C++ code that can be deployed into an embedded system. It is also capable of generating code for simulation, in order to check scenarios.

TASTD currently lacks supports for verification. Some work in that direction is in progress [36,37], where ASTD are extended with invariants that can be attached to automaton states and three other ASTD types (sequence, closure and guard), thus allowing to decompose the verification of properties into small parts. We hope that this new approach will help to simplify proof obligations. The refinement of ASTD actions into executable code must also be studied, in conjunction with ASTD refinement and invariant preservation.

References

1. Nganyewou Tidjon, L., Frappier, M., Leuschel, M., Mammar, A.: Extended algebraic state-transition diagrams. In: 2018 23rd International Conference on Engineering of Complex Computer Systems (ICECCS), Melbourne, Australia, pp. 146–155 (2018)
2. Hoare, C.A.R.: Communicating sequential processes. Commun. ACM **21**(8), 666–677 (1978)
3. Roscoe, B.: The Theory and Practice of Concurrency. Prentice Hall (1998)
4. Mikk, E., Lakhnechi, Y., Siegel, M.: Hierarchical automata as model for statecharts. In: Shyamasundar, R.K., Ueda, K. (eds.) ASIAN 1997. LNCS, vol. 1345, pp. 181–196. Springer, Heidelberg (1997). https://doi.org/10.1007/3-540-63875-X_52
5. Latella, D., Majzik, I., Massink, M.: Automatic verification of a behavioural subset of UML statechart diagrams using the SPIN model-checker. Formal Aspects Comput. **11**(6), 637–664 (1999)
6. Harel, D.: Statecharts: a visual formalism for complex systems. Sci. Comput. Program. **8**(3), 231–274 (1987)
7. de Azevedo Oliveira, D., Frappier, M.: TASTD: a real-time extension for ASTD. In: Glässer, U., Creissac Campos, J., Méry, D., Palanque, P. (eds.) ABZ 2023. LNCS, vol. 14010, pp. 142–159. Springer, Cham (2023). https://doi.org/10.1007/978-3-031-33163-3_11
8. de Azevedo Oliveira, D., Frappier, M.: Technical report 27 - extending ASTD with real-time. https://github.com/DiegoOliveiraUDES/astd-tech-report-27 (2023). Accessed 28 Jan 2023
9. MATLAB, Stateflow. https://www.mathworks.com/products/stateflow.html (2020)
10. Alur, R., Dill, D.L.: A theory of timed automata. Theoret. Comput. Sci. **126**(2), 183–235 (1994)
11. Schneider, S.: Concurrent and Real-Time Systems. John Wiley and Sons (2000)
12. Sun, J., Liu, Y., Dong, J.S., Liu, Y., Shi, L., André, É.: Modeling and verifying hierarchical real-time systems using stateful timed CSP. ACM Trans. Softw. Eng. Methodol. **22**(1), 3:1–3:29 (2013)
13. Sun, J., Liu, Y., Dong, J.S., Liu, Y., Shi, L., André, É.: Modeling and verifying hierarchical real-time systems using stateful timed CSP. ACM Trans. Software Eng. Methodol. (TOSEM) **22**(1), 1–29 (2013)
14. Tidjon, L.N., Frappier, M., Mammar, A.: Intrusion detection using ASTDs. In: Barolli, L., Amato, F., Moscato, F., Enokido, T., Takizawa, M. (eds) International Conference on Advanced Information Networking and Applications, pp. 1397–1411. Springer, Cham (2020). https://doi.org/10.1007/978-3-030-44041-1_118
15. Tidjon, L.N.: Formal modeling of intrusion detection systems, Ph.D. thesis, Institut Polytechnique de Paris; Université de Sherbrooke (Québec, Canada). https://theses.hal.science/tel-03137661 (2020)
16. Chaymae, E.J., Marc, F., Thibaud, E., Pierre-Martin, T.: Development of monitoring systems for anomaly detection using ASTD specifications. In: International Symposium on Theoretical Aspects of Software Engineering, pp. 274–289. Springer, Cham (2022). https://doi.org/10.1007/978-3-031-10363-6_19
17. de Azevedo Oliveira, D., Frappier, M.: Modelling an automotive software system with TASTD. In: Glässer, U., Creissac Campos, J., Méry, D., Palanque, P. (eds.) ABZ 2023. LNCS, vol. 14010, pp. 124–141. Springer, Cham (2023). https://doi.org/10.1007/978-3-031-33163-3_10

18. Ndouna, A.R., Frappier, M.: Modelling a mechanical lung ventilation system using TASTD. In: Bonfanti, S., Gargantini, A., Leuschel, M., Riccobene, E., Scandurra, P. (Eds.), Rigorous State-Based Methods - 10th International Conference, ABZ 2024, Bergamo, Italy, June 25-28, 2024, Proceedings, Vol. 14759 of Lecture Notes in Computer Science, pp. 324–340. Springer, Cham (2024). https://doi.org/10.1007/978-3-031-63790-2_26
19. Abrial, J.-R.: The B-Book: Assigning Programs to Meanings. Cambridge University Press, New York, NY, USA (1996)
20. Berghammer, R.: Relational specification of data types and programs, Universität der Bundeswehr München, Fak. für Informatik (1991)
21. Backhouse, R.C., van der Woude, J.: Demonic operators and monotype factors. Math. Struct. Comput. Sci. **3**(4), 417–433 (1993)
22. Abrial, J.: Modeling in Event-B. Cambridge University Press, Cambridge (2010)
23. Plotkin, G.D.: A structural approach to operational semantics. J. Log. Algebraic Methods Program. **60–61**, 17–139 (2004)
24. Balaban, M., Rosen, T.: Stcsp–structured temporal constraint satisfaction problems. Ann. Math. Artif. Intell. **25**, 35–67 (1999)
25. Gibson-Robinson, T., Armstrong, P., Boulgakov, A., Roscoe, A.W.: FDR3 — A modern refinement checker for CSP. In: Ábrahám, E., Havelund, K. (eds.) TACAS 2014. LNCS, vol. 8413, pp. 187–201. Springer, Heidelberg (2014). https://doi.org/10.1007/978-3-642-54862-8_13
26. Sun, J., Liu, Y., Dong, J.S., Pang, J.: PAT: towards flexible verification under fairness. In: Bouajjani, A., Maler, O. (eds.) CAV 2009. LNCS, vol. 5643, pp. 709–714. Springer, Heidelberg (2009). https://doi.org/10.1007/978-3-642-02658-4_59
27. Cavalcanti, A., et al.: Verified simulation for robotics. Sci. Comput. Program.**174**, 1–37 (2019)
28. Behrmann, G., David, A., Larsen, K.G.: A tutorial on UPPAAL. In: Bernardo, M., Corradini, F. (eds.) SFM-RT 2004. LNCS, vol. 3185, pp. 200–236. Springer, Heidelberg (2004). https://doi.org/10.1007/978-3-540-30080-9_7
29. André, É., Choppy, C., Reggio, G.: Activity diagrams patterns for modeling business processes. In: Lee, R. (eds) Software Engineering Research, Management and Applications, pp. 197–213. Springer, Cham (2014). https://doi.org/10.1007/978-3-319-00948-3_13
30. Mekki, A., Ghazel, M., Toguyeni, A.: Validating time-constrained systems using UML statecharts patterns and timed automata observers. In: Third International Workshop on Verification and Evaluation of Computer and Communication Systems (VECoS 2009), vol. 3, pp. 1–13 (2009)
31. Dong, J.S., Hao, P., Qin, S., Sun, J., Yi, W.: Timed automata patterns. IEEE Trans. Software Eng. **34**(6), 844–859 (2008)
32. Abrial, J.-R., Butler, M., Hallerstede, S., Hoang, T.S., Mehta, F., Voisin, L.: Rodin: an open toolset for modelling and reasoning in Event-B. STTT **12**(6), 447–466 (2010)
33. Börger, E., Stärk, R.: Abstract state machines: a method for high-level system design and analysis. In: Boca, P., Bowen, J., Siddiqi, J. (eds) Formal Methods: State of the Art and New Directions. Springer, London (2012). https://doi.org/10.1007/978-1-84882-736-3_3
34. Frappier, M., Gervais, F., Laleau, R., Milhau, J.: Refinement patterns for ASTDs. Formal Aspects Comput. **26**, 919–941 (2014)

35. Fayolle, T., Frappier, M., Laleau, R., Gervais, F.: Formal refinement of extended state machines. In: Derrick, J., Boiten, E.A., Reeves, S., (Eds.), Proceedings 17th International Workshop on Refinement, Refine@FM 2015, Oslo, Norway, 22nd June 2015, vol. 209 of EPTCS, pp. 1–16 (2015)
36. Cartellier, Q., Frappier, M., Mammar, A.: Proving local invariants in ASTDs. In: Li, Y., Tahar, S. (Eds), Formal Methods and Software Engineering - 24th International Conference on Formal Engineering Methods, ICFEM 2023, Brisbane, QLD, Australia, November 21-24, 2023, Proceedings, vol. 14308 of Lecture Notes in Computer Science, pp. 228–246. Springer, Singapore (2023). https://doi.org/10.1007/978-981-99-7584-6_14
37. Chen, C., Rivière, P., Singh, N.K., Dupont, G., Aït-Ameur, Y., Frappier, M.: A proof-based ground algebraic meta-model for reasoning on ASTD in event-b. In: 13th IEEE/ACM International Conference on Formal Methods in Software Engineering, FormaliSE@ICSE 2025, Ottawa, ON, Canada, April 27-28, 2025, pp. 46–57. IEEE (2025)
38. Abrial, J.-R., Butler, M., Hallerstede, S., Hoang, T.S., Mehta, F., Voisin, L.: Rodin: an open toolset for modelling and reasoning in event-b. Int. J. Softw. Tools Technol. Transf. **12**(6), 447–466 (2010)
39. Butler, M., Maamria, I.: Practical theory extension in event-B. In: Liu, Z., Woodcock, J., Zhu, H. (eds.) Theories of Programming and Formal Methods: Essays Dedicated to Jifeng He on the Occasion of His 70th Birthday, pp. 67–81. Springer, Berlin, Heidelberg (2013). https://doi.org/10.1007/978-3-642-39698-4_5
40. Hoang, T.S., Voisin, L., Salehi, A., Butler, M.J., Wilkinson, T., Beauger, N.: Theory plug-in for Rodin 3.x, CoRR abs/1701.08625 (2017). arXiv:1701.08625
41. Milhau, J.: Un processus formel d'intégration de politiques de contrôle d'accès dans les systèmes d'information, Theses, Université Paris-Est ; Université de Sherbrooke (Québec, Canada) (2011). https://theses.hal.science/tel-00674865
42. Fayolle, T.: Combinaison de méthodes formelles pour la spécification de systèmes industriels, Theses, Université Paris-Est ; Université de Sherbrooke (Québec, Canada) (2017). https://theses.hal.science/tel-01743832

Enhancing the Expressibility of ASM-Defined Classes of Algorithms with Event-B

Julien Cervelle, Frédéric Gervais, Pierre Valarcher, and Régine Laleau(✉)

Univ Paris Est Créteil, LACL, 94010 Créteil, France
{julien.cervelle,frederic.gervais,pierre.valarcher,laleau}@u-pec.fr

Abstract. Abstract State Machines (ASMs) provide a simple and expressive operational model in which algorithms are described as small-step transitions over rich states. However, when one aims at *classes* of algorithms (rather than individual algorithms), constraining only the underlying static algebra of primitive operations is fragile. In this paper we address this gap by combining the algebraic viewpoint of ASMs/EMAs with the proof-oriented discipline of the B method, and in particular Event-B.

We propose a lightweight framework in which the permitted operations of an algorithmic class are captured axiomatically (as a static algebra), while the class-defining global requirements are expressed and enforced via Event-B invariants and variants. We illustrate the approach on comparison based sorting, using the number of inversions as a logical progress measure: array updates that perform a corrective swap strictly decrease this measure, while non-modifying steps preserve it, making it possible to exclude "one-step sorters" and other algebra-compliant but incorrect control logics. We show how Rodin and the Theory Plug-in can encode the required mathematical vocabulary and discharge the associated proof obligations, yielding ASM-style operational steps that are correct by construction with respect to the intended class specification.

Keywords: ASM · Class of algorithms · Event-B · Theory Plug-in · Refinement

1 Introduction

The B method [1] and its event-based evolution Event-B [2] are proof-based formal methods for building systems which are *correct by construction*. They structure developments around explicit state, guarded operations/events, and a refinement discipline in which abstract models are gradually made more concrete while preserving formally stated properties. Central to this approach are invariants (safety) and variants/convergence arguments (progress/termination), which give rise to proof obligations discharged with tool support, notably Atelier B [4] and the Rodin platform [5]. Moreover, Rodin's Theory Plug-in [8] allows one to

A. Raschke et al. (Eds.): Egon Börger Festschrift, LNCS 16580, pp. 317–331, 2026.
https://doi.org/10.1007/978-3-032-24494-9_15

extend the modelling language with reusable mathematical vocabulary (types, operators, axioms, proved rules), making it possible to package domain-specific notions together with the lemmas needed for automation.

Abstract State Machines (ASMs) ([13,15]) provide a complementary, operationally oriented view of computation: algorithms are described as small-step state transitions over rich structures, driven by rules that produce parallel updates. ASMs are particularly well suited to capture algorithms at their "natural level of abstraction", and the Sequential Thesis argues that sequential algorithms can be simulated step-for-step by sequential ASMs [14]. However, when the goal is not merely to model an individual algorithm but to characterise a *class* of algorithms [9,10,12], restricting attention to a chosen static algebra of primitives is not sufficient: many well-formed ASM programs may use only the intended operations while failing to satisfy the global objective of the class (e.g., sorting). This observation motivates combining the operational expressiveness of ASMs with the class-level logical guarantees that B/Event-B can enforce.

The paper proceeds as follows. Section 2 recalls the ASM notions needed in the sequel. Section 3 introduces a comparison-based "sorting algorithm class" and uses it to illustrate the fragility of purely algebraic classification, then shows how progress can be captured by a logical measure based on the number of inversions, which naturally suggests an Event-B variant. Section 4 recalls the concepts of Event-B, Rodin and the Theory Plug-in needed to understand Sect. 5 that presents the Event-B modelling of the "sorting algorithm class" and explains how the Theory Plug-in is used to encode the required static vocabulary and supporting results, leading to an abstract Event-B machine that represents a generic sorting step together with mechanically checked proof obligations. We conclude with a discussion of limitations and perspectives.

2 Abstract State Machines: a Brief Definition

Abstract State Machines (ASMs), originally introduced by Yuri Gurevich under the name *Evolving Algebras* [13], provide a mathematically precise yet highly flexible model of computation. They capture algorithms at their "natural level of abstraction" by representing states as rich mathematical structures and transitions as parallel updates governed by simple rules.

2.1 States as Algebras

An ASM is defined over a *signature* Σ consisting of function symbols (which include constants as 0-ary functions). A *state* of the machine is a Σ-structure, that is, an algebra interpreting each function symbol of Σ over an underlying domain (or family of domains, in the many-sorted case).

In the context of this paper, we partition the signature into:

- **Static** function symbols, whose interpretation is fixed across all states (e.g., arithmetic operations, comparison, hardware primitives).

- **Dynamic** function symbols, whose interpretation may change from one state to the next (e.g., mutable variables, arrays, control flags).

Intuitively, the static part captures the "built-in" operations of the universe of discourse, while the dynamic part captures the evolving data of the computation.

2.2 Updates and Rules

The basic atomic action of an ASM is an *update* to the value of a dynamic function symbol at a given argument tuple. An update has the form

$$f(t_1, \ldots, t_n) := t_0$$

where f is a dynamic n-ary function symbol, and $t_0, \ldots, t_n$ are ground terms over the signature. Semantically, this means: in the next state, the value of f at the arguments given by $t_1, \ldots, t_n$ will become the value of t_0 in the current state; all other locations of f and all other function symbols are left unchanged.

ASM rules are built from such updates using a small set of constructors:

- **Guarded rules:**

  $$\texttt{if } \varphi \texttt{ then } R \texttt{ endif}$$

  where φ is a first-order formula over the current state, and R is a rule. The rule R is activated only if the guard φ holds.
- **Parallel composition:**

  $$R_1 \;||\; R_2$$

  which means that all updates produced by R_1 and R_2 are executed simultaneously in one step, provided they do not assign different values to the same location.
- (Optionally) **Choice and iteration** constructs, which are definable in terms of guarded and parallel rules in more elaborate ASM formalisms.

2.3 Small-Step Semantics and Runs

Given a fixed ASM program P (a finite, syntactically well-formed ASM rule) over a signature Σ, the operational semantics is defined as follows:

- At each step, starting from a current state S, the program P is evaluated in S.
- The evaluation of P yields a (finite) *update set*, i.e., a set of location/value pairs $f(\bar{a}) := v$.
- If the update set is *consistent* (no two updates assign different values to the same location), it is applied in parallel to S to produce the next state S'.

A *run* of an ASM is a (finite or infinite) sequence of states $S_0, S_1, S_2, \ldots$ such that each S_{t+1} results from applying the update set produced by P in state S_t. Though Yuri Gurevich did not provide a notion of initial value, it is common to consider that some symbols are interpreted as the input and the others are initialised with a default value.

2.4 Sequential Algorithms and the Sequential Thesis

The central claim of the ASM framework is that *every deterministic, sequential, step-by-step algorithm* can be modelled by an appropriate ASM whose states and transition rules reflect the algorithm's natural level of abstraction. This is captured in Gurevich's **Sequential Thesis** [14], which states that any sequential algorithm (under a precise axiomatization) can be simulated step-for-step by a sequential ASM.

In this sense, ASMs are not merely yet another machine model; they form a general, unifying semantic framework in which diverse computational paradigms (Turing machines, RAMs, high-level programs, hardware controllers, etc.) can be represented and compared within a single, algebraically grounded formalism.

3 Example: Characterizing the "Sorting Algorithm Class"

Let's attempt to define an ASM algebra for sorting an array of n elements. The core idea of a comparison-based sort is to compare elements and swap them if they are in the wrong order. This suggests a natural signature where 'swap' is a primitive operation on values.

An ASM state is an algebra over a given signature. Note that the domain has two sorts, the indices and the values.

- **Domains:** We need a domain of indices $D_{idx} = \{0, 1, \ldots, n-1\}$ and an ordered domain of values D_{val}. We also use a small domain of control states $D_{mode} = \{\texttt{OUTER\_LOOP}, \texttt{INNER\_LOOP}, \texttt{DONE}\}$.
- **Static Signature** (S_{sta})**:** These symbols have a fixed interpretation. They represent the unchanging toolkit for sorting.
  - Constants: $0, n-1 \in D_{idx}$.
  - Functions:
    $\texttt{*+1} : D_{idx} \to D_{idx}$, with usual semantics.
    $\texttt{*-1} : D_{idx} \to D_{idx}$, with usual semantics.
    $\texttt{*leq} : D_{val} \times D_{val} \to \{\text{true}, \text{false}\}$, the standard comparison.
    we consider also $<$, $\neg$ and $\wedge$ relational predicate (or function if we add the set *Bool* in domains.
- **Dynamic signature** (S_{dyn})**:** These symbols represent the evolving state of the computation.
  - $\texttt{c} : D_{idx} \to D_{val} \equiv D_{array}$, a dynamic function representing the array itself, the input.
  - $\texttt{i}, \texttt{j} : D_{idx}$, nullary functions (state variables) representing loop counters, initialized with 0.
  - $\texttt{mode} : D_{mode}$, a nullary function representing the control state, initialized with $\texttt{OUTER\_LOOP}$.

With this signature, a swap is accomplished as usually via a parallel update rule:

$$\mathsf{c}(i) := \mathsf{c}(j) \tag{1}$$

$$\texttt{||}\ \mathsf{c}(j) := \mathsf{c}(i) \tag{2}$$

3.1 An Example: Bubble Sort in ASM

Using this well-defined algebra, we can write a program for a slightly worse version of Bubble Sort. The algorithm, given in pseudo-code is:

```
for i from 0 to n-2 included
  for j from 0 to n-2 included
    if c[j] < c[j+1] then
       exchange c[j] and c[j+1]
    endif
  endfor
endfor
```

To be formally correct, this program must strictly use the functions provided in the static signature. The version below is a non-optimized Bubble Sort, which respects this constraint.

```
if mode = OUTER_LOOP and i < n-1 then
       j := 0
    || mode := INNER_LOOP
endif
||
if mode = OUTER_LOOP and not(i < n-1) then
    mode := DONE
endif
||
if mode = INNER_LOOP and j < n-1 then
       if not leq(c(j), c(j+1)) then
             c(j) :=  c(j+1)
          || c(j+1) := c(j)
       endif
    || j := j+1
endif
||
if mode = INNER_LOOP and not(j < n-1) then
       i := i+1
    || mode := OUTER_LOOP
endif
```

This ASM program correctly implements a variant of Bubble Sort. Notice that all operations on indices (increments, comparisons) now explicitly use the functions and constants from the static algebra.

3.2 Limitations: The Fragility of Classification

The power of ASMs to achieve a "literal identification" of an algorithmic class is fragile. The framework constrains the available primitive operations but places almost no constraints on the program's *control flow*. Even with our highly specialized and formally used "sorting algorithm class" we are not prevented from writing programs that are manifestly *not* sorting algorithms.

Indeed, an ASM which sets all the values of c to $c(0)$ gives a sorted array as output but is clearly not a sorting algorithm.

A partial answer can be given as follows. Firstly, one introduces c as 0-ary in D_{array} which prohibits tinkering with it directly. And one defines a swap function swap : $D_{array} \times D_{idx} \times D_{idx} \to D_{array}$ defined as:

```
swap(c,i,j) {
  if (c(j)<c(i)) then
    exchange c(i) and c(j)
  endif
}
```

Introducing such a specific (i.e., "restricted") swap operator does not, by itself, resolve the problem since the following, perfectly valid ASM program is still not a sorting algorithm:

```
if mode = OUTER_LOOP and not leq(c(0), c(0 +1)) then
          c(0)      := c(0 +1)
       || c(0 +1) := c(0)
endif
||
if mode = OUTER_LOOP  then mode := DONE endif
```

Yet, this is a first step since all ASM written using this signature are guaranteed to result an array with the same values and better ordered if the swap function was called on at least one unordered pair of values.

It is precisely to formalize and enforce such global properties that we turn to a method like Event-B. By allowing the explicit specification of invariants (properties that must always be true) and proving that each atomic operation (event) preserves them, Event-B provides a structured framework to ensure that a model adheres to a class-defining specification, offering a more robust path to identifying and building correct algorithms.

3.3 Expressing Progress via a Logical Measure

Above in this section, we just have established that restricting the static algebra is insufficient to characterize the class of sorting algorithms. The fault lies in the ASM program's control flow, which remains unconstrained. The key missing piece is a way to formally express the *purpose* of a sorting algorithm: to systematically reduce the disorder of the array until it is fully sorted (see [18]).

This notion of "progress" can be captured not by rules of execution, but by a logical property over the state of the machine. The idea is to define a **measure function** that quantifies the "disorder" of the array. For a program to be considered as a sorting algorithm, it must guarantee that this measure never increases and eventually reaches its minimum value (zero).

For comparison-based sorting, the canonical measure of disorder is the number of **inversions**. An inversion is a pair of array elements that are in the wrong order relative to each other. Formally, we define a measure function M which maps the current state of the array ($\mathtt{c}$) to a natural number:

$$M(\mathtt{c}) = |\{(k,l) \in D_{idx} \times D_{idx} \mid k < l \wedge \neg\mathtt{leq}(\mathtt{c}(k), \mathtt{c}(l))\}|$$

This function, M, counts the number of pairs of indices (k,l) where the element that comes first in the array is larger than the element that comes second. A fully sorted array has exactly 0 inversions. A reverse-sorted array has the maximum number of inversions.

Using this measure, we can state a crucial property that any valid comparison-based sorting algorithm must satisfy. Let $\mathtt{c}_t$ be the state of the array at a given step t, and $\mathtt{c}_{t+1}$ be the state after the ASM executes one step. A sorting program must satisfy the following property[1]:

$$M(\mathtt{c}_{t+1}) \leq M(\mathtt{c}_t)$$

Furthermore, any step that is intended to perform "useful work" (i.e., a swap) must decrease this measure:

- **For a swap step:** If the rule `(c(j), c(j+1))` $:=$ `swap(...)` is fired, it is because $\neg\mathtt{leq}(\mathtt{c}_t(j), \mathtt{c}_t(\mathtt{j+1})))$. This single swap corrects exactly one inversion, therefore guaranteeing that $M(\mathtt{c}_{t+1}) < M(\mathtt{c}_t)$.
- **For a swap preparing step (for instance looking for a maximum):** If the ASM rule only updates a counter (e.g., $\mathtt{j} := \mathtt{j+1}$), the array itself does not change. Thus, $\mathtt{c}_{t+1} = \mathtt{c}_t$, and the measure remains equal: $M(\mathtt{c}_{t+1}) = M(\mathtt{c}_t)$.

The correct Bubble Sort ASM program we showed earlier satisfies this property. In contrast, our non-sorting "one-step-sorter" program, while it may decrease the measure once, terminates without ensuring the measure is zero. More critically, one could easily write a malicious ASM program over the same algebra that swaps two elements that are *already* in the correct order, thereby *increasing* the inversion count and violating the progress property.

This demonstrates that the true identity of a sorting algorithm class is defined by two orthogonal components: an **algebra** of allowed operations and a **global dynamic property** of progress towards a goal. The ASM framework excels at defining the first, but offers no native mechanism to enforce the second. This is precisely the gap that Event-B is designed to fill, by integrating the specification and proof of such logical properties directly into the modelling process.

Remark. Note that some sorting algorithm, like heap sort, are not directly caught by this specification. Yet a heap is essentially a priority queue which can be used for sorting. One could try to define a class for priority queues.

[1] In formal methods, such a function that must strictly decrease over certain steps of the computation is known as a **variant** or **terminating measure**. It is the primary tool used to prove that an algorithm makes progress and eventually terminates.

4 Event-B, Rodin and the Theory Plug-in

The Event-B solution: Algebra plus specification. This is where the true value of a method like Event-B becomes apparent. It provides a framework to address both facets of the problem simultaneously:

1. **Defining the algebra:** The fixed hardware functions are modelled axiomatically in Event-B using 'CONSTANTS', 'SETS', and 'PROPERTIES'. This rigorously defines the static universe of operations, just as we did for our sorting algorithm class.
2. **Enforcing the logic:** Crucially, Event-B forces the developer to provide a high-level **specification** of the system's required behavior through logical properties, most notably **invariants** or **variants**. For instance, for a satellite, an invariant might be "the satellite's angular velocity must always remain within safe bounds". For the sorting algorithm, the goal would be expressed as a post-condition: "upon termination, the array is sorted and is a permutation of its initial state".

The development process in Event-B revolves around proving that each atomic action (an 'event', like one step of the Bubble Sort) preserves the system's invariants. This requirement to produce a formal proof moves the notion of correctness from a simple "syntactic adherence to an algebra" to a "provable satisfaction of a global specification". This duality—a fixed algebra of operations and a provable specification of global properties—provides the robust framework for literal identification that the ASM model alone cannot guarantee.

B is a formal method [1] that supports a large segment of the software development life cycle: specification, refinement and implementation. In B, specifications are organized into abstract machines (similar to classes or modules). State variables are modified only by means of substitutions. The initialization and the operations are specified in a generalization of Dijkstra's guarded command notation, called the Generalized Substitution Language (GSL), that allows the definition of non-deterministic substitutions. For instance, in an abstract machine, we can define an operation with guarded substitutions, which are of the form **any** x **where** A **then** S **end**, where x is a variable, A a first-order predicate on x, and S a substitution. Such a substitution is non-deterministic because x can be any value that satisfies predicate A. The abstract machine is then refined into concrete machines, by replacing non-deterministic substitutions with deterministic ones. At each refinement step, the operations are proved to satisfy their specification. Hence, through refinement steps and proofs, the final code is proved to be correct with respect to its specification. The B method is supported by the tool Atelier B [4].

Event-B [2] is an evolution of the B method to specify event-based systems. The main difference with respect to B is the ability of modelling full systems, including the environment and hardware behaviour. Thus, updates on the model state are described by means of guarded events. In Event-B, the definition of sets and constants are described in contexts while the variables and events are specified in machines. Rather than considering modular specifications, this approach recommends starting from an abstract main event, and then providing more and more details by adding new events and variables through successive refinement steps. Such new events refining the *skip* substitution (which does not change the state of the variables), this implies that they can only update the new variables introduced by refinements. Several properties are expected to be satisfied by refinement, in particular refined events are not inconsistent with respect to abstract events. From a tool viewpoint, these properties generate proof obligations to be discharged in order to ensure that this semantics of refinement is applied.

The Rodin platform [5] is an open source environment for Event-B which supports formal modelling, refinement and proof activities. Based on the IDE Eclipse, Rodin has been enriched with additional plugins for specific purposes like editing, animation, proof, etc. From a user viewpoint, each model in Rodin starts from a *Project* which is composed of *Machines* and *Contexts*. Concerning the proof activity, Rodin provides a proving perspective. For each machine and context, Rodin generates a set of proof obligations in order to verify properties like well-definedness, invariant preservation, action feasibility, convergence of events, deadlock freeness, data refinement, etc. One can refer to [7] for more details on proof obligations. The main automatic provers available for Rodin are **PP** (predicate prover) and **ML** (mono-lemma). There also exists **NewPP** directly developed within Rodin, while **PP** and **ML** come from Atelier-B [4], as external provers. Other external provers like SMT solvers can be added.

Among all the plugins developed for Rodin, we are mainly interested in the Theory Plug-in [8] which allows us to extend the mathematical modelling notation for Event-B and which provides support for reasoning about the extended language. Type parameters, like in programming languages, allows a theory to be instantiated for different types. For instance, one can define a theory for linear algebra with choosing a particular field. Datatypes are composed of types, a set of constructors and optionally destructors which can be recursive. In the Theory Plug-in, new operators can be defined either as an expression operator (the result of the operation has a value) or as a predicate operator (the result of the operation is an atomic formula), with an infix or a prefix notation. Operators may be associative or not, commutative or not. These operators can be defined either directly or in a recursive way on types. Axiomatic definitions are described by giving types, operators and axioms. New theorems can also be defined in a theory; they must then be proved using the proving perspective of Rodin. Inference rules can be used to infer new hypotheses, derive a goal into smaller goals or prove some sequents in the proof tree. Rewrite rules can be defined to substitute an expression by another one. These rules are also to be proved correct from the axioms.

The next section presents the modelling of the "sorting algorithm class" of Sect. 3 using Event-B, Rodin and the Theory Plug-in.

5 Modelling the "sorting Algorithm Class" in Event-B

5.1 Context and Theory

We specify a theory called "OrderedSet" to define sorted sets (Fig. 1). We do not provide the theory of indices as in Sect. 3 since it is clearer to use the prebuilt type of integers. Order relation axioms are included as examples but none is used in this project because the result which would use it is taken as an axiom.

Context "SortingAlgo_c" (Fig. 2) includes the constants and axioms (in the sense of Event-B). Here n is the size of the array, the function which counts the number of inversions and the function which returns the multiset of values in the array. We also add theorems which state that exchanging two unordered values in the array decreases the number of inversions and the exchanging values does not change the corresponding multiset. Though these theorem could be proved using Rodin, we prefer to admit them since they are known results.

Remark. Note that in the classical use of Event-B, which remains an industrial tool, it is quite often to add as axioms, theorems which come from the domain theories instead of proving them. This is what we do with axm3 and axm6. Of course, as when writing axioms, one has to pay close attention not to include contradiction. Yet, in industrial setting, it is sometime preferred to not spend time proving theorems, evident for mathematicians and not for proof assistants.

```
THEORY
  OrderedSet
AXIOMATIC DEFINITIONS
  xdb1
  TYPES
   OS
  OPERATORS
   •leq:  leq(x : OS, y : OS) PREDICATE INFIX
  AXIOMS
   reflexivity:  ∀x·x leq x
   transitivity:  ∀x,y,z·x leq y ∧ y leq z ⇒ x leq z
   antisymmetry:  ∀x,y·x leq y ∧ y leq x ⇒ x=y
END
```

Fig. 1. Theory OrderedSet.

5.2 Abstract Machine and Refinements

Using refinement allows us to enforce several properties to a step of computation. The abstract machine "SortingAlgo" (Fig. 3) declares the array to be sorted and contains one event "step" stating that Variable "array" is updated such that it is still an array with the same multiset of data. Note that the event is declared as "anticipated" ensuring that any refinement will preserve the multiset of data. This will be enforced in refinements by the "SIM" proof obligation, which consists

```
CONTEXT
  SortingAlgo_C
CONSTANTS
  n
  number_of_inversions
  multiset
AXIOMS
  axm2  :  n∈N ∧ n≥2
  axm1  :  number_of_inversions=(λf·f∈1‥n→OS | card({x↦y|x∈1‥n ∧ y∈1‥n ∧ x<y ∧ ¬f(x) leq f(y)}))
  axm3  :  ∀f·f∈1 ‥ n → OS ∧ number_of_inversions(f)=0 ⇒ (∀x,y·x∈1‥n ∧ y∈1‥n ∧ x<y ⇒ f(x) leq f(y))
  axm4  :  ∀f,a,b·f∈1 ‥ n → OS ∧ a∈1‥n ∧ b∈1‥n ∧ a<b ∧ ¬ f(a) leq f(b) ⇒
           number_of_inversions(f)>number_of_inversions(f  {a↦f(b),b↦f(a)})
  axm5  :  multiset=(λf·f∈1‥n→OS | (λs·s∈ran(f)| card({f∼[{s}]})))
  axm6  :  ∀f,a,b·f∈1 ‥ n → OS ∧ a∈1‥n ∧ b∈1‥n ⇒ multiset(f)=multiset(f  {a↦f(b),b↦f(a)})
END
```

Fig. 2. Context SortingAlgo_c.

```
MACHINE
  SortingAlgo
SEES
  SortingAlgo_C
VARIABLES
  array
INVARIANTS
  inv1  :  array∈1‥n → OS
EVENTS
  INITIALISATION  ≙
  STATUS
   ordinary
  BEGIN
   act1  :  array:∈1‥n → OS
  END

  step  ≙
  STATUS
   anticipated
  BEGIN
   act1  :  array:|array'∈1‥n→OS ∧ multiset(array)=multiset(array')
  END

END
```

Fig. 3. Abstract machine SortingAlgo.

in checking that the abstract action simulates the concrete one (see [7] for more details).

The first refinement "SortingAlgo2" (Fig. 4) ensures that each step is a swap and that it makes the array closest to a sorted array, decreasing the number of inversions. This is done with the variant "vrn1", the number of inversions, and the fact that Event "step" is convergent.

The second refinement "SortingAlgo2R" (Fig. 5) allows the algorithm to use several iterations to compute which inversion to perform. For instance, for Selection Sort, the algorithm must select the greatest element in a prefix of the array. We do this by adding the event "calc". As it refines "skip", it cannot change the

```
MACHINE
  SortingAlgo2
REFINES
  SortingAlgo
SEES
  SortingAlgo_C
VARIABLES
  array
INVARIANTS
  inv1  :   array∈1‥n → OS
VARIANTS
  vrn1  :   number_of_inversions(array)
EVENTS
  INITIALISATION  ≙
  STATUS
   ordinary
  BEGIN
   act1  :   array:∈1‥n → OS
  END

  step  ≙
  STATUS
   convergent
  REFINES
   step
  ANY
   x
   y
  WHERE
   grd1  :   x∈1‥n
   grd2  :   y∈1‥n
   grd3  :   x<y
   grd4  :   ¬ array(x) leq array(y)
  THEN
   act1  :   array≔array  {x ↦ array(y), y ↦ array(x)}
  END

END
```

Fig. 4. First refinement.

values of the variables of Machine "SortingAlgo2". To ensure that Event "calc" needs only a finite number of iterations, each Event "step" must give a bound on the number of iterations that can be performed, setting Variable "stepCount".

5.3 Caveat

To ensure that each algorithm actually sorts, something is missing: the guard of Event "step" could be too strong in a refinement and stop the process before the array is sorted.

We have two options. The first one is to add a proof obligation which ensures that as long as the variant is non 0 the event must have its guard true. This could be done from the development of the Plug-in called Deadlock-Freeness Theorems ([19]). One would just have to add in the hypotheses of the Deadlock-Freeness proof obligation, called "DLF" ([7]), that the variant is non 0.

```
MACHINE
  SortingAlgo2R
REFINES
  SortingAlgo2
SEES
  SortingAlgo_C
VARIABLES
  array
  stepCount
  chosenX
  chosenY
INVARIANTS
  inv1  :  stepCount∈ℕ
  inv2  :  chosenX∈1‥n
  inv3  :  chosenY∈1‥n
VARIANTS
  vrn1  :  stepCount
EVENTS
  INITIALISATION  ≙
   extended
  STATUS
   ordinary
  BEGIN
   act1  :  array:∈1‥n → OS
   act2  :  stepCount:∈ℕ
   act3  :  chosenX:∈1‥n
   act4  :  chosenY:∈1‥n
  END

  step  ≙
  STATUS
   ordinary
  REFINES
   step
  ANY
   maxCount
  WHERE
   grd1  :  chosenX<chosenY
   grd2  :  ¬ array(chosenX) leq array(chosenY)
   grd3  :  maxCount∈ℕ
  WITH
   x  :  x=chosenX
   y  :  y=chosenY
  THEN
   act1  :  array≔array  {chosenX ↦ array(chosenY), chosenY ↦ array(chosenX)}
   act2  :  stepCount≔maxCount
  END

  calc  ≙
  STATUS
   convergent
  ANY
   x
   y
  WHERE
   grd1  :  stepCount>0
   grd2  :  x∈1‥n
   grd3  :  y∈1‥n
  THEN
   act1  :  stepCount≔stepCount−1
   act2  :  chosenX≔x
   act3  :  chosenY≔y
  END

END
```

Fig. 5. Second refinement.

The other option is to derive a while-do-end algorithm applying the m-while rule ([6] and Chap. 15 of [2]), in order to combine Event "calc" and Event "step" together. In this algorithm the actions of Event "calc" are repeatedly executed until its guard is false. Event "step" corresponds to the final iteration of the loop. This is obviously the most elegant solution.

6 Conclusion

This paper highlights a fundamental limitation of using ASMs alone to define *classes* of algorithms: fixing a static algebra of allowed primitives (e.g., `leq`, `inc`, and swap-like updates) does not prevent the construction of well-formed programs whose control logic fails to realise the intended global goal. The "one-step sorter" example makes this fragility concrete: it respects the algebraic discipline but is not a sorting algorithm for arrays of size $n > 2$.

To address this, we advocate an Event-B-based characterisation in which an algebra of permitted operations is coupled with class-level logical obligations. Using Rodin and the Theory Plug-in, we show how the static vocabulary can be packaged as a theory/context layer, while invariants and a variant capture the essential safety and progress requirements. For comparison-based sorting, the number of inversions provides a natural progress measure: corrective swaps strictly decrease it, and non-modifying steps preserve it, enabling a robust notion of "being in the sorting class" that is independent of any particular algorithm (Bubble sort, etc.). The resulting abstract machine expresses a generic sorting step and is proved, by construction, to preserve the relevant properties.

The immediate next steps are to scale the approach beyond this first case study and to strengthen tool support. We plan to investigate systematic connections between ASM-like operational descriptions and Event-B refinements, ultimately supporting engineering workflows where class constraints and correctness arguments are carried throughout development.

References

1. Abrial, J.R.: The B-Book: assigning programs to meanings. Cambridge University Press (1996)
2. Abrial, J.R.: Modelling in Event-B - System and Software Engineering. Cambridge University Press (2010)
3. Abrial, J.-R., Mussat, L.: Introducing dynamic constraints in B. In: Bert, D. (ed.) B 1998. LNCS, vol. 1393, pp. 83–128. Springer, Heidelberg (1998). https://doi.org/10.1007/BFb0053357
4. Clearsy: Atelier B. https://www.atelierb.eu
5. Rodin. https://www.event-b.org
6. Cansell, D., Singh, N.K.: Correct-by-Construction synthesis of sequential algorithms. In: RODIN User and Developer Workshop, 25th June. Bergamo, Italy (2024)
7. Hoang, T.S.: An Introduction to the event-B modelling method in industrial deployment of system engineering methods, pp. 211–236. Springer-Verlag (2013)

8. Theory Plug-in. https://wiki.event-b.org/index.php/Theory_Plug-in
9. Börger, E.: Abstract state machines: a unifying view of models of computation and of system design frameworks. Ann. Pure Appl. Logic **133**(1–3), 149–171 (2005)
10. Grigorieff, S., Valarcher, P.: Evolving multialgebras unify all usual sequential computation models. In: STACS 2010, LIPIcs, vol. 5, pp. 417–428. Schloss Dagstuhl - Leibniz-Zentrum für Informatik (2010)
11. Grigorieff, S., Valarcher, P.: Functionals using bounded information and the dynamics of algorithms. In: LICS 2012, pp. 345–354. IEEE Computer Society (2012)
12. Grigorieff, S., Valarcher, P.: Classes of algorithms: formalization and comparison. Bulletin EATCS **107**, 95–127 (2012)
13. Gurevich, Y.: Evolving algebras 1993: Lipari guide. In: Specification and validation methods, pp. 9–36. Oxford University Press (1993)
14. Gurevich, Y.: Sequential abstract-state machines capture sequential algorithms. ACM Trans. Comput. Log. **1**(1), 77–111 (2000)
15. Boerger, E., Staerk, R.: Abstract state machines: a method for high-level system design and analysis. Springer-Verlag (2003)
16. Staerk, R., Schmid, J., Boerger, E.: Java and the Java Virtual Machine: definition. Validation. Springer-Verlag, Verification (2001)
17. Butler, et al.: Modelling and refinement in CODA. Electron. Proceed. Theor. Comput. Sci. (2013)
18. Knuth, D.E.: The art of computer programming. Sorting and Searching, vol. 3, 2nd edn., Addison–Wesley, Reading, MA (1998)
19. Yang, F., Jacquot, J.: An event-b plug-in for creating deadlock-freeness theorems. In: Proceedings of the 14th Brazilian Symposium on Formal Methods, São Paulo, Brazil. Brazilian Computer Society (2011)

Refinement-Centric Hazard Analysis with SHARCS: A Case Study Bridging Requirements and Formal Model

Asieh Salehi Fathabadi(✉), Colin Snook, Thai Son Hoang, and Michael Butler

School of Electronics and Computer Science (ECS), University of Southampton, Southampton, U.K.
{a.salehi,t.s.hoang,m.j.butler}@soton.ac.uk

Abstract. Safety and security analysis of critical systems demands approaches that are systematic at the requirements level and rigorous at the level of formal verification. SHARCS (Systematic Hierarchical Analysis of Requirements for Critical Systems) addresses this need through a refinement-centric hazard analysis, structuring system purposes, control actions, and constraints hierarchically. However, the transition from SHARCS analysis artefacts to formal models has so far remained largely implicit.

This paper extends SHARCS with systematic rules for constructing Event-B models, making the link between hazard analysis and formal modelling explicit. We define how SHARCS control abstractions, action analysis, and safety constraints are mapped to Event-B contexts, machines, events, invariants, and refinement steps. The approach is demonstrated through a railway level-crossing case study, showing how hazard analysis models can be treated as refinement-oriented ground models and progressively transformed into verifiable Event-B developments.

The resulting refinement-centric framework provides a traceable path from hazard identification to formal proof, reflecting core principles of faithful abstraction and stepwise refinement central to Egon Börger's work.

1 Introduction

Safety and security are key considerations in the design of critical systems. Traditional requirements analysis methods often rely heavily on human expertise and experience, which, while essential, can benefit from the rigour and formality of systematic approaches to ensure early detection and mitigation of potential issues. For instance, Systems Theoretic Process Analysis (STPA) [10] provides a systematic methodology to identify hazards by analysing how control actions might cause failures, but relies on human judgement to assess the impact of these actions. Conversely, formal techniques like Event-B [2] offer rigorous analysis through formal verification but lack the methodical hazard identification

A. Raschke et al. (Eds.): Egon Börger Festschrift, LNCS 16580, pp. 332–353, 2026.
https://doi.org/10.1007/978-3-032-24494-9_16

approach inherent to STPA, and practitioners often struggle to determine appropriate refinement strategies.

Background on SHARCS. We introduced the SHARCS approach (Systematic Hierarchical Analysis of Requirements for Critical Systems) in [4] to address the above-mentioned complementary limitations by synergising STPA with Event-B refinement. The key novelty of SHARCS lies in three integrated aspects:

1. **Hierarchical and Incremental Requirements Analysis:** Rather than attempting to analyse the requirements for an entire complex system at once, SHARCS structures the analysis hierarchically. Starting from abstract system-level purposes, it progressively introduces components and their interactions at each refinement level, systematically flowing down requirements from the system level to the component level. This hierarchical component design ensures that at each level, safety or security requirements are verified through formal modelling and proof.
2. **Control Abstraction Diagrams:** SHARCS introduces visual *control abstraction diagrams* that explicitly show agents, components, and control actions at each abstraction level. These diagrams serve as a bridge between requirements analysis and Event-B models, illustrating how abstract actions are refined by introducing intermediate components and states. Critically, these diagrams guide the discovery of appropriate refinement strategies by helping practitioners identify which abstractions to introduce at each level.
3. **Unified Safety and Security Framework:** Unlike approaches that treat safety and security separately, SHARCS provides a unified methodology applicable to both domains. By reapplying the hierarchical analysis process to each design component, SHARCS drives development from abstract system-level requirements to concrete component-level solutions, ensuring that both safety hazards and security vulnerabilities are systematically identified and mitigated.

The original SHARCS methodology [4] was demonstrated through the Tokeneer case study, a security-critical system requiring formal verification of access control mechanisms. While this demonstrated SHARCS effectiveness for security analysis, the methodology is equally applicable to safety-critical systems.

Contributions. This paper makes two principal contributions that extend and clarify the SHARCS methodology.

1. **Systematic construction rules.** While SHARCS provides a methodology for combining STPA with Event-B, the transition from analysis artefacts to formal models has remained largely implicit. This paper presents systematic rules that support the construction of Event-B models from SHARCS analysis elements:
   - Control abstraction diagrams → Event-B sets, variables, typing invariants, and events

  - Action analysis tables → Safety invariants, events, liveness properties, and refinement strategy

   These rules provide traceability from hazard identification to formal proof obligations and, we believe, make the refinement-based approach more accessible to practitioners. The systematic nature of the rules opens possibilities for future elaboration, improvement, and tool automation.
2. **Application to a safety-critical case study.** The Tokeneer security-critical case study [4] demonstrated SHARCS's applicability to security-critical systems with vulnerabilities, access control, and authentication concerns. To demonstrate that SHARCS is equally effective for safety-critical systems, we present a railway level-crossing case study. This safety case study involves different types of hazards (collision prevention), different system characteristics (physical interactions between trains, cars, and barriers), and different failure modes (mechanical failures, timing issues, detection failures). The case study shows how SHARCS hierarchical analysis naturally decomposes safety requirements from the system level (prevent train and car collisions) through component levels (barrier control, signal control, detection) to sub-component levels (sensors, actuators, indicators).

Together, these contributions provide developers with a rigorous and traceable analysis method that flows down critical system requirements to derived component requirements. They offer formal methods users a methodical approach to discover refinement strategies by selecting appropriate abstractions and requirements for each stage. Additionally, they enable domain experts to validate designs progressively through scenarios executed on abstract models, with explicit traceability between hazard analysis decisions and verified Event-B models.

Structure. The remainder of this paper is structured as follows. Section 2 presents the railway level-crossing safety case study, demonstrating an application of SHARCS to a safety-critical system. Section 3 presents systematic rules for the construction of Event-B models, using the case study's artefacts as concrete examples. Section 4 discusses related work, and Sect. 5 concludes with future directions.

2 Safety Analysis of a Railway Level Crossing

In this section, we present an application of SHARCS to a safety-critical railway level-crossing system, where a road intersects a railway line at the same crossing. The primary safety property is to ensure that there are no collisions, i.e., cars and trains do not use the crossing simultaneously. This case study will provide the artefacts, including control abstraction diagrams, action analysis tables, hierarchical component designs, and failure hierarchies, to illustrate the application of the systematic rules for constructing Event-B in Sect. 3.

There are three main phases of the SHARCS process:

1. System-level analysis and abstract modelling
2. Component level analysis and refinement modelling
3. Consolidation to produce the hierarchical component design and hierarchical failure analysis.

On Abstraction and Refinement. To provide a flavour of what we mean by abstraction and refinement in action analysis, consider Fig. 1. This shows a SHARCS *control abstraction diagram* for the level crossing system whose purpose is to ensure that cars and trains do not use the crossing simultaneously, thus avoiding collision between cars and trains. The solid arrows represent actions (*enter*, *leave*, etc.) performed by agents (*trains*, *cars*, etc.) on components (*crossing*, *barrier*, etc.). The model in Fig. 1 involves 3 agents, 7 components, and 15 actions. Now consider Fig. 2 which is an "abstraction" of Fig. 1 containing 2 agents, 1 component, and 4 actions. Rather than performing hazard analysis across all the actions of the more complex Fig. 1, we commence the analysis on the smaller number of actions of Fig. 2. We then incrementally consider additional components and associated actions and analyse those additional actions for potential hazards. In Sect. 3, we will show how these diagrams systematically lead to Event-B contexts, sets, constants, and events.

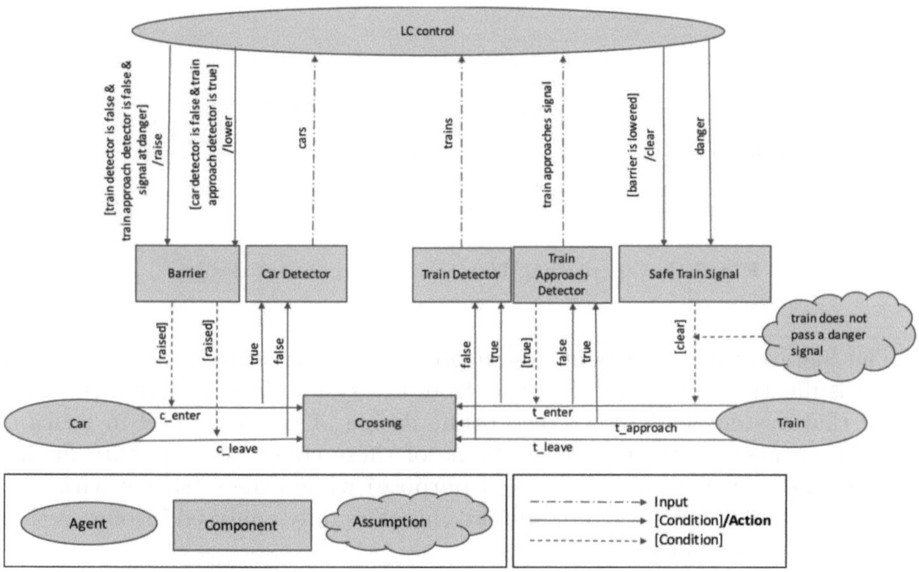

Fig. 1. Level Crossing: Control Abstraction Diagram.

On Consolidation. We present the diagrams of the consolidation phase next, in order to aid understanding of the SHARCS contribution in the case study analysis.

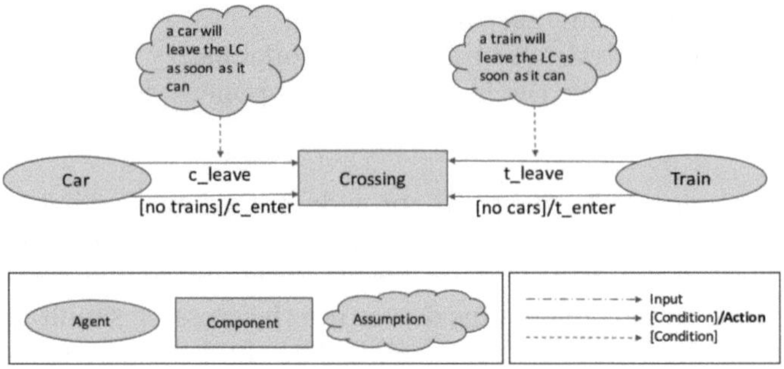

Fig. 2. System Level: Control Abstraction Diagram.

The hierarchical component design of the level crossing system, illustrated in Fig. 3 involves multiple components: the barrier component to stop cars when a train is passing, the detection component to identify cars on the crossing, and the signalling component to stop trains unless the crossing is clear. Further components include train detectors, train approach detectors, and traffic lights.

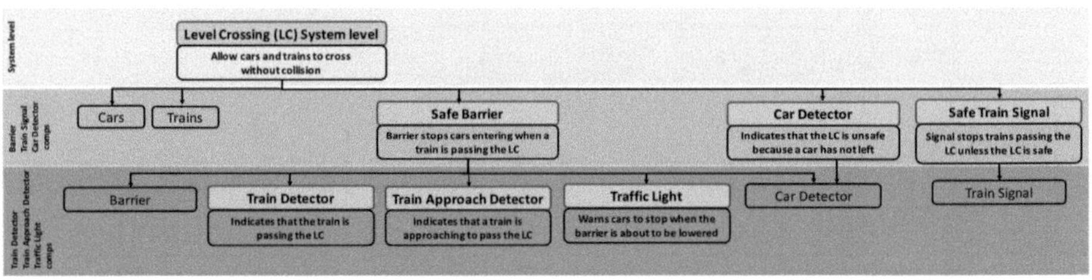

Fig. 3. Level crossing: hierarchical component design.

The hierarchical component design process as applied to the level crossing system is illustrated in Fig. 3. Starting from the system level purpose, the analysis of that system leads us to the outline design of the next level in terms of sub-components and their purpose. Some of these components require further analysis (those shown with a title and purpose) while others (shown with only a title) are assumed to be given, and are therefore only analysed insofar as they are used by their sibling components.

The purpose of the level crossing system is to allow cars and trains to cross without collision. High-level analysis of this system leads us to the design decision that, to achieve the system's purpose, we need some kind of safe barriers, car detectors and safe train signals (note that the prefix *safe* implies that these components are "abstract", with some extra functionality that we have yet to design). Analysis of the safe barrier in turn leads to the decision to use an ordinary (i.e. unintelligent) barrier, detectors and traffic lights. In summary, there are six control components in the level crossing design structure (over two levels): safe barrier, car detector, safe train signal, train detector, train approach detector and traffic light.

Failures at the immediate sub-component level could cause a failure at the higher level. Hence, in line with the hierarchical component design, starting from the top-level system failures, we have derived a hierarchy of failures as illustrated in Fig. 4. For example, a system-level failure of a train and a car using the crossing simultaneously ($F1$) breaks down into failures at the barrier ($FB1$), signalling ($FS1$), and car detection components ($FCD1$). This detailed analysis helps ensure comprehensive safety measures at each level of the design. In Sect. 3, we show how this failure hierarchy leads to the construction of safety invariants across Event-B refinement levels.

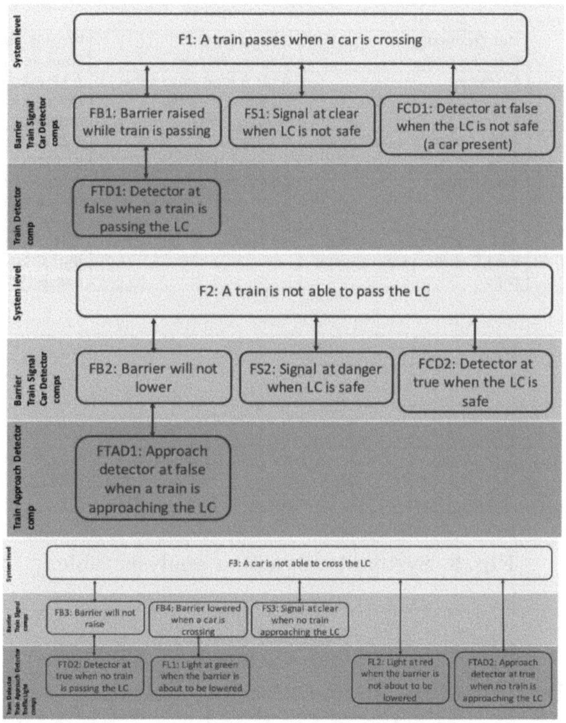

Fig. 4. Level crossing: hierarchical failures.

On System Level Analysis. The system and component level analyses both include control analysis (control abstraction diagram), action analysis (analysis table), formal modelling and verification and finally supporting identification of mechanisms for mitigating identified hazards in the next level.

The control abstraction diagram of the system level is shown in Fig. 2. The action analysis of the system level is presented in Fig. 5. An action analysis table is constructed to analyse all the possible actions that can occur at the system/component level and to identify the resulting failures. This leads to identification of conditions for controls that are intended to prevent failures in the system, followed by suggesting hazard mitigations to be introduced in the next level components: Barrier, Signal and Detector. As we will show in Sect. 3, each of these columns provides specific information that systematically guides the construction of Event-B models.

Level Crossing System level

Purpose: Allow cars and trains to cross without collision.

Actions: Trains can enter and leave the LC, Cars can enter and leave the LC.

Failures:
- **F1**: A train passes when a car is crossing
- **F2**: A train is not able to pass the LC
- **F3**: A car is not able to cross the LC

System Action	Not Occurring Causes Failure	Occurring Causes Failure	Wrong Timing or Order Causes Failure
Train enters the LC	No failure	**A12:** A train enters the LC when a car is crossing (*F1*)	**A13:** A train enters the LC before a car finishes crossing (*F1*)
Train leaves the LC	**A21:** A train does not leave (*F3*)	No failure	**A23:** A train does not leave before a car crosses (*F1*)
Car enters the LC	No failure	**A32:** A car enters the LC when a train is passing (*F1*)	**A33:** A car enters the LC before a train finishes passing (*F1*)
Car leaves the LC	**A41:** A car does not leave the LC when a train passes (*F2*)	No failure	**A43:** A car does not leave the LC before a train passes (*F1*)

Mitigations:
- ***Safe Barrier*** component stops cars entering when a train is passing. It should stop cars from before a train starts passing until after it finishes passing (addressing *A23, A32, A33*).
- ***Safe Train Signal*** component stops the train when a car is passing. It should only allow the train to pass when the barriers are closed AND the crossing is clear (addressing *A12, A13, A43*).
- ***Car detector*** component (assists the Safe Train Signal) indicates that the LC is unsafe because a car has not left (addressing *A13, A43*).
- ***Assumption*** a train will leave the LC as soon as it can (addressing A21)
- ***Assumption*** a car will leave the LC as soon as it can (addressing A41)
- ***Assumption*** a train will not enter the LC when the train signal is red (addressing A12)
- ***Assumption*** a car will not enter the LC when the barrier is lower (addressing A32)

Fig. 5. System level, action analysis table.

On Component Level Analysis. Here, the action analysis of two component levels, Barrier and Signal, are presented in Fig. 6 and Fig. 7, respectively.

The barrier component analysis in Fig. 6 introduces new actions (barrier raising/lowering) and new control constraints. The abstract action "car enters crossing" is refined by introducing intermediate barrier states. The signal component analysis in Fig. 7 similarly refines the train entry action by introducing signal states and detection mechanisms.

The Event-B models of the system, barrier, and signal level are included in the Appendix. In Sect. 3, we will present rules showing how these SHARCS artefacts, the control abstraction diagrams, and action analysis tables map to the Event-B constructs, guiding the construction of the Event-B models.

Safe Barrier			
Purpose: Barrier stops cars entering when a train is passing the LC, and allows cars entering when no train is passing the LC. **Actions:** Barrier can raise and lower.			
Failures: • **FB1**: Barrier raised while train is passing (causes *F1*) • **FB2**: Barrier will not lower (F2) • **FB3**: Barrier will not raise (F3) • **FB4**: Barrier lowered when a car is crossing (new)			
System Action	**Not Occurring Causes Failure**	**Occurring Causes Failure**	**Wrong Timing or Order Causes Failure**
Barrier raises	**AB11**: Barrier will not raise, when no train approaching or passing, preventing cars from crossing (FB3)	**AB12:** Barrier raises while train is passing (*FB1*)	**AB13:** Barrier raises before train leaves the LC (*FB1*)
Barrier lowers	**AB21**: Barrier will not lower, when a train approaching and no car crossing, preventing trains from passing (*FB2*)	**AB22:** Barrier lowers when a car is crossing the LC (*FB4*)	**AB23:** Barrier does not lower before train enters the LC (*FB1*)
Mitigations: • ***Train detector*** component indicates that the train is passing the LC (*AB12, AB13, AB11*) • ***Train approach detector*** component indicates that a train is approaching to pass the LC (*AB21, AB23*) • ***Car detector*** component indicates that no car is crossing (addressing AB21). • ***Traffic light*** component warns cars to stop when the barrier is about to be lowered (*AB22)*			

Fig. 6. Barrier component, action analysis table.

Safe Train Signal			
Purpose: Signal stops trains passing the LC unless the LC is safe (barrier lowered). **Actions:** Signal changes to clear or to danger			
Failures: • **FS1**: Signal at clear when LC is not safe (causes *F1*) • **FS2**: Signal at danger when the LC is safe (causes F2) • **FS3**: Signal at clear when no train approaching the LC (causes F3)			
System Action	**Not Occurring Causes Failure**	**Occurring Causes Failure**	**Wrong Timing or Order Causes Failure**
Signal changes to danger	**AS11**: Signal does not change to danger when LC is unsafe (*FS1*)	**AS12**: Signal changes to danger when the LC is safe (FS2)	**AS13**: Signal does not change to danger when no train approaching (FS3)
Signal changes to clear	**AS21**: Signal does not changes to clear when the LC is safe (FS2)	**AS22:** Signal changes to clear when LC is unsafe (*FS1*)	**AS23**: Signal changes to clear when no train approaching (FS3)
Mitigations: • ***Train approach detector*** component indicates that a train is approaching to pass the LC (*AS13, AS23*) • Train signal component is verified to ensure that the signal changes to, and remains at, danger when no train is approaching or the LC is unsafe (AS13, AS23, AS11, AS22) • Train signal component is verified to ensure that the signal changes to clear when a train is approaching and the LC is safe (AS12, AS21)			

Fig. 7. Signal component, action analysis table.

3 Rules for Constructing Event-B Models from SHARCS

Having presented the railway level-crossing case study with its SHARCS analysis artefacts in Sect. 2, we now present rules that make explicit how these artefacts map to Event-B formal models. The rules help to ensure the traceability from hazard analysis to formal verification. We use the level-crossing artefacts as concrete examples throughout.

3.1 Overview of the Approach

The Event-B construction process follows the hierarchical structure of SHARCS analysis, creating a refinement chain in Event-B that mirrors the abstraction levels in the hazard analysis. Each level of SHARCS analysis produces:

- a Control Abstraction Diagram (CAD) showing agents, components, and actions,
- an Action Analysis Table identifying hazards and control constraints,
- safety requirements derived from the analysis.

These artefacts guide the systematic construction of Event-B contexts (for static structure), machines (for dynamic behaviour), and refinement relationships (for hierarchical decomposition).

3.2 Capturing the Control Abstraction Diagram

The Control Abstraction Diagram (CAD) identifies the key entities and relationships at each abstraction level. The rules for capturing the CAD elements are the following:

Rule CAD-1 (Agent Definition): Each agent entity in the CAD is represented by a variable with its typing invariant in the corresponding Event-B machine.

The construction depends on whether the agent represents multiple instances or a single instance:

- *Single instance:* If an agent represents a single entity, the typing invariant specifies membership in a carrier set or predefined type, indicating the current state or identity of that single agent.
- *Multiple instances:* If an agent can have multiple instances (e.g., multiple trains, multiple cars), the typing invariant specifies that the variable is a subset of a carrier set or predefined types (such as BOOL, $\mathbb{Z}$). The variable represents the set of currently active agent instances.

For agents with non-predefined types, a carrier set in the Event-B context is also constructed. Multiple agents are also translated to the event parameter in the correspondence event, see Rule CAD-2.

Notation Convention: To distinguish between these cases in the CAD, we propose the following notation:

- `agent*` indicates multiple instances → represented by a subset typing invariant (e.g., $\texttt{variable} \subseteq \texttt{AGENT\_TYPE}$)

- `agent` indicates a single instance → represented by a membership typing invariant (e.g., `variable` ∈ `AGENT_TYPE` or `variable` ∈ `BOOL`)

Below is an example of this rule applied to *Car* and *Train*, which are multiple agents, introduced in the system level (Fig. 2):

```
CONTEXT c0
SETS
  CAR // Agent from CAD
  TRAIN // Agent from CAD
END

MACHINE m0
sees c0
variables
  cars // Agent from CAD
  trains // Agent from CAD
invariants
  @typeof−cars: cars ⊆ CAR // Agent from CAD
  @typeof−trains: trians ⊆ TRAIN // Agent from CAD
END
```

Rule CAD-2 (Component Definition): Components in the CAD follow the same construction approach as agents (Rule CAD-1). Each component entity is represented by a carrier set in the Event-B context and a variable with its typing invariant in the corresponding Event-B machine, using the same notation convention (`component*` for multiple instances, `component` for single instance).

Below is an example of this rule applied to *SafeBarrier*, which is a single component, introduced in the first level of refinement (Fig. 1):

```
CONTEXT c1
SETS
  BARRIER // Component from CAD
CONSTANTS
  Lowered
  Raised
AXIOMS
  @def_BARRIER: partition(BARRIER, {Lowered}, {Raised})
END

MACHINE m1
sees c1
variables
  cars // Agent from CAD
  trains // Agent from CAD
  barriers // Component from CAD
invariants
```

```
  @typeof−barriers: barriers : BARRIER // Component from CAD
END
```

Rule CAD-3 (Action Mapping): Each action arrow in the CAD between an agent to a component is represented by an Event-B event.

For example, the action *c_enter* in Fig. 2 is constructed as:

```
EVENT car_enters_LC
  ANY c // derived form Rule CAD−2 applied to "Car" mutiple agent
  WHERE
    // Guards derived from action analysis
  THEN
    // Actions derived from action analysis
END
```

Note that the *Car* multiple agent is translatable to an event parameter in this event.

The guards of events, like the above event, may strengthen at refinement level (barrier component is introduced), comparing with the abstract (system) level.

3.3 Capturing the Action Analysis Table

The Action Analysis Table (AAT) systematically examines each action to identify potential hazards. The table elements map to Event-B constructs as follows:

Rule AAT-1 (Failure to Safety Invariant): Failure conditions, representing the negation of the purpose, is represented by the same safety invariants derived from Rule AA-1.

The purpose and negation of the failures from Fig. 6 is formalised as safety invariants as below:

```
MACHINE m1
sees c1
...
invariants
  @safety_barriers_trains: barriers = Raised ⇒ trains = ∅ // negation of Failure
     FB1
  @safety_barriers_cars: barriers = Lowered ⇒ cars = ∅ // negation of Failure
     FB4
END
```

Rule AAT-2 (Action to Event): Each action under "System Action" column in the action analysis table corresponds to an Event-B event representing that state transition, which is the same as the action derived from Rule CAD-3.

Rule AAT-3 (Not Occurring Failures to Liveness): Scenarios where an action fails to occur causes a failure, "Not Occurring Causes Failure" column, are represented by liveness properties, typically verified through model checking techniques.

Rule AAT-4 (Occurring Failures to Guard): Scenarios where an action's occurrence causes a failure, "Occurring Causes Failure" column, are represented by event guards that prevent the action under unsafe conditions.

Rule AAT-5 (Wrong Timing/Order Failures to Sequencing): Scenarios where an action occurs at the wrong time/order, "Wrong Timing or Order Causes Failure" column, are represented by sequencing guards that enforce proper event control flow and ordering constraints.

Rule AAT-6 (Mitigation to Refinement): Mitigation strategies identified in the table guide the refinement structure, indicating which components, controls, and mechanisms should be introduced in subsequent refinement levels.

3.4 Summary of the Translation Rules

Table 1 provides a summary of the translation rules from SHARCS artefacts to Event-B constructs.

Table 1. SHARCS to Event-B Construction Rules

Rule	SHARCS Element	Event-B Translation
CAD-1	Agent	Carrier set in context and/or variable, typing invariant and/or event parameter in machine
CAD-2	Component	Carrier set in context and/or variable and typing invariant in machine
CAD-3	Action	Event in machine
AAT-1	Failure	Safety invariant in machine
AAT-2	Action	Event in machine
AAT-3	Not occurring failures	Liveness properties
AAT-4	Occurring failures	Event guard(s) in machine
AAT-5	Wrong timing/order failures	Sequencing event guards in machine
AAT-6	Mitigation	Refinement Strategy

3.5 Verification and Traceability

The systematic construction rules provide several benefits:

1. **Traceability:** Every Event-B construct can be traced back to its origin in the SHARCS analysis through the naming conventions and rule references.

2. **Completeness:** The rules ensure all identified hazards and control constraints are captured in the formal model.
3. **Proof Guidance:** The refinement structure derived from the SHARCS analysis provides natural proof decomposition, with each refinement level addressing specific component failures.
4. **Tool Support Potential:** The systematic nature of the rules makes them amenable to tool automation, potentially enabling automatic generation of Event-B models from the SHARCS analysis.

The proof obligations generated by Event-B verification establish that:

- Safety invariants are preserved by all events
- Refinements correctly satisfy the abstract model
- Component-level controls prevent system-level failures

4 Related Work and Comparison

The integration of safety analysis techniques with formal methods has been explored from various perspectives. Leveson's STPA [10] provides systematic hazard identification but lacks formal verification capabilities. Extensions such as STPA-Sec [13] and STPA-SafeSec [6] address security vulnerabilities but remain informal methodologies without rigorous verification.

Several works have combined STPA with formal methods. Howard et al. [9] augment STPA with Event-B to verify security requirements, while Colley and Butler [5] apply a similar approach for safety analysis. Abdulkhaleq et al. [1] formalize STPA requirements in temporal logic for model checking, and Hata et al. [8] model STPA constraints as pre/post conditions in VDM++. However, these approaches support only single-level analysis rather than hierarchical refinement, and the transition from STPA artefacts to formal models remains largely implicit.

Regarding translation approaches, Thomas and Leveson [11] define formal syntax for hazardous control actions from STPA, enabling automatic generation of model-based requirements. This work focuses on translating *from* STPA to requirements specifications but does not address translation *to* executable formal models with refinement. In contrast, approaches like [7] translate design notations (AADL) *to* Event-B, but structure refinement based on design language features rather than system-level hazard analysis. Similarly, [12] proposes lightweight integration between SysML and Event-B but does not yet incorporate refinement for gradual detail introduction.

Event-B refinement [2] provides a rigorous framework for stepwise system development with proof-based verification. However, finding appropriate abstractions and refinement strategies remains challenging. SHARCS addresses this by using systematic hazard analysis to derive refinement structures.

Our construction rules differ in three key aspects: (1) they bridge hazard analysis (STPA) with formal verification (Event-B) through explicit mappings,

(2) they preserve hierarchical structure from STPA through Event-B refinement chains, and (3) they provide bidirectional traceability, from analysis artefacts to formal constructs and back. This makes the refinement relationship between requirements-level hazard analysis and model-level verification explicit and systematic.

The notion of refinement-centric development aligns with Börger's Abstract State Machines approach [3], where faithful abstractions guide formal development. Our contribution makes this relationship explicit in the context of hazard-driven system design through the systematic translation rules.

5 Conclusion and Future Work

This paper has demonstrated SHARCS application to a safety-critical railway level-crossing system and presented a first systematic attempt at defining translation rules from SHARCS hazard analysis to Event-B formal models. The key contributions are:

1. **Safety-Critical Case Study:** A railway level-crossing analysis demonstrating SHARCS applicability to safety-critical systems, complementing the Tokeneer security case study. The case study shows hierarchical decomposition from system level through component levels with complete SHARCS artefacts.
2. **Systematic Construction Rules:** A systematic mapping from SHARCS artefacts (Control Abstraction Diagrams and Action Analysis Tables) to Event-B constructs (contexts, variables, invariants, events, and guards), derived from the case study and providing explicit traceability between hazard analysis and formal verification.
3. **Refinement-Centric Framework:** Construction rules that preserve the SHARCS hierarchical structure in Event-B refinement chains, ensuring the controls at the component level provably prevent system-level hazards.

The rules presented here represent an initial characterisation of a SHARCS analysis to Event-B mapping. While they demonstrate feasibility and provide explicit traceability, several avenues for future work remain:

- **Rule Elaboration:** Further refinement and extension of translation rules to cover additional SHARCS constructs, particularly for security-specific elements and more complex failure propagation patterns.
- **Tool Automation:** Development of automated tools to generate Event-B models from SHARCS artefacts, reducing manual effort and potential translation errors. The systematic nature of our rules provides a foundation for such automation.
- **Validation:** Application to larger industrial case studies with multiple refinement levels to validate scalability and identify areas for rule improvement.
- **Bidirectional Translation:** Exploring reverse translation from Event-B models back to SHARCS artefacts to support iterative refinement and design exploration.

- **Integration with Assurance:** Linking translation rules with safety/security assurance frameworks to provide evidence for certification processes.

By combining STPA's methodical hazard identification with Event-B's rigorous verification through explicit modelling rules, this work provides a foundation for making refinement-based hazard analysis more accessible and systematic for critical systems development.

A Event-B System Model

```
context c0
sets
  CAR  // The set of cars
  TRAIN // The set of trains
end
```

```
machine m0
sees c0
variables
  cars // The set of cars in the level crossing
  trains // The set of trains in the level crossing
invariants
  theorem @typeof−cars: cars ⊆ CAR
  theorem @typeof−trains: trains ⊆ TRAIN

  // There should be no collision
  @safety: trains = ∅ ∨ cars = ∅
events
  event INITIALISATION
  begin
   @init−cars: cars := ∅
   @init−trains: trains := ∅
  end

  /**
   * A car @c enters the level crossing.
   * Guards:
   * − @c is not yet in the level crossing
   * − There are no trains in the level crossing
   * Actions:
   * − @c is added to the set of cars in the level crossing.
   */
  event car_enters_LC
  any c where
```

```
 @grd1 : c ∉ cars
 @grd2 : trains = ∅
then
 @act1 : cars := cars ∪ {c}
end

/**
 * A car @c leaves the level crossing.
 * Guards:
 * – @c is in the level crossing
 * Actions:
 * – @c is removed from the set of cars in the level crossing.
 */
event car_leaves_LC
any c where
 @grd1 : c ∈ cars
then
 @act1 : cars := cars \ {c}
end

/**
 * A train @t enters the level crossing.
 * Guards:
 * – There are no trains in the level crossing
 * – There are no cars in the level crossing
 * Actions:
 * – @t is added to the set of trains in the level crossing.
 */
event train_enters_LC
any t where
 @grd1 : t ∈ TRAIN
 @grd2 : cars = ∅
then
 @act1 : trains := trains ∪ {t}
end

/**
 * A train @t leaves the level crossing.
 * Guards:
 * – @t is in the level crossing
 * Actions:
 * – @t is removed from the set of trains in the level crossing.
 */
event train_leaves_LC
any t where
```

```
  @grd1: t ∈ trains
 then
  @act1: trains := trains \ {t}
 end

end
```

B Event-B Safe Barrier Model

```
context c1
sets
 BARRIER
constants
 Lowered
 Raised
axioms
 @def−BARRIER: partition(BARRIER, {Lowered}, {Raised})
end
```

```
machine m1
refines m0
sees c0 c1
variables
 cars // The set of cars in the level crossing
 trains // The set of trains in the level crossing
 barriers // The status of the barriers: Lowered, Raised
invariants
 @safety−barriers_cars: barriers = Lowered ⇒ cars = ∅
 @safety−barriers_trains: barriers = Raised ⇒ trains = ∅
events
 event INITIALISATION extends INITIALISATION
 begin
  @init−barriers: barriers := Raised
 end

 /**
 * A car only can enter if the barriers are not Lowered
 */
 event car_enters_LC refines car_enters_LC
 any c where
  @grd1: c ∉ cars
  @grd2: barriers = Raised
 then
```

```
 @act1: cars := cars ∪ {c}
end

/**
 * A car only can leave if the barriers are not Lowered
 */
event car_leaves_LC extends car_leaves_LC
when
 @grd2: barriers = Raised
end

/**
 * A train only can safely enters the level crossing if the barriers are
    Lowered
 */
event train_enters_LC refines train_enters_LC
any t where
 @grd1: t ∈ TRAIN
 @grd2: barriers = Lowered
then
 @act1: trains := trains ∪ {t}
end

event train_leaves_LC extends train_leaves_LC
end

/**
 * Lowering the barrier from "raised" status
 * Guards:
 * – The barriers are raised
 * Actions:
 * – The barriers are lowered
 */
event barriers_lowers
when
 @grd1: barriers = Raised
 @grd2: cars = ∅
then
 @act1: barriers := Lowered
end

/**
 * Raising the barrier from "lowered" status
 * Guards:
```

```
* – The barriers are lowering
* – There are no trains
* Actions:
* – The barriers are raised
*/
event barriers_raises
when
 @grd1: barriers = Lowered
 @grd2: trains = ∅
then
 @act1: barriers := Raised
end

end
```

C Event-B Safe Train Signal Model

```
context c2
sets
 TRAIN_SIGNAL
constants
 SIGNAL_CLEAR
 SIGNAL_DANGER
axioms
 @def-TRAIN_SIGNAL: partition(TRAIN_SIGNAL, {SIGNAL_CLEAR}, {
    SIGNAL_DANGER})
end
```

```
machine m2
refines m1
sees c0 c1 c2
variables
 cars // The set of cars in the level crossing
 trains // The set of trains in the level crossing
 barriers // The status of the barriers: Lowered, Raised
 train_signal // The train signal
invariants
 @safe_train_signal: train_signal = SIGNAL_CLEAR ⇒ barriers = Lowered
events
 event INITIALISATION extends INITIALISATION
 begin
  @init-train_signal: train_signal := SIGNAL_DANGER
```

```
end

event car_enters_LC extends car_enters_LC
end

event car_leaves_LC extends car_leaves_LC
end

/**
 * A train @t enters the level crossing.
 * Guards:
 * – There are no trains in the level crossing
 * – The train signal is "Clear"
 * Actions:
 * – @t is added to the set of trains in the level crossing.
 */
event train_enters_LC refines train_enters_LC
any t where
 @grd1: t ∈ TRAIN
 @grd2: train_signal = SIGNAL_CLEAR
then
 @act1: trains := trains ∪ {t}
end

event train_leaves_LC extends train_leaves_LC
end

event barriers_lowers extends barriers_lowers
end

/**
 * The barriers are raising only when the train signal is "Danger"
 */
event barriers_raises extends barriers_raises
when
 @grd3: train_signal = SIGNAL_DANGER
end

/**
 * Train signal set to "Clear"
 * Guards:
 * – Train signal is current "Danger"
 * – There are no cars detected
 * – The barriers are Lowered
```

```
 * Actions:
 * – Train signal is set to "Clear"
 */
event train_signal_to_clear
when
 @grd1: train_signal = SIGNAL_DANGER
 @grd2: barriers = Lowered
then
 @act1: train_signal := SIGNAL_CLEAR
end

/**
 * Train signal set to "Danger"
 * Guards:
 * – Train signal is current "Clear"
 * Actions:
 * – Train signal is set to "Danger"
 */
event train_signal_to_danger
when
 @grd1: train_signal = SIGNAL_CLEAR
then
 @act1: train_signal := SIGNAL_DANGER
end

end
```

References

1. Abdulkhaleq, A., Wagner, S., Leveson, N.: A comprehensive safety engineering approach for software-intensive systems based on STPA. In: Procedia Engineering 128 (2015). Proceedings of the 3rd European STAMP Workshop 5–6 October 2015, Amsterdam, pp. 2–11. ISSN: 1877-7058.: https://doi.org/10.1016/j.proeng.2015.11.498, http://www.sciencedirect.com/science/article/pii/S1877705815038588
2. Abrial, J.R.: Modeling in Event-B: system and software engineering. Cambridge University Press (2010)
3. Börger, E.: The Abstract state machines method for high-level system design and analysis. In: Formal Methods: State of the Art and New Directions, pp. 79–116. Springer, London (2010) https://doi.org/10.1007/978-1-84882-736-3_3
4. Fathabadi, A.S., et al.: Systematic hierarchical analysis of requirements for critical systems. In: NASA Innovations in Systems and Software Engineering (2024)
5. Colley, J., Butler, M.: A formal, systematic approach to STPA using Event-B Refinement and Proof. In: 21th Safety Critical System Symposium (2013). https://eprints.soton.ac.uk/352155/
6. Friedberg, I., et al.: STPA-SafeSec: safety and security analysis for cyber-physical systems. J. Inf. Secur. Appl. **34**, 183–196 (2017). https://doi.org/10.1016/j.jisa.2016.05.008

7. Hadad, A.S.A., Ma, C., Ahmed, A.A.O.: Formal verification of AADL models by Event-B. IEEE Access **8**, pp. 72814–72834 (2020). https://doi.org/10.1109/ACCESS.2020.2987972
8. Hata et al.: Using hazard analysis STAMP/STPA in developing model-oriented formal specification toward reliable cloud service. In: 2015 International Conference on Platform Technology and Service, pp. 23–24 (2015)
9. Howard, G., et al.: A methodology for assuring the safety and security of critical infrastructure based on STPA and Event-B. Int. J. Crit. Comput. Based Syst. **9**(1/2), 56–75 (2019). https://doi.org/10.1504/IJCCBS.2019.098815
10. Leveson, N.G., Thomas, J.P.: STPA Handbook, Cambridge, MA USA (2018)
11. Thomas, J., Leveson, N.: Generating formal model-based safety requirements for complex, software-and human-intensive systems. In: Proceedings of the Twenty-first Safety-Critical Systems Symposium, Bristol, UK. Safety-Critical Systems Club (2013)
12. Thorburn, R., et al.: A lightweight approach to the concurrent use and integration of SysML and formal methods in systems design. In: Proceedings of the 25th International Conference on Model Driven Engineering Languages and Systems: Companion Proceedings, MODELS 2022, Montreal, Quebec, Canada, October 23-28, 2022. Ed. by Thomas Kühn and Vasco Sousa, pp. 83–84. ACM (2022). https://doi.org/10.1145/3550356.3559577
13. Young, W., Leveson, N.G.: Systems thinking for safety and security. In: Annual Computer Security Applications Conference, ACSAC '13, New Orleans, LA, USA, 9–13 December 2013. Ed. by Charles N. Payne Jr. ACM, pp. 1–8 (2013). https://doi.org/10.1145/2523649.2530277

Logic and Theory of Computation

Capturing Quantum Algorithms by Quantum Abstract State Machines

Flavio Ferrarotti[1(✉)] and Klaus-Dieter Schewe[2]

[1] Software Competence Center Hagenberg, Hagenberg, Austria
flavio.ferrarotti@scch.at
[2] Linz, Austria

Abstract. This paper introduces Quantum Abstract State Machines (Q-ASMs) as a rigorous method for the specification and analysis of quantum algorithms. While reification on a quantum computer is enabled, Q-ASMs also support the simulation on standard computers using probabilistic algorithms. Grover's search algorithm is used as an illustrative example. We further show that the framework is sufficiently general as to also express numerical algorithms based on nondigital quantum representations of real numbers.

Keywords: quantum computing · quantum algorithms · Abstract State Machines

1 Introduction

Computation theory as we know it is grounded in the encoding of any kind of information by words over some arbitrary alphabet [2]. It suffices to consider encodings by bits so that values of any basic data type are represented by bit strings. Registers and storage cells of any (standard) binary computer work with bit strings of some length n. The machine language of a processor provides finitely many elementary operations that are realised in hardware by logic gates, which usually process one or two bits.

Abstracting from this low-level picture we can design and analyse algorithms of all kinds on any level of abstraction using Abstract State Machines (ASMs), as proven by various behavioural theories, most importantly the theories of sequential, parallel, reflective and concurrent algorithms [5,8,12,18]. An easily comprehensible introduction to ASMs is provided by Börger [6], and extensions covering concurrent and reflective algorithms are contained in further monographs by Börger, Raschke and Gervasi [3,4].

The research of Flavio Ferrarotti was supported by the project QuantumReady (FFG grant no. 896217) within Quantum Austria, an initiative of BMBWF; by BMIMI, BMWET, the State of Upper Austria, and the State of Tyrol through the COMET Module Quantum Algorithm Engineering (FFG grant no. 923923); and by BMIMI, BMWET, and the State of Upper Austria within the SCCH competence center INTEGRATE (FFG grant no. 892418). All projects are managed by the Austrian Research Promotion Agency FFG.

A. Raschke et al. (Eds.): Egon Börger Festschrift, LNCS 16580, pp. 357–376, 2026.
https://doi.org/10.1007/978-3-032-24494-9_17

Quantum computing is grounded in the idea that states of a computer should be much more general than bit strings such that elementary operations can exploit special transformations that are enabled by the laws of quantum mechanics under very carefully controlled conditions [16]. Instead of bits, the states of which are either 0 or 1, we have to consider *quantum bits* (qubits), the states of which are given by any unit vector in a two-dimensional unitary vector space. The scalar product induces a norm with respect to which any Cauchy sequence will converge, so we obtain Hilbert spaces over complex numbers. Sequences of qubits are then vectors in higher dimensional Hilbert spaces defined by the tensor product of two-dimensional Hilbert spaces.

Beyond this general view, it is worth noting that quantum computation can accommodate different classes of representations. For example, integers may follow bit-based encodings, probabilistic choices can rely on geometric distributions, and even real numbers can be represented in a nondigital form using quantum states [15]. This diversity in representations highlights the need for a systematic way to organise and manage such encodings, which we address introducing a notion of quantum domains (qdomains for short). The specific operations available on a qdomain depend on the underlying quantum model; in the standard circuit model these operations are unitary, whereas other representations may permit additional primitive operations

Then the elementary operations on sequences of qubits can be defined by unitary transformations, in particular, the scalar products (and thus lengths and angles) are preserved. As with classical computation it is important to consider those unitary transformations that can be composed out of *(quantum) gates*, i.e., transformations defined on one or two qubits. In this way we can think of elementary operations in the standard quantum-circuit model as being realised by *quantum circuits*. This requirement is fundamental whenever a Q-ASM relies on that model, ensuring that operations are physically implementable. Later we illustrate that alternative quantum-information models may admit additional elementary operations.

Celebrated quantum algorithms using quantum representations of classical data (such as integers) are Grover's search algorithm [11] for searching through an unstructured data space to identify an element that satisfies a specific condition, and Shor's periodic finding algorithm [20] for determining the period of a periodic function. The latter one plays an essential role for fast prime factorisation, which can be applied to break an encryption [21] such as RSA.

A peculiarity with quantum computing concerns the generation of output. While it can be argued that loading sequences of qubits into registers and running elementary operations on them by using the corresponding quantum circuits can be done in a non-destructive way, this does not hold for output. The state of a qubit, i.e., the coefficients of the representing vector with respect to an orthonormal basis $\{|0\rangle, |1\rangle\}$ cannot be read as such. Instead, the output will be either $|0\rangle$ or $|1\rangle$, which underlie a Bernoulli distribution with probabilities determined by the absolute values of the complex coefficients (amplitudes). This limitation contrasts with the possibility of performing exact computations internally, for instance on real numbers represented in nondigital form by quantum states, where unitary operations combined with controlled copying of prepared states[1] enable deterministic manipulation of values until the final measurement.

As a consequence, every quantum algorithm is de facto probabilistic. For instance, Grover's algorithm determines the sought elements with a probability that is almost 1, but if an exact result is required, the algorithm should be coupled with a final test and repeated if necessary.

In order to obtain a higher-level view of quantum algorithms without reference to qubits we introduce Quantum Abstract State Machines (Q-ASMs) in this paper. We argue that the main difference is the need to provide qdomains, i.e., sets of values that are represented by sequences of qubits. With this we can preserve the view of states as Tarski structures that are manipulated by ASM rules. For the rules we can also preserve the ASM approach with the modification that basic operations are, in the standard setting, given by unitary transformations realised by quantum circuits, a fact that must be proven to ensure physical implementability. However, the Q-ASM framework itself is flexible: it allows one to incorporate additional elementary operations when these belong to the background quantum model under consideration. We make use of this flexibility later when discussing a nondigital specification of the arithmetic of real numbers. The gates in these circuits are assumed to be defined in the background of any Q-ASM [1]. Furthermore, if a Q-ASM is supposed to produce output, we obtain specifications of probabilistic algorithms, where the probabilistic behavior arises from quantum measurement according to the Born rule[2]. While our treatment of measurement follows the standard model, later examples will show that alternative models of quantum information may also provide non-unitary primitive operations at the representation level.

ASMs in general permit branching and unbounded parallelism, both of which rely on the evaluation of Boolean conditions. In a Q-ASM, each truth value should therefore be represented by a single qubit. The evaluation of a Boolean condition then yields `true` or `false` only probabilistically, with the distribution determined by the measurement of that qubit. As a consequence, every `if`- or `forall`-rule implicitly includes a random choice governed by the corresponding measurement statistics. Q-ASMs must therefore be formulated as probabilistic ASMs, in line with the approach proposed in [19].

This perspective is fundamentally different from the early work of Grädel and Nowack [10]. Their approach embeds quantum algorithms into the ASM framework without incorporating quantum measurement or probabilistic branching into the ASM semantics. Their Q-ASMs are defined as particular parallel

[1] The no-cloning theorem forbids duplicating an unknown quantum state, but if a state is known or prepared by the algorithm, additional copies can be created by re-preparing it. This allows parallel operations and can be integrated into circuit design before measurement.

[2] The Born rule states that the probability of obtaining a particular measurement outcome is given by the square of the amplitude of its projection onto the quantum state. For a state $|\psi\rangle = \sum_i \alpha_i |i\rangle$, the probability of observing basis state $|i\rangle$ is $|\alpha_i|^2$.

ASMs whose quantum behaviour is delegated entirely to background functions. All quantum effects, including superposition, interference, and especially measurement, are handled externally and atomically, while the ASM program itself remains deterministic. This effectively reduces quantum computation to classical parallelism equipped with stochastic oracles, obscuring the operational role of measurement and the probabilistic control flow inherent in quantum algorithms. The subsequent use of this framework in [7] thus raises concerns about its adequacy for capturing quantum computation at a meaningful level of abstraction.

The remainder of this paper is organised as follows. In Sect. 2 we introduce the basics of qubits and define qdomains, which provide the base sets for the interpretation of Q-ASM states and state transitions; this section also includes the definition of a q-domain for real numbers (represented in a nondigital form). This is followed by a presentation of unitary transformations and measurements in Sect. 3. Then Sect. 4 is dedicated to the introduction of Q-ASMs, which are quite analogous to standard ASMs with the difference that we exploit qdomains as base sets, elementary operations in the background that are defined by unitary transformations and shown to be realisable by quantum circuits, and foresee choice rules associated with probability distributions. In Sect. 5 we present a Q-ASM specification of Grover's search algorithm, for which we define the basic unitary operations on grounds of quantum gates in a Q-ASM background and use these in a fairly simple Q-ASM. Finally, Sect. 6 illustrates how Q-ASMs capture numerical algorithms operating over a q-domain of real number. These examples rely on an extended quantum-information model in which certain arithmetic primitives are provided by fixed circuits together with a non-unitary cloning operation. We conclude with a few final remarks in Sect. 7.

Throughout this paper we take a purely mathematical attitude towards quantum computing disregarding any link to quantum physics. In doing so our presentation assumes basic knowledge of linear algebra, in particular unitary vector spaces, i.e., vector spaces over the field of complex numbers that are equipped with a Hermitian, positive definite sesquilinear form (*scalar product*) [9,14]. Mathematical introductions to quantum computing can be found in the books by Mermin or Kitaev et al. [13,16].

2 Qubits and Quantum Domains

In this section, we introduce the fundamental mathematical structures underpinning quantum computing. States of quantum systems are described as vectors in a unitary vector space (or complex inner product space). A *unitary vector space* is a pair $(V, \langle \cdot, \cdot \rangle)$ comprising a vector space V over the field of complex numbers $\mathbb{C}$ and an *inner product* $\langle \cdot, \cdot \rangle : V \times V \to \mathbb{C}$. Thus, the following properties hold:

- *Hermitian symmetry*, i.e., for all $v, w \in V$ we have $\langle v, w \rangle = \overline{\langle w, v \rangle}$.
- *Sesquilinearity (semi-linearity in the first and linearity in the second argument)*, i.e., for all $u, v, w \in V$ and scalars $\alpha, \beta \in \mathbb{C}$ we have $\langle \alpha u + \beta v, w \rangle = \overline{\alpha} \langle u, w \rangle + \overline{\beta} \langle v, w \rangle$ and $\langle u, \alpha v + \beta w \rangle = \alpha \langle u, v \rangle + \beta \langle u, w \rangle$.

- *Positive definiteness*, i.e., for all $v \in V$, we have $\langle v, v \rangle \geq 0$ with equality iff $v = 0$.

The inner product induces a *norm* $\|v\| = \sqrt{\langle v, v \rangle}$ on the space, which satisfies the usual properties: $\|v\| \geq 0$, and $\|v\| = 0$ iff $v = 0$; $\|\alpha v\| = |\alpha|\|v\|$ for $\alpha \in \mathbb{C}$, and the triangle inequality $\|u + v\| \leq \|u\| + \|v\|$.

Moreover, the inner product defines the angle between two vectors: $\cos\theta = \frac{\mathrm{Re}(\langle u,v \rangle)}{\|u\|\|v\|}$, generalizing the real vector space notion of angle to the complex case. Two vectors u and v are *orthogonal* iff $\langle u, v \rangle = 0$.

The unitary vector spaces relevant for quantum computation are known as Hilbert spaces $\mathcal{H}^n = \mathbb{C}^{2^n}$, where the inner product of complex vectors $u = (u_1, \ldots, u_{2^n})$ and $v = (v_1, \ldots, v_{2^n})$ in such a space correspond to the direct generalization of the Euclidean dot product: $\langle u, v \rangle = \sum_{i=1}^{2^n} u_i \overline{v_i}$.

A valid quantum state must be a *unit vector* in a Hilbert spaces $\mathcal{H}^n$, i.e., $\|v\| = \langle v, v \rangle = 1$. This condition ensures that the total probability of all possible measurement outcomes sums to 1, which is a fundamental requirement in quantum mechanics.

From now on, we switch to *Dirac notation* (also called *bra-ket notation*), which is the standard notation adopted in this field. Then, complex column vectors (quantum states) in a Hilbert space $\mathcal{H}^n$ are denoted using *kets* $|\psi\rangle$ and their dual row vectors (Hermitian conjugate or complex conjugate transpose) using *bras* $\langle\psi|$. In this notation, the inner product of two quantum states $|\psi\rangle, |\phi\rangle \in \mathcal{H}^n$ is denoted as $\langle\psi|\phi\rangle$.

Qubits (short for *quantum bits*) are the fundamental unit of quantum information. Their states are represented by unit vectors in a Hilbert space. In particular, the state of a single qubit is a unit vector in $\mathcal{H} = \mathbb{C}^2$. In general, the state of an n-qubit system (or register) is a unit vector in a 2^n-dimensional Hilbert space $\mathcal{H}^n = \mathbb{C}^{2^n}$.

Any quantum state in the space $\mathcal{H}^n$ of an n-qubit system can be expressed as a unique linear combination of an *orthonormal basis*, i.e., we have 2^n vectors $\{|v_0\rangle, |v_1\rangle, \ldots, |v\rangle_{2^n-1}\}$ satisfying $\langle v_i|v_j\rangle = 0$ for $i \neq j$ (orthogonality) and $\langle v_i|v_j\rangle = 1$ for $i = j$ (normalization). Then any vector $|\psi\rangle \in \mathbb{C}^{2^n}$ can be written as a linear combination of these base vectors: $|\psi\rangle = \sum_{i=0}^{2^n-1} \alpha_i|v_i\rangle$ with $\alpha_i \in \mathbb{C}$.

The most commonly used orthonormal basis in quantum computing is the *computational basis*. For an n-qubit system, the standard basis vectors in $\mathbb{C}^{2^n}$ are $|b_1 b_2 \cdots b_n\rangle = |e_k\rangle$, where $k = \sum_{i=1}^{n} b_i 2^{n-i}$. Here, $|e_k\rangle$ denotes the unit vector in $\mathbb{C}^{2^n}$ with a 1 in the k-th position and 0 elsewhere.

In order to construct multi-qubit quantum states, we need an operation that combines two unitary vector spaces into a new, larger unitary vector space. This is achieved by tensor products. Let V and W be two vector spaces over a same field (e.g. $\mathbb{C}$), the *tensor product*, denoted $V \otimes W$, is a new vector space whose elements are formal linear combinations of pairs of vectors from V and W. If V has dimension m and W has dimension n, then the tensor product space has dimension $m \times n$.

For an n-qubits quantum system, each qubit's state space is $\mathbb{C}^2$, therefore the total space is $\mathcal{H}^{\otimes n} = \underbrace{\mathbb{C}^2 \otimes \mathbb{C}^2 \otimes \cdots \otimes \mathbb{C}^2}_{n \text{ times}} \cong \mathbb{C}^{2^n}$. In particular, given the computational basis $\{|0\rangle, |1\rangle\}$ for $\mathbb{C}^2$, then for an n-qubit system $\mathcal{H}^{\otimes n}$ the computational basis consists of 2^n states of the form $|b_1 b_2 \cdots b_n\rangle = |b_1\rangle \otimes |b_2\rangle \otimes \cdots \otimes |b_n\rangle$ with $b_i \in \{0, 1\}$. If for instance two quantum systems are in states $|\psi\rangle = \alpha_0|0\rangle + \alpha_1|1\rangle \in \mathbb{C}^2$ and $|\phi\rangle = \beta_0|0\rangle + \beta_1|1\rangle \in \mathbb{C}^2$, their combined state in $\mathbb{C}^2 \otimes \mathbb{C}^2$ is

$$|\psi\rangle \otimes |\phi\rangle = \alpha_0\beta_0|00\rangle + \alpha_0\beta_1|01\rangle + \alpha_1\beta_0|10\rangle + \alpha_1\beta_1|11\rangle .$$

A quantum state of an n-qubit system is *decomposable* (or *separable*) if it can be written as a tensor product of individual qubit states. For instance the state $|\psi\rangle = \big(\frac{1}{\sqrt{2}}|00\rangle + \frac{1}{\sqrt{2}}|10\rangle\big)$ is decomposable as it can be written as $|\psi\rangle = \big(\frac{1}{\sqrt{2}}|0\rangle + \frac{1}{\sqrt{2}}|1\rangle\big) \otimes |0\rangle$.

Separable states correspond to systems where the qubits behave independently. Quantum states that are *non-decomposable*, i.e., that cannot be written as a tensor product of individual qubit states, are called *entangled.* A prototypical example of an entangle two-qubit state is the Bell state $|\Phi^+\rangle = \frac{1}{\sqrt{2}}(|00\rangle + |11\rangle)$. Entanglement is essential for quantum speed-up. Indeed, Grover's search algorithm, which we use in this paper to illustrate Q-ASMs, relies on entanglement for computational advantage.

Quantum Domains. We introduce a key concept, which is necessary to define appropriate base sets for the interpretation of Q-ASM states and state transitions. A quantum domain (or *qdomain*) is a set of values (such as numbers, symbols, structured data, or even unit vectors in a unitary vector space) whose elements are represented by finite sequences of qubits in a direct limit Hilbert space. Formally, a qdomain Q consists of:

- A countable family of *finite-dimensional Hilbert spaces*:

$$\mathcal{H}^{\otimes 1} = \mathbb{C}^2 \subset \mathcal{H}^{\otimes 2} = \mathbb{C}^2 \otimes \mathbb{C}^2 \subset \mathcal{H}^{\otimes 3} = \mathbb{C}^2 \otimes \mathbb{C}^2 \otimes \mathbb{C}^2 \subset \cdots$$

- A *direct limit Hilbert space*: $\mathcal{H}_Q = \varinjlim \mathcal{H}^{\otimes n}$ containing all quantum states representing values in Q.
- An *encoding function* $\varphi_Q : Q \to \mathcal{H}_Q$ that maps each element in Q to a unique state in some $\mathcal{H}^{\otimes n}$ (with minimal n as needed).
- *Inclusion maps* $\iota_{n,n+1} : \mathcal{H}^{\otimes n} \to \mathcal{H}^{\otimes n+1}$ that extend encodings into larger spaces while maintaining consistency.

Note that a qdomain adapts to encode arbitrarily complex values by increasing the number of qubits used (*scalability*), uses representations of elements by quantum states (*quantum representation*), employs an injective encoding function φ_Q (*injectivity*), and if an encoding exists in $\mathcal{H}^{\otimes n}$, it also exists in all larger spaces (*closure under direct limits*).

As illustration, let us define a qdomain $Q_{\mathbb{Z}^+}$ for positive integers $\mathbb{Z}^+$. The considered countable finite-dimensional Hilbert spaces and the direct limit Hilbert space are the same as above. In fact, they are the same for every qdomain. The encoding function for this example is defined by:

$$\varphi_{\mathbb{Z}^+}(z) = |b_1 b_2 \cdots b_n\rangle \in \mathcal{H}^{\otimes n},$$

where n is the minimum number of qubits needed to store z in binary, i.e., $n = \lceil \log_2(z+1) \rceil$, and $b_1 b_2 \cdots b_n$ is the binary representation of z. In turn, the inclusion maps defined as

$$\iota_{n,n+1}(|b_1 b_2 \cdots b_n\rangle)) = |0 b_1 b_2 \cdots b_n\rangle$$

provide consistency across different $H^{\otimes n}$.

As further examples consider the rational domain $Q = \mathbb{Q}$, where each rational number $\frac{a}{b}$ (with a, b coprime) is encoded using a pair of binary sequences $\varphi_{\mathbb{Q}}(\frac{a}{b}) = |bin(a)\rangle \otimes |bin(b)\rangle$, or the symbolic domain $Q = \{A, B, C, \ldots\}$, where each symbol is mapped to a unique quantum state using a dictionary encoding.

Of course, sets of quantum states are also qdomains. For instance, if

$$Q = \{|\psi\rangle \in \mathcal{H}^{\otimes n} \mid n \geq 1 \wedge \langle\psi|\psi\rangle = 1\},.$$

then the encoding function can be defined as the identity, i.e., for each n-qubit state $|\psi\rangle$:

$$\varphi_Q(|\psi\rangle) = |\psi\rangle \in \mathcal{H}^{\otimes n}$$

If necessary, states can be padded via inclusion maps with extra qubits (set to $|0\rangle$) to fit into a larger Hilbert space.

A Quantum Domain for Real Numbers. We now define a qdomain whose elements are real numbers represented by quantum states. The construction is based on the nondigital real-number representation of Litvinov, Maslov and Shpiz [15], which encodes real values using four single-qubit mixed states. In order to conform strictly to our definition of qdomains, we represent these mixed states by suitable purified quantum states in a larger Hilbert space.

Pure and Mixed States. For a register with Hilbert space $\mathcal{H}^{\otimes n}$, a (pure or mixed) quantum state is mathematically described by a density operator ρ, i.e., a positive semidefinite, trace-1 operator on $\mathcal{H}^{\otimes n}$. A single-qubit mixed state yielding outcome $|1\rangle$ with probability $p \in [0,1]$ is given by

$$\rho(p) = \begin{pmatrix} 1-p & 0 \\ 0 & p \end{pmatrix}.$$

Every mixed state admits a *purification*, i.e., it can be realised as the reduced state of a pure state on a larger Hilbert space.

Purification of Single-qubit Mixed States. Let $\mathcal{H}_{\text{aux}} \cong \mathbb{C}^2$ be an auxiliary qubit. For each $p \in [0,1]$, define the pure state

$$|\psi(p)\rangle \;=\; \sqrt{1-p}\,|0\rangle \otimes |0\rangle \;+\; \sqrt{p}\,|1\rangle \otimes |1\rangle \;\in\; \mathcal{H} \otimes \mathcal{H}_{\text{aux}}.$$

Tracing out the auxiliary qubit yields the original mixed state:

$$\mathrm{Tr}_{\text{aux}}\big(|\psi(p)\rangle\langle\psi(p)|\big) \;=\; \rho(p).$$

Hilbert-space Carrier. As for all qdomains considered here, we use the inductive system of finite-dimensional Hilbert spaces

$$\mathcal{H}^{\otimes 1} \subseteq \mathcal{H}^{\otimes 2} \subseteq \mathcal{H}^{\otimes 3} \subseteq \cdots,$$

with direct limit $\mathcal{H}_Q = \varinjlim \mathcal{H}^{\otimes n}$. For $m \leq n$, the canonical embeddings are

$$\iota_{m,n}(\psi) \;=\; \psi \otimes |0\rangle^{\otimes(n-m)}.$$

Representation of Real Numbers. Let $X = \{x_1, x_2, x_3, x_4\}$ be four disjoint single-qubit registers, and let each register x_i be represented by the purified state $|\psi(p_i)\rangle$. For a real number $r \in \mathbb{R}$, choose any $d \in (0,1]$ with $|r|d \leq 1$ and set

$$p_1 = \tfrac{1+rd}{2}, \qquad p_2 = \tfrac{1-rd}{2}, \qquad p_3 = \tfrac{1+d}{2}, \qquad p_4 = \tfrac{1-d}{2}.$$

The real number r is encoded by the pure state

$$\varphi_{\mathbb{R}}(r) \;=\; |\psi(p_1)\rangle \otimes |\psi(p_2)\rangle \otimes |\psi(p_3)\rangle \otimes |\psi(p_4)\rangle \;\in\; \mathcal{H}^{\otimes 8} \subseteq \mathcal{H}_Q.$$

Decoding. Tracing out the auxiliary qubits yields four single-qubit mixed states $\rho(x_i) = \rho(p_i)$, and the represented real number is obtained via

$$r(\rho(X)) \;=\; \frac{\rho(x_1)_{11} - \rho(x_2)_{11}}{\rho(x_3)_{11} - \rho(x_4)_{11}}, \tag{1}$$

provided that the denominator is nonzero. By construction, $r(\varphi_{\mathbb{R}}(r)) = r$.

Definition (Qdomain of Real Numbers). The qdomain of real numbers is defined as

$$Q_{\mathbb{R}} \;=\; \big(\{\mathcal{H}^{\otimes n}\}_{n\geq 1},\, \mathcal{H}_Q,\, \varphi_{\mathbb{R}},\, \{\iota_{n,n+1}\}_{n\geq 1}\big),$$

where the encoding function $\varphi_{\mathbb{R}} : \mathbb{R} \to \mathcal{H}_Q$ is the injective map defined above.

As demonstrated in [15], basic arithmetic operations on these representations can be implemented by fixed quantum circuits. In the present setting, such circuits operate on the purified representations and induce the corresponding transformations on the associated mixed states.

Remark on Cloning. In the standard quantum circuit model, perfect cloning of an unknown quantum state is impossible (no-cloning theorem). In contrast, the model of [15] explicitly extends the standard circuit model by including a non-unitary cloning operation for single-qubit mixed states. This operation is used there in the construction of arithmetic circuits, but it is not required for the definition of the qdomain $Q_{\mathbb{R}}$ given above.

3 Unitary Transformations and Measurements

The elementary operations on qubits—and more generally on tensor products of qubit spaces—are defined by unitary transformations over the corresponding unitary vector space. This definition applies both at the level of individual qubits and to composite systems encoded in $\mathcal{H}^{\otimes n}$. Although in physical implementations these unitary operations are realized by one- or two-qubit gates, this level of hardware-specific detail is not essential for the development of quantum algorithms; rather, it is an implementation aspect. In an ideal quantum algorithm the abstract operations are unitary maps, and the precise behaviour of these gates is assumed to be exactly given by the mathematical model. In contrast, numerical simulations typically approximate unitary transformations, which is an important consideration when bridging theory and practice.

Let $\mathcal{H}$ be a Hilbert space with an inner product. A *unitary linear operator* is defined as a function $U : \mathcal{H} \to \mathcal{H}$ satisfying the following conditions:

- *Linearity:* For all $|\psi\rangle, |\phi\rangle \in \mathcal{H}$ and all scalars $a, b \in \mathbb{C}$ we have $U(a|\psi\rangle + b|\phi\rangle) = aU|\psi\rangle + bU|\phi\rangle$.
- *Preservation of the Inner Product:* For all $|\psi\rangle, |\phi\rangle \in \mathcal{H}$ we have $\langle U\psi|U\phi\rangle = \langle\psi|\phi\rangle$, which implies that also the norm is preserved, i.e., $\|U|\psi\rangle\| = \||\psi\rangle\|$ for all $|\psi\rangle \in \mathcal{H}$.
- *Invertibility and the Adjoint Condition:* The adjoint operator $U^\dagger$ is defined by the relation $\langle U\psi|\phi\rangle = \langle\psi|U^\dagger\phi\rangle$ for all $|\psi\rangle, |\phi\rangle \in \mathcal{H}$. A unitary operator satisfies $U^\dagger U = UU^\dagger = I$, where I is the identity operator on $\mathcal{H}$. This guarantees that U is invertible, with its inverse given by $U^{-1} = U^\dagger$.

Unitary transformations can naturally be considered as elementary operations acting on qdomains. More precisely, if $U : \mathcal{H}^{\otimes n} \to \mathcal{H}^{\otimes n}$ is a unitary operator, then for any quantum state $|\psi\rangle \in \mathcal{H}_Q$ (where $\mathcal{H}_Q$ is the direct limit Hilbert space of a qdomain Q), we get that $U|\psi\rangle \in \mathcal{H}_Q$ and the transformation is performed without loss of information, as it preserves both the structure and the norm of the state.

A basic example of an elementary single-qubit unitary transformation is given by the *Hadamard gate*, defined by

$$H = \frac{1}{\sqrt{2}} \begin{pmatrix} 1 & 1 \\ 1 & -1 \end{pmatrix}.$$

Its action on the basis states is

$$H|0\rangle = \frac{1}{\sqrt{2}}(|0\rangle + |1\rangle), \qquad H|1\rangle = \frac{1}{\sqrt{2}}(|0\rangle - |1\rangle).$$

Thus, a Hadamard transformation maps a basis state into an equal superposition of the two basis states. In particular, if applied to $|0\rangle$, it creates a balanced superposition where the probability amplitudes of $|0\rangle$ and $|1\rangle$ are both $1/\sqrt{2}$. This property is used in many quantum algorithms, such as Grover's search and the quantum Fourier transform, since it prepares coherent superpositions of computational basis states. Due to the linearity of quantum mechanics, subsequent unitary operations transform all amplitudes simultaneously, enabling interference effects that are essential for quantum speedups. Since H is real and symmetric, we have $H^\dagger = H$. Moreover, $H^2 = I$, hence $H^{-1} = H$. Therefore $H^\dagger = H^{-1}$, and thus H is unitary.

Another well known elementary unitary transformation, this time involving two qubits, is the one provided by the Controlled-NOT (CNOT) gate. It implements a conditional operation, flipping the state of the target qubit if and only if the control qubit is in the state $|1\rangle$; otherwise, it leaves the target qubit unchanged. We can define it by its action on the computational basis of $\mathcal{H}^{\otimes 2}$: $\text{CNOT}|00\rangle = |00\rangle$, $\text{CNOT}|01\rangle = |01\rangle$, $\text{CNOT}|10\rangle = |11\rangle$, and $\text{CNOT}|11\rangle = |10\rangle$. This gate is represented by the matrix:

$$\text{CNOT} = \begin{pmatrix} 1 & 0 & 0 & 0 \\ 0 & 1 & 0 & 0 \\ 0 & 0 & 0 & 1 \\ 0 & 0 & 1 & 0 \end{pmatrix}$$

This matrix is indeed unitary, which can be easily verified. This gate creates entanglement between qubits. When applied to a superposition state, it can produce non-separable (entangled) states. For instance, applying a Hadamard gate to the control qubit (assumed to be initially in a computational basis state) followed by a CNOT gate results in a Bell state, i.e., a maximally entangled state of two qubits. This feature is key for many quantum algorithms and protocols, including quantum teleportation and error correction.

Measurement operations in quantum computing are fundamentally different from classical measurements (memory read operations). When a quantum state is measured, it collapses to one of the basis states, and the outcome is probabilistic. The probabilities of the outcomes are determined by the amplitudes of the quantum state.

Measurement in quantum mechanics is modeled using a set $\{M_i\}$ of measurement operators acting on a Hilbert space, satisfying the completeness relation: $\sum_i M_i^\dagger M_i = I$. This condition guarantees that the total probability of all measurement outcomes is one. For a quantum state $|\psi\rangle$, the probability of obtaining the outcome i is given by: $P(i) = \langle\psi|M_i^\dagger M_i|\psi\rangle$. After the measurement yielding outcome i, the state collapses to $\frac{M_i|\psi\rangle}{\sqrt{P(i)}}$. This collapse process introduces inherent randomness into quantum measurement.

A von Neumann measurement is a special case of the above framework where each measurement operator is an orthogonal projector. In this case, we have: $M_i = P_i$, where P_i is a projector satisfying $P_i^2 = P_i$ and $P_i^\dagger = P_i$, and the projectors are mutually orthogonal, i.e., $P_i P_j = \delta_{ij} P_i$, and the completeness relation becomes: $\sum_i P_i = I$.

Von Neumann measurements correspond to measuring an observable represented by a Hermitian operator. The outcomes are exactly the eigenvalues of that operator, and the post-measurement states are the corresponding eigenstates. This framework is "ideal" in the sense that the measurement process is both repeatable (if measured immediately again, the same outcome is obtained) and yields maximal information about the observable (i.e., it reveals the precise eigenvalue of the observable, providing complete knowledge of the system's state in relation to that observable, with no remaining uncertainty).

In a single-qubit system, the computational basis is typically $\{|0\rangle, |1\rangle\}$. A state $|\psi\rangle = \alpha|0\rangle + \beta|1\rangle$ measured in this basis yields outcome $|0\rangle$ with probability $|\alpha|^2$ and $|1\rangle$ with probability $|\beta|^2$. This measurement is a von Neumann measurement because the operators are the projectors, i.e., $M_0 = |0\rangle\langle 0|$ and $M_1 = |1\rangle\langle 1|$. This is the standard, most intuitive basis for measurement, often used because of its simplicity and direct physical interpretation in many quantum computing architectures.

More generally, for an n-qubit system in the state $|\psi\rangle = \sum_{i=0}^{2^n-1} \alpha_i |i\rangle$, a measurement in the computational basis yields outcome $|i\rangle$ with probability $|\alpha_i|^2$, and the state collapses accordingly.

Quantum measurements are not restricted to the computational basis. One may choose any orthonormal basis for performing a von Neumann measurement. For instance, measuring in the Hadamard basis $\{|+\rangle, |-\rangle\}$ where:$|+\rangle = \frac{1}{\sqrt{2}}(|0\rangle + |1\rangle)$, $|-\rangle = \frac{1}{\sqrt{2}}(|0\rangle - |1\rangle)$, is equivalent to applying a Hadamard transformation to the state and then performing a measurement in the computational basis.

Beyond projective measurements, more general measurement schemes, such as positive operator-valued measures, allow for a broader range of measurement outcomes that are not necessarily orthogonal. The choice of measurement directly impacts the information extracted from a quantum system and plays a crucial role in the design and analysis of quantum algorithms.

4 Quantum Abstract State Machines

We will now proceed and define Q-ASMs as specific probabilistic ASMs. A (standard) ASM can be simply defined by a background, a signature and a rule. To support unbounded parallelism the background must fulfill the background postulate [8], i.e., it must provide an infinite set of reserve values, truth values and constructors for tuples and multisets as well as the basic operations associated with them. The signature is a finite set of function symbols, each associated with some fixed arity, and the rule is composed out of assignments, `if`- and `forall`-rules [6]. In addition, rules for bounded parallelism and `let`-rules can be defined as shortcuts.

In principle, Q-ASMs will be defined analogously. The *background* of a Q-ASM M is defined by a set $\mathcal{D}$ of quantum domains and operations on them. We assume that $\mathcal{D}$ is closed under products and injective limits, so arbitrary tuples and multisets can be constructed. In order to enable partial operations the background contains a specific constant *undef* that is not encoded by a qubit. Then for an operation o of arity n and arguments $x_1, \dots, x_n \in D \cup \{undef\}$, where D is a qdomain in the background we have $o(x_1, \dots, x_n) = undef$, whenever one of the x_i is *undef*.

Truth values are represented by single qubits. The background also contains by default all elementary quantum gates that take one or two qubits as arguments. With these it is possible to realise the standard Boolean operations on the truth values. All other operations provided by the background must be also defined by quantum circuits. In this way we can assume that background operations can be supported by some quantum processor that is realised by hardware. In case such hardware is not available the quantum gates must be simulated by probabilistic operations on standard hardware.

Finally, a Q-ASM preserves the existence of an infinite set of reserve values that can be imported when needed. All reserve values are represented by sequences of qubits.

The *signature* of a Q-ASM M is a finite set $\Upsilon = \{f_1, \dots, f_k\}$ of function symbols. Each f_i has an arity n_i. Same as for (standard) ASMs [6] f_i can be specified as *static* or *dynamic*. Among the dynamic function symbols some may be declared to be used exclusively for *output*. We write Υ_{dyn} for the set of dynamic function symbols and Υ_{out} for the set of output function symbols, thus $\Upsilon_{out} \subseteq \Upsilon_{dyn} \subseteq \Upsilon$.

The union $B = \bigcup_{D \in \mathcal{D}} D \cup \{undef\}$ is the *universe* of the Q-ASM M. Then a *state* of M is given by a family $\{f_{i,S}\}_{1 \le i \le k}$ of functions $f_{i,S} : (B - \{undef\})^{n_i} \to B$. In a state S a pair $\ell = (f_i, (v_1, \dots, v_{n_i}))$ with $v_j \in B - \{undef\}$ for all $1 \le j \le n_i$ is called a *location*, and we call v_0 the *value* of ℓ in the state S iff $f_{i,S}(v_1, \dots, v_{n_i}) = v_0$ holds, in which case we also write $\text{val}_S(\ell) = v_0$.

Note that in a state S of a Q-ASM M the arguments $v_1, \dots, v_{n_i}$ of a location ℓ as well as the value $\text{val}_S(\ell) = v_0$ (if different from *undef*) are elements of some qdomains in the background, i.e., each v_i is represented by a sequence of q_i qubits. The v_i can be accessed by using the projection operations on tuples provided by the background, and then subjected to other elementary operations, i.e., they can appear as input of quantum circuits that result in different sequences of qubits without exploiting any measurement.

A pair $u = (\ell, v)$ with a location ℓ of a state S and $v \in B$ for a dynamic function symbol is called an *update* in S, and a set of such updates is called an *update set*. We only consider finite update sets. An update set Δ is *consistent* iff for all $(\ell, v_1), (\ell, v_2) \in \Delta$ we have $v_1 = v_2$. For a consistent update set Δ in state S we define new state $S' = S + \Delta$ by $\text{val}_{S'}(\ell) = v$ for $(\ell, v) \in \Delta$, and $\text{val}_{S'}(\ell) = \text{val}_S(\ell)$ for all other locations of S. Furthermore, for inconsistent Δ we let $S + \Delta = S$. We call $S + \Delta$ the *successor* of S defined by Δ.

Note that there is the possibility of a clash, i.e., the existence of updates $(\ell, v_1), (\ell, v_2) \in \Delta$ with $v_1 \neq v_2$, in particular, as this may require measurements of qubits. This introduces some randomness in the definition of successor states.

For the definition of state transitions a Q-ASM applies a *rule*. In general, Q-ASM *rules* are constructed as follows:

- An assignment $f_i(t_1, \dots, t_{n_i}) := t_0$, where $f_i \in \Upsilon_{dyn}$ and the t_j are terms over Υ, the background operations and some set V of variables, is a rule;
- A branching rule (also called `if`-rule) has the form `if` φ `then` r_1 `else` r_2, where φ is a Boolean term and the r_i are rules;

- A (bounded) parallel rule (also called par-rule) has the form $r_1\|\dots\|r_n$ with rules r_i;
- An (unbounded) parallel rule (also called forall-rule) has the form forall $x \in D$ with $\varphi(x)$ do $r(x)$ with a qdomain D and a variable x that is free in the Boolean term $\varphi(x)$ and in the rule $r(x)$;
- A bounded random choice rule has the form choose with t : r_1 or r_2 with rules r_1, r_2 and a term t;
- An unbounded random choice rule has the form choose $x \in D$ with $t(x)$: $\varphi(x)$ do $r(x)$ with a qdomain D and a variable x that is free in the term $t(x)$, the Boolean term $\varphi(x)$ and in the rule $r(x)$.

The set $fr(r)$ of *free variables* of a Q-ASM rule r is defined as usual. Then the rule of a Q-ASM M is a Q-ASM rule r with $fr(r) = \emptyset$.

The informal meaning of Q-ASM rules is as follows. For an assignment $f_i(t_1,\dots,t_{n_i}) := t_0$ the terms t_j are evaluated in the current state S. Here we can assume that variables are bound to elements of the universe B different from *undef*. Then the location $(f_i,(\text{val}_S(t_1),\dots,\text{val}_S(t_{n_i})))$ is updated to $\text{val}_S(t_0)$, unless $f_i \in \Upsilon_{out}$. We can assume that such modifications are non-destructive, i.e., the states of the representing qubits are preserved. For an output location $(f_i,(\text{val}_S(t_1),\dots,\text{val}_S(t_{n_i})))$ with $f_i \in \Upsilon_{out}$, however, the qubits representing the $\text{val}_S(t_i)$ are measured and the corresponding output is produced.

For an if-rule if φ then r_1 else r_2 first the Boolean term φ is evaluated, which results in a single qubit. A measurement results in either $|0\rangle$ (false) or $|1\rangle$ (true), which underlie a Bernoulli distribution with some expectation value p. Then with a probability $1-p$ the rule r_1 is executed, or with probability p the rule r_2 is executed. That is, branching becomes a random choice.

For a par-rule $r_1\|\dots\|r_n$ all rules r_i are executed in parallel. For a forall-rule forall $x \in D$ with $\varphi(x)$ do $r(x)$ first for all x in the qdomain D the Boolean term $\varphi(x)$ is evaluated always resulting in a single qubit. A measurement of these qubits results in Bernoulli-distributions for $\{|0\rangle,|1\rangle\}$ with expectation value p_x. Then a subset $D' \subseteq D$ is selected with probability $\prod_{x\in D'}(1-p_x)\prod_{x\in D-D'} p_x$, and $r(x)$ is executed in parallel for all $x \in D'$.

For a bounded random choice rule choose with t r_1 or r_2 first the term t is evaluated, which should result in a value $p \in [0,1]$. If this is the case then either r_1 or r_2 is selected and executed. The selection underlies a Bernoulli distribution with expectation value p.

Finally, for a random choice rule choose $x \in D$ with $t(x)$: $\varphi(x)$ do $r(x)$ first for all x in the qdomain D the Boolean term $\varphi(x)$ is evaluated always resulting in a single qubit, a measurement of which results in $|0\rangle$ or $|1\rangle$ with a Bernoulli distribution with expectation value p_x. In addition, the term $t(x)$ is evaluated to result in a value $q_x \in [0,1]$. These values q_x define a distribution over D. Then with probability $(1-p_x)q_x$ the rule $r(x)$ is executed. Note that in this case the probabilities $(1-p_x)q_x$ for $x \in D$ do not add up to 1, so $\sum_{x\in D} p_x q_x$ is the probability that no x is chosen and the machine stops.

Formally, for a state S the rule r of a Q-ASM M yields a set of update sets $\boldsymbol{\Delta}_r^\theta(S)$ together with a probability distribution θ. This is defined by structural induction:

- For an assignment rule $f_i(t_1, \dots, t_{n_i}) := t_0$ with $f_i \notin \Upsilon_{out}$ we have $\boldsymbol{\Delta}_r^\theta(S) = \{\Delta\}$, where Δ contains a single update $((f_i, (\mathrm{val}_S(t_1), \dots, \mathrm{val}_S(t_{n_i}))), \mathrm{val}_S(t_0))$, and $\theta(\Delta) = 1$, i.e., the distribution θ is trivial.
- For an assignment rule $f_i(t_1, \dots, t_{n_i}) := t_0$ with $f_i \in \Upsilon_{out}$ the measurement of $\mathrm{val}_S(t_j)$ defines a set B_j of strings over $\{|0\rangle, |1\rangle\}$ of length m_j with a probability distribution θ_j that results from the Bernoulli distribution of the individual qubits used for the representation of $\mathrm{val}_S(t_i)$. With $\Delta_{b_0,\dots,b_{n_i}} = \{((f_i, (b_1, \dots, b_{n_i})), b_0)\}$ for $b_j \in B_j$ we get $\boldsymbol{\Delta}_r^\theta(S) = \{\Delta_{b_0,\dots,b_{n_i}} \mid b_j \in B_j \text{ for } 0 \le j \le n_i\}$, and the distribution θ is defined by $\theta(\Delta_{b_0,\dots,b_{n_i}}) = \prod_{j=0}^{n_i} \theta_j(b_j)$.
- For an **if**-rule **if** φ **then** r_1 **else** r_2 we get $\boldsymbol{\Delta}_r^\theta(S) = \boldsymbol{\Delta}_{r_1}^{\theta_1}(S) \cup \boldsymbol{\Delta}_{r_2}^{\theta_2}(S)$ with $\theta(\Delta) = p_i\theta_i(\Delta)$ for $\Delta \in \boldsymbol{\Delta}_{r_i}^{\theta_i}(S)$, where p_i is the probability of the measurement of $\mathrm{val}_S(\varphi)$ resulting in $|0\rangle$ or $|1\rangle$, respectively.
- For a **par**-rule $r_1\|\dots\|r_n$ we have $\boldsymbol{\Delta}_r^\theta(S) = \{\Delta_1 \cup \dots \cup \Delta_n \mid \Delta_i \in \boldsymbol{\Delta}_{r_i}^{\theta_i}(S)\}$ with $\theta(\Delta_1 \cup \dots \cup \Delta_n) = \prod_{i=1}^n \theta_i(\Delta_i)$.
- For a **forall**-rule **forall** $x \in D$ **with** $\varphi(x)$ **do** $r(x)$ we have $\boldsymbol{\Delta}_r^\theta(S) = \{\bigcup_{x\in D'} \Delta_x \mid \Delta_x \in \boldsymbol{\Delta}_{r(x)}^{\theta_x}(S),\ D' \subseteq D\}$ with $\theta(\bigcup_{x\in D'} \Delta_x) = \prod_{x\in D'}(1 - p_x)\theta_x(\Delta_x)\prod_{x\in D-D'} p_x$, where p_x is the probability of the measurement of $\mathrm{val}_S(\varphi(x))$ resulting in $|0\rangle$.
- For a bounded random choice rule **choose with** t r_1 **or** r_2 we have $\boldsymbol{\Delta}_r^\theta(S) = \boldsymbol{\Delta}_{r_1}^{\theta_1}(S) \cup \boldsymbol{\Delta}_{r_2}^{\theta_2}(S)$ with $\theta(\Delta) = p_i\theta_i(\Delta)$ for $\Delta \in \boldsymbol{\Delta}_{r_i}^{\theta_i}(S)$, where $p_1 = \mathrm{val}_S(t)$ and $p_2 = 1 - p_1$.
- For a random choice rule **choose** $x \in D$ **with** $t(x) : \varphi(x)$ **do** $r(x)$ we have $\boldsymbol{\Delta}_r^\theta(S) = \bigcup_{x\in D} \boldsymbol{\Delta}_{r(x)}^{\theta_x}(S)$ with $\theta(\Delta) = (1 - p_x)q_x\theta_x(\Delta)$ for $\Delta \in \boldsymbol{\Delta}_{r(x)}^{\theta_x}(S)$, where p_x is the probability of the measurement of $\mathrm{val}_S(\varphi(x))$ resulting in $|0\rangle$, and $q_x = \mathrm{val}_S(t(x))$.

Finally, a *run* of a Q-ASM M is a sequence $\varrho = S_0, S_1, \dots$ of states such that for all i we have $S_{i+1} = S_i + \Delta_i$ for some $\Delta_i \in \boldsymbol{\Delta}_r^{\theta_i}(S_i)$. The probability of such a run ϱ to be followed is $p_\varrho = \prod_{i\ge 0} \theta_i(\Delta_i)$.

5 Grover's Search Algorithm

Grover's search is a quantum algorithm that achieves speedup of quadratic order for unstructured search problems. It operates by iteratively amplifying the probability amplitude of the target solution within a search space. In this section, we present a formal specification of Grover's algorithm using Q-ASM. This algorithm is very well documented in the literature (see e.g., [13,16]). Therefore we assume familiarity with it.

Problem Formulation and Q-ASM Background. Given an unordered set (database) A of size $N = 2^n$, we assume a quantum domain Q_A that encodes elements of A. A Boolean function $f : Q_A \to \{0,1\}$ distinguishes a unique marked element x^* (i.e., $f(x^*) = 1$). The goal of Grover's algorithm is to identify x^* with high probability.

As detailed in the previous section, a Q-ASM state S is a collection of function interpretations defined over qdomains. These states are updated via rules that produce update sets Δ with associated probability distributions θ. Crucially, the following Q-ASM components are available in our background:

- *Quantum Domains:* In particular, we can define Q_A as the computational basis states in $\mathcal{H}^{\otimes n}$, as the size of A is 2^n.
- *Unitary Operations:* These include the Hadamard gate (H), the oracle O_f, and the diffusion operator D. All such operations are defined as unitary transformations on the Hilbert space $\mathcal{H}^{\otimes n}$.
- *Measurement Function:* A function $\mu : \mathcal{H}^{\otimes n} \to Q_A$ that extracts a classical result from the quantum state, modeled as a probabilistic update (see the treatment of output locations in Sect. 4).

Q-ASM Signature for Grover's Algorithm. The signature Υ for this specification comprises:

- A *dynamic nullary function symbol* ψ representing the current quantum state.
- *Static function symbols* for the unitary operations H, O_f, and D that act on ψ.
- A *measurement function symbol* μ (also static) to retrieve the output after the quantum evolution.

In a Q-ASM state S, ψ is an element of the universe B (as introduced in Sect. 4). Notice that Q_A must be a subset of B, and B should actually include all of $\mathcal{H}^{\otimes n}$. The update rules for ψ are applied via consistent update sets Δ that obey the probabilistic semantics.

Initialization: Preparing the Superposition. The algorithm starts by initializing the quantum state to a uniform superposition over all elements in Q_A:

$$\psi := H^{\otimes n}|0\rangle_n.$$

This assignment is a standard update rule in a Q-ASM (see Sect. 4, "Assignment Rule"). The Hadamard transformation $H^{\otimes n}$ is applied to the all-zero state $|0\rangle_n$, transforming ψ into the state $|s\rangle = H^{\otimes n}|0\rangle_n$. Note that the update set produced here is trivial (with probability 1) and every possible outcome of reading ψ is in the qdomain Q_A.

Oracle Operation and Unitary Update. The oracle O_f, which flips the phase of the marked element, is defined by its action on the computational basis:

$$O_f|x\rangle = (-1)^{f(x)}|x\rangle.$$

O_f is incorporated as a background unitary operator, consistent with the treatment of elementary operations in Sects. 3 and 4. Its application is modeled by an update that transforms ψ while preserving the state's norm and underlying structure. No measurement occurs at this stage, so the update remains a deterministic unitary evolution.

Iterative Amplitude Amplification. The core of Grover's algorithm is the repeated application of the combined unitary operation $D\,O_f$. This is specified by the Q-ASM rule:

$$\psi := D\,O_f\,\psi.$$

According to the Q-ASM semantics (Sect. 4), this update rule is processed by evaluating the right-hand side in the current state S. The combined operator $D\,O_f$ is itself a unitary transformation; therefore, its application updates ψ via a well-defined update set Δ, preserving the consistency of state transitions. The diffusion operator D, which inverts amplitudes about the mean, is defined as: $D = 2|s\rangle\langle s| - I$, where $|s\rangle = H^{\otimes n}|0\rangle_n$ is the uniform superposition over all $N = 2^n$ computational basis states. The rule is iterated approximately $\lfloor \frac{\pi}{4}\sqrt{N} \rfloor$ times. In the Q-ASM framework, such iterations can be seen as a sequence of update sets (each with trivial probability distributions when no measurement is involved) that cumulatively amplify the amplitude of the marked state.

Final Measurement and Extraction of the Marked Element. After sufficient iterations, the algorithm applies the measurement function to extract the marked element: $x^* := \mu(\psi)$.

This final step represents an output assignment as defined for output function symbols in Sect. 4. Unlike the unitary updates, the measurement involves collapsing the quantum state according to the Born rule. The Q-ASM semantics handle this via an update set where the update for ψ involves a probabilistic outcome, and the measurement function μ yields a classical result corresponding to one of the basis states. The probability of obtaining x^* is high due to the amplitude amplification achieved by the preceding iterations.

Refinement. The presented high-level specification of Grover's algorithm can be naturally refined up to the implementation level by means of one- and two-qubit (hardware) gates by following the usual schema, i.e., by realizing the subroutine that calculates f using standard one- and two-qubit gates as needed for the unitary transformation O_f. This of course will depend on the given function f. For the diffusion operator D, the refinement is known as it corresponds to its standard translation into one- and two-qubits unitary gates (see e.g. Sect. 4.3 in [16] for a detailed explanation).

Thus, Grover's algorithm is fully embedded within the ASM method, illustrating how quantum algorithms can be specified, analyzed, and eventually refined to low-level implementations, while still relying on the abstract yet rigorous Q-ASM framework presented in Sect. 4.

6 Numerical Algorithms over $Q_{\mathbb{R}}$

We illustrate how the qdomain $Q_{\mathbb{R}}$ supports standard numerical algorithms using only background quantum operations (implemented by fixed quantum circuits) on qdomain reals, and defers all observation to declared output measurements. Throughout, the background provides circuit-realised operations on $Q_{\mathbb{R}}$:

$$\mathrm{ADD},\ \mathrm{MUL},\ \mathrm{SMUL}_{\lambda}\ (\lambda \in \mathbb{R}),$$

and, where needed, quantum oracles O_f, O_g for function evaluation. Here ADD and MUL denote background quantum operations implementing addition and multiplication on qdomain reals, respectively. Given qdomain encodings $\psi_1, \psi_2 \in Q_{\mathbb{R}}$ representing real values r_1, r_2, the operations $\mathrm{ADD}(\psi_1, \psi_2)$ and $\mathrm{MUL}(\psi_1, \psi_2)$ yield qdomain encodings of $r_1 + r_2$ and $r_1 r_2$. Likewise, SMUL_{λ} denotes scalar multiplication by a classical real constant $\lambda \in \mathbb{R}$: given $\psi \in Q_{\mathbb{R}}$ representing r, the operation $\mathrm{SMUL}_{\lambda}(\psi)$ yields a qdomain encoding of λr. All these operations are realised by fixed quantum circuits acting on the underlying qubit encodings and are deterministic with respect to the abstract Q-ASM state, i.e., prior to any declared measurement.

Numerical Integration: Composite Trapezoidal Rule. Given $f : [a, b] \to \mathbb{R}$, a step count $N \in \mathbb{N}$, and an oracle O_f (acting on $Q_{\mathbb{R}}$), define

$$h := \mathrm{SMUL}_{1/N}\big(\mathrm{ADD}(b, \mathrm{SMUL}_{-1}(a))\big)$$

and initialise the accumulator

$$\psi_S := \mathrm{ADD}(O_f(a),\ O_f(b)).$$

For $k = 1, \ldots, N-1$, let

$$x_k = \mathrm{ADD}(a,\ \mathrm{SMUL}_k(h))$$

and update

$$\psi_S := \mathrm{ADD}\big(\psi_S,\ \mathrm{SMUL}_2(O_f(x_k))\big).$$

Set the (dynamic, output) symbol

$$\psi_{\mathrm{out}} \ :=\ \mathrm{SMUL}_{1/2}\big(\mathrm{MUL}(h, \psi_S)\big),$$

and declare ψ_{out} as output; its value is produced by a single measurement $\mu(\psi_{\mathrm{out}})$.

Function Approximation: Chebyshev/Clenshaw Evaluation. Assume a Chebyshev approximation $p_n(x) = \sum_{k=0}^{n} c_k T_k(x)$ on $[-1, 1]$ with coefficients $c_k \in Q_{\mathbb{R}}$, and input $\psi_x \in Q_{\mathbb{R}}$. Use Clenshaw's stable recurrence with two dynamic accumulators ψ_b, ψ_{b+1}, initialised to 0: For $k = 1, \ldots, N-1$, let

$$\psi_{\mathrm{tmp}} = \mathrm{ADD}\big(\mathrm{SMUL}_2(\mathrm{MUL}(\psi_x, \psi_b)),\ \mathrm{SMUL}_{-1}(\psi_{b+1})\big),$$

and update

$$\psi_{b+1} := \psi_b, \qquad \psi_b := \mathrm{ADD}(c_k, \psi_{\mathrm{tmp}}).$$

Finally set

$$\psi_{\mathrm{out}} \ :=\ \mathrm{ADD}\Big(\mathrm{SMUL}_{1/2}(c_0),\ \mathrm{MUL}(\psi_x, \psi_b)\Big),$$

declare ψ_{out} as output, and read it once via μ.

Initial-value ODE: Euler Method. Consider the initial-value problem

$$y'(t) = g(t, y), \qquad y(t_0) = y_0,$$

where $y(t)$ is an unknown function of t, $y'(t)$ is the derivative of y with respect to t (the rate of change of y at time t), $g(t, y)$ is a known function that specifies how the derivative depends on t and y, and $y(t_0) = y_0$ is the initial condition: the value of y at time $t = t_0$.

Let $h \in Q_{\mathbb{R}}$ be the step size, $M \in \mathbb{N}$ be the number of steps, and O_g be a unitary oracle implementing $(t, y) \mapsto g(t, y)$ on $Q_{\mathbb{R}} \times Q_{\mathbb{R}}$. Initialise the dynamic qdomain registers:

$$\psi_t := t_0, \qquad \psi_y := y_0.$$

For $m = 0, \ldots, M - 1$, perform the updates:

$$\psi_y := \text{ADD}\big(\psi_y, \text{MUL}(h, O_g(\psi_t, \psi_y))\big), \qquad \psi_t := \text{ADD}(\psi_t, h).$$

Finally, set $\psi_{\text{out}} := \psi_y$ and declare it as output, measured once via $\mu(\psi_{\text{out}})$.

Discussion. In all three cases, the Q-ASM specification uses only background quantum operations on $Q_{\mathbb{R}}$ (addition, multiplication, scaling, and oracles). The machine remains deterministic and non-destructive until a declared output location is measured by μ. All observation-induced randomness is confined to this final measurement.

7 Conclusion

In this paper we introduced Q-ASMs as specific probabilistic ASMs, which allow quantum algorithms to be specified and analysed on sufficiently high levels of abstraction. Q-ASMs are defined quite analogously to ASMs using signatures that are interpreted by Tarski structures. The main difference is that the base sets in this interpretation are considered to be quantum domains, i.e., elements are assumed to be encoded by sequences of qubits. Elementary operations on such domains are, in the standard setting, defined by unitary transformations that can be composed out of quantum gates, which are assumed to be part of the background of any Q-ASM. Furthermore, any use of Boolean conditions gives rise to a probabilistic choice.

While this work is just a first step towards a rigorous support for the development, validation and verification of quantum algorithms, we illustrated our key ideas on Grover's search algorithm and, more generally, showed that the framework is flexible enough to also express numerical algorithms based on nondigital quantum representations of real numbers. This flexibility demonstrates that Q-ASMs can accommodate not only the standard circuit model but also other models of quantum computation when equipped with the corresponding background operations. We intend to continue this work by addressing the theoretical foundations of quantum algorithms and providing an appropriate axiomatic definition of their class. Moreover, if a quantum algorithm is to be simulated by an algorithm running on a standard binary computer, it will be necessary to show how a random choice with a particular probability distribution can be refined by an algorithm that in the limit guarantees this distribution. For instance, the Metropolis algorithm is known to support this desired property [17].

References

1. Blass, A., Gurevich, Y.: Background of computation. Bull. EATCS **92**, 82–114 (2007)
2. Börger, E.: Berechenbarkeit, komplexität und logik –algorithmen, sprachen und kalküle unter besonderer berücksichtigung ihrer komplexität (3. Aufl.). Vieweg (1992)
3. Börger, E., Gervasi, V.: Structures of computing – a guide to practice-oriented theory. Springer (2024)
4. Börger, E., Raschke, A.: Modeling companion for software practitioners. Springer, Heidelberg (2018). https://doi.org/10.1007/978-3-662-56641-1_9
5. Börger, E., Schewe, K.-D.: Concurrent Abstract State Machines. Acta Inf. **53**(5), 469–492 (2016)
6. Börger, E., Stärk, R.: Abstract State Machines. Springer-Verlag, Berlin Heidelberg New York (2003)
7. Ferrarotti, F., González, S.: ASM specification and refinement of a quantum algorithm. In: Raschke, A., Riccobene, E., Schewe, K.-D., (eds.) Logic, Computation and Rigorous Methods - Essays Dedicated to Egon Börger on the Occasion of His 75th Birthday, vol. 12750 of Lecture Notes in Computer Science, pp. 135–146. Springer (2021)
8. Ferrarotti, F., Schewe, K.-D., Tec, L., Wang, Q.: A new thesis concerning synchronised parallel computing - simplified parallel ASM thesis. Theor. Comp. Sci. **649**, 25–53 (2016)
9. Fischer, G.: Lineare Algebra, 18th edn. Springer Spektrum, Wiesbaden (2014)
10. Grädel, E., Nowack, A.: Quantum Computing and Abstract State Machines. In: Börger, E., Gargantini, A., Riccobene, E. (eds.) ASM 2003. LNCS, vol. 2589, pp. 309–323. Springer, Heidelberg (2003). https://doi.org/10.1007/3-540-36498-6_18
11. Grover, L.K.: A fast quantum mechanical algorithm for database search. In: Miller, G.L. (ed.) Proceedings of the Twenty-Eighth Annual ACM Symposium on the Theory of Computing (STOC 1996), pp. 212–219. ACM (1996)
12. Gurevich, Y.: Sequential abstract-state machines capture sequential algorithms. ACM Trans. Comp. Logic **1**(1), 77–111 (2000)
13. Kitaev, A.Y., Shen, A.H., Vyalyi, M.N.: Classical and Quantum Computation. American Mathematical Society, Providence, Rhode Island (2000)
14. Lang, S.: Linear Algebra, 3rd edn. Springer, New York (1987)
15. Litvinov, G.L., Maslov, V.P., Shpiz, G.B.: Nondigital implementation of the arithmetic of real numbers. Math. Notes **70**(1), 53–60 (2001)
16. Mermin, N.D.: Quantum computer science: an introduction. Cambridge University Press, Cambridge (2007)
17. Metropolis, N., Rosenbluth, A.W., Rosenbluth, M.N., Teller, A.H., Teller, E.: Equation of state calculations by fast computing machines. J. Chem. Phys. **21**(6), 1087–1092 (1953)

18. Schewe, K.-D., Ferrarotti, F.: Behavioural theory of reflective algorithms I: reflective sequential algorithms. Sci. Comput. Program. **223**, 102864 (2022)
19. Schewe, K.-D., Ferrarotti, F., Tec, L., Wang, Q.: Towards a behavioural theory for random parallel computing. In: Beierle, C., Brewka, G., Thimm, M., (eds.) Computational Models of Rationality – Essays Dedicated to Gabriele Kern-Isberner on the Occasion of Her 60th Birthday, vol. 29 of Tributes, pp. 365–373. College Publications (2016)
20. Shor, P.W.: Algorithms for quantum computation: discrete logarithms and factoring. In: 35th Annual Symposium on Foundations of Computer Science (FOCS 1994), pp. 124–134. IEEE Computer Society (1994)
21. Shor, P.W.: Polynomial-time algorithms for prime factorization and discrete logarithms on a quantum computer. SIAM J. Comput. **26**(5), 1484–1509 (1997)

Inductive Nonmonotonic Reasoning Based on Defeasible and Indefeasible Beliefs

Christoph Beierle[1](✉), Alexander Hahn[2], Gabriele Kern-Isberner[2], and Lars-Phillip Spiegel[1]

[1] FernUniversität in Hagen, 58097 Hagen, Germany
{christoph.beierle,lars-phillip.spiegel}@fernuni-hagen.de
[2] TU Dortmund University, 44227 Dortmund, Germany
{alexander.hahn,gabriele.kern-isberner}@tu-dortmund.de

Abstract. In this paper we address nonmonotonic reasoning from belief bases that may contain both defeasible beliefs expressed by conditionals of the form "*If A then usually B*", and indefeasible beliefs of the form "*A holds*". We present different notions of consistency and give an overview of established inference methods extended to conditional belief bases that may be only weakly consistent. We then extend the concept of inductive inference operator for belief bases with conditionals to belief bases containing both conditionals and facts; such an inference operator extends the beliefs given explicitly in a belief base to an inference relation. After illustrating that belief bases with facts are more informative than belief bases which only contain conditionals, we show how nonmonotonic reasoning from belief bases with conditionals and facts can be systematically reduced to reasoning from belief bases containing only conditionals. This reduction yields extensions of inductive inference operators to belief bases with facts. Corresponding extensions of p-entailment, system Z, lexicographic inference, c-inference, and system W for belief bases with facts are presented. Note that implementations of all these inference operators are available in the library underlying the online reasoning platform InfOCF-Web.

Keywords: Conditional · Conditional belief base · Nonmonotonic reasoning · Inductive inference operator · Defeasible belief · Indefeasible belief · Strongly consistent · Weakly consistent

1 Introduction

In formal studies of knowledge representation and reasoning, the beliefs of intelligent agents are often modelled using logical formulas. When the underlying logic is monotonic, adding a formula to the set of beliefs does not invalidate any conclusions drawn from the unextended set of beliefs. However, this monotonic behaviour, a core characteristic of classical logic, does not match the plausible

A. Raschke et al. (Eds.): Egon Börger Festschrift, LNCS 16580, pp. 377–397, 2026.
https://doi.org/10.1007/978-3-032-24494-9_18

reasoning humans do in everyday life, where reasonable conclusions must be drawn in the presence of uncertain or incomplete information. In contrast, in a nonmotonic inference relation, we can have that A entails B, but adding further information C to A might cause that $A \wedge C$ does not entail B any more. The prototypical example for illustrating this phenomen is the so-called *penguin triangle*: if we know that Tweety is a bird, we plausibly conclude that Tweety can fly. However, if we get the additional information that Tweety is a penguin, we withdraw this entailment and we do no longer infer that Tweety can fly.

For dealing with plausible beliefs and for studying nonmonotonic reasoning, conditionals of the form "*If A then usually B*", being entities of a three-valued nature [20] and going well beyond classical logic, are used. Such conditionals, which we formally represent by $(B|A)$, establish a plausible, but uncertain and defeasible connection between the antecedent A and the consequent B. Various semantics have been proposed for conditional belief bases consisting of a finite set of such conditionals, including ϵ- or p-entailment, [1,22] Lewis' system of spheres [39], conditional objects evaluated by using boolean intervals [18], possibility distributions [12], ranking functions [41,42], rational closure or system Z [37,40], special classes of ranking functions like c-representations [31], or system W [35]. Common to all these semantics is that they involve a plausibility relation among the underlying propositional interpretations, which are often referred to as *worlds*. The core idea is that a conditional $(B|A)$ is accepted if its verification $A \wedge B$ is strictly more plausible than its falsification $A \wedge \neg B$.

A set of conditional beliefs can be formally represented by a binary relation $\mid\!\sim$ on propositional formulas, where $A \mid\!\sim B$ represents that A (defeasibly) entails B; this relation is called inference relation or entailment relation. Inductive inference [33] is the process of completing a given conditional belief base Δ, containing explicitly given beliefs accepted by an agent, to an inference relation representing the agent's complete set of conditional beliefs.

In this paper, we study belief bases that in addition to defeasible conditionals also contain indefeasible beliefs of the form A *holds* (with certainty). For the treatment of such conditionals, we employ two different notions of consistency [22,30], and give an overview of some established inductive inference operators that have been extended to cover also belief bases that are not strongly, but only weakly consistent. While there are approaches where conditionals that cannot be verified have been used for representing indefeasible beliefs [16,21], we show why it is better to add explicitly represented factual beliefs to a belief base. We extend the concept of inductive inference [33] to belief bases with facts. While from a modelling perspective, it is advantageous and more adequate to use strongly consistent belief bases with facts, on a lower level of abstraction, reasoning with weakly consistent belief bases containing only conditionals can be used. We present a general transformation mapping a belief base with facts to a conditional belief base having only conditionals, and we identify two basic postulates guaranteeing that this transformation yields inference-equivalent results. This reduction, yielding extensions of inductive inference operators to belief bases with facts, is illustrated by corresponding extensions of p-entailment [1,22], system Z [40], lexicographic inference [38], c-inference [6,7], and system W [35]. Implementations of all these inference operators are available in the library underlying the online reasoning platform InfOCF-Web[1] [9,10].

This paper relies on and extends our previous work on conditional belief bases. We employed Börger's method for high-level system design and analysis [13–15], which is based on Gurevich's notion of abstract state machines (ASMs) [25], for specifying, refining, and verifying various belief management operations on conditional belief bases [2–5,8,11].

The rest of this paper is organized as follows. After presenting some required basics in Sect. 2, we recall and illustrate the concept of inductive inference from conditional belief bases in Sect. 3. In Sect. 4, we investigate the modelling of indefeasible beliefs with self-contradictory conditionals and propose two basic postulates an inductive inference operator should satisfy with respect to such conditionals. In Sect. 5, we introduce belief bases with facts and conditionals, and extend the concept of inductive inference operator correspondingly. In particular, we develop a general approach for obtaining an inductive inference operator, which is able to deal also with facts representing indefeasible beliefs, from an inductive inference operator for belief bases consisting only of conditionals representing defeasible beliefs. In Sect. 6, we conclude and point out further work.

2 Background

A *(propositional) signature* is a finite set Σ of propositional variables. Assuming an underlying signature Σ, we denote the resulting propositional language by $\mathcal{L}_\Sigma$. Usually, we denote elements of signatures with lowercase letters $a, b, c, \ldots$ and formulas with uppercase letters $A, B, C, \ldots$. We may denote a conjunction $A \wedge B$ by AB and a negation $\neg A$ by $\overline{A}$ for brevity of notation. The material implication $A \rightarrow B$ abbreviates $\neg A \vee B$, and a double-negated formula $\neg\neg A$ is identified with A. The set of interpretations over the underlying signature is denoted as Ω_Σ. Interpretations are also called *worlds* and Ω_Σ the *universe*. An interpretation $\omega \in \Omega_\Sigma$ is a *model* of a formula $A \in \mathcal{L}$ if A holds in ω, denoted as $\omega \models A$. The set of models of a formula (over a signature Σ) is denoted as $Mod_\Sigma(A) = \{\omega \in \Omega_\Sigma \mid \omega \models A\}$ or short as Ω_A. The subscript Σ in Ω_Σ, $\mathcal{L}_\Sigma$, and $Mod_\Sigma(A)$ can be omitted if the signature is clear from the context or if the underlying signature is not relevant. A formula A *(classically) entails* a formula B, denoted by $A \models B$, if $\Omega_A \subseteq \Omega_B$. By slight abuse of notation, we sometimes interpret worlds as the corresponding complete conjunction of all elements in the signature in either positive or negated form.

A *conditional* $(B|A)$ connects two formulas A, B and represents the rule "If A then usually B", where A is called the *antecedent* and B the *consequent* of the conditional. The conditional language is denoted as $(\mathcal{L}|\mathcal{L})_\Sigma = \{(B|A) \mid A, B \in \mathcal{L}_\Sigma\}$. We use a three-valued semantics of conditionals in this paper going back to de Finetti [20]. For a world ω a conditional $(B|A)$ is either *verified* by ω if $\omega \models AB$, *falsified* by ω if $\omega \models A\overline{B}$, or *not applicable* to ω if $\omega \models \overline{A}$. Popular

[1] https://www.fernuni-hagen.de/wbs/research/infocf-web/.

models for conditionals are *ranking functions* (also called *ordinal conditional functions*, OCF) [41,42] and *total preorders* (TPO) on Ω_Σ [17]. An OCF $\kappa : \Omega_\Sigma \rightarrow \mathbb{N} \cup \{\infty\}$ maps worlds to a *rank* such that at least one world has rank 0, i.e., $\kappa^{-1}(0) \neq \emptyset$. OCFs have been first introduced by Spohn [41] in a more general form. The intuition is that worlds with lower ranks are more plausible than worlds with higher ranks; worlds with rank ∞ are considered infeasible. OCFs are lifted to formulas by setting $\kappa(A) = \min\{\omega \mid \omega \models A\}$, i.e., by mapping a formula A to the smallest rank of a model of A, or to ∞ if A has no models. An OCF κ over Σ is a model of a conditional $(B|A) \in (\mathcal{L}|\mathcal{L})_\Sigma$, denoted as $\kappa \models (B|A)$, if

$$\kappa \models (B|A) \quad \text{iff} \quad \kappa(A) = \infty \text{ or } \kappa(AB) < \kappa(A\overline{B}) \tag{1}$$

holds. Thus, $\kappa \models (B|A)$ if according to κ, either the antecedent of the conditional is infeasible, or the verification of the conditional is strictly more plausible than its falsification.

3 Inductive Inference From Conditional Belief Bases

For explicitly representing a set of beliefs of the form *"If A then usually B"*, a conditional belief base can be used.

Definition 1 (conditional belief base). *Let Σ be a signature. A finite set of conditionals $\Delta \subseteq (\mathcal{L}|\mathcal{L})_\Sigma$ is called a* conditional belief base.

Throughout the paper, we will use the classic penguin triangle for illustration.

Example 2 (Δ_{pen}). Let the propositional variables in $\Sigma = \{b, p, f\}$ represent birds, penguins, and flying, and let the conditional belief base

$$\Delta_{pen} = \{(f|b), (\overline{f}|p), (b|p)\}$$

represent the beliefs that birds usually fly, that penguins usually do not fly, and that penguins are usually birds.

Ranking functions constitute one of the different semantic frameworks that have been proposed for conditional belief bases (e.g. [12,36,39]).

Definition 3 (models of conditional belief bases). *An OCF κ is a* model *of a conditional belief base Δ, denoted as $\kappa \models \Delta$, if $\kappa \models (B|A)$ for all $(B|A) \in \Delta$; κ is* admissible *(for Δ) if additionally $\kappa(A) < \infty$ for all $(B|A) \in \Delta$.*

Example 4 (Δ_{pen}, cont.). An admissible model κ for the conditional belief base Δ_{pen} from Example 2 needs to satisfy $\kappa(bf) < \kappa(b\overline{f})$, $\kappa(p\overline{f}) < \kappa(pf)$, and $\kappa(pb) < \kappa(p\overline{b})$. An example for such a ranking model κ is given in Table 1. Note that this specific model κ is admissible for Δ_{pen} because both $\kappa(b) \neq \infty$ and $\kappa(p) \neq \infty$ hold.

Table 1. Example ranking function as a model for the belief base Δ_{pen} for Example 4. The symbols ✓ and × indicate which conditionals are verified (✓) or falsified (×) by each world.

ω	$(f\|b)$	$(\overline{f}\|p)$	$(b\|p)$	$\kappa(\omega)$
$\overline{p}\,\overline{b}\,\overline{f}$				3
$\overline{p}\,\overline{b}\,f$				4
$\overline{p}\,b\,\overline{f}$	×			2
$\overline{p}\,b\,f$	✓			0
$p\,\overline{b}\,\overline{f}$		✓	×	5
$p\,\overline{b}\,f$		×	×	6
$p\,b\,\overline{f}$	×	✓	✓	1
$p\,b\,f$	✓	×	✓	2

In the literature, often only admissible models are taken into account, leading to a rather strong notion of consistency [22]. The distinction between admissible models and other models of Δ in Definition 3 allows us to distinguish two different notions of consistency [29].

Definition 5 (consistency of conditional belief bases). *A conditional belief base Δ is* weakly consistent *if it has a model κ, and Δ is* strongly consistent *if it has a model κ that is admissible for Δ.*

Note that Δ is strongly consistent iff it has a model κ that assigns to every world at least some plausibility [30], i.e., iff $\kappa^{-1}(\infty) = \emptyset$. Therefore, if Δ has an admissible model, then it also has an admissible model in which assigning the rank ∞ to any world is completely avoided.

Because every strongly consistent conditional belief base Δ is also weakly consistent, in the following, we may call Δ consistent if it is strongly or weakly consistent.

While a conditional belief base Δ contains explicitly given beliefs, the complete set of conditional beliefs of an agent is assumed to be formally captured by a binary relation $\mid\!\sim$ on propositional formulas. Then $A \mid\!\sim B$ represents that A (defeasibly) entails B; this relation is called *inference relation* or *entailment relation.* Because we consider defeasible or nonmonotonic entailment, it may be the case that there are formulas A, B, C with both $A \mid\!\sim B$ and $AC \not\mid\!\sim B$: Given more specific information, the agent might revoke a conclusion that was drawn based on more general information.

Different sets of properties for inference relations have been suggested, and often the set of postulates called *system P* [1,36] is considered as the minimal requirement for nonmonotonic inference relations. The postulates of system P are displayed in Fig. 1. Inference relations satisfying system P are called *preferential inference relations.* For details we refer to [1,36].

Every ranking function κ induces a preferential inference relation $\mid\!\sim_\kappa$ via

$$A \mid\!\sim_\kappa B \quad \text{iff} \quad \kappa(A) = \infty \text{ or } \kappa(AB) < \kappa(A\overline{B}) \quad \text{iff} \quad \kappa \models (B|A) \qquad (2)$$

(REF)	*Reflexivity*	for all $A \in \mathcal{L}$ it holds that $A \mid\!\sim A$
(LLE)	*Left Logical Equivalence*	$A \equiv B$ and $B \mid\!\sim C$ imply $A \mid\!\sim C$
(RW)	*Right weakening*	$B \models C$ and $A \mid\!\sim B$ imply $A \mid\!\sim C$
(CM)	*Cautious Monotony*	$A \mid\!\sim B$ and $A \mid\!\sim C$ imply $AB \mid\!\sim C$
(CUT)		$A \mid\!\sim B$ and $AB \mid\!\sim C$ imply $A \mid\!\sim C$
(OR)		$A \mid\!\sim C$ and $B \mid\!\sim C$ imply $(A \vee B) \mid\!\sim C$

Fig. 1. The system P postulates for nonmonotonic inference relations.

Note that the condition $\kappa(A) = \infty$ in (2) ensures that system P's reflexivity axiom—(REF): $A \mid\!\sim_{\kappa} A$—is satisfied also for $A \equiv \bot$.

Inductive inference is the process of completing a given belief base to an inference relation. To formally capture this for conditional belief bases, the concept of inductive inference operators was introduced [33]. While the original formulation of an inductive inference operator [33] implicitly assumes all given belief bases to be strongly consistent, the definition can be used to cover also weakly consistent conditional belief bases.

Definition 6 (inductive inference operator for conditional belief bases Δ [33]). *An* inductive inference operator *is a mapping* $C : \Delta \mapsto \mid\!\sim_{\Delta}$ *that maps a consistent belief base* Δ *to an inference relation such that direct inference (DI) and trivial vacuity (TV) hold:*

(DI) *If* $(B|A) \in \Delta$, *then* $A \mid\!\sim_{\Delta} B$.
(TV) *If* $\Delta = \emptyset$ *and* $A \mid\!\sim_{\Delta} B$, *then* $A \models B$.

Note that the assumption of strong consistency of Δ for an inductive inference operator in [33] prevents that Δ may contain a conditional which cannot be verified. The generalization to weakly consistent belief bases used in Definition 6 ensures that an inductive inference operator C can be applied to, e.g., a weakly consistent Δ with $(\bot|A) \in \Delta$ and that $A \mid\!\sim_{\Delta} \bot \in C(\Delta)$.

If no confusion arises, we may simply use $\mid\!\sim$ to denote the inductive inference operator mapping Δ to $\mid\!\sim_{\Delta}$. Furthermore, we may also consider inductive inference operators that are defined on strongly consistent belief bases only. We will talk explicitly about an inductive inference operator for weakly consistent belief bases when we want to emphasize that it is essential that $\mid\!\sim$ can be applied also to weakly consistent belief bases.

An inductive inference operator C is *preferential* if every inference relation $\mid\!\sim_{\Delta}$ in the image of C satisfies system P. Examples of preferential inductive inference operators are:

p-entailment $\mid\!\sim^{p}$ [1,22] considers all models of a belief base and is the most cautious preferential inductive inference operator. It can be characterized by system P because it licenses precisely the inferences that can be obtained by iteratively applying the rules of system P [18,37];

system Z $\mathrel{|\!\sim}^{z}$ [22] determines the uniquely defined minimal model of Δ, and it coincides with rational closure [37];

lexicographic inference $\mathrel{|\!\sim}^{lx}$ [38] employs a comparison of the number of conditionals falsified by a world, and it extends rational closure;

c-inference $\mathrel{|\!\sim}^{c}$ [6,7] considers all c-representations which are special ranking functions obtained by summing up natural number impacts assigned to falsified conditionals [31,32];

system W $\mathrel{|\!\sim}^{w}$ [34,35] is based on a preferred structure on worlds, and it captures both c-inference and system Z and thus rational closure.

The axioms of system P, and also the definition of p-entailment given by

$$A \mathrel{|\!\sim}^{p}_{\Delta} B \quad \text{iff} \quad A \mathrel{|\!\sim}_{\kappa} B \text{ for every model } \kappa \text{ of } \Delta, \tag{3}$$

cover strongly as well as weakly consistent conditional belief bases.

The definition of system Z is often given only for strongly consistent conditional belief bases [22]. Also the Z-partition of a conditional belief base as the core building block of system Z was first defined for strongly consistent conditional belief bases by Pearl [40]. It was extended by Goldszmidt and Pearl [23] for covering also weakly consistent conditional belief bases.

Definition 7 ((extended) Z-partition [23,40]**).** *A conditional $(B|A)$ is* tolerated *by a set of conditionals $\Delta = \{(B_1|A_1), \ldots, (B_n|A_n)\}$ if there is a world $\omega \in \Omega$ such that ω verifies $(B|A)$ and ω does not falsify any conditional in Δ, i.e., $\omega \models AB$ and $\omega \models \bigwedge_{i=1}^{n}(\overline{A_i} \vee B_i)$.*

The (extended) Z-partition *$EZP(\Delta) = (\Delta^0, \ldots, \Delta^k, \Delta^\infty)$ of a conditional belief base Δ is the ordered partition of Δ constructed by letting Δ^i be the inclusion maximal subset of $\Delta \setminus \bigcup_{j=0}^{i-1} \Delta^j$ that is tolerated by $\Delta \setminus \bigcup_{j=0}^{i-1} \Delta^j$ until $\Delta^{k+1} = \emptyset$. The set Δ^∞ is the remaining set of conditionals containing no conditional tolerated by Δ^∞.*

Example 8 (Δ_{pen}, cont.). Consider again the belief base Δ_{pen} from Example 2. We now construct the extended Z-partition $EZP(\Delta_{pen})$ according to Definition 7. To check the toleration of the conditionals, observe the verifications and falsifications in Table 1. The conditional $(f|b)$ can be verified without falsifying any conditional in Δ_{pen}. Therefore, $(f|b) \in \Delta^0$. However, the conditional $(\overline{f}|p)$ cannot be verified without falsifying $(f|b)$ or $(b|p)$, and $(b|p)$ cannot be verified without falsifying $(f|b)$ or $(\overline{f}|p)$. Hence, $(\overline{f}|p) \notin \Delta^0$ and $(b|p) \notin \Delta^0$. For Δ^1, observe that $(\overline{f}|p)$ and $(b|p)$ tolerate each other since they can be verified at the same time by the world $pb\overline{f}$. Therefore, $\Delta^1 = \{(\overline{f}|p), (b|p)\}$. In summary, we have

$$EZP(\Delta_{pen}) = (\Delta^0 = \{(f|b)\},\ \Delta^1 = \{(\overline{f}|p), (b|p)\},\ \Delta^\infty = \emptyset).$$

Note that the set Δ^∞ is empty since after constructing Δ^1, no conditionals remain that do not tolerate each other.

Because the Δ^i are chosen to be inclusion-maximal, $EZP(\Delta)$ is unique [40]. It can be used for checking the consistency of a conditional belief base.

Proposition 9 ([23,28]). *Let $\Delta = \{(B_1|A_1), \ldots, (B_n|A_n)\}$ be a conditional belief base, and let $EZP(\Delta) = (\Delta^0, \ldots, \Delta^k, \Delta^\infty)$ be its extended Z-partition.*

(1.) *Δ is strongly consistent iff $\Delta^\infty = \emptyset$.*
(2.) *Δ is weakly consistent iff $\Delta^\infty \neq \Delta$ or $A_1 \vee \cdots \vee A_n \not\equiv \top$.*
(3.) *Δ is not weakly consistent iff $\Delta^\infty = \Delta$ and $A_1 \vee \cdots \vee A_n \equiv \top$.*

With the help of Proposition 9, we can conclude after the construction of $EZP(\Delta_{pen})$ in Example 8 that the belief base Δ_{pen} is strongly consistent.

The following definition is an extension of system Z for covering also weakly consistent belief bases.

Definition 10 ((extended) system Z [23]**).** *Let Δ be a weakly consistent belief base with $EZP(\Delta) = (\Delta^0, \ldots, \Delta^k, \Delta^\infty)$. The (extended) Z-ranking function κ^z_Δ is defined as follows: For $\omega \in \Omega$, if a conditional in Δ^∞ is applicable to ω define $\kappa^z_\Delta(\omega) = \infty$. If not, let Δ^j be the last element in $EZP(\Delta)$ that contains a conditional falsified by ω. Then let $\kappa^z_\Delta(\omega) = j + 1$. If ω does not falsify any conditional in Δ, then let $\kappa^z_\Delta(\omega) = 0$.* (Extended) system Z *maps Δ to the inference relation $\mathrel{|\!\sim}^z_\Delta$ induced by κ^z_Δ according to Eq.* (2).

Table 2. System Z-ranking function for the belief base Δ_{pen} for Example 11. The symbols ✓ and × indicate which conditionals are verified (✓) or falsified (×) by each world.

ω	$(f\|b)$	$(\overline{f}\|p)$	$(b\|p)$	$\kappa^z_{\Delta_{pen}}(\omega)$
$\overline{p}\,\overline{b}\,\overline{f}$				0
$\overline{p}\,\overline{b}\,f$				0
$\overline{p}\,b\,\overline{f}$	×			1
$\overline{p}\,b\,f$	✓			0
$p\,\overline{b}\,\overline{f}$		✓	×	2
$p\,\overline{b}\,f$		×	×	2
$p\,b\,\overline{f}$	×	✓	✓	1
$p\,b\,f$	✓	×	✓	2

Example 11 (Δ_{pen}, cont.). The Z-ranking function $\kappa^z_{\Delta_{pen}}$ for Δ_{pen} can be computed by considering the Z-partition $EZP(\Delta_{pen})$ from Example 8 together with the falsification behavior of the worlds given in Table 2. The function $\kappa^z_{\Delta_{pen}}$ is also given in the table.

With the Z-ranking function $\kappa^z_{\Delta_{pen}}$, we are now able to answer inference queries on the basis of Δ_{pen} according to system Z. For instance, we can infer that flying animals are usually not penguins ($f \mathrel{|\!\sim}^z_{\Delta_{pen}} \overline{p}$) since $\kappa^z_{\Delta_{pen}}(f\overline{p}) = 0 < 1 = \kappa^z_{\Delta_{pen}}(fp)$.

For every weakly consistent belief base Δ, the OCF κ^z_Δ is a model of Δ; moreover, κ^z_Δ is the unique Pareto-minimal model of Δ. For strongly consistent belief bases, extended system Z coincides with system Z as defined in [22,40].

The original definition of lexicographic inference [38] ensures that $\mathrel|\!\!\!\sim^{lx}$ is an inductive inference operator for strongly consistent belief bases. For dealing with weakly consistent belief bases, a slight adaptation of lexicographic inference for guaranteeing direct inference (DI) is required, ensuring that $\mathrel|\!\!\!\sim^{lx}$ is also an inductive inference operator for weakly consistent belief bases [26]. We give the slightly adapted definition here.

Definition 12 ($<^{lx}_\Delta$, lexicographic inference, $\mathrel|\!\!\!\sim^{lx}_\Delta$ [26,38]). *The* lexicographic ordering *on two vectors in* $\mathbb{N}_0^n$ *is defined by* $(v_1, \ldots, v_n) <^{lx} (w_1, \ldots, w_n)$ *iff there is a* $k \in \{1, \ldots, n\}$ *such that* $v_k < w_k$ *and* $v_j = w_j$ *for* $j = k+1, \ldots, n$.

Let Δ *be a belief base with* $EZP(\Delta) = (\Delta^0, \ldots, \Delta^k, \Delta^\infty)$, *and let, for* $i \in \{1, \ldots, k, \infty\}$, $\xi^i(\omega) = \{(B|A) \in \Delta^i \mid \omega \models A\overline{B}\}$. *The binary relation* $<^{lx}_\Delta \subseteq \Omega_\Sigma \times \Omega_\Sigma$ *induced by* Δ *is defined by, for any* $\omega, \omega' \in \Omega_\Sigma$,

$$\omega <^{lx}_\Delta \omega' \quad \text{iff} \quad (|\xi^1(\omega)|, \ldots, |\xi^k(\omega)|, |\xi^\infty(\omega)|) <^{lx} (|\xi^1(\omega')|, \ldots, |\xi^k(\omega')|, |\xi^\infty(\omega')|).$$

For formulas $F, G \in \mathcal{L}_\Sigma$ *we define*

$$F <^{lx}_\Delta G \quad \text{iff} \quad \min(Mod_\Sigma(F), <^{lx}_\Delta) <^{lx}_\Delta \min(Mod_\Sigma(G), <^{lx}_\Delta)$$

where $\min(S, <)$ *denotes the set of minimal objects in* S *with respect to the ordering* $<$. *Then* A lexicographically entails B *(in the context of* Δ*), denoted* $A \mathrel|\!\!\!\sim^{lx}_\Delta B$, *if* $\xi^\infty(\omega) \neq \emptyset$ *for all* $\omega \in Mod_\Sigma(A)$ *or* $AB <^{lx}_\Delta A\overline{B}$. *Lexicographic entailment maps each* Δ *to* $\mathrel|\!\!\!\sim^{lx}_\Delta$.

An extension of c-inference, originally defined only on strongly consistent belief bases [6,7], has recently been extended to weakly consistent belief bases [27,28]. This extension of c-inference is obtained by considering extended c-representations which result from taking impacts for falsified conditionals from $\mathbb{N} \cup \{\infty\}$ (instead of just from $\mathbb{N}$) into account.

Also system W was originally defined only for strongly consistent belief bases [35]. An extension to weakly consistent belief bases has been introduced by restricting the underlying preferred structure of worlds to those worlds that are not infeasible [26,30].

Note that for every inductive inference operator mentioned above, the corresponding extension to weakly consistent belief bases is conservative in the sense that its restriction to strongly consistent belief bases coincides with the original version.

4 Belief Bases with Self-contradictory Conditionals

Within the rich body of research in nonmonotonic reasoning, a main focus is on reasoning from belief bases consisting only of defeasible conditionals, while the additional explicit representation of indefeasible facts [19,24,36] has attracted less attention. Several authors (e.g. [16,21]) use conditionals of the form $(\bot|\overline{A})$ to force all worlds satisfying $\overline{A}$ to be infeasible, with the intention of making A a strict belief.

Note that $(\bot|\overline{A})$ is a self-contradictory conditional because every world satisfying the antecedent $\overline{A}$ falsifies $(\bot|\overline{A})$. Therefore, $(\bot|\overline{A})$ is a conditional that cannot be verified by any world.

Example 13 (Δ_{pen}, cont.). In Δ_{pen}, the relationship between penguins and birds is modelled by the conditional $(b|p)$, representing the defeasible belief that penguins *are usually* birds. This modelling permits the existence of exceptional non-bird penguins. Instead, if the belief base should encode the factual belief that penguins *are* birds, using $(b|p)$ would be too lax because there should be no feasible world in which a penguin is not a bird. For achieving this, the conditional $(\bot|\neg(p \rightarrow b))$, or equivalently the conditional $(\bot|p\overline{b})$, can be used. Replacing $(b|p)$ in Δ_{pen} with $(\bot|p\overline{b}))$ yields:

$$\Delta'_{pen} = \{(f|b), (\overline{f}|p), (\bot|p\overline{b})\}$$

Note that Δ'_{pen}, in contrast to Δ_{pen}, is not strongly consistent, but only weakly consistent. In general, no conditional belief base using a modelling with self-contradictory conditionals as in Example 13 can be strongly consistent.

Let us apply the inductive inference operator C for conditional belief bases given by $C : \Delta \mapsto \{A \mathrel{|\!\sim}_\Delta B \mid (B|A) \in \Delta\}$ to Δ'_{pen}. It is easy to verify that C satisfies (DI) and (TV) and is thus an inductive inference operator. Note that $C(\Delta'_{pen})$ contains neither $\top \mathrel{|\!\sim}_\Delta p \rightarrow b$ nor the logically equivalent entailment $\top \mathrel{|\!\sim}_\Delta \overline{p} \vee b$. Therefore, we propose the following postulate for inductive inference operators for conditional belief bases ensuring that an agent plausibly believes the opposite of what she deems to be infeasible according to a self-contradictory conditional in her belief base.

(SF) An inductive inference operator $C : \Delta \mapsto \mathrel{|\!\sim}_\Delta$ for conditional belief bases satisfies *acceptance of self-contradictory conditionals* (SF) iff $(\bot|\overline{A}) \in \Delta$ implies $\top \mathrel{|\!\sim}_\Delta A$.

Furthermore, if Δ contains only self-contradictory conditionals, the following postulate ensures that an inductive inference operator for conditional belief bases does not entail anything which cannot be deduced via classical logic.

(SFO) An inductive inference operator $C : \Delta \mapsto \mathrel{|\!\sim}_\Delta$ for conditional belief bases satisfies *acceptance of self-contradictory conditionals only* (SFO) iff $\Delta = \{(\bot|\overline{A_1}), \ldots, (\bot|\overline{A_m})\}$ being weakly consistent and $A \mathrel{|\!\sim}_\Delta B$ together imply $\{A_1, \ldots, A_m\} \cup \{A\} \models B$.

5 Belief Bases with Facts

As illustrated in the previous section, using self-contradictory conditionals like $(\bot|\overline{A})$ in a conditional belief base Δ implies that checking Δ for strong consistency does not yield any additional information because we already know that Δwill fail this check. Furthermore, if Δ additionally contains both the conditionals $(B|\overline{A'})$ and $(\overline{B}|\overline{A'})$, all worlds satisfying $\overline{A'}$ are forced to be infeasible. However, the latter may be an effect of an unintended inconsistency within the set of conditionals that cannot be detected by any of the consistency tests according to Proposition 9. Even more, such an inconsistency may be not represented explicitly within the conditionals of a belief base, but it may surface only after applying nonmonotonic entailments on the conditionals. Therefore, from a modelling point of view, instead of using self-contradictory conditionals in a belief base, it is desirable to distinguish a set Φ of facts representing indefeasible beliefs and a set Δ of conditionals representing defeasible beliefs.

Definition 14 (belief base with facts). *Let Σ be a signature.*

- *A finite set of formulas $\Phi \subseteq \mathcal{L}_\Sigma$ is called a* factual belief base.
- *$\Gamma = \langle \Phi, \Delta \rangle$ is called a* belief base *if Φ is a factual belief base over Σ and Δ is a conditional belief base over Σ.*

Example 15 (Γ_{pen}). The penguin example with the factual belief that penguins *are* birds can be represented as the following belief base with facts:

$$\Gamma_{pen} = \langle \{p \rightarrow b\}, \{(f|b), (\overline{f}|p)\} \rangle$$

In analogy to an inductive inference operator for conditional belief bases (Definition 6), the strict beliefs Φ and the defeasible beliefs Δ given explicitly in a belief base $\Gamma = \langle \Phi, \Delta \rangle$ can inductively be completed to a nonmonotonic inference relation. Just as for conditional belief bases, this inductive completion of Γ can be done in many different ways. As a minimal requirement for this completion, we adapt the concept of inductive inference operator by taking the factual beliefs into account.

Definition 16 (inductive inference operator for belief bases $\langle \Phi, \Delta \rangle$). *An* inductive inference operator for belief bases with facts *is a mapping $C : \Gamma \mapsto {\mid\!\sim}_\Gamma$ that maps a consistent belief base $\Gamma = \langle \Phi, \Delta \rangle$ to an inference relation such that direct inference (DI-F) and trivial vacuity (TV-F) in the presence of facts hold:*

(DI-F) *If $A \in \Phi$ then $\top {\mid\!\sim}_\Gamma A$, and if $(B|A) \in \Delta$ then $A {\mid\!\sim}_\Gamma B$.*
(TV-F) *If $\Delta = \emptyset$ and $A {\mid\!\sim}_\Gamma B$ then $\Phi \cup \{A\} \models B$.*

Note that the restriction of an inductive inference operator $C : \Gamma \mapsto {\mid\!\sim}_\Gamma$ to belief bases with an empty factual belief base, i.e., $\Gamma = \langle \emptyset, \Delta \rangle$, yields an inductive inference operator for conditional belief bases as given in Definition 6. Vice versa, the restriction of $C : \Gamma \mapsto {\mid\!\sim}_\Gamma$ to belief bases with an empty set of conditionals, i.e., $\Gamma = \langle \Phi, \emptyset \rangle$, yields an inductive inference operator such that the elements of Φ are entailed, and all other inferences licensed by this operator can be obtained by deduction from Φ in classical logic.

Given an inductive inference operator C for conditional belief bases, the question arises how to extend C to cover also belief bases with factual information. The concept of inductive inference given in Definitions 6 and 16 provides a general framework and guideline, covering also borderline cases like the operator mapping $\Gamma = \langle \Phi, \Delta \rangle$ to the relation $\{\top \mathrel{|\!\!\sim}_\Gamma A \mid A \in \Phi\} \cup \{A \mathrel{|\!\!\sim}_\Gamma B \mid (B|A) \in \Delta\}$. For answering the question of how to deal with additional factual information in a systematic and general way, we introduce the concept of embedding a belief base with facts and conditionals into a belief base containing only conditionals.

Definition 17 (conditional embedding of a belief base, $\theta(\boldsymbol{\Gamma})$). *The* conditional embedding *of a belief base with facts $\Gamma = \langle \Phi, \Delta \rangle$ is given by the conditional belief base:*

$$\theta(\Gamma) = \{(\bot|\overline{A}) \mid A \in \Phi\} \cup \Delta \tag{4}$$

Another approach of encoding propositional beliefs in a purely conditional belief base is to represent a proposition A by a conditional with a tautology as its antecedent, yielding the *defeasible embedding* of $\Gamma = \langle \Phi, \Delta \rangle$ given by $\theta^{def}(\Gamma) = \{(A|\top) \mid A \in \Phi\} \cup \Delta$. But note that there is a fundamental difference between encoding a propositional belief A as a *fact* via $(\bot|\overline{A})$ and encoding it as a *plausible belief* via $(A|\top)$. In the first case, all worlds ω satisfying $\overline{A}$ will be assigned rank ∞ by all models κ of Γ, and also $\kappa'(\omega) = \infty$ for every model κ' of $\theta(\Gamma)$. However, in the second case, A is only deemed to be most plausible and usually, there will be models κ'' of $\theta^{def}(\Gamma)$ with $\kappa''(\omega) < \infty$ for some ω with $\omega \models \overline{A}$. In principle, our approach allows for both possibilities but requires careful knowledge engineering, distinguishing clearly between facts vs. plausible beliefs. Only propositional beliefs that hold with certainty should be included in the facts Φ.

Table 3. Ranking functions for Example 18.

ω	$\kappa_1(\omega)$	$\kappa_2(\omega)$	$\kappa_3(\omega)$
$\overline{p}\,\overline{b}\,\overline{f}$	0	0	0
$\overline{p}\,\overline{b}\,f$	0	0	0
$\overline{p}\,b\,\overline{f}$	1	1	1
$\overline{p}\,b\,f$	0	0	0
$p\,\overline{b}\,\overline{f}$	∞	1	2
$p\,\overline{b}\,f$	∞	2	2
$p\,b\,\overline{f}$	1	1	1
$p\,b\,f$	2	2	2

Example 18 (Γ_{pen}, cont.). Consider again the belief base Γ_{pen} from Example 15. The strict resp. defeasible embeddings are given as follows:

$$\theta(\Gamma_{pen}) = \{(\bot|p\overline{b}), (f|b), (\overline{f}|p)\},$$
$$\theta^{def}(\Gamma_{pen}) = \{(p \to b|\top), (f|b), (\overline{f}|p)\}.$$

Via (extended) system Z, one obtains the ranking functions κ_1 for $\theta(\Gamma_{pen})$, which equals $\Delta'_{pen}$from Example 13, κ_2 for $\theta^{def}(\Gamma_{pen})$, and κ_3 for Δ_{pen} from Example 2 (see Table 3). While κ_1 is a non-admissible model of $\theta(\Gamma_{\mathrm{peng}})$, the ranking function κ_2 is an admissible model of $\theta^{def}(\Gamma_{\mathrm{peng}})$. According to κ_1, non-bird penguins are infeasible: $\kappa_1(p\overline{b}) = \infty$. According to κ_2, penguin birds and non-bird penguins are equally plausible: $\kappa_2(pb) = \kappa_2(p\overline{b}) = 1$. For κ_3, non-bird penguins are feasible, but less plausible than penguin birds: $\kappa_3(pb) = 1 < 2 = \kappa_3(p\overline{b})$.

Based on the strict embedding θ, we now define a mapping Θ on inductive inference operators.

Definition 19 ($\boldsymbol{\Theta}$(C)). *Let $C : \Delta \mapsto \mathrel{|\!\sim}_\Delta$ be an inductive inference operator for conditional belief bases. Then $\Theta(C)$ is the function*

$$\Theta(C) : \Gamma \mapsto \mathrel{|\!\sim}_\Gamma \quad \textit{with} \quad \mathrel{|\!\sim}_\Gamma = C(\theta(\Gamma)). \tag{5}$$

Note that the overloading of the symbol $\mathrel{|\!\sim}$ in Definition 19 does not cause any conflict because the index of $\mathrel{|\!\sim}$ uniquely determines whether it refers to the image of C or to the image of $\Theta(C)$. An immediate consequence of Definition 19 is the equation

$$\mathrel{|\!\sim}_\Gamma \; = \mathrel{|\!\sim}_{\theta(\Gamma)} \tag{6}$$

where the left-hand side of (6) refers to the image of $\Theta(C)$ and the right-hand side of (6) refers to the image of C.

To ensure that $\Theta(C)$ is an inductive inference operator for belief bases with facts and conditionals, it suffices to require C to satisfy some reasonable postulates.

Proposition 20. *Let $C : \Delta \mapsto \mathrel{|\!\sim}_\Delta$ be an inductive inference operator for (weakly consistent) conditional belief bases. If C satisfies (SF) and (SFO) then $\Theta(C)$ is an inductive inference operator for belief bases with facts and conditionals.*

Proof. Let $C : \Delta \mapsto \mathrel{|\!\sim}_\Delta$ be an inductive inference operator for (weakly consistent) conditional belief bases that satisfies (SF) and (SFO). We need to show that $\Theta(C)$ satisfies (DI-F) and (TV-F).

We show (DI-F) first. Let $\Gamma = \langle \Phi, \Delta \rangle$ be a belief base with facts and conditionals and let $A \in \Phi$. Then $(\bot|\overline{A}) \in \theta(\Gamma)$. With (SF) satisfied by C, it follows that $\top \mathrel{|\!\sim}_{\theta(\Gamma)} A$, and with (6) it follows that $\top \mathrel{|\!\sim}_\Gamma A$. Next, let $(B|A) \in \Delta$. Then $(B|A) \in \theta(\Gamma)$. With (DI) satisfied by C, it follows that $A \mathrel{|\!\sim}_{\theta(\Gamma)} B$ and therefore by (6), it follows that $A \mathrel{|\!\sim}_\Gamma B$. Thus $\Theta(C)$ satisfies (DI-F).

We show (TV-F) next. Let $\Gamma = \langle \Phi, \Delta \rangle$ be a belief base with facts and conditionals where $\Delta = \emptyset$. Then $\theta(\Gamma) = \{(\bot|\overline{A_i}) \mid A_i \in \Phi\}$. Assume now that $\theta(\Gamma)$ is weakly consistent and that $A \mathrel{|\!\sim}_\Gamma B$. We need to show $\Phi \cup \{A\} \models B$. This is a direct consequence of (SFO) and therefore $\Theta(C)$ satisfies (TV-F). □

The most skeptical preferential inductive inference operator satisfies (SF).

Proposition 21. *p-entailment satisfies (SF).*

Proof. Let $(\bot|\overline{A}) \in \Delta$. We need to show $\top \mathrel{|\!\sim}^p_\Delta A$. We show this by showing that $\kappa(A) < \kappa(\overline{A})$ for all models of Δ (cf. (3)). Consider any OCF κ with $\kappa \models \Delta$. Due to $\kappa \models (\bot|\overline{A})$ we have that $\kappa(\overline{A}) = \infty$. Then it follows that $\kappa(A) = 0$, because $\min\{\kappa(A), \kappa(\overline{A})\} = 0$. Then $\kappa(A) < \kappa(\overline{A})$ and therefore $\top \mathrel{|\!\sim}^p_\Delta A$. □

Next, we show that every preferential inductive inference operator satisfies (SF).

Proposition 22. *Every inductive inference operator $C : \Delta \mapsto \mathrel{|\!\sim}_\Delta$ with $\mathrel{|\!\sim}^p_\Delta \subseteq \mathrel{|\!\sim}_\Delta$ satisfies (SF).*

Proof. Let $(\bot|\overline{A}) \in \Delta$. Then with Proposition 21 we have $\top \mathrel{|\!\sim}^p_\Delta A$. Because $\mathrel{|\!\sim}^p_\Delta \subseteq \mathrel{|\!\sim}_\Delta$ it follows that $\top \mathrel{|\!\sim}_\Delta A$. □

For the following, it will be helpful to show that lexicographic inference, being a rather bold inductive inference operator, satisfies (SFO).

Proposition 23. *Lexicographic inference satisfies (SFO).*

Proof. Let $\Delta = \{(\bot|\overline{A_1}), \dots, (\bot|\overline{A_m})\}$ be weakly consistent. Then $EZP(\Delta) = (\Delta^0, \Delta^\infty)$ with $\Delta^0 = \emptyset$ and $\Delta^\infty = \Delta$. Now let $A \mathrel{|\!\sim}^{lx}_\Delta B$. We need to show that $\{A_1, \dots, A_n, A\} \models B$. We show this by showing that $\{A_1, \dots, A_n, A\} \cup \{\overline{B}\}$ is unsatisfiable. Due to $A \mathrel{|\!\sim}^{lx}_\Delta B$ there are two cases. If $\xi^\infty(\omega) \neq \emptyset$ for all ω with $\omega \models A$ then $\{A_1, \dots, A_n, A\}$ is unsatisfiable. Thus assume the second case, i.e., $AB <^{lx}_\Delta A\overline{B}$. Towards a contradiction, assume $\{A_1, \dots, A_n, A, \overline{B}\}$ is satisfiable. Then there is some world $\omega \in \Omega$ with $\omega \models \{A_1, \dots, A_n, A, \overline{B}\}$. Because $\omega \models \{A_1, \dots, A_n\}$, ω does not falsify any conditionals in Δ. Then there can be no $\omega' \in \Omega$ with $\omega' <^{lx}_\Delta \omega$. But since $\omega \models A\overline{B}$, this is a contradiction to the assumption that $AB <^{lx}_\Delta A\overline{B}$. Thus $\{A_1, \dots, A_n, A, \overline{B}\}$ is unsatisfiable and therefore $\{A_1, \dots, A_n, A\} \models B$. □

Every inductive inference operator extended by lexicographic inference also satisfies (SFO).

Proposition 24. *Every inductive inference operator $C : \Delta \mapsto \mathrel{|\!\sim}_\Delta$ with $\mathrel{|\!\sim}_\Delta \subseteq \mathrel{|\!\sim}^{lx}$ satisfies (SFO).*

Proof. Let $\Delta = \{(\bot|\overline{A_1}), \dots, (\bot|\overline{A_m})\}$ be weakly consistent. With Proposition 23 we have that $A \mathrel{|\!\sim}^{lx}_\Delta B$ implies $\{A_1, \dots, A_n, A\} \models B$. Because $\mathrel{|\!\sim}_\Delta \subseteq \mathrel{|\!\sim}^{lx}$, it follows that $A \mathrel{|\!\sim}_\Delta B$ implies $A \mathrel{|\!\sim}^{lx}_\Delta B$ and therefore $\{A_1, \dots, A_n, A\} \models B$. □

With Propositions 22 and 24, it is now easy to show that all inductive inference operators discussed in this paper satisfy (SF) and (SFO).

Proposition 25. *p-Entailment, system Z, lexicographic inference, c-inference and system W satisfy (SF) and (SFO).*

Proof. (SF) follows from Proposition 22 and the fact that, for $\mid\!\sim \in \{\mid\!\sim^{z}, \mid\!\sim^{lx}, \mid\!\sim^{c}, \mid\!\sim^{w}\}$, $\mid\!\sim$ is preferential and thus $\mid\!\sim^{p} \subseteq \mid\!\sim$. (SFO) follows from Proposition 24 and the fact that, for $\mid\!\sim' \in \{\mid\!\sim^{p}, \mid\!\sim^{z}, \mid\!\sim^{c}, \mid\!\sim^{w}\}$, lexicographic inference is an extension of $\mid\!\sim'$ and thus $\mid\!\sim' \subseteq \mid\!\sim^{lx}$ [26]. □

As a consequence of Proposition 20 we get the following observation stating that $\Theta(C)$ is a conservative extension of C.

Proposition 26. *Let C be an inductive inference operator satisfying (SF) and (SFO), and let $\Gamma = \langle \Phi, \Delta \rangle$. If $\Phi = \emptyset$ then $C(\Delta) = \Theta(C)(\Gamma)$.*

Note that the claim $C(\Delta) = \Theta(C)(\Gamma)$ if $\Phi = \emptyset$ in Proposition 26 for an inductive inference operator C can also be transferred to the level of belief bases, i.e., for the conditional embedding θ, the equation $\theta(\langle \emptyset, \Delta \rangle) = \Delta$ holds.

OCFs can be used not only as models for conditional belief bases, but also for factual belief bases and for belief bases containing both facts and conditionals. We first define OCF models of a propositional formula.

Definition 27. *Let Σ be a signature. An OCF κ over Σ. is a* model *of a formula $A \in \mathcal{L}_{\Sigma}$, denoted as $\kappa \Vdash A$, if $\kappa(\overline{A}) = \infty$.*

Proposition 28. *If $\kappa \Vdash A$ then $\kappa(A) = 0$ and $\kappa(\omega) = \infty$ for all $\omega \in \Omega_{\Sigma}$ with $\omega \models \overline{A}$.*

Proof. This prop is an immediate consequence of the observation that $\min\{\kappa(F), \kappa(\overline{F})\} = 0$ for all OCFs κ over Σ and all formulas $F \in \mathcal{L}_{\Sigma}$. □

OCF models and admissible OCF models of a belief base with factual information constitute a refinement of OCF models of conditional belief bases (Definition 3).

Definition 29 (models of belief bases with facts). *Let Σ be a signature, let Φ be a factual belief base over Σ, let $\Gamma = \langle \Phi, \Delta \rangle$, and let κ be an OCF over Σ.*

- *κ is a* model *of Φ, denoted as $\kappa \models \Phi$, if $\kappa \Vdash A$ for all $A \in \Phi$.*
- *κ is a* model *of $\Gamma = \langle \Phi, \Delta \rangle$, denoted as $\kappa \models \langle \Phi, \Delta \rangle$, if $\kappa \models \Phi$ and $\kappa \models \Delta$; κ is* admissible *(for $\langle \Phi, \Delta \rangle$) if additionally $\kappa(A) < \infty$ for all $(B|A) \in \Delta$.*

The following definition extends the consistency notions for conditional belief bases to belief bases with facts.

Definition 30 (consistency of belief bases with facts). *A factual belief base Φ is* consistent (with respect to OCFs) *if it has a model κ.*

A belief base $\Gamma = \langle \Phi, \Delta \rangle$ is weakly consistent *if it has a model κ. Γ is* strongly consistent *if it has a model κ that is admissible for Γ.*

We will say that Γ is consistent if it is strongly or weakly consistent. Consistency of a factual belief base Φ representing strict beliefs corresponds to the consistency of Φ in classical logic and it thus can be checked with the methods available for classical logic.

Proposition 31. *Let Φ be a factual belief base. Then Φ is consistent (with respect to OCFs) iff Φ is consistent with respect to classical logic.*

For a belief base with facts, employment of the embedding θ yields a method for determining its consistency status.

Proposition 32. *Let $\Gamma = \langle \Phi, \Delta \rangle$ be a belief base and let $EZP(\theta(\Gamma)) = (\theta(\Gamma)^1, \ldots, \theta(\Gamma)^k, \theta(\Gamma)^\infty)$.*

- *Γ is weakly consistent iff Φ is consistent and $\theta(\Gamma)$ is weakly consistent.*
- *Γ is strongly consistent iff Φ is consistent, $\theta(\Gamma)$ is weakly consistent, and $\Delta \cap \theta(\Gamma)^\infty = \emptyset$.*

Proof. The first point follows from the fact that Γ has a model iff $\theta(\Gamma)$ has a model by construction.

For the second point, we show both directions of the iff separately:

"$\Rightarrow$": Assume Γ is strongly consistent. Then there is some κ such that $\kappa \models \Gamma$ and κ is admissible for Γ. The existence of κ implies that Φ is consistent and that $\theta(\Gamma)$ is weakly consistent. We show that $\Delta \cap \theta(\Gamma)^\infty = \emptyset$ via contradiction. Assume there was $(B|A) \in \Delta \cap \theta(\Gamma)^\infty$. Then $\kappa^z_\Gamma(AB) = \infty$. This implies $\kappa^z_\Gamma(A) = \infty$ because $\kappa^z_\Gamma \models (B|A)$. Because κ^z_Γ is the unique minimal ranking function modeling Γ [22], for all models κ of Δ it must hold that $\kappa(A) = \infty$. But then there would be no admissible model of Γ, contradiction.

"$\Leftarrow$": Assume Φ is consistent, $\theta(\Gamma)$ is weakly consistent, and $\Delta \cap \theta(\Gamma)^\infty = \emptyset$. We show that Γ is strongly consistent by showing that κ^z_Γ is an admissible model of Γ. First, κ^z_Γ is a model of Γ because Φ is consistent and $\theta(\Gamma)$ is weakly consistent. Next, observe that $\Delta \cap \theta(\Gamma)^\infty = \emptyset$ implies $\theta(\Gamma)^\infty = \{(\bot|\overline{F}) \mid F \in \Phi\}$. Thus, for all $F \in \Phi$, we have $\kappa^z_\Gamma(\overline{F}) = \infty$. We now only need to show that $\kappa^z_\Gamma(A) < \infty$ for all $(B|A) \in \Delta$. If there is an $\omega \in \Omega$ with $\omega \models A$ and $\omega \models \Phi$ this immediately follows per construction. Towards a contradiction, assume now that there were no such ω. Then for all ω' with $\omega' \models A$ it must be the case that $\omega' \not\models \Phi$. But then, by construction, $(B|A) \in \theta(\Gamma)^\infty$, contradiction. □

As a side note, the condition $\Delta \cap \theta(\Gamma)^\infty = \emptyset$ in Proposition 32 implies that Δ is strongly consistent. We illustrate that our general approach of generating an inductive inference operator for belief bases with facts in Proposition 20 works for both kinds of consistency with the following example.

Example 33. Let $\Gamma_{eagle} = \langle \{\overline{p}, p \to b, e \to b\}, \{(f|b), (\overline{f}|p)\} \rangle$ extend Γ_{peng} by the facts that eagles are birds and by the observation that we are not dealing with penguins. Then $EZP(\theta(\Gamma)) = (\theta(\Gamma)^0, \theta(\Gamma)^\infty)$ with $\theta(\Gamma)^0 = \{(f|b)\}$ und $\theta(\Gamma)^\infty = \{(\bot|p), (\bot|p\overline{b}), (\bot|e\overline{f}), (\overline{f}|p)\}$. Because $\Delta \cap \theta(\Gamma)^\infty \neq \emptyset$, it is the case that Γ is not strongly consistent. Nevertheless we can still do inference about eagles with this belief base utilizing our embedding and Proposition 20. For example, we get $e \mid\!\sim^z_{\theta(\Gamma_{eagle})} f$.

We now compare our generic construction of an inductive inference operator for belief bases with facts in Proposition 20 with the definition of system Z for facts and conditionals given by Eiter and Lukasiewicz [19]. In order to distinguish the two different constructions, we will denote the latter by $\kappa^{z'}$ in the following definition, but use our notation otherwise.

Definition 34 (system Z with facts [19]**).** *Let $\Gamma = \langle \Phi, \Delta \rangle$ be a strongly consistent belief base with facts and conditionals. Γ tolerates a conditional $(B|A)$ if there is $\omega \in \Omega$ with $\omega \models AB$, $\omega \not\models C\overline{D}$ for all $(D|C) \in \Delta$, and $\omega \models F$ for all $F \in \Phi$. Let $EZP(\Gamma) = (\Delta^0, \ldots, \Delta^k, \Delta^\infty)$ be defined utilizing this tolerance notion. Note that $\Delta^\infty = \emptyset$ because Γ is strongly consistent. The system Z ranking function $\kappa^{z'}_\Gamma$ is then defined as follows: For $\omega \in \Omega$, if $\omega \not\models \Phi$ then $\kappa^{z'}_\Gamma(\omega) = \infty$. If $\omega \models \Phi$ then $\kappa^{z'}_\Gamma$ is defined analogously to Definition 10. The inference relation $\mid\!\sim^{z'}_\Gamma$ is then obtained via* (2).

Definition 34 differs from the approach obtained via Proposition 20 in that it only handles strongly consistent belief bases. Furthermore, for $\kappa^{z'}_\Gamma$ the facts are considered separately from the conditionals and are not included in the ordered partition. Nevertheless, the specific approach for system Z in [19] coincides with our general transformation approach.

Proposition 35. *System Z with facts as given in Definition 34 [19] coincides with the conditional embedding construction applied to system Z, i.e., for every strongly consistent belief base Γ with facts, we have, for all worlds ω:*

$$\kappa^{z'}_\Gamma(\omega) = \kappa^{z}_{\theta(\Gamma)}(\omega)$$

Proof. Let $\Gamma = \langle \Phi, \Delta \rangle$ be a strongly consistent belief base with facts. We need to show $\kappa^{z'}_\Gamma(\omega) = \kappa^{z}_{\theta(\Gamma)}(\omega)$ for all $\omega \in \Omega$. First, we show (†): Γ tolerates $(B|A)$ iff $\theta(\Gamma)$ tolerates $(B|A)$.

"⇒": Let $\langle \Phi, \Delta \rangle$ tolerate $(B|A)$. Then there is a world ω with $\omega \models AB$ and $\omega \not\models C\overline{D}$ for all $(D|C) \in \Delta$ and $\omega \not\models \overline{F}$ for all $F \in \Phi$. Then $\omega \not\models C'\overline{D'}$ for all $(D|C) \in \theta(\Gamma)$, because by definition $\theta(\Gamma) = \Delta \cup \{(\bot|\overline{F}) \mid F \in \Phi\}$ and thus $\theta(\Gamma)$ tolerates $(B|A)$. The other direction is analogous.

Now we show that $\kappa^{z'}_\Gamma(\omega) = \kappa^{z}_{\theta(\Gamma)}(\omega)$ for all $\omega \in \Omega$. Let $EZP(\Gamma) = (\Delta^1, \ldots, \Delta^k, \Delta^\infty)$ and $EZP(\theta(\Gamma)) = (\theta(\Gamma)^1, \ldots, \theta(\Gamma)^k, \theta(\Gamma)^\infty)$. Because Γ is strongly consistent also Δ is strongly consistent and thus $\Delta^\infty = \emptyset$. Note that, by construction and due to (†), $\theta(\Gamma)^\infty = \{(\bot|\overline{F}) \mid F \in \Phi\}$ and $\theta(\Gamma)^i = \Delta^i$ for $i \in \{0, \ldots, k\}$. Now let $\omega \models \overline{F}$ for some $F \in \Phi$. Then $\kappa^{z'}_\Gamma(\omega) = \infty$ per definition. Because ω must then falsify $(\bot|\overline{F}) \in \theta(\Gamma)^\infty$ we have $\kappa^{z}_{\theta(\Gamma)}(\omega) = \infty$ as well. In the case that $\omega \models \Phi$ the definitions coincide and $\kappa^{z}_\Gamma(\omega) = \kappa^{z}_{\theta(\Gamma)}(\omega)$ follows immediately from the fact that $\theta(\Gamma)^i = \Delta^i$ for $i \in \{0, \ldots, k\}$. □

In this section, we have investigated inductive inference operators for belief bases with facts. In particular, we have shown how an inductive inference operator for such belief bases can be constructed systematically from an inductive inference operator for conditional belief bases by utilizing a conditional embedding of factual beliefs.

6 Conclusions and Future Work

In this paper, we studied inductive inference from belief bases containing both indefeasible beliefs represented by facts and defeasible beliefs represented by conditionals. We argued that instead of using self-contradictory conditionals that cannot be verified for the modelling of indefeasible beliefs, it is preferable and more adequate to use an explicit factual representation. We proposed two basic postulates for an inductive inference operator for conditional belief bases ensuring that the general transformation method developed in this paper yields an inductive inference operator for belief bases with both facts and conditionals. Implementations of algorithms checking the different notions of consistency for conditional belief bases and for belief bases with facts corresponding to the respective propositions in this paper are available in the library InfOCF underlying the online reasoning platform InfOCF-Web [9,10]. InfOCF also provides implementations for the inductive inference operators p-entailment, system Z, lexicographic inference, c-inference, and system W discussed in this paper.

Our future work includes empirical evaluations of modelling using conditional belief bases with facts. We are currently also working on the consolidation of inconsistency in a weakly consistent conditional belief base Δ by identifying the reasons for inconsistency in Δ and developing methods for transforming Δ into an inferentially equivalent belief base with facts and a strongly consistent set of conditionals.

Acknowledgments. This work was supported by the Deutsche Forschungsgemeinschaft (DFG, German Research Foundation), project number 512363537, grant BE 1700/12-1 awarded to Christoph Beierle and grant KE 1413/15-1 awarded to Gabriele Kern-Isberner. Alexander Hahn was supported by grant KE 1413/15-1, and Lars-Phillip Spiegel was supported by grant BE 1700/12-1.

References

1. Adams, E.W.: The Logic of Conditionals: An Application of Probability to Deductive Logic. Synthese Library. Springer Science+Business Media, Dordrecht, NL (1975)
2. Beierle, C., Kern-Isberner, G.: Modelling conditional knowledge discovery and belief revision by abstract state machines. In: Börger, E., Gargantini, A., Riccobene, E. (eds.) ASM 2003. LNCS, vol. 2589, pp. 186–203. Springer, Heidelberg (2003). https://doi.org/10.1007/3-540-36498-6_10
3. Beierle, C., Kern-Isberner, G.: On the modelling of an agent's epistemic state and its dynamic changes. Electron. Commun. Eur. Assoc. Softw. Sci. Technol. **12**, 1–17 (2008). https://doi.org/10.14279/TUJ.ECEASST.12.234
4. Beierle, C., Kern-Isberner, G.: A verified AsmL implementation of belief revision. In: Börger, E., Butler, M., Bowen, J.P., Boca, P. (eds.) ABZ 2008. LNCS, vol. 5238, pp. 98–111. Springer, Heidelberg (2008). https://doi.org/10.1007/978-3-540-87603-8_9

5. Beierle, C., Kern-Isberner, G., Koch, N.: A high-level implementation of a system for automated reasoning with default rules (system description). In: Armando, A., Baumgartner, P., Dowek, G. (eds.) IJCAR 2008. LNCS (LNAI), vol. 5195, pp. 147–153. Springer, Heidelberg (2008). https://doi.org/10.1007/978-3-540-71070-7_12
6. Beierle, C., Eichhorn, C., Kern-Isberner, G., Kutsch, S.: Properties of skeptical c-inference for conditional knowledge bases and its realization as a constraint satisfaction problem. Ann. Math. Artif. Intell. **83**(3-4), 247–275 (2018). https://doi.org/10.1007/s10472-017-9571-9
7. Beierle, C., Eichhorn, C., Kern-Isberner, G., Kutsch, S.: Properties and interrelationships of skeptical, weakly skeptical, and credulous inference induced by classes of minimal models. Artif. Intell. **297**, 103489 (2021). https://doi.org/10.1016/j.artint.2021.103489
8. Beierle, C., Haldimann, J., Kern-Isberner, G.: Semantic splitting of conditional belief bases. In: Raschke, A., Riccobene, E., Schewe, K.-D. (eds.) Logic, Computation and Rigorous Methods. LNCS, vol. 12750, pp. 82–95. Springer, Cham (2021). https://doi.org/10.1007/978-3-030-76020-5_5
9. Beierle, C., et al.: Scaling up reasoning from conditional belief bases. In: Destercke, S., Martinez, M.V., Sanfilippo, G. (eds.) SUM 2024. LNCS, vol. 15350, pp. 29–44. Springer, Cham (2024). https://doi.org/10.1007/978-3-031-76235-2_3
10. Beierle, C., Haldimann, J., Sanin, A., Spang, A., Spiegel, L., von Berg, M.: The InfOCF library for reasoning with conditional belief bases. In: Casini, G., Dundua, B., Kutsia, T. (eds.) JELIA 2025, Part II. LNAI, vol. 16094, pp. 19–27. Springer, Cham (2025). https://doi.org/10.1007/978-3-032-04590-4_2
11. Beierle, C., Kutsch, S., Kern-Isberner, G.: From concepts in non-monotonic reasoning to high-level implementations using Abstract State Machines and functional programming. In: Mashkoor, A., Wang, Q., Thalheim, B. (eds.) Models: Concepts, Theory, Logic, Reasoning and Semantics - Essays Dedicated to Klaus-Dieter Schewe on the Occasion of his 60th Birthday, pp. 286–310. College Publications (2018)
12. Benferhat, S., Dubois, D., Prade, H.: Possibilistic and standard probabilistic semantics of conditional knowledge bases. J. Logic Comput. **9**(6), 873–895 (1999)
13. Börger, E., Stärk, R.: Abstract State Machines: A Method for High-Level System Design and Analysis. Springer, Cham (2003)
14. Börger, E.: The ASM refinement method. Formal Aspects Comput. **15**(2–3), 237–257 (2003). https://doi.org/10.1007/s00165-003-0012-7
15. Börger, E., Raschke, A.: Modeling Companion for Software Practitioners. Springer, Cham (2018). https://doi.org/10.1007/978-3-662-56641-1
16. Casini, G., Meyer, T., Varzinczak, I.: Taking defeasible entailment beyond rational closure. In: Calimeri, F., Leone, N., Manna, M. (eds.) JELIA 2019. LNCS (LNAI), vol. 11468, pp. 182–197. Springer, Cham (2019). https://doi.org/10.1007/978-3-030-19570-0_12
17. Darwiche, A., Pearl, J.: On the logic of iterated belief revision. Artif. Intell. **89**(1–2), 1–29 (1997)
18. Dubois, D., Prade, H.: Conditional objects as nonmonotonic consequence relationships. Special Issue on Conditional Event Algebra. IEEE Trans. Syst. Man Cybern. **24**(12), 1724–1740 (1994)
19. Eiter, T., Lukasiewicz, T.: Complexity results for structure-based causality. Artif. Intell. **142**(1), 53–89 (2002)

20. de Finetti, B.: La prévision, ses lois logiques et ses sources subjectives. Ann. Inst. H. Poincaré **7**(1), 1–68 (1937). Engl. transl. *Theory of Probability*, J. Wiley & Sons, 1974
21. Giordano, L., Gliozzi, V., Olivetti, N., Pozzato, G.L.: Semantic characterization of rational closure: from propositional logic to description logics. Artif. Intell. **226**, 1–33 (2015). https://doi.org/10.1016/j.artint.2015.05.001
22. Goldszmidt, M., Pearl, J.: Qualitative probabilities for default reasoning, belief revision, and causal modeling. Artif. Intell. **84**, 57–112 (1996)
23. Goldszmidt, M., Pearl, J.: On the relation between rational closure and system-z. In: Proceedings of the Third International Workshop on Nonmonotonic Reasoning, 31 May–3 June, pp. 130–140 (1990)
24. Goldszmidt, M., Pearl, J.: On the consistency of defeasible databases. Artif. Intell. **52**(2), 121–149 (1991)
25. Gurevich, Y.: Evolving algebras 1993: Lipari guide. In: Börger, E. (ed.) Specification and Validation Methods, pp. 9–36. Oxford University Press (1995)
26. Haldimann, J., Beierle, C.: Approximations of system W for inference from strongly and weakly consistent belief bases. Int. J. Approx. Reason. **175**, 109295 (2024). https://doi.org/10.1016/j.ijar.2024.109295
27. Haldimann, J., Beierle, C., Kern-Isberner, G.: Syntax splitting and reasoning from weakly consistent conditional belief bases with C-inference. In: Meier, A., Ortiz, M. (eds.) FoIKS 2024. LNCS, vol. 14589, pp. 85–103. Springer, Cham (2024). https://doi.org/10.1007/978-3-031-56940-1_5
28. Haldimann, J., Beierle, C., Kern-Isberner, G.: Inductive inference from weakly consistent belief bases. Knowl. Eng. Rev. **40**(e8), 1–32 (2025). https://doi.org/10.1017/S0269888925100088
29. Haldimann, J., Beierle, C., Kern-Isberner, G., Meyer, T.: Conditionals, infeasible worlds, and reasoning with system W. In: Chun, S.A., Franklin, M. (eds.) Proceedings of the Thirty-Sixth International Florida Artificial Intelligence Research Society Conference (2023). https://doi.org/10.32473/flairs.36.133268
30. Haldimann, J., Beierle, C., Kern-Isberner, G., Meyer, T.: Reasoning with system W and infeasible worlds. Ann. Math. Artif. Intell. **93**(5), 665–698 (2025). https://doi.org/10.1007/S10472-025-09982-W
31. Kern-Isberner, G.: Conditionals in Nonmonotonic Reasoning and Belief Revision. LNAI, vol. 2087. Springer, Cham (2001)
32. Kern-Isberner, G.: A thorough axiomatization of a principle of conditional preservation in belief revision. Ann. Math. Artif. Intell. **40**(1–2), 127–164 (2004)
33. Kern-Isberner, G., Beierle, C., Brewka, G.: Syntax splitting = relevance + independence: new postulates for nonmonotonic reasoning from conditional belief bases. In: Calvanese, D., Erdem, E., Thielscher, M. (eds.) Principles of Knowledge Representation and Reasoning: Proceedings of the 17th International Conference, KR 2020, pp. 560–571. IJCAI Organization (2020). https://doi.org/10.24963/kr.2020/56
34. Komo, C., Beierle, C.: Nonmonotonic inferences with qualitative conditionals based on preferred structures on worlds. In: Schmid, U., Klügl, F., Wolter, D. (eds.) KI 2020. LNCS (LNAI), vol. 12325, pp. 102–115. Springer, Cham (2020). https://doi.org/10.1007/978-3-030-58285-2_8
35. Komo, C., Beierle, C.: Nonmonotonic reasoning from conditional knowledge bases with system W. Ann. Math. Artif. Intell. **90**(1), 107–144 (2022). https://doi.org/10.1007/s10472-021-09777-9
36. Kraus, S., Lehmann, D., Magidor, M.: Nonmonotonic reasoning, preferential models and cumulative logics. Artif. Intell. **44**(1–2), 167–207 (1990)

37. Lehmann, D., Magidor, M.: What does a conditional knowledge base entail? Artif. Intell. **55**, 1–60 (1992)
38. Lehmann, D.: Another perspective on default reasoning. Ann. Math. Artif. Intell. **15**(1), 61–82 (1995)
39. Lewis, D.: Counterfactuals. Harvard University Press, Cambridge (1973)
40. Pearl, J.: System Z: a natural ordering of defaults with tractable applications to nonmonotonic reasoning. In: Proceedings of the 3rd Conference on Theoretical Aspects of Reasoning About Knowledge (TARK 1990), pp. 121–135. Morgan Kaufmann Publication Inc., San Francisco, CA, USA (1990)
41. Spohn, W.: Ordinal conditional functions: a dynamic theory of epistemic states. In: Harper, W., Skyrms, B. (eds.) Causation in Decision, Belief Change, and Statistics, II, pp. 105–134. Kluwer Academic Publishers (1988)
42. Spohn, W.: The Laws of Belief: Ranking Theory and Its Philosophical Applications. Oxford University Press, Oxford (2012)

Non-deterministic Algorithms – Capture By Abstract State Machines

Klaus-Dieter Schewe[1(✉)] and Flavio Ferrarotti[2]

[1] Linz, Austria
kd.schewe@gmail.com

[2] Software Competence Center Hagenberg, Hagenberg im Mühlkreis, Austria
flavio.ferrarotti@scch.at

Abstract. An axiomatic definition of non-deterministic algorithms by four postulates is motivated covering branching time, abstract states, background and bounded exploration with a slicing condition. Then it is shown that Abstract State Machines with choice rules specify such algorithms. Furthermore, a proof is given that every algorithm as stipulated by the postulates can always be step-by-step simulated by a behaviourally equivalent ASM with the same signature and background. This behavioural theory is rounded up by discussing special cases, where parallelism, choices or both are bounded, which in all cases is captured by a simplification of the bounded exploration postulate.

Keywords: behavioural theory · non-deterministic algorithm · bounded exploration · slicing · Abstract State Machine

1 Introduction

Over the last 40 years the Abstract State Machines (ASMs) method has achieved remarkable results in the effective and efficient development of provably correct soft- and hardware systems. Ferrarotti et al. present a historical survey in [10]. In this they also emphasise that the origins of the ASM method lie in the theory of computation starting with Gurevich's "new thesis", which aimed to sharpen Church's thesis [16]. According to this thesis every computational system can be faithfully simulated by an appropriate dynamic structure taking also the finiteness of resources into account. These dynamic structures became known as *evolving algebras* with a first full description in the Lipari guide [17]. After several successful applications in practice evolving algebras were renamed as ASMs to emphasise the focus on abstract states defined by Tarski structures that are subject of changes by means of machines with finite control as elaborated in detail in the ASM book [9].

Going one step further the new thesis became subject of mathematical proofs. For these it is necessary to provide first a precise definition of some class of computational systems. This was first done for sequential algorithms [18], which

A. Raschke et al. (Eds.): Egon Börger Festschrift, LNCS 16580, pp. 398–417, 2026.
https://doi.org/10.1007/978-3-032-24494-9_19

are defined axiomatically by three postulates comprising sequential time requiring that algorithms have states and a state transition function, abstract states requiring that states are universal algebras over some signature plus closure under isomorphisms, and bounded exploration requiring the existence of a set W of ground terms—called *bounded exploration witness*—such that the update sets that characterise state transitions are uniquely determined by the values of the terms in W. There is an implicit fourth *background* postulate requiring that a value *undef* as well as truth values and the usual operators on them are available in the base set of every state.

The proof that sequential ASMs capture the class of sequential algorithms motivated the notion of *behavioural theories*. In general, a behavioural theory provides an abstract definition of a class of computational systems by a set of postulates, a definition of an abstract machine model, and the proof that the class of algorithms is captured by the abstract machine model. That is, each instance of the machine model satisfies the postulates, and conversely, each algorithm in the class as stipulated by the postulates can be step-by-step simulated by a behaviourally equivalent abstract machine. In this way Gurevich's seminal "sequential ASM thesis" is the behavioural theory of sequential algorithms, the ur-instance of behavioural theories.

The ideas underlying the sequential ASM thesis have been generalised to various other classes of algorithms starting with parallel algorithms that are captured by parallel ASMs with the main extension by unbounded parallelism [1,2]. The thesis also makes use of elaborated background structures [3]. The original "parallel ASM thesis" proven by Blass and Gurevich was simplified by Ferrarotti et al. [12], who developed a different axiomatisation with only four postulates capturing again *sequential time*, *abstract states*, *background* and *bounded exploration*. The key feature is the use of multiset comprehension terms in the definition of bounded exploration witnesses. Other behavioural theories cover recursive algorithms [8], concurrent algorithms [4], bulk synchronous parallel algorithms [13], and reflective sequential and parallel algorithms [19,20].

The abstract machine model in each of these behavioural theories, i.e. a specific class of ASMs, can be used directly for rigorous specifications as shown in the ASM book [9], which has been complemented by the modelling companion [7] featuring among others ambient and concurrent ASMs, and a monograph on structures of computing [6] featuring among others reflection in programming languages. Specifications with ASMs are further subjected to rigorous and flexible refinement [5].

However, these behavioural theories do not cover non-deterministic or random algorithms with the exception of a small add-on to the theory of sequential algorithms [18] showing that sequential ASMs extended by bounded choice capture bounded choice non-deterministic algorithms, i.e. algorithms, where choices depend on the algorithm, but not on the state. The only changes to the postulates is the replacement of the sequential time postulate by a branching time postulate, and a corresponding extension to the abstract state postulate. Furthermore, concurrent algorithms are non-deterministic as a result of unpredictable start- and end-times of the steps of agents, though each agent may behave deterministically [4].

Gurevich provides several arguments, why non-determinism should be considered relevant for algorithms not only as high-level abstraction. Most importantly he argues that choices are de facto made by the environment rather than the algorithm itself. We may add another justification for non-determinism: for problem solving algorithms, in particular for decision problems, non-determinism can be seen as search with the possibility of backtracking in case a chosen direction of the algorithm does not lead to success.

Contribution. This article is dedicated to a behavioural theory of (single-agent) non-deterministic algorithms. We start from the simplified parallel ASM thesis [12] and discuss what needs to be changed to cover also unbounded choices. In addition to branching time and small changes to the abstract states the key difference will concern bounded exploration witnesses, which become sets of multiset comprehension terms, where the terms are again multiset comprehension terms. We will then show that non-deterministic algorithms as stipulated by these postulates are captured by non-deterministic ASMs. For this we will exploit the deep results about indistinguishable update tuples in the simplified parallel ASM thesis. Based on this result we will investigate also the special cases, where parallelism or choices or both are bounded. All cases lead to a simplification of the bounded exploration postulate, in the last case being equivalent to Gurevich's result.

Organisation of the Article. Section 2 is dedicated to the definition and motivation of the four postulates by means of which we define non-deterministic algorithms. In Sect. 3 we recall basic definitions of non-deterministic ASMs. In Sect. 4 we first prove that non-deterministic ASMs always satisfy the postulates, i.e. they define non-deterministic algorithms as stipulated by the postulates. We also prove the converse that each non-deterministic algorithm can be step-by-step simulated by a behaviourally equivalent ASM. To some extent we can exploit results from the simplified parallel ASM thesis [12]. In Sect. 5 we discuss special cases, when parallelism or choices are bounded and independent from states. We conclude with a brief summary in Sect. 6.

2 Defining Postulates for Non-deterministic Algorithms

We start with motivating and defining postulates that define the class of non-deterministic algorithms. In all existing behavioural theories for sequential, parallel, concurrent algorithms and others we assume that an algorithm $\mathcal{A}$ comprises a set $\mathcal{S}$ of states, a subset $\mathcal{I} \subseteq \mathcal{S}$ of initial states and a state transition function τ. As non-deterministic algorithms involve choices, we must have a *state transition relation* $\tau \subseteq \mathcal{S} \times \mathcal{S}$ instead. This defines the following first postulate for non-deterministic algorithms.

Postulate 1 (Branching Time). A non-deterministic algorithm $\mathcal{A}$ comprises a set of states $\mathcal{S}$, a set of initial states $\mathcal{I} \subseteq \mathcal{S}$ and a state transition relation $\tau \subseteq \mathcal{S} \times \mathcal{S}$.

Then for states S and S' with $\tau(S, S')$ we call S' a *successor state* of S. Let $\tau(S) = \{S' \mid (S, S') \in \tau\}$ denote the set of successor states of the state S. With Postulate 1 we already get the definition of a *run* of $\mathcal{A}$ as a sequence of states $S_0, S_1, \dots$ with $S_0 \in \mathcal{I}$ and $\tau(S_i, S_{i+1})$ for all $i \geq 0$. Algorithms $\mathcal{A}$ and $\mathcal{A}'$ with the same runs are called *behaviourally equivalent.*

We can preserve the notion of state from the parallel ASM thesis [1,12]. For this consider a *signature* Υ, i.e. a finite set of function symbols, where each $f \in \Upsilon$ has some fixed arity n_f. Given a set B, we can define a *structure* S over Υ as a family of functions $f_S : B^{n_f} \to B$ (for all $f \in \Upsilon$). Then B is called the *base set* of the structure S. In order to permit also partial functions, we can simply assume the presence of a special value $\mathit{undef} \in B$ and request $f_S(b_1, \dots, b_{n_f}) = \mathit{undef}$, whenever one of the b_i is undef.

An *isomorphism* between Υ-structures S and S' is a bijection $\sigma : B \to B'$ between the corresponding base sets with $\sigma(\mathit{undef}) = \mathit{undef}$ such that $f_{S'}(\sigma(b_1), \dots, \sigma(b_{n_f})) = \sigma(f_S(b_1, \dots, b_{n_f}))$ holds for all $b_1, \dots, b_{n_f} \in B$. With this we can formulate the following second postulate for non-deterministic algorithms.

Postulate 2 (Abstract State). There exists a signature Υ such that all states $S \in \mathcal{S}$ of a non-deterministic algorithm $\mathcal{A}$ are Υ-structures, and the sets $\mathcal{S}, \mathcal{I}$ are closed under isomorphisms. Whenever $\tau(S, S')$ holds, the states S and S' have the same base set. For any isomorphism σ defined on state S, whenever $\tau(S, S')$ holds we also get $\tau(\sigma(S), \sigma(S'))$.

With Postulate 2 we already get the means to analyse differences between states, for which we use the notion of update sets. For a function symbol $f \in \Upsilon$ of arity n and values $b_1, \dots, b_n \in B$ for the base set B of some state S we call the pair $\ell = (f, (b_1, \dots, b_n))$ a *location* of S, and $b_0 = f_S(b_1, \dots, b_n)$ is called the *value* of this location in S, which we also denote as $\mathrm{val}_S(\ell)$. An *update* in S is a pair (ℓ, v) with a location ℓ of S and a value $v \in B$.

An *update set* in S is a set of such updates. An update set Δ in S is called *consistent* iff for all $(\ell, v_1), (\ell, v_2) \in \Delta$ we have $v_1 = v_2$, in other words, there can only be a unique update value for any location. For consistent Δ we define the state $S' = S + \Delta$ by $\mathrm{val}_{S'}(\ell) = v$ for $(\ell, v) \in \Delta$ and $\mathrm{val}_{S'}(\ell) = \mathrm{val}_S(\ell)$ for all other locations. We extend this definition by $S + \Delta = S$ for inconsistent Δ. The following lemma is well known [18, Lemma 5.1].

Lemma 2.1. *For any two states S, S' with the same base set B there exists a unique minimal consistent update set $\Delta(S, S')$ with $S' = S + \Delta(S, S')$.*

As we are dealing with algorithms, we must ensure that update sets are always finite. As discussed in the context of the logic of parallel ASMs [14] this can be formally achieved by exploiting meta-finite structures [15]. With finite update sets it will always be the case that almost all locations in states of some run have the same value as in the initial state of that run.

For the remainder of this article let $\boldsymbol{\Delta}(S) = \{\Delta(S, S') \mid \tau(S, S')\}$ denote the *set of update sets* on the state S. Each $\Delta \in \boldsymbol{\Delta}(S)$ defines a successor state $S' = S + \Delta$ of the state S and vice versa.

In every algorithm we make implicit assumptions about values in base sets and functions on them that are available in every state. In existing behavioural theories we refer to this as the *background*. For instance, we already mentioned the value *undef*. Backgrounds in general have been investigated in depth by Blass and Gurevich [3]. For non-deterministic algorithms we can stick to the same background requirements as used for synchronous parallel algorithms [12], which leads to the following third postulate.

Postulate 3 (Background). Each state contains:

- truth values **true** and **false** and the Boolean operations on them;
- a special value *undef*;
- the equality predicate =;
- all ordered pairs as well as binary function symbols (x, y) for pairing and unary projection functions π_1, π_2 for extracting the first and second components of a pair;
- all finite multisets together the empty multiset $\langle\rangle$, singletons $\langle x\rangle$, binary sum $x \oplus y$, and general sum $\bigoplus x$ as well as functions *TheUnique* and *AsSet*.

In a multiset $x \oplus y$ the multiplicity of a value v is the sum of the multiplicities of v in x and y, respectively. Analogously, the multiplicity of a value v in $\bigoplus x$, where x is a multiset of multisets, is the sum of all multiplicities in the elements of x; otherwise the general sum is not defined. We have $\mathit{TheUnique}(\langle x\rangle) = x$ and $\mathit{TheUnique}(x) = \mathit{undef}$ for all x that are not singleton multisets. $\mathit{AsSet}(x)$ is the multiset that has the same elements as the multiset x, but all with multiplicity 1 (so this multiset is in fact a set).

The decisive observation underlying the sequential ASM thesis [18] as well as the (simplified) parallel ASM thesis [12] is that the behaviour of a sequential or parallel algorithm, respectively, is completely determined by some finite specification. This specification must contain terms defined over the signature Υ, which are evaluated in a state in order to build the successor state. Hence there must exist a finite set of terms—ground terms in the case of the sequential thesis, multiset comprehension terms in case of the parallel thesis—that determine the update set, the application of which will result in the successor state.

For non-deterministic algorithms the same argument applies with the difference that there are several successor states. The evaluation of multiset comprehension terms in a state gives rise to a multiset, and the varying size of these can be exploited to capture unbounded parallelism, where the number of parallel branches depends on the state. Then multiset comprehension terms could also capture the varying number of possible successor states. We therefore define *witness terms* as a double multiset comprehension terms of the form

$$\alpha = \langle \beta(y_1, \dots, y_q) \mid \psi(y_1, \dots, y_q) \rangle \ , \tag{1}$$

where $\beta(y_1, \dots, y_q)$ is a multiset comprehension term of the form

$$\beta(y_1, \dots, y_q) = \langle (t_0, \dots, t_n) \mid \varphi(x_1, \dots, x_r, y_1, \dots, y_q) \rangle \ ,$$

where the x_i and y_j are the only variables appearing in the terms t_k.

Informally, the inner condition φ is meant to capture parallelism, whereas the outer condition ψ is to capture choices. In order to distinguish these options from each other, we consider the effect of strengthening conditions for parallel branches or choices. In the case of parallelism the number of parallel branches can be reduced and consequently update sets would be reduced to subsets, while the number of update sets remains unchanged. In the case of choice update sets could only be discarded as a whole. Therefore, we consider *sliced witness terms* of the form

$$\alpha' = \langle \beta(y_1, \dots, y_q) \mid \psi(y_1, \dots, y_q) \wedge \chi(y_1, \dots, y_q) \rangle \tag{2}$$

with some condition χ for a witness term α as in (1). The only requirement for the condition χ is that the set of its free variables is a subset of the set of free variables of ψ. With this we get the following fourth postulate for non-deterministic algorithms.

Postulate 4 (Bounded Exploration). For a non-deterministic algorithm $\mathcal{A}$ there exists a finite set W of witness terms such that for all states S, S' that coincide on W, i.e. $\text{val}_S(\alpha) = \text{val}_{S'}(\alpha)$ holds for all $\alpha \in W$, we have $\boldsymbol{\Delta}(S) = \boldsymbol{\Delta}(S')$. In addition, if W is replaced by W' containing sliced witness terms α' for all $\alpha \in W$, then this defines another non-deterministic algorithm $\mathcal{A}'$ with the same signature and background as $\mathcal{A}$ such that $\boldsymbol{\Delta}^{\mathcal{A}'}(S) \subseteq \boldsymbol{\Delta}^{\mathcal{A}}(S)$ holds for all states S.

Here we use superscripts $\mathcal{A}$ and $\mathcal{A}'$, respectively, to distinguish between sets of update sets associated with $\mathcal{A}$ and $\mathcal{A}'$. The set W of witness terms will be called a *bounded exploration witness.* Note that the slicing preserves the states, but reduces the successor states and consequently also the runs, which is what we should expect if we restrict choices.

3 Abstract State Machines

We use non-deterministic Abstract State Machines (ASMs) as defined in [9] with background extensions as in [12] as the abstract machine model in our theory. We recall a few basic definitions, then show that ASMs define non-deterministic algorithms.

States of a (non-deterministic) ASM M result from the interpretation of a signature Υ, which is defined as in the previous section. The interpretation comprises a base set B as well as functions $f_S : B^{n_f} \to B$ for all function symbols $f \in \Upsilon$, where n_f denotes the arity of f. We also require that M has a background, which contains truth values **true** and **false**, a special value *undef*, and non-negative integers. Each base set B used to define states must contain these values, and $f_S(b_1, \dots, b_{n_f}) = \mathit{undef}$ must hold, whenever at least one of the values $b_i \in B$ is *undef*. Furthermore, base sets must be closed under a finite multiset constructor $\langle \cdot \rangle$ and under pairing $(\cdot)$. The empty multiset $\langle\rangle$ must also be an element of B.

In this way we obtain the set $\mathcal{S}$ of all states of M, for which we further request closure under isomorphisms. Certain states in $\mathcal{S}$ are declared to be initial states, which defines a set $\mathcal{I}$ of initial states, for which we request also closure under isomorphisms. The background of M further contains the equality predicate $=$, the Boolean operators on truth values, the basic arithmetic operators on integers, the projection operator π_i for pairs, and the multiset operators $\oplus$ for binary sums, $\bigoplus$ for general sum, as well as functions *TheUnique* and *AsSet*.

Then the signature Υ of M, the background of M and an arbitrary set V of variables define the set of *terms* of M in the usual way. This includes tuple terms defined as shortcuts for nested pairing and multiset comprehension terms $\langle t(x_1, \dots, x_n) \mid \varphi(x_1, \dots, x_n) \rangle$ with variables x_i and terms t and φ; the latter one should be Boolean, i.e. its evaluation in a state with respect to a given variable assignment should result in a truth value. Let $\mathbb{T}_M(V)$ denote the set of terms of M with variables in V. For every term t the *set* $fr(t)$ *of free variables* is defined as usual. State transitions of M are defined by means of rules as follows:

- ***skip*** is a rule, called *skip rule*.
- For $f \in \Upsilon$ and terms $t_0, t_1, \dots, t_{n_f}$ the expression $f(t_1, \dots, t_{n_f}) := t_0$ is a rule, called *assignment rule*.
- For a Boolean term φ and rules r_1 and r_2 the expression

$$\textbf{if } \varphi \textbf{ then } r_1 \textbf{ else } r_2$$

  is a rule, called *conditional rule*.
- For a Boolean term φ with free variables $x_1, \dots, x_k$ and a rule r with free variables among the x_i the expression

$$\textbf{forall } x_1, \dots, x_k : \varphi(x_1, \dots, x_k) \textbf{ do } r(x_1, \dots, x_k)$$

  is a rule, called *parallel rule*.
- For a Boolean term ψ with free variables $x_1, \dots, x_k$ and a rule r with free variable among the $x_1, \dots, x_k$ the expression

$$\textbf{choose } x_1, \dots, x_k : \psi(x_1, \dots, x_k) \textbf{ do } r(x_1, \dots, x_k)$$

  is a rule, called *choice rule*.

In order to avoid ambiguities the free use of parentheses is permitted. Furthermore, common shortcuts can be used, e.g. omitting **else** r_2 for the case of a skip rule r_2. The set of *free variables* in a rule is defined as usual. The semantics of rules is defined by a set of update sets $\boldsymbol{\Delta}_{r,\sigma}(S)$ for a state S with base set B and a variable assignment $\sigma : V \to B$:

- For a skip rule we have $\boldsymbol{\Delta}_{skip,\sigma}(S) = \{\emptyset\}$.
- For an assignment rule $f(t_1, \dots, t_{n_f}) := t_0$ we have $\boldsymbol{\Delta}_{r,\sigma}(S) = \{\Delta\}$ with $\Delta = \{((f, (\text{val}_{S,\sigma}(t_1), \dots, \text{val}_{S,\sigma}(t_{n_f}))), \text{val}_{S,\sigma}(t_0))\}$.
- For a conditional rule **if** φ **then** r_1 **else** r_2 we have $\boldsymbol{\Delta}_{r,\sigma}(S) = \boldsymbol{\Delta}_{r_1,\sigma}(S)$ in case $\text{val}_{S,\sigma}(\varphi) = \textbf{true}$ holds, and $\boldsymbol{\Delta}_{r,\sigma}(S) = \boldsymbol{\Delta}_{r_2,\sigma}(S)$ otherwise.
- For a parallel rule **forall** $x_1, \dots, x_k : \varphi(x_1, \dots, x_k)$ **do** $r'(x_1, \dots, x_k)$ we have

$$\boldsymbol{\Delta}_{r,\sigma}(S) = \Big\{ \bigcup_{\substack{(a_1,\dots,a_k) \\ \text{val}_{S,\sigma[x_1 \mapsto a_1,\dots,x_k \mapsto a_k]}(\varphi)=\textbf{true}}} \Delta_{(a_1,\dots,a_k)} \mid \Delta_{(a_1,\dots,a_k)} \in \boldsymbol{\Delta}_{r',\sigma[x_1 \mapsto a_1,\dots,x_k \mapsto a_k]}(S) \text{ for all } (a_1, \dots, a_k) \text{ with } \text{val}_{S,\sigma[x_1 \mapsto a_1,\dots,x_k \mapsto a_k]}(\varphi) = \textbf{true} \Big\} .$$

- For a choice rule **choose** $x_1, \dots, x_k : \psi(x_1, \dots, x_k)$ **do** $r'(x_1, \dots, x_k)$ we have

$$\boldsymbol{\Delta}_{r,\sigma}(S) = \bigcup_{\substack{(a_1,\dots,a_k) \\ \text{val}_{S,\sigma[x_1 \mapsto a_1,\dots,x_k \mapsto a_k]}(\psi)=\textbf{true}}} \boldsymbol{\Delta}_{r',\sigma[x_1 \mapsto a_1,\dots,x_k \mapsto a_k]}(S) .$$

Then a non-deterministic ASM M comprises a background as defined above, a signature Υ defining the set $\mathcal{S}$ of states and the subset $\mathcal{I}$ of initial states, and a closed rule r. This defines the state transition relation τ_M of M with $\tau_M(S, S')$ iff there exists some update set[1] $\Delta \in \boldsymbol{\Delta}_r(S)$ with $S + \Delta = S'$.

4 The Non-deterministic ASM Thesis

We will now address the capture of non-deterministic algorithms by ASMs. First we show that the algorithms defined by non-deterministic ASMs define algorithms as stipulated by Postulates 1–4. Then we proceed showing also the converse of Theorem 4.1.

Theorem 4.1 (Plausibility). *Every non-deterministic ASM satisfies the defining postulates for non-deterministic algorithms.*

Proof. The requirements of the abstract state and background postulates are built into the definition of non-deterministic ASMs, so there is nothing to show. In particular, the sets $\mathcal{S}$ and $\mathcal{I}$ of states and initial states of M are well-defined. Furthermore, τ_M defines the state transition relation, which shows the branching time postulate.

So it remains to show the satisfaction of the bounded exploration postulate. For this we construct a standard bounded exploration witness W_r from the rule r of M. This is done by structural recursion as follows:

[1] We can omit the variable assignment σ, because the rule r is closed.

(1) If r is a **skip** rule, then we have $W_r = \{\langle\langle () \mid \mathbf{true}\rangle \mid \mathbf{true}\rangle\}$.
(2) If r is an assignment rule $f(t_1,\dots,t_n) := t_0$, then we have

$$W_r = \{\langle\langle (t_0,\dots,t_n) \mid \mathbf{true}\rangle \mid \mathbf{true}\rangle\} .$$

(3) If r is a conditional rule **if** φ **then** r_1 **else** r_2, we have

$$W_r = \Big\{\langle\langle \varphi \mid \mathbf{true}\rangle \mid \mathbf{true}\rangle\Big\} \cup \Big\{\langle\langle t \mid \psi \wedge \varphi\rangle \mid \chi\rangle \mid \langle\langle t \mid \psi\rangle \mid \chi\rangle \in W_{r_1}\Big\}$$
$$\cup \Big\{\langle\langle t \mid \psi \wedge \neg\varphi\rangle \mid \chi\rangle \mid \langle\langle t \mid \psi\rangle \mid \chi\rangle \in W_{r_2}\Big\} .$$

(4) If r is a parallel rule **forall** $x_1,\dots,x_k : \varphi$ **do** $r'(x_1,\dots,x_k)$, we have

$$W_r = \Big\{\langle\langle t \mid \psi \wedge \varphi(x_1,\dots,x_k)\rangle \mid \chi\rangle \mid \langle\langle t \mid \psi\rangle \mid \chi\rangle \in W_{r'(x_1,\dots,x_k)}\Big\}$$
$$\cup \Big\{\langle\langle \varphi(x_1,\dots,x_k) \mid \mathbf{true}\rangle \mid \mathbf{true}\rangle\Big\} .$$

(5) If r is a choice rule **choose** $x_1,\dots,x_k : \varphi$ **do** r', we have

$$W_r = \Big\{\langle\langle t \mid \psi\rangle \mid \chi \wedge \varphi(x_1,\dots,x_k)\rangle \mid \langle\langle t \mid \psi\rangle \mid \chi\rangle \in W_{r'(x_1,\dots,x_k)}\Big\}$$
$$\cup \Big\{\langle\langle \varphi(x_1,\dots,x_k) \mid \mathbf{true}\rangle \mid \mathbf{true}\rangle\Big\} .$$

We first show that states that coincide on W yield the same sets of update sets. For this we use structural induction on the rule r, so let S_1 and S_2 be two states of M and let $\zeta : V \to B$ be a variable assignment on the set V of free variables of a rule r. Assume that with ζ the states S_1, S_2 coincide on W.

(1) Let r be a **skip** rule. Then we always have $\boldsymbol{\Delta}_{r,\zeta}(S_1) = \{\emptyset\} = \boldsymbol{\Delta}_{r,\zeta}(S_2)$.
(2) If r is an assignment rule $f(t_1,\dots,t_n) := t_0$ with $V = \bigcup_{0\le i\le n} fr(t_i)$, we get

$$\mathrm{val}_{S_i,\zeta}(\langle\langle (t_0,\dots,t_n) \mid \mathbf{true}\rangle \mid \mathbf{true}\rangle) = \langle\langle (\mathrm{val}_{S_i,\zeta}(t_0),\dots,\mathrm{val}_{S_i,\zeta}(t_n))\rangle\rangle .$$

Consider the locations $\ell_i = (f, (\mathrm{val}_{S_i,\zeta}(t_1),\dots,\mathrm{val}_{S_i,\zeta}(t_n)))$ and the values $b_i = \mathrm{val}_{S_i,\zeta}(t_0)$. As S_1 and S_2 coincide on W_r using ζ, we have $\ell_1 = \ell_2$ and $b_1 = b_2$, hence $\boldsymbol{\Delta}_{r,\zeta}(S_1) = \{\{(\ell_1, b_1)\}\} = \{\{(\ell_2, b_2)\}\} = \boldsymbol{\Delta}_{r,\zeta}(S_2)$.
(3) Let r be a conditional rule **if** φ **then** r_1 **else** r_2, and let $V_0 = fr(\varphi)$, $V_1 = fr(r_1)$ and $V_2 = fr(r_2)$. Let $\zeta : V_0 \cup V_1 \cup V_2 \to B$ be a variable assignment. As $\langle\langle \varphi \mid \mathbf{true}\rangle \mid \mathbf{true}\rangle \in W_r$, we have $val_{S_i,\zeta}(\varphi) = \mathbf{true}$ for both $i \in \{1,2\}$ or $val_{S_i,\zeta}(\varphi) = \mathbf{false}$ for both $i \in \{1,2\}$.
Condider the first case. Then with ζ S_1, S_2 coincide on $\langle\langle t \mid \psi \wedge \varphi\rangle \mid \chi\rangle$ for all $\langle\langle t \mid \psi\rangle \mid \chi\rangle \in W_{r_1}$, hence they also coincide on W_{r_1}. By induction $\boldsymbol{\Delta}_{r_1,\zeta}(S_1) = \boldsymbol{\Delta}_{r_1,\zeta}(S_2)$, and by definition $\boldsymbol{\Delta}_{r,\zeta}(S_i) = \boldsymbol{\Delta}_{r_1,\zeta}(S_i)$ holds, from which the claim follows immediately.
Analogously, in the second case S_1, S_2 coincide on $\langle\langle t \mid \psi \wedge \neg\varphi\rangle \mid \chi\rangle$ for all $\langle\langle t \mid \psi\rangle \mid \chi\rangle \in W_{r_2}$, hence they also coincide on W_{r_2}. By induction $\boldsymbol{\Delta}_{r_2,\zeta}(S_1) = \boldsymbol{\Delta}_{r_2,\zeta}(S_2)$, and by definition $\boldsymbol{\Delta}_{r,\zeta}(S_i) = \boldsymbol{\Delta}_{r_2,\zeta}(S_i)$ holds, from which the claim follows immediately.

(4) Let r be a parallel rule **forall** $x_1, \dots, x_k : \varphi$ **do** $r'(x_1, \dots, x_k)$, and for $V_0 = fr(t)$ and $V = fr(r(v))$ let $\zeta : (V \cup V_0) - \{v\} \to B$ be a variable assignment. As $\langle\langle \varphi(x_1, \dots, x_k) \mid \mathbf{true} \rangle \mid \mathbf{true} \rangle \in W_r$, we have that

$$B = \{(a_1, \dots, a_k) \mid val_{S_i, \zeta[x_1 \mapsto a_1, \dots, x_k \mapsto a_k]}(\varphi) = \mathbf{true}\}$$

is the same set of tuples for both $i \in \{1, 2\}$.
As S_1, S_2 with ζ coincide on $\langle\langle t \mid \psi \wedge \varphi(x_1, \dots, x_k) \rangle \mid \chi \rangle$ for all $\langle\langle t \mid \psi \rangle \mid \chi \rangle \in W_{r'(x_1, \dots, x_k)}$, they also coincide on $W_{r'(a_1, \dots, a_k)}$ for all $(a_1, \dots, a_k) \in B$. Hence by induction we have $\boldsymbol{\Delta}_{r'(a_1, \dots, a_k)}(S_1) = \boldsymbol{\Delta}_{r'(a_1, \dots, a_k)}(S_2)$ for all $(a_1, \dots, a_k) \in B$. By definition

$$\boldsymbol{\Delta}_{r,\zeta}(S_i) = \Big\{ \bigcup_{(a_1, \dots, a_k) \in B} \Delta_{(a_1, \dots, a_k)} \mid \Delta_{(a_1, \dots, a_k)} \in \boldsymbol{\Delta}_{r'(a_1, \dots, a_k)}(S_i) \Big\}$$

for $i \in \{1, 2\}$, which immediately implies the claim.

(5) Let r be a choice rule **choose** $x_1, \dots, x_k : \varphi$ **do** r' with $V_0 = fr(t)$, $V = fr(r(v))$, and let $\zeta : (V \cup V_0) - \{v\} \to B$ be a variable assignment. As in the previous case we have $\langle\langle \varphi(x_1, \dots, x_k) \mid \mathbf{true} \rangle \mid \mathbf{true} \rangle \in W_r$, and hence the set

$$B = \{(a_1, \dots, a_k) \mid val_{S_i, \zeta[x_1 \mapsto a_1, \dots, x_k \mapsto a_k]}(\varphi) = \mathbf{true}\}$$

of tuples is the same for both $i \in \{1, 2\}$.
As S_1, S_2 with ζ coincide on $\langle\langle t \mid \psi \rangle \mid \chi \wedge \varphi(x_1, \dots, x_k) \rangle$ for all $\langle\langle t \mid \psi \rangle \mid \chi \rangle \in W_{r'(x_1, \dots, x_k)}$, they also coincide on $W_{r'(a_1, \dots, a_k)}$ for all $(a_1, \dots, a_k) \in B$. By induction we get $\boldsymbol{\Delta}_{r'(a_1, \dots, a_k)}(S_1) = \boldsymbol{\Delta}_{r'(a_1, \dots, a_k)}(S_2)$ for all $(a_1, \dots, a_k) \in B$. By definition

$$\boldsymbol{\Delta}_{r,\zeta}(S_i) = \bigcup_{(a_1, \dots, a_k) \in B} \boldsymbol{\Delta}_{r'(a_1, \dots, a_k)}(S_i)$$

for $i \in \{1, 2\}$, which immediately implies the claim.

Concerning the slicing condition in Postulate 4 any slicing of a witness term $\alpha \in W_r$ corresponds to a strengthening of a choice subrule by replacing the condition $\psi(y_1, \dots, y_q)$ by $\psi(y_1, \dots, y_q) \wedge \chi(y_1, \dots, y_q)$. Hence we obtain a modified rule r', and the ASM defined by this rule yields sets of update sets $\boldsymbol{\Delta}_{r'}(S) \subseteq \boldsymbol{\Delta}_r(S)$. □

Theorem 4.2 (Capture). *For every non-deterministic algorithm $\mathcal{A}$ there exists a behaviourally equivalent ASM M.*

For the proof of this theorem we want to exploit as much as possible the related behavioural theory of parallel algorithms [12], so we summarise a few essential results without repeating the proofs. A *parallel algorithm* is defined by for postulates:

Sequential Time. A parallel algorithm $\mathcal{A}$ has a set $\mathcal{S}$ of states, a set $\mathcal{I} \subseteq \mathcal{S}$ of initial states, and a state transition function $\tau : \mathcal{S} \to \mathcal{S}$.

Abstract State. There exists a signature Υ such that all states $S \in \mathcal{S}$ are Υ-structures. The sets $\mathcal{S}$ and $\mathcal{I}$ are closed under isomorphisms. The successor state $\tau(S)$ of every state S has the same base set as S. Any isomorphism between states S and S' is also an isomorphism between $\tau(S)$ and $\tau(S')$.

Background. The background requirements are the same as in Postulate 3.

Bounded Exploration. There exists a finite set W of multiset comprehension terms of the form $\alpha = \langle (t_1, \dots, t_n) \mid \varphi \rangle$ such that for all states S, S' that coincide on W we have $\Delta_{\mathcal{A}}(S) = \Delta_{\mathcal{A}}(S')$, where $\Delta_{\mathcal{A}}(S)$ is the unique minimal consistent update set with $\tau(S) = S + \Delta(S)$ (see Lemma 2.1).

If we fix a *bounded exploration witness* W, assuming without loss of generality that W is closed under subterms, then for every state S and $\alpha \in W$ we obtain a multiset $\text{val}_S(\alpha)$ of tuples of values of the base set of S. Any $b \in B$ that appears in one such tuple is called a *critical value* in state S. A tuple of such critical values is called a *critical tuple*. The following sequence of lemmata was proven in [12].

Lemma 4.1 **([12, Lemma 7.1]).** *For every state S, if $((f,(a_1,\dots,a_n)),a_0)$ is an update in $\Delta_{\mathcal{A}}(S)$, then $\bar{a} = (a_0,\dots,a_n)$ is a critical tuple in S.*

Lemma 4.2 **([12, Lemma 7.5]).** *Let $\mathcal{A}$ be a parallel algorithm, S a state of $\mathcal{A}$, and let $\bar{a} = (a_0,\dots,a_r)$, and let $(f,(a_1,\dots,a_r),a_0) \in \Delta_{\mathcal{A}}(S)$. For every $(r+1)$-tuple of critical values $\bar{b} = (b_0,\dots,b_r)$ with $tp^{\mathrm{FO}_{wo=}}_{S|_W}(\bar{b}) = tp^{\mathrm{FO}_{wo=}}_{S|_W}(\bar{a})$ the update $(f,(b_1,\dots,b_r),b_0)$ also belongs to $\Delta_{\mathcal{A}}(S)$.*

Here $S|_W$ denotes a relational structure defined by the bounded exploration witness W of $\mathcal{A}$. The vocabulary of $S|_W$ is $\Sigma_W = \{R_{\alpha_1},\dots,R_{\alpha_m}\}$ for $W = \{\alpha_1,\dots,\alpha_m\}$. For $\alpha_i = \langle (t_0,\dots,t_n) \mid \varphi_i(x_1,\dots,x_r)\rangle$ the relation symbol R_{α_i} has arity $n+2$ and the following interpretation:

$$\begin{aligned} R^{S|_W}_{\alpha_i} = \{(b_0,\dots,b_{n_i}, j\cdot b_0\cdots b_{n_i}\cdot a_1\cdots a_{r_i}) \mid{} & (a_1,\dots,a_{r_i}) \in B^{r_i},\\ & \mathbf{S} \models \varphi_i(x_1,\dots,x_{r_i})[a_1,\dots,a_{r_i}] \text{ and}\\ & \text{val}_{S,\mu[x_1\mapsto a_1,\dots,x_{r_i}\mapsto a_{r_i}]}(t_0) = b_0,\dots,\text{val}_{\mathbf{S},\mu[x_1\mapsto a_1,\dots,x_{r_i}\mapsto a_{r_i}]}(t_{n_i}) = b_{n_i}\}, \end{aligned}$$

where $j\cdot b_0\cdots b_{n_i}\cdot a_1\cdots a_{r_i}$ denotes a value in B such that the set of these values for fixed $b_0,\dots,b_{n_i}$ is in one-one correspondence to the set of tuples $(a_1,\dots,a_{r_i})$ satisfying the required conditions for the evaluation of φ_i and t_k $(0 \le k \le n_i)$. An element a_i belongs to the domain of $S|_W$ iff for some $\alpha_i \in W$ there is a $\bar{a} \in R^{S|_W}_{\alpha_i}(\bar{a})$ such that a_i appears in $\bar{a}$.

Furthermore, $tp^{\mathrm{FO}_{wo=}}_{S|_W}(\bar{a})$ denotes the *type* of the tuple $\bar{a}$ in first-order logic without equality with respect to the structure $S|_W$, i.e. the set of all formulae satisfied by $\bar{a}$ in the structure $S|_W$.

In a nutshell, the lemma states that for every critical tuple $\bar{a}$ that defines an update in some update set any other critical tuple $\bar{b}$ with the same type also defines an update (for the same function symbol f) in the very same update set.

Lemma 4.3 ([12, **Lemma 7.6**]). *For every relational vocabulary Σ with no constants, every finite structure S of schema Σ, every $r \geq 0$ and every r-tuple $\bar{a}$ over S there is a formula $\chi \in tp_S^{\mathrm{FO}_{wo=}}(\bar{a})$ such that for any finite relational structure S' of schema Σ and every r-tuple $\bar{b}$ over S' we have $S' \models \chi[\bar{b}]$ iff $tp_S^{\mathrm{FO}_{wo=}}(\bar{a}) = tp_{S'}^{\mathrm{FO}_{wo=}}(\bar{b})$.*

The formula χ in Lemma 4.3 is called an *isolating formula* of the type $tp_S^{\mathrm{FO}_{wo=}}(\bar{a})$. Given a formula χ which isolates the $\mathrm{FO}_{wo=}$-type of a critical tuple $\bar{a}$ in a critical structure $S|_W$, we can write an equivalent term t_χ which evaluates to true in S only for those tuples which have the same $\mathrm{FO}_{wo=}$-type as $\bar{a}$ in $S|_W$.

Lemma 4.4 ([12, **Lemma 7.7**]). *Let S be a state of a parallel algorithm $\mathcal{A}$ of signature Σ with a bounded exploration witness W and let $\bar{a}$ be an r-tuple in $(S|_W)^r$ and χ an isolating formula for the $\mathrm{FO}_{wo=}$-type of $\bar{a}$ in $S|_W$. Then there is a term t_χ over Σ such that for every $\bar{b} \in (S|_W)^r$ we have*

$$\mathrm{val}_{S,\mu[\bar{x}\mapsto\bar{b}]}(t_\chi) = \mathit{true} \quad \textit{iff} \quad S|_W \models \chi[\bar{b}].$$

The term t_χ in Lemma 4.4 is called an *isolating term* of the type $tp_S^{\mathrm{FO}_{wo=}}(\bar{a})$. With isolating terms we easily obtain a rule r_S with $\Delta_{r_S}(S) = \Delta_{\mathcal{A}}(S)$. The rule r_S is a bounded parallel combination of parallel rules of the form

$$\textbf{forall}\ x_0, x_1, \ldots, x_r : t_\chi^{\bar{a}}(x_0, x_1, \ldots, x_r)\ \textbf{do}\ f(x_1, \ldots, x_r) := x_0$$

for all $\bar{a} = (a_0, a_1, \ldots, a_r) \in (S|_W)^{r+1}$ with $(f, (a_1, \ldots, a_r), a_0) \in \Delta_{\mathcal{A}}(S)$, where $t_\chi^{\bar{a}}(x_0, x_1, \ldots, x_r)$ is an isolating term of the critical tuple $\bar{a}$.

Lemma 4.5 ([12, **Cor. 7.8**]). *If S is a state of the parallel algorithm $\mathcal{A}$ and W is a bounded exploration witness for $\mathcal{A}$, then $\Delta_{r_S}(S) = \Delta_{\mathcal{A}}(S)$.*

We will exploit that these lemmata only depend on the bounded exploration witness W, i.e. a set of multiset comprehension terms, and a critical tuple $\bar{a}$ for it. This generality is what we need for non-deterministic algorithms.

From now on let $\mathcal{A}$ denote again a non-deterministic algorithm as defined by Postulates 1–4. We fix a bounded exploration witness W for $\mathcal{A}$, and without loss of generality we can assume that it is closed under subterms.

First consider a single state S with base set B and the set of update sets $\boldsymbol{\Delta}_{\mathcal{A}}(S)$. For $\alpha \in W$ the evaluation in S yields a multiset of multisets U, where U contains tuples $(b_0, \ldots, b_n)$ of values $b_i \in B$. Each such value b_i is called a *W-critical value* in S, and a *W-critical tuple* is a tuple of W-critical values. First we can show that the values appearing in the updates in one of the update sets in $\boldsymbol{\Delta}_{\mathcal{A}}(S)$ are again critical values.

Lemma 4.6. *For every state S, if $((f, (a_1, \ldots, a_n)), a_0)$ is an update in $\Delta \in \boldsymbol{\Delta}_{\mathcal{A}}(S)$, then $\bar{a} = (a_0, \ldots, a_n)$ is a W-critical tuple in S.*

Proof. Assume that a_i is not W-critical. Then choose a structure S_1 by replacing a_i by a fresh value b without changing anything else. Then S_1 is isomorphic to S and thus a state by Postulate 2.

Let $\alpha \in W$ be a witness term. Then we must have $\text{val}_S(\alpha) = \text{val}_{S_1}(\alpha)$, hence S and S_1 coincide on W. Postulate 4 implies $\boldsymbol{\Delta}_{\mathcal{A}}(S) = \boldsymbol{\Delta}_{\mathcal{A}}(S_1)$ and hence $(f(a_1, \dots, a_n), a_0) \in \Delta \in \boldsymbol{\Delta}_{\mathcal{A}}(S_1)$. However, a_i does not appear in the structure S_1 and thus cannot appear in $\Delta \in \boldsymbol{\Delta}_{\mathcal{A}}(S_1)$, which gives a contradiction. □

The slicing condition in Postulate 4 ensures that there exists a set W' of sliced witness terms such that for the corresponding algorithm $\mathcal{A}'$ we get $\boldsymbol{\Delta}_{\mathcal{A}'}(S) = \{\Delta\}$. If $\alpha = \langle \beta(y_1, \dots, y_q) \mid \psi(y_1, \dots, y_q) \rangle \in W$ is sliced by $\alpha' = \langle \beta(y_1, \dots, y_q) \mid \psi(y_1, \dots, y_q) \wedge \chi(y_1, \dots, y_q) \rangle \in W'$, then we get a q-tuple $\bar{b}_\alpha$, such that the concatenation $\bar{b}$ of all these tuples for those $\alpha \in W$ such that slicing is needed for the reduction to Δ as the only update set. We call $\bar{b}$ a *characterising tuple* for the update set $\Delta \in \boldsymbol{\Delta}_{\mathcal{A}}(S)$. As ψ and χ have the same free variables, characterising tuples are W^c-critical, where

$$W^c = \{\langle (y_1, \dots, y_q) \mid \psi(y_1, \dots, y_q) \rangle \mid \exists \alpha \in W. \alpha = \langle \beta(y_1, \dots, y_q) \mid \psi(y_1, \dots, y_q) \rangle\}$$

is a set of multiset comprehension terms derived from W.

Then we can think of the step of the algorithm $\mathcal{A}$ in state S being the sequence of two substeps. In the first step the different characterising tuples for the possible successor states are determined in parallel and stored in some temporary locations. Then in a second step one of these characterising tuples is chosen, and the corresponding update set is built and applied.

The first step corresponds to a parallel algorithm $\mathcal{A}^c$ with bounded exploration witness W^c, such that the characterising tuples $\bar{b}$ of any update set are W^c-critical tuples. In the second step we can think of using modified locations: if $\bar{a}$ is a critical tuple with respect to W that defines an update with function symbol f in $\Delta \in \boldsymbol{\Delta}_{\mathcal{A}}(S)$ and $\bar{b}$ characterises Δ, then we use a new function symbol $\tilde{f}$ such that $\bar{b}$ is included in the locations used in Δ. This second step (for fixed $\bar{b}$) corresponds to a parallel algorithm $\mathcal{A}^p$ with bounded exploration witness

$$W^p = \Big\{ \Big\langle (t_1, \dots, t_n, y_1, \dots, y_p) \mid \varphi(x_1, \dots, x_k) \wedge \psi(y_1, \dots, y_q) \Big\rangle \mid \\ \langle\langle (t_1, \dots, t_n) \mid \varphi(x_1, \dots, x_k) \rangle \mid \psi(y_1, \dots, y_q) \rangle \in W \Big\}$$

and the concatenated tuple $\bar{a}\bar{b}$ is W^p-critical. We then can apply the results for parallel algorithms, which give us isolating terms $t_\chi^{\bar{b}}$ and $t_\chi^{\bar{a}\bar{b}}$ for $\mathcal{A}^c$ and $\mathcal{A}^p$, respectively. With these we can define a rule

$$\begin{aligned} &\textbf{choose } y_1, \dots, y_p : t_\chi^{\bar{b}}(y_1, \dots, y_q) \textbf{ do} \\ &\quad \textbf{forall } x_0, \dots, x_k : t_\chi^{\bar{a}\bar{b}}(x_0, \dots, x_k, y_1, \dots, y_q) \textbf{ do } f(x_1, \dots, x_k) := x_0 \end{aligned} \tag{3}$$

With these we define a rule r_S as the parallel composition of all rules as in (3) for all characterising tuples $\bar{b}$ and all update-defining tuples in the corresponding update sets.

Lemma 4.7. *If S is a state of the non-deterministic algorithm $\mathcal{A}$, W is a bounded exploration witness for $\mathcal{A}$ and r_S is the rule above with respect to W, then we get $\boldsymbol{\Delta}_{r_S}(S) = \boldsymbol{\Delta}_{\mathcal{A}}(S)$.*

Proof. By definition, one update set $\Delta \in \boldsymbol{\Delta}_{r_S}(S)$ is characterised by $\bar{b}$, and $((f,(a_1,\dots,a_k)),a_0)$ is an update in Δ. Then due to the construction of isolating terms the parallel rule yields also all updates $((f,(a_1',\dots,a_k')),a_0')$, where the type of $\bar{a}'\bar{b}$ (for $\bar{a}' = (a_0',\dots,a_k')$) is the same as the type of $\bar{a}\bar{b}$ (with respect to W^p). As r_S is the parallel composition of rules as defined by (3). the rule r_S yields the complete update set Δ.

Analogously, due to the construction of isolating terms, the choice rule yields all characterising tuples $\bar{b}$ for the update sets in $\boldsymbol{\Delta}_{\mathcal{A}}(S)$, which implies $\boldsymbol{\Delta}_{r_S}(S) = \boldsymbol{\Delta}_{\mathcal{A}}(S)$ as claimed. □

Now we have rules r_S for every state S of the given algorithm $\mathcal{A}$, which yield the set of update sets in that state. However, there are infinitely many states $S \in \mathcal{S}$ and we need a single rule to obtain a behaviourally equivalent ASM. Therefore, we exploit again the bounded exploration witness to obtain an equivalence relation on $\mathcal{S}$ with only finitely many equivalence classes such that only the rules for representatives of each equivalence class are needed.

For a state S define an equivalence relation $\sim_S$ on the bounded exploration witness W by $\alpha \sim_S \alpha'$ iff $\text{val}_S(\alpha) = \text{val}_S(\alpha')$. Then call two states S, S' W-*similar* iff $\sim_S = \sim_{S'}$ holds. As $\sim_S$ defines a partition of W, there can only be finitely many different equivalence relations, and consequently the number of W-similarity classes is also finite. Then we show the following three lemmata.

Lemma 4.8. *Let S be a state of $\mathcal{A}$ and let S_1, S_2 be isomorphic states of $\mathcal{A}$. If $\boldsymbol{\Delta}_{r_S}(S_1) = \boldsymbol{\Delta}_{\mathcal{A}}(S_1)$ holds, then also $\boldsymbol{\Delta}_{r_S}(S_2) = \boldsymbol{\Delta}_{\mathcal{A}}(S_2)$.*

Proof. Let σ be an isomorphism with $\sigma(S_1) = S_2$. As σ is a bijection between the base sets B_1 and B_2 of the states S_1 and S_2, respectively, it can be extended to locations, updates, update sets and also sets of update sets, hence $\sigma(\boldsymbol{\Delta}_{\mathcal{A}}(S_1)) = \boldsymbol{\Delta}_{\mathcal{A}}(S_2)$ holds. Then we get $\boldsymbol{\Delta}_{r_S}(S_2) = \sigma(\boldsymbol{\Delta}_{r_S}(S_1)) = \sigma(\boldsymbol{\Delta}_{\mathcal{A}}(S_1)) = \boldsymbol{\Delta}_{\mathcal{A}}(S_2)$ as claimed. □

Lemma 4.9. *If S, S' are states of $\mathcal{A}$ that coincide on the bounded exploration witness W, then we get $\boldsymbol{\Delta}_{r_S}(S') = \boldsymbol{\Delta}_{\mathcal{A}}(S')$.*

Proof. By Postulate 4 we have $\boldsymbol{\Delta}_{\mathcal{A}}(S) = \boldsymbol{\Delta}_{\mathcal{A}}(S')$. With Lemma 4.7 we get $\boldsymbol{\Delta}_{r_{S'}}(S') = \boldsymbol{\Delta}_{\mathcal{A}}(S')$. Furthermore, the relational structures $S\mid_{W^p}$ and $S'\mid_{W^p}$ must be isomorphic, and the isomorphism ζ maps critical values to critical values. Therefore, for every update $((f,(a_1,\dots,a_n),a_0)) \in \Delta \in \boldsymbol{\Delta}(S)$ the type $tp^{\mathrm{FO}_{wo=}}_{S|_{W^p}}(\bar{a}\bar{b})$ coincides with the type $tp^{\mathrm{FO}_{wo=}}_{S'|_{W^p}}(\bar{a}\bar{b})$, where $\bar{b}$ is a characterising tuple for Δ and the same holds for the type of $\bar{b}$ with respect to structures $S|_{W^c}$ and $S'|_{W^c}$. Hence $r_S = r_{S'}$ holds by construction of the rule r_S, and we get $\boldsymbol{\Delta}_{r_S}(S') = \boldsymbol{\Delta}_{r_{S'}}(S')$. Combining these equalities implies the claim. □

Lemma 4.10 (W-similarity). *If $\mathcal{A}$ is a non-deterministic algorithm with bounded exploration witness W and S, S' are W-similar states, then $\boldsymbol{\Delta}_{r_S}(S') = \boldsymbol{\Delta}_{\mathcal{A}}(S')$ holds.*

Proof. Without loss of generality we can assume that the base sets B, B' of S and S', respectively, are disjoint. Otherwise, we can replace S' by an isomorphic copy $\sigma(S')$, prove the lemma for this state instead, so we get $\boldsymbol{\Delta}_{r_S}(\sigma(S')) = \boldsymbol{\Delta}_{\mathcal{A}}(\sigma(S'))$ and apply Lemma 4.8 to show the claim.

Now due to Lemma 4.8 it suffices to show the claim for a state $\bar{S}$ that is isomorphic to S'. So we construct an isomorphism ζ with $\zeta(\text{val}_{S'}(\alpha)) = \text{val}_S(\alpha)$ for all $\alpha \in W$, and consider $\bar{S} = \zeta(S')$. This is possible, because S and S' are disjoint and W-similar.

Then by construction S and $\bar{S}$ coincide on W, so we get $\boldsymbol{\Delta}_{r_S}(\bar{S}) = \boldsymbol{\Delta}_{\mathcal{A}}(\bar{S})$ by Lemma 4.9, which completes the proof. □

Finally, as there are only finitely many W-similarity classes, we choose representatives $S_1, \dots, S_r$ for these. Then for $1 \le i \le r$ there exists a condition φ_i, which is satisfied in S_i, but not in the other states S_j, so we can define a rule r as a bounded parallel composition of conditional rules **if** φ_i **then** r_{S_i}. Then it is rather straightforward to show that for this rule we get $\boldsymbol{\Delta}(S) = \boldsymbol{\Delta}_{\mathcal{A}}(S)$, which completes the proof of Theorem 4.2.

5 Special Cases

Theorems and 4.1 and 4.2 provide a behavioural theory of non-deterministic algorithms for the general case, where parallelism and choices are both unbounded, i.e. the state determines the number of successor states as well as the number of parallel branches leading to each of these. We now look at the cases where parallelism is bounded, i.e. the number of parallel branches in a state does not depend on the state, or choice is bounded, i.e. the number of successor states does not depend on the state. The third case, where both parallelism and choice are bounded should result in a characterisation that is equivalent to the one given by Gurevich [18] (see also [9, p.307]). Clearly, in all three cases the Postulates 1, 2 and 3 will be preserved, so we can concentrate on bounded exploration.

5.1 Bounded Parallelism

We consider first the case of bounded parallelism, so we preserve unbounded choice. For deterministic algorithms the case of bounded parallelism is covered by the sequential ASM thesis [18] with sets of (ground) terms as bounded exploration witnesses. It is therefore justified to consider *bounded parallel witness terms* as multiset comprehension terms of the form

$$\alpha = \langle (t_0, \dots, t_n) \mid \psi(y_1, \dots, y_q) \rangle \ , \tag{4}$$

where the $t_i = t_i(y_1, \dots, y_q)$ are terms t with variables among the y_j, i.e. we just have multiset comprehension terms. Then the slicing of such terms α gives rise to terms of the form

$$\alpha' = \langle\!\langle (t_0, \dots, t_n) \mid \psi(y_1, \dots, y_q) \wedge \chi(y_1, \dots, y_q) \rangle\!\rangle \tag{5}$$

with some condition χ. With this we get the following modified bounded exploration postulate for non-deterministic, bounded parallel algorithms.

Postulate 5 (Bounded Parallel Bounded Exploration). For a non-deterministic, bounded parallel algorithm $\mathcal{A}$ there exists a finite set W of bounded parallel witness terms such that for all states S, S' that coincide on W, i.e. $\mathrm{val}_S(\alpha) = \mathrm{val}_{S'}(\alpha)$ holds for all $\alpha \in W$, we have $\boldsymbol{\Delta}(S) = \boldsymbol{\Delta}(S')$. In addition, if W is replaced by W' containing sliced witness terms α' for all $\alpha \in W$, then this defines another non-deterministic algorithm $\mathcal{A}'$ with the same signature and background as $\mathcal{A}$ such that $\boldsymbol{\Delta}^{\mathcal{A}'}(S) \subseteq \boldsymbol{\Delta}^{\mathcal{A}}(S)$ holds for all states S.

We obtain bounded parallel ASMs, if we replace parallel rules by *bounded parallel rules* (for short: *par rules*) of the form **par** $r_1 \dots r_k$ with rules r_i. The set $\boldsymbol{\Delta}_{r,\sigma}(S)$ of update sets of a par rule r in state S for some variable assignment σ then becomes

$$\boldsymbol{\Delta}_{r,\sigma}(S) = \{ \Delta_1 \cup \dots \cup \Delta_k \mid \Delta_i \in \boldsymbol{\Delta}_{r_i,\sigma}(S) \text{ for all } 1 \le i \le k \}$$

and the construction of a set of bounded parallel witness terms becomes $W_r = \bigcup_{1 \le i \le k} W_{r_i}$. This is equivalent to what we get from the definitions in Sects. 3 and 4, if we take into account that a par rule **par** $r_1 \dots r_k$ is only a shortcut for a parallel rule **forall** $x \in \{1, \dots, k\}$ **do** $r(x)$, where $r(x)$ is a nested conditional rule

$$\textbf{if } x = 1 \textbf{ then } r_1 \textbf{ else } (\textbf{if } x = 2 \textbf{ then } r_2 \textbf{ else } (\dots \\ (\textbf{if } x = k-1 \textbf{ then } r_{k-1} \textbf{ else } r_k) \dots)) .$$

With these simplifications the proof of Theorem 4.1 also shows the following corollary.

Corollary 5.1. *Every non-deterministic bounded parallel ASM satisfies the defining Postulates 1, 2, 3 and 5 for non-deterministic bounded parallel algorithms.*

With the following corollary we obtain a complete behavioural theory for non-deterministic bounded parallel algorithms.

Corollary 5.2. *For every non-deterministic bounded parallel algorithm $\mathcal{A}$ as stipulated by the Postulates 1, 2, 3 and 5 there exists a behaviourally equivalent non-deterministic bounded parallel ASM M.*

Proof. We proceed as in the proof of Theorem 4.2 with the difference that the complex construction of isolating terms is only needed for characterising tuples $\bar{b}$, but not for update tuples $\bar{a} = (a_0, \dots, a_n)$ with $((f, (a_1, \dots, a_n)), a_0) \in \Delta \in$

$\boldsymbol{\Delta}_{\mathcal{A}}(S)$ for an update set Δ characterised by $\bar{b}$. As the parallelism is bounded, the definition of W^p degenerates to

$$W^p = \Big\{ \langle (t_0, \ldots, t_n, y_1, \ldots, y_q) \mid \psi(y_1, \ldots, y_q) \rangle \mid \\ \langle (t_0, \ldots, t_n) \mid \psi(y_1, \ldots, y_q) \rangle \in W \Big\} .$$

Then we can exploit Corollary 6.6 of the sequential ASM thesis, which guarantees that there is a rule $r_S^{\bar{b}}$ with $\Delta_{r_S^{\bar{b}}}(S) = \Delta$ [18]. These rules are par rules composed out of assignment rules. With these we obtain rules r_S as parallel composition of rules

$$\textbf{choose } y_1, \ldots, y_p : t_\chi^{\bar{b}}(y_1, \ldots, y_q) \textbf{ do } r_S^{(y_1, \ldots, y_q)}$$

for the different characterising tuples $\bar{b}$ of state S. As in Lemma 4.7 we get $\boldsymbol{\Delta}_{r_S}(S) = \boldsymbol{\Delta}_{\mathcal{A}}(S)$.

In order to combine the rules r_S for all states S to a single rule r with $\boldsymbol{\Delta}_r(S) = \boldsymbol{\Delta}_{\mathcal{A}}(S)$ for all S we exploit again W-similarity as for the proof of Lemma 4.10, which completes the proof in the same way as for Theorem 4.2. □

5.2 Bounded Choice

Next let us consider the case of bounded choice, but we preserve unbounded parallelism. Following our argumentation above the outer multiset comprehension is not required, so *bounded choice witness terms* are simply finite unions $U_1 \cup \cdots \cup U_q$ of sets U_i of multiset comprehension terms, and slicing degenerates to taking subsets $U_{i_1} \cup \cdots \cup U_{i_p}$ with $i_j \in \{1, \ldots, q\}$. With this we get the following modified bounded exploration postulate for bounded choice non-deterministic algorithms.

Postulate 6 (Bounded Choice Bounded Exploration). For a bounded choice non-deterministic algorithm $\mathcal{A}$ there exists a finite set W of bounded choice witness terms such that for all states S, S' that coincide on W, i.e. $\text{val}_S(\alpha) = \text{val}_{S'}(\alpha)$ holds for all $\alpha \in W$, we have $\boldsymbol{\Delta}(S) = \boldsymbol{\Delta}(S')$. In addition, if W is replaced by W' containing sliced witness terms α' for all $\alpha \in W$, then this defines another non-deterministic algorithm $\mathcal{A}'$ with the same signature and background as $\mathcal{A}$ such that $\boldsymbol{\Delta}^{\mathcal{A}'}(S) \subseteq \boldsymbol{\Delta}^{\mathcal{A}}(S)$ holds for all states S.

We obtain bounded choice ASMs by replacing general choice rules by *bounded choice rules* of the form **choose** $r_1 \ldots r_k$, i.e. one of the rules r_i is chosen. The set $\boldsymbol{\Delta}_{r,\sigma}(S)$ of update sets of a bounded choice rule r in state S for some variable assignment σ then becomes

$$\boldsymbol{\Delta}_{r,\sigma}(S) = \bigcup_{i=1}^{k} \boldsymbol{\Delta}_{r_i,\sigma}(S)$$

and the construction of a set of bounded choice witness terms becomes

$$W_r = W_{r_1} \cup \dots \cup W_{r_k} .$$

This is again equivalent to what we get from the definitions in Sects. 3 and 4, if we take into account that a rule **choose** $r_1 \dots r_k$ is only a shortcut for a choice rule **choose** $x \in \{1, \dots, k\}$ **do** $r(x)$, where $r(x)$ is again the nested conditional rule

$$\textbf{if } x = 1 \textbf{ then } r_1 \textbf{ else } (\textbf{if } x = 2 \textbf{ then } r_2 \textbf{ else } (\dots \\ (\textbf{if } x = k-1 \textbf{ then } r_{k-1} \textbf{ else } r_k) \dots)) .$$

With these simplifications the proof of Theorem 4.1 also shows the following corollary.

Corollary 5.3. *Every bounded choice ASM satisfies the defining Postulates 1, 2, 3 and 6 for bounded choice non-deterministic algorithms.*

The converse holds as well, so we obtain a complete behavioural theory for bounded choice non-deterministic algorithms.

Corollary 5.4. *For every bounded choice non-deterministic algorithm $\mathcal{A}$ as stipulated by the Postulates 1, 2, 3 and 6 there exists a behaviourally equivalent bounded choice non-deterministic ASM M.*

Proof. We proceed as in the proof of Theorem 4.2 with the difference that the complex construction of isolating terms is only needed for update tuples $\bar{a} = (a_0, \dots, a_n)$ with $((f, (a_1, \dots, a_n)), a_0) \in \Delta_i$ with $1 \le i \le k$, where $\boldsymbol{\Delta}_{\mathcal{A}}(S) = \{\Delta_1, \dots, \Delta_k\}$. The construction in the proof of Theorem 4.2 then simplifies to a rule r_S as a parallel composition of rules

$$\textbf{choose} \dots \textbf{forall } x_0, \dots, x_k : t_{\chi}^{\bar{a}_i}(x_1, \dots, x_k) \textbf{ do } f(x_1, \dots, x_k) := x_0 \ \dots ,$$

for $1 \le i \le k$.

As in Lemma 4.7 we get $\boldsymbol{\Delta}_{r_S}(S) = \boldsymbol{\Delta}_{\mathcal{A}}(S)$. Then we exploit W-similarity as for the proof of Lemma 4.10 to construct a single rule r with $\boldsymbol{\Delta}_r(S) = \boldsymbol{\Delta}_{\mathcal{A}}(S)$ for all S, which completes the proof. □

Let us finally consider that case, where both parallelism and choice are bounded. Combining the considerations for the previous two special cases, bounded exploration witnesses in this case degenerate to finite sets of grounds terms. There is no need for a slicing condition, as critical values result from the evaluation of the witness terms, and there are only finitely many. It is therefore always clear to which update set $\Delta \in \boldsymbol{\Delta}_{\mathcal{A}}(S)$ an update $((f, (a_1, \dots, a_n)), a_0)$ belongs.

Postulate 7 (Bounded Choice/Parallel Bounded Exploration). For a bounded choice, bounded parallel non-deterministic algorithm $\mathcal{A}$ there exists a finite set W of ground terms such that for all states S, S' that coincide on W we have $\boldsymbol{\Delta}(S) = \boldsymbol{\Delta}(S')$.

For bounded choice, bounded parallel ASM M the defining rule can only exploit par rules and bounded choice rules, but neither forall nor general choice rules. The proofs of the following two corollaries is then straightforward, as we only need to exploit the sequential ASM thesis.

Corollary 5.5. *Every bounded choice, bounded parallel ASM satisfies the defining Postulates 1, 2, 3 and 7 for bounded choice, bounded parallel non-deterministic algorithms.*

Corollary 5.6. *For every bounded choice, bounded parallel non-deterministic algorithm $\mathcal{A}$ as stipulated by the Postulates 1, 2, 3 and 7 there exists a behaviourally equivalent bounded choice, bounded parallel non-deterministic ASM M.*

6 Concluding Remarks

We motivated and defined four postulates that define the class of non-deterministic parallel algorithms, for which choices are essential. We then showed that this class of algorithms is captured by non-deterministic Abstract State Machines, which constitutes a behavioural theory of non-deterministic algorithms. The proof was surprisingly simple, because we could exploit the deep results of the behavioural theory of synchronous parallel algorithms [12], in particular the fact that any two tuples that are indistinguishable by the algorithm either define both updates for the same function symbol or both do not. In [11] the results have been generalised to probabilistic algorithms, where choices underlie some probability distribution.

We also discussed special cases, when the parallelism, the choice or both are bounded, which results in simplified theories. In fact, the bounded exploration postulate becomes simpler. For the case of bounded choice bounded parallel algorithm the simplification is equivalent to the long known result that is covered in the sequential ASM thesis [18] (see also [9, Sect. 7.2.2]).

Acknowledgments. The work of Flavio Ferrarotti has been funded by the Federal Ministry for Innovation, Mobility and Infrastructure (BMIMI), the Federal Ministry for Economy, Energy and Tourism (BMWET), and the State of Upper Austria in the frame of the COMET Module Dependable Production Environments with Software Security (DEPS) (FFG grant no. 888338) and the SCCH competence center INTEGRATE (FFG grant no. 892418) within the COMET - Competence Centers for Excellent Technologies Programme managed by Austrian Research Promotion Agency FFG.

Disclosure of Interests. The authors have no competing interests to declare that are relevant to the content of this article.

References

1. Blass, A., Gurevich, Y.: Abstract State Machines capture parallel algorithms. ACM Trans. Comput. Logic **4**(4), 578–651 (2003)

2. Blass, A., Gurevich, Y.: Abstract State Machines capture parallel algorithms: correction and extension. ACM Trans. Comput. Logic **9**(3) (2008)
3. Blass, A., Gurevich, Y.: Background of computation. Bulletin EATCS **92**, 82–114 (2007)
4. Börger, E., Schewe, K.-D.: Concurrent abstract state machines. Acta Informatica **53**(5), 469–492 (2015). https://doi.org/10.1007/s00236-015-0249-7
5. Börger, E.: The ASM refinement method. Formal Aspects Comput. **15**(2-3), 237–257 (2003). https://doi.org/10.1007/S00165-003-0012-7
6. Börger, E., Gervasi, V.: Structures of Computing – A Guide to Practice-Oriented Theory. Springer, Cham (2024). https://doi.org/10.1007/978-3-031-54358-6
7. Börger, E., Raschke, A.: Modeling Companion for Software Practitioners. Springer, Cham (2018). https://doi.org/10.1007/978-3-662-56641-1
8. Börger, E., Schewe, K.D.: A behavioural theory of recursive algorithms. Fund. Inform. **177**(1), 1–37 (2020)
9. Börger, E., Stärk, R.: Abstract State Machines. Springer, Heidelberg (2003)
10. Ferrarotti, F., Gervasi, V., Raschke, A., Schewe, K.D.: The Abstract State Machines method (2025). submitted for publication
11. Ferrarotti, F., Schewe, K.D.: A behavioural theory of probabilistic algorithms using probabilistic Abstract State Machines (2025). submitted for publication
12. Ferrarotti, F., Schewe, K.D., Tec, L., Wang, Q.: A new thesis concerning synchronised parallel computing - simplified parallel ASM thesis. Theor. Comp. Sci. **649**, 25–53 (2016). https://doi.org/10.1016/j.tcs.2016.08.013
13. Ferrarotti, F., González, S., Schewe, K.D.: BSP abstract state machines capture bulk synchronous parallel computations. Sci. Comput. Program. **184** (2019). https://doi.org/10.1016/j.scico.2019.102319
14. Ferrarotti, F., Schewe, K.D., Tec, L., Wang, Q.: A complete logic for database abstract state machines. Logic J. IGPL **25**(5), 700–740 (2017)
15. Grädel, E., Gurevich, Y.: Metafinite model theory. Inf. Comput. **140**(1), 26–81 (1998)
16. Gurevich, Y.: A new thesis. Abstracts, American Mathematical Society p. 317 (1985). abstract 85T-68-203
17. Gurevich, Y.: Evolving algebras 1993: Lipari Guide. In: Specification and Validation Methods, pp. 9–36. Oxford University Press (1995)
18. Gurevich, Y.: Sequential abstract-state machines capture sequential algorithms. ACM Trans. Comp. Logic **1**(1), 77–111 (2000)
19. Schewe, K.D., Ferrarotti, F.: Behavioural theory of reflective algorithms I: reflective sequential algorithms. Sci. Comput. Program. **223**, 102864 (2022). https://doi.org/10.1016/J.SCICO.2022.102864
20. Schewe, K.D., Ferrarotti, F.: Behavioural theory of reflective algorithms II: reflective parallel algorithms (2025). http://arxiv.org/abs/2508.09053

Modelling

Establishing Language-Backed Modelling

Bernhard Thalheim(✉)

Christian Albrechts University Kiel, 24118 Kiel, Germany
bernhard.thalheim@email.uni-kiel.de

Abstract. Modelling in Computer Science and many other disciplines is very often language-based. That is why modelling languages have become a universal tool that we take for granted without looking too closely or even questioning it. Languages often have a diabolical connection to certain mathematical structures, such as set theory. Modelling languages are based on notions of mostly simple first-order constructors and a corresponding simple construction theory, although better constructors have been well researched. A typical example of hard language binding is database structure modelling. Furthermore, it is also important to gain a better understanding of meta-abstraction. In this paper, we highlight the challenges, pitfalls, and resulting obstacles of such hard language binding and present some solutions to improve the situation.

Keywords: model · modelling · database structure model · languages

1 Languages Enable and Hinder Modelling

The article falls within the scope of science, art, and practice of models, modeling as a craft, and systematic model studies as a discipline. We do not want to introduce ***modelology*** here or go into detail, which is why we would like to refer to and use the following terminology from [39]:

Definition 1 (Model notion). A model is a well-formed, adequate, and dependable instrument that acceptably represents 'something' (called origin as a source, archetype, starting point) and that functions properly in usage scenarios in accordance with the concerns of a community of practice (CoP) for given application cases in a situation.

The notion 'model' is used very flexibly in Computer Science. On the one hand, intuitive *pre-models* are used to express a momentary opinion or belief. *Proto-models* go a step further and express views with a certain degree of conviction and are intended to satisfy at least some representation and communication requirements. Definition 1 goes further and requires that a models presents some comprehension with a well-founded certainty and reliability. *Rich models* go beyond this and also partially incorporate their background.

Models should simplify origins and be parsimonious. In modelling, we therefore prefer languages that are both simple and easy to understand, in as graphical

A. Raschke et al. (Eds.): Egon Börger Festschrift, LNCS 16580, pp. 421–444, 2026.
https://doi.org/10.1007/978-3-032-24494-9_20

a form as possible. Despite their suitability, the extent to which constructs can be simplified and expanded again is less important. This brings us to low-structured models that display everything at once and in its entirety, i.e. very large models appear very quickly.

1.1 Typical Lacunas in Database Modelling

A DBMS should enable data in often highly complex applications to be managed completely, sufficiently precisely and efficiently. It should be possible to persistently enter data into systems, query and combine it efficiently, and detect and correct errors. We usually follow a data-structure-first principle and then expect high-performance system support for all processes, especially queries.

Here Only Structure Modelling. We will limit ourselves here to structural modelling for object-relational databases and leave aside the functionality of database systems. This focus alone already gives rise to many limitations that must be overcome in order to fully utilise the technology. The use of constructors, at least first-order constructors, has become established practice in database modelling, which raises the question of whether this is sufficient and appropriate for the application.

Many, but by no means all, natural languages favour a state-oriented style of representation, whereby processes are mapped using sophisticated grammatical constructions and internal syntactic relationships. Database languages take this state orientation to the extreme.

Language-Backed Modelling. Computer Science is full of fundamentalistic wrong turns[1]

that have become increasingly entrenched and that should be broken down so that Computer Science can become a science. We want to look at one of these wrong turns for structural modelling and ask ourselves whether alternative solutions could be offered here. Since Computer Science is language-loving and languages have their own peculiarities, one may wonder whether the choice of language allows for many things but also restricts or even prohibits others.

In addition, one wants to be able to understand models quickly and easily in terms of their well-formedness, which is usually visualised in planar dimensions. Visualising complex systems is a formidable challenge.

Language Unstructuredness Hinders Modelling. It is convenient to model in languages with as few universal constructs as possible, which only need to be

[1] We borrow this term from W. Reisig, who used it to refer to cardinal errors in classical modelling – especially UML-based modelling – (Workshop Modellierung 2023, Fribourg). We now know of two dozen such aberrations. Particularly prominent in the database area are: object-oriented databases, active databases, object identifiers, schema-free (i.e. model-free) database structures, bus-based data ocean pumping instead of database engines, and also data marts.

applied once for each model element. Even for natural languages, this simple structuring is not sufficient as soon as one wants to express oneself in a more precise or poetic way. Typical expressive structures are higher-order subordinate clauses by great writers and scientific texts. Models should be less complicated than the origins, but at the same time they must be precise enough to enable users to realise their particular concern sufficiently. This lesson is well known, but little attention is paid to it.

The Syntax-First Nightmare. Computer Science is based, among other things, on (mostly first-order) predicate logic and thus inherits its assumptions and incapacities that lead to problems. With the AI hype, this misguided approach continues and deepens all the distortions. One of these aberrations is the definition of languages according to the principle of

syntax-first – semantics-on-top-of-syntax – and – pragmatics-sometime-later (if at all), in which syntax and semantics are separated and layered, even though this is not the case in natural languages and certainly not in applications.

As a typical example the database design on relational language basis can be considered, where first relatively primitive syntactic constructs are used and everything specific is shifted into the semantics, e.g. by a complicated and partially unmanageable bunch of almost hundred different kinds of integrity constraints [35]. All of these kinds of constraints are needed but often simply not used. In addition, these kinds of constraints remain general, but require different implementation methods for each of their sub-kinds [42].

1.2 The Storyline of This Paper

In this paper, we want to examine the principles of structure modelling against the backdrop of increasingly complex systems. We therefore first identify some challenges that need to be approached differently today than in the early days of DBMS technology. These challenges demonstrate how deeply Computer Science is permeated by unquestioned paradigms, tacitly accepted principles, and problematic assumptions. One can partially agree with P. Graham and many others [1,14] that there is still a long way to go before Computer Science becomes a science. Modeling as a lore is no exception here, but rather even less well-founded, even for the modeling of computational processes. In the sequel, we focus on two of these challenges in the database area, illustrate them and propose solutions that can be used to solve such problems.

2 Challenges of Low-Structured Languages

With the expansion of database technology to more complex applications, some paradigms became problematic. For example, flat first-order constructs were no longer sufficient, as challenged by OLTP-OLAP warehouse solutions [22]. On the other hand, we need meta-considerations that go beyond linguistic considerations. Applications can hardly be considered at one level of detail and data granularity anymore. We must also break away from the rigid focus on syntax first.

2.1 Higher-Order Constructors

Models should be usable for the concern at hand. This would also imply that there should be a uniform level of detail and that only this level of detail should be used. At the latest when dealing with large sizes that are difficult for humans to comprehend, we must consider different forms of refinement. Languages tempt us to assume that we only need one type of detail. The complexity of origins and problems shows that this can never work.

First-Order Only. Representations in natural and formal languages are often rule-based, so that one assumes that a single application of constructors is sufficient to construct sentences or even entire texts. Therefore, one may only need a single application. That is why people in Computer Science believe in one-shot compositions. OLAP applications running on OLTP database systems show that this assumption must be rather incorrect.

On the other hand, Computer Science is model-obsessed simply because of the size and complexity of the systems for users, who cannot even begin to comprehend this size and complexity in a single step. We probably need a gradual, layered development of systems depending on the simplicity required for consideration.

Problem (A): Constructors of any order.
Would it not make sense to also consider higher-order constructors?

With the extended entity-relationship model [36], we have already allowed higher orders for both attribute and relationship types, as long as this is manageable and technologically feasible. We should therefore set about enriching these constructs.

The Set Abberation of Smith/Smith and Followers. To represent database structures, [33]'s central work was based on the paradigm to consider only sets, so that a set of instances was understood as a class and the undefined term 'class' was simply understood as a set. This paradigm leads to two pitfalls. First, specialization then simply becomes a subset of a class and generalization becomes a superset of a class, whereby the semantics of this construction are simply forgotten and, at the same time, generalization is then only the inverse of specialization. Second, the association of different classes is simply mislabeled as aggregation. This abbreviation is followed by the 'discovery' of a power set.

The set paradigm leads to yet another confusing shortcoming. Classes become extensions of intensions, even though intensions actually make statements about extensions and are therefore actually a meta-construct or at least a model element.

Problem (B): Sophistication of generalisation and specialisation.
Can generalisation and specialisation be mathematically justified without limiting oneself to sets or power sets? What is the sense and meaning of these first-order constructors?

Set semantics are only the first, rather simplistic approach. Reducing to set algebras also does not lead to an understanding of multiple applications of specialisation or even the rarely considered generalisation. There are two alternatives with a *multi-level approach*: on the one hand, specialisation as a detail extension [13] (or, inverted, as detail refinement) and, on the other hand, as classification [21] (or, inverted, as simple generalisation or, if applicable, power set). In the second approach, at least the coherence of deep and multiple specialisation is maintained.

Problem (C): Semantics for constructor application.
Should the constructor concept be linked not only to syntax but also to semantics from the outset, so that additional integrity conditions are not maintained from the outset?

Neither collections nor other mathematical structures were used for the combinations of elements, which is why many constructions require work-around. Added to this is the total disregard for mathematical set theory. Similar mistakes were also made with object orientation, in which a class has not only structural attributes but also methods. One need only recall the discussions on covariance and contra-variance, as well as on object identifiers (see, for example, [2,30]).

2.2 Meta-(Meta-(Meta-))Variety

With UML and, above all, standardisation efforts, different levels of abstraction were introduced for languages. A meta-level should then define forms of language utterances. Meta-meta-levels above the meta-level can also be introduced as forms of composition for meta-languages. Then linguistic expressions are from level $\mathcal{M}_0$. The language with its composition is meta-level $\mathcal{M}_1$. Since models and application meanings in Computer Science are usually language-based, it is now assumed that the same levels apply to models and meanings, which is a grave mistake and misuse of levels. It is also often postulated that there is no meta-meta-meta level $\mathcal{M}_4$ [47].

Various Notions of 'Meta'. A key question is what 'meta' actually means. 'Meta' describes the nature and essence of the constructions used. The term 'meta' is used in various meanings in Computer Science:

(1) 'Meta-' is concerned with the conceptions behind something.
(2) 'Meta-' is based on joint consideration and safeguarding by an implicit background, e.g. personal knowledge, knowing, and familiarity.
(3) 'Meta-'-things are formed by classification abstraction.
(4) 'Meta-' also means to be more comprehensive.
(5) 'Meta-' means something that is more than usual or goes above and beyond.

(6) 'Meta-' also means situations after/beyond/beside/advanced according to the current situation.
(7) 'Meta-' means to be outside the normal limits of something. Etc. etc.
Up to now, we consider 'meta'^{1}, 'meta'^{2}, 'meta'^{3}, but not yet 'meta'^{4} or 'meta'^{5}.]

Problem (D): Problem-oriented versions of 'meta'.
Is it possible to find a sufficiently plausible form of 'meta' depending on the nature and essence of an item?

We should assume that 'meta' should be based on the main characteristics of an item, but we need a more detailed description for this.

Meta for Languages, Meaning, and Models. In the context of modelling, we see three different items:

(1) the modelling languages used as instrumentarium for creating models;
(2) background and the knowing of the specific meaning, sense, and significance of the constructs used within an application by the CoP;
(3) the model prescribed by the concern for a collection of origins.
Instruments (e.g. languages) should be effective, efficient and methodically usable as enabler. They have a composition, i.e. a form and a supporting functionality for using the instrument. Implicit personal knowledge and the knowing should reflect the area of application.

This means that the meaning and thus the explanation of an item in the application is more likely to be borrowed from the application with the relevant perspectives of the CoP. The background also includes the negative aspects, which are not reflected in the model but which help to determine the model content. These three sides are closely related to and represents the essence, nature, meaning, and significance of all elements and even the models themselves to be fully understood within a CoP. Models rather tend to follow the purpose for their existence, i.e. the main dimensions are their use *for what*, for treating *what*, with the intention *for what.*

Problem (E): Characterising nature and essence of an item.
Can we distinguish between the levels of abstraction based on the nature and essence of an item?

If the answer is positive according to the criterion of nature and essence then we have a way of dealing with the levels of abstraction.

The Level of 'Meta'-abstraction. An abstraction can be based on another abstraction, depending on the type of abstraction. We must therefore consider the extent to which such an abstraction process can be continued iteratively. In modelling languages, it is assumed that continuation is not possible beyond level 2 [47]. Even for instrumentation, and especially for languages, one should at least define level 2 more precisely, beyond pure intuition. With [46], we should perhaps also question this and, for modeling purposes, at least consider the fourth level of meta-abstraction.

Problem (F): Levels of 'meta' abstraction.
Isn't there also a meta-abstraction level 3 or even 4?

Abstraction level 2 is certainly a good starting point. But there must be further levels that allow us to better grasp the nature of an item. We must ask ourselves what abstraction levels two, three, and four could mean for models and background and the knowing.

2.3 Macro-, Meso and Micro-constructs

In most cases, structuring and, in many cases, modeling assume that there is a finest and at the same time sufficient unique level of detail. In order to discuss coarser structures, OLTP-OLAP applications assumed that the finest detail is provided by OLTP data and that the coarsening can then be provided via derivations with queries (e.g. [17]). However, there are many applications, e.g., in medicine, where the coarse data is available first and the finer data, e.g., for explanation, has to be added later if necessary.

Competition of Refinement and Coarsement. Modeling is often understood in a top-down manner. We start with a rough representation, narrow down parts of it, and then consider the refinement of these respective parts, hoping that coherence with other parts and the entire system can be maintained. With ASM refinements, this approach was also given a theoretical foundation.

There are at least four other approaches to database structure modeling [36]: bottom-up with coarsening, mixed tactics toggling between top-down and bottom-up, controlled tactics such as modular design with design-by-units, and inside-out such as the oil stain method. For this reason, we need methods that thrive on and benefit from the competition between refinement and coarsening.
Problem (G): Refinement and coarsement as two sides of the same coin.
Can refinement and coarsening be fully justified as a mixed tactic alongside other tactics?

In addition, refinement can also be used as a basis for explanations and justifications, for example, without this being implemented in systems. Refined data is used to provide an explanation of data when necessary.

Phenotype or Genotype? Depending on the required granularity, the perspectives of user groups, and the feasibility of maintaining relationships, different forms of analysis can be considered. There are models that can be represented in detail as micro models. There is a component view via meso models, in which a system is first viewed as a schema of separable components. There are also macro models that first model a system as such, as in [28], and only then consider description etc. models. This distinction can be considered even more finely, as in the human heart model for analyzing drug effects [16]: micro at the protein level, micro/meso at the gene level, meso at the cell level, meso/macro at the cell tissue level, and macro at the physical functional level whereby each of these model suites must be considered separately, using rather different and

difficult to associate mechanisms such as structural representations or partial differential equations. Model suites [40] are auxiliary constructions consisting of well-associated and coherent collections of models.
Problem (H): Makro-models and meso-models need a foundation.
Is it possible to consider different forms of abstraction simultaneously and coherently, as in a model suite?

The introduction of Turbo-ASM [6] already provided a mechanism for considering micro and micro/meso specifications in mutual context. With meso modeling, however, we often abandon the apparatus of refinement. With meso and, even more so, macro models, we are changing not only the instrumentation but also the perspective and concern in modeling.

Foldable and Expandable Inner-Structures in Models. Models quickly become very large and very detailed due to performance requirements and the necessary spectrum. For example, database schemas with well over ten thousand entity, relationship, and attribute types are created, which greatly exceeds human comprehension, although it is also known that even 30 entity and relationship types are too much for the reader to take in. For this reason, it has become common practice, at least for complex applications, to introduce folding and expanding mechanisms based on the accordion principle (e.g. zoom in, zoom out), whereby only what is really necessary is represented, depending on the form of viewpoints, and all links to other parts of a schema are only hinted at. This approach is well known to practitioners, but has been almost completely overlooked by theorists, even though it is based on the container construction [32,41] and a manifestation of components as meso-schemata [4,10,31].

Components are a typical meso-structure for modularisation. Components become the main building blocks of a system. They are used for handling of the main data. The association among components is based on 'connector' types (called hinge or bridge types) that enable in associating the components in a variable fashion. Components then form a skeleton.

If one understands architecture as a conceptual model consisting of interdependent components and considers its structure, then OLTP-OLAP architectures [22] are an example of macro-structures, at least for tracking data changes in the derived OLAP analysis structures. This example in particular shows that terms are enriched by macro- and meso-semantics and pragmatics. They use the same word for quite different attributes, e.g. in the case of a selection based on a query. This means we have to question the same-meaning-forever paradigm.
Problem (I): Foldable constructions.
Should we really only use simple structures with a minimum number of constructors?

Even if one adheres to the syntax-first paradigm, one is left completely confused when one realises that the meaning of the same name for an attribute can vary greatly in the context of specialisations and generalisations [3]. For example, price is used in Fig. 1 as an attribute for a car's list price that depends on countries, but in sales it is a negotiated price, which may even include further specific agreements resulting from the customer relationship. In addition, an attribute value can be overwritten during generalisation or specialisation in a dependent type of higher order, or it may not be overwritten. This is specified by an inheritance pattern for a constructor.

The simplest way to support this would be to allow the specific meaning of each component already used in a construction to be changed when a higher order type is introduced. So far, this mechanism is only known for directives [45] in prescription models.

2.4 Syntax-First Semantics-on-Top-of-Syntax

One of the most difficult principles is the primary focus on the *syntax-first – semantics-on-top-of-syntax principle*. Not only does this lead to wild and barely controllable semantics, it is also uncommon in natural languages and especially in disciplinary languages, which require, for example, the refinement of words into terms and terminologies in domain-oriented languages. The syntax-first principle is, however, specific to the generally preferred form of first-order predicate logic, which was adopted in Computer Science without any other options.

Integrating Syntax and Semantics. This syntax-first principle also leads to interesting self-restrictions. For example, functional and inclusion constraints cannot be axiomatized and therefore cannot be adequately treated deductively in first-order predicate logic, but they can be axiomatised in simple second-order predicate logic [15]. The literature still maintains that the two constraints cannot be axiomatized together. Furthermore, it is believed that each of these types of constraints only requires a rough specification. There are four subtypes of functional constraints, which must be clearly distinguished at the latest during implementation [42].

We postulate that at least syntax and semantics, if not pragmatics as well, must be understood and treated as a whole in order to avoid later implementations that are difficult to understand and maintain. At least this is known to database implementation insiders who have to fix implementation errors.

Database structure models are based on syntactic constructs to which local semantics and constraints are subsequently assigned and, in exceptional cases, at least schema environment semantics. In order to reduce the problems of local semantics, a questionable normalisation is performed for the local constructs without sufficiently including the context. Global normalisation is actually required [43].

Problem (J): Co-development of syntax and semantics.

Is it possible to develop construction mechanisms that, analogous to natural languages, allow for a coherent simultaneous consideration of syntax and semantics?

Pragmatics and Meaning Support Is an Essential Dimension. Modelling usually only uses *proto-models*, whose dependability is only implicitly assumed. Even if the dependability or, where applicable, only the quality of models is given, an essential component is missing in the model: an explanation of the meaning, sense, and significance of model elements together with the model specification.

There are two well-developed mechanisms for developing '*rich models*': firstly, the conceptualisation of all model elements through additional adjuncts and meaning from the application area, as in conceptual modelling [25], and secondly, the use of background models with which meaning, sense, and significance are sufficiently and completely associated with the foreground model.

Conceptual modelling attempts, at least to a certain extent, to assign notions as the (application) meaning of elements using the terms (or at least meaningful words) employed. A concept is then underlaid with a notion from the field of application and also with a term from a terminology.

Rich models therefore also include pragmatics from both the application domain and the CoP-specific pragmatics.

Problem (K): Rich models in a linguistic setting.
Can one systematically develop rich models in order to be able to convey both pragmatics and the necessary partial body of knowledge on which theoretical basis?

A classic form of coherent development is the triptych approach [26], in which models are specified using terms from terminological languages whose meanings are derived primarily from knowing and expertise in the field of application.

3 Higher-Order Constructors Revisited

The constructor concept with an onetime application of this constructor to elements is only the beginning. Onetime use even hinders modelling and forces the use of auxiliary constructions as a work-around solution. For all constructors, Frege's concept of compositionalism applies only syntactically, not semantically – contrary to the opinion in Computer Science – due to the specific internal semantics associated with the constructor that are added with a constructor.

A Small Example. To illustrate solutions to our challenges, we will use a simple example from [27]. For further discussion of solutions to the first two challenges, we considered recording different types of products such as books and cars as base or kernel types. Books have a serial number, as do cars, with an numbering system following different patterns. Subclasses could be, for example, special books such as *Harry Potter 4*.

We will use the example in Fig. 1 in this and next Section step by step to illustrate solutions for the first two challenges. This form of representation can be understood as a "natural representation" or *natural model*, where the user finds his world again and does not have to align himself with the system world, e.g. with schema non-redundancy restriction.

3.1 Schemes for Constructor Application

We will first introduce o refined version of the classic form of the constructor notion and then show how this definition can be expanded for application.

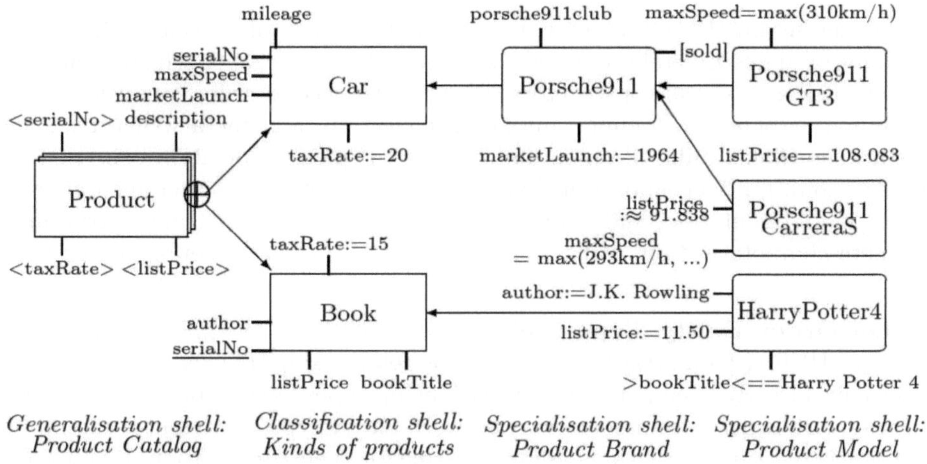

Fig. 1. Reconsidering specialisation and generalisation.

Definition 2 (Classic structural constructor notion refined). *A* structural constructor *is an algebraic expression for a composite with composition components and with correctness criteria for application of the constructor that are enforced through rules for validation of correctness.*

The semantics of the composite consists of the constructor semantics and additional current deployment semantics and pragmatics.

Constructors are supported by functions such as selectors *for retrieval among components and* modificators *for retrieval and enforcement of changes from the composite to its components.*

Composites may have several representation forms and default rules.

The correctness criteria also include preconditions for the applicability of the constructor and postconditions for the acceptance of the application results. Formalisation of composites and composition constructors can be based on [24]. Each constructor combines the semantics and meaning of its components and also adds its own semantics and meaning to the composites. So far, so good. But this notion considers a composite to be standalone without context. Even with models, this context must be considered together with the execution of a constructor in order to maintain the connection in the model. To do this, graph grammars [11] are generalised.

Definition 3 (Application of a structural constructor in a model). *Given a model* $\mathtt{M}$ *with its submodel* $\mathtt{M}_1$ *which contains the components* $C_1, ..., C_n$ *with their environments* $\mathcal{E}(C_i)$, ..., $\mathcal{E}(C_n)$.

The application of a constructor $\mathcal{C}$ *to* $\mathtt{M}_1$ *is a transformation in which* $C_1, ..., C_n$ *are replaced by the composite* $\mathfrak{C}(C_1, ..., C_n)$ *in such a way that the environment relationship is preserved, resulting in a submodel* $\mathtt{M}_2$ *that replaces* $\mathtt{M}_1$ *in* $\mathtt{M}$.

Depending on the constructor, the components may also occur in M_2, occur partially, or are completely replaced. OLAP constructors [23] or schema transformations [24] are typical constructors. We consider second-order constructors for renaming, association, folding, unfolding, collection, and meta-structures such as star, snowflake, bulk, lifespan, and context. Typical association constructors are sum, join, product, and meet. Lifespan meta-structures are incremental, evolution, loop, circulation, and network meta-structures. Context meta-structures are meta-characterisation, utilisation-recording, and quality meta-structures.

Higher-Order Entity Types. With the extension of the ER modeling language to HERM [36], stratified schemes for relationship, cluster, and attribute types have already been permitted. Relationship types have a construction order starting with order 1 for associations between entity types. Attributes should be well-bracketed Fitch structures as guiding rule for their composition. If you want to distinguish between generalization and specialization, specializations can also be layered, as in the above example with *Porsche911* and *Porsche911GT3*.

We therefore also introduce such an order for entity types, starting with order 0 for core types and then order i+1 for further specialisations (represented by rectangles with rounded corners). With such an ordering for all types, a potency concept becomes superfluous.

Construction Constraints. A constructor cannot be applied arbitrarily, but is restricted by correctness conditions. The orthogonality of possible constructor applications is rather an exception. The classic Church-Rosser property for the application of term rewriting rules cannot therefore be required.

A typical example is HERM where model elements are layered and subject to an order, so that a meta-rule of the following form is used and thus cyclic schemata are avoided:

A type of order k can only use types of lower order. An entity type has an order of 0. A relationship type has an order of at least 1. Attribute types are described by well-bracketed structure expressions.

You could consider the order for the individual types of schema elements or include it in the schema as a whole.

3.2 Generalisation and Specialisation in HERM

Generalisation and specialisation follow different desiterata for the existence of corresponding objects for types considered. Products combine the two kernel types and only exist if they can be assigned to at least one of the kernel types. Specialisation is a linguistic construct, so that there are three orthogonal dimensions [38]: syntactic specialisation as an extension of the assumed types, semantic specialisation through logical restrictions, and pragmatic specialisation based on application and the perspectives of the CoP. This means that there are also seven types of IsA subtypes, not just one. Specialisation can also enable the assignment of roles. Specialisations can also be multiple and encompass different facets.

Generalisation is an abstraction and therefore eliminates specific aspects of its components. One must consider at least half a dozen different kinds of abstractions for generalisation. To make it manageable, we assume that the components of a generalisation are disjoint (see $\bigoplus$).

For instance, the *Product* type can be used independently as a new type or as a generalisation of kernel types without loosing the identifiers provided by the component types. Figure 1 uses the second variant.

We could also simplify generalisation and specialisation by viewing them as unary relationship types. However, we want to focus more on the difference between these two constructs, so we will use the double box instead of the cluster type and the weak entity type representation for specialisations. In both cases, we can use the order restriction for the constructor in order to avoid cycles in a schema.

3.3 Constructors with Expansion Directives

Database modelling languages may well use a small set of constructs, such as entity types for things of interest, relationship types for associations between types, cluster types for generalisations, subtype types for specialisations, and attribute types for recording characteristics or properties.

Due to the value inheritance during specialisation, the *myPorsche911 CarreraS* also has corresponding values for attributes such as *listPrice*, *marketLaunch* and *taxRate*. For generalisation, *serialNo* is then taken from the base types and can be distinguished because different numbering schemes apply to the base types. The value for *listPrice* for *Book* can be overwritten by *listPrice := 11.50* for *HarryPotter4*. For now, we consider six different kinds of attributes:

(a) flexible attributes with a specific value (*serialNo* in *Book*),
(b) invisible attributes with a fixed value for the type and thus class (*bookTitle* in *HarryPotter4*),
(c) attributes with a suggested value (*listPrice* in *Porsche99CarraraS*),
(d) attributes with an inherited value (*taxRate* in *Product*),
(e) attributes with functional treatment, e.g. by aggregation function (*maxSpeed* in *Porsche911GT3*),
(f) attributes with flexible value through aggregation function application (*sold* in *Porsche911*), and (g) attributes whose value can still be changed during specialisation (*listPrice* in *HarryPotter4*).

Value Inheritance Pattern and Controlled Redundancy. Until now, description models have been used in Computer Science as blueprints for system development and programming. However, such models also serve other purposes, such as discussion in a CoP, coordination of viewpoints, screening, deliberation, exploration, surveying, understanding, and comprehension, as well as separability into components.

Blueprint models are subject to the strict requirement of minimal redundancy of all types, which then leads to the unnatural requirement that an attribute belongs to exactly one type and is not redundantly carried in other types. Natural models then carry attributes such as *taxRate* in a controllable redundant manner.

With this kind of controlled redundancy, we can then also derive inheritance patterns for instantiation in databases and use these patterns for DBMS technology to achieve low-redundancy storage. Analogous patterns are also used in value inheritance for passed-on values such as <*serialNumber*>.

4 The 'Meta' Problem Resolved

Computer Science has become accustomed to interpreting 'meta' solely from a linguistic perspective. There are also other uses of 'meta'. For the design, we remember the concept of meta-data of data according to F.F. Kramer [19]. In addition to (1) the specification of coding or (2) structuring and functioning, this results in four further dimensions: (3) provenance as a reference to the CoP for development and use,

(4) context in which the element is placed,

(5) meaning of these data, and

(6) significance and sense within a given application.

These six dimensions then allow a model of a meta-date to be created. This raises the question of whether, analogous to the meta-data concept, such meta-characterisations can also be developed for models.

4.1 The Three Dimensions for 'Meta' in Modelling

The second notion used for meta-data of data is at a minimum accepted in Computer Science, although it is surprising to notice that meta-data deals with five additional negelected sides. Further, we have already considered the seven variants of the notion of 'meta' and should ask ourselves whether a proper understanding of 'meta' exists. With the triptych approach [26], the accompanying information for a model was split into two components: On the one hand, the enabling instrumentation, e.g. with languages, is considered. On the other hand, the dimension of support from the application landscape and the discipline, which is usually assumed implicitly and mostly not specified, is made visible. In Computer Science, the language dimension is placed solely in the foreground. The background dimension is deliberately concealed as a given. This amputation deprives a model of its legitimacy for further use after its initial application, which is one reason for the declining acceptance of modelling as a discipline. The consideration of specialised domain-specific languages or AI-backed model generation do not eliminate this mutilation.

We start from the world of things. Depending on the perspective, there are then different manifestations in modelling, as indicated in Fig. 2:

$*$ The language dimension describes abstraction levels precisely for languages as an instrument of typical instrument abstractions, e.g. in line with a central need for successful communication and intuitively comprehensible description. In the first abstraction level $\mathcal{M}_1$, representation serves as linguistic abstraction

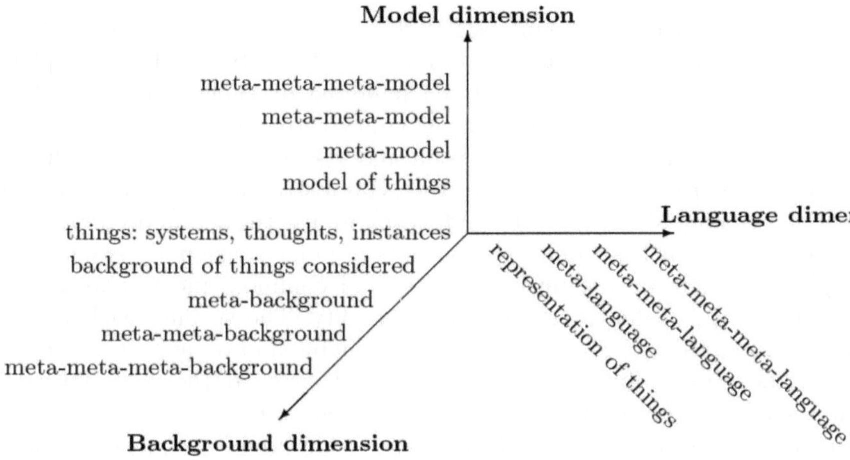

Fig. 2. Dimensions for meta-treatment in modelling.

of things (e.g. systems, thoughts, instances) at $\mathcal{M}_0$ (thing etc. as considered and declared). At $\mathcal{M}_1$ level, the form of expressions is pragmatism-/utility-oriented, canonised like a corset, participant-/community-dependent, and interwoven. Depending on the CoP, specific forms of presentation are also pragmatically preferred, e.g. ER or HERM structures. The instrument, like a language, follows certain rules for well-structured expression due to $\mathcal{M}_2$ (meta-language), at least in the form supporting a craftsman, e.g. frames and pattern, constraints for well-formedness, principles of expression, and the way of representation. For example, the database description follows a series of well-formedness rules such as recursive and layered type definition. The next level of abstraction $\mathcal{M}_3$ (meta-meta-language) then also provides the language reasoning and representation style, the strategic methodology and the moulds for instrumentation. Languages, therefore, also follow a certain language culture and doctrine (called epistemology, ethics, and aesthetics in [46]) at the fourth level $\mathcal{M}_4$ (meta-meta-meta-language).

$*$ Modelling also starts with the things on $\mathcal{M}_0$. These are represented in a model on $\mathcal{M}_1$ (model level) and also use disciplinary modelling assumptions. In database modelling, we also draw on reference solutions for similar problems. The $\mathcal{M}_2$ level represents means for forming models depending on the selected kind or category of models (meta-model level). A typical aid provided by the instrumentation is tried-and-tested stereotypes, pattern, and templates. This is also used to configure models for $\mathcal{M}_1$. At the $\mathcal{M}_3$ level, epistemological and strategic methodologies and moulds are provided so that meta-models for $\mathcal{M}_2$ can be used to create from a constellation at $\mathcal{M}_3$. The $\mathcal{M}_4$ level, in turn, establishes the culture and doctrine for general access to modelling.

$*$ The extent of one's or of CoP's perception, understanding, knowledge, or vision (horizon, purview, range, reach, scope) is the explicit or implicit background dimension, grounding, and reflected insight about knowledge, about paradigms, the disciplinary matrix according to L. Fleck [8] (or T. Kuhn [20]), the personal or CoP world view, and the handling of knowledge. In syntax-oriented modelling, this supporting dimension is suppressed or relegated to the background. Rich models such as conceptual models are then used to explicitly represent the background dimension. In the $\mathcal{M}_0$ abstraction level, we draw on the narrative meaning of things. In the $\mathcal{M}_1$ level, we use the actual used knowing and knowledge, notions that underpin concepts in models, the understanding in given application, normal life business rules, and common understood knowledge practice in the realm of understanding reality. The specific background, knowledge, and familiarity is clarified, made available and organised in $\mathcal{M}_2$ by the general background, by the enlightened world view, by the accepted rules including the adaptation mechanisms, which are underpinned by empirical, specialist and disciplinary knowledge. $\mathcal{M}_3$ and $\mathcal{M}_4$ background is usually overlooked or at least taken for granted. $\mathcal{M}_3$ is background, grounding, and reflected insight about knowledge, about paradigms, the disciplinary matrix, the world view of the CoP, pedigree, acknowledged philosophy in the background, and the handling of knowledge. With the $\mathcal{M}_4$ level, we make use of the systemic culture, norms, postulates, ethics, wisdom, regulations, aesthetics, and skills of the application world.

Applying Meta-Leveling. We are already familiar with this leveling, for example, from the representation of data structures with HERM. In addition to publications, there is also a fully formulated two-year course program in HERM teaching. Things are presented structurally in the language dimension. A professional extension is the consideration of representative sample data from the application at $\mathcal{M}_0$ level. For presentation, various HERM schemata are used in the $\mathcal{M}_1$ level, which follow the HERM construction principles of the meta level $\mathcal{M}_2$ of HERM. Rarely will there be a single structure that encompasses all sides, although global-as-design strategies are often enforced. This systematic construction is supported by HERM grammar, configurators, rules for ortho-normalised presentation, constraint and exception handlers, maximes, principles, embeddings into technology or platform, tactical pragmatism rules for selection of the kind of types for model elements, patterns, etc. from $\mathcal{M}_2$. This also includes the adornment with directives and pragmas for model elements [45].

The $\mathcal{M}_3$ level provides the constellation setting, the underlying mathematics, background theories, paradigms and especially the disciplinary matrix of object-relational database structuring, quality control and guarantee methods, equivalent representations, and folding, e.g. theories of higher-order types, exception handling approaches, flexible redundancy treatment, collection semantics for entity types or reference semantics for relationship types, sophisticated typing as described above, directive-based constraint management, incompleteness or incoherence handling, etc.

The HERM language philosophy and doctrine is given in $\mathcal{M}_4$ as a way of thinking and the culture behind this kind of database structure representation and world views in landscape of application worlds. Another typical meta-language rule is the use of attributes as a tree with a root. As in any natural language, such meta-language rules define a grammar according to which only linguistically correct expressions can be considered well-formed. We already know from languages that meta-languages also contain rules for the use of constructs. It should be noted that even at the $\mathcal{M}_1$ level, more than one model is considered, i.e. a model suite. Following [12] for system consideration, we use coherently at this level a system model, a system description model, an informative model for concise and informative description, and a series of different models depending on the aspect under consideration, such as process models.

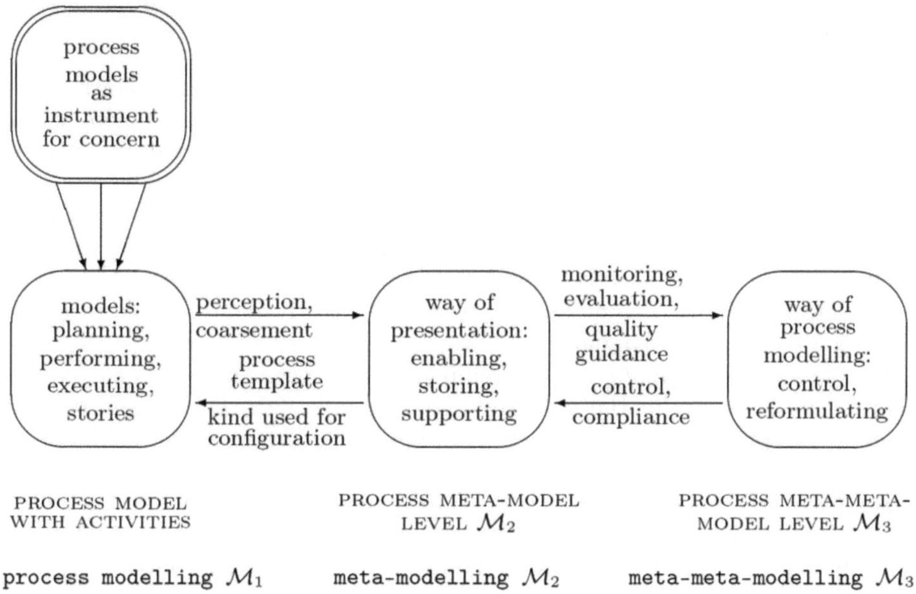

Fig. 3. The meta-control mould for meta-reasoning (rephrased from [44]

Another process-oriented example is a general system structure [9,44] for the meta levels in Fig. 3. We distinguish the process level, the meta-modelling level that contains the modelling methods level with rules the selection of process specification language, and the meta-meta-modelling level that contains the abstraction to meta-modelling methods and controls. This approach is similar to government and binding [7] where the utterance playout is based on a second layer playout selection for the utterance that is again ruled by controller for settling the kind of utterance and its general form.

4.2 Meta-Meta-Model Stereotypes

We have already established that the meta-abstraction mechanism for models is different from that for languages and the inherited knowledge used in the model.

Meta-models define how a model can be compiled, harmonised, and semantically and pragmatically well-founded. This also explains what can and cannot be declared as a model.

Meta-meta-models, on the other hand, describe the strategic orientation of a model using a disciplinary matrix, philosophy, systematics of model construction, configurable and refinable stereotypes, generic forms of models, variations and variants forms, and orientation based on the constellation of models. We can also describe this meta-meta level in terms of model nature and essence and use it to set guidelines for the modelling process, e.g. how a model is formed and functionally equipped.

It seems that a more precise description of the $\mathcal{M}_3$ level is difficult or even impossible. However, we can describe the description using different approaches to $\mathcal{M}_3$ modelling, e.g. the following few ones:

- *Software development $\mathcal{M}_3$ stereotype:* Software development follows a specific development methodology for system and software development within a working system paradigm and is also oriented towards executable, precise, and analysable models.
- *Hardware development $\mathcal{M}_3$ stereotype:* Hardware utilises prefabricated and reliable micro-components of the highest quality, which offer basic functionality such as I/O connectivity with a specialised protocol. These basic components can be used to create complex and directly interpretable programs using a composition language.
- *Component $\mathcal{M}_3$ stereotype:* The architecture stereotype can also be expanded into a model suite for the individual components with their interface model and the corresponding interface coupling [34]. Components compete for resources.
- *Analysis $\mathcal{M}_3$ stereotype:* Program analysis focuses on specific quality characteristics such as precision or liveliness. It can also include validation/-verification/testing/debugging/explanation methods. The models usually require background models of considered application cases.
- *Business process declaration $\mathcal{M}_3$ stereotype:* Business processes follow the business activity style and thus the perspectives of use by various natural and artificial agents with different profiles and portfolios as well as date massives, obligations, roles, and responsibilities. They require 3C collaboration.
- *Platform $\mathcal{M}_3$ stereotype:* A software-hardware platform and technology dictate a specific type of programming and an implicitly specified mindset (e.g. object-oriented, parallel, functional, imperative, procedural, declarative, symbolic, set processing). Models must then follow this style and also the characteristics of the platform.
- *Macro-Meso-Micro $\mathcal{M}_3$ stereotype:* Systems are separated at a macro level with macro states, limited at a meso level using paradigms and principles of realisation and platforms, and then described at a micro level [29]. Macro- and meso-models are relatively independent, analogous to specific implementation variants for transactions (updates in-place, in-local, in-private, etc.).

The stereotype list is very incomplete. Additionally, stereotypes are not used individually in isolation, but often in a mixture of different primary and secondary stereotypes. Each of these stereotypes adopts – mostly implicitly – the mindset in specific areas of application.

4.3 The $\mathcal{M}_0$–$\mathcal{M}_1$ Abberation

One of the seductive Computer Science narratives for databases postulates that $\mathcal{M}_0$ data must follow the model structure at the $\mathcal{M}_1$ level. Such rigidity benefits the programmer, but is counterproductive for the interface. With the introduction of constructors, it is now possible to use different equivalent representation mechanisms as a natural model for all users, as a personal model for individual users, and also as a programmer model. XML pursues a further approach with thing-oriented representation, so that, for example, *MyPorsche911CarreraS* is characterised both by an object-related *serialNo*, *maxSpeed*, *marketLaunch*, *price paid* (hidden in *tax*), etc., as well as the current *mileage*, while objects represented in *Porsche911GT3* at the dealer do not necessarily have to have a *mileage*.

We can observe the same aberration for the other $\mathcal{M}_i$ levels. The use of natural languages teaches us that Computer Science does not need this *one-size-fits-all* narrative (one coding, one representation pattern, ...). One of the reasons why interoperability has failed is because of such unnatural restrictions. With the introduction of graph databases, we have learned that it is not the individual thing-related representation that makes sense, but rather that things must be viewed in their context and also represented directly in this way. This also eliminates problematic integrity constraints and overcomes the overemphasis on local normalisation instead of global normalisation.

5 Conclusion

Computer Science is a model-loving science in which hardly anything can be done without models. At the same time, models are only a quickly used tool that can be forgotten relatively quickly after use, that is no longer modified in the further course of software development, and that then serves only for illustration or wall decoration. A systematic science of models, the modelling as an activity and the use of models, and systematics of modelling exists only in its infancy or – more advanced – for specific modelling languages such as ASM [5] or information systems development [36]. Overlooking the potential of models is another example where Computer Science has taken a wrong turn. Another misconception is the almost exclusive focus on modelling languages and graphical representations, e.g. as domain-oriented languages and diagrams. With ***modelology*** as a science, practice, craft, and art of models, of modelling activities and of the systematic study of modelling, we aim to close this gap (see the threescore papers in [39]).

Summarising. After analysing the shortcomings of current modelling theory, we have limited ourselves to two solutions for constructor theory and meta-abstractions (problems (A)–(F)). The solutions are relatively straightforward. Expressive constructors have long been common in mathematics. Explicit consideration of the background, and in particular of the paradigms assumed from the outset at the meta-meta layer and principles at the meta layer, has advanced science. The explicit integration of the background dimension prevents models from becoming dishonest.

Database Challenges. The challenges and problems ((G)–(K)) can also be addressed despite their omission in research to date. The simultaneous consideration of micro-, meso- and macro-structures in database applications has led to the simplification and enrichment of application systems, e.g. in OLAP [23] and data mining [18] – at least as a starting point for a solution (G)-(I). In Computer Science, physical system representations push syntax to the foreground and semantics and pragmatics into the background. Modelling can help here. With rich models problems (K) can also be solved.

Repairing Imperfections of Wrong Turns. We have used database modelling to demonstrate solutions to challenges, although a similar and equally adequate solution can be found in other areas. Making language more flexible and considering behaviour can break down the rigidity of a state-oriented approach. Simple and unstructured language can only be a starting point. More complex and complicated contexts require different forms of presentation and also an internal structuring of sentences. The co-design of structure, functionality, distribution and interactivity [36] has already demonstrated how to escape the syntax-first trap. Some of the challenges have arisen from technological hubris, formalisation issues, and the programming environment, which is why we need to take a closer look in future.

Applying Modelology for System Development. In Computer Science, the potential and capability of models continues to be underestimated or even attributed to a kind of "intelligence" that leads to really poor system quality without any documentation. Models are still used as quick and rough drafts for describing systems or for declaration of specification languages, mostly in the syntax-only variant. Such blueprints should, however, be sufficiently precise and robust at the same time. With the current kind of use of models, much of the potential of this mental instrument is not even close to being exploited. In *modelology* [39], on the other hand, the questions of 'what', 'how', 'when', 'where', 'why' 'for whom', etc. are asked first and explicitly in both positive and negative form, so that one also understands the instrumentality and the model nature including the added value of models. The development of models can therefore be mastered systematically by observing all essential quality requirements and understanding the background postulates, tool principles and assumptions made.

Models are not isolated, as in aspect-driven representation in software engineering, but are developed as a *model suite* of coherent and well-associated models at different levels of abstraction. It is not the individual model that is refined, but rather the model suite, depending on the scope, perspective and concerns. Model suites allow for both an overall view and a detailed examination of individual aspects in the sub-models, including all exploratory modifications. This allows intuitive, well-founded, rich, and even ad hoc models to be treated in an integrated and revisable manner. It also allows representations to be kept consistent depending on user perspectives and interaction.

Currently, modelling in Computer Science is carried out more as a secondary task, which quickly turns models into disposable goods. Yet another crucial wrong turn. The value of models is, however, increasing through further development of the models in a variety of forms. This means that ken, knowledge, and expertise are explicitly written into the models.

Acknowledgement. The richness of the ASM approach is far wider than currently conceived and elaborated. The approach is awaiting integration with many other subdisciplines. For instance, ASM modelling can be enriched with many ideas from modelology. A presentation of potential applications compared to ASM achievements conducted over more than 30 years would be a great contribution to science. With the exception of a few comments, we have omitted direct references to this rich body of ASM knowledge.

Dedication. We dedicate this work to **Egon Börger**, to whom we are indebted not only for his enormous contribution to the fundamentals of Computer Science, but also for his application of ASM to co-develop BPMN's semi-semantics into a complete and greatly simplified theory [37].

MMM Contribution. This work has emerged from the many MMM [2](MMM is an acronym that stands for the three components of a theory and practice of model-based science: M(odels)–(to_)M(odel_and_use)–(systematic_)M(odelling).) discussions since 2009 with the Kiel club till 2020 and the seven online MMM clubs since 2020, in addition to the email discussions. We would like to thank all colleagues for their contributions to modelology and their suggestions (especially Sergey Stupnikov for his remark on Fig. 2), as well as their critical questions and closer examination.

References

1. Abelson, H., Sussman, G.J.: Structure and Interpretation of Computer Programs, 2nd edn. MIT Press, Cambridge (1996)
2. Beeri, C., Thalheim, B.: Identification as a primitive of database models. In: Proceedings of FoMLaDO'98, pp. 19–36. Kluwer, London (1999)
3. Bense, H., Thalheim, B., Zeh, T.: A category system for data properties. In: Arai, K. (ed.) FICC 2025. LNNS, vol. 1283, pp. 674–691. Springer, Cham (2025). https://doi.org/10.1007/978-3-031-84457-7_42
4. Berg, K., Kalinichenko, L.: Modeling facilities for the component-based software development method. In: Proceedings of ADBIS'96, pp. 10–20, Moscow (1996)

5. Börger, E., Raschke, A.: Modeling Companion for Software Practitioners. Springer, Cham (2018). https://doi.org/10.1007/978-3-662-56641-1
6. Börger, E., Stärk, R.: Abstract State Machines - A Method for High-level System Design and Analysis. Springer, Heidelberg (2003). https://doi.org/10.1007/978-3-642-18216-7
7. Chomsky, N.: Some Concepts and Consequences of the Theory of Government and Binding. MIT Press, Cambridge (1982)
8. Cohen, R.S., Schnelle, T. (eds.) Cognition and Fact: Materials on Ludwik Fleck, volume 87 of Boston Studies in the Philosophy of Science. Dortrecht, Reidel (1986)
9. Cox, M.T., Raja, A. (eds.): Metareasoning - Thinking About Thinking. MIT Press, Cambridge (2011)
10. Dahanayake, A.: How to catch a moonbeam: from model-ware to component-ware software product engineering. In: Dahanayake, A., Pastor, O., Thalheim, B. (eds.) M2P 2020. CCIS, vol. 1401, pp. 47–66. Springer, Cham (2021). https://doi.org/10.1007/978-3-030-72696-6_2
11. Ehrig, H., Engels, G., Kreowski, H.-J., Rozenberg, G. (eds.) Handbook of Graph Grammars and Computing by Graph Transformations. Vol. 2: Applications, Languages and Tools. World Scientific, Singapore (1999)
12. Fischer, J., Møller-Pedersen, B., Prinz, A., Thalheim, B.: Models versus model descriptions. In: Dahanayake, A., Pastor, O., Thalheim, B. (eds.) M2P 2020. CCIS, vol. 1401, pp. 67–89. Springer, Cham (2021). https://doi.org/10.1007/978-3-030-72696-6_3
13. Frank, U.: Toward a unified conception of multi-level modelling: advanced requirements. In: Proceedings of MODELS 2018 Workshops, volume 2245 of CEUR Workshop Proceedings, pp. 718–727. CEUR-WS.org (2018)
14. Graham, P.: Hackers and Painters - Big Ideas from the Computer Age. O'Reilly (2004)
15. Hannula, M., Kontinen, J.: A finite axiomatization of conditional independence and inclusion dependencies. In: Beierle, C., Meghini, C. (eds.) FoIKS 2014. LNCS, vol. 8367, pp. 211–229. Springer, Cham (2014). https://doi.org/10.1007/978-3-319-04939-7_10
16. Hunter, P.J.: Heart modeling, computational physiology and the IUPS Physiome project. In: Parent, C., Schewe, K.-D., Storey, V.C., Thalheim, B. (eds.) ER 2007. LNCS, vol. 4801, pp. 21–21. Springer, Heidelberg (2007). https://doi.org/10.1007/978-3-540-75563-0_2
17. Inmon, W.H., Zachman, J.A., Geiger, J.G.: Data Stores, Data Warehousing and the Zachman Framework. McGraw Hill, New York (1997)
18. Jannaschk, K.: Infrastruktur für ein Data Mining Design Framework: eine Untersuchung mit Fallbeispielen. Ph.D. thesis, University of Kiel, Germany (2017)
19. Kramer, F.F.: Ein allgemeiner Ansatz zur Metadaten-Verwaltung. Ph.D. thesis, Christian-Albrechts University of Kiel, Technical Faculty, Kiel (2018)
20. Kuhn, T.: The Structure of Scientific Revolutions. University of Chicago Press, Chicago, Illinois, 2nd, Enlarged, with Postscript Edition (1970)
21. Kühne, T.: Multi-dimensional multi-level modeling. Softw. Syst. Model. **21**(2), 543–559 (2022)
22. Lenz, H.-J., Thalheim, B.: OLTP-OLAP schemes for sound applications. In: TEAA 2005. LNCS, vol. 3888, pp. 99–113. Springer, Trondheim (2005)
23. Lenz, H.-J., Thalheim, B.: A formal framework of aggregation for the OLAP-OLTP model. J. UCS **15**(1), 273–303 (2009)
24. Ma, H., Noack, R., Schewe, K.-D., Thalheim, B.: Using meta-structures in database design. Informatica **34**, 387–403 (2010)

25. Mayr, H.C., Storey, V.C., Thalheim, B.: The meaning of modeling concepts: the left triptych wing. In: Information Modelling and Knowledge Bases XXXVII, volume 418 of Frontiers in Artificial Intelligence and Applications, pp. 255–273. IOS Press (2026)
26. Mayr, H.C., Thalheim, B.: The triptych of conceptual modeling - a framework for a better understanding of conceptual modeling. Softw. Syst. Model. **20**(1), 7–24 (2021)
27. Neumayr, B., Schrefl, M., Thalheim, B.: Hetero-homogeneous hierarchies in data warehouses. In: APCCM, volume 110 of CRPIT, pp. 61–70. Australian Computer Society (2010)
28. Prinz, A., Møller-Pedersen, B., Fischer, J., Thalheim, B.: Understanding Modelling and Programming. Springer, Cham (2024). https://doi.org/10.1007/978-3-031-71280-7
29. Prinz, A., Thalheim, B.: Operational semantics of transactions. In: ADC 2003, volume 17 of CRPIT, pp. 169–179. Australian Computer Society (2003)
30. Schewe, K.-D.: The specification of data-intensive application systems. Advanced Ph.D. (Habilitation thesis), Brandenburg University of Technology at Cottbus, Faculty of Mathematics, Natural Sciences and Computer Science (1994)
31. Schewe, K.-D., Thalheim, B.: Component-driven engineering of database applications. In: APCCM'06, volume 49 of CRPIT, pp. 105–114 (2006)
32. Schewe, K.-D., Thalheim, B.: Design and Development of Web Information Systems. Springer, Cham (2019). https://doi.org/10.1007/978-3-662-58824-6
33. Smith, J.M., Smith, D.C.P.: Database abstractions: aggregation and generalization. ACM TODS **2**(2), 105–133 (1977)
34. Sünbül, A.: Architectural design of evolutionary software systems in continuous software engineering. Ph.D. thesis, TU Berlin, Germany (2001)
35. Thalheim, B.: Dependencies in Relational Databases. Teubner, Leipzig (1991)
36. Thalheim, B.: Entity-Relationship Modeling - Foundations of Database Technology. Springer, Berlin (2000). https://doi.org/10.1007/978-3-662-04058-4
37. Thalheim, B.: BPMN and beyond business process modelling notation, workflow modelling, functionality of systems (Collection of papers, esp. with E. Börger) (2009). https://www.researchgate.net/ (search keyphrase: "BPMN and Beyond Thalheim"). Assessed 14 Dec 2025
38. Thalheim, B.: Specialization and generalization. In: Liu, L., Özsu, M.T. (eds.) Encyclopedia of Database Systems, pp. 2746–2747. Springer, Boston (2009). https://doi.org/10.1007/978-0-387-39940-9_175
39. Thalheim, B.: Models, to model, and modelling. In: Collections of Papers on Modelling. https://www.researchgate.net (search keyphrase "Towards a theory of models, especially conceptual models and modelling"), also academia.edu, 2009-2025
40. Thalheim, B.: The Conceptual Framework to Multi-Layered Database Modelling based on Model Suites, volume 206 of Frontiers in Artificial Intelligence and Applications, pp. 116–134. IOS Press (2010)
41. Thalheim, B.: Web information systems: collection of BTU and CAU papers (2003–2009). https://www.researchgate.net/ (search keyphrase: "Web Information Systems: Analysis, Design, Development, and Implementation of Business Sites, Collaboration Sites, Edutainment (e-Learning) Sites, and Infotainment (Information) Sites") (2010)
42. Thalheim, B.: Semiotics in databases. In: Schewe, K.-D., Singh, N.K. (eds.) MEDI 2019. LNCS, vol. 11815, pp. 3–19. Springer, Cham (2019). https://doi.org/10.1007/978-3-030-32065-2_1

43. Thalheim, B.: Schema optimisation instead of (local) normalisation. In: Herzig, A., Kontinen, J. (eds.) FoIKS 2020. LNCS, vol. 12012, pp. 281–300. Springer, Cham (2020). https://doi.org/10.1007/978-3-030-39951-1_17
44. Thalheim, B.: Model-based reasoning for investigating the heart capability. In: Lohff, B., Schaefer, J. (eds.) Cardio-Physiology Challenging Empirical Philosophy, vol. II, pp. 162–199. BoD, Norderstedt (2022)
45. Thalheim, B.: Science and practice of modelling. In: Meer, K., Rabinovich, A., Ravve, E., Villaveces, A. (eds.) Model Theory, Computer Science, and Graph Polynomials. Trends in Mathematics, pp. 525–540. Springer, Cham (2025). https://doi.org/10.1007/978-3-031-86319-6_29
46. Van Gigch, J.P.: Metadecisions: Rehabilitating Epistemology. Springer, New York (2003). https://doi.org/10.1007/978-1-4615-0097-1
47. Wedekind, H., Ortner, E., Inhetveen, R.: Informatik als Grundbildung. Informatik-Spektrum **27**(2), 172–180 (2004). https://doi.org/10.1007/s00287-004-0383-z

Modeling and Implementing Human-Centered Digital Twins

Albert Fleischmann[1] and Christian Stary[2(✉)]

[1] InterAktiv Business Consulting, Pfaffenhofen, Germany
Albert.Fleischmann@interaktiv.expert
[2] Institute of Business Informatics, Johannes Kepler University Linz, Altenberger Straße 69, 4040 Linz, Austria
Christian.Stary@jku.at

Abstract. In this paper, we investigate the semantically correct modeling and implementation of Digital Twins (DTs), particularly the connections between digital representations, physical objects, and human actors. The semantically correct implementation of DTs using Abstract State Machines (ASMs) enables the transparent and intuitive development of complex systems, especially Cyber-Physical Systems. We discuss the human-centered definition, representation, refinement, validation, and implementation of Digital Twins and their physical counterparts. This is based on behavioral models from Subject-oriented Business Process Management (S-BPM) and ASM-based execution patterns. The models offer not only an intuitive diagrammatic notation and the step-by-step refinement to executable system specifications, but also the structured configuration and the dynamic adaptation to changing operating conditions. The ASM-based interpretation of DT models captures all the execution capabilities required to control the behavior of a Cyber-Physical System (CPS) at runtime. Hence, the approach fully integrates DT design with cyber-physical operations in the sense of context-aware development of socio-technical systems in dynamic environments. The ASM specifications' executable code allows to check DTs whether they meet the required behavior prior to operation.

Keywords: Digital Twin (DT) · Abstract State Machine (ASM) · Formal semantics · Cyber-Physical System (CPS) · Socio-technical Systems · Validation · Specification · Design-integrated engineering

1 Introduction

The increased propagation of Cyber-Physical Systems (CPSs) leads to increased complexity in system development and operation. It affects economy and everyday life, not only in terms of digitally transforming technological infrastructures, but rather in terms of establishing novel ecosystems that increasingly involve humans as designers aside their role of users. Thereby, complexity is caused by the heterogeneity of CPS components and their dynamic connectivity. A variety

A. Raschke et al. (Eds.): Egon Börger Festschrift, LNCS 16580, pp. 445–468, 2026.
https://doi.org/10.1007/978-3-032-24494-9_21

of experts, including sensor, robot, and software specialists need to contribute to the development of CPSs, and need to understand design specifications and runtime processes.

Albeit the heterogeneity of (proprietary) components, their autonomy plays a crucial role – each part should be able to operate stand-alone while being connected with other components. CPSs need to be dynamically adaptable, due to the current volatility of ecosystems and steady technological progress. Adaptation challenges developers, providers, and users. Digital Twins (DTs) can handle the resulting complexity. They are digital representations that have the capability to accompany the design and engineering process of CPSs, control them at runtime, and support the continuous adaption of their behavior: "A digital twin is a set of virtual information constructs that mimics the structure, context, and behavior of a natural, engineered, or social system (or system-of-systems), is dynamically updated with data from its physical twin, has a predictive capability, and informs decisions that realize value. The bidirectional interaction between the virtual and the physical is central to the digital twin" [12].

In this paper we take a systems' engineering and systems thinking perspective when addressing the design and operation of a human-centered DT. As Kasser in his 2021 INCOSE lecture [10] states, systems engineering captures "a set of problem-solving tools for remedying complexity" and needs to "deal with parts and their interaction as a whole" (the cited statements stem from the presented slides). Rather than "isolating parts to understand behavior" in conventional thinking, systems thinking needs to be applied to "explore [the] emergent nature of the system as a whole".

Systems thinking includes several perspectives, namely a scientific, external, internal, progressive, and a quantitative one [10]. For holistic engineering of DTs, not only the big picture and operational elements (concerning the What) from an external perspective needs to be included, but also functional ones. They concern the How. They need to be integrated with structural elements from the internal (analytic) perspective as well as the temporal dimension from a progressive perspective. In the lecture Kasser argues that Systems Engineering is the best way to tackle the problem of handling the complexity of socio-technical systems in a cost-effective and timely manner. We follow this integrative approach in the context of DT-based development of CPSs designed for humans.

The paper is structured as follows: Sect. 2 details the background and concept of DTs. Sections 3, 4 and 5 provide requirements for DT model construction and implementation, and subject-oriented concepts to meet them. Abstract State Machines (ASMs) are motivated for semantically correct specification and operation of DTs. Section 6 concludes the paper with the insights to take away and several topics for future research.

2 Digital Twins Becoming Digital Triplets for Socio-technical System Development

In this section, we develop a systems perspective on Digital Twins (DTs) that bridges the physical, digital, and human domains. We describe the traditional

DT concept and its explicit extension to include the human dimension relevant for design and operation. Furthermore, we demonstrate how it applies across the product life-cycle to define and understand system behavior [17].

Figure 1 shows the extended definition of DTs as we use it in this article. We explicitly enrich the basic understanding of DTs through integrating and defining the role of human entities. Referring to a device or system, humans are involved. They either interact with the physical entity or the virtual model. Consequently, DTs become a digital triplet. Therefore, we prefer to use the term socio-technical when referring to CPSs.

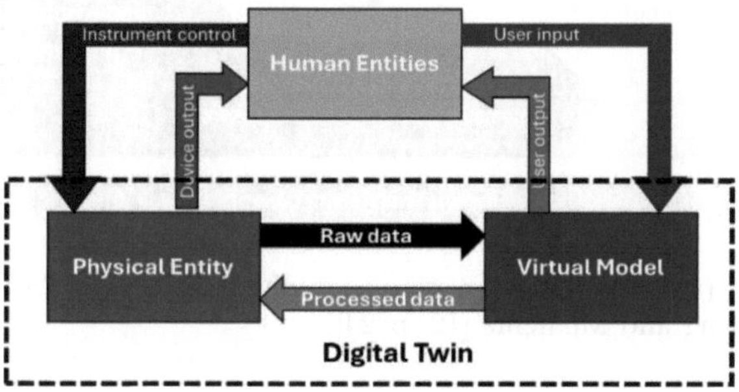

Fig. 1. Extending the Digital Twin to a Digital Triplet.

The basic components of Digital Triplets as shown in Fig. 1 are (i) a physical entity, (ii) a virtual model, (iii) human entities, and (iv) connections between the physical entity, human entities, and the virtual model. Figure 2 details the operation of the resulting ecosystem where "information flows bidirectionally between the virtual representation and physical counterpart. These information flows may be through automated processes, human-driven processes, or a combination of the two" [12, p. 24]

The traditional dimensions of DT model construction still do not consider human entities explicitly. They rather refer to (cf. [17]):

- Geometry: It describes the geometric shape and assembly relationships of the physical entity.
- Physics: It refers to the properties and constraints of the physical entities.
- Behavior: It concerns the dynamically occurring states of the physical entity in relationship to the virtual model and human entities.
- Rules: They are grounded in historical data to make the system smarter.
- Human interaction: This aspect refers to the parametrization and human control of the virtual and physical entities.

Figure 3 shows an example of a Digital Triplet featuring human-oriented DTs. It concerns a traffic management system as socio-technical CPS. The figure shows the three model dimensions. The geometry and the physics of the intersection

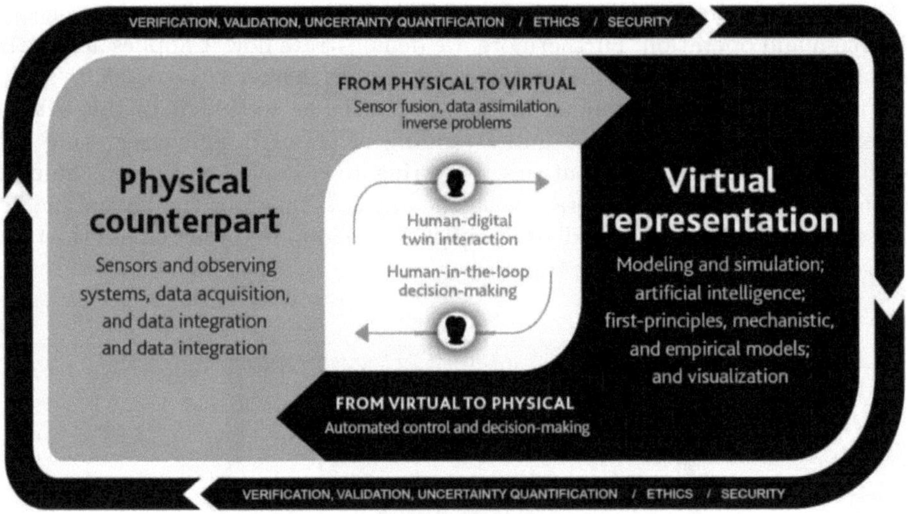

Fig. 2. The DT as part of a DT ecosystem as understood by the National Academy of Sciences, Engineering and Medicine [12, p. 24].

is part of the physical entity. The physical entity includes sensors which detect whether a vehicle is approaching the crossing. The sensors cause an event which is sent to the virtual system which evaluates the event and causes a reaction. This reaction can be to switch the traffic lights affecting human behavior at the crossing.

In this work we consider the geometry and physical aspects of a Digital Triplet as part of its implementation. We focus on the functional aspects which are covered by the behavior and rule properties. With respect to our example we need first to consider the sequence in which the traffic lights switch on and off which lamps as part of the design process. During the implementation phase we then specify who or which entity will execute which part of the behavior defined in an abstract model.

3 Modeling and Implementing Digital Triplets

Based on the dimensions of model construction outlined in Sect. 2 for the DT life cycle, several aspects of Digital Triplets modeling and development have to be considered [17]:

- Model assembly
- Model fusion
- Model verification
- Model modification
- Model management
- Statistics' analysis toward the DT modeling

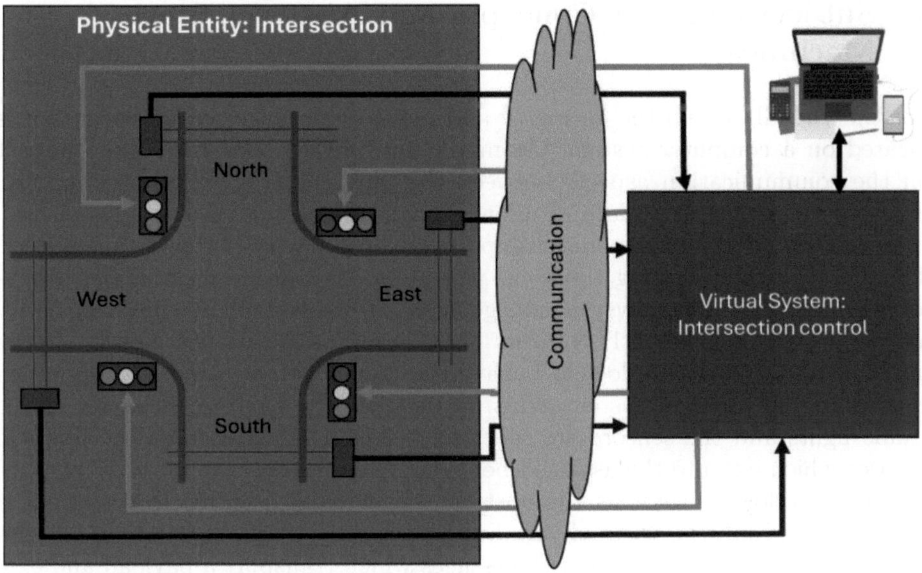

Fig. 3. Intersection control as example of a Digital Twin system.

Based on these aspects of modeling and implementation of DT, fundamental requirements for modeling concepts and languages can be derived. In a Digital Triplet physical, human, and virtual elements exchange information to monitor, simulate, predict, diagnose and control the state and behavior of the socio-technical system. In general, socio-technical systems have a complex structure with many parts which interact with each other to synchronize their various tasks. In order to handle such complex structures, several modeling and implementation features have been proposed, e.g. [8,15–17]:

- *Hierarchy of subsystems*: It supports model assembly, model fusion, model modification, and model management.
- *Loosely coupling of subsystems*: It supports model assembly, model fusion, model modification, and model management.
- *Concurrency*: It supports model assembly, model fusion, model modification, and model management.
- *State transitions*: They support model verification, and model modification.
- *Effective event handling*: It supports model verification, and model modification.

A variety of modeling languages provides concepts to meet the requirements for handling models mentioned above, however, to different extent. An overview on modeling concepts can be found in [5].

4 Subject-oriented Concepts and Abstract State Machines

For the virtual system the geometry and physics are not essential because it is located on a computer system. Geometry and physics may have some impact on the communication aspects between the physical and virtual system, e.g., different values for wear data or allowed environment temperature. In general, these aspects do not have a major impact on the behavior of the virtual system. Therefore, in the following the focus will be on the specification of the behavior logic of DTs. The physical and geometrical aspects of the physical entity are described independently from its behavioral and functional aspects. In the implementation step the logical behavior is connected with the corresponding entities of the physical system. This means that the abstract behavior of the traffic lights and the sensors are specified before it is assigned to the physical entities which execute the assigned behavior.

In the following sections the abstract behavior of a traffic light system is described in a subject-oriented way. Subjects are the active elements of a socio-technical systems. They exchange messages which transport a payload and execute actions on objects. Objects are entities on which operations (actions) are defined. These operations can either change the state of an object or return the control to the entity which initiates that operation.

Internally, a subject uses objects for its tasks. The behavior specification of a subject contains the sequence of messages and their payload. It also contains the operations that need to be executed on specific objects and how the results of these actions influence the further behavior. If a subject or an object is specified, it is left open how it will be implemented. A subject is an abstract and active entity described by its behavior and the object used. Objects are entities which have states and offer operations which change the state of an object or deliver the current state of an object.

4.1 Structure of Subject-oriented Models

This section defines a model. The presented sample model is for organizing traffic flow on a road crossing. All functional aspects are considered step by step. The implementation aspects which transfer the functional model into a triplet are introduced in the implementation phase (see Sect. 5).

The specification of a subject-oriented model representing a DT consists of the Subject Interaction Diagram (SID) and the Subject Behavior Diagram (SBD).

Subject Interaction Diagram (SID). The traffic light control system consists of three subsystems. Figure 4 shows these subsystems. Messages are exchanged between these subsystems. These interactions are described as connecting lines between the subsystems. Each line between subsystems represents sets of interactions.

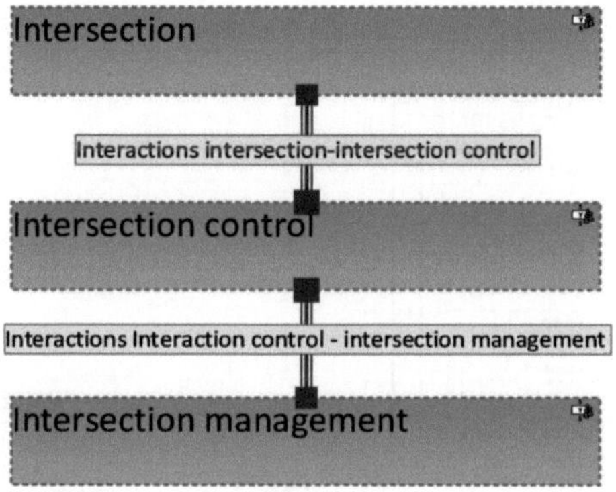

Fig. 4. Subsystems of the traffic light control system.

The intersection subsystem covers aspects directly related to intersections, such as traffic lights and car sensors. The subsystem intersection control describes how to control intersection equipment, such as traffic lights and sensors. The subsystem intersection management captures management aspects, such as time periods, for controlling the flow of traffic.

Each subsystem will now be examined in more detail. Figure 5 shows the Subject Behavior Diagram (SBD) of the "Intersection" subsystem. This subsystem consists of the "Intersection Steering System" subject and contains four subsystems: "North," "East," "South," and "West." The subject "Intersection Steering System" receives the messages "Switch On," "Switch Off," and "Interaction Parameters" from the subject "Intersection Interface" and sends the message "Car Traffic Data" to it. This subject is part of the "Intersection Control" subsystem. These messages belong to the interaction set "Interactions Intersection-Intersection Control" shown in Fig. 4. Subjects which are part of another subsystem than the considered subsystem are called external subjects.

The subject "Intersection Steering System" communicates with the subjects "North road", "East road", "South road", and "West road". These subjects are part of the subsystems "North", "East", "South", and "West".

Figure 6 shows the communication structure of the "North" subsystem. The East, South, and West subsystems are structured analogously. Figure 7 shows the Subject Interaction Diagram of the subsystem "Intersection Control". The subject "Intersection Interface" which was an external interface of the subsystem "Intersection" communicates with the subject "Intersection steering system" which is now an external subject because it belongs to the "intersection" subsystem.

The "Intersection Controller" subject turns the intersection steering system on or off by sending "switch on" or "switch off" messages. The payload of the "Intersection Parameters" message contains intersection control parameters, such as the duration of the green and red phases. The "Intersection Controller" forwards the "Car Traffic Data" message to the "Intersection Manage-

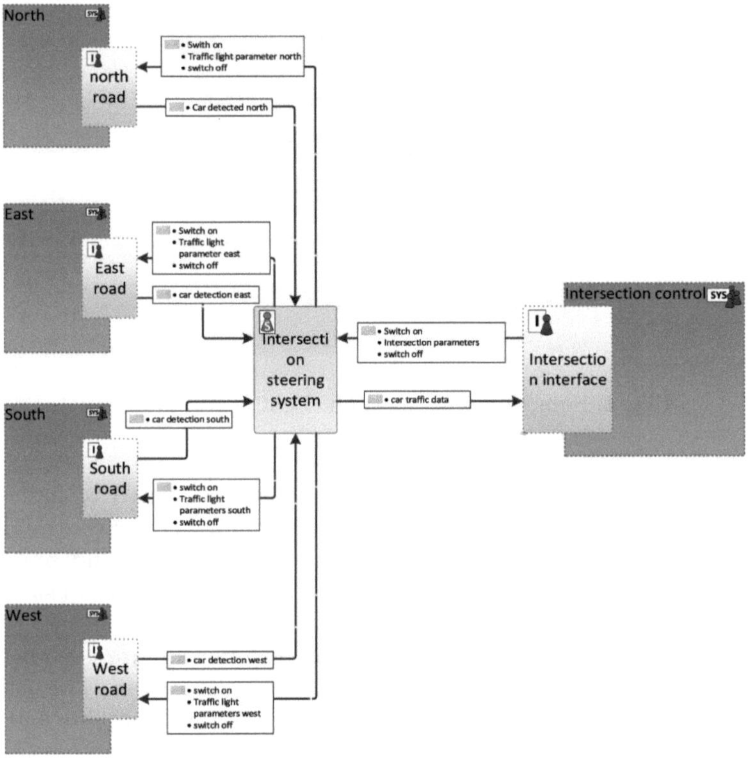

Fig. 5. Detailed structure of Intersection subsystem.

ment Interface," which then forwards it to the external "Intersection Manager," which is part of the "Intersection Management" subsystem. The "Intersection Control" subsystem coordinates the intersection's functions with the functions of "Intersection Management" which integrates the section's functions into the overarching objectives of traffic flow management. The latter may include several intersections.

Figure 8 shows the interaction diagram for the "Intersection Management" subsystem. This subsystem creates intersection control parameters based on intersection traffic data collected by sensors and input from people responsible for organizing traffic flow. The "Intersection Manager" receives the "Car Traffic" message, which is forwarded to the "Transaction Traffic Data Management" subject. This subject stores the data. The "Intersection manager" can be asked for historical traffic data by sending the "get intersection data" message. The requested data are provided to the "Intersection Manager" as the payload of the"Intersection Data" message.

Additionally, the "Intersection Manager" can be asked for various inputs from traffic management personnel. The management personal input is handled by the subject "Human Interface".

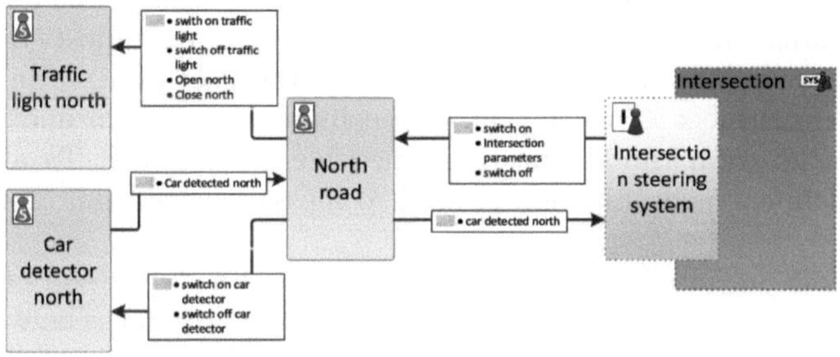

Fig. 6. Communication structure of traffic light subsystem North as subsystem of the Intersection system.

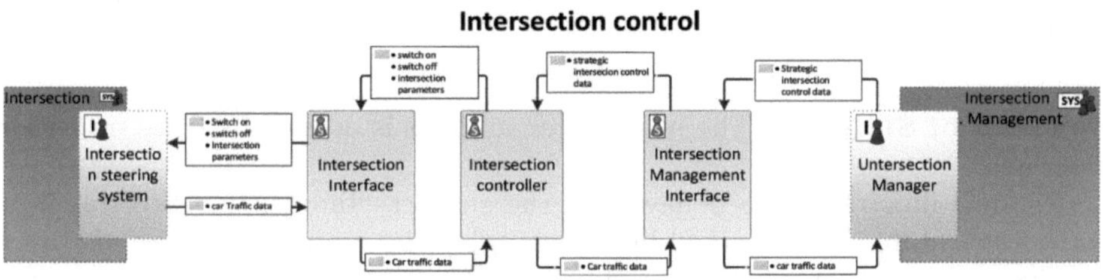

Fig. 7. Subject Interaction Diagram of the "Interaction Control" subsystem.

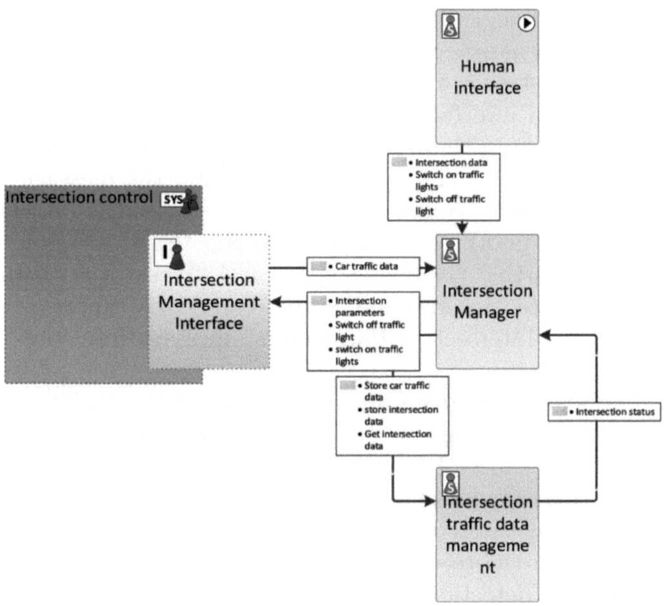

Fig. 8. Subject Interaction Diagram of the "Intersection Management" subsystem.

Message Exchange and Synchronization To organize their cooperation, subjects exchange messages. These messages can transport objects from one subject to another. Related to message exchange is the synchronization of subjects' execution. If a subject is waiting for a specific message from another subject, it stops its execution thread until the message is available. To allow a flexible way to define synchronization related to message exchange, input pools are introduced.

Input pools are intelligent mailboxes with a defined size and other properties. These properties help specify the communication interfaces between physical devices, virtual entities, and human entities in an abstract way. For example, if messages must be exchanged synchronously, i.e. the sending entity stops executing its thread until the receiving entity has accepted the message, the input pool for this message has the size zero. For other messages from other subjects the input pool may have another size. Details about this input pool concept are described in [7].

Behavior of Subjects. The behavior of subjects is defined by state transition diagrams.

Figure 9 illustrates the behavior of the subject "Intersection Steering System". Each state is represented by a rectangle. There are three types of states. Receive states are represented by red rectangles with a small "R" in the upper left corner. Send states are represented by green rectangles with a small "S" in the upper left corner. Internal states are represented by yellow rectangles with a small 'D" in the upper left corner. The start state of a behavior description is marked with a small triangle in the upper right corner. Receive and send states are also labeled with a name.

In Fig. 9, the start state is a receive state with the name "Switch on". In this state, the "Intersection interface" subject expects the "Switch on" message. If this message is available in the input pool, the transition to the "North" state is executed. This state is a send state. In this state, the message "Switch on" must be sent to the subject "North Road." If the message can be sent (deposited in the receiver's input pool), the transition to the "East" state is executed. In the state sequence "North," "East," "South," and "West," the traffic lights turn on. In the receive state "Intersection Parameters," the "Intersection Steering System" receives the "Intersection Parameters" message from the "Intersection Interface."

The time periods of the green and red phases of the traffic lights, etc. are contained in the payload of this message. In the internal state "Calculate direction parameters", the values of the traffic light parameters for each traffic light are derived. Once this calculation is finished, the "Parameters Calculated" transition is executed. In the subsequent send states, these parameter values are sent to each traffic light. In the receive state "Car Detection", the "Car Detection" message from the car detection subjects is expected. These messages are forwarded to the "Intersection interface" subject. If, in the "Car detection" state, the message "Car detection" from the car detection subjects are expected. These messages are forwarded to the subject “Intersection interface”. If in state “Car detection” the message “Switch off” is received the traffic lights are switched off in the succeeding states “North”,”East”,”South” and “West”. After these state sequence, the end state “End” is reached.

These messages are forwarded to the subject “Intersection Interface”. If the “Car Detection” state receives the “Switch Off” message, the traffic lights are switched off in the succeeding states: “North,” “East,” “South,” and “West.” After this sequence of states, the final state, “End”, is reached.‘

Figure 10 shows the behavior of the subject “North Road.” The “Intersection Steering System” exchanges messages with this subject. In the start state, “Switch on traffic light,” the subject “North Road” receives the message “Switch on.” Then, the standard behavior sequence is executed. In the “Wait close time” receive state, no message is expected. Receiving messages can be controlled by timeouts. This means that if an expected message is not available within a defined time period, the timeout transition is executed. In the “Wait for close time” state, no message is expected, and the execution thread stops here for the defined time period. This time period is the red time.

The main behavior of the subject, “Behavior North”, is supplemented by exception-handling behaviors. Both exception handlers begin in the “All states” state. This means these exception handlers are activated in all states. One exception handler controls the “Switch off” message from the subject “Intersection Steering System.” When this message arrives, the main behavior is interrupted, regardless of the state in which the main behavior is executing. Now the behavior defined in the exception handler is executed. Independent in which state of the main behavior the “Switch off” message is received the exception handler behavior is executed in which the traffic light “North” is switched off and the end state is reached.

The second exception handler handles the message “Car detected north” from the subject “Car detector north”. This means the message is forwarded to the subject “Intersection Steering System” and the main behavior continues in the state in which the exception arose.

Figure 11 shows the behavior of subject “Human Interface”. The internal functions (Yellow rectangles) represent the internal functions to “Calculate” the intersection parameters, e.g., red phase time periods. The function “Input of intersection parameters” calculates the initial intersection control parameters. In the implementation phase this function is executed by a human. However, in the model user inputs are considered as the execution of a function.

Objects in Subject-oriented Models. Subjects exchange messages which are used to synchronize their cooperation and to transport objects which have to be handed over from one subject to another to fulfill their tasks. Objects can be virtual or physical. In the abstract behavior model as it is defined in the section above all objects are considered as virtual entities. The state of an object is represented by values of variables. Message payloads are copies of these

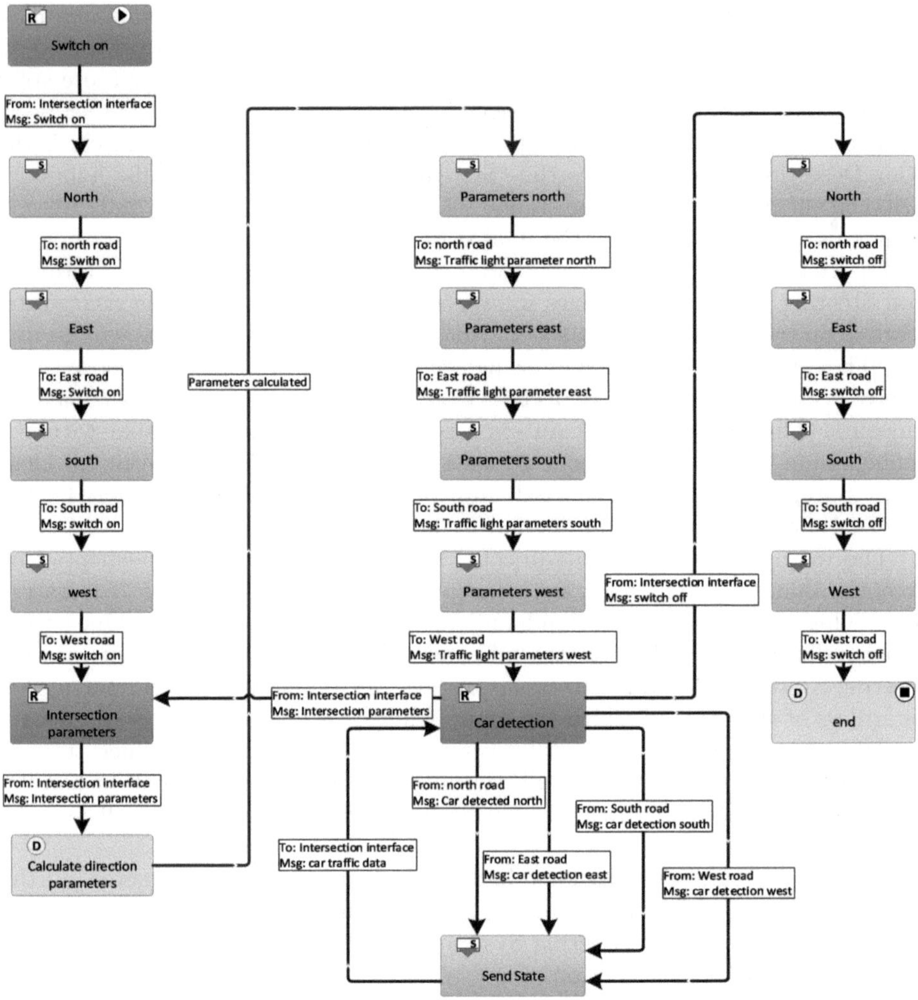

Fig. 9. Subject Behavior Diagram of the subject "Intersection Steering System".

values. Figure 12 shows the payload of message the message "Intersection data". This payload is of the "Intersection control parameters" type.

An internal object of the type "Intersection control parameter" is used by the subject "Human Interface" (see Fig. 13). This object is used in the state "Input of Intersection Parameters". This operation is used to define the values of the complex object "Intersection control parameter". Figure 14 shows the dialog in which the usage of the internal object is assigned to state "Input of intersection parameters". How the internal object is changed is normally described in natural language. In our example this operation on the internal object is executed by humans who type in the object values.

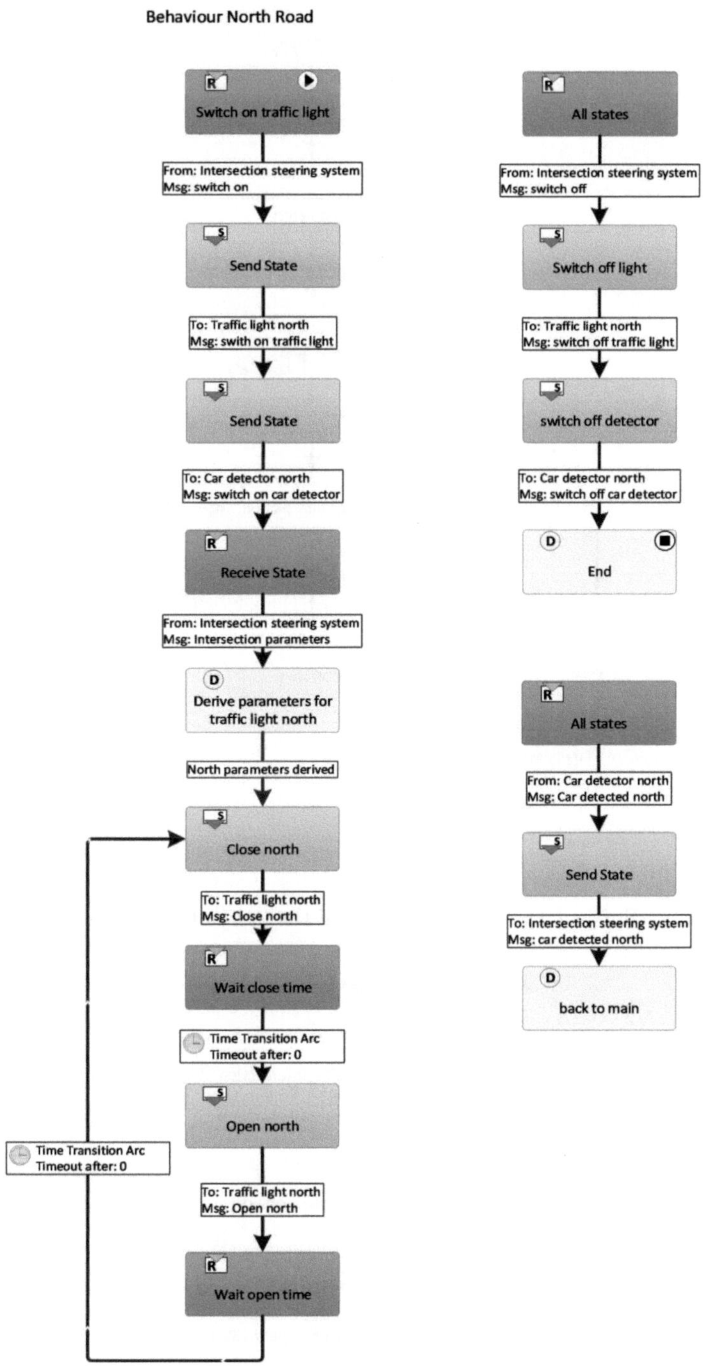

Fig. 10. Subject Behavior Diagram of the subject "North road".

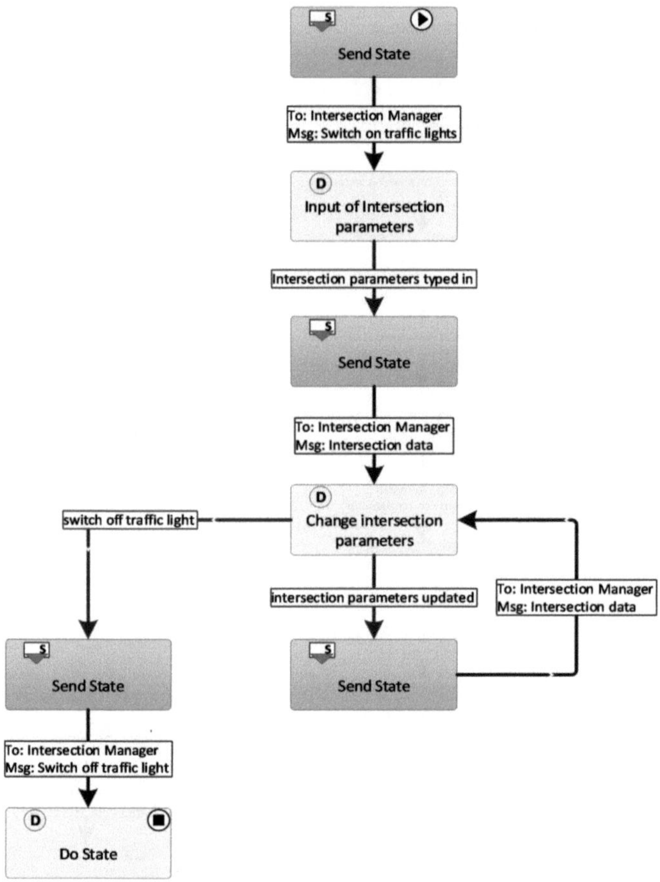

Fig. 11. Subject Behavior Diagram of the subject "Human Interface"

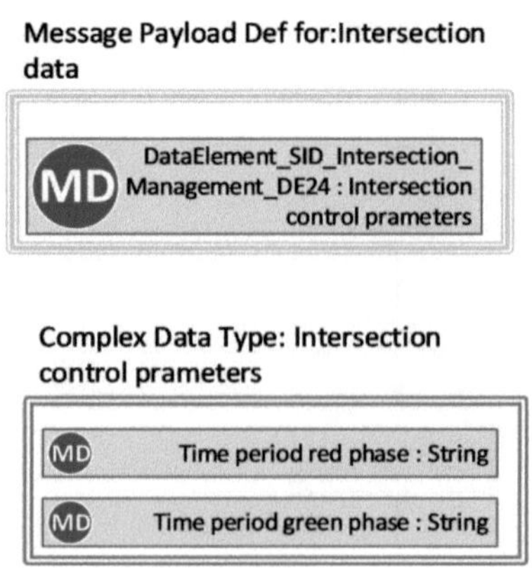

Fig. 12. Data objects used in the subsystem "Intersection Management".

In the state "Transfer intersection parameters" the message "Intersection data" is sent. As described above this message has a payload of the type "Intersection control parameters" which is the same type as the internal object of the subject "Human Interface". The values of the internal object are mapped to the message payload (see Fig. 15). The receiving subject copies the values of the payload to an internal object of the same type.

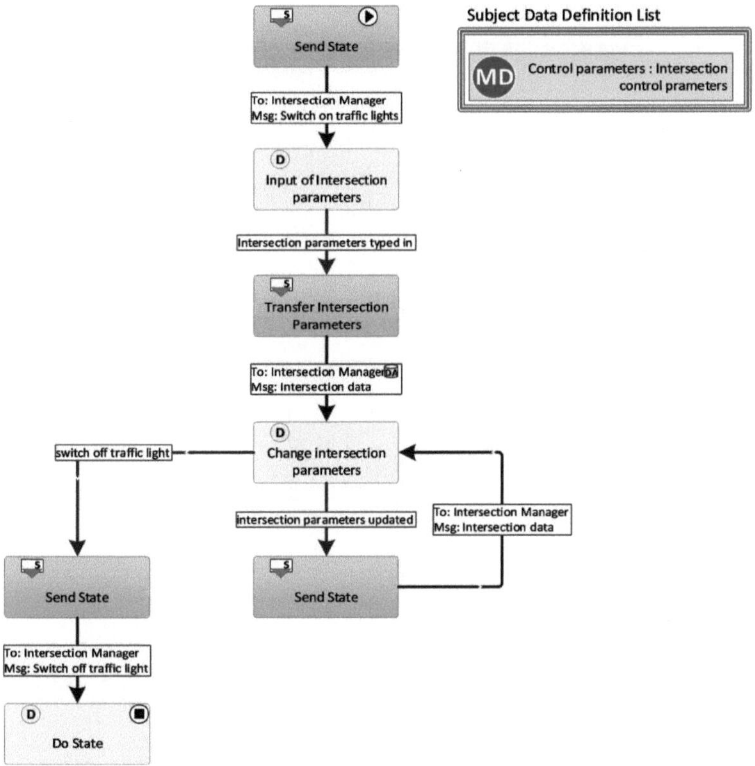

Fig. 13. Data objects used in the subject "Human Interface".

4.2 Execution Semantics of Subjects Defined by ASMs

Subject-oriented models as described in the previous sections are stored in an OWL based standard. This OWL standard specifies the core elements of subject-oriented models and the relationships between them.

Figure 16 shows a visualization of a segment of the OWL standard with model elements for describing Subject Behavior Diagrams (Behavior Describing Components). The depicted structure is included in the standard ontology for subject-oriented models.

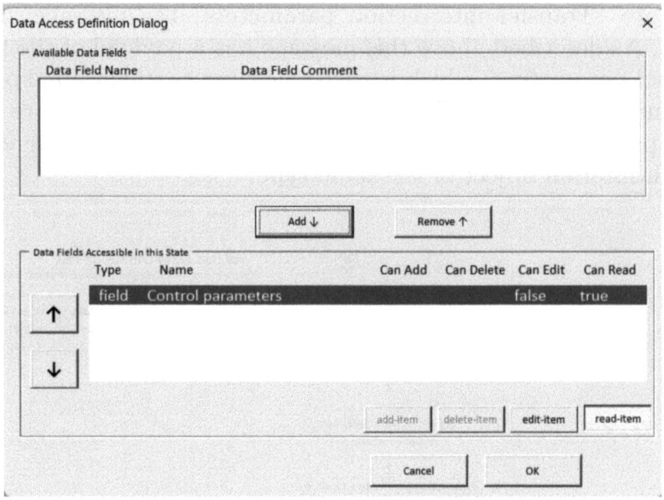

Fig. 14. Usage of internal object "Control Parameters" in state "Input of intersection parameters".

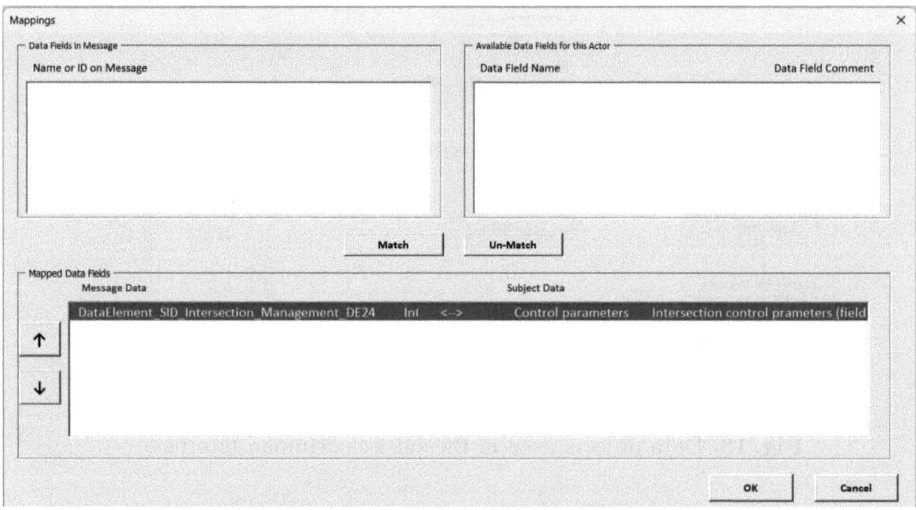

Fig. 15. Values of internal of object are mapped to payload parameters.

However, specifying the static model structure is only half of what is formally necessary for the straightforward digitalization of processes. The second important aspect is a formal specification of the execution semantics of a modeling language. That is, a uniform definition of a workflow engine's behavior would have when executing a corresponding process model, so that any engine conforming to the specification would execute the same model by 100%.

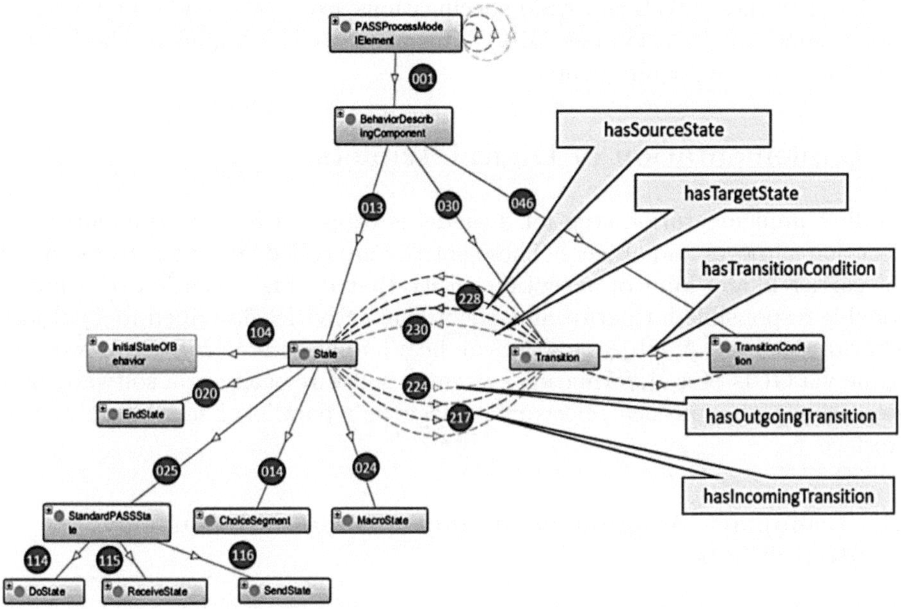

Fig. 16. OWL structure of subject oriented models.

```
Behavior_subj(D) = {Behavior(subj, node) | node ∈ Node(D)}
Behavior(subj, state) =
    if SID_state(subj) = state then
        if Completed(subj, service(state), state) then
            let edge = select_Edge({e ∈ OutEdge(state) | ExitCond(e)(subj, state)})
                Proceed(subj, service(target(edge)), target(edge))
        else Perform(subj, service(state), state)
    where
        Proceed(subj, X, node) =
            SID_state(subj) := node
            Start(subj, X, node)
```

Fig. 17. Part of the Formal Execution Semantics Specification of subject oriented models in ASM Notation - Excerpt from Börger [2].

For subject-oriented models, such a specification exists based on the Abstract State Machine (ASM) formalism (see [1–3]). Figure 17 shows an excerpt of the various ASMs that together form the formal execution specification for an interpreter intended to execute Subject Behavior Diagrams (SBDs).

The significance of both standard specifications – the Standard Subject-Oriented Ontology/OWL for the static model structure and interpreter specification for the dynamic specification in business process modeling and management execution aspects of PASS – arises from their combination, as described in [3].

Based on these OWL and ASM specifications, executable code can be derived from a model specification (see [4,6]). This allows to check models whether they meet the behavior requirements.

5 Implementation of Digital Triplets

The first implementation step for a model is to assign real existing entities for execution subjects and objects. These entities are called subject carriers. A subject carrier is any kind of execution entity that during execution of a process model is responsible for performing the actual activities described in a subject's behavior diagram. A subject carrier can be a human interacting with a workflow engine via GUIs of an information system, a software entity or a software entity interacting with a physical/electronic device via a parallel or serial input/output interface.

5.1 Exemplary Assignment of Implementation Technology to Subjects

The following sections describe the behavior of the intersection control system. This specification does not include how or by whom this behavior is executed. The first implementation step is to define the technology used to execute the behavior of a subject. Figure 18 and Fig. 19 show the assignment of executors to the subjects "Traffic Light North", "Car Detector North", and "North Road." The "Traffic light North" subject is executed by a traffic light as we know it in daily life. This means that the behavior of this subject is executed by a physical device. The subject "Car detector North" is also executed by a related physical device.

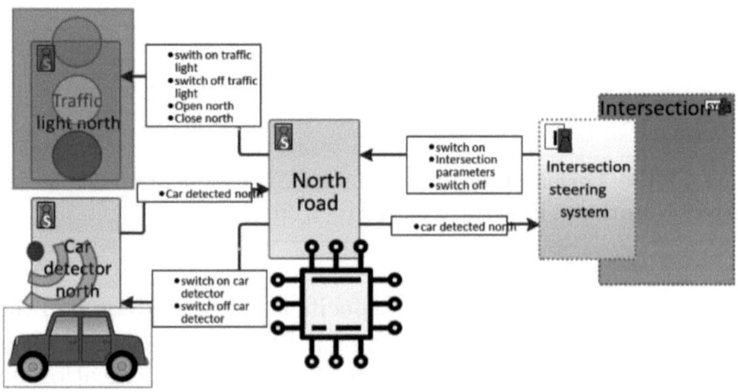

Fig. 18. Assigning executors to subjects in the subsystem "Intersection".

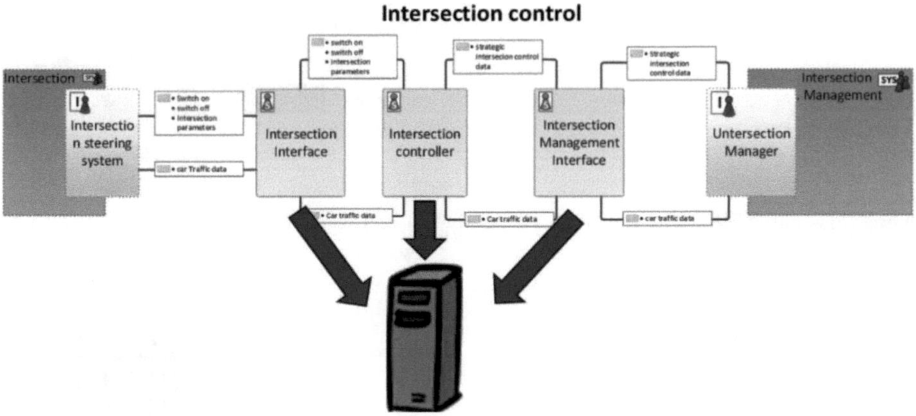

Fig. 19. Assigning executors in the subsystem "Intersection Control".

The subject "North Road" is run by an electronic controller. The controller turns the traffic light lamps on and off and receives electrical pulses from the car detector. This communication is realized through corresponding parallel or serial input/output (PIO or SIO) circuits.

Figure 20 shows the assignment of the subject Human Interface to executors. This subject is executed by software and humans. This means that the behavior is driven by a software which requires some inputs from users via a screen. The function executed at the internal state "Input of Intersection parameters" (see Fig. 13) assigns the corresponding values to the internal object "Intersection control parameters". This function is implemented by requesting input from a user.

5.2 General Concept to Assign Implementation Technologies to Subjects

The abstract model has to be embedded in its context - the subjects have to be assigned to executors/actors. These executors can be physical, virtual, or human entities. If the behavior is assigned to an executor the defined behavior is executed. In Sect. 5.1 it is shown which executors are assigned to which subjects. This is done in an ad hoc manner. It is recommended to create a structural model of the context. This context model shows the various executors and their relationship. Figure 21 shows the basic structure of the context of a Digital Triplet. More or less it is the constituting structure of a triplet. A triplet is embedded in a context consisting of physical, virtual and human entities.

Each constituting entity type is structured in more detail. Figure 22 shows the structure of the physical system of the intersection control system. The physical context has four functional subsystems. These subsystems consist of functional units, and each functional unit is implemented by an Executor/Actor.

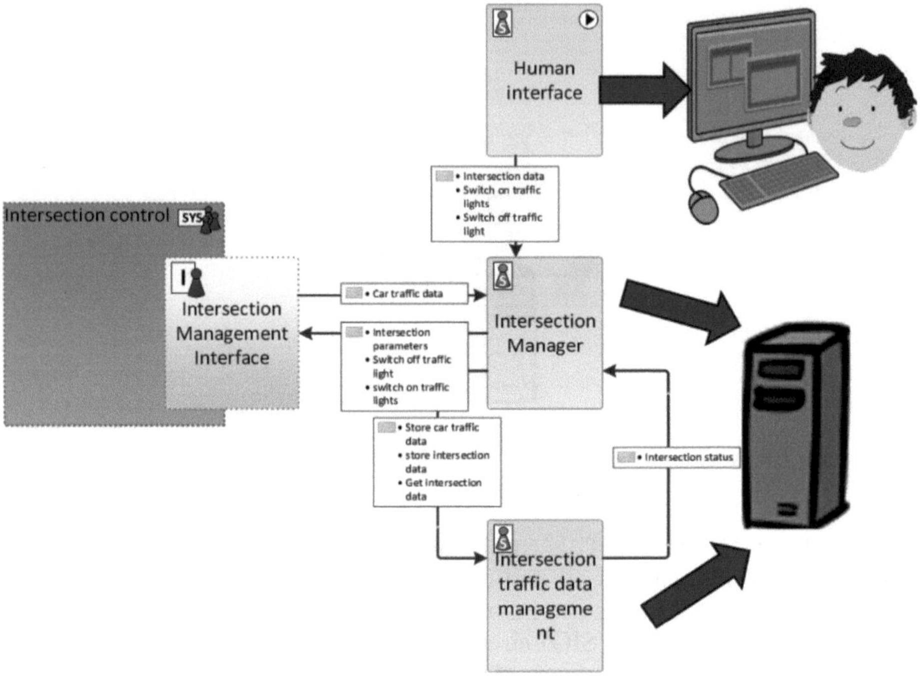

Fig. 20. Assigning executors in the subsystem "Intersection Management".

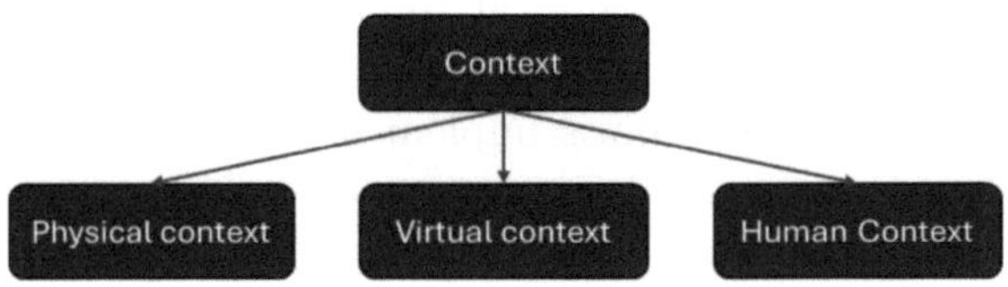

Fig. 21. General structure of the context of a virtual triplet.

These executors are mapped to subjects. They follow the behavior as specified in the subject model. Figure 23 shows the deployment of subjects on computer systems. These are the virtual entities of the intersection management system. They are implemented by software.

The most complex context aspects of a virtual triplet are the human aspects. Physical and virtual entities are mapped to their executor for "ever". This is not the case for human entities. Various people may handle the required input. Employees are in vacation and during that time colleagues may take over their tasks. When people leave the organization, other persons are hired. This means the human aspects of the context continuously change and the assignment to human executors must be very flexible. In [13,14], a highly flexible method and corresponding tools are described. In Fig. 24, however, a simple situation is

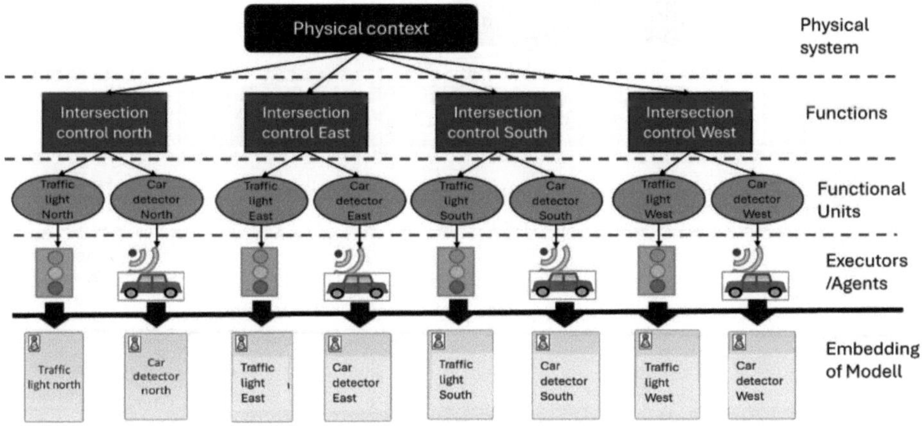

Fig. 22. Physical entities of the traffic light system.

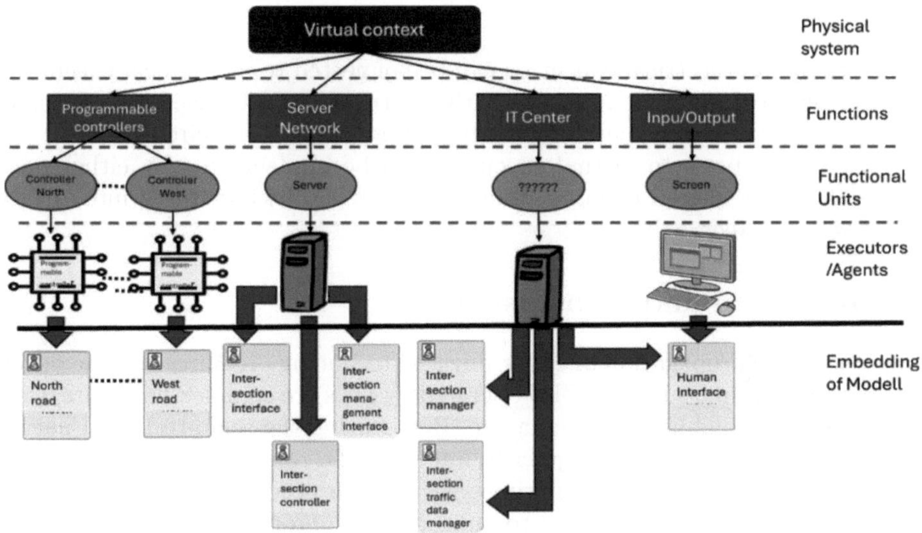

Fig. 23. Deployment of virtual entities on computer systems.

described. There is a single person who types in the intersection control parameters.

5.3 Implementation of the Communication Between Executors/Actors

In this context, the implementation of interaction between subjects is related to different types of executors. These implementations can be widespread. The interaction between physical executors depends on their physical attributes and

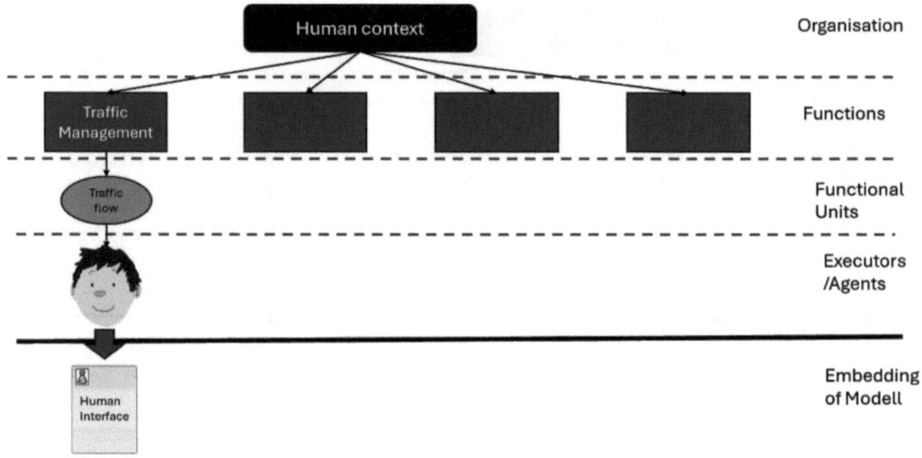

Fig. 24. Organizational context of a virtual triplet.

can be complex. Electrical executors can be connected to mechanical executors. When a physical executor interacts with a virtual executor, electronic circuits must be applied, such as parallel or serial input/output (IO) circuits.

Interactions between virtual executors can be implemented by either message exchange or shared memory. Human entities can be integrated into virtual executors via screens.

6 Discussion and Conclusion

The continuous propagation of cyber-physical technology requires specific development and runtime support. CPS operated by DTs are complex hardware/software systems of highly dynamic nature. Recognizing the socio-technical nature of these systems requires to explicitly integrate the role of humans, designing, using, or operating CPS. Any runtime specification needs to be coherently connected to design representations to tune physical processes with digital ones preserving human control.

The presented design-integrated engineering of human-centered DTs has its focus on interaction and data exchange between networked components and human users, taking into account their operational context. Stakeholders acting in specific roles need to elaborate how they access the digital and physical components which trigger data collections and exchanges. It implements the understanding of DTs as 'active software systems' that rely on 'a set of models and a set of digital shadows, both of which are purposefully updated on a regular basis, provides a set of *services* to use both purposefully with respect to the original system, and can send information about the environment and control commands to the original system' [11, p. 3f].

The development challenge is not only to recognize the context of use, and thus structure design. It may further lead to layering abstractions [9], but still rely on technology-independent processing to ensure accurate execution. Both, developers and users can benefit from design and runtime approaches that enable a unifying view on CPS and allow for validation and implementation-independent execution before operation. DTs support digital representations that accompany design, engineering, runtime control and adaptive behavior.

ASM specifications support formally correct processing and system execution based on semantic model checking. The ASM specification provides the behavior of any workflow engine when executing a subject-oriented DT model. Aligned with the OWL structure of subject-oriented models, ASM specifications enable deriving executable code from a model specification. This finally features system evaluation through DT models when checking whether human needs in terms of behavior requirements can be met.

References

1. Börger, E., Gervasi, V.: Structures of Computing: a Guide to Practice-Oriented Theory. Springer, Cham (2024)
2. Börger, Egon: A Subject-Oriented Interpreter Model for S-BPM. In: Fleischmann, A., Schmidt, W., Stary, C., Obermeier, S., Börger, E. (eds.) Subject-Oriented Business Process Management, chap. Appendix B, pp. 18–66. Springer, Berlin, Heidelberg (2012). https://doi.org/10.1007/978-3-642-32392-8
3. Elstermann, M., Krenn, F.: The semantic exchange standard for subject-oriented process models. In: Proceedings of the 10th International Conference on Subject-Oriented Business Process Management, pp. 1–8. ACM, New York, NY, USA (2018). https://doi.org/10.1145/3178248.3178257
4. Elstermann, M., Wolski, A.: mapping execution and model semantics for subject-oriented process models. In: Subject-Oriented Business Process Management. The Digital Workplace – Nucleus of Transformation. S-BPM ONE 2020, pp. 46–59. Springer, Cham (2020). https://doi.org/10.1007/978-3-030-64351-5_4
5. Embley, D.W., Thalheim, B.: Handbook of Conceptual Modeling. Springer, Berlin, Heidelberg (2011). https://doi.org/10.1007/978-3-642-15865-0
6. Fleischmann, A., Borgert, S., Elstermann, M., Krenn, F., Singer, R.: An overview of S-BPM-oriented tool suites. In: Proceedings of the 9th International Conference on Subject-oriented Business Process Management. ACM, New York, NY, USA (2017)
7. Fleischmann, A., Schmidt, W., Stary, C., Obermeier, S., Börger, E.: Subject-Oriented Business Process Management. Springer, Heidelberg (2012). https://doi.org/10.1007/978-3-642-32392-8
8. Hassija, V., et al.: A survey on digital twins: enabling technologies, use cases, application, open issues, and more. IEEE J. Sel. Areas Sens. **2**, 84–107 (2025). https://doi.org/10.1109/JSAS.2024.3523856
9. Jost, T.E., Heininger, R., Stary, C.: Layering abstractions for design-integrated engineering of cyber-physical systems. In: Lyu, Z. (ed.) Handbook of Digital Twins, pp. 221–237. CRC Press, Boca Raton (2024). https://doi.org/10.1201/9781003425724-17
10. Kasser, J.E.: System's Thinking as it Applies to Systems Engineering (2021). https://www.youtube.com/watch?v=exng0hUlzOk

11. Michael, J., et al.: Integrating models of civil structures in digital twins: state-of-the-art and challenges. J. Infrastruct. Intell. Resilience **3**(3), 100100 (2024). https://doi.org/10.1016/j.iintel.2024.100100
12. National Academies of Sciences, Engineering, and Medicine: The Digital Twin Landscape. In: Foundational Research Gaps and Future Directions for Digital Twins, chap. 2, pp. 21–48. The National Academies Press, Washington, DC, USA (2024). https://doi.org/10.17226/26894, https://www.nationalacademies.org/read/26894/chapter/4
13. Schaller, T.: Organisationsverwaltung in CSCW-Systemen. Ph.D. thesis, Universtiät Bamberg, Bamberg (1998)
14. Schaller, T., Fleischmann, A.: Mapping of agents to subjects in S-BPM. In: Subject-Oriented Business Process Management. Process Customer Satisfaction and Process Excellence. S-BPM ONE 2025, pp. 19–34. Springer, Cham (2026). https://doi.org/10.1007/978-3-032-04944-5_2
15. Segovia, M., Garcia-Alfaro, J.: Design, modeling and implementation of digital twins. Sensors **22**(14), 5396 (2022). https://doi.org/10.3390/s22145396
16. Stary, C., Elstermann, M., Fleischmann, A., Schmidt, W.: Behavior-centered digital-twin design for dynamic cyber-physical system development. Complex Syst. Inf. Model. Quart. (CSIMQ) (30), 31–52 (2022). https://doi.org/10.7250/CSIMQ.2022-30.02
17. Tao, F., Xiao, B., Qi, Q., Cheng, J., Ji, P.: Digital twin modeling. J. Manuf. Syst. **64**, 372–389 (2022). https://doi.org/10.1016/j.jmsy.2022.06.015

Author Index

A

Ait-Ameur, Yamine 201

B

Banach, Richard 249
Baugh, John 249
Beierle, Christoph 377
Bodeveix, Jean-Paul 201
Bombarda, Andrea 30
Bonfanti, Silvia 30
Bowen, Jonathan P. 16
Braghin, Chiara 76
Butler, Michael 332

C

Castillo, Giuseppe Del 152
Cervelle, Julien 317
Chen, Christophe 201

D

Dupont, Guillaume 201

F

Fares, Elie 201
Fathabadi, Asieh Salehi 332
Ferrarotti, Flavio 357, 398
Filali, Mamoun 201
Fleischmann, Albert 445
Frappier, Marc 295

G

Gargantini, Angelo 30
Gervais, Frédéric 317
Gervasi, Vincenzo 176
Grieu, Anne 201

H

Hahn, Alexander 377
Hoang, Thai Son 332

K

Kang, Eunsuk 249
Kern-Isberner, Gabriele 377
Kühn, Thomas 126

L

Laleau, Régine 317
Langmaack, Hans 3
Leuschel, Michael 273

M

Mendil, Ismail 201
Méry, Dominique 223
Miraglia, Federico 176

O

Ober, Iulian 106
Oliveira, Diego de Azevedo 295

P

Pantel, Marc 201
Pellegrinelli, Nico 30
Pribyl, Felix 49
Prinz, Andreas 106

R

Raschke, Alexander 3
Reif, Wolfgang 49
Riccobene, Elvinia 76
Rivière, Peter 201

S

Sabinus, Edward 126
Schellhorn, Gerhard 49
Schewe, Klaus-Dieter 3, 357, 398
Sherratt, Edel 106
Singh, Neeraj Kumar 201
Snook, Colin 332
Spiegel, Lars-Phillip 377
Stary, Christian 445

A. Raschke et al. (Eds.): Egon Börger Festschrift, LNCS 16580, pp. 469–470, 2026.
https://doi.org/10.1007/978-3-032-24494-9

T
Thalheim, Bernhard 3, 421

V
Valarcher, Pierre 317
Verdier, Guillaume 201

W
Weißbach, Mandy 126

Z
Zimmermann, Wolf 126

MIX
Papier aus verantwortungsvollen Quellen
Paper from responsible sources
FSC® C105338
FSC
www.fsc.org

If you have any concerns about our products,
you can contact us on
ProductSafety@springernature.com

In case Publisher is established outside the EU,
the EU authorized representative is:
Springer Nature Customer Service Center GmbH
Europaplatz 3, 69115 Heidelberg, Germany

Printed by Libri Plureos GmbH
in Hamburg, Germany